CRISIS IN
AMERICAN
INSTITUTIONS

CRISIS IN
AMERICAN
INSTITUTIONS

EDITED BY
JEROME H. SKOLNICK
ELLIOTT CURRIE
University of California, Berkeley

Boston

Little, Brown and Company

CONTENTS

INTRODUCTION
Approaches to Social Problems   1

PART 1
SYSTEM-WIDE PROBLEMS

Chapter 1
INEQUALITY   19

GABRIEL KOLKO   *The Unchanging Pattern of Inequality*   23

PHILIP M. STERN   *How 381 Super-Rich Americans Managed
Not to Pay a Cent in Taxes Last Year*   32

PAUL JACOBS   *Keeping the Poor Poor*   42

BERNARD BECK   *Bedbugs, Stench, Dampness,
and Immorality: A Review Essay
on Recent Literature About Poverty*   53

Chapter 2
RACISM   70

HAROLD M. BARON   *Black Powerlessness in Chicago*   74

JULIUS JACOBSON   *Union Conservatism:
A Barrier to Racial Equality*   84

LEE RAINWATER   *The Revolt of the Dirty-Workers*   99

ROBERT BLAUNER   *Internal Colonialism and Ghetto Revolt*   103

Chapter 3
CORPORATE POWER   122

JOHN KENNETH GALBRAITH   *The Corporation*   127

RALPH NADER   *GM and the Auto Industry:
The Threat of Corporate Collectivism*   137

NICHOLAS JOHNSON   *The Silent Screen*   147

v

Chapter 4
MILITARIZATION   156

SELECTIVE SERVICE SYSTEM   *Channeling*   162
GENERAL DAVID M. SHOUP   *The New American Militarism*   168
RICHARD F. KAUFMAN   *The Military-Industrial Complex*   178
RICHARD DUDMAN   *Agent Meany*   192
RICHARD J. BARNET   *The National-Security Managers*   198

PART 2
INSTITUTIONS IN CRISIS

Chapter 5
EDUCATION   213

The Schools   213

EDGAR Z. FRIEDENBERG   *Status and Role in Education*   217
DAVID ROGERS   *110 Livingston Street*   228
JONATHAN KOZOL   *Death at an Early Age*   239
ROBERT A. DENTLER   *For Local Control in the Schools*   245

The Universities   251

MICHAEL MACCOBY   *Government, Scientists,
and the Priorities of Science*   257

RODNEY T. HARTNETT   *College and University Trustees:
Their Backgrounds, Roles, and
Educational Attitudes*   266

SHELDON WOLIN
JOHN SCHAAR   *Berkeley: The Battle of People's Park*   281

BARBARA RASKIN   *Federal City College:
Militancy in Microcosm*   294

STUDY COMMISSION ON
UNIVERSITY GOVERNANCE   *Education and Society:
The Need for Reconsideration*   305

Chapter 6
SOCIAL SERVICES 310

Health 310

ROBERT COLES
HARRY HUGE   *"Black Lung": Mining as a Way of Death*   314

ELIZABETH B. DREW   *Going Hungry in America:
Government's Failure*   322

ELINOR LANGER   *The Shame of American Medicine*   336

Welfare 346

JACOBUS tenBROEK   *The Two Nations: Differential Moral
Values in Welfare Law and Administration*   350

RICHARD M. ELMAN   *Brownleaf's Story*   361

RICHARD A. CLOWARD
RICHARD M. ELMAN   *Poverty, Injustice,
and the Welfare State*   367

Chapter 7
JUSTICE 387

The Police 387

PAUL CHEVIGNY   *Force, Arrest, and Cover Charges*   393

NICHOLAS PILEGGI   *"Gestapo" or "Elite"?
The Tactical Patrol Force*   402

IRVING LOUIS HOROWITZ   *Reactionary Immortality:
The Private Life in Public Testimony
of John Edgar Hoover*   411

Criminal Law and Corrections 420

SANFORD H. KADISH   *The Crisis of Overcriminalization*   425

ANTHONY M. PLATT   *The Rise of the Child-Saving Movement:
A Study in Social Policy and Correctional Reform*   442

ROBERT MARTINSON   *The Age of Treatment: Some
Implications of the Custody-Treatment Dimension*   463

CRISIS IN
AMERICAN
INSTITUTIONS

INTRODUCTION

Approaches to Social Problems

When social scientists produce books on social problems, they face a dilemma, which they usually try to resolve in an introductory essay: how to justify their choice of what is to be considered a "problem" and what is not. For, by selecting certain social phenomena and not others as problems, the social scientist offers a particular vision of what is wrong with his society and, at least by implication, of what ought to be done about it. This inevitably involves making judgments about matters of great moral and political importance, and this involvement fits badly with the common conception of science as a matter of cool and purely technical judgment.

The dilemma usually is resolved by arguing that the choice of problems is dictated by impersonal, scientific criteria which are, in themselves, devoid of moral or political significance. This stance rescues the social scientist from charges of bias, while supporting his claim to a special scientific expertise. We find this argument unconvincing. In the following pages we intend to show why, by examining some themes in the history of the literature of social problems.

Much contemporary work in social problems has been guided by a reaction against the unabashed and unexamined moralism of early American social science. As C. Wright Mills and others have argued, most among the earliest theorists of social problems or social "pathology" had small-town backgrounds. Their texts in social problems consisted mainly in a moral critique of the city and its evils, and an affirmation of the values of an earlier, more agrarian and homogeneous America. Sociology was closely tied to social work and other ameliorative professions.[1]

[1] C. Wright Mills, "The Professional Ideology of the Social Pathologists," in Irving L. Horowitz, ed., *Power, Politics, and People: the Collected Essays of C. Wright Mills* (New York: Ballantine Books, 1963).

When, however, the simple link between small-town Protestant morals and the study of social problems began to break down, the dilemma in the study of social problems began to appear. Sociology, especially its "applied" areas, began to detach itself from the social workers and the ministers and claim for itself special, scientific status. As this occurred, the relationship between social science and social values became critical: if sociology could no longer assume its basic values, where would it get them, and how, if at all, could "science" justify meddling in people's lives in the name of attacking "social problems"?

The most frequent answer given by writers on social problems, ancient and recent, may be seen in these "definitions of the field." Social problems are:

> Any difficulty or misbehavior of a fairly large number of persons which we wish to remove or correct.[2]

> What people think they are.[3]

> Whenever people begin to say, isn't it awful! why don't they do something about it?[4]

> Conditions which affect sizeable proportions of the population, which are out of harmony with the values of a significant segment of the population, and which people feel can be improved or eliminated.[5]

These definitions have a major element in common, the idea that social problems are matters of popular definition. No condition is a problem unless a defined number of people in the world say it is. A distinction is therefore to be made between "objective" and "subjective" aspects of social problems, and, according to these theorists, it is this difference which makes social problems amenable to "scientific" study. Since we are merely taking, as our starting point, the definitions of the problem that "other people," "society," or "significant segments of the population" provide, we are no longer in the position of "moralizing" about objective conditions. Thus, scientific objectivity derives its sanction from collective consensus.

This perspective dominates the current literature on social problems. The advantage of this approach should be clear, though the approach itself may seem overly relativistic and lacking in intellectual direction.

[2] Lawrence K. Frank, "Social Problems," *American Journal of Sociology,* vol. 30 (January, 1925), p. 463.
[3] Richard C. Fuller and Richard R. Myers, "The Natural History of a Social Problem," *American Sociological Review,* vol. 6 (June, 1941), p. 320.
[4] Paul B. Horton and Gerald R. Leslie, *The Sociology of Social Problems* (New York: Appleton-Century-Crofts, 1955), p. 6.
[5] Arnold M. Rose, "Theory for the Study of Social Problems," *Social Problems,* vol. 4 (January, 1957), p. 190.

Employing such a conception, the social scientist can establish himself as a specialist, but avoid the charge of introducing his own biases. He can legitimize his own structuring of the social world into the problematic and the not problematic as a *scientific* endeavor.

This position is misleading. It is truer to say that this "subjective" approach provides a ritual smokescreen behind which social scientists of very different persuasions can rationalize their presentation of "problems," which have been selected for complex reasons, which may indeed have something to do with public definitions; but the social world and its prospects are ultimately defined by the social scientist himself, who no less than anyone else is immersed in the concerns of his time.

These points can be clarified if we look at some of the work of the early social problem writers. Willard Waller, in an influential paper published in 1936 called "Social Problems and the Mores,"[6] was one of the first and most perceptive theorists to attempt to develop a "scientific" approach to social problems. Waller began by asserting the radically subjective character of social problems:

> Value judgments are the formal causes of social problems, just as the law is the formal cause of crime.[7]

But it is not clear from this statement *whose* value judgments are to be determinative. This basic issue constantly recurs in the field of social problems: which social classes or groups are offered a hearing? Whose definitions of the "problems" count, and whose do not?[8]

Another question is raised when Waller considers remedies for poverty:

> A simpleton would suggest that the remedy for poverty in the midst of plenty is to redistribute income. We reject this solution at once because it would interfere with the institution of private property, would destroy the incentive for thrift and hard work and disjoint the entire economic system.[9]

Waller's extremely important question is: What is *left out* in the writer's definition of the things to be considered as problems? What features of society are going to be taken for granted as the framework *within* which problems will be defined and resolved? In this case, of course, the taken-for-granted framework is an unmodified system of private property and its attendant social relations.

[6] Willard Waller, "Social Problems and the Mores," *American Sociological Review*, vol. 1 (December, 1936).

[7] *Ibid.*, p. 925.

[8] This point is considered in depth by Howard S. Becker in "Whose Side Are We On?," *Social Problems*, vol. 14 (Winter, 1967).

[9] Waller, *op. cit.*, p. 926.

Waller did not naively accept these values. On the contrary, he made a vital point, that "social problems are not solved because people do not want to solve them";[10] they were problems mainly because of peoples' unwillingness to alter the basic conditions from which they sprang. Thus:

> venereal disease becomes a social problem in that it arises from our family institutions and also in that the medical means which could be used to prevent it, which would unquestionably be fairly effective, cannot be employed for fear of altering the mores of chastity.[11]

This suggests that social problems are, in the broadest sense, *political* problems, reflecting the opposed views of conflicting groups. For Waller, the important conflict was that between the "humanitarian mores" — the values of the do-gooder and reformer — and "organizational mores" — the "mores upon which the social order is founded, the mores of private property and individualism, the mores of the monogamous family, Christianity, and nationalism."[12]

Waller believed that a truly scientific approach to social problems would have to rise above both sets of mores to develop a neutral perspective all its own. But this seems opposed to Waller's own recognition that approaches to social problems always operate, at least implicitly, on a conception of basic social conditions within which discourse on problems is to take place; and such conceptions are based not on scientific analysis, but on the values held by specific groups. In Waller's time, those conditions were recognized as "private property and individualism . . . the monogamous family, Christianity, and nationalism." In later treatments of social problems, the basic conditions are rarely acknowledged so explicitly, but are not otherwise much changed. For the most prominent characteristic of social problems writing in the United States is its tacit acceptance of the structure of American society, and its corollary restriction of "problems" to maladjustments *within* that structure.

II

This tendency is seen clearly in more recent works. Books on social problems conceived in the 1950's reflect social and political concerns which now appear strange, or at least overdrawn. It is not an exaggeration to say that the shadow of McCarthyism and the general national hysteria over the "Communist menace" permeates this literature. Thus, Horton and Leslie's text on *The Sociology of Social Problems*[13] contains a major

---

[10] *Ibid.*, p. 928.
[11] *Ibid.*, p. 927.
[12] *Ibid.*, p. 924.
[13] Horton and Leslie, *op. cit.*

section on "Civil Liberties and Subversion," in which the authors' interpretation of the problematic aspects of American life is strongly influenced by the preoccupations of the 1950's.

Horton and Leslie see the "American Heritage of Liberty" as under attack from both Left and Right, from both monolithic Communism and overzealous attempts to defend our way of life from it. Their position is resolutely "liberal" and centrist. They claim a "scientific" objectivity, yet they are quite capable of a deep moral critique of people whose politics are "extreme," whether Right or Left:

> Most extremists are deviants. Most extremists show a fanatical preoccupation with their cause, a suspicious distrust of other people in general, a disinterest in normal pursuits, recreations, and small talk, and a strong tendency to divide other people into enemies and allies.[14]

In this statement, scientific judgment is permeated and directed by a preference for "normality," moderation, even "small talk," political and personal preferences not uncommon in an age noted for its "Silent Generation." Among the authors' eight "Rational Proposals for Preserving Liberty and Security" are these:

> An adequate national defense is, needless to say, necessary in a world where an international revolutionary movement is joined to an aggressive major power. This is a military problem, not a sociological problem, and is not discussed here.
> Counterespionage is essential. Highly trained professional agencies such as the FBI and the Central Intelligence Agency can do this efficiently and without endangering personal liberties of citizens. If headline-hunting congressmen, Legion officials, or other amateurs turn G-man, they merely scare off any real spies and destroy the counterespionage efforts of the professionals.[15]

Notice that the military and intelligence services themselves are, in this treatment, entirely exempt from classification as problems relevant for social science. Questions about the operation of these agencies are conceived to be internal and technical; it is presumed that they are doing their job as best they can, for they are, after all, our first lines of defense.

In a section on "Questions and Projects," the authors ask:

> How have conservatives or reactionaries sometimes given unintentional assistance to the Communists? How have liberals sometimes given unintentional assistance to the Communists?[16]

14 *Ibid.*, p. 517.
15 *Ibid.*, p. 520.
16 *Ibid.*, p. 523.

Most of these concerns seem somewhat out of place today. Certainly, uncritically accepting the "purely military" nature of defense problems, the expertise of the CIA and FBI, and the imagery of the monolithic and implacable "Communists" reflect preoccupations that were widespread at the time. Yet they do not *merely* reflect their time; rather, they structure it, define its problems, and defend that definition against others at least equally plausible.

Moreover, the authors seek to define the possibilities of social change and the role of social scientists in promoting it. Horton and Leslie argue that the resolution of social problems "nearly always involves sweeping institutional changes" — thus debunking the conservative notion that social problems are primarily problems of individuals — *but also* that such changes are costly and difficult and therefore "it is unrealistic to expect that these problems will be solved easily or quickly . . . basic solutions of social problems will come slowly, if at all. Meanwhile, however, considerable *amelioration* or 'improvement' may be possible" — thus debunking the impatient and those demanding major changes, now.[17]

Social change must be gradual and "realistic"; it must also be guided by experts. The authors insist — contrary to all visible signs — that their role, and that of social experts in general, is merely to show the layman how to get what he already values. But in this role, it is folly for the layman to *question* the expert. Horton and Leslie write that:

> When experts are *agreed* upon the futility of one policy or the soundness of another, it is sheer stupidity for the layman to disagree.[18]

A moderate, cold war "liberalism" and gradualism, a fear of "extremism" and of an international Communist conspiracy — all these are offered not as moral and political positions but as part of the social scientist's stock in trade, his expertise. Indeed, they are very nearly equated with a serious approach to social problems. The sturdy entrepreneurial and Protestant values presented in Waller's paper of the 1930's give way, in Horton and Leslie's text of the 1950's to a dessicated and diffuse demand for moderation, anti-Communism, and "normal pursuits."

Thus, the selection of problems, strategies, solutions, and change is a creative act by the social problems theorist, acting within — but also upon — the preconceptions and concerns of his time. The social problems books of the 1960's differ from those of the 1950's partly because of a changing relationship between social science and the agencies of social policy and social control.

17 *Ibid.*, p. 12.
18 *Ibid.*, p. 19.

III

Merton and Nisbet's *Contemporary Social Problems*[19] is a product of the beginning of the 1960's, the period of the New Frontier which produced a significant shift in the direction of social commitment. People were becoming aware of an "underdeveloped" world abroad and a "disadvantaged" or "deprived" world at home, both unhappily excluded from the benefits of an age of general affluence and well-being. New agencies of social improvement and amelioration were created at home and abroad, recruiting many people with some training in social science. A critique of old-style "welfare" efforts began to develop, along with the rising notion of "helping people help themselves," whether in Nigeria, Harlem, or Appalachia. The idea of inclusion, of participation, in the American way of life, became predominant. From a slightly different vantage, the idea emerged as "development" or "modernization." The common strand linking "participation" and "development" is the extension of technological and intellectual resources of established American institutions into excluded, deprived, or underdeveloped places and groups, with the general aim of uplift. An intervention-minded government combined with an energetic social science, on a scale unprecedented in this country. Significantly, this merger brought social science together with the *federal* government, at a time when the federal government was looked to for major and progressive social change.

In this period — very brief, as it turned out — social problems often were seen as problems of being left out, "left behind," as the people of Appalachia were described, "traditional" like the Mexican-Americans, "transitional" like the American Indians, or even "premodern," like most Africans and some Asians. For social problems theory, the result was a "conservative" theory, or metatheory, of American society as a whole, coupled with a "liberal" critique of the conditions hindering the extension of the American way to all, and a highly developed sense of the expert's importance in directing this extension.

These views are apparent in Nisbet's introduction to *Contemporary Social Problems*. For Nisbet, social problems are problematic because they "represent interruptions in the expected or desired scheme of things; violations of the right or the proper, as a society defines these qualities; dislocations in the social patterns and relationships that a society cherishes."[20] Here the common "subjective" approach to social problems becomes more than usually conservative, more explicitly an orientation to "society's" view of the good and proper, and therefore less "relativistic." This ten-

[19] Robert K. Merton and Robert A. Nisbet, eds., *Contemporary Social Problems* (New York: Harcourt, Brace and World, 1961).
[20] Robert A. Nisbet, "The Study of Social Problems," in *Ibid.*, p. 4.

dency toward conservative imagery in theory is coupled with an assessment of the American situation which is in keeping with the spirit of
intervention:

> In America today we live in what is often called an affluent society.
> It is a society characterized by imposing command of physical re-
> sources, high standards of private consumption, effective main-
> tenance of public order and security, freedom from most of the
> uncertainties of life that plagued our ancestors, and relatively high
> levels of humanitarianism. There are also, of course, squalid slums,
> both urban and rural; occasional epidemics of disease; sudden erup-
> tions of violence or bigotry, even in the most civilized of commu-
> nities; people for whom the struggle for food and shelter yet remains
> obsessing and precarious. Thus, we are not free of social problems,
> and some of them seem to grow almost in direct proportion to our
> affluence.[21]

Thus, Nisbet is well aware that America has not yet solved all its "problems," indeed that some seem to come with the generally glittering package that is America in the twentieth century. Yet the "problems" are
conceived as peripheral, as existing in the backwaters of society in
"occasional eruptions," and squalid pockets where modern institutions
have not fully penetrated.

By contrast, during the same period, C. W. Mills called the United
States an "overdeveloped" society,[22] a conception which may well be
more appropriate for a society that has fouled its landscape, polluted its
water and air, rendered its cities increasingly uninhabitable, that annually
slaughters tens of thousands with its overpowered automobiles; and must
pay wealthy farmers not to produce while millions do not get enough to
eat.

Like earlier theorists, Nisbet sharply separated the role of the scientific
student of social problems from that of other concerned people. The scientist as a scientist should not engage in moral exhortation or political
action, but should concentrate on understanding. This does not mean,
for Nisbet, that the scientist must be a relativist, for he is "as interested
as the next citizen in making the protection of society his first responsibility, in seeing society reach higher levels of moral decency, and, when
necessary, in promoting such legal actions as are necessary in the short
run for protection or decency."[23]

Surely, this is an instance of a "scientific" stance masking a feeling for
vaguely defined values — here, "social protection" and "moral decency"

[21] *Ibid.*, p. 5.
[22] C. Wright Mills, quoted in Irving L. Horowitz, introduction to *Power, Politics,
and People, op. cit.*, p. 8.
[23] Nisbet, *op. cit.*, p. 9.

— which in turn structure the kinds of phenomena that will be selected as "social problems." In this instance, problems are selected according to whether or not they offend the values of social stability — that is, values associated with the conservative tradition in social thought.

Thus, problems are repeatedly equated with "dislocations and deviations";[24] they are problems of "dissensus." Indeed, the entire book is divided into two sections, one of which deals with "deviant behavior" and the other with "social disorganization." The articles in the text are not all of a piece. A paper by Weiss and Riesman on the problems of work takes a different view on what constitutes a "problem"; the authors declare that "social forms which tend toward the suppression or frustration of meaning and purpose in life are inferior forms, whether or not they tend toward disorganization."[25] But several papers show a tendency to accept the contours of existing institutions and to phrase the problems as if combating disorganization *within* them. Perhaps the clearest illustration of this tendency appears in Janowitz's essay dealing with problems of the military establishment:

> It is self-evident that the military establishment, the armed forces, and their administrative organizations have become and will remain important institutions of United States society. The distinctive forms of military organization must be analyzed in order to understand the typical sources of personal and social disorganization found in military life.[26]

The existence of a large military establishment is beyond the critical purview of the sociologist. He is most interested not in the effect of the military on national life, but in the problems of maladjustment within the military apparatus. Moreover, the author promotes one of several possible conceptions of the role of the military in American life:

> The peacetime military establishment is a complex organization with multiple functions. Its major tasks are to maintain strategic deterrent forces and limited war forces so as to reduce the possibility of future wars. The armed forces have also become involved in a wide variety of logistical, research, and training activities. In the current international scene, they must take on many politico-military duties, including military assistance to allied powers. . . .[27]

Such an approach implies that the phenomenon which, later on in this book, we call "militarizaton," is beyond dispute or analysis. In addition,

---

[24] *Ibid.*, p. 12.

[25] Robert S. Weiss and David Riesman, "Social Problems and Disorganization in the World of Work," in Merton and Nisbet, *op. cit.*, p. 464.

[26] Morris Janowitz, "The Military Establishment; Organization and Disorganization," in Merton and Nisbet, *op. cit.*, p. 515.

[27] *Ibid.*, p. 516.

it reflects a specific, limited-war ideology of the military purpose. Accordingly, the chief problems of the military system in the cold war period, for Janowitz, are the individual and organizational problems connected with the need to maintain constant readiness.

Of course, the general feeling about the international situation then was greatly different from the popular feeling some years later, and Janowitz's analysis of military problems somewhat reflects national preoccupations. Far fewer critics attacked the military's role then, as Janowitz's mention of the Selective Service System makes clear:

> Overt opposition to the system, even political criticism of its injustices, is virtually absent.[28]

Yet this sort of analysis is more than a reflection; it is also a choice. The acceptance of the place of the military in American society leads to the enlistment of the resources of social science in the service of military ends. Thus Janowitz recognizes changes in the requirements of military discipline:

> The shock technique of assimilation was an essential element of the older forms of discipline based on authoritarian domination. It probably had some utility . . . with the development of military organizations based on group consensus, some training procedures have had to be modified. New procedures of assimilation stress positive attachments and group loyalties . . . it is more a process of fostering positive incentives and group loyalties through a team concept.[29]

The issue has become how to assimilate the recruit into the military and how to manipulate his group attachments for the military's organizational purposes. The analyst stops short of inquiring critically *just what* the recruit is to be assimilated into. The effect of primary-group relations on morale under cold war conditions is much discussed but nowhere do we find discussion of the cold war.

This leads us to reassert a principle: one can tell a great deal about an approach to social problems by considering what it leaves out.

IV

Robert Merton's epilogue to *Contemporary Social Problems*, called "Social Problems and Sociological Theory," is a major attempt to give theoretical definition to the field of social problems. Merton again distinguishes between ordinary conceptions of social problems and the "technical sense

[28] *Ibid.*, p. 528.
[29] *Ibid.*, pp. 533–534.

in which the sociologist employs the term."[30] He considers the "first and basic ingredient of a social problem" to be "any substantial discrepancy between socially shared standards and actual conditions of social life."[31] Merton is well aware that different interests are present in society and that therefore definitions of social problems are likely to be contested — "one group's problem will be another group's asset" — and more specifically that "those occupying strategic positions of authority and power of course carry more weight than others in deciding social policy and so, among other things, in identifying for the rest what are to be taken as significant departures from social standards."[32]

But, according to Merton, this does not mean that the sociologist of social problems must succumb to relativism *or* abandon his position as a scientific student of society's problems. The way out of the dilemma is to conceive of a distinction between "manifest" and "latent" social problems — the latter problems also "at odds with the values of the group" but not recognized as such. Thus, the task of the sociologist is to uncover the latent problematic aspects of existing institutions and policies; in this way, "sociological inquiry does make men increasingly accountable for the outcome of their collective and institutionalized actions."[33]

This is a useful and important distinction in many ways, and the demand that social science make men accountable for their actions is a healthy departure from the spurious relativism of some earlier theorists. But the distinction between manifest and latent problems does not do what Merton says it does: it does not make the choice of problems a technical or "neutral" one. In fact, Merton's approach is best seen as providing a rationale for evaluating and criticizing particular policies and structures within a presumably consensual society whose basic values and directions are not seen as problematic.

We can easily agree with Merton that "to confine the study of social problems to only those circumstances that are expressly defined as problems in the society is arbitrarily to discard a complement of conditions that are also dysfunctional to values held by people in that society."[34] But beyond that there are the issues of a society's values, its culture or lack of culture, its fundamental orientations. These may be examined and criticized as transcending the amorphous "values held by people in that society." To take an obvious example, the values "held by" the German people under Nazi rule may be criticized in terms of traditional western

---

[30] Robert K. Merton, "Social Problems and Sociological Theory," in Merton and Nisbet, *op. cit.*, p. 701.
[31] *Ibid.*, p. 702.
[32] *Ibid.*, p. 706.
[33] *Ibid.*, p. 710.
[34] *Ibid.*, p. 711.

values. Merton's approach altogether is a dem and for the active intervention by social scientists in solving problems on the fringes of an assumed
consensus on broad social goals. It promotes — again — the conception
of the social scientist as expert in fitting people into the American main
stream and in pointing out how certain existing institutions and patterns
block this kind of integration, leading to all manner of deviant and disruptive behavior.

This renders the social scientist a responsible citizen rather than a mere
social critic or ideologue:

> Under the philosophy intrinsic to the distinction between manifest
> and latent social problems, the sociologist neither abdicates his intel-
> lectual and professional responsibilities nor usurps the position of
> sitting in moral judgment on his fellow men.[35]

But what does this "philosophy" mean except that the sociologist is to
function as an expert within "socially shared standards"? Unfortunately,
this combination can produce an alignment of "expertise" and "professionalism" with dominant values and interests masquerading as societal
consensus. Such an alignment can serve as the vehicle for a sophisticated
brand of moral intervention justified by referring to an asserted agreement
on the fundamentals. Both deviant behavior and social disorganization
— hence social problems in general — are defined as disruptions of a social stability in which the question of the adequacy of social life is not
raised:

> Whereas social disorganization refers to faults in the arrangement
> and working of social statuses and roles, deviant behavior refers to
> conduct that departs significantly from the norms set for people in
> their social statuses.[36]

It is not, as some critics have suggested, that this kind of analysis suggests
that whatever is, is right. But it does ultimately rest on some notion of
societal consensus as the measuring-rod against which "problems" are to
be assessed, and its proponents insist on taking an important role in interpreting that consensus. Moreover, this expertise may conflict with what
people themselves feel to be their problems, and if so, the expert wins.
Merton argues that:

> We cannot take for granted a reasonably correct public imagery of
> social problems; of their scale, distribution, causation, consequences
> and persistence or change . . . popular perceptions are no safe
> guide to the magnitude of a social problem.[37]

[35] *Ibid.*, p. 712.
[36] *Ibid.*, p. 723.
[37] *Ibid.*, pp. 712–713.

The corollary is that the sociologist's imagery of social problems is at least "reasonably correct," even, perhaps, where segments of the public strongly object to having their problems defined, or redefined, for them.

This approach to social problems, then, is a rationale for the moral expert in some position to make his expertise heard and felt. It promotes the idea that social problems are somehow technical. Merton suggests that "the kind of social problem that is dominated by social disorganization results from instrumental and technical flaws in the social system. The system comes to operate less efficiently than it realistically might. . . ."[38] If the problems are technical, then it is reasonable to consider the social scientist as a technician and his intervention as untainted by partisan concerns. The difficulty is that the position of the social scientist as technician is highly ambiguous in Merton's approach. It is never clear whether he merely reflects, or helps to shape, those "socially shared standards"; nor is it at all clear just whose standards they are. The implication is that similarly trained social scientists and indeed, all intelligent people, would agree on the *nature* of social problems, if not necessarily on their extent or their remedies. That, of course, is simply not true.

V

Social scientists, then, study social problems from the vantage point of committed people striving to make sense of the society in which they find themselves. There is nothing wrong with that, but it should not be mislabeled "disinterested" inquiry. Indeed, the idea that science must be divorced from social values is a peculiar one; it trivializes and dehumanizes the idea of science. We do not advocate the replacement of a fake "objectivity" with a mindless rejection of scientific standards. But the scientific value of a work of social analysis must lie in the quality of its arguments and its evidence, not in the fact that it springs from the mind of a properly credentialed "expert," claiming a spurious detachment.

In fact, much of the best in social science *is* best precisely because it ignores some of the sillier criteria that are recurrently imposed in "official" definitions of the field. Nowhere is this more true than in the study of social problems. As John Seeley has suggested, the work social scientists actually do in studying social problems is not nearly so sterile and circumscribed as their own definitions of what they are doing suggest. Though they claim merely to "take" their social problems, social scientists actually "make" them. In general, we are all better off for that. But, as Seeley has said, this leaves the social scientist with the "awful responsibility" of becoming a social critic.[39]

[38] *Ibid.*, p. 723.
[39] John R. Seeley, "The Making and Taking of Problems," in *The Americanization of the Unconscious* (New York: Science House, 1967).

Among the responsibilities introduced by this recognition is the requirement that we state with some clarity where our basic sympathies lie. This does not necessarily mean that we must "take sides," as some sociologists have suggested.[40] It does mean that we ought to try to acknowledge the basic values which form the sources of our interest in certain "problems." For the fact is that, as we have seen, many social problems authors adopt and incorporate values and presuppositions which usually remain unacknowledged. Most social problems work focuses on those groups and individuals who have failed to "make it" within the existing social structure: deviants, dropouts, the disaffected and disadvantaged, and not widely or consistently on the institutions which make up that structure. This point has been made before. Although the author of nearly every recent book on social problems describes his work as "sociological" in that he attempts to find social sources for problems, the treatment — and the solution — usually returns to the symptoms: criminals, not the law; mental illness, not the quality of life; the culture of the poor, not the predations of the rich; and so on, through a generally predictable assortment of "problems." The traditional social problems text is a hodgepodge; structural problems like poverty and symptomatic problems like delinquency or mental illness are thrown together indiscriminately, frequently along with collective protest and other responses to structural issues. It all implies that anything that disturbs the routine functioning of society-as-it-is, is a "problem."

But a society is not a conglomeration of disconnected problems; it is a structure of institutions in a particular relationship to each other at a particular time in history. It stands to reason that the special function of a *social* analysis of social problems is to begin here, in a society's institutions, values, and basic processes.

VI

For at least two reasons it can be argued that an institutional or systematic approach to social problems is particularly appropriate for social science. One is practical, even pragmatic, having to do with the division of intellectual labor. If social scientists do not study institutional decay and inadequacy, who will? The question is not trivial; frequently, perhaps especially in the United States, large areas of institutional life have gone unexplored and unexamined. Let us consider two examples: until very recently we knew almost nothing about the police, the courts, and other "social control" institutions; and we know next to nothing about the structure of that phenomenon we loosely call "racism." We have very, very

[40] See Becker, *op. cit.*

few critical analyses of the business system, of the military establishment, and so on. Some of these gaps in knowledge are accidental, but most reflect the historic tendency for American social science to abdicate the function of institutional criticism.

This abdication is reflected in our selection of readings. Many are the work of social scientists; many are not. And there is a pattern; in the sections dealing with the largest, most "established" of institutions, such as the corporation and the military, the balance shifts away from social scientists toward journalists and social critics.

A case can be made, then, that as *social* analysts it is our calling to examine critically the basic institutions and processes of society, and that historically this calling has been seriously neglected.

A second reason for focusing on institutional problems has to do with the values that we feel are appropriate to a democratic society. Democratic conceptions of society have always held that institutions exist to serve man, and that, therefore, they must be accountable to men. Where they fail to meet the tests imposed on them, democratic theory holds that they ought to be changed. Authoritarian governments, religious regimes, and reformatories, among other social systems, hold the opposite: in case of misalignment between individuals or groups and the "system," the individuals or groups are to be changed or otherwise made unproblematic. Somewhere between these conceptions lies the working ideology of conventional social problems theory.

Conventional and democratic conceptions of social problems have different practical consequences for the lives of individuals and the relationship of individuals to established authority. This should be obvious; to focus on the individual or group generates only those conceptual tools which can guide intervention in the lives of individuals, or the culture or attitudes of groups. Such intervention is basically abhorrent to democratic views of the world, for it violates group autonomy and individual integrity. It places the intervener in a position fraught with manipulative and coercive possibilities, a theme taken up and expanded in several of our readings. On the other hand, by concentrating on institutions we make possible the development of theory and explanation of a kind which in turn makes possible strategies of *institutional* change.

All writers on social problems agree that things qualify as "problems" only when it is felt that something can be done about them. And much of the conflict between approaches to social problems can be reduced to differences in their understanding of those which among contemporary conditions are needless impositions of human suffering, and which are fundamental facts basic to social existence, elements of the human condition about which nothing can be done. To speak of something as a "problem" is to bring it out of the realm of the inevitable or the tacitly accepted, take away its "sacred" character, and suggest that it need not be the way it is. To focus on institutions in this way is to open them to public scrutiny and to insist on the responsibility for change. More generally, such an approach holds those in positions of authority, power, and influence accountable for their actions.

In this way, theory connects closely with social policy. It is this connection which guides our selection of articles and supporting material, for we have selected areas of institutional life that are matters not only of public concern but, of public decision-making, of public policy.

Not long ago it was fashionable to say that affluent America no longer had any major political problems; that it had only technical problems.[41] Recent events have surely shattered that rather smug conception. Very nearly the opposite has become true; problems formerly considered wholly technical in nature have become *political* problems, contested public issues. This is especially true of those institutions covered in our Part 2. Police work, medical care, "reform" movements, the welfare establishment, teaching, university research, all are "professional" fields which are coming under increasing public scrutiny and criticism. In short, we are no longer willing to leave these areas to the experts; they are far too important and touch our lives too deeply.

Likewise, the issues in Part 1 are problems of public policy which, however, transcend particular institutions; they are master processes affecting, in one way or another, many institutions at once and constituting basic trends of contemporary American society. Our aim here is to introduce the reader to the systematic aspects of social problems, and to avoid the frequent implication of social problems books that society's problems are unrelated to one another or to the fundamental social processes, and may be dealt with piecemeal.

In approaching social problems in this way, our aim is twofold: to introduce the reader to some problematic aspects of American society about which the traditional social problems book says little or nothing, and to promote a way of looking at society — a critical view — which can be applied to other areas of social life not treated here, and can become a part of the student's continuing intellectual equipment.

[41] An influential book in this tradition is Daniel Bell's *The End of Ideology; On the Exhaustion of Political Ideas in the Fifties* (New York: Free Press, 1962).

PART

SYSTEM-WIDE
PROBLEMS 1

INEQUALITY 1

Poverty is periodically rediscovered in America. The latest rediscovery took place around the beginning of the 1960's and culminated in the war on poverty. This was shocking; it came when many people, including numerous social scientists, had gotten used to celebrating the rapidly approaching end of income disparities in the United States and other western democracies. The belief in diminishing economic inequality served as a major element in a more general argument portraying these countries as having solved the basic political problems accompanying industrialization. Accordingly, such problems as remained were problems of "piecemeal technology."[1]

The American poor were doubtless aware that this celebration was premature. The poor, however, had little voice in public affairs. The fact of continuing poverty had to be "rediscovered" by the better-off to become a matter of "national" concern. When this happened, two conceptions of the meaning and causes of poverty emerged. Both, in general, agreed on the dimensions of the problem; both agreed on the necessity for social action aimed at ameliorating it. Beyond this, the agreement ended.

According to one view, poverty demonstrated the failure of modernization to affect certain segments of the population. Nonetheless, America was still to be considered an

[1] Karl Popper, quoted in Daniel Bell, *The End of Ideology; On the Exhaustion of Political Ideas in the Fifties* (New York: Free Press, 1962), p. 312.

"affluent" society and a forerunner of the relatively smooth social and economic development which might become the pattern for less fortunate nations to follow. Poverty meant that there were underdeveloped sections of the United States that had to be brought up to par with the rest of the country. This could be accomplished through a combination of popular good will and governmental action. The envisoned governmental action took several forms, but generally involved two aspects; piecemeal and minor assaults on the problems of social structure, and fairly major attacks on the culture and habits of the poor. Priorities stemmed from a general satisfaction with the direction of American society, coupled with a distaste for the squalor and moral chaos felt to characterize the condition of poverty.

By the second view, poverty was one aspect of a *system* of maldistribution of income which was not only characteristic of, but integral to, American society. This system had changed very little over the years and showed few signs of changing in the foreseeable future. The poverty of many and the astounding wealth of some were intimately related parts of a whole. Significant change would require a fundamental assault on that whole. Speculations as to the cultural deficiencies of the poor were only a mask for the refusal to confront basic problems of social organization.

Among the earliest books of the 1960's to take this perspective was Gabriel Kolko's *Wealth and Power in America,* first published in 1962. Kolko sought to show not only that there had been no appreciable change in the distribution of income in America since at least the early part of this century, but also that the scope of income inequality was such that it "permeates every aspect of the lives of the American populace — poor and rich alike."[2]

In the selection reprinted here, Kolko argues that, contrary to conventional belief, there has been no trend toward equality of incomes in the United States between 1910 and 1959. Kolko's data for the years up to 1937 are

[2] Gabriel Kolko, *Wealth and Power in America* (New York: Praeger, 1962), p. 111.

controversial,[3] but most studies independently support his conclusions on the stability of income patterns from about 1941 on. Kolko suggests that the phenomenon of postwar affluence may be attributed to the pronounced rise in income shares of the second and third highest income tenths — groups composed largely of managerial and professional people. Finally, Kolko directs our attention to the many sources of "hidden" income available to the corporate wealthy.

The discussion of social sources of disparities between rich and poor continues in Philip Stern's analysis of the failure of our most frequently touted instrument of income redistribution, the graduated income tax. In non-socialist countries, the income tax is often considered the great equalizer, the agency through which a competitive, acquisitive society mitigates its tendency to produce the very rich and the very poor. But, as Stern shows, the very, very rich pay proportionately fewer taxes than those with one tenth the income, and about the same proportion as those with average incomes. Many of the "super-rich" pay no income taxes at all. Through a variety of loopholes, the very rich can hold back billions of dollars of funds, while the rest of us are urged to contribute more and yet more through surtaxes, and while federal programs costing relatively miniscule amounts are scuttled right and left on grounds of extravagance. And taxlessness among the rich is increasing, whereas over two million people living below the poverty line continue to pay their share.

As Stern makes clear, the source of this phenomenon is not mystical; the rich are better organized and, unsurprisingly, better financed. They are therefore able to operate as an enormously effective political pressure group. Perhaps nowhere is the contention that social problems are, at bottom, political problems better shown.

In Jacobs's paper, we are given an analysis of the way the system operates at the other end. An entire specialized

[3] For discussions of these issues, see S. M. Miller and Martin Rein, "Poverty, Inequality, and Policy," in Howard S. Becker, ed., *Social Problems; A Modern Approach* (New York: Wiley, 1967); Ben B. Seligman, Introduction to *Poverty as a Public Issue* (New York: Free Press, 1965).

economic system — the "poverty market" and its agencies — operates to ensure that the poor pay more and receive less. This paper reveals compellingly that the better-off enjoy advantages which are rarely recognized, but which make all the difference between security and insecurity, well-being and anxiety. And on the other side, there is a cumulative, vicious-circle quality to the condition of having very little money whereby poverty becomes a self-perpetuating system. Simply, economic life is very different for the poor, and much more difficult — something often ignored in studies of their culture and aspirations. If the poor are different, it is in the last analysis because they have less money.

The failure of much of the recent concern over poverty to boldly confront this fact is a major concern of Bernard Beck's review of recent writing on poverty. Beck suggests that several ambiguities surround the renewed concern for the poor. Who are the "we" whose idealism is continually appealed to? And when "we" get hold of a certain amount of funds and encouragement, as in the war on poverty, is "our" intervention guided by anything other than a traditional concern for meddling in the lives of the poor, without altering the *system* which routinely generates poverty? Do such enterprises as the war on poverty represent anything more than another, more sophisticated, attempt on "our" part to impose middle class values on the poor? Beck argues that a genuinely serious "war" on poverty will have as its "target population" not the poor themselves, but the respectables; not the habits of the poor, but the inequities of the system. Such an approach would have the supreme advantage of not requiring moral intervention into people's lives; but as Beck suggests pessimistically, "we" may not be prepared for that kind of sacrifice.

GABRIEL KOLKO   *The Unchanging Pattern*
of Inequality

A radically unequal distribution of income has been characteristic of
the American social structure since at least 1910, and despite minor year-
to-year fluctuations in the shares of the income-tenths, no significant trend
toward income equality has appeared. This, in brief, is the deduction that
can be made from a study of the table on page 24.

Throughout the 1950's, the income of the top tenth was larger than the
total for the bottom five income-tenths — about the same relationship as
existed in 1910 and 1918. The income share of the richest tenth has
dropped only slightly, if at all, since 1910. The average percentage of the
national personal income before taxes, received by this group was about
one-eighth less in 1950–59 than in 1910–41, omitting the exceptional years
1921 and 1929. This loss, however, disappears when the 1950–59 figures
are corrected to allow for their exclusion of all forms of income-in-kind
and the very substantial understatement of income by the wealthy, both
of which are consequences of the post-1941 expansion in income taxation.

While the income share of the richest tenth has remained large and virtually constant over the past half century, the two lowest income-tenths
have experienced a sharp decline. In 1910, the combined income shares of
the two poorest income-tenths were about one-quarter that of the richest
tenth; by 1959, their share had dropped to one-seventh. During this same
period, the percentage of the next-lowest tenth also decreased, while the
fourth and fifth from the lowest tenths (the sixth- and seventh-ranking)
neither gained nor lost ground appreciably. Together these five groups,
which constitute the poorer half of the U.S. population, received 27 per
cent of the national personal income in 1910, but only 23 per cent in 1959.
Thus, for the only segments of the population in which a gain could indicate progress toward economic democracy, there has been no increase in
the percentage share of the national income.

The only significant rises in income distribution have occurred in the
second- and third-richest income-tenths. Their combined shares increased
more than one-quarter from 1910 to 1959, and by the end of that period
their combined income share was almost equal to that of the richest tenth.
It should be noted, however, that their gain was made almost entirely

From *Wealth and Power in America* by Gabriel Kolko. Reprinted by permission of
Frederick A. Praeger, Inc. and Thames and Hudson, Ltd.

Percentage of National Personal Income,
Before Taxes, Received by Each Income-Tenth[a]

	Highest tenth	2nd	3rd	4th	5th	6th	7th	8th	9th	Lowest tenth
1910	33.9	12.3	10.2	8.8	8.0	7.0	6.0	5.5	4.9	3.4
1918	34.5	12.9	9.6	8.7	7.7	7.2	6.9	5.7	4.4	2.4
1921	38.2	12.8	10.5	8.9	7.4	6.5	5.9	4.6	3.2	2.0
1929	39.0	12.3	9.8	9.0	7.9	6.5	5.5	4.6	3.6	1.8
1934	33.6	13.1	11.0	9.4	8.2	7.3	6.2	5.3	3.8	2.1
1937	34.4	14.1	11.7	10.1	8.5	7.2	6.0	4.4	2.6	1.0
1941	34.0	16.0	12.0	10.0	9.0	7.0	5.0	4.0	2.0	1.0
1945	29.0	16.0	13.0	11.0	9.0	7.0	6.0	5.0	3.0	1.0
1946	32.0	15.0	12.0	10.0	9.0	7.0	6.0	5.0	3.0	1.0
1947	33.5	14.8	11.7	9.9	8.5	7.1	5.8	4.4	3.1	1.2
1948	30.9	14.7	11.9	10.1	8.8	7.5	6.3	5.0	3.3	1.4
1949	29.8	15.5	12.5	10.6	9.1	7.7	6.2	4.7	3.1	0.8
1950	28.7	15.4	12.7	10.8	9.3	7.8	6.3	4.9	3.2	0.9
1951	30.9	15.0	12.3	10.6	8.9	7.6	6.3	4.7	2.9	0.8
1952	29.5	15.3	12.4	10.6	9.1	7.7	6.4	4.9	3.1	1.0
1953	31.4	14.8	11.9	10.3	8.9	7.6	6.2	4.7	3.0	1.2
1954	29.3	15.3	12.4	10.7	9.1	7.7	6.4	4.8	3.1	1.2
1955	29.7	15.7	12.7	10.8	9.1	7.7	6.1	4.5	2.7	1.0
1956	30.6	15.3	12.3	10.5	9.0	7.6	6.1	4.5	2.8	1.3
1957	29.4	15.5	12.7	10.8	9.2	7.7	6.1	4.5	2.9	1.3
1958	27.1	16.3	13.2	11.0	9.4	7.8	6.2	4.6	3.1	1.3
1959	28.9	15.8	12.7	10.7	9.2	7.8	6.3	4.6	2.9	1.1

[a] "Recipients" for 1910–37 and "spending units" for 1941–59.

Source: Data for 1910–37 are from National Industrial Conference Board, *Studies in Enterprise and Social Progress* (New York: National Industrial Conference Board, 1939), p. 125. Data for 1941–59 were calculated by the Survey Research Center. Figures for 1941–46 are available in rounded form only. Previously unpublished data for 1947–58 are reproduced by permission of the Board of Governors of the Federal Reserve System, and data for 1959 by permission of the Survey Research Center.

during the Depression years of the 1930's. Further, this group is largely made up of persons in occupations such as professionals, small business-men, top clerical workers, and lesser managers, with rising salary or wage incomes and low unemployment, and by no means was in urgent need of a greater share of the national income.

Many recent explanations of rising real and dollar incomes in the lower-income groups since 1939 or 1941, which have been utilized to provide the occurrence of a radical and purportedly permanent income redistribution, ignore the fact that these increases reflect increased em-ployment, not an alteration in the basic distribution structure.

Prior to World War II, it was commonly assumed that the different phases of the business cycle affected the distribution of income — that relative income inequality rose when unemployment rose. However, the relationship between employment trends and income is more important in the study of real income and dollar earnings than in the study of income distribution. During an upward trend in unemployment, the *dollar earnings* of the lowest-income classes decline much more rapidly than those of the other groups, and during an upswing in employment, both the dollar earnings and real income of the lowest-income classes rise much more rapidly than those of the higher-income groups. During full employment, the rate at which the dollar income of the poorer classes increases generally keeps pace with the rate of rise for the highest classes (although occasionally falling slightly behind — as from 1948 to the early 1950's).[1]

However, even the pre-1941 data show that once common generalizations on the correlation between employment trends and income distribution did not always hold true. The income share of the highest tenth increased sharply in 1929, during a period of only moderately high employment. More important, even in the period of comparative full employment since 1941, the income shares of the poorer half of the nation have either declined or remained stable.

EXPENSE ACCOUNTS — INCOME-IN-KIND
FOR CORPORATE EXECUTIVES

Material on money income must be supplemented by data on distribution of income-in-kind among income classes to arrive at more nearly accurate figures for total income and income inequality.

Extensive data show that in 1941 the total dollar value of income-in-kind for urban families was relatively insignificant, ranging from $155 for families earning less than $500, to $457 for those earning more than $10,000. For farm families, income-in-kind ranged in value from $417 for those earning less than $500, to $719 for those earning more than $3,000. Each tenth of farm consumer-units received roughly the same value in home-produced food, but the richest third received about one-half the rental value in housing.[2] Thus, except for those with extremely small earn-

---

[1] Detailed data on this trend can be found in Selma Goldsmith, *et al.*, "Size Distribution of Income Since the Mid-Thirties," *Review of Economics and Statistics*, February, 1954, pp. 1–32; Jesse Burkhead. "Living Standards and Productivity," *Review of Economics and Statistics*, August, 1951, p. 247; *Monthly Labor Review*, September, 1942, p. 421.

[2] Bureau of Labor Statistics, *Family Spending and Saving in Wartime* (Washington, D.C.: Government Printing Office, 1945), Bulletin No. 822, p. 94; and Nathan M. Koffsky and Jeanne E. Lear, "Size Distribution of Farm Operators' Income in 1946," *Studies in Income and Wealth* (New York: National Bureau of Economic Research, 1951), XIII, 243. In 1935–36, the distribution of income-in-kind among the nation's families was about equal for food; but for housing it was very much greater among the rich. See National Resources Committee, *Consumer Expenditures in the United States* (Washington, D.C.: Government Printing Office, 1939), p. 79.

ings, income-in-kind was only a minor factor in farm incomes in 1941.

In the ensuing twenty years, the value of home-grown food has been declining consistently for the farmer, from about one-fifth of his cash income in 1941, to about one-tenth in the early postwar period. The farmer purchased 28 per cent of his total food consumption in 1923; he purchased 60 per cent in 1955. The farm population has declined radically since World War II, and its share of the national disposable income since 1945 dropped by more than half, to 3.7 per cent in 1956; and in 1957 farm food- and fuel-in-kind was equal to only 0.5 per cent of the national personal income. Clearly, the role of farm income-in-kind in the national income distribution is now of no great importance.[3]

Among urban consumers in the lowest tenths, income-in-kind has been mainly relief goods, and these have become inconsequential with the advent of full — if sporadically so — employment.

Meanwhile, as income-in-kind declined in value for farm and low-income families, it gained new prominence in the highest income-tenth, and especially the top 5 per cent of the spending units. Here it takes the form of the expense account and other executive benefits. A by-product of the steeper Federal personal and corporate tax rates instituted in 1941, the expense account is now an acknowledged form of executive remuneration. In 1959, a Harvard Business School study revealed that two-thirds of corporate executives regarded their expense accounts as tax-free compensation.

Legally, a corporation can deduct as expenses only bills incurred in the "ordinary and necessary" course of business, but the fact that a corporation in the top tax bracket is only 48 cents out of pocket for every dollar it deducts from its Federal tax bill has led to some broad interpretations of business costs. Especially at the extremes, in closely owned or very widely diffused corporations, extravagant use has been made of income-in-kind for management. The *Wall Street Journal* frequently mentions such items as $300-a-day hotel suites, $10,000-to-$25,000 parties, executive penthouses with marble walls and gold faucets. According to one *Wall Street Journal* report: "Hidden hunting lodges are one of the 'fringe benefits' awaiting officials who succeed in working their way up to the executive suite of a good many U.S. corporations. Other impressive prizes: sharing use of yachts, private planes and railroad cars, jaunts to exotic watering places and spectacular soirées — all paid for by the corporation. . . . Companies maintaining private retreats, planes and other facilities for fun or luxurious traveling generally report they are necessary to the conduct of their business. . . . This is the prime reason for some companies maintaining such facilities, though perhaps not for others. Even in the

[3] Department of Agriculture, *1957 Agricultural Outlook Charts* (Washington, D.C.: Government Printing Office, 1956), p. 30.

former case, executives generally manage to get considerable enjoyment from their firms' luxury properties. . . . In this way, a good many executives whose fortune-building efforts are impaired by today's high taxes still are enjoying the frills enjoyed by the Mellons, Morgans and Baruchs."[4]

Company-provided luxuries are obvious indicators of a man's position in the hierarchy. For the top corporate elite, they generally include a company car, a gas credit card, vacations, excellent medical care, country-club memberships, dining and entertainment, and the cash difference between expense allowances and actual expenditures. Lesser corporate personnel receive lesser benefits, according to their rank.

In 1954, 37 per cent of the Cadillacs registered in Manhattan and 20 per cent of those registered in Philadelphia were in the names of businesses. Some 80 per cent of the check totals of the most expensive restaurants and 30 to 40 per cent of Broadway theater tickets are covered by expense accounts. Most of the items charged to Diners' Club, American Express, and other luxury credit-card clubs by members, who numbered well over a million in 1958, are paid for by businesses.[5]

One-half of the executives in small companies and one-third of those in large companies are reimbursed for their expenses in social clubs and organizations. More than one-half of the executives in small firms and more than one-quarter of those in large companies are provided with private automobiles. One-fifth of the large corporations have their own country clubs and resorts for their executives.

Gifts received by executives — particularly those influential in purchasing — from personnel in other corporations are another type of income-in-kind. For Christmas, 1959, such giving accounted for $300 million — all tax deductible as business expenses.

Since nearly two-fifths of the top executives do not have to account to anyone for their expenses, and more than three-fifths are given no yardsticks to limit themselves, it is possible for executives to treat themselves to unusual indulgences, and from time to time some of these are revealed to the public — often in the form of advice on expense-account opportunities as suggested in the pages of business publications. One corporation president spent $17,000 of company funds on an African safari; another charged to business expenses $65,000 in jewelry, $22,000 in liquor, $35,000 in night-club tabs, $25,000 in gifts, and $16,000 in boat outlays.

[4] *Wall Street Journal,* March 18, 1958, p. 1; also p. 1 on the following dates: October 29, November 11 and 13, 1957; February 14, and 21, March 13 and 18, 1958.
[5] William H. Whyte, Jr., "The Cadillac Phenomenon," *Fortune,* February, 1955, pp. 106–11; "Expense Accounts: A $5 Billion Tax Deduction, and Growing," *U.S. News & World Report,* August 16, 1957, pp. 83–88; Ernest Havemann, "The Expense Account Aristocracy," *Life,* March 9, 1953, pp. 140–42; Harvey S. Berman, "He's on an Expense Account," *Challenge,* March, 1956, pp. 55–58. For credit cards, see Robert Bendiner, "Credit Cards: The Thirty-Day Tycoons," *The Reporter,* February 5, 1959, pp. 26–30.

In scope and value, the income-in-kind of the rich presents a sharp contrast to the surplus flour, corn meal, rice, and butter provided as relief goods to the poor.[6]

An unofficial Treasury Department estimate in August, 1957, placed the annual total for corporate expense-account outlays at more than $5 billion, and possibly as high as $10 billion.[7] Certainly a portion of this total was in reality income-in-kind received by members of the top income-tenth. If only one-third of this amount is considered income-in-kind for the top tenth, it would add at least 1 percentage point to this group's share of the national income in 1956.

Although existing statistics do not allow us to calculate precisely the percentage of total expense-account outlays that represent personal income-in-kind, they are sufficient to indicate that income-in-kind was an item of major consequence to the share of the top income-tenth, especially to the style of living enjoyed by many of the richest members of the economic elite.

EVASIONS AND ERRORS: $30 BILLION-PLUS

The existing data on income distribution fail to account for a significant proportion of money income because of underreporting on tax returns and nonreporting to interviewers. Since automatic payroll deductions withhold the amount of money due for Federal income taxes, persons wholly dependent on wages or salary for their incomes — and this includes the vast majority of urban low- and middle-income earners — have little reason to underreport their incomes to data collectors. Whatever payroll earnings are underreported or nonreported are probably to be found in very small companies where executives or owners are in a position to alter their required earnings statements.

However, professionals, businessmen, and others receiving cash payments for their services are in an especially advantageous position to underreport their income on tax returns. Roughly one-half of unreported entrepreneurial income represented farm income, the better part of which probably went to low-income earners.[8] The unreported half going to

---

[6] "Expense Accounts," *Harvard Business Review*, March–April, 1960, pp. 16, 172; Randolph Paul, *Taxation in the United States* (Boston: Little, Brown & Co., 1954), p. 618; *U.S. News & World Report*, August 16, 1957, p. 87; also "Expense Account Scandal," *ibid.*, January 25, 1960, pp. 50–56.

[7] *Ibid.*, August 16, 1957, p. 83; and V. Henry Rothschild and Rudolf Sobernheim, "Expense Accounts for Executives," *Yale Law Journal*, July, 1958.

[8] See C. Harry Kahn, "Entrepreneurial Income," *38th Annual Report, National Bureau of Economic Research, 1958*, pp. 84–85. On the other hand, Frederick D. Stocker and John C. Ellickson, "How Fully Do Farmers Report Their Incomes?" *National Tax Journal*, June, 1959, pp. 116–26, claim that tax evasion by farmers in 1952 was only 18 per cent of their income, 16 per cent in 1953, and 13 per cent in 1955

businessmen and professionals probably went to those already earning enough to underreport their incomes without arousing the suspicion of tax auditors. The result is ultimately indicative of an understatement of income by the upper tenths in tax and other statistics.

Refusal to report income data to interviewers also leads to an understating of income by the highest groups. Non-reporting is almost exclusively confined to the upper brackets. A 1941 Bureau of Labor Statistics study found that "the non-reporting rate tended to be higher in blocks with higher rent levels and with larger proportions of families at upper-income levels, ranging from about 1 per cent at the under $1,000 level to 35 per cent at the $10,000 and over level."[9]

Nondeclaration of income to avoid taxes is illegal, but it is so widespread that no study of income distribution can ignore it. Between 1950 and 1953, the number of Federal income-tax returns reporting high incomes *declined,* a fact that the National Bureau of Economic Research, in view of "the almost certain increase in upper bracket salaries," found "puzzling" and meriting "close investigation."[10]

In 1957, only 91 per cent of the national personal money income was reported on individual income-tax returns, somewhat more than the 86 per cent for 1944–46. The missing sum of 1957 — $27.7 billion — comprised 3 per cent ($7.1 billion) of wages and salaries paid, 14 per cent ($1.6 billion) of distributed dividends, 58 per cent ($5.5 billion) of interest, and 27 per cent ($10.8 billion) of entrepreneurial income — the income of nonsalaried professionals, unincorporated businesses, and farmers.[11] About the same amount of personal income is unreported in Census and Survey Research Center data. Obviously, the omission of income of this magnitude — especially if a large segment of it belongs in any single income-tenth — could produce a crucial distortion in the resulting income-distribution figures.

— or no larger than for most occupational classes. Data given in C. Harry Kahn, "Coverage of Entrepreneurial Income on Federal Tax Returns" in U.S. House of Representatives, Committee on Ways and Means, *Tax Revision Compendium,* 86th Cong., 1st Sess. (Washington, D.C.: Government Printing Office, 1959), pp. 11, 1449, show that 56 per cent of the undeclared entrepreneurial income in 1957 was accounted for by the business and professional classes.

[9] Robert Wasson, Abner Hurwitz, and Irving Schweiger, "Field Surveys of Consumer Income — An Appraisal," *Studies in Income and Wealth,* XIII, 518.

[10] National Bureau of Economic Research, *The National Economic Accounts of the United States* (Washington, D.C.: Government Printing Office, 1958), p. 110.

[11] Daniel M. Holland and C. Harry Kahn, "Comparison of Personal and Taxable Income," in U.S. Senate, Joint Committee on the Economic Report, *Federal Tax Policy for Economic Growth and Stability,* 84th Cong., 1st Sess. (Washington, D.C.: Government Printing Office, 1955), p. 320; Goldsmith, "Appraisal of Basic Data . . . ," *op. cit.,* p. 302; Daniel M. Holland, "Unreporting of Dividends and Interest on Tax Returns," *Tax Revision Compendium,* II, 1399, 1403, 1418; Kahn, "Coverage of Entrepreneurial Income on Federal Tax Returns," *ibid.,* II, 1439–61.

In 1952, spending units earning more than $10,000 owned more than 80 per cent of the publicly held stock. So it is highly probable that spending in the top tenth — in that year, those earning more than $7,090 — received most of the unreported dividend income.[12] The Bureau of Internal Revenue's sample audit of 1948 tax returns showed that those reporting $25,000-plus in income accounted for 7.2 per cent of all returns with dividend errors and 38.4 per cent of the dollar value of all errors, and that those reporting $7,000-plus in income accounted for 40.7 per cent of all returns with dividend errors and 73.6 per cent of the dollar value of all errors.[13] Most interest-bearing savings, bonds, notes, etc., are owned by the top income-tenth, and thus a large segment of undeclared income in this category must be allocated to the economic elite. The 1948 tax audit found 52.6 per cent of the dollar value of interest errors in the returns for the $7,000-plus bracket, the top income-tenth.[14]

A good part of the existing income-distribution statistics fails to account for income earned in the corporate sector of the economy and — quite legally — not distributed to the owners of stock because of their desire to avoid high tax rates. But any nondistribution of corporate profits directly affects the income of the top income-tenth — especially of that small group within it that, as I will later show in detail, owns the vast bulk of stock. The relative importance of dividends grows with income, and above the $100,000 level, dividends are substantially larger than salary or wages. Since tax avoidance has become a primary concern of the highest income classes, especially since 1941, corporations increasingly retain dividends instead of distributing them. As Harvard economist William Crum has put it, "A group of wealthy directors owning stock in a closely held corporation may vote to retain earnings not so much because of the needs of the business as on account of the large surtaxes for which they would be personally liable were these earnings disbursed."[15] In 1923–29, corporations withheld 27 per cent of their net profits; in 1946–59 the figure was 51 per cent.[16] Had 1946–59 corporate profits been distributed

[12] George Katona, et al., "Stock Ownership Among American Families," *Michigan Business Review,* January, 1953, p. 14.

[13] Calculated from data in Bureau of Internal Revenue, *The Audit Control Program: A Summary of Preliminary Results* (Washington, D.C.: Government Printing Office, 1951), p. 20. Holland, "Unreporting of Dividends and Interest . . . ," *op. cit.,* p. 1415, claims that the $7,000-plus returns accounted for 66 per cent of the missing dividends and 38 per cent of the interest.

[14] Bureau of Internal Revenue, *op. cit.,* p. 21. Lower-income returns generally report most of their interest receipts. See Lawrence H. Seltzer, *Interest as a Source of Personal Income and Tax Revenue* (New York: National Bureau of Economic Research, 1955), Occasional Paper 51, pp. 1257–58.

[15] William Crum, et al., *Fiscal Planning for Total War* (New York National Bureau of Economic Research, 1942), p. 278.

[16] Lawrence H. Seltzer, *The Nature and Tax Treatment of Capital Gains and Losses* (New York: National Bureau of Economic Research, 1951), p. 221; data for 1946–59 from *Economic Report of the President — 1960,* p. 220.

at the 1923–29 rate, an average of $4.7 billion more in dividends would have been paid out annually to individuals, nearly all of them in the top income-tenth.

In this way, the economic elite can spread their dividend incomes evenly during fluctuations in the business cycle. Or they can increase the market value of their stock; then, if they sell it in the future, they will pay taxes on their profits at the much lower capital-gains rate. Corporations themselves have furthered this policy of personal tax avoidance since 1941 by sharply increased understatement and nonreporting of profits, accomplished by such devices as charging capital expenditures to current income. Thus the corporations represent vast income reserves for the economic elite.[17]

If 1950 corporate profits had been distributed at the 1923–29 rate, the top income-tenth would have received 32 per cent rather than 29 per cent of the personal income. For 1952, they would have received 30 per cent rather than 29 per cent. In any postwar year, profits undistributed after allowing for a reasonable rate of corporate savings and self-financing would have added 1 to 4 percentage points to the share of the richest tenth. The value of corporate expense-account income-in-kind would have added at least 1 percentage point. Undeclared income, very conservatively assigning only one-third to one-half of it to the top tenth, would have added an additional 3 to 5 percentage points. Thus in 1952, for example, the top income-tenth actually accounted for at least 34 per cent of all personal income rather than 29 per cent. . . .

[17] *Montgomery's Federal Taxes* (35th ed.; New York: The Ronald Press Company, 1954), Part 5, p. 37. For corporate tax evasion, see Raymond W. Goldsmith. *A Study of Saving in the United States* (Princeton, N.J.: Princeton University Press, 1955). I, 969, II, 549–50; and William F. Hellmuth, Jr., "The Corporate Income Tax Base," *Tax Revision Compendium*, I, 283–316.

PHILIP M. STERN   *How 381*
                          Super-Rich Americans
                  Managed Not to Pay a Cent
                          in Taxes Last Year

There are, in this land, some 381 rich or super-rich Americans who can
look back upon April 15, 1968, with satisfaction, if not smugness — and
who are probably facing this Tuesday's midnight tax deadline with near
or total equanimity. The reason: even though each had an income in excess of $100,000, not one of the 381 paid a penny of Federal income tax
last April. Indeed, 21 of them had incomes of more than $1-million in
1967 but contrived to pass the 1968 deadline wholly unscathed. And they
are likely to have equal success this year.

In 1966, four lucky Americans, each of whom drew an income in excess
of $5-million, clearly escaped taxation. Even that achievement was
dwarfed by the gentleman who a few years ago enjoyed an income of
more than $20-million and shared not a penny of it with Internal Revenue.

Such tax avoidance exploits are dramatically on the rise. In just 12
years' time, taxlessness among those with incomes of more than $1-million
has increased five-fold; for those with incomes greater than $200,000,
there has been a seven-fold increase — far outstripping the growth in the
number of people in each category.

Some of these facts were disclosed to Congress last January by outgoing
Treasury Secretary Joseph Barr, when he issued his now-famous warning
of a "taxpayers' revolt" if such tax avoidance is permitted to continue.
Barr's revelation has not been kindly received by the incoming Administration, one of whose tax officials has denounced it as "inflammatory" and
"unprofessional." The existence of tax-free millionaires and multimillionaires, this official observed, is "not necessarily meaningful."

Judging from the public response evoked by Barr's statement (20 times
as many pro-tax-reform letters received by the Treasury Department this
February as compared with last), the issue of taxlessness among the hy-
peraffluent is of considerable interest to Americans of far more modest
means. That includes 2.2 million who live below the official "poverty line"

($2,200 for a married couple), and yet pay some taxes, and those in the $7,000 to $20,000 income range. As Barr noted, these 35 million taxpayers pay half of all the individual income taxes the Treasury receives, and their taxes are generally based on the "fully ordinary rates" found on page 11 of the Form 1040 instructions.

That rate schedule, which calls for paying increasingly stiff rates as income rises, leaves the inescapable impression that the richer a person is, the greater the share of his income goes to the U.S. Treasury. But in the economic stratosphere, the actuality is strikingly different. According to Government figures for recent years, the facts are that —

1. More than a thousand taxpayers with incomes over $200,000 paid the same proportion of their total income in taxes as did the typical person in the $15,000–$20,000 group.

2. The bulk of taxpayers in the $500,000 to $1-million income group paid as small a proportion of their incomes in taxes as did most taxpayers with average incomes only one-twentieth as great (i.e., those in the $20,000 to $50,000 category).

3. The topmost income group — those with incomes of more than $5-million a year — paid only half as much tax, proportionately, as those with one-tenth as much income.

As such figures indicate, the supposedly "inflammatory" Mr. Barr was actually telling only part of the story of the tax avoidance success of the very rich. The official statistics he used make no mention, for example, of the huge amounts of income which the wealthy are permitted, in computing their taxes, to treat as if nonexistent. Most conspicuously, half of all "capital gains" (profits from the sale of property — stocks, real estate, etc.) may be entirely ignored for tax purposes.[1] For the super-rich, this brings immense comfort. Among those listed as having incomes over $5-million, average income was $9-million, and two-thirds of that sum was in capital gains. Thus, on the average, $3-million per taxpayer was entirely outside the reach of the tax collector. All told, about $13-billion is excluded from taxable income annually in this manner, at a yearly cost of $4.5-billion. As if this were not a sufficiently generous tax treatment of capital gains, the law permits total escape from the gains tax on stocks held until death and passed on to one's heirs. (At least $15-billion escapes the gains tax in this manner each year, depriving the Treasury of about $2.5-billion in revenue.)

[1] The other half is taxed at rates no higher than 50 per cent. Thus, no matter how great a person's other income, or how stupendous his capital gains, the tax on those gains is never more than 25 per cent (50 per cent of half the gain) — about the same top rate as a family with a taxable income of around $12,000. This is in acute disharmony with the "ability to pay" principle that supposedly underlies the American graduated income tax.

In addition to the capital-gains exclusion, interest from state and local bonds, doesn't even have to be reported on tax returns — a fact that put the late Mrs. Horace Dodge, owner of $56-million worth of such bonds, in a position to enjoy more than $1.5-million of this income without even filing a return.

Moreover, Secretary Barr spoke only of the wholly untaxed multimillionaires, omitting the many others who, while paying some taxes, manage to pay far less than is called for under the regular rate schedule. For example, that schedule seems to call for those with incomes of $1-million and more to pay about 65 per cent of that income in taxes, yet more than two-thirds of the multimillionaires in that group contrive to pay less than 30 per cent, for a tax saving of $350,000 on each million dollars of income.

Chairman Wilbur Mills of the taxwriting House Ways and Means Committee has said he intends to have his group look into the tax returns of those agile persons with wholly untaxed incomes of more than $200,000, to see how they manage their escape. But actually the get-away routes are far from secret, having been written into the public tax laws by the predecessors of the Mills group. Moreover, the specific tax avoidance maneuvers employed by actual taxpayers (as taken from their returns) have recently been published in a Treasury Department study, from which the following cases of Messrs. A through K have been taken.

For a man not gainfully employed (no wages or salaries reported), Mr. A fared handsomely, with an income of just under $11-million, almost all of it from dividends (indicating stock holdings of about $300-million). Not a penny of this impressive income went to the U.S. Treasury because of the "unlimited charitable deduction." Mr. A is one of about 70 Americans who have earned an exemption from the usual 30 per cent ceiling on charitable deductions. He did so by giving to charity for eight years the equivalent of 90 per cent of his taxable income.[2] Having won the right to an unlimited charitable deduction, Mr. A was able to cancel out nearly all of his taxable income in one stroke: the gift to charity (quite likely the A Family Foundation) of stock valued at $10.5-million. So great was Mr. A's wealth, however, that this act of prodigious generosity was barely noticeable; it represented only 3 per cent of his total holdings; in an average year, stock market rises would more than make up the gift, so that Mr. A would end the year richer than ever.

Had Mr. A been subject to the ordinary charitable deduction ceiling of 30 per cent, he would have had to pay a tax of about $5-million. But the unlimited charitable deduction, plus a few hundred thousand of other

---

[2] This seemingly difficult feat can be accomplished with a puny gift to charity in the case of an oil tycoon, for example, who uses some special deductions to reduce his taxable income to negligible proportions.

deductions (for state and local taxes, investment management fees, etc.) reduced his taxable income to zero and spared him that annoyance.

Actually, Mr. A's total tax saving was even greater, for the stock he donated had risen greatly in value since he had inherited it from father or grandfather. If he had sold the stock and given cash to charity, he would have had to pay a $2-million capital gains tax on the $8-million increase in the stock's value. But the tax laws are generous: they give him credit for the increase, but forgive him the tax on it.

At the end of the whole transaction, Mr. A's net outlay is only $3.5-million (the $10.5-million gift minus the two-part tax saving of $7-million). And he has the full enjoyment of the $5-million in cold, here-and-now cash spending money that otherwise would have gone to the United States Treasury.

The untaxed increase in the value of gifts to charity sometimes reaches impressive proportions. One donor got a $201,000 deduction for stock worth just $181 when he received it; another received a deduction of $21.6-million, up from $467,000. His total tax saving (or added "take home pay," if one can put it that way): $16-million — $11-million in the income tax he wholly avoided plus an added $5-million in the forgiven capital gains tax, which he would have had to pay if he had sold the stock. The same benefits would have been available if Mr. A's donation had been in the form of a presciently purchased painting that had skyrocketed in value. And if the gift had consisted of nonvoting stock in the family-held company (as is sometimes the case), Mr. A's generosity would not even have diluted his control of the firm.

While Mr. A cleanly avoided all taxes, Mr. G was less tidy about canceling out his $1,284,718 of income and suffered the indignity of paying $383 in taxes — about three-hundredths of 1 per cent of his total income. (By contrast, the typical unmarried individual earning $1,700 would pay 7 per cent of his income in taxes.)

Almost all of Mr. G's income was in those familiar capital gains, half of which can legally be ignored for tax purposes. Thus his deduction-finding task was reduced by some $600,000. Evidently the charitable deduction had little appeal to Mr. G: of his $1,284,000 income, only $463 went to charity. Instead, this credit-worthy individual found no difficulty in off-setting most of that $600,000 by borrowing about $10-million, on which the interest payments (all deductible) came to $588,000. But for this deduction, Mr. G would have had to pay a tax on his $600,000 taxable income of about 65 cents on the dollar. Thus, in a sense, the Treasury was underwriting 65 per cent of his borrowing costs; his net out-of-pocket outlay (taking this tax saving into account) was therefore only 35 cents on the dollar. Moreover, Congress, often so parsimonious with Government funds, has sanctioned a profligate use of the Treasury in cases such as this, for there is nothing in the tax laws to prevent Mr. G from taking his $10-million of borrowings, the interest on which is partially financed by the Government, and investing them in such a way as to generate even more tax-favored income, causing further incursions on the Treasury.

He might, for example, secure a 100 per cent loan on a new $10-million building and turn it into what is aptly called a tax "shelter." Ignoring the fact that he does not have a penny of his own in the building, and according him all the benefits of a full cash owner, the law permits Mr. G to assume, for tax purposes, that the building is wearing out (depreciating) much faster in the early years of its life than in its later years. This fiction, sometimes called a fast tax write-off, produces huge depreciation deductions ($800,000 in the first year, in this case), far exceeding the building's rental income and leaving generous excess deductions to "shelter," or offset, income Mr. G derives from other sources.

The use of that very escape route brought great tax joy to Mr. J who, despite a total income of $1,433,000, was able with a straight face to tell the Treasury that his income for tax purposes was a *minus* $3,000. His real estate "losses" of $864,000 exceeded his taxable income, and he was allowed to apply that $3,000 "loss" to the reduction of his taxable income in other years. Nor is the tax-free Mr. J unique. The Treasury Department, on studying 13 wealthy real estate operators, found that nine of them had succeeded in reducing their taxes to zero and two others to less than $25.

The tax returns of these multimillionaire tycoons would suggest they are atrocious businessmen, since their mammoth investments in motels and shopping centers appear consistently to produce devastating "losses." The same impression may be derived from the returns of the so-called "gentleman farmers" whose business sense seems only to fail them when they turn to farming. Those in the $100,000-to-$1-million income group who invested in nonfarm ventures showed profits outweighing losses by a 5-to-1 ratio. But those in that same, supposedly sophisticated income group who went into farm ventures reported "losses" outweighing profits by a 3-to-1 margin.

These "losses" are incurred by top-bracket city folk (stock brokers are replacing show business luminaries as the most avid "gentleman farmers") who invest in, say, herds of breeding cattle or in citrus groves. While the herd or grove is maturing, there is no income, but lots of fully deductible expenses, creating a protective "shelter" for nonfarm income earned in Hollywood or on Wall Street. And here again, the bulk of these expenses are in "tax dollars" which would otherwise have gone to the Treasury. In the case of Mr. K, whose seemingly egregious business sense led him to incur a farm "loss" on the year of $450,000, the shelter was sufficient to keep the tax collector from laying a finger on his $738,203 of income. (As usual, the exclusion of a quarter of a million dollars of capital gains greatly facilitated the tax-avoidance feat.)

Co-beneficiaries of the special farm tax provision are the promoters and farm "managers" who take care of the herd or grove for a fee (tax deductible, of course, to the investor) and who unabashedly encourage high-bracket Wall Street cowboys to take full advantage of the U.S. Treasury for their own enrichment. "Citrus Tax Angles," a publication emanating from a promotion group in Redlands, Calif., tells the prospective investor that, after two years of tax saving, he "more than recaptures" his original outlay, "and he still has title to appreciating real estate [the citrus grove]. Think of it — tax dollars were used to purchase the property and are the only dollars invested."

Partly out of concern that such tax blandishments are artificially boosting farm land prices, the Treasury Department and some rural Congressmen have proposed a $15,000 limit on farm "loss" deductions by city folk, a suggestion branded by retired Brig. Gen. H. L. Oppenheimer, the most celebrated promoter of tax-loss cattle breeding, as "principally motivated by a 'soak-the-rich' philosophy and the socialistic desire to bring all take-home incomes down to the same level."

Sometimes, beneath the land where tax-saving cattle graze, there lies oil. Such, apparently, was the case with Mr. I, who combined a spectacular lack of success in farming (incurring a "loss" of some $828,000) with an $865,000 special oil deduction ("percentage depletion") and was thus able to protect every penny of his $1,313,000 net income from the hands of the tax collector. Under the depletion law, 27½ per cent of the income from an oil well is not taxable.

In addition to his depletion allowance, Mr. I enjoyed a $125,000 deduction for "intangible drilling expenses," a tax prerequisite less well known than percentage depletion but, to many oil investors, far more useful. Unlike the ordinary capital investment — say, in a machine — which is deducted gradually over the useful life of the machine, most of the cost of drilling an oil well can be deducted immediately. This privilege accounts for the recent dramatic growth of what Barron's Magazine has termed "a tax-sheltered venture . . . enjoying mounting popularity on Wall Street: the oil-drilling participation fund." Such funds are apparently tailored to investors more interested in tax savings than oil discovery, since they usually involve drilling in unproven, "wild-cat" areas where the odds against finding oil are something like 14 to 1.

The intangible drilling deduction is considered especially handy by those oil tycoons with an apparent aversion (or phobia) to paying any Federal income taxes — ever. One oil man has given standing instructions to his tax attorney to "drill up" any potentially taxable income that may loom on his financial horizon. Others are said to guide their drilling deci-

sions with monthly warnings from computers as to income needing "shelter" from Internal Revenue. One oil magnate managed to avoid paying
any taxes over an entire 12-year period, during which he sold at least $50-
million worth of oil.

Such consistent avoiders of taxation must be the object of special envy
and resentment from those of modest incomes who are deeply opposed to
the Vietnam war, and who long to withhold part of all of their taxes as a
protest of conscience. But while they are barred from doing so by the
danger of heavy fine or imprisonment, 381 of the super-rich were able
to achieve the same result last year, wholly within the law.

One proposal for ending total tax avoidance, favored by the late Robert
Kennedy and espoused by officials of the outgoing Johnson Administration, would impose a minimum tax on the well-to-do, applicable to their
total income, that total to include the now-excluded half of capital gains,
state and local bond interest, the special oil-depletion deductions and
the presently untaxed increase in the value of gifts to charity.

The suggestion has been criticized from all sides. It is strongly opposed
by the new Nixon team in the Treasury Department on the ground that
it would not accomplish the objective of taxing all wealthy persons. The
Nixon tax experts are said to be looking for better ways of ending inequities in the tax system.

The minimum-tax idea as proposed by the Treasury also draws criticism from tax reformers. Former Internal Revenue Commissioner Morti-
mer Caplin points out that it leaves two escape routes unaffected — the
"intangible" oil deduction and the "fast writeoff" on buildings. Unless
these routes are closed, Caplin says, there might still be 21 untaxed multimillionaires.

More generally, tax reform purists do not like the blanket approach embodied in the proposal; they are critical of the Treasury's failure to tackle
head-on the specific loopholes. Those who had high hopes in 1961, when
the leading exponent of tax reform, Harvard Law Professor Stanley Surrey,
took over the Treasury's tax affairs, are puzzled as to why, after eight years
of Surrey's administration, the Treasury remains silent on, or is still "studying" these long-standing, costly, well-known favors.

Surrey did bequeath his successors a study highlighting one often-over-
looked aspect of tax perferences. Because the loopholes permit the leak-
age of revenue that would otherwise come into the Treasury, they are
just as expensive and contribute just as much to budget deficits, as do
conventional spending programs for which Congress votes the funds each
year. For example, were it not for the special tax provisions for oil and
gas, the Treasury would net an added $1.6-billion in revenues annually.
In this sense, says Surrey, each tax loophole is really a "tax expenditure,"
but it is hidden (it doesn't show up in the President's budget), and

neither the President nor the Congress makes any annual judgment as to its benefits or how it fits into current national priorities.

This has great importance now, when President Nixon is pressing his resistant Cabinet departments to reduce rather than increase the spending levels proposed by their Democratic predecessors. If the oil and gas exploration "subsidy" were an appropriated item, as are the farm subsidies that are part of the Agriculture Department budget, the $1.6-billion would presumably be charged to the budget of the Government department concerned with natural resource development, the Interior Department, and Interior Secretary Hickel would be examining it critically against other natural resource programs as he tries to comply with the President's budget-cutting edict. But because the oil subsidy is a hidden "tax expenditure," it is immune from such scrutiny — even though it has remained unchanged for over 40 years (during which circumstances and technology have altered greatly) and even though a recently released study states that the $1.6-billion "expenditure" is netting the nation only about $150-million in added oil reserves.

The same is true of the "fast tax writeoffs" for real estate, which now represent an annual "tax expenditure" of $750-million — only $50-million of which is spent on the most urgent building need, low-cost housing.

All told, the Surrey study states, such hidden "tax expenditures" now total a minimum of $60-billion a year — one-third the size of the conventional budget. Yet they remain seemingly immune from both Presidential and Congressional budget-cutting impulses while Congressionally appropriated programs such as the Job Corps (reportedly destined for a $120-million cut) remain exposed and vulnerable.

Mr. Nixon and his advisers seem intent on even greater use of "tax expenditures," via tax incentives to stimulate private participation in job training and low-cost housing. These, rather than any major reform program, will receive the Administration's attention this year.

Loophole-closing has never been a favored political pastime in America. Congress has behaved as though it had a phobia against it and to date has proved adept only at opening the loopholes wider and for more and more groups. Even Presidents, who have a national constituency and a national responsibility, have shown little feel for curbing tax avoidance. Modest efforts were made by F.D.R. in the thirties (after the disclosure that many owners of large yachts were paying no taxes), Harry Truman in 1950 and John F. Kennedy in 1961 and 1963. But in all cases, these Presidents marched up Capitol Hill and then marched down again, having failed to close any basic loophole.

Presidential skittishness about facing the tax-reform issue reached a notable height in the closing days of President Johnson's term. Under Congressional mandate to propose a loophole-closing program and with nothing political but his name in history to worry about, Mr. Johnson not only refused to endorse the Treasury Department's reform proposals but even declined to allow them to be made public before he had left office—even though those proposals, as noted, sidestepped virtually every tax favor of any consequence. When the Treasury "package" was reluctantly made public by Congress, it was quickly disavowed by the new Treasury officials of the Nixon Administration, who have indicated they will look for their own ways to foster tax equity and are said to be floundering for a course of action as they begin to sense the muscle of the various pressure groups involved.

Why has tax reform fared so abysmally? The answer boils down to this simple fact: those who benefit from a given tax favor are generally cohesive, well organized, superbly financed and endowed with all the energy and zeal that the threat of losing tens, if not hundreds, of millions of dollars can provide. By contrast, those who favor closing a given loophole are usually diffuse, unorganized, largely inarticulate — and perhaps fearful of pressing too hard for reforms lest Congress begin to frown on their own particular tax preferences. The loophole-closing efforts of most labor unions (whose members enjoy tax-free treatment of billions in medical, pension and other fringe benefits) have been less than zealous, although logically the unions should be the leading opponents of tax favors to the rich. A few days ago, the A.F.L.-C.I.O. did call on Congress to impose higher taxes on "the loophole set"; yet a few weeks earlier, the huge union rebuffed a group of reform-minded Congressmen and refused to put up a penny to organize a citizens' tax-protest movement.

As indicated earlier, Secretary Barr's revelation of the untaxed wealthy has inspired an outpouring of mail to Congressmen, but it is only a trickle compared with the torrents stimulated in just a few weeks' time in 1962 by the savings and loan associations, when a tax provision inimical to the associations seemed likely to pass. (It was defeated, thanks to the outpouring of mail.) And when a single industry, such as oil and gas, enjoys an annual tax subsidy as huge as $1.6-billion, the expenditure of even a minute fraction of that amount to insure continued congressional (and even Presidential) sympathy for the depletion allowance must be reckoned as an extremely lucrative "investment." (In the closing days of a hard-fought off-year campaign some years ago, several Western-state senatorial candidates were offered campaign contributions provided they would pledge themselves in favor of the depletion allowance.)

As the corpses of past reform efforts attest, the battle against the loopholes is an acutely uneven contest. In my own view, the balance will not shift materially unless there comes to pass (a) some form of publicly financed support for political campaigns, so that candidates are not so heavily dependent on contributions from special-interest groups (as even the most public-spirited are today), and (b) a broad public protest against the tax favors enjoyed by the wealthy and by large corporations.

But the latter will not come to pass, I believe, as long as the loophole closers continue to address the basic tax preferences obliquely rather than head-on. A case in point is a 13-point reform bill favored by a group of Congressmen headed by Wisconsin's Democratic Representative Henry Reuss. By far the most venturesome plan put forward this year, it has the enticement of offering an alternative to the 10 per cent surtax extension (it plugs enough loopholes to raise the same amount of revenue as the surtax — which wholly bypasses the untaxed multimillionaires). Yet the Reuss package merely favors reducing the oil-depletion allowance, rather than repealing it outright (in favor, perhaps, of a Congressionally appropriated oil exploration subsidy, should that prove necessary). By failing to question the *principle* of the depletion allowance, they are inhibited from asking why oil investors are so special as to require what amounts to a double deduction on their investment (the intangible deductions plus the depletion allowance) or why a multibillion-dollar exploration incentive is needed in a nation so oil rich that it permits some oil states to limit artificially the amount of oil produced.

Similarly, the Reuss group favors closing certain escape routes (the real estate and farm "losses," for example) that depend on the special capital gains tax. But the Congressmen have avoided any head-on confrontation with the preferential capital gains tax itself — that is, with the *principle* of according favored treatment to one kind of income. They have thus denied themselves the chance to pose such basic and popularly understandable questions as:

Why should the work of money be so vastly favored over the work of men? Why should a lawyer or doctor or engineer pay more taxes on dollars *he* works to earn than an investor pays on dollars, that others may earn *for* him? Why is a dollar of capital-gains income different from a dollar of earned income when it comes to buying food or shoes — or yachts — or, for that matter, paying taxes?[3]

Many tax reformers argue that frontal assaults on such sacred cows as the depletion allowance and the capital-gains tax are "politically unrealistic." Yet the dismal fate of most reform efforts suggests that, on the contrary, it is the indirect and cautious approach that has proved politically impractical, by its failure to pose questions and issues simple enough to spark widespread public protest against the loopholes.

Tax reform is not necessarily a partisan matter. In the opinion of Re-

---

[3] It is true that capital gains often reflect several years' build-up in value, and it would be unfair to tax them as if they had been entirely earned in the year they are realized. But this is a problem the tax laws have faced in other areas and solved through so-called "income averaging."

publican members of the House Ways and Means Committee (which handles tax legislation for the House), "The need for a thorough overhauling of our tax system. . . is one of our most pressing national problems." And according to the chairman of that committee, Arkansas Democrat Wilbur Mills, "We can no longer afford to defer serious, large-scale efforts to revise our Federal tax system."

Each of those statements has a contemporary ring. The first was made in 1943; the second in 1958. But the sweeping tax reform of which they spoke in such urgent terms is still a thing of the future. In fact, as noted earlier, the extent of total tax avoidance among the very rich has risen greatly since Congressman Mills spoke the words quoted above.

Reformers and the general public have sometimes tended to be intimidated by the immense complexity of the tax laws. But the tax question really boils down, ultimately, to a simple question: Who pays how much? Twenty-one multimillionaires pay nothing, while two million persons below the poverty line pay something. The public response to that plain fact may encourage the would-be reformers to confront head-on both the tax "experts" and their largely unquestioned Conventional Wisdoms.

PAUL JACOBS   *Keeping the Poor Poor*

Let me begin with a true story about how, for some poor people, pineapple juice tasted not sweet, but salty. At regular intervals, pineapple juice canneries must clean out the pipes that carry the juice from the crushing to the canning rooms. To do this, a salt solution is forced through the pipes and then flushed out before the new canning process starts again. A few years ago, one large cannery went through this cleaning operation and began running juice again before it was discovered that the pipes had not been totally purged of the salt solution. But, by that time, thousands of gallons of pineapple juice, all of it slightly salty, had already been processed and canned.

The cans, unlabeled, were sold at a very low price to a food distributor who specializes in handling offbrand and reject merchandise for sale in

From *New Politics*, Vol. 5, pp. 3–16, 19–20, 25–27. Reprinted by permission.

poor neighborhoods and communities. The distributor put a label on the cans and retailed them for about half the usual price for that size, making a very good profit for himself. Across the label was printed, "NO SWEET-ENER ADDED," certainly an accurate statement of the juice's condition.

In both a real and symbolic sense, this otherwise trivial incident involving the sale of salty pineapple juice is characteristic of the relationships of the poor to society. The merchandise would have had little or no monetary value outside the poverty market. It seemed cheap to those who purchased it, although in reality, considering its actual value, it was very expensive. No complaints about the saltiness of the juice were recorded, and its sale was justified by the distributor on the basis that even though the merchandise was imperfect, it was at least available to the poor who might not otherwise have been able to buy any.

Precisely the same set of characteristics are true for most of the life of the poor. As David Caplovitz has clearly demonstrated in his study, *The Poor Pay More*, not only do the poor pay more proportionately for what they get, but what they get for more money is often of inferior quality. Thus, the poverty market can be an extremely profitable one for those who specialize in selling to it, although the rewards are tempered by high risks.

The overall dimensions of the poverty market are reasonably well established. It includes approximately 35,000,000 people divided into seven million families and four million unrelated individuals. Their total income is estimated at $28,000,000,000. (Oscar Gass in *Commentary*.) But the poor dispose of this income in their own distinctive ways.

To begin with, those who constitute the poverty class spend different proportions of their income for food, shelter, clothing and medical care than are spent by the remaining four-fifths of the population. Nearly 29% of the average poor person's income goes into food expenditures, while those whose income exceeds $4,000 a year spend less than 24% of it for food. The cost of shelter for the poor is more than 29% of their incomes, in contrast to the 17% expended by those in the higher income brackets. Ironically, too, although the poor spend a higher proportion of their income for housing, what they get in exchange is always worse than similarly priced — or even lower priced — middle-income housing.

The differences between the expenditures of the poor and other income groups on clothing and medical care are even sharper: the poor spend one half as much of their income on clothing as do their economic betters, but a higher proportion on medical care, which, in accordance with the iron law of poverty, is almost always bad. And because the poor have far less money to spend, they are at the same time in much greater debt relative to their income than the middle and upper income brackets. (Interestingly enough, the only items on which both the poor and the rich spend the same proportion of their respective incomes are gifts and contributions.)

The food the poor eat is different from that purchased by the other segments of the population, even taking into account regional preferences; they seek recreation in different ways; they buy in different kinds of stores, although the prices they pay may be just as high or higher, and they buy some items, such as cockroach powder, rarely used by the rest of the consumers. Their overriding economic concerns are short-term rather than long-range ones, for they must worry about whether or not they will have enough money tomorrow rather than after retirement.

Yet these statistical differences do not adequately reflect the fact that poverty creates not only a different life style but a different emotional set as well. Anxiety and uncertainty, derived from their economic situation, dominate the orientation of the poor to the world.

Because of their anxiety and uncertainty certain social types unknown to us become prominent in the lives of the poor. The "mouse man" or the "six-for-fiver," for example, are familiar characters in many poor neighborhoods, just as the "mouse house" (loan company) is an important part of the appliance and automobile buying pattern of the poor. And although the "policy" industry is estimated to take in a quarter of a billion dollars annually in New York City alone, the "collectors" who can be found on every Harlem street corner will rarely be seen on the quiet streets of Riverdale. "Collectors" and "mouse men" live on the economic anxiety. of the poor, without whom they could not thrive.

How large this anxiety factor looms in the lives of the poor is illustrated in almost all the problems they face. As we all know too well from our daily lives, the automobile is one of the most ubiquitous features of American material culture, and the quiet humming of its engine a great source of pride to its owner. But the battered, old cars of the poor are noisy, and the sound of a loud engine rattle, an increasingly noisy rod, or a grinding bearing strikes panic in the hearts of the poor. If their car breaks down on the highway, or if it will not start in the morning, they cannot call the auto club. What may be merely a nuisance to others is a major disaster to them; they are caught in a trap from which they cannot escape without paying a great price. Generally, they cannot afford to have their cars fixed, but without a car many of them cannot go to work or look for employment, the two primary functions for which they need a car. And so, after they have found a relative or friend who will tow their disabled car back to their homes, they are forced to try fixing it themselves. (Public libraries get much less use in poor neighborhoods than in other areas, but what little use is made of them includes the frequent borrowing of do-it-yourself repair manuals.)

However, unlike the Model T or Model A Ford, the modern car is not likely to be fixed by anyone except a skilled mechanic. Indeed, if I have no other criterion by which to judge the character of a strange neighborhood, the number of junked cars on the streets or in yards serves as an accurate measure; the more abandoned cars, the poorer the area. After a while, the rusty and broken-down monuments of junk become so much a part of the landscape of poverty that no one even notices their presence.

When the poor must somehow face up to purchasing another car, the magnitude of the problem is likely to be overwhelming. Since approximately 60% of all the cars purchased in the U.S. are bought on time, automobile financing is a big business. And, as might be expected, the poor buy far more used than new cars: in 1962, only 9% of the new cars purchased on installment payments were bought by people whose income was below $3,000, but 40% of all the used cars were sold in the poverty market, 75% of them at less than $500. (University of Michigan Survey Research Center, Survey of Customer Finances.)

The cheapest way to buy a car — by means of a personal bank loan — is rarely open to the poor. In order to secure such a loan, at a simple interest rate, the prospective borrower must put up some collateral, such as stocks, a savings account, or property — assets rarely held by the poor as a matter of definition.

The next cheapest method is to get a bank loan on the car. For this, the bank usually requires a down payment of one-third to one-fourth in cash; then it will finance the car, holding a chattel mortgage on it until all the payments have been completed. The interest rates for such loans vary from 4% to 6%, depending on whether the bank also purchases paper from dealers, in which case the dealers must be protected. (The dealer will normally try to get 6% interest from buyers, although he will bargain about these rates and settle for 5.5% or even 5%. Then he will sell the sales contract to the banks for 4% keeping the balance in his own reserve funds.)

Recently, I purchased a new car, and the contrast between the way in which that transaction was carried on and what happens when a poor person does the same thing, was most revealing. After I picked out the car I wanted, I called a bank for some information about their low-cost loans. But instead of getting merely information, I got the loan, by telephone, in the space of about five to seven minutes. The bank official asked me where I lived, and after I gave him the address, which is in a "good" section of the city, he asked me if I owned my house. When I replied in the affirmative, he then inquired where I held charge accounts. After I named the stores, which were obviously all "good" ones by his standards, he asked the the purchase price of the car and how much I was going to pay in cash. When I told him I would be paying between a quarter and a third down, he informed me I could have the loan without even having to come to the bank. And not once did he ask me what my income was, for my economic position — indeed my entire life pattern — was evident from my residential location and my choice of stores and my tone of voice.

The pattern of life for the poor is equally clear to him; and so poor people are rarely able to get car loans directly from banks, even if they apply in person. Banks don't like to make small loans, for the administrative costs are too high; and they are reluctant to make loans to people whose income is uncertain or whose credit rating is less than exemplary. To the poor, a bank is the place where the teller scowls as he cashes a welfare check and charges 25¢ for the service.

In Los Angeles recently, 8,067 interviews were conducted among all income groups to obtain data concerning the use of banks. Almost 18% of the families questioned refused to reveal their income, but 9.1% of those who did said they earned less than $250 a month; of this group 47% had checking accounts and 51% had savings accounts — somewhat higher percentages than the national average for this income level. (The bank that made the survey believes the reason for this was that the sample included a large proportion of retired people whose cash income may be below $250, but whose real income is higher.) Seventy-three per cent of those in the $250–$650 a month group and 91% in the $650–$1,000 a month group had checking accounts.

Quite apart from the wide gap in the use of checking accounts between the poor and other groups, the data also revealed that the bank is not a place in which the poor conduct much business. For instance, 24% of all the families in the sample had obtained a loan within the two years prior to the survey, but only 8% of the poor had received such loans.

Whatever business the poor do have in banks is likely to involve savings accounts: branch banks located in poor neighborhoods usually have many more savings accounts than checking accounts. Indeed, the poor use their savings accounts as others use their checking accounts; their frequent withdrawals and deposits distinguish branch banks in poor neighborhoods from those located elsewhere.

But for many of the poor, a bank is far too intimidating a place even when they can afford to patronize it. I suspect, too, that the notion that some impersonal agency is keeping a permanent record of one's residence and of how much money one has, keeps away those who are worried about being found by the skip tracers who work for collection or welfare agencies.

The practice of paying bills by check as a matter of routine scarcely exists for the poor. Instead, more than half pay cash or use money orders, purchased either at the post office or, equally likely, from the liquor stores or gas stations which sell the commercial variety.

The commercial money order business has developed in response to the peculiar need of the poverty market, where marginality is so dominant a theme. Unlike the money orders obtainable in the post office or the banks, commercial ones vary in price, depending on whether the location in which they are sold produces a high or low volume. But even if they are more expensive than bank or postal money orders, they are more convenient for the poor since they can be purchased in handy locations at night or on weekends. Moreover, they do not involve the permanent records associated with a checking account.

The commercial money order business is a fairly simple one. The company maintains an account in a regular bank and the money order it sells is treated like a check; that is, the bank assumes no responsibility for the transaction beyond what is normal for bank and depositor. This fact is not usually clear to the poor; for the bank's name appears on the money order, which enhances the legitimacy of the transaction. Most of the companies operating in this field are legitimate, but occasionally one does go out of business, leaving the holder of the money order without recourse.

Commercial money order companies are not regulated by state or federal agencies, and thus can charge whatever price they believe the market will bear. As a result, the rates vary; a company in a "good" location, one with a high volume of sales, can charge higher rates than one in an area where people rely upon post office money orders or checking accounts. And since these commercial money orders are used almost exclusively to pay bills, they provide another illustration of the dictum that the poor, who can least afford it, pay more, even if only to pay their bills.

That basic principle operates throughout the lives of the poor, no matter what other differences may exist among them. Thus, unless they belong to credit unions, they must finance any substantial purchases through dealers or through finance companies whose rates vary enormously, depending upon what they find the traffic will bear.

Finance company rates *are* incredible. There is no point in going into a detailed analysis of their operations for these have been explored and documented by the Congress. (No action has been taken, incidentally, to reduce the exorbitant rates of interest exacted from the poor.) Instead, let me use but one example of the possible range. If a middle-class person borrows $2,500 from a bank on a 36-month personal loan, it will cost him $238.16; financing the purchase of a car at the usual rate of 6% will cost him $449.84 for the same period of time. At a loan company, a "mouse house," the normal charge is $674.84. Thus, for the privilege of borrowing the same sum of money, a man with savings or other assets pays $346.68 less than the one without resources.

Not only do the poor pay more for credit, they also run greater risk of losing their purchases. Dealers will normally extend credit to any prospective purchaser so long as he has no record of repossession, even though he may already be in debt to a number of finance companies, as are so many of the poor. So long as the buyer can make a down payment, either with his own money or by getting a loan from a "mouse house," the dealer will sell the commodity. However, if the buyer gets laid off or has an emergency drain on income and falls 30 days behind in payments without attempting to contact whoever is holding the contract, an inexorable process starts. The contract holder hires a "recovery outfit," a company which has the legal authority, under the terms of the contract, to simply repossess the car or television set in any way it can. Normally, in the case of a car, this is done either at the debtor's place of work or at home, late at night, while he is asleep. Appliances or furniture are simply removed from the home.

Once the property is back in the possession of the mortgage holder, the debtor is offered the opportunity to get it back by making up the payments. If he cannot pay, he is sent a "5 day letter" which by law gives him five days to either pay up or refinance, at additional interest charges, of course.

If the debtor does neither, the property reverts to the mortgage holder, who then resells it. After the repossessed item has been sold, the mortgage holder will attempt to recover from the customer the difference between the unpaid balance and the price the property brought at resale. The recovery attempt is made by a collection agency which gets ½ of whatever is recovered. The agency goes to court, routinely, to obtain orders to attach the wages of debtors. Just as routinely, the court issues these orders merely on the presentation of the contract and the record of payments, but without notification to the buyer or his representative. The court order is then presented to the debtor's employer, who must go to the administrative expense of withholding the amount specified from the employee's wages and paying it over to the agency. Very often, the employer simply fires the employee rather than be bothered.

The same process operates regardless of the purchaser's income. Obviously, the chances are much greater that the poor, who are generally not well-educated, and whose income is low and irregular, will get caught up in the endless series of credit traps. From the dealer or finance company's viewpoint, the justification for their very high interest rates lies in the risk that the purchaser will be unable to make his payments and will skip town.

Normally, if a credit manager has losses of more than 1% a year, he is in danger of losing his own job, for he is apparently using bad judgment about who represents a good credit risk. Yet in some parts of the poverty market, a credit manager who loses less than 10% or 12% of his customers is considered equally lacking in judgment; he, obviously, is setting too rigorous standards and is thus keeping away potential customers.

The 10% or 12% loss rate is taken into account when the retail price is established on an item to be sold within the poverty market. In the jewelry industry, for example, a normal markup is 100%, but for jewelry sold to the poor, this markup often goes to 300% and even higher. Thus, as a rule, a ring, for which a jewelry store pays a $50 wholesale price, is sold for $100 on a cash or short-term credit basis. That same ring will retail for $300 in the poverty market, where the credit jeweler will attempt to get as large a down payment as possible in order to protect himself against the possibility of default on future weekly payments. If the customer can be persuaded to make a $60 down payment, the retailer will have covered the price of the ring and made a modest profit. From then on everything he receives helps swell his profit rate.

The fact that the retailer wants a large number of customers who will enter into such credit arrangements requires that his credit standards be considerably lower than those established by the merchant who caters to middle- and upper-income families. The credit manager in the poverty market demands of his customer only a fixed place of residence and a fixed income, no matter how small, either from a job or from some government agency. In fact, what the retailer is selling is credit itself, and his efforts are bent on trying to keep the customer always in debt to him. He attempts, wherever possible, to draw the customer into the store to make the weekly payments so that he can continue to sell additional merchandise, often by displaying tempting "bargain" items close to the payment counter. In these transactions the price is quoted as a dollar a week rather than some fixed total sum, and the new purchases are urged on the customer on the basis that it will only mean continuing to pay the dollar a week. Every effort is expended to keep the customer on the books continuously in a state of delicate equilibrium in which the desire for goods will outweigh the anxiety associated with the perpetual need to keep up payments.

My own experience living among the poor has been a vivid demonstration of the axiom that the poor pay more, proportionately, in exchange for less. The food stores in poor neighborhoods are more monopolistic than stores in other areas. For one thing, the poor are simply less mobile than middle-class people; shopping around for bargains by bus is much more difficult than shopping by car. The poor are less likely to leave their own neighborhoods and less likely to make a large-scale expenditure on food at any one time. The amount of money they spend on food is the only nonfixed item in their budgets. Thus, they must buy it daily, and never in the larger amounts on which they save money; for what they spend on food may be the carfare they will need tomorrow to get their sick kids to the hospital. It is this need to keep the food budget in a fluid state that accounts, in part, for the low rate of participation in the food stamp programs: families on welfare, or with uncertain income, cannot spend a sizable sum of money at one time, especially at the beginning of the month when rent, utilities, and other fixed-cost items must be paid.

The kinds of food they buy also reveal the great differences between their life styles and those of the other groups. The poor buy markedly less meat, poultry, eggs, dairy products, fruits, and vegetables than do those in higher income brackets. The only items which they buy in significantly greater amounts are grain products. Dried beans, bread, spaghetti, macaroni, and other starches are what the poor use to fill their stomachs, while their children drink far more soda pop than milk.

Those who specialize in selling in the poverty market can count on certain other characteristic patterns of behavior among their customers. Middle-income people tend to read advertising about sales and to take advantage of them; not so the poor. Nor do they readily buy secondhand merchandise: the Goodwill stores are patronized more by bohemians and the middle class than by the poor. They do not save trading stamps as avidly as middle-class families, and they do not participate in "giveaway" programs. They combine an inability to discern real value with a psychic need to buy something new and a financial incapacity to buy more than they require for their immediate purpose. Welfare recipients are often at the mercy of retailers who demand that a fixed amount of goods be purchased before they will cash a relief check. Even worse, they may insist, as a condition of cashing welfare checks, that their customers buy slow-moving items for which the hapless consumer may have little or no use. When that happens, the poor have no choice, for usually they require the cash as quickly as they can get it because some other pressing need is at their throats.

Vulnerability to exploitation of their pervasive anxiety is only one of many special characteristics of the economic situation of the poor. Their economic milieu is also marked by the fact that different kinds of goods and services are available to them than to those in other circumstances. This is, in part, a reflection of their distinctive value system, but to some extent their values are shaped, in turn, by their consumer choices. For instance, reading a morning newspaper (while drinking their non-salty pineapple juice) is a commonplace, routine act for most Americans, but it is not a characteristic pattern of the poor. Instead, they watch television, and listen to the radio, and these media, almost exclusively, mold their view of the world.

. . . Bad economic circumstances force the poor into seeking abnormal solutions to those economic problems which create far more anxiety for them than the same problems do for the rest of society. Indeed, pitifully few responses are available to what is the basic fact of economic life amongst the poor: that more money must go out each month to pay a myriad of bills from rent and utilities, to furniture payments, to automobile installments, than comes in from wages, salaries or welfare payments. And since income is capricious while the monthly bills must constantly be met, anxiety is always present; by law, the consequences of non-payment are inevitable: eviction, the gas shut off, the car or furniture repossessed. Thus, for example, a working mother, without a husband, may have to leave her job because of the unreliability of baby sitters. Once this happens, she and her children are caught in a whirlpool which will suck them all down into despair.

Many people — most, perhaps — who are not poor also go into debt for consumer items such as cars, furniture or appliances, medical care, clothing, jewelry, and so on. But if the low-wage earner is out of work for an extended period, or if his wife loses her job, the very delicate balance between wages and debts is upset and the family gets into real trouble.

When he falls behind in installment payments, a characteristic response of the low-income person is to go to a finance company to "consolidate" his debts and to undertake a series of single monthly payments, presumably according to his ability to pay. As we know, the interest rates are outrageous, but most people in these straits seem to have few alternatives indeed.

For those whose debts continue to escalate despite consolidation, or for those who cannot even get credit from the finance companies, only slender choices remain. One is to give their children away, a practice common among urban Negroes who have simply adapted a Southern rural custom and out of the same economic motives. If a mother cannot support her children, she will "give" them to a relative, usually the child's grandparents, to raise. Usually, she is expected to provide some money for the child's upkeep, but frequently, of course, she cannot. . . .

More unique to the poor is a sense of gratitude for what others assume to be their natural due. For example, they view installment buying as a privilege to which they are not really entitled — because they do not feel worthy of receiving the fruits of the society. As a result, they are much less likely to grow indignant over the exploitative rates of interest and carrying charges they pay for the right to use merchandise which is not paid for in full. As a consequence of this attitude, the poor are much better customers than the rich from the retailer's point of view: they are not so quick to complain about the quality of the merchandise; they are much more easily intimidated; and they shop far less carefully. The notion of depending upon an organization such as Consumers Union to help protect their interests is completely meaningless to the poor; it assumes a degree of self-consciousness about themselves as consumers which they do not have as yet.

How can the poor become more self-conscious, self-interested consumers? It does little good to educate them about what foods make up a proper nutritional balance when their food budget fails to match the requirements, or when it remains the only item which gives them any financial flexibility. Indeed, the whole notion of a budget implies some ability to plan ahead, to project actions on the basis of a stable income which is enough to meet the reasonable demands put upon it. But the income of the poor is either capricious or inadequate — or both — and only the demands made upon it are stable, fixed by forces and institutions over which they have little or no measure of control.

Thus, I am somewhat pessimistic about the value of educational programs directed toward helping the poor become better consumers. What good will it do to convince the Indians of the Pima reservation in Arizona that their children should drink less pop and eat more meat when very few of the mud "sandwich" houses on the reservation have either electricity or water? Milk and meat spoil in the hot Arizona summer unless they are refrigerated; soda pop and beans do not. What the Pima Indians need is either to cease being poor or to become much more aware of their rights despite their poverty. Such an awareness can come, I believe, only as part of a *general* rise in their living standards, or of a *general* awakening to their rights through some form of political action. . . .

All of us are born into a state of anxiety, and many, or even most, of us must cope, throughout our lives, with deep-rooted feelings of personal inadequacy. For the poor, these feelings are continuously reinforced by the economic circumstances in which they live and by their relationships with the rest of society. In an egalitarian society where everyone is living in poverty, being poor generates neither much anxiety nor strong feelings of inadequacy. But in a society such as ours, which measures achievement primarily by financial and material standards, to be poor is to be scorned by others, and even worse, by one's own self. It is for this reason that in America the taste and smell of poverty are so sour.

BERNARD BECK   *Bedbugs, Stench, Dampness,*
and Immorality: A Review Essay
on Recent Literature About Poverty

> TROFIMOV: . . . They all look serious, have grim expressions, speak of weighty matters, and philosophize; and meanwhile anyone can see that the workers eat abominably, sleep without pillows, thirty or forty to a room, and everywhere there are bedbugs, stench, dampness, and immorality. . . . It's obvious that all our fine talk is merely to delude ourselves and others. Show me the day nurseries they are always talking about — and where are the reading rooms? They only write about them in novels, but in reality they don't exist. There is nothing but filth, vulgarity, asiaticism. . . . I'm afraid of serious countenances, I don't like them, I'm afraid of serious conversations. We'd do better to remain silent.

I

It is no surprise that a large number of books have appeared in the past two years dealing with poverty. Concern with (and usually for) the poor has become respectable, even fashionable. The publication of thought-provoking books for lay readers, leading to the discovery of the political potency of the issue, has produced a great deal of public activity accompanied by funds available to those concerned with poverty, if not always to the poor themselves. And if the social sciences and other institutionalized, professional establishments were negligent in their attention to the subject, as some have suggested, recent hyperactivity in these quarters may compensate for any previous neglect.[1]

It is appropriate after this period of abundance of scholarly and professional works about poverty to attempt a general overview and stock-taking of the whole product and of individual contributions. But this attempt may not be lightly undertaken. Several circumstances promise trouble. To begin with, there is a thick, interstitial glue composed of expressions

From *Social Problems*, Vol. 15, No 1, pp. 101–114. Reprinted by permission of The Society for the Study of Social Problems and the author.
The quotation is from *The Cherry Orchard*, Act II, 1904; from *The Major Plays* by Anton Chekhov, translated by Ann Dunnigan. Copyright © 1964 by Ann Dunnigan. Reprinted by permission of The New American Library, Inc., New York.
[1] See the exchange between Jack L. Roach and Everett C. Hughes, *American Journal of Sociology*, LXXI (July 1965), pp. 68–77.

of concern, outrage, and compassion; profferings of credentials of ideological purity, sober realism, professional expertise, and hip, inside
championship of underdogs; exhortations to optimism or pessimism; stern
calls for loin-girding and foundation-rebuilding; and pious invocation of
ideals, dreams and the American Way. The profitable substance of fact,
analysis, proposal, and criticism is often so immersed in this glue as to be
hard to reach. These books seem more hortatory than expository, a point
that will occupy us a little later.

In the second place, there is ample evidence of great sincerity, diligence,
and competence, making it hard for a reviewer to be the least bit contrary
without giving the appearance of a cynicism born of callowness. It is also
hard to give proper credit without becoming maudlin. When so many
serious and admirable writers ponder so deeply on a matter so grave, there
is a temptation to respectful silence.

In the third place, the timing of such a review seems inapt. For although there has barely been time for a general appraisal of this literature,
the mood of the nation, of its politics, and of the public activities which
define the context of a discussion of poverty have all changed sufficiently
to make a great deal of it, especially the programmatic parts, seem out of
date. Although many of these books were published less than a year ago,
the hopes seem benighted, the fears understated, and the determination
quixotic. The new departures have foundered in old hang-ups. Freshness
and innovation have worn away to reveal the same old stodginess and
temporizing. Is it worthwhile now to pick over the thoughts addressed
to a different nation at another time?

But the final, weightiest, most personal source of uneasiness lies in the
very subject itself. In the recent concern with poverty, the urgency of the
problem has substituted for the clarity of the issues; experiencing an
impulse to act has substituted for the soundness of a vision. Poverty has
also elicited from professional writers a strong dose of that reforming
pronoun "We," through which the writer globalizes his particular approach into a fantasy of omnipotence which harnesses all the power of
society to his plan. This fictitious We will get more attention below.

Suffice it to say here that in a confused and motley area where public
commitment and personal engagement are so much at stake, reflection and
detachment, necessary to the critical project, are perhaps neither welcome
nor at home, giving only an impression of dandyism. Nevertheless, the
very importance of the subject, its implication with cherished values and
social pieties, demand a hard look. The accidents of timing make the
retrospective interpretation of the programmatic work of the recent past
particularly provoking for the general study of social reactions to social
problems as well as for the study of this particular problem. Moreover,
there seem to be some points worth making about this literature which
are neither carping nor apologetic. I will mention several points which

seem to me to characterize these books generally and make specific comments about particular books in that context.

II

The recent literature on poverty contains quite a few titles aimed directly at a public ready for information and inspiration. They include then-Senator Humphrey's *War on Poverty*,[2] an Establishment primer; Shostak and Gomberg's collection *New Perspectives on Poverty*,[3] an independent attempt to keep the war on poverty honest; and the various anthologies with their hearts in the right place by Ferman, Kornbluh, and Haber (*Poverty in America*);[4] Will and Vatter (*Poverty in Affluence*);[5] Herman P. Miller (*Poverty: American Style*);[6] and Hannah H. Meissner (*Poverty in the Affluent Society*).[7]

In a more professional and less hortatory vein are the results of various conferences of concerned scientists and specialists. Even these are not merely academic studies of poverty as a phenomenon, but display commitment to value positions and action projects inextricably merged with analysis. Among them are Margaret Gordon, *Poverty in America*,[8] Leo Fishman, *Poverty Amid Affluence*,[9] and the Florence Heller School Colloquia for 1963–64, *Poverty and Dependency*.[10] Finally, there is a new introduction written by Harold Wilensky for the Free Press paperback edition of his book with Charles Lebeaux, *Industrial Society and Social Welfare*.[11] This new introduction is similar to the offerings in the second group, although its scope is wider than poverty alone. This is a somewhat arbitrary sample of books in the poverty field, but I doubt that additions or substitutions would produce very different conclusions.[12]

[2] Hubert H. Humphrey, *War on Poverty*, New York: McGraw-Hill, 1964.

[3] Arthur B. Shostak and William Gomberg, editors, *New Perspectives on Poverty*, Englewood Cliffs, N.J.: Prentice-Hall, 1965.

[4] Louis A. Ferman, Joyce L. Kornbluh, and Alan Haber, editors, *Poverty in America*, Ann Arbor: University of Michigan Press, 1965.

[5] Robert E. Will and Harold G. Vatter, editors, *Poverty in Affluence*, New York: Harcourt, Brace and World, 1965.

[6] Herman P. Miller, editor, *Poverty: American Style*, Belmont, California: Wadsworth, 1966.

[7] Hannah H. Meissner, editor, *Poverty in the Affluent Society*, New York: Harper and Row, 1966.

[8] Margaret S. Gordon, editor, *Poverty in America*, San Francisco: Chandler, 1965.

[9] Leo Fishman, editor, *Poverty Amid Affluence*, New Haven: Yale University Press, 1966.

[10] Florence Heller Graduate School for Advanced Studies in Social Welfare, Colloquia: 1963–64, *Poverty and Dependency*, Waltham, Mass.: Brandeis University, 1965.

[11] Harold L. Wilensky and Charles N. Lebeaux, *Industrial Society and Social Welfare*, New York: Free Press, 1965.

[12] The similarity of the titles of most of these works, relieved only by marginal differentiation, reflects a sameness in outlook with corresponding minor attempts at individuation.

One interesting and commendable aspect of these books taken in a body is the consistent attention they give to the history of poverty as a social problem, to the ideological setting in which it provoked concern, and to the specification of the variety and social basis of perspectives on the subject. There is an element of honest self-disclosure in these works which reflects the increased awareness of commentators that problems do not exist in an ideological and historical vacuum. It is especially nice to have these books as documents of the poverty problem as well as analyses of it, since the problem has declined in headline value in the short time since they appeared.

The documentation compensates for the confusion generated, for the lay reader and for the specialist, by the inconclusive discussions of definitions. The conventions of academic writing seem to require that a delimitation of the subject matter under the label "poverty" is due to the careful reader. This is the approach that would be required if poverty were to be used as a general, theoretical term for use in the analysis of all societies or social systems. But the social histories make it clear that poverty is to be treated as an institutionally and historically bounded issue in public discourse, instead. Therefore, the specialist is interested in definition-like specifications in discussing poverty. These specifications include the answers to the following questions: What kinds of difficulties should we think of eliminating when we think of poverty? By what standards can we tell how bad things are, how much better we are making them, and when we are entitled to feel we have achieved a significant change? The first of these questions is descriptive rather than stipulative, and is usually met by a report about the human costs of being poor. The second is evaluative and usually elicits the statistical problem of determining a "poverty line" which is used as the anchor point for judgments. Ultimately, the definition of poverty in use is the definition of the problem by concerned members of society, not the definition of the concept by interested scientific investigators. In short, it is a folk-concept rather than a technical term.

If we can take the "definitions" or other specifications of poverty as evidence of the social concerns and projects which the writers want to deal with under the poverty label, then these are the ends which are most strongly represented in the effort to eliminate poverty: the improvement of the quality of life of the poor, the optimization of national profiles of income distribution and output allocation, the relief of the population as a whole from the repugnant by-products of poverty populations, and the revitalizing of American public life and democratic values. Most commentators would hasten to say that each of these implies the others and that concentration on one aspect does not mean indifference to the others. Nevertheless, from section to section in any book, and from book to book, there is variation in the focus of attention. Moreover, it has not been shown that the most effective way to any of these must lead also to the others, except as an article of faith. It is possible to imagine that the quality of life of the poor might improve at the cost of increased depredations by poverty populations on the other members of society, or that the revitalization of public life might mean an increase in conflict which could interfere with a consensus on income distribution.

The possible incompatibility of specific ends reflects underlying differences in the attitudes of poverty warriors toward poor people. The interim ideology makes it possible for all kinds of attitudes to appear effectively the same. But there is a counter-tendency for poverty writers to validate their own credentials by debunking "conventional" approaches to poverty. The result is a set of positions defined in opposition to a variety of straw men. Thus Will and Vatter are committed to the elimination of poverty, not merely to its amelioration.[13] Similarly, Shostak and Gomberg stand for thoroughgoing revision of the entire social structure, not merely for a patch job on a poverty-generating society which continues basically unchanged until the next crisis of public conscience.[14] Many non-official writers call for true self-determination for the poor as opposed to the same old patronizing interference by middle-class reformers.[15] At the same time, hard-nosed macro-analysts reject the romantic idealization of the poor as a creative social force and urge effective official action to get the job done.[16]

Although everyone is sympathetic to the situation of the poor, there are varieties of sympathy. The picture is complicated by the fact that the poor have other social characteristics as well. Some of them are Negroes; some are criminals; some are violent; some are stupid; some are old; some are orphans. Although Simmel wrote that the poor are only related to society by their poverty, the American poor are socially located in ways which are often more salient for social attitudes.[17] Sympathy can be based, in general, on a view of the poor as helpless victims, as embarrassing errors, as unanticipated hazards, or as embattled heroes. In the current attack on poverty, these differences only provide ammunition for methodological in-fighting, but in the future they could be sharpened into major opposing positions in public discourse.

It should also be clear that inconsistencies between attitudes can appear as ambivalences in the approach of any particular writer. Other implicit

[13] Will and Vatter, *op. cit.*, Preface.

[14] Arthur Shostak, "An Overview of Current Administration Policy" in Shostak and Gomberg, *op. cit.*, pp. 128–133.

[15] Paul Jacobs, "Discussion" of a paper by Frank Riessman in Gordon, *op. cit.*, pp. 413–417.

[16] See Wilensky, *op. cit.*, pp. xliv-xlviii.

[17] Georg Simmel, "The Poor," *Social Problems,* 13 (Fall 1965), pp. 118–140.

ambivalences are also present in this literature. One of the most important arises from the very social history and documentation which makes these works valuable. Several editors and authors have thought to include material about social approaches to poverty in earlier periods and the development of the problem to the present. Thus we have in Meissner's collection a report on the treatment of poverty in New York at the turn of the century, an excerpt from the Pittsburgh Survey (1905–1909), a selection from Robert Hunter (1904);[18] and Leo Fishman offers an article by Oscar Handlin on poverty since the Civil War.[19]

An unanticipated effect of these historical perspectives is to raise a doubt as to whether the ingenuity of the most recent proposals for overcoming poverty actually reflects anything new. Selections designed to show the age and persistence of the problems of poverty also indicate that we do not understand much more about dealing with it than in the past. No ideological impetus for the current war on poverty is more compelling or fresher than Bernard Shaw's argument as reproduced in Miller's collection.[20] Meanwhile, the magnitude of the poverty problem, both absolutely and relatively, has steadily declined.

In trying to strike exactly the right note of alarm and optimism, many books convince the reader that poverty is pressing and intolerable and at the same time limited and diminishing. The balance of sentiments is delicate, but the logic of the arguments is not consistent. In particular, it is necessary to show not only that poverty should be combatted more rapidly, but that concerted efforts can quicken the pace. An additional perspective impelling us to renewed efforts is developed by Wilensky: the comparison of American efforts with the investment of other western nations.[21] Yet the English observers of poverty in that active welfare society raise the same doubts and concerns, as in Peter Townsend's contribution to the Florence Heller Colloquia.[22]

The discussion of the urgency of the poverty problem seems more often to rest on the descriptions alone. The extent and difficulty of the problem is a secondary issue. It is the accounts of the misery and hopelessness of the poor, the stories of their reverses at the hands of the ordinary agencies of modern society, the listing of their unmet needs and absent resources that bear the weight of persuasion. It is only after our indignation has been aroused by unsmiling, underfed children, resigned, unemployed fathers, deserted, desperate mothers, that further details are brought in to channel our determinations to help.

[18] Meissner, *op. cit.*, pp. 4–20.
[19] Fishman, *op. cit.*, pp. 3–17.
[20] Miller, *op. cit.*, pp. 27–29.
[21] Wilensky, *op. cit.*, pp. ix–x.
[22] *Poverty and Dependency, op. cit.*, Peter Townsend, "The Scale and Meaning of Poverty in Contemporary Western Society," pp. 1–16.

As I mentioned above, the books under consideration fall into two broad categories — one set reports the work of professional social scientists and another set introduces the general reader to the subject. Each of these categories merits specific comments.

In the first category, special note should be taken of the collection edited by Leo Fishman. This volume, alone among all the rest, is single-mindedly devoted to analysis and description of poverty as a phenomenon. It puts to one side the instruction of attitudes and the planning of programs. A consistent and undistracted account of this type is an indispensable foundation for all excursions into social action. Here in one book is a meaty general survey of poverty as a subject matter rather than as an issue. The selections composing it are, on the whole, very good.

The collection by Margaret Gordon is also fundamental and substantial, but in another direction. Here are presented the range of serious programs actually contemplated by persons who have a chance of implementing them. With a few exceptions, attitudinizing is eschewed in favor of detailed presentation of plans. Whether or not these represent the best approaches, they certainly represent the most likely ones. Unfortunately, the book took shape too early to give attention to the recent range of direct income payment proposals which have come from all ideological sides. The Gordon book, by the way, serves as a basic source of materials for some of the collections addressed to the general public. The general impression which remains is, as Frank Fernbach concludes his article, "The greatest challenge we face is not a lack of knowledge about what should be done to mount a war on poverty, it is whether Americans now have the will to wage this war and to win it."[23] That will must be expressed in society's resources, mainly money and human effort, and must be freed from the encumbering reservations of the ideologies which have dominated public life until now. Pessimists have begun to think that the answer to Fernbach's challenge has already begun to come in; its import is, "not this time around."

Wilensky's new introduction and the papers in the Florence Heller Colloquia are too diverse to be easily summarized, but they are thoughtful and original pieces by reliable students. S. M. Miller is particularly noteworthy for his continuing effort to place action on and by the poor in a proper political context.[24]

Turning to the second category of books, I want to make some summary comments. The books have a common specialized character. They are intended to introduce the subject of poverty to the general reader and to

[23] Frank L. Fernbach, "Policies Affecting Income Distribution," in Gordon, *op. cit.*, p. 127.
[24] S. M. Miller, "Poverty, Professionals and Politics," in *Poverty and Dependency*, pp. 44–58.

orient him to the enterprise of getting rid of it. Thus the question to be raised about them is not whether they contribute to our understanding of poverty, but whether they represent fairly and persuasively what is already understood. Furthermore, they must be judged on how well they motivate the uninitiated reader to wholesome and beneficial attitudes and actions. In other words the criteria for judgment must first be those of rhetoric rather than analysis.

These cautionary words are necessary because at first reading I missed the coherence, conceptual order, and abstention from attitudes which would be standard equipment in works for theoretical or professional training purposes. Thus, definitions of poverty appear only as far as needed to generate compassionate concern or to roughly locate targets for that concern. Views on the sources or circumstances of poverty appear which are incompatible or mutually unrelated, but there is hardly an attempt to accommodate them to one another or to synthesize a common point of view. Different authors are clearly talking about different situations under the common rubric of "poverty," yet the ambiguity is neither discussed nor resolved. There is hardly a declarative statement about poverty or its surrounding circumstances which is not immediately surrounded by indications as to whether it should be applauded or deplored, e.g., the undeveloped future orientation of the poor. In many cases, description occurs only in terms which have been defined in an evaluative context (e.g., the personality of poor people is discussed as strong or weak, ennobled or stunted, rather than merely described as a type of personality organization, if such it is). Finally, the separate accounts of the ills to be remedied, the preconditions to an effective remedy; and the proposed remedies are sometimes ludicrously inappropriate to one another. A sober practicum would not display a cycle of mutually reinforcing evils, resistant to all ameliorative efforts, call for the total reordering of society at large as a prerequisite, and then suggest birth control pamphlets or teachers with kindly attitudes as the program of action.

The rhetoric of inciting to action, however, includes all these features as reasonable and effective gambits. Definition and consistent development of arguments are aimed at the focussing of concern rather than at clarification. Incompatible and unrelated viewpoints are aimed at stimulating serious soul-searching, not at generating coherent accounts. Value-couched descriptions are intended to mobilize attitudes more than to provide data. Sections on problems, preconditions, and programs are meant not only to communicate urgency, difficulty, and the need for participation, but also the opportunities available to the aroused reader for concrete contributions. These are works of propaganda, then, in a non-pejorative sense of the word, and should be judged as such.

Nevertheless, there is a great deal of informative and thoughtful material in these books. They cannot be understood as attempts to analyze poverty as a phenomenon nor to lay a firm foundation for value discussions of the most professional kind, but they are still useful as sources of information, historical, documentary, statistical, ideological, and reportorial. The polemical articles, which are numerous, are often of the highest quality and topical interest. The reader who is uninstructed about poverty will find a taste of most of the kinds of questions which poverty has raised in the minds of recent American thinkers.

III

The specific questions raised by these books lead to more general considerations about the study of poverty. I should like to mention here four different matters suggested by reading over all these works. They are, in order, the use of the fictitious We; the rejuvenation of deprived perspectives; the limited range of approaches to poverty; and the emergence of the poor as new aborigines.

The Use of the Fictitious We. Time and again in the writing on poverty, there appears a type of statement which suggests that in dealing with the problem posed by Them (the poor), We should do some particular thing. (Capitalization is mine.) Howard S. Becker in his recent presidential address to the Society for the Study of Social Problems asked whose side we are on.[25] In much of the poverty literature, there is no question of choosing one of the available sides; "we" implies one of the sides from the beginning. Even writers whose sympathy is clearly with the underdog poor as opposed to the respectable society which defines them as a problem use "we" to mean the respectables and "they" to mean the poor.

This identification with the top dogs is not selling out; it is simple honesty. The literature does come from respectable middle-class persons, in general, and the audiences to which it is addressed are similarly respectable and middle-class. In practical terms, to be sure, these respectables are the ones who have to be convinced to permit and to sponsor activity in behalf of the poor (at least within the strategic limits most social problems professionals place on themselves). The effect of using this facile We is a one-sidedness in planning programs and anticipating changes.

The consensus implied by We is rarely borne out by the facts. It is misleading to make plans that We can use in dealing with Them, because the major problems for poverty warriors are not negotiating with the poor, but negotiating with various sectors of the respectable society which are supposedly our teammates in We. This kind of talk holds out an offer that we cannot deliver on. We are not in a position to bring about the actions and

[25] Howard S. Becker, "Whose Side Are We On?" *Social Problems,* 14 (Winter 1967), pp. 239–247.

commitments which we bravely assert to be our part of the process of eliminating poverty. Thus, if We commit ourselves to true equality of opportunity, we can make certain changes in Their attitudes toward job-holding. Our thoughts are directed to the changes that can be made in attitudes toward job-holding, but there is not much professional savvy devoted to the problem of getting We to make the commitment. It is time for social problems analysts and applied social scientists generally to face the fact that we have less impact on the segments of society we claim to represent than we do on our target populations.

In truth, the only We we belong to is the relatively small and powerless (although somewhat influential) one containing those who are professionally or culturally involved in the social progress ideology. We are painfully aware that the values of the poor are at odds with the ones we recommend. But are the respectable segments as close to recommended values as our rhetoric suggests?

The Rejuvenation of Derived Perspectives. There is a special poignancy about the hearty invocation of We which is revealed by a comparison of the recent focus on poverty with the older project of attacking "social problems." Poverty emerged as an issue at a time when the social problems professional faced depressing problems of his own.

To begin with, in spite of a high level of dedication in his work and occasional eloquence in his exhortations to respectable society, the outcomes were often disappointing. The problems did not abate; on the contrary they seemed to increase out of all control. The promising directions and hopeful attitudes did not spark an outbreak of public enthusiasm and support. Many workers resigned themselves to an agonizingly slow rate of change, to stinginess and inattentiveness from powerful agents, to aborted applications of far-reaching plans. Like old maids, their vigor subsided and they suffered from lack of response. Some fell into cynicism, self-pity, or blind ritualism. The conditions they labored so long and sincerely to combat remained as pernicious and widespread as ever. Their remedies did not work or could not be sufficiently implemented to receive a fair test.

In addition, in recent years, the study of social problems has encountered certain difficulties from critics. The criticism directed against practice in the same problem areas has been even more severe. Social problems specialists, it was suggested, were patronizing, supporters of the status quo, moral entrepreneurs. Their motives were suspect, their judgments were open to question, they often interfered with the viable patterns of the people they claimed to be helping. The complex fabric of unspoken assumptions which used to be shared by author and reader of this literature appears to be more frayed and threadbare these days. It is no longer obvious that all right-thinking men must react with the same pity or indignation, that the direction of amelioration is defined by the statement of the problem situation, that the location of expertise and moral legitimacy is unambiguous.

To people working under these handicaps, the war on poverty offered the possibility of relief. The rise of recent interest in the poverty problem seemed to open new areas to students and practitioners. In addition, there appeared a new social resolve to seriously attack conditions which had been allowed to continue without proper attention. Money, legitimacy, encouragement, prestige, even glamour were to accompany this new assault on poverty. A great volume of programs, analyses, and calls to arms issued from the professional community. The tone of much of this product, especially when directed to the lay public, was didactic and promised new leadership in the crusade against poverty.

But the poverty rubric covered many discussions of the same social problems which had occupied students in this field before, like family disorganization, deviance, alienation, racial discrimination, and for which the same suggested remedies were offered. That is to say, a large part of the problems literature dealing with poverty was identical to the problems literature before poverty became a hot issue. Instead of new departures, we found business as usual. By and large the new label "poverty" covered the same ground as the old label "social problems."

There is no reason to suppose that the treatments and remedies suggested in that older literature were inappropriate in the new context. But progress in the old areas of concern, using the old remedies, had not been encouraging, and certainly fell short of the avowed goal of eliminating the problems in a finite, specifiable future. The slow, cumulative processes suggested in the old literature did not seem to gibe with the language of the Blitzkrieg on poverty. On the other hand, such a concentration of effort and resources had never been available before to problems specialists. Under the guise of anti-poverty programs, the old anti-problem techniques might finally get a fair test.

There is some evidence that the war on poverty has been used by various agencies as the occasion for instituting and funding the programs that they had in mind for years but could never support until recently. In this context it makes sense that so many commentators emphasize that raising the income of the poor is not a solution to poverty, but that a broad spectrum of interventions in every facet of the life of the poor was necessary. A great deal of money was to be spent, but not by being fed into the pockets of the poor. Instead they were to be exposed to family and individual counseling, resocialization, constructive therapeutic programs of education, recreation, and cultural endeavor. Organizations were to be formed, and the poor were to be introduced to a host of new experiences which would have a profound, subtle effect in reorienting them to a dif-

ferent pattern of existence complete with new aspirations and new standards of self-judgment. These are the projects which dedicated social
problems treaters had been itching to promote for a long time, but had
always been too busy, too understaffed, too poor to realize. The spectacle
of the misery of the poor was used as basis to justify the implementation
of long-delayed plans to a previously indifferent nation. These programs
are on the whole commendable, but they are not news.

There is an added benefit for social problems students working under
the poverty label. The attack on poverty seems to be free of the criticism
and suspicion that have fallen on the motives and value assumptions of
writers in the other social problems fields. Poverty, of all modern social
problems, seems to be the most defensible. The hoped-for outcome of
programs of reform seem to be the most worthy of respect. If you involve
yourself in the War on Poverty, do you not avoid the imputation of repressive authoritarianism laid on some who battle crime, delinquency, and
deviation? the imputation of moral prudery laid on some who oppose lax-
ness and decay? the imputation of depersonalizing manipulativeness laid
on some who fight disease? In the area of poverty, the attitude of middle-
class progressive meliorism could still be, not only respectable, but exemplary.

Certainly, the poverty literature shows a general turning away from
doubting introspection toward externalized accusation directed at society
at large. Its tone suggests that reluctance to interfere is not a product of
scruples but of mealy-mouthedness, that eagerness for action is not self-
aggrandizement but emergency rescue tactics. The poverty warriors have
the freedom to act in the confidence of their sentiments and the assurance
of the justice of their actions. The powerful forces of public definition
have taken them off the defensive and made them instead the center of
legitimate activity (at least until as recently as a year ago).

There was a great deal to be happy about in those developments. It
was time these programs were given the trial they deserved, on a scale
which might produce effectiveness. It was also time for the defensiveness
to give way to dedication. It was especially time for humane sentiments
to find humane outlets. At the same time, the demands of an intolerable
situation should not be used as a pretext for comfortable people to indulge
themselves in authoritarian imperiousness or pious postures. And the delayed application of old plans should not be confused with innovations of
perspective. It is at least encouraging for social problems workers to see
how many reasonable and untried plans were available when public willingness grew to use them.

The Limited Range of Approaches to Poverty. The fictitious character
of the We appearing in poverty writing shows up also in the inadequacies
of the proposals advanced for dealing with poverty. The evidence is con-

vincing that poverty is a problem which afflicts its victims in a wide variety of mutually reinforcing and viciously cycling ways. The poor have to bear not only the burden of insufficient resources in the present, but also the legacy of missed opportunities, snowballing misfortunes, barren associations, rudimentary cultural repertoires, shadowed reputations, bleak futures. Their physical health is undermined, their mental composure is precarious, their family connections are fragmented, their learning is stunted, their habitations are wretched, their habits are repulsive, and their lives are made up of isolation, brutalization, and unconsciousness. There is no point of leverage for change in more wholesome directions. All aspects of life conspire to destroy an attempt in any direction.

The society which surrounds them, moreover, has organized its routines around the expectation that they will remain as wretched in the future as they have been in the past. In fact, to make a place for them requires, we are told, a complete change of our attitudes and actions toward the poor. We must rearrange our social structure to give them encouragements and opportunities they cannot get now. And our sentiments about the poor and the meaning of poverty must change so as to lift its stigma. The problem of the poor, then, is made up of the interlocking limitations of their lives combined with the rejection and exclusion we impose on them.

What then is necessary to attack these problems? While all writers are careful to say that there are no easy answers, the tentative suggestions that often are put forth are still ludicrously inadequate to dealing with the awesome problems they are directed against.

Four different kinds of limitations can be cited: the failure to deal with the problem of scale; the failure to treat respectable society as a target population of poverty programs; the failure to transcend implicit assumptions about the scope of feasible programs in order to exploit the full gamut of possibilities; and the illusion that it is possible to study or attack poverty without dealing with the independent facts of public life on which the poverty situation is contingent (e.g., at present, the war in Vietnam).

To begin with, programs envisioned as a final remedy for poverty cannot be immediately extrapolated from successes with a handful of individuals. The citation of promising pilot projects is common. But the kinds of morale and individual effectiveness that can occur in a pilot project are exactly the features that we expect to be routinely absent in huge programs aimed at millions of people.

The conduct of the welfare establishment comes in for a good share of bad-mouthing. It is labelled conservative, bureaucratic, punitive, inefficient, heartless, degrading to clients. It is accused of paternalism and cynicism. But neither the case workers nor the administrators of welfare institutions characteristically begin as monsters. Nor is the unwieldy organization of welfare the result of sorcery. There is reason to predict that when the promising programs of the present day are institutionalized on a mass basis, with the corresponding requirements of maintaining morale, keeping open the pipelines for funds, recruiting new generations of workers, they will bog down in the same difficulties. Something more is required for a fresh approach than admonitions to renewed dedication and human sentiments. Those methods have been tried often in the past. Nor is it impressive to revile paternalism in welfare agencies because we *really* know what the poor need.

In the second place, a good deal of the attention devoted to helping the poor and planning for them should be diverted to helping respectable people so that they discover the benefits of allowing the poor to reenter society. This is the very consensus implied in the confident use of We language, but we have almost no programs of sociological sophistication for achieving it.

Why do so many proposals involve major intrusions into the lives of the poor, while so few suggest even minor alterations in the arrangements of the non-poor? We are warned often enough that a real end to poverty will require investments and commitments which we have not historically been accustomed to; we must regard complacently major alterations in our ordinary social routine; we must assign praise and blame on some new, nonpunitive basis. But these general strictures never appear as the subject of specific proposals. We hear the details of store front employment agencies for the poor, but no concrete proposals for effecting necessary changes among the secure.

How politic are even the most daring of these proposals! They seem to have been delicately fashioned within the bounds of the feasible. There is always a disclaimer to the effect that other major changes must occur if these specific programs are to work. Somehow, the United States must persuade itself not to spend huge amounts on war and the military. Then we can raise the salaries of social workers, increase payments, open more training centers, etc. The tasks described in the premises are herculean, but are not planned. Only the relatively minor conclusions are spelled out. Perhaps it occurs to us that if these imposing preconditions could be met, it would hardly be necessary to spell out these programs so bravely.

The same innocence is apparent in discussing the role of racial inequality on poverty problems. If we were all to commit ourselves to equal rights, then certain concrete attacks on the problems of ghetto Negroes could be made. But if the first monumental condition could be achieved, would not the other problems of the ghetto immediately diminish to a great extent?

In the third place, there is insufficient adventurousness in poverty programs when compared to the major changes they presuppose. If such preconditions can be offered deadpan, then why not offer a full range of bold alternatives, if only as a setting for the ones that will finally look most attractive? There is a wide range of alternatives proposed for the development problems of backward nations; why are we so niggardly in thinking about our own? Why not a plan for expropriations of slum businesses and whole slum neighborhoods? Or for the deliberate and concerted use of block-busting? In American society these suggestions are, of course, irresponsible. But there is an irresponsibility also in speaking as though poverty were only a problem of the poor, requiring programs only dealing with the poor.

Finally, even in the study of poverty we too often proceed on the understanding that poverty is a separable sphere of social life with an internal dynamic of its own, discoverable by observation of the poor. It is a truism that poverty is a situation of interdependence between the poor and the comfortable, although it is not always kept in mind in actual studies. But in addition, more attention needs to be paid to factors seemingly divorced from the setting of poverty which have great determining effect on what can and cannot happen to and for the poor. How can the current situation of the poor and of official programs aimed at them be understood, without considering how decisions on the allocation of public resources and energies in general are made? Are riots in the ghettoes of our cities more or less associated with the fortunes of the war on poverty than battles in the villages of Vietnam? Can we claim to make a scholarly study of an area of social life when such important parameters appear in none of our models?

The Emergence of the New Aborigines. Once the We, however, fictitious, is formed in the discourse of poverty writers, it generates a strong notion about the nature of Them. There is a certain formal similarity between our relationship to the poor and the relationship of expanding European societies to the "aboriginal" populations which turned up as embarrassing by-products of the inclusion of new territories in their spheres of activity. In spite of the most admirable attitudes we can muster, the poor remain "our natives," in the strongest senses of each of those words. Our most compelling experience of the poor, the one which leads to the attempts to define poverty and specify a poverty line, is our confrontation with the bizarre, reduced, and miserable circumstances of their daily lives. Poverty is, first and foremost, misery.[26] As in the speech of Trofimov, composed by Chekhov in 1904, the thing which alarms us about

[26] Excuse the interlingual pun.

the poor is the fact they fail to display the trappings of civilization, the routine cues which reassures us in our lives that we are doing all right. Moreover, these beings, alien in their lack of these cues, are indissolubly tied to us and our social enterprise. In the pursuit of our ordinary, proper activities, this scandal has been generated and will not go away. To reverse the old saying, if you're all right, you're white; the poor are our white man's burden.

By defining the poor as a separate population with a special social fate, we make it possible for ourselves to deal with them and confront their problems as a job of elimination. But at the same time we set them apart into a category of extraordinariness where customary rules of interaction and respect are suspended. To be poor is no longer to be one of us. Intervention in their affairs becomes noble instead of rude. Lecturing them on tactics becomes idealistic rather than snotty. The poverty warrior represents succor rather than interference.

One approach to poverty that may avoid this process of differentiation relies on the manipulation of external factors, mainly labor market and income distribution, in the routine workings of society. These manipulations require little concern with the identity and social honor of the poor, little in the way of special statuses and rules of treatment. Resources are made available and opportunities provided on the plausible theory that the poor, like other men, will use them.

A special word of commendation should go to the proponents, in whatever form, of the guaranteed annual income. Whether the details of this plan are worked out in satisfactory fashion or not, it is reassuring that someone had the idea that one way to help people who do not have sufficient resources to live at a prescribed level is to give them those resources. If you go by most of the proposed remedies for poverty, you would never know that these were people whose basic problem was not having enough money.

The only problems in this approach (apart from the basic one of whether it will actually work) are those involved in winning the permission of the ordinary, respectable segments of society for the diversion of resources and the invocation of legitimate sanctions. As I have mentioned before, this is no simple matter.

One intriguing possibility of the aboriginal image of the poor is that its very defects will produce positive consequences which a more correct attitude would not. Non-official workers with poor people have increasingly emphasized the development of political consciousness. The very fact of being lumped into a category of alienness by the declared enemies of poverty might contribute to the formation of a cohesive and powerful *Klasse für sich*, a party, if not an army, of the wretched. But the formation could occur in defiant opposition to respectable meliorists rather than in grateful cooperation. Such a force might compel the compliance of society at large which poverty workers seem unable to obtain. It might penetrate to some of the refractory preconditions of thoroughgoing change.

But will We like it if We see it? Or will this indirectly positive result be one We fear and deplore? It would make an interesting case of an intended, unrecognized function.[27] However interesting the possibility, the facts of our society may require realistic students to class it with the sort of fantasy to be found only in an opera for beggars.

[27] See Marion J. Levy, Jr., *The Structure of Society,* Princeton: Princeton University Press, 1952, pp. 87–88.

RACISM 2

It has long been accepted that "race relations" constitutes an American social problem. But it is only recently that the conception of a *system* of racism having deep roots in American institutions has become widespread. A legacy of an unreflective postwar optimism about American society was the idea that racial prejudice and discrimination, like many other problematic aspects of national life, were destined to disappear in the not-so-distant future. A number of sources fed this belief.

One was the increasing volume of civil rights legislation, which first appeared with Roosevelt's establishment of a Fair Employment Practices Commission in 1942, continued with Truman's executive order desegregating the armed forces in 1948, the famous school desegregation decisions of 1954, and so on. For many people, this seemed to signify the increasing willingness of the federal government to take positive action toward reversing the effects of several hundred years of discrimination.

Another source was the typical phrasing of issues in social theory. Most of the postwar work on race relations saw the problem in terms of *attitudes* and its resolution in terms of combatting these attitudes. The dominant conception was the notion of prejudice. A number of classic studies of the 1930's had considered the system of relationships between blacks and whites in American communities; among them John Dollard's *Caste and Class in a Southern Town* and Drake and Cayton's *Black Metrop-*

70

olis.[1] But the general trend in later work was to view racism as a property not of structures, but of individuals.

Several related ideas accompanied this approach. First was a tendency to see racial problems as problems primarily of specific geographical regions and social groups — that is, of the South and of the less educated and lower, or lower-middle class white. Research on prejudiced attitudes tended to support this interpretation. Second, since regional backwardness was breaking down under the pressure of industrialization and urbanization, and since such negatively related characteristics as education were increasing and being extended to lower and lower strata, the social supports of prejudice were crumbling and we could look forward to continuous improvement in race relations.[2] Therefore (third), change would come as a result of attitude modification within existing structures and institutions. Finally, the consistent implication was that racial prejudice and discrimination were basically un-American — in the double sense of being foreign to American values (the American Creed, as Gunnar Myrdal[3] characterized it), and a cancerous and alien growth on the body politic.

Several things conspired to modify this analysis. If any one could be singled out, it was the growing awareness of the depth of racial discrimination and powerlessness in the North — coupled with the admission that conventional civil rights legislation was inadequate to overcome racism. All this was dramatically demonstrated in the urban uprisings of the 1960's.

The result of this recognition has been numerous attempts to reinterpret the meaning of racism in America and a belief that racism is a systematic phenomenon, not

[1] John Dollard, *Caste and Class in a Southern Town* (Garden City, N.Y.: Doubleday Anchor, 1949); St. Clair Drake and Horace R. Cayton, *Black Metropolis: A Study of Negro Life in a Northern City* (New York: Harper Torchbooks, Rev. Ed., 1962).

[2] For an example of this kind of analysis see Arnold M. Rose, "Race and Minority Relations," in Robert K. Merton and Robert A. Nisbet, eds., *Contemporary Social Problems* (New York: Harcourt, Brace and World, 1961).

[3] Gunnar Myrdal, *An American Dilemma* (New York: Harper and Row, 1962).

confined to any region or group, but extending deep into every major American institution. Racism implies not merely negative attitudes, but fundamentally flawed structures.

This, in turn, has led to a greater concern for problems of *power* in the analysis of race relations. As it became apparent that major institutions of American society were more intractable than expected, it was no longer possible to place much faith in attitude change as an agency of fundamental social change. The problem of change was increasingly seen as a question of power, and at the same time, the source of disadvantage was seen as the limited access to positions of authority and decision-making.

Black exclusion from such positions is discussed in detail by Harold Baron in his study of black powerlessness in Chicago. Not only are blacks gravely under-represented in decision-making positions, but where they are represented, their actual power is minimal. Control over decision-making means control over all matters about which decisions are made. Consequently, as Baron suggests, Chicago's balance of power makes it as "white" as Mississippi.

Included in the new recognition of the depth of racism was the rejection of an earlier argument that black Americans would follow the path by other "immigrant" groups into the mainstream of society through existing channels of social mobility. As the Kerner Commission, among other investigations, concluded, this analysis failed to consider the changing economic and job structure, the historical differences in the way blacks, compared to other groups, arrived in this country, and the changed significance of the labor movement. Collective action through labor organization was critical in raising the opportunities and living standards of most previously settled ethnic groups; their achievement of security and well-being did not come about accidentally or fatefully, but through concerted political struggle.

Changes in the labor movement, therefore, can be critical in their effect on the life chances of groups. Julius Jacobson's discussion of union conservatism shows that this traditional avenue of political action has historically been very nearly closed to blacks. The conservatism of most contemporary labor has meant that, by and large, despite rhetorical support, union leadership has tended consistently to take the side of order versus change, of established authority versus democratic aspirations. For the black worker, the unions have become merely another racist institution, barely distinguishable from the rest, an obstacle to, not an agency for, change.

The short selection by Lee Rainwater explores an aspect of racism that is often obscured, the role of society's "dirty workers" in maintaining the system. The division of labor has traditionally resulted in white optimism about the racial situation. Most whites have had little occasion for intimate contact with the routine operation of social control in the ghettos. But as Rainwater suggests, it is characteristic of racism that it depletes and degrades not only the oppressed, but also the institutions of the dominant society. These become emptied of their original purpose — education, welfare, and so on — and are reduced more and more to control or custodial functions. These effects of racism illuminate the behavior of those personnel charged with the dirty works; to understand *them,* we need to realize that they are at the forefront of a particularly unpleasant system, pressured from both sides.

In "Internal Colonialism and Ghetto Revolt," Robert Blauner attempts to provide a theoretical framework to explain the phenomenon of American racism and relate it to its historical origins. Blauner argues that to comprehend the meaning of the urban revolts of the 1960's, we must take seriously the conception — advanced also by Malcolm X, Kenneth Clark,[4] and others — that the black communities are best seen as internal colonies, arising from the worldwide expansion of white European power and relating to the dominant society in a way that is analogous to the typical colonial situation. According to this analysis, the ghetto disorders are not senseless outbursts, but prim-

[4] Malcolm X, *Malcolm X Speaks,* George Breitman, ed. (New York: Grove Press, 1966); Kenneth B. Clark, *Dark Ghetto: Dilemmas of Social Power* (New York: Harper Torchbooks, 1965).

itive forms of political rebellion. And Blauner maintains that recognition of the colonial character of racism means that it is difficult to be optimistic about the near future; decolonization is bound to be accompanied by intense and sometimes violent conflict.

HAROLD M. BARON   *Black Powerlessness*
                                                 in Chicago

Until recently, the three principal targets of the civil-rights movement in the North were discrimination and inferior conditions in (1) housing for Negroes, (2) jobs for Negroes, and (3) the education of Negroes. But after failing to bring about major changes, many Negroes realized that one reason the status quo in housing, jobs, and education continues is that *the black community lacks control over decision-making*. Negroes remain second-class citizens partly because of the discrimination of individual whites, but mainly because of the way whites control the major institutions of our society. And therefore the fourth major goal of Negro organizations and the civil-rights movement has become the acquisition of power.

It was because of this concern with power for black people that, more than two years ago, the Chicago Urban League — a social-welfare organization dedicated to changing institutions so as to achieve full racial equality — started to study the decision-making apparatus in Cook County, Ill., and particularly how it affects or ignores Negro citizens. (Cook County takes in the city of Chicago, and two-thirds of the population of the surrounding suburban ring included in the Chicago Standard Metropolitan Statistical area.) Among the questions we posed were:

What is the extent of Negro exclusion from policy-making positions in Chicago?

Where Negroes *are* in policy-making positions, what type of positions are these, and where are Negroes in greatest number and authority?

With Harriet Stulman, Richard Rothstein, and Rennard Davis. Copyright © by TRANS-action Magazine, New Brunswick, New Jersey. Reprinted by permission.

Do Negroes in policy-making positions represent the interests of the Negro community? and

How might an increase in the percentage of Negro policy-makers affect socio-economic conditions for Negroes in general?

What we found was that in 1965 some 20 per cent of the people in Cook County were Negro, and 28 per cent of the people in Chicago were Negro. Yet the representations of Negroes in policy-making positions was minimal. Of the top 10,997 policy-making positions in the major Cook County institutions included in our study, Negroes occupied only 285 — or 2.6 per cent.

In government (see Table 1), out of a total of 1088 policy-making positions Negroes held just 58. This 5 per cent is about one-fourth of the percentage of Negroes in the total county population. Of the 364 elective posts in the survey, however, Negroes occupied 29, or 8 per cent, indicat-

TABLE 1   *The Exclusion of Negroes from Government: Policy-Making Positions in the Cook County Public Sector (1965)*

	Policy-making positions	Positions held by Negroes	%
1. Elected officials			
U.S. House of Representatives	13	1	8
State legislature	120	10	8
Cook County — nonjudicial	34	3	9
Chicago — nonjudicial	59	7	12
Cook County — judicial	138	8	6
Total:	364	29	8
2. Appointive supervisory boards			
Total:	77	10	13
3. Local administrative positions			
City of Chicago	156	2	1
Chicago Board of Education	72	7	9
Metropolitan Sanitary District	7	0	0
Cook County government	13	1	8
Total:	248	10	4
4. Federal government			
Civil service	368	8	2
Presidential appointments	31	1	3
Total:	399	9	2
Grand total:	1088	58	5

ing that the franchise has helped give Negroes representation. Yet Negroes had the most positions, percentagewise, on appointed supervisory boards, such as the Board of Education and the Chicago Housing Authority. There they occupied 10 of the 77 policy-making positions, or about 13 per cent.

Negroes were better represented on appointed supervisory boards and in elected (nonjudicial) offices than they were in local administrative positions, or in important federal jobs based in Chicago. Thus, Negroes held 12 per cent of the nonjudicial elected posts in Chicago's government, but only a little over 1 per cent of the appointive policy-making positions in the city administration. The same anomaly appears at the federal level. There is one Negro out of the 13 U.S. Congressmen from Cook County (8 per cent), but Negroes held only one out of 31 Presidential appointments (3 per cent), and eight of the 368 top federal civil-service posts (2 per cent).

Nonetheless, Negroes have — proportionately — two-and-half-times as many important posts in the public sector as they have in the private sector. As Table 2 indicates, Negroes are virtually barred from policy-making positions in the large organizations that dominate the private institutions in the Chicago area. Out of a total of 9909 positions, Negroes fill a mere 227. This 2 per cent representation is only one-tenth of the proportionate Negro population.

The whitest form of policy-making in Chicago is in the control of economic enterprises. Out of 6838 positions identified in business corporations, Negroes held only 42 (six-tenths of 1 per cent). Thirty-five of these were in insurance, where Negroes occupy 6 per cent of the 533 posts. But all 35 were in two all-Negro insurance firms. The other seven positions were in four smaller banks. In banks in general, Negroes occupied three-tenths of 1 per cent of the policy posts. There were no Negro policy-makers at all in manufacturing, communications, transportation, utilities, and trade corporations.

Out of the 372 companies we studied, the Negro-owned insurance companies were the only ones dominated by blacks (see Table 3). And if we had used the same stringent criteria for banks and insurance companies that we used for nonfinancial institutions, there would have been no black policy-makers in the business sector at all.

Now, amazingly enough, Chicago has proportionately more Negro-controlled businesses, larger than neighborhood operations, than any other major city in the North. Therefore, similar surveys in other Northern metropolitan areas would turn up an even smaller percentage of Negro policy-makers in the business world.

The legal profession, represented by corporate law firms, had no Negroes at high policy levels. We are convinced that the same situation would be found in other professions, such as advertising and engineering.

TABLE 2   *The Exclusion of Negroes from*
Private Institutions: Policy-Making
Positions in the Cook County Private Sector (*1965*)

	Policy-making positions	Positions held by Negroes	%
1. Business corporations			
Banks	2258	7	a
Insurance	533	35	6
Nonfinancial corporations	4047	0	0
Total:	6838	42	a
2. Legal profession			
Total:	757	0	0
3. Universities[b]			
Total:	380	5	1
4. Voluntary organizations			
Business and professional	324	3	1
Welfare and religious	791	69	9
Total:	1115	72	6
5. Labor unions			
Internationals	94	15	16
District councils	211	20	9
Locals	514	73	14
Total:	819	108	13
Grand total:	9909	227	2
Grand total for public and private sectors:	10,997	285	2

a Below 1 per cent.
b Includes the University of Illinois, which is a public body.

The very prestigious universities — the University of Chicago, Northwestern University, Loyola University, DePaul University, Roosevelt University, the Illinois Institute of Technology, and the University of Illinois (the only public university of the seven) — had a negligible 1 per cent Negro representation. Most of these universities had few Negro students, faculty members, or administrators. Five of the seven had no Negro policy-makers. The University of Illinois had one. Roosevelt University, the sole institution that had a number of Negroes at the top, was the newest, and the one with the least public support. When this university was founded, its leaders had made a forthright stand on racial questions and a firm commitment to liberal principles.

We included these major universities in our survey because other institutions — public and private — have been placing increasingly greater

TABLE 3   *The Exclusion of Negroes from*
Private Establishments: Percentage of
Negro Policy-Makers in the Cook County
Private Sector by Establishment (1965)

	Total estab-lish-ments	None	Percentage of Negro policy-makers			
			1–5%	6–15%	16–50%	51%+
1. Business corporations						
Banks	102	98	0	4	0	0
Insurance	30	28	0	0	0	2
Nonfinancial corporations	240	240	0	0	0	0
2. Legal professions	54	54	0	0	0	0
3. Universities[a]	7	5	0	2	0	0
4. Voluntary organizations						
Business and professional	5	3	2	0	0	0
Welfare and religious	14	2	4	7	1	0
5. Labor unions						
Internationals	4	0	1	1	2	0
District councils	23	13	0	5	5	0
Locals	33	14	2	8	7	2
Total:	512	457	9	27	15	4

[a] Includes the University of Illinois, which is a public body.

value on them. Every year hundreds of millions of dollars in endowment and operating funds are given to the Chicago-area schools. After all, their research activities, and their training of skilled personnel, are considered a key to the region's economic growth. One indication of the tremendous influence these universities have is that they have determined the nature of urban renewal more than any other institutional group in Chicago (aside from the city government). Without a doubt, the universities have real — not nominal — power. And perhaps it is a reflection of this real power that only five out of 380 policy-making positions in these universities are held by Negroes.

The exclusion of Negroes from the private sector carries over to its voluntary organizations: Negroes are found in only 1 per cent of the posts there. It is in the voluntary associations that it is easiest to make symbolic concessions to the black community by giving token representation, yet even here Negroes were underrepresented — which highlights the fundamental norms of the entire sector.

The sectors and individual groups in the Chicago area with the highest Negro representation were those with a Negro constituency — elective offices, supervisory boards, labor unions, and religious and welfare organizations. These four groups accounted for 216 of the posts held by Negroes, or 75 per cent, although these four groups have only 19 per cent of all the policy-making positions we studied. Labor unions had a larger percentage — 13 per cent — than any other institution in the private sector. In welfare and religious organizations, whose constituents were often largely Negro, Negroes occupied 8 per cent of the positions, the same percentage of the elected public offices they held.

Now, either the black constituency elected the Negroes directly (in the case of elective offices and trade unions); or the Negroes were appointed to posts in an operation whose clients were largely Negro (principal of a Negro school, for example); or Negroes were given token representation on bodies that had a broad public purpose (like religious organizations). By "token representation," we mean — following James Q. Wilson — that "he is a man chosen because a Negro is 'needed' in order to legitimate [but not direct] whatever decisions are made by the agency."

Of the three ways a black constituency had of getting itself represented, the most important was the first. The statistics clearly show the importance of the Negro vote. The elected political offices and the elected trade-union offices account for only 11 per cent of all the policy-making positions in Cook County. Yet almost half of all the Negro policy-makers were found in these two areas — 137 out of 285.

Nonetheless, even in the major areas where Negro representation was the greatest — labor unions, elective offices, supervisory boards, and religious and welfare organizations — many institutions still excluded Negroes from positions of authority.

There are, of course, few Negroes in the building-trade unions, most of which bar Negroes from membership. Only two out of the 12 building-trade-union organizations we studied had even one Negro in a decisive slot. These two Negroes made up a mere one and a half per cent of the policy-making positions in the building-trade unions.

The greatest degree of black representation was found in the former C.I.O. industrial unions. Only one-fourth of these units in the survey totally excluded Negroes from leadership. In almost half, the percentage of Negro policy-makers was over 15 per cent — which is above token levels.

The former A.F. of L. unions (not including those in the building trades) had a higher rate of exclusion than those of the C.I.O. Two-fifths of these A.F. of L. unions had no Negroes at all in policy-making posts. But one-third of this group had leaderships that were 15 per cent or more Negro. And the only two black-controlled locals large enough to be included in this study were in A.F. of L. unions.

In elective offices, the Negro vote certainly does give Negroes some representation — though far below their proportionate number. In public administration, however, where advancement to policy-making offices comes through appointment and influence, Negroes are all but excluded from decisive posts, at both the federal and local levels. Although a very high percentage of all Negro professionals are in public service, they do not reach the top.

The only major governmental operation that had a goodly number of Negroes at the upper level of the bureaucratic hierarchy was the public-school system. Nine per cent of the top positions were occupied by Negroes. This unique situation is the result of some fairly recent appointments, made as concessions after an intense civil-rights campaign directed at the Chicago Board of Education. In this instance, one can consider these civil-rights actions as a proxy for Negro votes. Still, this high-level representation in the Chicago school hierarchy did not seem to reflect any uniform policy of including Negroes in management. At the level of principalship that was not included as a policy-making position in this study, only 3 per cent of the positions were occupied by blacks.

The voluntary welfare and religious associations that were sufficiently important to be included in the study usually had at least a few Negro policy-makers. Only two out of 14 bodies had no Negroes in policy positions (see Table 3), while four organizations had token representation — below 5 per cent. None had a Negro majority in the key posts. Only the Chicago Urban League (with 43 per cent) had Negroes in more than 15 per cent of its policy slots. If individual religious denominations had been among the organizations counted in the survey, there would have been some black-dominated groups. As it was, Negro representation in the United Protestant Federation, which *was* included, came largely from the traditionally Negro denominations. It is of interest to note that, in recent years, Protestant groups have provided some of the few instances in which Negroes have been elected to important offices by a constituency that was overwhelmingly white.

Not only were Negroes grossly underrepresented in Chicago's policy-making posts, but even where represented they had less power than white policy-makers. The fact is that *the number of posts held by Negroes tended to be inversely related to the power vested in these positions — the more powerful the post, the fewer the black policy-makers.*

As we have seen, Negroes were virtually excluded from policy-making in the single most powerful institutional sector — the business world. In *all* sectors, they were generally placed in positions in which the authority was delegated from a higher administrator, or divided among a board. Rarely were Negroes in positions of ultimate authority, either as chief executive or as top board officer.

When Negroes ran for a board or for a judicial office on a slate, their number had been limited by the political parties apportioning out the nominations. The percentage of Negroes on such boards or (especially) in judicial offices tended to run lower than the number of Negroes in legislative posts, for which Negroes run individually.

It is also true that no Negro has *ever* been elected to one of the key city-wide or county-wide executive positions, such as Mayor, City Clerk, or President of the Cook County Board. These are the positions with the greatest power and patronage.

In welfare agencies, where Negroes have token representation, they are virtually excluded from the key posts of executive director. Only five of the 135 directors of medium and of large welfare agencies were Negro.

Now, it was in the trade-union sector that the highest percentage of Negroes had policy posts — 13 per cent. We asked several experts on the Chicago trade-union movement to list the number of Negroes among the 100 most powerful trade unionists in the area. Among the 100 people they named, the number of Negroes ranged from two to five. This did not surprise us, for it was compatible with our general knowledge of the number of Negroes with truly powerful posts in other sectors.

A RULE OF THUMB ON NEGRO POWER

All in all, then, we would suggest the following rule of thumb: *The actual power vested in Negro policy-makers is about one-third as great as the percentage of the posts they hold.*

Thus when Negroes elected other Negroes to office, these officers tended to represent small constituencies. For example, the greatest number of Negroes in legislative posts came from relatively small districts that happen to have black majorities. Indeed, according to Cook County tradition, Negroes simply do not hold legislative posts in city, state, or federal government *unless* they represent a district that is mostly black. No district with Negroes in the minority had a Negro representative, even when Negroes constituted the single largest ethnic group. And some districts with a Negro majority had a *white* representative.

Then too, the smaller the district, the more likely it would be homogeneous, and the greater the chances of its having a black majority that could return a Negro to office. In the Chicago area, consequently, Negroes were best represented on the City Council, which is based on 50 relatively small wards, each representing about 70,000 people; Negroes were represented most poorly in the U.S. House of Representatives, for which there are only nine rather large districts in Chicago, each representing about 500,000 people.

Most of the government policy-making posts that Negroes had been appointed to were in operations that had a large Negro clientele, if not

a majority — as in the case of the Chicago public schools; or in operations that had largely Negro personnel, as in the case of the post office.
On the appointed supervisory boards, in fact, those with as many as two
Negro members were the Chicago Board of Education and the Board
of Health, both of which serve very large numbers of Negroes.

This limiting of Negro policy-makers to Negro constituencies was quite
as evident in the private sector. Three of the four banks with Negroes in
policy-making posts were in Negro neighborhoods; and two were the
smallest of the 102 banks we studied, and the other two were not much
larger. The two insurance firms had mainly Negro clients, and were
among the smallest of the 30 studied. In the voluntary organizations, the
more they served Negroes, the higher the percentage of Negroes on their
boards (although representation was by no means proportionate). Thus,
the five Negro executive directors of welfare organizations we studied
headed all-Negro constituencies: Three directed moderate-sized neighborhood settlements in the ghetto; one directed a virtually all-Negro hospital;
and one directed an interracial agency that had traditionally had a Negro
executive.

Still another way of limiting the power of Negro policy-makers, we
discovered, was by "processing" them. Public and private institutions, as
indicated, tend to have a token representation of Negroes. And many
Negroes in these positions have totally identified with the traditional
values and goals of the institution, regardless of what they mean to the
mass of Negroes. Some of these Negro policy-makers, because of their
small numbers and lack of an independent source of power, are neutralized. Others, if they are firm in representing the needs and outlook of
the black community, are isolated. The two Negro members of the Chicago Board of Education represented these extremes. Mrs. Wendell
Green, a longtime Board member and the elderly widow of a former
judge, had been the most diehard supporter of Benjamin Willis, the former
Schools Superintendent, through all of his fights against the civil-rights
movement. The other Negro — Warren Bacon, a business executive —
sympathized with the campaign against inferior, segregated housing and,
as a result, has been largely isolated on the Board. He was rarely consulted on critical questions. His vote was usually cast with a small minority, and sometimes alone.

The fact is that the norms and traditions of *any* organization or enterprise limit the amount of power held by black policy-makers. It is no
longer bold to assert that the major institutions and organizations of our
society have an operational bias that is racist, even though their *official*
policies may be the opposite. The Negro policy-maker in one of these
institutions (or in a small black-controlled organization dependent upon
these institutions, such as the head of a trade-union local) has a certain

degree of conflict. If he goes along with the institution, from which he gains power and prestige, he ends up by implementing operations that restrict his minority group. Edward Banfield and James Q. Wilson have neatly pinpointed this dilemma in the political sphere:

> Not only are few Negroes elected to office, but those who are elected generally find it necessary to be politicians first and Negroes second. If they are to stay in office, they must soft-pedal the racial issues that are of the most concern to Negroes as Negroes.

This pattern is seen in the failure of William Dawson, Cook County's one Negro Congressman, to obtain many Presidential appointments or top federal civil-service posts for Negroes. Theoretically he is in a more strategic position to influence government operations than any other Chicago-based Congressman, since he has 23 years' seniority and holds the important chairmanship of the Government Operations Committee. Yet in 1965 Negroes held only 2 per cent of the top federal jobs in Chicago.

Any examination of the real power of Negroes in Chicago requires an examination of the strongest single organization in the Negro community — the Democratic Party. Wilson's study, *Negro Politics*, points out that the strength and cohesiveness of the Negro Democratic organization is largely dependent upon the strength of the total Cook County Democratic organization. The Negro organization is a "sub-machine" within the larger machine that dominates the city. The Negro sub-machine, however, has basically settled for lesser patronage positions and political favors, rather than using its considerable strength to try to make or change policy. Therefore, this Negro organization avoids controversial questions, and seeks to avoid differences with the central organization on such vital issues as urban renewal and the schools.

In short, then, not only are Negroes underrepresented in the major policy-making positions in Cook County, but even where represented their actual power is restricted, or their representatives fail to work for the long-term interests of their constituency. It is therefore safe to estimate that Negroes really hold less than 1 per cent of the effective power in Chicago metropolitan area. Realistically, the power structure of Chicago is hardly less white than that of Mississippi.

From these figures it is clear that, at this time, Negroes in the Chicago area lack the power to make changes in the areas of housing, jobs, and education. The basic subjugation of the black community, however, would not end if there were simply more Negroes in policy-making posts. We have seen the prevalence of tokenism, of whites' choosing Negro leaders who are conservative, of their boxing in Negro leaders who are proved to be liberal, of their giving these leaders less actual power than they give themselves.

Our analysis suggests that the best way to increase both the number *and* the power of Negro policy-makers is through unifying the black constituency. Access to policy-making positions could come through both the development of large, black-controlled organizations, and through getting Negroes into white-dominated organizations. If the constituency lacks its own clear set of goals and policies, however, things will surely remain the same. For success depends not just upon formal unity, but upon the nature of the goals set by the black community. In this situation, the overcoming of black powerlessness seems to require the development of a self-conscious community that has the means to determine its own interests, and the cohesiveness to command the loyalty of its representatives. We can safely predict that more and more Negroes will be moved into policy-making positions. The fundamental conflict, therefore, will take place between their co-optation into the established institutions and their accountability to a black constituency.

JULIUS JACOBSON   *Union Conservatism:*
A Barrier to Racial Equality

Some may attempt to define our system in terms of private investment in corporate enterprise, where goods are produced for sale at profit.

But, as I see it, the distinguishing feature of this American system is its emphasis on people, on freedom, on free institutions, and on the opportunity for betterment. The Bill of Rights, the Constitution, and our educational system are all integral parts of our economic order and more essential to it than the stock exchange or any corporate board.

The above quotation from a speech provides a clue to understanding why the Negro masses today, on the whole, have an attitude that covers the narrow range from indifference to pronounced hostility toward the American trade union movement. For this speech, with its dubious prop-

From *The Negro and the American Labor Movement,* edited by Julius Jacobson. Copyright © 1968 by Julius Jacobson. Reprinted by permission of Doubleday and Company, Inc.

osition that the Bill of Rights is more fundamental to the American economic system than the stock exchange and corporate boards, and its
Fourth of July tribute to our system's alleged emphasis on "the oppor-
tunity for betterment," is from the formal address of an American labor
leader of some note, not a banker. And it is not from an address by Samuel
Gompers at the turn of the century to a convocation of the National Civic
Federation (an early alliance of bankers, AFL leaders, and public figures)
but from one delivered by George Meany, President of the American
Federation of Labor-Congress of Industrial Organizations, to the Fiftieth
Anniversary World Convocation of the National Industrial Conference
Board in New York City in September 1966.

While Meany's thoughts on the American system are crudely put, they
are not his alone. They are shared, among others, by a whole school of
American sociology which has been saying essentially the same thing for
many years, though, of course, with far greater sophistication and artful-
ness. According to this school, America is not dominated by an economic
class; there are, so the theory goes, no real hard and fast economic classes
in America — this is the land of "social mobility" (or, as Meany would
put it, there is "opportunity for betterment"). Since there are no economic
classes, there can be no class struggle. Since there is no class struggle,
there is no room for "ideologies" which reflect the special social and political needs and aspirations to power of an economic class. This rather
euphoric view of America does not deny that there are antagonisms in
American life, such as sectional differences or ethnic conflicts. But given
the positive "distinguishing features" of the American system, these differences can be amicably settled through a give-and-take process of
compromise and the judicious intervention of enlightened government.
Militancy or "extremist" programs and actions are decried as being in-
jurious to all.

One difficulty with the "end of ideology" theory of a classless America,
especially as popularized, consciously or not, by George Meany, is that it
does not correspond to the real world. Here, we can only note the credibility gap between the theory and the reality of life for the vast majority
of twenty million Negro Americans. A detailed account is not needed; we
need only remember that the lot of the Negroes, after all the promises and
good resolutions, remains one of economic, social, political, and personal
discrimination and humiliation. They have an unemployment rate double
that of whites (one out of every three Negro youths is unemployed) and
the disproportion continues to grow. In the ten-year period following the
merger of the AFL and CIO has been a decline in Negro family income
relative to whites (from 56 per cent to 53 per cent). Approximately one
half of Negro families have an annual income of less than $4500 a year.
Nearly one fourth of the Negroes in Los Angeles are poverty-stricken,
and this appalling figure is lower than in many other urban areas. (This

is based on federal government definitions of poverty, which are under-stated.) By any meaningful, relative definition of poverty, there are, in absolute numbers, more poor Negroes today than during the Great De-pression. Also, while integration is the law of the land, segregation remains the reality, North and South, and the ghetto continues to grow while homes continue to deteriorate. But the measure of oppression can never be gauged by statistics. The frustration, anger, and sorrow pro-duced by bigotry and racism do not lend themselves to statistical surveys. One thing is certain: the victims of racism can hardly be placated by such assurances as "our educational system" is an "integral part of our economic order"; nor, we suspect, would Meany's assurances that this is not a profit-motivated corporate economy carry the ring of truth if told to a Negro worker taking home less than fifty dollars a week in a New York City sweatshop, with poverty wages protected by an AFL-CIO contract.

Fortunately, oppression not only breeds misery, it also inspires resis-tance. We need only point to the multifaceted Negro revolution which began nearly fifteen years ago. Unfortunately, this resistance does not always receive the support it should from its "natural allies." The union movement is a prime case in point.

Actually, the union movement in this country has never fully met its responsibility to the Negro people in general, or to the Negro worker in particular. The early history of the American Federation of Labor reveals little more than contempt for the Negro worker, motivated in large mea-sure by racial prejudice among AFL affiliates (the United Mine Workers is an important exception) and in the Gompers leadership.

However, even if the AFL were not guilty of racist policies, it probably could not have had a major impact on the conditions of life of Negro workers, especially in the earliest years of the century. The AFL was primarily a federation of craftsmen organized on the basis of their various skills. This narrow form of organization gave it the strength to survive anti-union pressure from employers in a period when industrial unionism was simply not the order of the day. The large corporations, particularly in steel, had enormous financial resources and allies in all levels and branches of government; they could buy armies of Pinkerton men, judges, politicians, and strikebreakers. They were simply too powerful for the nascent industrial unions to take permanent hold. This was made tragically clear in the Great Steel Strike of 1919 and in the events of the next decade, which witnessed not only the collapse of industrial unionism and near-demise of the once powerful United Mine Workers, but also the decline of long-established craft unions. By 1933 the unions could claim only a membership of two and a quarter million, and even that figure was arrived at by inflating numbers and crediting membership to unions that existed only on paper. The bulk of AFL affiliates which survived the massive open-shop drives of the twenties were the most racially oriented craft unions, such as those in the building trades. On the other hand, the AFL unions that were the first to succumb to the anti-labor offensive were the weak all-Negro "federal" locals directly affiliated with the AFL Executive Council. Thus by 1930 a generous estimate of total Negro membership in the AFL was around fifty thousand.

To say that the AFL could not have successfully transformed itself into an industrial union in this period, organizing the millions of white and Negro laborers in mass-production industries, is not to rationalize its racial policies, which had deleterious effects on Negro workers, white workers, and the trade union movement. There *were* thousands of Negro crafts-men ignored by the AFL; others were kept in segregated locals. And no less damaging was the fact that in strikebound plants employers found it easier to recruit strikebreakers among Negroes who never developed a trade union consciousness and could see no reason why they should for-sake a much needed day's pay for the sake of a white man's union.

The American Dream crumbled in the crash of '29. Despair and hunger supplanted the self-confidence of the twenties. The large corporations remained powerful, but less so. The union-busting drives of the twenties, euphemistically called the American Plan, could no longer rally public opinion as before, nor could the corporations depend to the same extent on the assistance of congenial Presidents, Attorney Generals, and judges. The unskilled, culturally divided immigrant workers of earlier decades were now largely replaced by a more culturally integrated work force — it was "Americanized." New economic circumstances interacting with a heightened political and social consciousness forged in the Depression created, at last, the proper soil to nourish the cause of industrial unionism. Relentless pressure was exerted within the AFL to focus its efforts on the organization of steel, packing house, rubber, etc. The effort was naturally resisted by the most powerful AFL leaders, who clung desperately to their principles of craft organization.

Those trade unionists determined to plant the union flag in mass-pro-duction industries realized that they could not succeed without winning the support of Negro workers, who constituted a significant and cohesive percentage of the work force. This the industrially oriented unionists proceeded to do. But it was not only necessity that promoted their efforts to win Negro support and build democratic, interracial unions. Much of the personnel for the Committee for Industrial Organization was provided by John L. Lewis' United Mine Workers with its relatively equalitarian traditions on the race issue (although, in practice, many UMW locals were not free of segregationist practices). In addition to UMW organizers, the ranks of early CIO activists were swelled by a color-ful phalanx of equalitarian, socially conscious militants — Socialists, Trotskyists, Lovestoneites, independent radicals, ex-Wobblies, ex-members of the Detroit-based Proletarian[1] — all of whom worked to overcome Negro resistance to unionization and, at least, to neutralize white workers' resistance to Negroes. Some of these radicals had been members of the UMW, but opposed to Lewis. Lewis, who ruled the UMW with an iron fist, drove the opposition leaders out of the union and out of the industry. But they were among the most talented and courageous men in the union movement and he felt obliged to call upon them to take leading posts in the CIO drive. Frank Brophy, for example, accepted Lewis' invitation to act as Secretary for the top Committee of Five. By 1937, when the Committee was expelled by the AFL and became the Congress of Industrial Organizations, it had thirty-two incipient internationals.

Given the special political problems posed by the campaign to organize the mass-production industries, the greater political bent of those who led the CIO drive and the need for welfare legislation to protect the interests of mass-production workers, the CIO was soon committed to social programs and political campaigns. These, in turn, acted as further incentives to seek the support of Negro workers in the unions, directly involving them in the unions' internal and political affairs, and, in addition, to seek out and solidify an alliance of the CIO and a host of Negro organizations. In the legislative program of the early CIO a high priority was given to civil rights causes.

If only out of self-interest, competitively motivated, the AFL loosened some of its racial barriers, made new overtures to Negro organizations, paid lip service to civil rights programs and some legislation, and generally tried to project the image of a movement that abhorred bigotry and racist practices.

The CIO-Negro alliance managed to hold together throughout the war. However, some friction was created by the actions of Communists, who had become an extremely powerful force in the CIO. The Communists, out of allegiance to the Russo-American alliance, emerged as the extreme right wing of the labor movement. They advocated the speed-up, proposed incentive pay, denounced strikes, defended the proposal for a labor draft, and announced that it was the duty of workers "to force better profits on unwilling employers." They also made it quite explicit that they were prepared to sacrifice the rights of Negroes in the interests of the war. Thus, Negro leaders, who could see no contradiction between the fight against Hitlerism and the continued struggle for civil rights and fair employment practices at home, were roundly denounced by Communist

[1] The Communist Party was opposed to the formation of the CIO and did not bring the Party-led unions into the organization until the spring of 1937. However, many individual Communists, in advance of their more cautious Party, were swept along by the rising tide of industrial unionism and played a prominent role in 1935–36.

leaders. Most notably, the March on Washington Movement, which under the leadership of A. Philip Randolph, threatened to assemble in Washington in a mass demonstration to protest job discrimination, was subjected to Communist vilification. Randolph was described as "a Fascist helping defeatism." The attitude of the Communists provoked Willard S. Townsend, the Negro President of the CIO-affiliated United Transport Service Employees, to note that "the present line of the Communist carpetbaggers on the Negro question . . . is indistinguishable from that of many of our southern poll taxers and carpetbaggers." Had the Communist line been adopted by the CIO during the war, the alliance with the Negro organizations might have ended then and there.

While the record of the CIO was a marked improvement over what had been, it was not without blemish. There were instances of segregationist acts, particularly in Southern locals, and it did not aggressively pursue in action the equalitarian policies it advocated during the war years (e.g., it failed to support the March on Washington Movement). In the immediate postwar period when the AFL tried to counter the CIO "Operation Dixie" with its own organizing drive in the South, it tried to project an equalitarian image before Negro workers with attacks on the racial practices of CIO unions. The criticism was hypocritical, but not all of it was fanciful. Most serious is that the efforts of the CIO leadership to raise the rank and file to its own level of equalitarian consciousness were inadequate.

The alliance of Negro and labor organizations, particularly the CIO, continued in the postwar period. A tribute to its effectiveness was Truman's surprise victory in the 1948 presidential election. But the extent to which organized labor went all-out for Truman's victory was symptomatic of a creeping inner malaise in the trade union movement that eventually deepened the gulf between organized labor and the Negro working class. This malaise was the increasing political conservatism and bureaucratization of the CIO. The reasons for this devolution cannot be detailed here. But the fact must be recognized. Postwar evidence of this retrograde change is the support given to Truman in 1948, the manner in which the CIO purged its ranks of Communist-led unions, its response to the McCarthyite madness, and the fact that its alliance with traditional Negro organizations took place within the framework of the Democratic Party, involving further alliances and deals with corrupt city machines.

In the enthusiasm generated by its successful campaign for Truman, the CIO compromised its political autonomy and conveniently overlooked the anti-labor record of its candidate. From a lesser evil, Truman emerged as a positive good. Yet, to give but one instance of his record, it was Truman who responded to a series of massive strikes in the spring of 1946 (one year after VE Day, and six months after Japan surrendered) with strikebreaking proposals that might have given pause even to a Coolidge or a Harding. He proposed that in strikebound plants taken over by the federal government, authority be granted to induct strikers into the Army and imprison strike leaders. Though the labor draft provision was removed from the bill (not by Truman) and the bill never enacted into law, it reveals the conservative temper of the man supported by the CIO two years later as a hard-hitting champion of the oppressed.

Nor did the CIO take full and honest public cognizance of the fact that it was the Truman Administration that provided the prelude to McCarthyism. As for the Wisconsin Senator himself, one would be hard put to find a CIO document clearly exposing McCarthy as a dangerous demagogue and decrying the alarming erosion of democratic liberties in the early fifties. Indeed, the CIO seemed to take a lesson from McCarthy when it came to dealing with the Communist threat inside the CIO. Of course, Communists presented a real menace to the CIO while the threat of the American Communist Party to the American "way of life" was largely the diabolical product of McCarthy's morbid fancy. Nevertheless, the CIO leadership, operating under the pressures of the cold war and having grown cynical and conservative where democracy was concerned, removed its Communist threat in the most expeditious bureaucratic fashion — it simply expelled the Communist-led unions. That was in 1950. It was a far cry from the manner in which several CIO unions had earlier handled the Communist issue. The most notable contrast was provided by Walter Reuther, who led a militant faction in the UAW to victory over a powerfully entrenched Communist and fellow-traveling machine. Reuther's faction defeated the Communists not with organizational edicts or the crude epithets of "red-baiting" but with an attack from the left, exposing the basically reactionary nature of the Communist movement and its readiness to sacrifice democratic principles and basic trade union objectives in order to further Party-dictated Stalinist political objectives. The difference between Reuther's methods and those used by the CIO as a whole was far greater than the mere two-year difference in time implies.

Despite the endless bill of grievances that could be drawn against the AFL and the CIO by those concerned with political and trade union democracy, hope and enthusiasm were revived by their merger in 1955. A unified labor movement of fifteen million including one and a half million Negroes could provide a dynamic new force in America. This seemed justified by the initial efforts of the AFL-CIO to rid itself of utterly corrupt and gangster-ridden affiliates. The movement would continue to reform itself at the same time that it engaged in dramatic campaigns to organize the South, concerned itself with the serious problem of attracting white-collar workers, became again a pole of attraction for the idealistic young, and, in general, would emerge as a viable instrument for political and economic democratization.

The fusion itself might not precipitate the sought-after change in the labor movement. But there was the upheaval in the Negro and civil rights movements that was already a year in ferment. It was clear that Negro consciousness and militancy would grow; new forces would develop in the civil rights movement; and in the struggle even traditional, conservative Negro organizations would develop a more active, militant character. Surely, the unified labor movement would feel obliged to move along with the changing times if only to keep in step and maintain its alliance with the Negro organizations. At the very least, along with eliminating racketeering unions from the house of labor, it would conduct an uncompromising campaign to cleanse itself of discriminatory racial practices — particularly in the old-line AFL craft organizations.

These were not unreasonable expectations. But they proved too high. Instead, after thirteen years the unified labor movement is encased by a bureaucratic encrustation as impenetrable to change as high-tensile armor plating to buckshot. Even Walter Reuther is obliged to recognize this publicly. Speaking before a special convention of the United Automobile Workers held in April 1967, Reuther delivered a blistering attack on the AFL-CIO leadership in which he summed up his view that "in the eleven years of the merger we believe that the AFL-CIO has become stagnant and is vegetating. I say, to put it simply and understandably, it has an acute case of hardening of the arteries."

However, every bureaucratic institution has its intellectual apologists. The union movement is no exception. Thus books and articles in great profusion have recently appeared to counter the charge that the union movement is dying spiritually. In answer to the critics of organized labor, one finds the usual litany of statistics, quotations from resolutions about civil rights, financial reports, accounts of labor contributions to welfare legislation in the past and commitment to carry on in the same spirit in the future — only better. The real issues are thereby skirted, or obscured. A major symptom of the AFL-CIO's malaise is its inability to attract the young and idealistic. Yet one of the saving graces of this decade is that in the younger generation today there are thousands of young people prepared to lay their bodies on the line for idealistic causes. Few of them have found their way into the labor movement. There are exceptions, such as the involvement of hundreds of youngsters in the struggle to organize the California agricultural workers. Even here, what is instructive is that the youngsters who assisted in the organization and strike responded to the appeal of the Mexican workers with greater zeal than did the upper echelons of the AFL-CIO.

The truth that must be confronted is that the young see nothing idealistic in the labor movement as a whole. There was little to inspire enthusiasm in the AFL-CIO support of the Bay of Pigs adventure or in Meany's dash from his television set to the telephone on October 22, 1962 to wire President Kennedy "the support of the entire labor movement" for his action in the missile crisis that threatened the world with nuclear annihilation. Young people could not be expected to appreciate the heartiness of the labor movement's applause for Johnson's invasion of the Dominican Republic and they are not likely to be moved by reports that at its 1967 Executive Council gathering in Bal Harbour organized labor is again on record with a hawklike position on Vietnam. What is more, young people will hardly be impressed by the Executive Council's assessment hailing social progress under Johnson as "a record unsurpassed in any period of democratic government."

On domestic issues, the AFL-CIO stance is that of moderate liberalism; on foreign policy issues, it is that of rightwing reaction. But what of its internal life and organization? A fair and objective characterization of its internal structure is — authoritarian and corrupted. There are exceptions, of course — in both directions: some unions permit a degree of democracy while others veer in a totalitarian direction. It is interesting to note that in the various charts and statistics found in the literature on the labor movement today there is nothing on salaries and expenses of officers. This is not a trifling question, since the extent to which a union officer will enrich himself is a fair index of the quality of his organization. Perhaps this is why it is seldom mentioned that in recent years wages in AFL-CIO affiliates for union notables run to over $100,000 a year (plus expenses). Most damning, though, is that few unions will tolerate opposition. This is true not only of the old-line craft unions but of industrial unions as well, where to organize opposition — even to voice it — entails the risk of the loss of one's job or physical assault or both. These hard facts of life usually go unnoticed in much of the current apologias on the labor movement.

In the civil rights revolution, the trade union movement has not been able to move beyond the limits of its bureaucratic, socially conservative mentality. It has been unable to meet the special needs and problems of the Negro working class because it cannot truly recognize its existence. Left to its own resources, it cannot eliminate discriminatory practices within the house of labor since it refuses to acknowledge how widespread they are. Given its conservative temper and intolerance, it cannot accept constructive criticism from within or outside its ranks. It is insensitive to changing moods because it doesn't really care enough.

This bureaucratic inertia is harmful not only to the civil rights cause but for the organizational needs of the AFL-CIO itself. For example,

the AFL-CIO's ability to conduct a major organizational drive in the
South is limited since a massive drive there requires more than money; it
calls for a missionary spirit in the ranks which is possible only if the
leadership encourages membership participation in union affairs. A
frightening prospect for labor autocrats!

On paper and in resolutions the AFL-CIO is committed to racial
equality in a most general way. One test of its sincerity is how it responds
to various calls to action from the civil rights movement. Take the March
on Washington of 1963, designed to further the cause of civil rights legislation. It won the support and sponsorship of an extraordinarily wide section of civil rights organizations, liberal groups, churches, and a few
unions with large Negro memberships. Notorious for its absence from
the list of sponsors or supporters was the AFL-CIO. This was not an
oversight. The AFL-CIO Executive Council discussed the March and
refused to endorse it. More than that, it refused to recommend that
affiliated unions give their endorsement, leaving it instead to "individual
union determination."

On the issue of "preferential hiring" of Negro workers the AFL-CIO
position is as undistinguished as on other civil rights demands. The call
for "preferential" treatment for weak or oppressed or disadvantaged
minorities is in principle thoroughly democratic, though the term "preferential" lends itself to demagogic abuse, of which the Meany leadership
has taken full advantage. It is, in fact, widely applied in the United
States. The graduated income tax, for example, is a form of preferential
treatment for low-income groups. With the exception of a few crackpots,
no one has recently denounced the tax system for discriminating in favor
of those with lower incomes.

To illustrate the point by another analogy: if in the thirties the demand
had been raised that immigration quotas be revised so that German Jews
be given preference over other nationalities because of their uniquely
disadvantaged position, would anyone with an ounce of humanity have
raised the cry that such "preferential" treatment was unfair because it
would have discriminated against or inconvenienced Englishmen or
Swedes also seeking to emigrate to the United States?

What, then, is either extreme or unfair in the demand that Negro
workers who have so long been oppressed be partially compensated for
crimes against them (including crimes by racist unions which deprived
them of a livelihood) by giving them preferential consideration in hiring
practices?

One might argue that the slogan of preferential hiring is a poor one to
raise, from a tactical point of view, but this is not the sole objection of
the AFL-CIO, which has made it a matter of principle. As Meany expressed it in testimony to the House Judiciary Committee in 1963, pref-

erential hiring is a "pitfall" since it "would merely replace one kind of discrimination with another." What upsets labor leaders about a perfectly moderate, democratic demand is that it is too radical for their tastes (just as the moderate March on Washington was too radical to endorse) and, no less important, if preferential hiring were practiced on a wide scale it might tend to correct the racial imbalance of racist unions, thereby threatening the power of entrenched leaderships. There are a number of unions with little to fear on this score since they already have written into their constitutions provisions that prohibit members from running for national office unless they have held office for a specific number of years previously!

If the AFL-CIO Executive Council could not find room in its heart to endorse the Washington March with its moderate demands, one can hardly expect Meany or his fellows to have kind words for the advocates of Black Power. Nonetheless, the level and style of their repudiation of Black Power shed light on their lack of compassion and understanding.

In a letter to A. Philip Randolph, written in October 1966, praising the Negro labor leader for repudiating Black Power concepts, Meany had the following to say:

> Your restatement of commitment to the attainment of racial justice by the democratic process, your repudiation of the strategies of violence, reprisals or vigilantism, your reaffirmation of the goals of integration commends itself to every thinking American.
>
> You and I agree that extremism is the antithesis of democracy and extremism by advocates of justice for America's minority population cannot be countenanced any more than extremism by advocates of white supremacy.

To dispute the legitimacy of Black Power is one thing. To equate, however, the extremism of the victims with the extremism of their oppressors is bewildering. But if Meany's letter ignores the difference between the two, it at least has the virtue of being restrained. It was, after all, a letter to Randolph.

However, a month before Meany sent his letter, another union leader discussed Black Power at greater length in the union press. Excerpts follow:

> Somehow or other I can't accept the proposition that a bunch of hoodlums who hurl rocks at bypassers, throw gasoline torches into buildings, and upturn and set fire to parked cars are freedom fighters and not just plain bums out for a spree of violence. . . .
>
> In support of this weighted balance of favor toward Negroes I offer the testimony of Cicero, Illinois, where a whole community of stupid whites massed to commit racist violence against a cluster

of do-and-dare Negro Yahoos. The latter were mobilized under the auspices of the Student Nonviolent Coordinating Committee, a group composed of violent nonstudents at present dominated by a character named Stokely Carmichael, who, I understand, passed a course in surliness *cum laude*, and was accorded the honorary title of B. P. for "Black Power." . . .

However, I've got news for Mr. Carmichael, the reputed author of the Black Power slogan. The Negro goons who go on racist rampages know exactly what Black Power means. To them it means the chance to go on a spree of violence with a testimonial as a "freedom fighter" for a cover; a chance to do pillaging and looting with little likelihood of punishment. . . .

How is it possible for a trade unionist to describe with such malice Negroes who raise the slogan of Black Power because they despair of ever being accepted as equals by whites?

It is true, of course, that many Black Power advocates have fallen victim to an inverted kind of racism. But even here, how can anyone confuse the pain and anguish of black people treated as less than human with the cruelty and howls of their white tormentors?

What adds to the significance of these coarse descriptions of Negro protest is that they did not appear in the press of some old, conservative, hard-bitten craft union but were printed in *The Hat Worker*, written by its editor, Jack Rich, and published by the old-time socialistic Millinery Workers International.

That the AFL-CIO leadership has grown calloused and is becoming irrelevant to the lives of the Negro masses was demonstrated by its response to the urban racial upheavals in the summer of 1967. It could not grasp that these were more than "riots" (though less than revolutions). The best that George Meany could do in his 1967 Labor Day message was to call for legislative programs and anti-poverty moneys that would "strike at the evils which breed riots." At the same time, Meany — who so well reflects the temper and consciousness of the trade union leadership as a whole — associated the "riots" with "The criminal madness of a few . . ." as he inveighed against "The mindless riots of this unhappy summer [which] cannot be condoned. Arson, looting, and murder have no relations to civil rights; they are criminal wrongs and an affront to the very ideals which motivate the quest for a better society."

In his plea for law and order President Meany is somewhat confused about who was murdering whom in these "mindless riots"; eighty dead black bodies — men, women, children — in Detroit and Newark suggest that Meany's accusing finger is pointing in the wrong direction. Such false accusations, along with shallowness and conservativism, typified the reaction among trade union leaders. These are postures which can only retard the cause of racial justice, hinder the cause of trade unionism, and widen the breach between organized labor and the Negro people.

Much has been written in criticism and defense of the internal racial practices of the AFL-CIO. One thing to which all agree: racial discrimination exists inside major international unions affiliated with the Federation. In dispute are how deep and extensive it is and how to combat it.

In discussing the problem several years ago, President Meany maintained that:

> We have never at any time tried to gloss over the short-comings of unionism on the subject of equal opportunity. Yes, some of our members take a wrongheaded view. . . . But we in the labor movement publicly deplore these few holdouts against justice. We do our utmost to bring them around to the right side. And at the same time, the employers — who actually do the hiring — escape in many instances with no criticism whatever.

It is a disingenuous performance. It is a matter of record that the AFL-CIO tried to minimize, or gloss over, these shortcomings and union leaders were loath to discuss, much less deplore, them in public. Of special interest is Meany's passing the blame on to employers. No one doubts that employers discriminate. Nevertheless, it is no less true that in innumerable cases it is the unions that, in effect, do the hiring and the discriminating while individual employers are often prepared to employ Negroes. That is the way it works in many of the building craft unions. One of the more widely publicized union-versus-Negro worker battles recently waged is illustrative.

In New Rochelle, a suburb of New York City, a new shopping center was being build recently until work was stopped as a result of a dispute between civil rights organizations and the discriminatory building trades unions. At issue was the fact that these unions have no Negro members, nor do they accept Negro apprentices for training. New Rochelle has a large Negro population with many unemployed Negro workers. The R. H. Macy Company, whose building is the largest in the center, publicly offered to pay some of the cost involved in training Negro apprentices since the dispute caused the entire building project to come to a full halt. To be sure, Macy's management was not altruistic — just realistic. But it is an employer in this case, as in many others, who was willing to break the race barrier. The unions, however, remain obdurate in their racial policies. Charges of discriminatory practices against Negroes by Local 501 of the International Brotherhood of Electrical Workers, Local 38 of the Sheet Metal Workers and Local 86 of the Plumbers Union were brought before the New York State Commission for Human Rights by the New Rochelle Human Rights Commission. On November 15, 1967, the State Commission found the electrical and sheet metal locals guilty of discriminatory practices against Negroes.

According to the Commission, the business agent for Local 501 of the IBEW admitted that in his thirty-nine years of union membership he had never known of a Negro apprentice or journeyman in the local.

Meany maintains that the AFL-CIO is doing its utmost to eliminate discriminatory practices. This claim is somewhat weakened when, a few minutes later, he notes that "we are the only one, among civil rights forces, which has openly called for legislation for the correction of short-comings in its own ranks."

It is never made clear which are the other civil rights forces requiring correction of shortcomings. More important here, why should the AFL-CIO have to rely so heavily on legislation to eliminate discrimination in its own house? If the CIO could expel unions for being Communist-controlled and the merged union movement found it possible to expel affiliates for corruption, why can't the AFL-CIO establish its own forceful legislation and discipline to overcome discriminatory practices in its own organization?

Moreover, the problem of union discrimination is much broader than Meany suggests. This mounting evidence is that not "some" members take a wrongheaded view but that the bulk of the union movement, on one level or another, follows discriminatory policies, and has successfully resisted the minimal internal union pressures and heavier external effort to bring full equality into the labor movement. A detailed account is not possible here, but at the very least we can point to the recent findings of the New York City Commission on Human Rights.

After conducting a series of hearings on allegations of racial discrimination in the building trade unions in 1963, the Commission reported:

> A pattern of exclusion exists in a substantial portion of the building construction industry, effectively barring nonwhites from participating in this area of the city's economic life.

In March 1967 the Commission ended another series of hearings on the construction industry, and its sixty-four-page report reveals only minimal variations from the 1963 pattern. There are two major exceptions to this pattern of exclusion — the electricians' and carpenters' unions.

Bolstering these conclusions is a study recently completed by the department of economics at the University of Texas for the Office of Manpower Policy, Evaluation and Research of the U.S. Labor Department. Entitled "Negro Participation in Apprenticeship Programs," the report is a survey of union practices in eleven major cities across the country, including New York.

Between March 1963 and March 1966, the report reveals, the Elevator

Constructors Union in New York City admitted only two nonwhites to its apprenticeship training program. Local 2, Plumbers Union (Manhattan) admitted only nine. (This is the local of which President Meany is still a member.) It admitted no nonwhite apprentices at all during 1965–66. Local 1, Plumbers Union (Brooklyn and Queens) admitted twenty-two nonwhites to its apprenticeship program between 1963 and 1966, but in the 1965–66 period only six nonwhites were admitted to the program.

The report shows that considerable progress has been made by the Carpenters District Council and the International Brotherhood of Electrical Workers, Local 3. Between March 1963 and March 1966, 630 nonwhites were admitted to the carpenters' apprenticeship program and, during the same period, the IBEW admitted 275 nonwhites. The number of nonwhites admitted to apprenticeship by the electricians is particularly important, the Texas report says, because of "the fact that the U. S. Census of 1960 reported only 79 Negro electrical apprentices in the entire nation."

Sheet Metal Workers Local 28 admitted no nonwhites until 1966. It is a glaring example of the bitterness with which some craft unions resist democratic racial practices. It took the courts to order Local 28 to hold apprenticeship training tests. Those passing the tests would then have to be taken into the union's apprenticeship training program. Before the court decision the sheet metal workers' apprenticeship training program had worked on a father-son basis, which, in effect, excluded Negroes.

Under court order, the tests were given at the New York University testing center. A number of Negro youths applied for the tests and, in preparation for the difficult examinations, were tutored in a special program set up by the Workers Defense League. When the test results were revealed, nine of the top scores were Negroes, and twenty-six out of the top sixty were Negroes. Local 28 was legally obliged to take them into the union as apprentices-trainees. Embittered by the prospect of Negro apprentices, the local refused to take them in, suggesting that Negroes who scored so high could have done so only if they cheated. At this point the State Commission on Human Rights went to court and successfully enjoined Local 28 from denying the Negro youths their rights. Apparently the discriminatory craft unions want to have it both ways: on the one hand, they argue that one reason Negroes are not found in the craft unions is that they do not have the skills; on the other hand, when Negroes prove that they do have the skills, it is argued that they must have cheated. At the time of this writing it is not certain whether Local 28 will continue its efforts in the courts to bar Negro trainees from its apprenticeship program.

One final point on the question of union attitudes toward the Negro worker in particular and the Negro in general. What is so damaging to the union posture is the evident racist attitudes of its rank and file. There is little room to doubt that a high percentage of the American working class — above all, the industrial proletariat, many of them union members — is violently racist. To arrive at this conclusion, we need not turn to interviews or questionnaires. We need only refer to newspapers and television to see that it is in work-class districts — in Chicago, Cicero, Cleveland, etc. — that Negro demonstrators have encountered the most hysterical and violent opposition from whites.

The racist attitudes of American workers are a social problem, with roots that are deep and complex. The unions are certainly not responsible for this state of affairs. The AFL-CIO does not preach discrimination. On the contrary, its formal educational material invariably advances the ideas of racial equality and nothing said here is intended to detract from what the labor movement has contributed to civil rights legislation. The point is that the good that the union movement does is primarily on an elitist level, i.e., it is done from above. There has been no corresponding effort to bring the principles of racial equality home to the rank and file. For this reason, the union movement, bureaucratized and elitist, must assume its share of responsibility for the racial savagery and ignorance exhibited by so many rank-and-file workers.

LEE RAINWATER   *The Revolt*
of the Dirty-Workers

Schoolteachers, social workers, and policemen in a number of major cities have recently gone on strike, or resigned en masse, or taken mass sick leaves. These events bring to mind the works of Everett C. Hughes, the man who established the investigation of work, occupations, and professions as a major area of social research. In "Good People and Dirty Work," Everett Hughes analyzed some of the societal and social-psychological factors in Germany that fostered the mass murder of concentration-camp victims. He was particularly concerned with the link between the cadre that actually carried out the dirty work and the Germans in general, who were "ignorant" of and silent about what went on in the concentration camps. As in much social-science research, Hughes was able to use an extreme, almost unique social event to advance our understanding of much more common processes. The German murderers raised much more general questions about how societies go about handling situations in which repressive action is considered necessary, but few citizens are willing to do what they want done.

The Germans' anti-Semitism made them feel that "something must be done about the Jews," which in turn led them to covertly delegate to the S.S. the task of doing that something. It then became important to the Germans to fuzz over the gory details, to conceal from themselves, as well as from others, exactly what was being done. Hughes suggested that this is a typical way societies deal with out-groups:

> The greater their social distance from us the more we leave in the hands of others a sort of mandate by default to deal with them on our behalf. . . . Perhaps we give them an unconscious mandate to go beyond anything we ourselves would care to do, or even to acknowledge. I venture to suggest that the higher and more expert functionaries who act in our behalf represent something of a distillation of what we may consider our public wishes, while some of the others show a sort of concentrate of those impulses of which we are, or wish to be, less aware.

This shameful work that nevertheless must be done is, then (morally) "dirty work."

It is easy to see the same processes operating in the deeply felt American ambivalence toward the police. But the process operates much more broadly. In our world, there is a large out-group — a separate nation of ghetto Negroes whom most white Americans feel must be controlled and confined. Yet those same white Americans are deeply ashamed and uncertain about *how* Negroes are controlled and confined, and they prefer to conceal from themselves much of the detail of how the doers of this dirty work actually go about their assigned tasks.

As the urban ghettos have grown, so has the cohort of functionaries who receive the covert assignment to "keep the colored out of our way." In the process, many institutions officially designed to further well-being and opportunity have become perverted into institutions of custody and constraint. Social-welfare workers find that their profession, designed to help, has been perverted into one designed to spy and to punish. More dramatically, the schools have become custodial institutions in which less and less learning takes place. To conceal their failure, year-in and year-out the schools promote students who have learned less than they should. The proliferation of policemen in schools, of special schools for "incorrigible" children, and the like, testify to the prisonlike functions that undergird the educational rhetoric and increasingly call into question the national ideology that "education" cures all ills.

Americans are, in general, indifferent to the welfare of their public functionaries — witness the notoriously poor prestige and salaries of these functionaries. This indifference has been so great that those recruited for many public-service jobs tend to be people who are not the main breadwinners of their families, or who regard public-service work as temporary, or who are motivated more by a desire for security than by the usual American expectation of affluence. And, in the same way, society's indifference has served to blunt the drive of public-service workers for equitable compensation and for a reasonable recognition of their right to collective bargaining.

As the ghettos in this country grow, a new dimension is added, a dimension of silence and ignorance about exactly what these functionaries are expected to do, and how in fact they do carry out society's covert orders to control and cool out those who must be excluded from ordinary society. If the teachers, social workers, and cops were ever to spell out in detail what their duties are in order to justify their wage demands, they would threaten the delicate balance preserved by silence about their assigned dirty work — no one wants to learn that they are striking for "combat pay."

But the dirty-workers *are* striking — for increased pay, of course, but also for other demands that are more directly related to the dangers of dirty work, and to the disrespect society insists on giving to those who do its tacit bidding. The New York teachers, for example, openly and directly challenged the implicit understanding that it is more important for them to be custodians than for them to be teachers. It is gradually dawning on all of these public servants that both their official public tasks (to educate, to protect the citizens, to look after the welfare of the dependent) and their covert tasks (to control Negroes and make them as invisible as possible) are impossible to achieve.

The dirty-workers are increasingly caught between the silent middle class, which wants them to do the dirty work and keep quiet about it, and the objects of that dirty work, who refuse to continue to take it lying down. Individual revolts confront the teachers with the problems of the "blackboard jungle," the police with the problem of "disrespect for law and order," and the welfare workers with the problem of their charges' feigned stupidity and real deception. These civilian colonial armies find their right to respect from their charges challenged at every turn, and often they must carry out their daily duties with fear for their physical safety.

Equally ominous for the dirty-workers is the organized Negro challenge to their legitimacy. Not only must they cope with individual resistance to their ministrations, but also, more and more, with militant and insistent local civil-rights groups that expose their failures and tax them with their abrogation of their professional responsibilities to teach, to protect, to help.

It is encouraging that those expected to do the dirty work are rebelling. But it is really too much to expect that they will admit their own individual culpability, at least as long as the rest of us won't. Even so, the more the teachers, the police, and the welfare workers insist on the impossibility of their tasks, the more that society at large, and its political leaders, will have to confront the fact that our tacit understandings about the dirty work that is to be done are no longer adequate.

Of course there are dangers, too. The police are our internal hawks, and they might win — and there are also hawks among schoolteachers (they want unruly children kicked out of school) and welfare workers (who want to escalate the attack on welfare chiselers). As dangerous in the long run, perhaps, are the doves — the teachers and the social workers who want to save the ghetto through education and casework (or that form of neighborhood casework called "community action"). Should either the ghetto hawks or doves carry the day, their victory could become the basis for a new tacit understanding about dirty work, one that would save the country from paying the price it is apparently most reluctant to pay — the price of providing economic resources and open, decent housing to Negroes, so there is no longer a ghetto that requires dirty-workers.

ROBERT BLAUNER   *Internal Colonialism and*
                                                Ghetto Revolt

It is becoming almost fashionable to analyze American racial conflict
today in terms of the colonial analogy. I shall argue in this paper that
the utility of this perspective depends upon a distinction between colonization as a process and colonialism as a social, economic, and political
system. It is the experience of colonization that Afro-Americans share
with many of the non-white people of the world. But this subjugation
has taken place in a societal context that differs in important respects
from the situation of "classical colonialism." In the body of this essay I
shall look at some major developments in Black protest — the urban riots,
cultural nationalism, and the movement for ghetto control — as collective
responses to colonized status. Viewing our domestic situation as a special
form of colonization outside a context of a colonial system will help explain some of the dilemmas and ambiguities within these movements.

The present crisis in American life has brought about changes in social
perspectives and the questioning of long accepted frameworks. Intellectuals and social scientists have been forced by the pressure of events to
look at old definitions of the character of our society, the role of racism,
and the workings of basic institutions. The depth and volatility of contemporary racial conflict challenge sociologists in particular to question
the adequacy of theoretical models by which we have explained American
race relations in the past.

For a long time the distinctiveness of the Negro situations among the
ethnic minorities was placed in terms of color, and the systematic discrimination that follows from our deep-seated racial prejudices. This was
sometimes called the caste theory, and while provocative, it missed es-

From *Social Problems*, Vol. 16, No. 4, pp. 393–408. Reprinted by permission of The
Society for the Study of Social Problems and the author.

This is a revised version of a paper delivered at the University of California Centen-
nial Program, "Studies in Violence," Los Angeles, June 1, 1968. For criticisms and ideas
that have improved an earlier draft, I am indebted to Robert Wood, Lincoln Bergman,
and Gary Marx. As a good colonialist I have probably restated (read: stolen) more
ideas from the writings of Kenneth Clark, Stokely Carmichael, Frantz Fanon, and
especially such contributors to the Black Panther Party (Oakland) newspaper as Huey
Newton, Bobby Seale, Eldridge Cleaver, and Kathleen Cleaver than I have appro-
priately credited or generated myself. In self-defense I should state that I began working somewhat independently on a colonial analysis of American race relations in the
fall of 1965; see my "Whitewash Over Watts: The Failure of the McCone Report,"
Trans-action, 3 (March–April, 1966), pp. 3–9, 54.

sential and dynamic features of American race relations. In the past ten years there has been a tendency to view Afro-Americans as another ethnic group not basically different in experience from previous ethnics and whose "immigration" condition in the North would in time follow their upward course. The inadequacy of this model is now clear — even the Kerner Report devotes a chapter to criticizing this analogy. A more recent (though hardly new) approach views the essence of racial subordination in economic class terms: Black people as an underclass are to a degree specially exploited and to a degree economically dispensable in an automating society. Important as are economic factors, the power of race and racism in America cannot be sufficiently explained through class analysis. Into this theory vacuum steps the model of internal colonialism. Problematic and imprecise as it is, it gives hope of becoming a framework that can integrate the insights of caste and racism, ethnicity, culture, and economic exploitation into an overall conceptual scheme. At the same time, the danger of the colonial model is the imposition of an artificial analogy which might keep us from facing up to the fact (to quote Harold Cruse) that "the American black and white social phenomenon is a uniquely new world thing."[1]

During the late 1950's, identification with African nations and other colonial or formerly colonized peoples grew in importance among Black militants.[2] As a result the U.S. was increasingly seen as a colonial power and the concept of domestic colonialism was introduced into the political analysis and rhetoric of militant nationalists. During the same period Black social theorists began developing this frame of reference for explaining American realities. As early as 1962, Cruse characterized race relations in this country as "domestic colonialism."[3] Three years later in *Dark Ghetto*, Kenneth Clark demonstrated how the political, economic, and social structure of Harlem was essentially that of a colony.[4] Finally in 1967, a full-blown elaboration of "internal colonialism" provided the theoretical framework for Carmichael and Hamilton's widely read *Black Power*.[5] The following year the colonial analogy gained currency and

[1] Harold Cruse, *Rebellion or Revolution*, New York: 1968, p. 214.

[2] Nationalism, including an orientation toward Africa, is no new development. It has been a constant tendency within Afro-American politics. See Cruse, *ibid.*, esp. chaps. 5–7.

[3] This was six years before the publication of *The Crisis of the Negro Intellectual*, New York: Morrow, 1968, which brought Cruse into prominence. Thus the 1962 article was not widely read until its reprinting in Cruse's essays, *Rebellion or Revolution, op. cit.*

[4] Kenneth Clark, *Dark Ghetto*, New York: Harper and Row, 1965. Clark's analysis first appeared a year earlier in *Youth in the Ghetto*, New York: Haryou Associates, 1964.

[5] Stokely Carmichael and Charles Hamilton, *Black Power*, New York: Random House, 1967.

new "respectability" when Senator McCarthy habitually referred to Black Americans as a colonized people during his campaign. While the rhetoric of internal colonialism was catching on, other social scientists began to raise questions about its appropriateness as a scheme of analysis.

The colonial analysis has been rejected as obscurantist and misleading by scholars who point to the significant differences in history and social-political conditions between our domestic patterns and what took place in Africa and India. Colonialism traditionally refers to the establishment of domination over a geographically external political unit, most often inhabited by people of a different race and culture, where this domination is political and economic, and the colony exists subordinated to and dependent upon the mother country. Typically the colonizers exploit the land, the raw materials, the labor, and other resources of the colonized nation; in addition a formal recognition is given to the difference in power, autonomy, and political status, and various agencies are set up to maintain this subordination. Seemingly the analogy must be stretched beyond usefulness if the American version is to be forced into this model. For here we are talking about group relations within a society; the mother country — colony separation in geography is absent. Though whites certainly colonized the territory of the original Americans, internal colonization of Afro-Americans did not involve the settlement of whites in any land that was unequivocably Black. And unlike the colonial situation, there has been no formal recognition of differing power since slavery was abolished outside the South. Classic colonialism involved the control and exploitation of the majority of a nation by a minority of outsiders. Whereas in America the people who are oppressed were themselves originally outsiders and are a numerical minority.

This conventional critique of "internal colonialism" is useful in pointing to the differences between our domestic patterns and the overseas situation. But in its bold attack it tends to lose sight of common experiences that have been historically shared by the most subjugated racial minorities in America and non-white peoples in some other parts of the world. For understanding the most dramatic recent developments on the race scene, this common core element — which I shall call colonization — may be more important than the undeniable divergences between the two contexts.

The common features ultimately relate to the fact that the classical colonialism of the imperialist era and American racism developed out of the same historical situation and reflected a common world economic and power stratification. The slave trade for the most part preceded the imperialist partition and economic exploitation of Africa, and in fact may have been a necessary prerequisite for colonial conquest — since it helped deplete and pacify Africa, undermining the resistance to direct occupation. Slavery contributed one of the basic raw materials for the textile industry which provided much of the capital for the West's industrial development and need for economic expansionism. The essential condition for both American slavery and European colonialism was the power domination and the technological superiority of the Western world in its relation to peoples of non-Western and non-white origins. This objective supremacy in technology and military power buttressed the West's sense of cultural superiority, laying the basis for racist ideologies that were elaborated to justify control and exploitation of non-white people. Thus because classical colonialism and America's internal version developed out of a similar balance of technological, cultural, and power relations, a common *process* of social oppression characterized the racial patterns in the two contexts — despite the variation in political and social structure.

There appear to be four basic components of the colonization complex. The first refers to how the racial group enters into the dominant society (whether colonial power or not). Colonization begins with a forced, involuntary entry. Second, there is an impact on the culture and social organization of the colonized people which is more than just a result of such "natural" processes as contact and acculturation. The colonizing power carries out a policy which constrains, transforms, or destroys indigenous values, orientations, and ways of life. Third, colonization involves a relationship by which members of the colonized group tend to be administered by representatives of the dominant power. There is an experience of being managed and manipulated by outsiders in terms of ethnic status.

A final fundament of colonization is racism. Racism is a principle of social domination by which a group seen as inferior or different in terms of alleged biological characteristics is exploited, controlled, and oppressed socially and psychically by a superordinate group. Except for the marginal case of Japanese imperialism, the major examples of colonialism have involved the subjugation of non-white Asian, African, and Latin American peoples by white European powers. Thus racism has generally accompanied colonialism. Race prejudice can exist without colonization — the experience of Asian-American minorities is a case in point — but racism as a system of domination is part of the complex of colonization.

The concept of colonization stresses the enormous fatefulness of the historical factor, namely the manner in which a minority group becomes a part of the dominant society.[6] The crucial difference between the colonized Americans and the ethnic immigrant minorities is that the latter

[6] As Eldridge Cleaver reminds us, "Black people are a stolen people held in a colonial status on stolen land, and any analysis which does not acknowledge the colonial status of black people cannot hope to deal with the real problem." "The Land Question," *Ramparts*, 6 (May, 1968), p. 51.

have always been able to operate fairly competitively within that relatively open section of the social and economic order because these groups
came voluntarily in search of a better life, because their movements in
society were not administratively controlled, and because they transformed their culture at their own pace — giving up ethnic values and institutions when it was seen as a desirable exchange for improvements in
social position.

In present-day America, a major device of Black colonization is the
powerless ghetto. As Kenneth Clark describes the situation:

> Ghettoes are the consequence of the imposition of external power
> and the institutionalization of powerlessness. In this respect, they
> are in fact social, political, educational, and above all — economic
> colonies. Those confined within the ghetto walls are subject peo-
> ples. They are victims of the greed, cruelty, insensitivity, guilt and
> fear of their masters. . . .
>
> The community can best be described in terms of the analogy of
> a powerless colony. Its political leadership is divided, and all but
> one or two of its political leaders are shortsighted and dependent
> upon the larger political power structure. Its social agencies are
> financially precarious and dependent upon sources of support out-
> side the community. Its churches are isolated or dependent. Its
> economy is dominated by small businesses which are largely owned
> by absentee owners, and its tenements and other real property are
> also owned by absentee landlords.
>
> Under a system of centralization, Harlem's schools are controlled
> by forces outside of the community. Programs and policies are su-
> pervised and determined by individuals who do not live in the com-
> munity. . . .[7]

Of course many ethnic groups in America have lived in ghettoes. What
make the Black ghettoes an expression of colonized status are three special features. First, the ethnic ghettoes arose more from voluntary choice,
both in the sense of the choice to immigrate to America and the decision
to live among one's fellow ethnics. Second, the immigrant ghettoes
tended to be a one- and two-generation phenomenon; they were actually
way-stations in the process of acculturation and assimilation. When they
continue to persist as in the case of San Francisco's Chinatown, it is because they are big business for the ethnics themselves and there is a new
stream of immigrants. The Black ghetto on the other hand has been a
more permanent phenomenon, although some individuals do escape it.
But most relevant is the third point. European ethnic groups like the
Poles, Italians, and Jews generally only experienced a brief period, often
less than a generation, during which their residential buildings, commer-

7 *Youth in the Ghetto, op. cit.,* pp. 10–11; 79–80.

cial stores, and other enterprises were owned by outsiders. The Chinese and Japanese faced handicaps of color prejudice that were almost as strong as the Blacks faced, but very soon gained control of their internal communities, because their traditional ethnic culture and social organization had not been destroyed by slavery and internal colonization. But Afro-Americans are distinct in the extent to which their segregated communities have remained controlled economically, politically, and administratively from the outside. One indicator of this difference is the estimate that the "income of Chinese-Americans from Chinese-owned businesses is in proportion to their numbers 45 times as great as the income of Negroes from Negro-owned businesses."[8] But what is true of business is also true for the other social institutions that operate within the ghetto. The educators, policemen, social workers, politicians, and others who administer the affairs of ghetto residents are typically whites who live outside the Black community. Thus the ghetto plays a strategic role as the focus for the administration by outsiders which is also essential to the structure of overseas colonialism.[9]

The colonial status of the Negro community goes beyond the issue of ownership and decision-making within Black neighborhoods. The Afro-American population in most cities has very little influence on the power structure and institutions of the larger metropolis, despite the fact that in numerical terms, Blacks tend to be the most sizeable of the various interest groups. A recent analysis of policy-making in Chicago estimates that "Negroes really hold less than 1 per cent of the effective power in the Chicago metropolitan area. [Negroes are 20 per cent of Cook County's population.] Realistically the power structure of Chicago is hardly less white than that of Mississippi."[10]

---

[8] N. Glazer and R. P. Moynihan, *Beyond the Melting Pot*, Cambridge, Mass.: M.I.T., 1963, p. 37.

[9] "When we speak of Negro social disabilities under capitalism . . . we refer to the fact that he does not own anything — *even what is ownable in his own community*. Thus to fight for black liberation *is to fight for his right to own*. The Negro is politically compromised today because he owns nothing. He has little voice in the affairs of state because he owns nothing. The fundamental reason why the Negro bourgeois-democratic revolution has been aborted is because American capitalism has prevented the development of a black class of capitalist owners of institutions and economic tools. To take one crucial example, Negro radicals today are severely hampered in their tasks of educating the black masses on political issues because Negroes do not own any of the necessary means of propaganda and communication. The Negro owns no printing presses, he has no stake in the networks of the means of communication. Inside his own communities he does not own the house he lives in, the property he lives on, nor the wholesale and retail sources from which he buys his commodities. He does not own the edifices in which he enjoys culture and entertainment or in which he socializes. In capitalist society, an individual or group that does not own anything is powerless." H. Cruse, "Behind the Black Power Slogan," in Cruse, *Rebellion or Revolution, op. cit.*, pp. 238–39.

[10] Harold M. Baron, "Black Powerlessness in Chicago," *Trans-action*, 6 (Nov., 1968), pp. 27–33.

Colonization outside of a traditional colonial structure has its own special conditions. The group culture and social structure of the colonized in America is less developed; it is also less autonomous. In addition, the colonized are a numerical minority, and furthermore they are ghettoized more totally and are more dispersed than people under classic colonialism. Though these realities affect the magnitude and direction of response, it is my basic thesis that the most important expressions of protest in the Black community during the recent years reflect the colonized status of Afro-America. Riots, programs of separation, politics of community control, the Black revolutionary movements, and cultural nationalism each represent a different strategy of attack on domestic colonialism in America. Let us now examine some of these movements.

RIOT OR REVOLT?

The so-called riots are being increasingly recognized as a preliminary if primitive form of mass rebellion against a colonial status. There is still a tendency to absorb their meaning within the conventional scope of assimilation-integration politics: some commentators stress the material motives involved in looting as a sign that the rioters want to join America's middle-class affluence just like everyone else. That motives are mixed and often unconscious, that Black people want good furniture and television sets like whites is beside the point. The guiding impulse in most major outbreaks has not been integration with American society, but an attempt to stake out a sphere of control by moving against that society and destroying the symbols of its oppression.

In my critique of the McCone report I observed that the rioters were asserting a claim to territoriality, an unorganized and rather inchoate attempt to gain control over their community or "turf."[11] In succeeding disorders also the thrust of the action has been the attempt to clear out an alien presence, white men and officials, rather than a drive to kill whites as in a conventional race riot. The main attacks have been directed at the property of white business men and at the police who operate in the Black community "like an army of occupation" protecting the interests of outside exploiters and maintaining the domination over the ghetto by the central metropolitan power structure.[12] The Kerner report misleads when it attempts to explain riots in terms of integration: "What the riots appear to be seeking was fuller participation in the social order and the

[11] R. Blauner, "Whitewash Over Watts," op. cit.

[12] "The police function to support and enforce the interests of the dominant political, social, and economic interests of the town" is a statement made by a former police scholar and official, according to A. Neiderhoffer, Behind the Shield, New York: Doubleday, 1967 as cited by Gary T. Marx, "Civil Disorder and the Agents of Control," Journal of Social Issues, forthcoming.

material benefits enjoyed by the majority of American citizens. Rather than rejecting the American system, they were anxious to obtain a place for themselves in it."[13] More accurately, the revolts pointed to alienation from this system on the part of many poor and also not-so-poor Blacks. The sacredness of private property, that unconsciously accepted bulwark of our social arrangements, was rejected; people who looted apparently without guilt generally remarked that they were taking things that "really belonged" to them anyway.[14] Obviously the society's bases of legitimacy and authority have been attacked. Law and order has long been viewed as the white man's law and order by Afro-Americans; but now this perspective characteristic of a colonized people is out in the open. And the Kerner Report's own data question how well ghetto rebels are buying the system: In Newark only 33 per cent of self-reported rioters said they thought this country was worth fighting for in the event of a major war; in the Detroit sample the figure was 55 per cent.[15]

One of the most significant consequences of the process of colonization is a weakening of the colonized's individual and collective will to resist his oppression. It has been easier to contain and control Black ghettoes because communal bonds and group solidarity have been weakened through divisions among leadership, failures of organization, and a general dispiritment that accompanies social oppression. The riots are a signal that the will to resist has broken the mold of accommodation. In some cities, as in Watts, they also represented nascent movements toward community identity. In several riot-torn ghettoes the outbursts have stimulated new organizations and movements. If it is true that the riot phenomenon of 1964–68 has passed its peak, its historical import may be more for the "internal" organizing momentum generated than for any profound "external" response of the larger society facing up to underlying causes.

Despite the appeal of Frantz Fanon to young Black revolutionaries, America is not Algeria. It is difficult to foresee how riots in our cities can play a role equivalent to rioting in the colonial situation as an integral phase in a movement for national liberation. In 1968 some militant groups (for example, the Black Panther Party in Oakland) had concluded that ghetto riots were self-defeating of the lives and interests of Black people in the present balance of organization and gunpower, though they had served a role to stimulate both Black consciousness and white awareness

[13] Report of the National Advisory Commission on Civil Disorders, N.Y.: Bantam, March, 1968, p. 7.

[14] This kind of attitude has a long history among American Negroes. During slavery, Blacks used the same rationalization to justify stealing from their masters. Appropriating things from the master was viewed as "*taking* part of his property for the benefit of another part; whereas *stealing* referred to appropriating something from another slave, an offense that was not condoned." Kenneth Stampp, *The Peculiar Institution*, Vintage, 1956, p. 127.

[15] Report of the National Advisory Commission on Civil Disorders, *op. cit.*, p. 178.

of the depths of racial crisis. Such militants have been influential in "cooling" their communities during periods of high riot potential. Theoretically oriented Black radicals see riots as spontaneous mass behavior which must be replaced by a revolutionary organization and consciousness. But despite the differences in objective conditions, the violence of the 1960's seems to serve the same psychic function, assertions of dignity and manhood for young Blacks in urban ghettoes, as it did for the colonized of North Africa described by Fanon and Memmi.[16]

CULTURAL NATIONALISM

Cultural conflict is generic to the colonial relation because colonization involves the domination of Western technological values over the more communal cultures of non-Western peoples. Colonialism played havoc with the national integrity of the peoples it brought under its sway. Of course, all traditional cultures are threatened by industrialism, the city, and modernization in communication, transportation, health, and education. What is special are the political and administrative decisions of colonizers in managing and controlling colonized peoples. The boundaries of African colonies, for example, were drawn to suit the political conveniences of the European nations without regard to the social organization and cultures of African tribes and kingdoms. Thus Nigeria as blocked out by the British included the Yorubas and the Ibos, whose civil war today is a residuum of the colonialist's disrespect for the integrity of indigenous cultures.

The most total destruction of culture in the colonization process took place not in traditional colonialism but in America. As Frazier stressed, the integral cultures of the diverse African peoples who furnished the slave trade were destroyed because slaves from different tribes, kingdoms, and linguistic groups were purposely separated to maximize domination and control. Thus language, religion, and national loyalties were lost in North America much more completely than in the Caribbean and Brazil where slavery developed somewhat differently. Thus on this key point America's internal colonization has been more total and extreme than situations of classic colonialism. For the British in India and the European powers in Africa were not able — as outnumbered minorities — to destroy the national and tribal cultures of the colonized. Recall that American slavery lasted 250 years and its racist aftermath another 100. Colonial dependency in the case of British Kenya and French Algeria lasted only 77 and 125 years respectively. In the wake of this more drastic uprooting and destruction of culture and social organization, much more

[16] Frantz Fanon, *Wretched of the Earth,* New York: Grove, 1963; Albert Memmi, *The Colonizer and the Colonized,* Boston: Beacon, 1967.

powerful agencies of social, political, and psychological domination developed in the American case.

> Colonial control of many peoples inhabiting the colonies was more a goal than a fact, and at Independence there were undoubtedly fairly large numbers of Africans who had never seen a colonial administrator. The gradual process of extension of control from the administrative center on the African coast contrasts sharply with the total uprooting involved in the slave trade and the totalitarian aspects of slavery in the United States. Whether or not Elkins is correct in treating slavery as a total institution, it undoubtedly had a far more radical and pervasive impact on American slaves than did colonialism on the vast majority of Africans.[17]

Yet a similar cultural process unfolds in both contexts of colonialism. To the extent that they are involved in the larger society and economy, the colonized are caught up in a conflict between two cultures. Fanon has described how the assimilation-oriented schools of Martinique taught him to reject his own culture and Blackness in favor of Westernized, French, and white values.[18] Both the colonized elites under traditional colonialism and perhaps the majority of Afro-Americans today experience a parallel split in identity, cultural loyalty, and political orientation.[19]

The colonizers use their culture to socialize the colonized elites (intellectuals, politicians, and middle class) into an identification with the colonial system. Because Western culture has the prestige, the power, and the key to open the limited opportunity that a minority of the colonized may achieve, the first reaction seems to be an acceptance of the dominant values. Call it brainwashing as the Black Muslims put it; call it identifying with the aggressor if you prefer Freudian terminology; call it a natural response to the hope and belief that integration and democratization can really take place if you favor a more commonsense explanation, this initial acceptance in time crumbles on the realities of racism and colonialism. The colonized, seeing that his success within colonialism is at the expense of his group and his own inner identity, moves radically toward a rejection of the Western culture and develops a nationalist outlook that celebrates his people and their traditions. As Memmi describes it:

> Assimilation being abandoned, the colonized's liberation must be carried out through a recovery of self and of autonomous dignity. Attempts at imitating the colonizer required self-denial; the colo-

---

[17] Robert Wood, "Colonialism in Africa and America: Some Conceptual Considerations," December, 1967, unpublished paper.

[18] F. Fanon, *Black Skins, White Masks,* New York: Grove, 1967.

[19] Harold Cruse has described how these two themes of integration with the larger society and identification with ethnic nationality have struggled within the political and cultural movements of Negro Americans. *The Crisis of the Negro Intellectual, op. cit.*

nizer's rejection is the indispensible prelude to self-discovery. That accusing and annihilating image must be shaken off; oppression must be attacked boldly since it is impossible to go around it. After having been rejected for so long by the colonizer, the day has come when it is the colonized who must refuse the colonizer.[20]

Memmi's book, *The Colonizer and the Colonized,* is based on his experience as a Tunisian Jew in a marginal position between the French and the colonized Arab majority. The uncanny parallels between the North African situation he describes and the course of Black-white relations in our society is the best impressionist argument I know for the thesis that we have a colonized group and a colonizing system in America. His discussion of why even the most radical French anti-colonialist cannot participate in the struggle of the colonized is directly applicable to the situation of the white liberal and radical vis-à-vis the Black movement. His portrait of the colonized is as good an analysis of the psychology behind Black Power and Black nationalism as anything that has been written in the U.S. Consider for example:

> Considered en bloc as *them, they,* or *those,* different from every point of view, homogeneous in a radical heterogeneity, the colonized reacts by rejecting all the colonizers en bloc. The distinction between deed and intent has no great significance in the colonial situation. In the eyes of the colonized, all Europeans in the colonies are de facto colonizers, and whether they want to be or not, they are colonizers in some ways. By their privileged economic position, by belonging to the political system of oppression, or by participating in an effectively negative complex toward the colonized, they are colonizers. . . . They are supporters or at least unconscious accomplices of that great collective aggression of Europe.[21]

> The same passion which made him admire and absorb Europe shall make him assert his differences; since those differences, after all, are within him and correctly constitute his true self.[22]

> The important thing now is to rebuild his people, whatever be their authentic nature; to reforge their unity, communicate with it, and to feel that they belong.[23]

Cultural revitalization movements play a key role in anti-colonial movements. They follow an inner necessity and logic of their own that comes from the consequences of colonialism on groups and personal identities;

[20] Memmi, *op. cit.,* p. 128.
[21] *Ibid.,* p. 130.
[22] *Ibid.,* p. 132.
[23] *Ibid.,* p. 134.

they are also essential to provide the solidarity which the political or military phase of the anti-colonial revolution requires. In the U.S. an Afro-American culture has been developing since slavery out of the ingredients of African world-views, the experience of bondage, Southern values and customs, migration and the Northern lower-class ghettoes, and most importantly, the political history of the Black population in its struggle against racism.[24] That Afro-Americans are moving toward cultural nationalism in a period when ethnic loyalties tend to be weak (and perhaps on the decline) in this country is another confirmation of the unique colonized position of the Black group. (A similar nationalism seems to be growing among American Indians and Mexican-Americans.)

THE MOVEMENT FOR GHETTO CONTROL

The call for Black Power unites a number of varied movements and tendencies.[25] Though no clear-cut program has yet emerged, the most important emphasis seems to be the movement for control of the ghetto. Black leaders and organizations are increasingly concerned with owning and controlling those institutions that exist within or impinge upon their community. The colonial model provides a key to the understanding of this movement, and indeed ghetto control advocates have increasingly invoked the language of colonialism in pressing for local home rule. The framework of anti-colonialism explains why the struggle for poor people's or community control of poverty programs has been more central in many cities than the content of these programs and why it has been crucial to exclude whites from leadership positions in Black organizations.

The key institutions that anti-colonialists want to take over or control are business, social services, schools, and the police. Though many spokesmen have advocated the exclusion of white landlords and small businessmen from the ghetto, this program has evidently not struck fire with the Black population and little concrete movement toward economic expropriation has yet developed. Welfare recipients have organized in many cities to protect their rights and gain a greater voice in the decisions that

[24] In another essay, I argue against the standard sociological position that denies the existence of an ethnic Afro-American culture and I expand on the above themes. The concept of "Soul" is astonishingly parallel in content to the mystique of "Negritude" in Africa; the Pan-African culture movement has its parallel in the burgeoning Black culture mood in Afro-American communities. See "Black Culture: Myth or Reality" in Peter Rose, editor, *Americans From Africa*, Atherton, 1969.

[25] Scholars and social commentators, Black and white alike, disagree in interpreting the contemporary Black Power movement. The issues concern whether this is a new development in Black protest or an old tendency revised; whether the movement is radical, revolutionary, reformist, or conservative; and whether this orientation is unique to Afro-Americans or essentially a Black parallel to other ethnic group strategies for collective mobility. For an interesting discussion of Black Power as a modernized version of Booker T. Washington's separatism and economism, see Harold Cruse, *Rebellion or Revolution, op. cit.*, pp. 193–258.

affect them, but whole communities have not yet been able to mount direct action against welfare colonialism. Thus schools and the police seem now to be the burning issues of ghetto control politics.

During the past few years there has been a dramatic shift from educational integration as the primary goal to that of community control of the schools. Afro-Americans are demanding their own school boards, with the power to hire and fire principals and teachers and to construct a curriculum which would be relevant to the special needs and culture style of ghetto youth. Especially active in high schools and colleges have been Black students, whose protests have centered on the incorporation of Black Power and Black culture into the educational system. Consider how similar is the spirit behind these developments to the attitude of the colonized North African toward European education:

> He will prefer a long period of educational mistakes to the continu-
> ance of the colonizer's school organization. He will choose institu-
> tional disorder in order to destroy the institutions built by the colo-
> nizer as soon as possible. There we will see, indeed a reactive drive
> of profound protest. He will no longer owe anything to the colonizer
> and will have definitely broken with him.[26]

Protest and institutional disorder over the issue of school control came to a head in 1968 in New York City. The procrastination in the Albany State legislature, the several crippling strikes called by the teachers union, and the almost frenzied response of Jewish organizations makes it clear that decolonization of education faces the resistance of powerful vested interests.[27] The situation is too dynamic at present to assess probable future results. However, it can be safely predicted that some form of school decentralization will be institutionalized in New York, and the movement for community control of education will spread to more cities.

This movement reflects some of the problems and ambiguities that stem from the situation of colonization outside an immediate colonial context. The Afro-American community is not parallel in structure to the communities of colonized nations under traditional colonialism. The significant difference here is the lack of fully developed indigenous institutions besides the church. Outside of some areas of the South there is really no Black economy, and most Afro-Americans are inevitably caught up in the larger society's structure of occupations, education, and mass communication. Thus the ethnic nationalist orientation which reflects the reality of colonization exists alongside an integrationist orientation which corresponds to the reality that the institutions of the larger society are much

[26] Memmi, op. cit., pp. 137–138.
[27] For the New York school conflict see Jason Epstein, "The Politics of School Decentralization," New York Review of Books, June 6, 1968, pp. 26–32; and "The New York City School Revolt," ibid., 11, no. 6, pp. 37–41.

more developed than those of the incipient nation.[28] As would be expected the movement for school control reflects both tendencies. The militant leaders who spearhead such local movements may be primarily motivated by the desire to gain control over the community's institutions — they are anti-colonialists first and foremost. Many parents who support them may share this goal also, but the majority are probably more concerned about creating a new education that will enable their children to "make it" in the society and the economy as a whole — they know that the present school system fails ghetto children and does not prepare them for participation in American life.

There is a growing recognition that the police are the most crucial institution maintaining the colonized status of Black Americans. And of all establishment institutions, police departments probably include the highest proportion of individual racists. This is no accident since central to the workings of racism (an essential component of colonization) are attacks on the humanity and dignity of the subject group. Through their normal routines the police constrict Afro-Americans to Black neighborhoods by harassing and questioning them when found outside the ghetto; they break up groups of youth congregating on corners or in cars without any provocation; and they continue to use offensive and racist language no matter how many inter-group understanding seminars have been built into the police academy. They also shoot to kill ghetto residents for alleged crimes such as car thefts and running from police officers.[29]

Police are key agents in the power equation as well as the drama of dehumanization. In the final analysis they do the dirty work for the larger system by restricting the striking back of Black rebels to skirmishes inside the ghetto, thus deflecting energies and attacks from the communities and institutions of the larger power structure. In a historical review, Gary Marx notes that since the French revolution, police and other authorities

[28] This dual split in the politics and psyche of the Black American was poetically described by Du Bois in his *Souls of Black Folk*, and more recently has been insightfully analyzed by Harold Cruse in *The Crisis of the Negro Intellectual, op. cit.* Cruse has also characterized the problem of the Black community as that of underdevelopment.

[29] A recent survey of police finds "that in the predominantly Negro areas of several large cities, many of the police perceive the residents as basically hostile, especially the youth and adolescents. A lack of public support — from citizens, from courts, and from laws — is the policeman's major complaint. But some of the public criticism can be traced to the activities in which he engages day by day, and perhaps to the tone in which he enforces the 'law' in the Negro neighborhoods. Most frequently he is 'called upon' to intervene in domestic quarrels and break up loitering groups. He stops and frisks two or three times as many people as are carrying dangerous weapons or are actual criminals, and almost half of these don't wish to cooperate with the policeman's efforts." Peter Rossi, *et al.*, "Between Black and White — The Faces of American Institutions and the Ghetto," in Supplemental Studies for The National Advisory Commission on Civil Disorders, July 1968, p. 114.

have killed large numbers of demonstrators and rioters; the rebellious "rabble" rarely destroys human life. The same pattern has been repeated in America's recent revolts.[30] Journalistic accounts appearing in the press recently suggest that police see themselves as defending the interests of white people against a tide of Black insurgence; furthermore the majority of whites appear to view "blue power" in this light. There is probably no other opinion on which the races are as far apart today as they are on the question of attitudes toward the police.

In many cases set off by a confrontation between a policeman and a Black citizen, the ghetto uprising have dramatized the role of law enforcement and the issue of police brutality. In their aftermath, movements have arisen to contain police activity. One of the first was the Community Alert Patrol in Los Angeles, a method of policing the police in order to keep them honest and constrain their violations of personal dignity. This was the first tactic of the Black Panther Party which originated in Oakland, perhaps the most significant group to challenge the police role in maintaining the ghetto as a colony. The Panthers' later policy of openly carrying guns (a legally protected right) and their intention of defending themselves against police aggression has brought on a series of confrontations with the Oakland police department. All indications are that the authorities intend to destroy the Panthers by shooting, framing up, or legally harassing their leadership — diverting the group's energies away from its primary purpose of self-defense and organization of the Black community to that of legal defense and gaining support in the white community.

There are three major approaches to "police colonialism" that correspond to reformist and revolutionary readings of the situation. The most elementary and also superficial sees colonialism in the fact that ghettoes are overwhelmingly patrolled by white rather than by Black officers. The proposal — supported today by many police departments — to increase the number of Blacks on local forces to something like their distribution in the city would then make it possible to reduce the use of white cops in the ghetto. This reform should be supported, for a variety of obvious reasons, but it does not get to the heart of the police role as agents of colonization.

---

[30] "In the Gordon Riots of 1780 demonstrators destroyed property and freed prisoners, but did not seem to kill anyone, while authorities killed several hundred rioters and hung an additional 25. In the Rebellion Riots of the French Revolution, though several hundred rioters were killed, they killed no one. Up to the end of the Summer of 1967, this pattern had clearly been repeated, as police, not rioters, were responsible for most of the more than 100 deaths that have occurred. Similarly, in a related context, the more than 100 civil rights murders of recent years have been matched by almost no murders of racist whites." G. Marx, "Civil Disorders and the Agents of Social Control," *op. cit.*

The Kerner Report documents the fact that in some cases Black policemen can be as brutal as their white counterparts. The Report does not tell us who polices the ghetto, but they have compiled the proportion of Negroes on the forces of the major cities. In some cities the disparity is so striking that white police inevitably dominate ghetto patrols. (In Oakland 31 per cent of the population and only 4 per cent of the police are Black; in Detroit the figures are 39 per cent and 5 per cent; and in New Orleans 41 and 4.) In other cities, however, the proportion of Black cops is approaching the distribution in the city: Philadelphia 29 per cent and 20 per cent; Chicago 27 per cent and 17 per cent.[31] These figures also suggest that both the extent and the pattern of colonization may vary from one city to another. It would be useful to study how Black communities differ in degree of control over internal institutions as well as in economic and political power in the metropolitan area.

A second demand which gets more to the issue is that police should live in the communities they patrol. The idea here is that Black cops who lived in the ghetto would have to be accountable to the community; if they came on like white cops then "the brothers would take care of business" and make their lives miserable. The third or maximalist position is based on the premise that the police play no positive role in the ghettoes. It calls for the withdrawal of metropolitan officers from Black communities and the substitution of an autonomous indigenous force that would maintain order without oppressing the population. The precise relationship between such an independent police, the city and county law enforcement agencies, a ghetto governing body that would supervise and finance it, and especially the law itself is yet unclear. It is unlikely that we will soon face these problems directly as they have arisen in the case of New York's schools. Of all the programs of decolonization, police autonomy will be most resisted. It gets to the heart of how the state functions to control and contain the Black community through delegating the legitimate use of violence to police authority.

The various "Black Power" programs that are aimed at gaining control of individual ghettoes — buying up property and businesses, running the schools through community boards, taking over anti-poverty programs and other social agencies, diminishing the arbitrary power of the police — can serve to revitalize the institutions of the ghetto and build up an economic, professional, and political power base. These programs seem

[31] Report of the National Advisory Commission on Civil Disorders, *op. cit.*, p. 321. That Black officers nevertheless would make a difference is suggested by data from one of the supplemental studies to the Kerner Report. They found Negro policemen working in the ghettoes considerably more sympathetic to the community and its social problems than their white counterparts. Peter Rossi, *et al.*, "Between Black and White — The Faces of American Institutions in the Ghetto," *op. cit.*, chap. 6.

limited; we do not know at present if they are enough in themselves to end colonized status.[32] But they are certainly a necessary first step.

THE ROLE OF WHITES

What makes the Kerner Report a less-than-radical document is its superficial treatment of racism and its reluctance to confront the colonized relationship between Black people and the larger society. The report emphasizes the attitudes and feelings that make up white racism, rather than the system of privilege and control which is the heart of the matter.[33] With all its discussion of the ghetto and its problems, it never faces the question of the stake that white Americans have in racism and ghettoization.

This is not a simple question, but this paper should not end with the impression that police are the major villains. All white Americans gain some privileges and advantage from the colonization of Black communities.[34] The majority of whites also lose something from this oppression and division in society. Serious research should be directed to the ways in which white individuals and institutions are tied into the ghetto. In closing let me suggest some possible parameters.

1. It is my guess that only a small minority of whites make a direct economic profit from ghetto colonization. This is hopeful in that the ouster of white businessmen may become politically feasible. Much more significant, however, are the private and corporate interests in the land and residential property of the Black community; their holdings and influence on urban decision-making must be exposed and combated.

2. A much larger minority have occupational and professional interests in the present arrangements. The Kerner Commission reports that 1.3 million non-white men would have to be up-graded occupationally in order to make the Black job distribution roughly similar to the white. They advocate this without mentioning that 1.3 million specially privileged white workers would lose in the bargain.[35] In addition there are

[32] Eldridge Cleaver has called this first stage of the anti-colonial movement *community* liberation in contrast to a more long-range goal of *national* liberation. E. Cleaver, "Community Imperialism," Black Panther Party newspaper, 2 (May 18, 1968).

[33] For a discussion of this failure to deal with racism, see Gary T. Marx, "Report of the National Commission: The Analysis of Disorder or Disorderly Analysis," 1968, unpublished paper.

[34] Such a statement is easier to assert than to document but I am attempting the latter in a forthcoming book tentatively titled *White Racism, Black Culture,* to be published by Little, Brown, 1970.

[35] Report of the National Advisory Commission on Civil Disorders, *op. cit.,* pp. 253–256.

those professionals who carry out what Lee Rainwater has called the
"dirty work" of administering the lives of the ghetto poor: the social
workers, the school teachers, the urban development people, and of course
the police.[36] The social problems of the Black community will ultimately
be solved only by people and organizations from that community; thus
the emphasis within these professions must shift toward training such a
cadre of minority personnel. Social scientists who teach and study problems of race and poverty likewise have an obligation to replace themselves
by bringing into the graduate schools and college faculties men of color
who will become the future experts in these areas. For cultural and
intellectual imperialism is as real as welfare colonialism, though it is currently screened behind such unassailable shibboleths as universalism and
the objectivity of scientific inquiry.

3. Without downgrading the vested interests of profit and profession,
the real nitty-gritty elements of the white stake are political power and
bureaucratic security. Whereas few whites have much understanding
of the realities of race relations and ghetto life, I think most give tacit or
at least subconscious support for the containment and control of the Black
population. Whereas most whites have extremely distorted images of
Black Power, many — if not most — would still be frightened by actual
Black political power. Racial groups and identities are real in American
life; white Americans sense they are on top, and they fear possible reprisals or disruptions were power to be more equalized. There seems to be a
paranoid fear in the white psyche of Black dominance; the belief that
Black autonomy would mean unbridled license is so ingrained that such
reasonable outcomes as Black political majorities and independent Black
police forces will be bitterly resisted.

On this level the major mass bulwark of colonization is the administrative need for bureaucratic security so that the middle classes can go about
their life and business in peace and quiet. The Black militant movement
is a threat to the orderly procedures by which bureaucracies and suburbs
manage their existence, and I think today there are more people who feel
a stake in conventional procedures than there are those who gain directly
from racism. For in their fight for institutional control, the colonized will
not play by the white rules of the game. These administrative rules have
kept them down and out of the system; therefore they have no necessary
intention of running institutions in the image of the white middle class.

The liberal, humanist value that violence is the worst sin cannot be defended today if one is committed squarely against racism and for
self-determination. For some violence is almost inevitable in the decoloni-

[36] Lee Rainwater, "The Revolt of the Dirty-Workers," *Trans-action*, 5 (Nov., 1967),
pp. 2, 64.

zation process; unfortunately racism in America has been so effective that the greatest power Afro-Americans (and perhaps also Mexican-Americans) wield today is the power to disrupt. If we are going to swing with these revolutionary times and at least respond positively to the anti-colonial movement, we will have to learn to live with conflict, confrontation, constant change, and what may be real or apparent chaos and disorder.

A positive response from the white majority needs to be in two major directions at the same time. First, community liberation movements should be supported in every way by pulling out white instruments of direct control and exploitation and substituting technical assistance to the community when this is asked for. But it is not enough to relate affirmatively to the nationalist movement for ghetto control without at the same time radically opening doors for full participation in the institutions of the mainstream. Otherwise the liberal and radical position is little different than the traditional segregationist. Freedom in the special conditions of American colonization means that the colonized must have the choice between participation in the larger society and in their own independent structures.

CORPORATE POWER

The corporation is a legal organization which allows a business to use the capital of a number of persons, called shareholders. The modern large corporation has three elements: in addition to the shareholders, it has a board of directors, and officers of the board of directors who are usually responsible solely to the board. The officers — or management — actually run the corporation. For many years students of corporations have observed that the owner of the corporation — the shareholders — have very little control over the policies of the corporation. In the modern industrial corporation control is exercised by a virtually omnipotent management. Bayless Manning remarks:

> In 1932, Berle and Means vivisected the modern corporation. They found a virtually omnipotent management and an impotent shareholdership. A quarter-century of unparalleled corporate law reform intervenes. In 1958, Livingston surveyed the lot of the shareholder in a reformed world — a world of SEC regulation, extensive disclosure requirements, elaborate proxy machinery, Security Exchange self-discipline, Corporate Good Citizenship, Peoples Capitalism Corporate Democracy. His findings? A virtually omnipotent management and an impotent shareholdership.[1]

[1] Bayless Manning, quoted in Melvin Aron Eisenberg, "The Legal Roles of Shareholders and Management in Modern Corporate Decision-Making," *California Law Review*, Vol. 57, No. 1 (January, 1969), pp. 23–24.

Thus, the industrial wealth of the United States is concentrated in the hands of several hundred corporations (as Galbraith writes in the introduction to this section); and within those corporations, a relatively small number of persons occupying positions as officers make major policy decisions regarding the industrial expansion of the United States.

The economic power of these corporations is enormous.

> Today approximately 50 per cent of American manufacturing — that is everything other than finance and transportation — is held by about 150 corporations reckoned, at least, by asset values. If finance and transportation are included, the total increases. If a rather larger group is taken, the statistics would probably show that about two-thirds of the economically productive assets of the United States, excluding agriculture, are owned by a group of not more than 500 corporations. This is actual asset ownership. . . . But in terms of power, without regard to asset positions, not only do 500 corporations control two-thirds of the non-farm economy but . . . a still smaller group has the ultimate decision-making power. This is, I think, the highest concentration of economic power in recorded history. Since the United States carries on not quite half of the manufacturing production of the entire world today, these 500 groupings — each with its own little dominating pyramid within it — represent a concentration of power over economics which makes the medieval feudal system look like a Sunday-school party. In sheer economic power this has gone far beyond anything we have yet seen.[2]

Contrary to the classical economic theory, according to which corporations are responsive to the demands of the market, these giant corporations are themselves able to determine the demands of the market. As Galbraith points out, the planning required in a corporation as large as General Motors or United States Steel approximates the planning that would be required in a large American state or in a major country: "The revenues of General Motors in

[2] A. A. Berle, "Economic Power and the Free Society," in Andrew Hacker, ed., *The Corporation Take-Over* (New York: Harper and Row, 1964), pp. 101–102.

1963 were 50 times those of Nevada, eight times those of
New York and slightly less than one-fifth of those of the
federal government." Corporations of this size cannot afford to "retool" in response to demand; they must take
measures — such as mass advertising of products — to
control demand.

One source of corporate decision-making is in what Galbraith calls "the technostructure." Galbraith considers this
technostructure, which "embraces all who bring specialized knowledge, talent or experience to group decision-
making" the guiding intelligence of the major corporate
enterprises." Yet, the output of the technostructure, like
that of the computer, depends upon the programs that are
put into it. For example, if management wants to know
how to maximize profits on the automobile, it may learn
from specialists within the technostructure that an avertis-
ing campaign responsive to underlying sexual motives will
be more productive of demand than an emphasis on increased safety. So, automobiles possessed tail fins before
they had seat belts. Still, corporate management sets the
goals of corporate activity. The technostructure can operate as a decision-making forum only in response to major
policies. The analysis of corporate or management decision-making incurs a problem. A distinction is too rarely
drawn between implementation decisions and policy decisions, the latter involving fundamental assumptions about
the purposes of the organization. In the large corporation,
the management makes the policy decisions, the decisions
concerning goals. As to means, management usually ratifies
decisions formulated by the hierarchy of the technostructure.

Since many decisions are often made on technical
grounds, it may appear presumptuous for shareholders
or the general public to demand a voice in their creation.
It can be said that the average layman doesn't have the
ability to make a considered judgment on technical issues.
However, the major decisions made by boards of manage-
ments are assumptions about the purposes of the organization that affect the public in general, and influence
the industrial growth of the nation, foreign policy, domes-

tic affairs — in short, the quality of national, and sometimes international, life.

Whereas other legal scholars of the corporation have
concentrated on the relationship between management
and the shareholder when they discuss corporate responsibility, Ralph Nader has aroused public concern over the
relationship between the large industrial corporation and
the interests of the American public as a whole. Nader,
whose book *Unsafe at Any Speed*[3] spurred the nation to
some long overdue reforms in automobile safety, has gone
on to press Congress and executive agencies on a variety
of consumer causes including radiation hazards, meat inspection, environmental pollution, and public noise.
Nader's basic assumptions differ from those of most corporate managers. They believe in maximizing the profits
of the corporation. For them this goal is the principal end
of corporate activity. Nader has a different outlook. Corporations are a formidable, if not central, feature of the
social, economic, and political life of the nation, and corporate activity is necessarily within the public domain.
When one corporation such as General Motors can have
fifty times as much revenue as one of the United States,
it seems that controls ought to be established to guarantee
that its performance accord with the public interest. In
the article reprinted below, for example, Nader uses the
automobile industry as an example. It has been seriously
deficient on this score. It has failed to move ahead on safety
standards; it has been secretive about the costs involved
in various parts, thus preventing the consumer from making a considered judgment as to which he would prefer
and which he would not; it has failed to acknowledge the
high repair rate of automobiles and that high profits derive
from part replacement; it has been laggard in the field of
air pollution, though the internal combustion engine has
been heavily responsible for that pollution; it has engaged
in market researches of questionable validity, which probe
the unconscious desires of the consumer but do not respect
his integrity as a decision-making citizen. Finally, by its

[3] Ralph Nader, *Unsafe At Any Speed* (New York: Grossman, 1965).

strong dependence on an entrenched technostructure, it
has failed to be creative and innovative in offering technical improvement in the automobile.

Nader's overall criticism, however, is not unlike that of
Galbraith. Galbraith's book *The New Industrial State*
challenges the "free enterprise" assumptions of conservative economists. He observes that economic models developed by conservative economists work only for a small
portion of the economy. Major industrial corporations are
an exception to these models. Therefore, Galbraith challenges conservative economic theories. The exceptions
are more influential than the rule, and a theory which cannot take the major exceptions into account is operating in a
kind of dream world, especially when the exceptions constitute such entities as General Motors, Bell Telephone and
United States Steel.

Nader makes a similar point when he demonstrates that
actual corporate behavior is distant from the norm of free
enterprise contemplated by those economists who profess
to believe in the free enterprise system. There is, in fact,
little competition. There are interlocking directorates
within the same industry, and there is an elite of corporate
managers and corporate law firms maximizing industry
profits, with little regard for the general public.

The communications industry provides yet another illustration of tight and centralized corporate control. This
industry is discussed in an article by Federal Communications Commissioner Nicholas Johnson. Johnson presents a
view of the television industry in which a few top executives from the major networks set the standards for the programming that is to be offered to the entire American
public. Johnson argues that *government* censorship is far
less of a problem than *network* censorship and offers numerous examples to prove his contention. The media and
other big corporations are so large, so profitable, and so
politically powerful that they are a part of the public
domain — rather like state and local governments: "Large
corporations have both the incentive and the power to
control the information reaching the citizenry of our free
society. Thus, while the public was shown miles of film

about the horrifying events of the war in Vietnam television revealed little if anything about the multi-billion
dollar corporate profits that the war produced." Government policy becomes the subject of criticism, as it should
be: but corporate policy is offered de facto immunity,
because it is rarely given a hearing over the airways.

All three authors suggest that the large corporation is
a form of "private government," which has power and influence far beyond that ordinarily considered in the legal
concept of the corporation. We have a Bill of Rights to
protect us from the excesses of government officials: the
question that this section raises is how to obtain a similar
bill of rights to protect us from the excesses of the private
governments managed by corporate officials?

JOHN KENNETH GALBRAITH   *The Corporation*

Few subjects of earnest inquiry have been more unproductive than study
of the modern large corporation. The reasons are clear. A vivid image of
what *should* exist acts as a surrogate for reality. Pursuit of the image then
prevents pursuit of the reality.

For purposes of scholarly inquiry, the corporation has a sharp legal
image. Its purpose is to do business as an individual would but with the
added ability to assemble and use the capital of several or numerous
persons. In consequence, it can undertake tasks beyond the reach of any
single person. And it protects those who supply capital by limiting their
liability to the amount of their original investment, insuring them a vote
on the significant affairs of the enterprise, defining the powers and the
responsibilities of directors and officers, and giving them access to the
courts to redress grievance. Apart from its ability to mobilize capital and
its lessened association with the active life of any individual, the corporation is not deemed to differ functionally from the individual proprietorship

or partnership. Its purpose, like theirs, is to conduct business on equitable terms with other businesses and make money for the owners.

Such corporations do exist and in large numbers. But one wonders if the natural interest of the student of economics is the local paving firm or body repair shop. Or is it General Motors and Standard Oil of New Jersey and General Electric?

But these firms depart sharply from the legal image. In none of these firms is the capital pooled by original investors appreciable; in each it could be paid off by a few hours' or a few days' earnings. In none does the individual stockholder pretend to power. In all three cases, the corporation is far more influential in the markets in which it buys materials, components and labor and in which it sells its finished products than is commonly imagined to be the case with the individual proprietorship.

In consequence, nearly all study of the corporation has been concerned with its deviation from its legal or formal image. This image — that of "an association of persons into an autonomous legal unit with a distinct legal personality that enables it to carry on business, own property and contract debts"[1] — is highly normative. It is what a corporation should be. When the modern corporation disenfranchises its stockholders, grows to gargantuan size, expands into wholly unrelated activities, is a monopoly where it buys and a monopoly where it sells, something is wrong.

That the largest and most famous corporations, those whose names are household words and whose heads are accorded the most distinguished honors by their fellow businessmen, should be considered abnormal must seem a little dubious.

Additionally, it must be evident that General Motors does not have much in common with the Massachusetts Institute of Technology professors who pool their personal funds and what they can borrow from the banks and their friends to supply some erudite item to the Department of Defense and thus, in their modest way, help to defend the country and participate in capital gains. Their enterprise, created, owned and directed by themselves and exploiting the advantages of the corporate form, approaches the established image. General Motors as clearly does not.

The answer is that there is no such thing as a corporation. Rather there are several kinds of corporations all deriving from a common but very loose framework. Some are subject to the market; others reflect varying degrees of adaptation to the requirements of planning and the needs of the technostructure. The person who sets out to study buildings on Manhattan on the assumption that all are alike will have difficulty in passing from the surviving brownstones to the skyscrapers. And he will handicap himself even more if he imagines that all buildings should be like brown-

---

[1] Harry G. Guthmann and Herbert E. Dougall, *Corporate Financial Policy*, Second Edition (New York: Prentice-Hall, Inc., 1948), p. 9.

stones and have load-carrying walls and that others are abnormal. So with corporations.

2

The most obvious requirement of effective planning is large size. This, we have seen, allows the firm to accept market uncertainty where it cannot be eliminated; to eliminate markets on which otherwise it would be excessively dependent; to control other markets in which it buys and sells; and it is very nearly indispensable for participation in that part of the economy, characterized by exacting technology and comprehensive planning, where the only buyer is the Federal Government.

That corporations accommodate well to this need for size has scarcely to be stressed. They can, and have, become very large. But because of the odor of abnormality, this adaptation is not stressed. The head of the largest corporation is automatically accorded precedence at all business conventions, meetings and other business rites and festivals. He is complimented for his intelligence, vision, courage, progressiveness and for the remarkable rate of growth of his firm under his direction. But the great size of his firm — the value of its assets or the number of its employees — is not praised although this is its most striking feature.

Nothing so characterizes the industrial system as the scale of the modern corporate enterprise. In 1962 the five largest industrial corporations in the United States, with combined assets in excess of $36 billion, possessed over 12 per cent of all assets used in manufacturing. The fifty largest corporations had over a third of all manufacturing assets. The 500 largest had well over two-thirds. Corporations with assets in excess of $10,000,000, some 2000 in all, accounted for about 80 per cent of all the resources used in manufacturing in the United States.[2] In the mid nineteen-fifties, 28 corporations provided approximately 10 per cent of all employment in manufacturing, mining and retail and wholesale trade. Twenty-three corporations provided 15 per cent of all the employment in manufacturing. In the first half of the decade (June 1950–June 1956) a hundred firms received two-thirds by value of all defense contracts; ten

[2] Hearings before the Subcommittee on Antitrust and Monopoly of the Committee of the Judiciary, United States Senate, Eighty-Eighth Congress, Second Session, Pursuant to S. Res. 262. Part I. *Economic Concentration. Overall and Conglomerate Aspects* (1964), p. 113. Data on the concentration of industrial activity in the hands of large firms, and especially any that seem to show an increase in concentration, sustain a controversy in the United States that, at times, reaches mildly pathological proportions. The reason is that much of the argument between those who see the market as a viable institution and those who feel that it is succumbing to monpolistic influences has long turned on these figures. These figures are thus defended or attacked according to predilection. However, the general orders of magnitude given here are not subject to serious question.

firms received one third.[3] In 1960 four corporations accounted for an estimated 22 per cent of all industrial research and development expenditure. Three hundred and eighty-four corporations employing 5,000 or more workers accounted for 85 per cent of these expenditures; 260,000 firms employing fewer than 1,000 accounted for only 7 per cent.[4]

Planning is a function that is associated in most minds with the state. If the corporation is the basic planning unit, it is appropriate that the scale of operations of the largest should approximate those of government. This they do, In 1965, three industrial corporations, General Motors, Standard Oil of New Jersey and Ford Motor Company, had more gross income than all of the farms in the country. The income of General Motors, of $20.7 billion, about equaled that of the three million smallest farms in the country — around ninety per cent of all farms. The gross revenues of each of the three corporations just mentioned far exceed those of any single state. The revenues of General Motors in 1963 were fifty times those of Nevada, eight times those of New York and slightly less than one-fifth those of the Federal Government.[5]

Economists have anciently quarreled over the reasons for the great size of the modern corporations. Is it because size is essential in order to reap the economics of modern large scale production?[6] Is it, more insidiously, because the big firm wishes to exercise monopoly power in its markets? The present analysis allows both parties to the dispute to be partly right. The firm must be large enough to carry the large capital commitments of modern technology. It must also be large enough to control its markets. But the present view also explains what the older explanations don't explain. That is, why General Motors is not only large enough to afford the best size of automobile plant but is large enough to afford a dozen or more of the best size; and why it is large enough to produce things as diverse as aircraft engines and refrigerators, which cannot be explained by the economies of scale; and why, though it is large enough to have the market power associated with monopoly, consumers do not seriously complain of exploitation. The size of General Motors is in the service not of monopoly or the economies of scale but of planning. And for this

---

[3] Carl Kaysen, "The Corporation: How Much Power? What Scope?" in *The Corporation in Modern Society*, Edward S. Mason, ed. (Cambridge: Harvard University Press, 1959), pp. 86–87.

[4] M. A. Adelman, Hearings before the Subcommittee on Antitrust and Monopoly of the Committee on the Judiciary, United States Senate, Eighty-Ninth Congress, First Session, Pursuant to S. Res. 70. Part III. *Economic Concentration. Concentration, Invention and Innovation* (1965), pp. 1139–1140.

[5] Data from *Fortune*, U.S. Department of Agriculture and *Statistical Abstract of the United States*.

[6] Cf. Joe S. Bain, "Economics of Scale, Concentration and the Condition of Entry in Twenty Manufacturing Industries," *The American Economic Review*, Vol. XLIV, No. 1. (March, 1954).

planning — control of supply, control of demand, provision of capital, minimization of risk—there is no clear upper limit to the desirable size. It could be that the bigger the better. The corporate form accommodates to this need. Quite clearly it allows the firm to be very, very large.

3

The corporation also accommodates itself admirably to the needs of the technostructure. This, we have seen, is an apparatus for group decision — for pooling and testing the information provided by numerous individuals to reach decisions that are beyond the knowledge of any one. It requires, we have also seen, a high measure of autonomy. It is vulnerable to any intervention by external authority for, given the nature of the group decision-making and the problems being solved, such external authority will always be incompletely informed and hence arbitrary. If problems were susceptible to decision by individuals, no group would be involved.

One possible source of such intervention is the state. The corporate charter, however, accords the corporation a large area of independent action in the conduct of its affairs. And this freedom is defended as a sacred right. Nothing in American business attitudes is so iniquitous as government interference in the *internal* affairs of the corporation. The safeguards here, both in law and custom, are great. There is equally vehement resistance to any invasion by trade unions of the prerogatives of management.

There is also, however, the danger of intervention by the owners — by the stockholders. Their exclusion is not secured by law or sanctified by custom. On the contrary, either directly or through the agency of the Board of Directors, their power is guaranteed. But being legal does not make it benign. Exercise of such power on substantive questions requiring group decision would be as damaging as any other. So the stockholder too must be excluded.

In part this has been accomplished by the simple attrition of the stockholder's power as death and the distribution of estates, the diversifying instincts of trusts and foundations, the distributional effects of property settlements and alimony, and the artistic, philanthropic and social enjoyments of non-functional heirs all distribute the stock of any corporation to more and more hands. This process works rapidly and the distribution need by no means be complete to separate the stockholder from all effective power. In the mid nineteen-twenties, in the first case to draw wide public attention to this tendency, it became known that Colonel Robert W. Stewart, the Chairman of the Board of Directors of the Standard Oil Company of Indiana, had, in concert with some of the men who later won immortality as the architects of the Teapot Dome and Elk Hills transactions, organized a highly specialized enterprise in Canada called the Continental Trading Company. This company had the sole function of buying crude oil from Colonel E. A. Humphreys, owner of the rich Mexica field in east central Texas, and reselling it to companies controlled by the same individuals, including Standard Oil of Indiana, at a markup of twenty-five cents a barrel. It was an excellent business. No costs were involved, other than a small percentage to the Canadian lawyer who served as a figurehead and went hunting in Africa whenever wanted for questioning, and for mailing back the proceeds after they had been converted into Liberty Bonds. (If some of these had not been used, carelessly, to bribe Secretary of the Interior Albert B. Fall and others to pay the deficit of the Republican National Committee, Continental might have forever remained unknown as was unquestionably intended.) It was Colonel Stewart's later contention that he had always intended to turn over the profit to Standard Oil of Indiana. But, absentmindedly, he had allowed the bonds to remain in his own possession for many years and had cashed some of the coupons. In 1929 Standard of Indiana was only eighteen years distant from the decree which had broken up the Standard Oil empire of John D. Rockefeller of which it had been an important part. The Rockefellers still owned 14.9 per cent of the voting stock of the Indiana Company and were deemed to have the controlling interest. They reacted sternly to the outrage; the elder Rockefeller had, on notable occasions, imposed a somewhat similar levy on his competitors, but never on his own company. With the aid of the publicity generated by the Teapot Dome scandal, his own high standing in the financial community, his brother-in-law Winthrop W. Aldrich, who solicited proxies, and a very large expenditure of money, John D. Rockefeller, Jr., was able to oust the Colonel, although not by a wide margin.[7] (The latter had the full support of his Board of Directors.) In the absence of the scandal and his ample resources, Rockefeller, it was realized with some shock, would have had little hope.

In most other large corporations, the chance for exerting such power would have been less and it has become increasingly less with the passage of time. Professor Gordon's prewar study of the 176 largest corporations showed that at least half of their stock was held in blocks of less than one per cent of the total outstanding. In less than a third of the companies was there a stockholder interest large enough to allow potential control, i.e., the election of a Board of Directors, and "the number of companies in which any large degree of *active* leadership is associated with consider-

[7] Cf. Adolf A. Berle, Jr. and Gardner C. Means, *The Modern Corporation and Private Property* (New York: Macmillan, 1934), pp. 82–83. Of the 8,465,299 shares represented, Rockefeller got the votes of 5,510,313. Stewart retired on a pension of $75,000 a year. M. R. Werner and John Starr, *Teapot Dome* (New York: The Viking Press, Inc., 1959), pp. 274–275.

able ownership is certainly even smaller."[8] That was a quarter of a century ago; the dispersion of stock ownership, which was then much greater for the older railroad corporations than for newer industrial corporations, has almost certainly continued.[9] It means that to change control more stockholders must be persuaded, against the advice of management, to vote their stock for someone whom, in the nature of the case, they do not know and will not be disposed to trust. The effort must also contend with the tendency of the indifferent to give proxies to management. It is also in face of the requirement that the loser of a proxy battle, if he is an outsider, must pay the cost. And it must contend finally with the alternative, always available to the dissatisfied stockholder, of simply selling his stock. Corporate size, the passage of time and the dispersion of stock ownership do not disenfranchise the stockholder. Rather, he can vote but his vote is valueless.

4

To be secure in its autonomy, the technostructure also needs to have a source of new capital to which it can turn without having, as a *quid pro quo*, to surrender any authority over its own decisions. Here capital abundance enters as a factor. A bank, insurance company or investment banker cannot make control of decision, actual or potential, a condition of a loan or security underwriting if funds are readily available from another and more permissive source and if there is vigorous competition for the business.

The complexity of modern technological and planning decisions also protects the technostructure from outside interference. The country banker, out of his experience and knowledge of the business, can readily interpose his judgment, as against that of a farmer, on the prospects for feeder cattle — and does. Not even the most self-confident financier would wish to question the judgment of General Electric engineers, product planners, stylists, market researchers and sales executives on the culturally advanced toaster. . . . By taking decisions away from individuals and locating them deeply within the technostructure, technology and planning thus remove them from the influence of outsiders.

---

[8] R. A. Gordon, *Business Leadership in the Large Corporation* (Washington: Brookings, 1945), Chapter II. The median holdings of management were 2.1 per cent of the stock. In 56 per cent of the companies, management owned less than one per cent; in only 16 of the companies did it own as much as 20 per cent of the stock outstanding. A more recent study by Mabel Newcomer, *The Big Business Executive* (New York: Columbia University Press, 1955), showed that by 1952 there had been a further reduction in management holdings.

[9] This is explicitly confirmed by a study by R. J. Larner, "The 200 Largest Nonfinancial Corporations," *The American Economic Review*, Vol. LVI, No. 4, Part 1 (September 1966), pp. 777–787.

But the corporation accords a much more specific protection to the technostructure. That is by providing it with a source of capital, derived from its own earnings, that is wholly under its own control. No banker can attach conditions as to how retained earnings are to be used. Nor can any other outsider. No one, the normally innocuous stockholder apart, has the right to ask about an investment from retained earnings that turns out badly. It is hard to overestimate the importance of the shift in power that is associated with availability of such a source of capital. Few other developments can have more fundamentally altered the character of capitalism. It is hardly surprising that retained earnings of corporations have become such an overwhelmingly important source of capital.

5

There remains one final source of danger to the autonomy of the technostructure. That arises with a failure of earnings. Then there are no retained earnings. If new plant is needed or working capital must be replenished, there will have to be appeal to bankers or other outsiders. This will be under circumstances, i.e., the fact that the firm is showing losses, when the right of such outsiders to inquire and to intervene will have to be conceded. They cannot be told to mind their own business. Thus does a shortage of capital, though limited in time and place, promptly revive the power of the capitalist. And it is in times of such failure of earnings, and then only, that the stockholder of the large corporation can be aroused. In large corporations, battles for control have been rare in recent times. And in all notable cases involving large corporations — the New York Central, Loew's, TWA, the New England railroads, Wheeling Steel, Curtis Publishing — the firm in contention was doing badly at the time. If revenues are above some minimum — they need not be at their maximum for no one will know what that is — creditors cannot intervene and stockholders cannot be aroused.

Here too the corporation, and the industrial system generally, have adapted effectively to the needs of the technostructure, though, surprisingly, the nature of the adaptation has been little noticed. The adaptation is, simply, that big corporations do not lose money. In 1957, a year of mild recession in the United States, not one of the one hundred largest industrial corporations failed to return a profit. Only one of the largest two hundred finished the year in the red. Seven years later in 1964, a prosperous year by general agreement, all of the first hundred again made money; only two among the first two hundred had losses and only seven among the first five hundred. None of the fifty largest merchandising firms — Sears, Roebuck, A & P, Safeway, et al. — failed to return a profit. Nor, predictably, did any of the fifty largest utilities. And among the fifty largest transportation companies only three railroads and the momentarily unfortunate Eastern Airlines, failed to make money.[10]

The American business liturgy has long intoned that this is a profit and loss economy. "The American competitive enterprise system is an acknowledged profit and loss system, the hope of profits being the incentive and the fear of loss being the spur."[11] This may be so. But it is not true of that organized part of the economy in which a developed technostructure is able to protect its profits by planning. Nor is it true of the United States Steel Corporation, author of the sentence just cited, which has not had losses for a quarter of a century.

6

As always, no strong case is improved by overstatement. Among the two hundred largest corporations in the United States — those that form the heart of the industrial system — there are a few in which owners exercise any important influence on decisions. And this influence decreases year by year. But there are exceptions. Some owners — the du Pont, and in lesser measure the Firestone and Ford, families are examples — participate, or have participated, actively in management. Thus they earn influence by being part of the technostructure and their influence is unquestionably increased by their ownership. Others, through position on the Board of Directors, have power in the selection of management — in decision on those who make decisions. And yet others may inform themselves and intervene substantively on individual decisions — a merger, a plant acquisition or the launching of a new line.

In the last case, however, there must always be question as to how the individual is deciding and how much has been decided for him by the group which has provided the relevant information; the danger of confusing ratification with decision must again be emphasized. And in all circumstances it is important to realize that corporate ceremony more or less deliberately disguises the reality. This deserves a final word.

Corporate liturgy strongly emphasizes the power of the Board of Directors and ultimately, thus, of the stockholders they are assumed to represent. The rites which attest this point are conducted with much solemnity; no one allows himself to be cynical as to their substance. Heavy dockets, replete with data, are submitted to the Board. Time is allowed for study. Recommendations are appended. Given the extent and group character of the preparation, rejection would be unthinkable. The Board, nonetheless, is left with the impression that it has made a decision.

10 *The Fortune Directory*, August, 1958, August, 1965.
11 United States Steel Corporation. *Annual Report, 1958.*

Corporate procedure also allows the Board to act on financial transactions — changes in capital structure, declaration of dividends, authorization of lines of credit. These, given the control by the technostructure of its sources of savings and capital supply, are frequently the most routine and derivative of decisions. But as elsewhere noted, any association with large sums of money conveys an impression of power. It brings it to mind for the same traditional reasons as does a detachment of soldiers.

With even greater unction although with less plausibility, corporate ceremony seeks also to give the stockholders an impression of power. When stockholders are (or were) in control of a company, stockholders' meetings are an occasion of scant ceremony. The majority is voted in and the minority is voted out, with such concessions as may seem strategic, and all understand the process involved. As stockholders cease to have influence, however, efforts are made to disguise this nullity. Their convenience is considered in selecting the place of meeting. They are presented with handsomely printed reports, the preparation of which is now a specialized business. Products and even plants are inspected. During the proceedings, as in the report, there are repetitive references to *your* company. Officers listen, with every evidence of attention, to highly irrelevant suggestions of wholly uninformed participants and assure them that these will be considered with the greatest care. Votes of thanks from women stockholders in print dresses owning ten shares "for the excellent skill with which you run *our* company" are received by the management with well-simulated gratitude. All present show stern disapproval of critics. No important stockholders are present. No decisions are taken. The annual meeting of the large American corporation is, perhaps, our most elaborate exercise in popular illusion.

In 1956 upwards of 100,000 stockholders of Bethlehem Steel returned proxies to a management committee. These were voted routinely for a slate of directors selected by management exclusively from among its own members. The following colloquy occurred in Washington the following year:

> SENATOR KEFAUVER: The exhibit shows that the members of the Board of Directors paid themselves $6,499,000 in 1956.
>
> MR. HOMER (President of Bethlehem Steel Corporation): I wish to interpose there, Senator, we did not pay ourselves. I wish that term would not be used.
>
> SENATOR KEFAUVER: Very well, approved by the stockholders.
>
> MR. HOMER: That is better.[12]

---

[12] U.S. Congress, Hearings on Administered Prices, Part II. *Steel,* p. 562.

RALPH NADER

GM and the
Auto Industry: The Threat
of Corporate Collectivism

Getting around on the ground in private transport is America's biggest business. Whether in input-output analysis or simple aggregate data, the automobile industry stands as the private economic activity with the greatest multiplier effect for the rest of the economy. The industry consumed eleven per cent of the aluminum, twenty per cent of the steel, thirty-five per cent of the zinc, fifty per cent of the lead, and more than sixty per cent of the rubber used in the United States in 1967.

The automobile industry's capacity for insatiable depletion of public and private pocketbooks can be painful. One of every six retail dollars goes to buy or provide for motor vehicles. More than a hundred billion dollars a year are expended on new cars, used cars, gasoline, tires, auto repair and replacement parts, auto insurance and finance, the construction and upkeep of roads, and other supportive facilities. Numerous ancillary industries and public services rely on the continuous multi-million volume production of America's most visible industrial art form.

It is often said by auto industry boosters that one of every six business establishments is dependent on the purchase and use of motor vehicles. In terms of unused capacity, fuel consumption per passenger, injuries and pollution, and total time loss of passengers, automotive travel is probably the most wasteful and inefficient mode of travel by industrial man. This is not to mention the highway lobby's appropriation and gross misuse of urban land for highway belts and its stifling of investment in mass transit. Yet, automobiles will be here for some time to come, and the market structure, performance, and profits of an industry that so dominates the economy and is in turn so dominated by one corporation — General Motors — demand careful scrutiny to determine if it is functioning in the best interests of the public.

The domestic automobile industry is composed of four companies, three of which account for more than ninety-seven per cent of the domestic car market. General Motors delivered 54.7 per cent of the North American-type passenger cars sold in the United States last year. In most of the postwar period, GM's share of the market has consistently been between fifty and fifty-five per cent of the domestic market.

Reprinted by permission from *The Progressive,* Madison, Wisconsin.

The dimensions of the world's largest industrial giant require some statistical etching. For 1967, the company's net sales reached $20,026,000,000, the third highest in its history. Net income was reported at $1,627,000,000, down from $1,793,000,000 for 1966, and still a distance from its profit record of $2,126,000,000 in 1965 (4.7 per cent of the total of U.S. corporate after-tax earnings).

First half reports for 1968 pointed to at least a near record for GM sales and profits. Its profit rate is regularly far higher than that of other auto manufacturers. GM's shares of total domestic automobile manufacture sales and earnings for 1966 were 52 per cent and 69 per cent respectively. For the period 1947–1966, GM's profits after taxes averaged 22.7 per cent return on net worth, almost twice the 12.2 per cent national average. This is the most conservative estimate, based on GM's accounting practices, which understate its income.

The very size and diversity of GM provides an awesome leverage against any competitors. General Motors Acceptance Corporation, the company's wholesale and retail financing subsidiary, is the single largest seller of short-term commercial paper with such outstandings rivaling the U.S. Treasury itself. Motors Insurance Corporation, a wholly owned subsidiary of GMAC, is one of the nation's largest underwriters of physical damage insurance.

The nearly 13,000 substantial GM dealers, whom GM has made financially dependent upon it by its policy of dealer exclusivity, comprise a powerful force at the retail level to further GM's hegemony. Bending dealers to their will has resulted in a greater and greater captive or exclusive market for parts and accessories (trumpeted publicly by the saturation advertising campaign to "KEEP YOUR CAR ALL GM") and has put a merciless squeeze or squeeze-out on independent manufacturers and wholesalers.

Power begets power. The former chief of the Justice Department's Anti-trust Division, Donald Turner, in June, 1966, spoke on the anti-competitive effects of advertising flowing from firms possessing inordinate market power in their industry. GM's annual advertising budget exceeds $200 million, touting, among other things, excellence and "genuineness" of their parts. With a liquidity position in excess of three billion dollars distributed in variable proportions among more than 100 of the country's largest banks, GM exerts a powerful influence in the world of finance. Considerations other than economics dictate such geographical placement.

Flexibility in the exercise of market power by GM is facilitated by keeping its financial reporting on the most general level. GM publishes only consolidated figures on its operations, refusing to break down its profits and financial data by divisions. Close observers of GM's operations indicate that one reason for such non-disclosure is that exceptionally high profits are made from its spare parts and accessories business — a particularly sensitive fact in view of the fancification, poor durability, and expensive replacement (owing to original design decisions) of various portions of its automobiles.

Another reason for no divisional reporting is to cover up which lines are subsidizing other company activities for the purpose of driving competitors out of business. Non-disclosure of divisional operations relates also to the spectacular profit rate, even for GM, of certain divisions. The Cadillac division, for example, before the construction of its new plant in the early 1960's, is reliably reported to have had a return in investment of more than 100 per cent *after* taxes. One can imagine the reaction of a Cadillac purchaser on learning that little more goes into a Cadillac than a top-line Buick or a fully equipped Chevrolet, in terms of production cost.

Perhaps the most intriguing expression of inordinate market power is GM's long established practice of a target rate of profit. The method used is basically similar to that of a public utility, except that GM sets its own upper limit several orders of magnitude above the average utility and there is no public supervision of its cost formulations and pricing practices. To set its target rate of return, ranging from fifteen to twenty per cent on net worth but always managing to exceed it substantially, GM has to possess the market power requisite for fixing its prices in advance of the new model year without having to concern itself with the possible effects of competitive pricing on its planned percentage profits and on its share of the market.

Analysis of the yearly outcome of GM's pricing formula suggests that a sufficient margin is taken into account to cover estimated income taxes. Income tax rates have not affected GM's rate of return. Taxes for GM have been treated as another cost which it can pass on to its customers. After taxes, the 1929 rate of return was 36.2 per cent, while the 1950 rate of return was 37.5 per cent on average stockholders' investment; in 1950 GM made a pre-tax profit of 77.4 per cent to earn 37.5 per cent after taxes.

In an article that appeared in *The Corporate Director* (July, 1956), the American Institute of Management marveled at GM's phenomenal rate of return:

> The astonishing fact emerges . . . that, from 1949 through 1955, the average rate of operating profit [net sales less cost of sales, selling and administrative expense and depreciation] in proportion to total assets employed, including debt, has exceeded forty per cent per annum. The operating profit on net stock and surplus, defined to include minority interest and special reserves, has exceeded fifty-five per cent per annum in the average of these years. It has averaged 140 per cent of the average net plant account in these same years.

At the 1955 rate of profit, the AIM noted that GM's net earnings (after interest and income taxes) were sufficient to recoup the company's entire net plant investment in two years. AIM took note that this kind of return is "in fact, a continuing characteristic of the enterprise, being equaled or bettered in twelve of the preceding twenty years."

The price leadership of GM *vis-à-vis* Ford and Chrysler, for example, is indicative of its power. On occasion Ford and Chrysler have announced their annual model prices before GM, but they generally have to adapt closely to GM's prices if they guessed wrong. In 1957, Ford guessed wrong and *raised* its prices to meet GM's.

There is even less incentive to compete on price, under a target pricing policy by the dominant firm in the industry, when that firm has pursued a product policy that emphasizes nonprice competition. With little price competition at the producer level and with the camouflaging complexities of financing, and trade-in gimmicks, the emphasis long ago shifted to the area of style, intimations of aggression, power, vacation-land image, and the "personality" of the particular make or model.

The bulk of the communication process between auto company and customer stresses these themes and garnishes them with animistic appellations taken from the mountains, jungles, and ocean depths. In the attenuated competition of a tight oligopoly, the range of competition is continually narrowed as each company competes more and more about less and less. In this game GM has excelled. It has led the way with wraparound windshields, hard-top models, protruding dash panels, low profile vehicles (partly through tire size reduction), dagger fins and ornaments, and other creative lethalities which the other domestic companies felt compelled to emulate.

As George Romney said ten years ago, when he was head of American Motors, GM's share of the market was so great that its styles determined the modernity of American cars. The stage was repeatedly set for what economists call "protective imitation." On the other side of vehicle design, although disc brakes and radial ply tires were available on some mass production cars in Europe as early as 1953 and 1949 respectively, only when GM, commencing in 1965, tiptoed into these radical offerings, as extra cost options, did the other companies follow suit.

Clearly, a competitive industry would have seen one or more companies forge ahead here with such tested innovations. But again and again, one hears and has heard the plaint of Ford and Chrysler personnel bemoaning the risks attendant upon not following the product leadership of GM. GM's planning in these price and product areas is made possible, of course, by the effective insulation from a critical consuming body having available real choices whose differences are revealed at the point of sale. Again, Romney stated it candidly:

> When you get an inadequate number of companies in an indus-
> try, the customer ceases to be king. He begins to be dictated to
> by the concepts that a few have as to what he ought to have. . . .

The domestic industry is no more competitive than it was a decade ago, although the operation of the auto safety law has the potential to provide a discernible point of sale differentiation in terms of safety performance that may stimulate some safety competition. One worsening area is that the price of entry into automobile production with national distribution most certainly has gone up from the figure of one billion dollars estimated by Romney in 1958. Very high barriers to entry, including the exclusive dealer franchise, help preserve the status quo.

The history and attainments of GM's market power make it a classic candidate for anti-trust enforcement under the Sherman and Clayton Acts. In law and in economics there are solid grounds for proceeding toward dissolution or divestiture of General Motors under the two anti-trust laws. The only obstacle is political. How ironic indeed, for the political power of highly concentrated economic firms was a fundamental concern of the Republican Congress that passed the Sherman Anti-trust Act in 1890. History has come full circle, when General Motors can succeed in transforming a *fait accompli* into *de facto* immunity from this basic anti-trust action.

This is not the place for a detailed legal analysis of such an action. It is enough to say that General Motors passes the test of unreasonable market power in terms of its size and the source of that power growth through mergers and acquisitions of more than 100 companies, including the Olds Motor Works, Cadillac Motor Company, and Fisher Body. The Standard Oil, Alcoa, and Dupont cases, among others, are relevant authoritative interpretations of the anti-trust laws for application to the GM situation.

The Justice Department knows, more than anyone, the case against General Motors. Beginning near the end of the Eisenhower Administration and continuing into the Kennedy and Johnson Administrations, Anti-trust Division lawyers conducted a detailed examination into the company's anti-competitive and monopolistic behavior, both vertically and horizontally. A grand jury was convened in New York for eighteen months. In May, 1966, a 120-page memorandum, together with a 104-page draft complaint, was completed by the staff. Succeeding inquiries to the Department of Justice have received the same reply: "The matter is still under study." Anti-trust chiefs come and go, and the reply remains the same.

There are skeptics who say, "What difference does it make whether there are four or eight domestic automobile companies, or whether GM remains as is or is subjected to dissolution or divestiture proceedings?"

I maintain that it makes a great deal of difference. Before giving my reasons, I should like to itemize a few of the many deficiencies associated with the auto industry's performance so there is a clearer idea of the gap between performance and promise:

1. The auto industry has been mired in a rut of technological stagnation unparalleled in a consumer goods industry. The record would have been worse were it not for innovations pressed on a reluctant industry by suppliers and European manufacturers. Henry Ford II and Donald Frey, Ford vice president, have recognized this lack of product innovation in public addresses. Professor Richard Morse of MIT recently sharply criticized the auto industry for neglecting research and development, particularly in engine innovation.

Auto thefts have been a serious problem for decades; yet only [in 1969 did] the auto industry begin to adopt some long-standing engineering "fixes" that make cars difficult to steal. All the published research on crash safety by the industry since 1920 can be digested in a day's reading.

In the safety area generally, research and development facilities and manpower allocations have been almost insignificant. The most impressive evidence of this situation is available in the public docket of the National Highway Safety Bureau. This docket is full of statements about what automobile companies cannot do, what they do not know, and what they are unable even to measure. Under the pressures of modest, proposed safety standards, the companies owned up to their barren heritage, in marked contrast to their previous self-congratulatory catatonia. With the advent of the safety law, a capability for safety innovation is being built up slowly. Competition may be induced by legal compulsion in this area.

2. An institutionalized, Byzantine-like secrecy has been nurtured by the leading auto companies. Several purposes are thereby served. One is the myth that secrecy is necessary to preserve the bitter competition between companies. This has to be a big joke in Detroit, where there are few auto secrets. Secrecy is really directed against the public pursuant to the tried precepts that concealing the facts prevents the criticisms.

Just how phony is their continual plea of confidentiality for competitive reasons can be judged by an episode during the Kefauver hearings on administered prices. The big three auto companies turned down the Subcommittee request for a listing of materials costs on grounds that disclosure would place them at a serious competitive disadvantage. American Motors supplied the subcommittee with figures of their cost of materials and components. (The year was 1958 and AMC had its best years to come.) The companies know each others costs, if not to the fourth decimal point. But if the public knew, for example, that the direct and indirect labor cost of a medium priced car does not exceed $300, the handy pretext of wage increases employed by management for raising car prices would tend to diminish to its real, not fancied, significance.

3. Because it conflicted with GM's sales formula of visible obsolescence and invisible permanence, safety became encapsuled in a slogan that was merchandised: *"Safety doesn't sell."* Taking safety out of the competitive race occurred years ago and the consumer was never asked. His choice was made for him by corporate planning. To illustrate this, consider the argument that safety can be incorporated as part of competitive behavior. Safety is mostly engineered into the vehicle and is not visible to a consumer's supposed aesthetic rejection. Better brakes, tires, handling, safer instrument panels, steering columns, and door locks are all "passive" safety features hardly in the category of engaging a car buyer. Viewed as an innovative segment of product quality, it becomes part of vehicular progress, not a nasty nuisance.

A few safety features were add-on components and required passenger cooperation. The companies deliberately ignored these features (seat belts were prominent in aviation in the 1920's) and when they could no longer ignore them offered some as optional extra-cost equipment with very little communication of their protective qualities. Later they added seat belts as standard equipment, but their unnecessarily awkward design and installation (reflecting low seat and door pillar strength in part) impeded usage. Finally, by requirement of law for 1968 cars, shoulder harnesses of the most discommodious design were installed over the objections of General Motors.

In a classic episode of corporate deception, General Motors, in the summer of 1967, hastily forgot its own graphic displays of the shoulder harnesses' superior safety shown in the lobby of its Detroit headquarters (in May) and dispatched some misleading films to Washington in a last ditch attempt to get rid of the "spaghetti" (as harnesses are derisively called by auto stylists) for at least another year. The attempt failed, in no small part because one small auto manufacturer, Volvo, produced data on some 25,000 accidents involving Volvos equipped with harnesses that convincingly established the safety of their harnesses in even high speed collisions. This was a lesson in the benefits of competitive dissent because there was diversity. For decades millions of unrestrained flying objects called Americans were flung inside their vehicles, crushing bones and ending life, because the industry's leaders focused competition toward variations of stylistic pornography instead of toward engineering integrity. (The policy of delivering style as standard equipment and safety as extra cost option is still hanging on wherever possible in the industry.)

4. One of the neglected needs is that of breathing pure air. Roughly half of the nation's air pollution proceeds from the internal combustion

engine and its emissions of hydrocarbon, carbon monoxide, nitrogen oxides, and lead. Here, once again, it was not the industry that defined the problem but a professor (Haagen-Smit) at Cal Tech, who observed the connection between photochemical smog and auto emissions in 1951.

The agonizing experience of Los Angeles County and the state of California in trying to move the auto industry toward less polluting engines has been told elsewhere. Here one may note that the Anti-trust Division of the Justice Department thought there was enough serious evidence of concerted and collusive behavior by the domestic auto companies in restraining the development and marketing of auto exhaust control systems to keep a grand jury busy for eighteen months. But just as a ground-breaking suit for "product fixing" was about to be filed, the expected criminal action was dropped over the dissent of Government counsel who handled the proceedings before the grand jury. This was in January, 1968. A civil complaint ("go and sin no more" relief) was to be instituted instead. As of this day, there has been no action at all.

A particularly clear illustration of continuing industry intransigence on pollution-free engines was afforded [May, 1968] during Senate hearings on steam cars. Testimony by GM and Ford was so patently misleading that independent authorities in the room blinked with incredulity. These company statements could be ascribed to ignorance, but it would be more accurate to describe them as exercises in corporate prevarication.

5. Even in the area of supposed consumer acceptance, that of product differentiation over style, comforts and gadgetry, the industry maintains an aversion to factual disclosure.

Would the consumer crave for styling changes if he knew that they are costing him at least $700 of the price of his new car? Especially if he had a choice of not having them and saving the difference?

Do consumers really want those chrome eyebrows, called bumpers, whose chief function appears to be self-protection or the fostering of a multi-million dollar industry selling bumper guards to make up for stylistic idiocy? Ask them after they see that $200 repair bill following a three mile-per-hour crash into another car while parking.

Was there a clamor by consumers to put eyelids on Cougars, particularly the kinds of eyelids that sometimes refuse to flutter open at night (such a defect led to the recall of 85,000 Cougars last spring)? These eyelids were standard equipment.

What popular demonstration demanded hidden windshield wipers and the consequent freezing problem in northern climates?

Do consumers know that, when asked to buy a fully-tinted windshield, they are paying more in order to see substantially less?

How about the discomfort in just getting in and out of cars and in having sufficient head room for many passengers while seated?

6. What of the internal democracy of these corporations? Like any bureaucratic structure staffed by professionals with allegedly professional missions conflicting with prevailing corporate dictates, the climate can suppress or liberate, be fair or be unjust, be accountable, or be a buckpasser. The practices of exploiting the employed inventor or insuring the indemnification of directors have weakened incentive and responsibility.

Too often, those who wish to change an institution place an exclusive emphasis on external controls. Clearly, Ford's Donald Frey (himself an engineer and former professor) was thinking of problems internal to the industry's environment when he wrote:

> It's a sad commentary, but some of the most reactionary people in industry are engineers. Fresh new departures that require creative thinking and innovation can wind up in the file marked NIH — NOT INVENTED HERE. It is up to management to prevent this waste by creative engineering organizations that are mentally attuned to trying the new.

Old line conservatives, believing in the open market and free enterprise, instead of the controlled market and closed enterprise characteristic of modern day oligopolies, might recommend some old-fashioned competition for meeting human needs of sober design, health and safety, economical operation and repair. Meaningful competition has a good deal of motivational force.

Looking over these less than optimum practices, it is apparent that anti-trust is relevant more in a structural rather than a strictly substantive sense. By fostering competition, it increases the probability of diversity, dissent, and risk-taking. It also attenuates the fear of the giant by the intermediates or the midgets. Anti-trust enforcement has other points to commend it. It is law; it has traditions deep in both conservative and liberal thinking; it has doctrines of great flexibility resembling the common law more than statutory law. Above all, anti-trust enforcement articulates the ideal of decentralized economic power and is a marvelous engine for disclosure of inaccessible facts having a spin-off into supplementary reforms which must be undertaken to do the tasks that anti-trust action is not equipped to perform.

It is instructive that while corporate planning seeks to obtain security at the expense of consumer or market sovereignty and at the expense of needed anti-trust enforcement, more and more managers are wondering how to generate innovation just to solve the problems that they define as important for commercial success. Studies of innovation find a strong and unyielding contribution by the individual inventor or small business unit. The cause of auto safety has suffered grievously because of the unjust and unsupportive environment for the lone inventor who is still the main source of creativity in the world of automobiles, although he rarely receives the recognition.

I have urged that anti-trust needed a constituency that supported its active enforcement. This is a constituency not just of professional manpower but of legal reforms and tools. Corporate accountability must necessarily be fostered with a variety of controls and incentives. These range from disclosure requirements, effective sanctions, determining the scope of corporate involvement in political campaigns, more independent roles by professional engineering, scientific and medical societies, a comprehensive rewriting of corporate charters for large corporations, and other reforms to take the myth out of people's capitalism and put the people in it.

In many ways these problems have deepened because of unchecked corporate concentrations. In 1965, the Assistant Attorney General for Anti-trust, William Orrick, described the broader motivations behind the anti-trust laws in a manner often conveniently forgotten by those who give lip service to these laws:

> The Sherman Act in 1890, the Clayton Act in 1914, the Celler-Kefauver Act in 1950 reflected Congressional fear of the political power that might be wielded by our largest corporations; fear of the inability of the small businessman to survive and prosper in an economy dominated by huge corporate structures; fear of the absence of shareholder democracy in the big corporations; fear of local concerns being acquired by national companies operated by absentee management unresponsive to local problems. . . . Finally, and perhaps most important of all, Congress' dedication to anti-trust goals as a means of preserving our way of life has always rested on its recognition that concentration of industrial power may lead to the police state.

The atrophy of anti-trust enforcement and the absence of sufficient appreciation for its doctrines can be appraised by the surprise with which the following selections will be met:

On March 8, 1956, President Eisenhower's Anti-trust chief, Stanley N. Barnes, urged General Motors voluntarily to give up one or more of its automobile divisions in order to lessen a dangerous concentration in the industry.

In the late 1940's, Henry C. Simons, one of the leading advocates of the "Chicago school of economics" and free-enterprise economics in the United States, wrote that reasonable monopoly is a contradiction in terms. There can be no such thing. Wide dispersion of political and economic power is the only foundation on which a democratic, free-enterprise system can long exist. The role of government, in Professor Simons' view, was to (1) maintain active competition within a general framework of free-enterprise rules of the game so as to stimulate efficiency and to disperse economic power; and to (2) own and operate directly those few industries where competition cannot be made to function effectively. He specifically urged these steps that are at least as urgent as they were two decades ago:

Federal incorporation of all private corporations.

Forbidding any manufacturing or merchandising corporation to own stock in any other such corporation.

An upper limit on the asset size of all corporations, far below the size of the present giants.

Provision that no firm may be big enough to dominate its industry, the Federal Trade Commission to determine this size limit in each industry.

Complete prohibition of interlocking directorates, except between unrelated industries.

Simplification of corporate securities to two simple types, to minimize the possibility of hidden or indirect control of corporations.

The distance of corporate behavior and influence from these norms declared by Orrick and Simons is the measure of the intensity of the radicalism of corporate collectivism. For if radicalism be defined as the operational aberration from the traditional and acknowledged norms of a society and if its intensity be gauged by the power of that aberration, then the issue is industrial autocracy and the corporate state. This is the real challenge to the consumer.

NICHOLAS JOHNSON   *The Silent Screen*

Julian Goodman, president of NBC, believes that television "is now under threat of restriction and control." Frank Stanton, president of CBS, says that "attempts are being made to block us." Elmer Lower, president of ABC News, thinks he may "face the prospect of some form of censorship."

I agree. Censorship *is* a serious problem in our country. My only dispute with these network officials involves just *who* is doing the censoring. They apparently believe it's the Government. I disagree.

NBC recently cut Robert Montgomery's statements off the air when,

Reprinted from *TV Guide,* July 5, 1969 by permission of the author.

during the Johnny Carson show, he mentioned a CBS station being investigated by the Federal Communications Commission. Folk singer Joan Baez was silenced by CBS when she wished to express her views about the Selective Service System on the Smothers Brothers show. Now, of course, the entire show has been canceled — notwithstanding the high ratings and its writers' . . . Emmy. Sure there's censorship. But let's not be fooled into mistaking its source.

For at the same time that network officials are keeping off your television screens anything they find inconsistent with their corporate profits or personal philosophies, the FCC has been repeatedly defending their First Amendment rights against Government censorship. Just recently, for example, the FCC ruled — over strong protests — that the networks' coverage of the Chicago Democratic convention was protected by the Constitution's "freedom of the press" clause. In other decisions, the Commission refused to penalize radio station WBAI in New York for broadcasting an allegedly anti-Semitic poem, or a CBS-owned station for televising a "pot party."

Many broadcasters are fighting, not for *free* speech, but for *profitable* speech. In the WBAI case, for example, one of the industry's leading spokesmen, Broadcasting magazine, actually urged that WBAI be *punished* by the FCC — and on the same editorial page professed outrage that stations might not have an unlimited right to broadcast profitable commercials for cigarettes which may result in illness or death.

This country is a great experiment. For close to 200 years we have been testing whether it is possible for an educated and informed people to govern themselves. All considered, the experiment has worked pretty well. We've had our frustrations and disappointments as a Nation, but no one has been able to come up with a better system, and most of the newer nations still look to us as a model.

Central to our system, however, is the concept of an educated and an informed people. As Thomas Jefferson said, "The way to prevent error is to give the people full information of their affairs." Our founding fathers were familiar with censorship by the King of England. They were going to replace a king with a representative Congress. But they were concerned lest any American institution become powerful enough to impede the flow of information to the people. So they provided in the First Amendment that "*Congress* shall make no law . . . abridging the freedom of speech. . . ." Why "Congress"? I believe they assumed Congress would be the only body powerful enough to abridge free speech. They were wrong.

A lot has happened to the creation and control of information in this country since 1789. That was an age of town meetings and handbills. Today most information comes from the three broadcasting networks,

ABC, CBS and NBC, and the two wire services, Associated Press and United Press International. As Professor John Kenneth Galbraith has reminded us in "The New Industrial State," 70 years ago the large corporation confined itself to mass production in heavy industry. "Now," he writes, "it also sells groceries, mills grain, publishes newspapers and provides public entertainment, all activities that were once the province of the individual proprietor or the insignificant firm."

It is easy for us to forget how large, profitable and politically powerful some corporations have become. In 1948 about half of all manufacturing assets in the United States were controlled by 200 corporations; today a mere 100 corporations hold that power. A single corporation such as American Telephone & Telegraph (one of the FCC's many regulated companies) controls the wages and working conditions of 870,000 employees, purchases each year some $3.5 billion in goods and services, has assets of $37 billion, and has annual gross revenues in excess of $14 billion. This gross revenue is several times larger than the combined budgets of all the Federal regulatory commissions, the Federal court system, and the U.S. Congress; larger than the budget of each of the 50 states; a larger operation, indeed, than all but very few foreign governments.

I am not suggesting that large corporations are inherently evil. Not at all. They have created much of our wealth. I am merely urging that we be aware of the fact that large corporations have both the incentive and the power to control the information reaching the citizenry of our free society.

Sometimes corporate pressures to control what you see on television are just plain silly. For example, in his book "TV — The Big Picture," Stan Opotowsky reports that "Ford deleted a shot of the New York skyline because it showed the Chrysler building. . . . A breakfast-food sponsor deleted the line 'She eats too much' from a play because, as far as the breakfast-food company was concerned, nobody could ever eat too much." Often, however, corporate tampering with the product of honest and capable journalists and creative writers and performers can be quite serious. Sometimes there is a deliberate alteration of content; sometimes needed information is squeezed out by more profitable "entertainment" programming.

On February 10, 1966, the Senate was conducting hearings on the Vietnam war. Fred Friendly, who was president of CBS News at the time, wanted you to be able to watch those hearings. His network management did not permit you to watch. If you were watching CBS that day you saw instead of George Kennan's views, opposing the Vietnam war, the fifth CBS rerun of I Love Lucy. Fred Friendly quit CBS because of this decision, and subseqently wrote "Due to Circumstances Beyond Our Control" to tell the story. He began his book with the quotation, "What the

American people don't know can kill them." Indeed it can. In Vietnam, about 35,000 so far. We have been shown miles of film from Vietnam, it's true. But how much has television told you about the multibillion-dollar corporate profits from that war?

There are many other situations in which censorship exists side-by-side with large profits — and disease or death. The tobacco industry spends about $250 million a year on radio and television commercials designed to associate cigarette smoking, especially by the young, with fishing, football, the fresh air of the great outdoors, sexual prowess, and all other desirable attributes of a fun-packed adult world. In exchange for this investment, the industry sells on the order of $9 billion worth of cigarettes a year. Would it really surprise you to learn that the broadcasting industry has been less than eager to tell you about the health hazards of cigarette smoking? It shouldn't. Just recently, for example, a United States congressman alleged that the president of the National Association of Broadcasters had suppressed from Congress and the American public revealing information about the "substantial appeal to youth" of radio and television cigarette commercials. The relation of this forgetfulness to profits is clear: cigarette advertising provides the largest single source of television's revenue, about 8 per cent.

The FCC has ruled that broadcasters can't present one point of view on a controversial issue and censor all others just to serve their own beliefs and profits. The "Fairness Doctrine" requires that all viewpoints be presented. The FCC applied this doctrine to cigarette commercials. And what was the response of the broadcasting industry? It fought the decision with all the economic and political strength at its command. It has finally gone all the way to the Supreme Court to argue that a doctrine which limits its power to keep *all* information about the health hazards of cigarette smoking from the American people is a violation of broadcasters' First Amendment rights!

Or how about the 50,000 people who die each year on our highways? Their deaths are due to many causes, of course, including their own intoxication and carelessness. But how many television stations told you — either before or after Ralph Nader came along — that most auto-safety engineers agree virtually *all* those lives could be saved if our cars were designed properly? Nader, in *Unsafe at Any Speed*, speculates about "the impact which the massive sums spent ($361,006,000 in 1964 on auto advertising alone) have on the communication media's attention to vehicle safety design."

Television certainly didn't take the lead in telling us about unfit meat, fish and poultry. (Chet Huntley was found to have been editorializing *against* the Wholesome Meat Act at a time when he and his business partners were heavy investors in the cattle and meat business!) Bryce Rucker, in "The First Freedom," notes that:

> Networks generally have underplayed or ignored events and statements unfavorable to food processors and soap manufacturers. Recent examples are the short shrift given Senate subcommittee hearings on, and comments favorable to, the 1966 "truth in packaging" bill and the high cost of food processing. Could it be that such behavior reflects concern for the best interests of, say, the top-50 grocery-products advertisers, who spent $1,314,893,000 in TV in 1965, 52.3 percent of TV's total advertising income?

What could be more essential than information about potentially harmful food and drugs?

All Americans are concerned about "the crime problem." Have you ever stopped to wonder why the only crimes most of us hear about are, in the words of the Presidential Commission on Law Enforcement and Administration of Justice, "the crimes that are the easiest for the poor and the disadvantaged to commit . . ."? What we haven't been told is that much of the crime in the United States is "white-collar" crime; that the rich steal as much or more than the poor. As the Crime Commission report defined it:

> The "white-collar" criminal is the broker who distributes fraudulent securities, the builder who deliberately uses defective material, the corporation executive who conspires to fix prices, the legislator who peddles his influence and vote for private gain, or the banker who misappropriates funds. . . .

Did you ever find out from television, for example, that a *single* recent price-fixing case involved a "robbery" from the American people of more money than was taken in *all* the country's robberies, burglaries and larcenies during the years of that criminal price fixing? The crime commission declared that "it is essential that the public becomes aware of the seriousness of business crime." Why is it the news media do not tell you about *these* threats to "law and order"?

One could go on and on. The inherent dangers in cyclamates (the artificial sweeteners in soft drinks) have been so widely discussed in Sweden that the government is considering prohibiting their use. The danger is scarcely known [until 1969] to the average American. Most of the Nation's 160,000 coal miners have "black lung" disease (the disintegration of the lung from coal dust) in one form or another. Mine operators may refuse to pay for fresh-air masks — or support workmen's compensation legislation. Some television stations in coal-mining areas have, until recently, refused to televise programs offered them by doctors about this serious health hazard. Reports differ, and no one knows for sure, but one current sampling showed that 20 per cent of the color TV sets studied were emitting excess X-ray radiation. Natural-gas pipelines are exploding as predicted. And did you know that the life expectancy of the average American adult male has been *declining* in recent years? The list goes on almost without end.

Note what each of these items has in common: (1) human death, disease, dismemberment or degradation, (2) great profit for manufacturers, advertisers and broadcasters, and (3) the deliberate withholding of needed information from the public.

Many pressures produce such censorship. Some are deliberate, some come about through default. But all have come, not from Government, but from private corporations with something to sell. Charles Tower, chairman of the National Association of Broadcasters Television Board, recently wrote a letter to *The New York Times,* criticizing its attack on CBS for "censoring" the social commentary on the Smothers Brothers show. He said,

> There is a world of difference between the deletion of program material by Government command and the deletion by a private party [such as a broadcaster]. . . . Deletion by Government command is censorship. . . . Deletion of material by private parties . . . is not censorship.

Another *Times* reader wrote in answer to Mr. Tower:

> Mr. Tower's distinction . . . is spurious. The essence of censorship is the suppression of a particular point of view . . . over the channels of the mass media, and the question of who does the censoring is one of form only. . . .

He's right. The results *are* the same. You and I are equally kept in ignorance, ill-prepared to "prevent error," and to engage in the process of self-governing which Thomas Jefferson envisioned — regardless of *who* does the censoring.

A number of talented people *within* the broadcasting industry recognize its failings. One of the Nation's leading black announcers told me of his first job as a disc jockey. He was handed a stack of records, but forbidden to read any news over the air. Said his boss: "You're not going to educate the Negroes of this community at my expense." A high ABC network executive was recently quoted in the pages of *TV GUIDE* as saying, "There are many vital issues that we won't go near. We censor ourselves." Eric Sevareid has said of the pressures involved in putting together a network news show: "The ultimate sensation is that of being bitten to death by ducks." And the executive editor of the *San Francisco Chronicle* has warned: "The press is in danger. Not the exciting kind of Hollywood danger, but of dissolving into a gray mass of nonideas." For it is also a form of censorship to so completely clog the public's airwaves with tasteless gruel that there is no time left for quality entertainment and social commentary, no time "to give the people full information of their affairs." Mason Williams, the multitalented one-time writer for the Smothers Brothers, has left television in disgust and written a poem about his experiences with "The Censor," who, he says in conclusion,

> Snips out
> The rough talk
> The unpopular opinion
> Or anything with teeth
> And renders
> A pattern of ideas
> Full of holes
> A doily
> For your mind[1]

Your mind. *My* mind. The mind of America.

The Rolling Stones said it long ago:

> When I'm drivin' in my car,
> When the man comes on the radio,
> He's tellin' me more and more
> About some useless information . . .
> Supposed to fire my imagination? . . .
> I can't get no satisfaction![2]

Many Americans are trying to *say* something to each other. But the media haven't been listening. And you haven't been told. So some have turned to violence as a means of being heard. All you've been shown are the dramatic pictures; you know there's "something happening." But, like the Everyman of Bob Dylan's song, "You don't know what it is, do you, Mr. Jones?" The "Silent Screen" of television has left you in ignorance as to what it's all about.

The time may soon come when the media will have to listen. From many directions come suggestions for change. Law professor Jerome Barron says the courts should recognize a "public right of access to the mass media." Free speech in this age of television, he believes, requires

[1] From The Mason Williams Reading Matter (Doubleday & Co., Inc.).
[2] Copyright © Immediate Music Inc., 1965. Written by Mick Jagger & Keith Richards. Used by permission. All rights reserved. International copyright secured.

that citizens with something to say be permitted to say it over radio and television. Suppose you approach a television station with a "commercial" you have prepared either supporting or protesting the President's conduct of the Vietnamese war. It may no longer be sufficient for the station to say to you, "Sorry, we don't like your views, so we won't broadcast your announcement" — as a San Francisco station did last year to those trying to express their point of view regarding a *ballot proposition!* As the U.S. Supreme Court said a few days ago in the Red Lion case, upholding the constitutionality of the FCC's Fairness Doctrine:

> There is no sanctuary in the First Amendment for unlimited private censorship operating in a medium not open to all. Freedom of the press from governmental interference under the First Amendment does not sanction repression of that freedom by private interests.

It is too early to know the full, ultimate impact of this decision.

In Holland, any group that can get 15,000 persons to support its list of proposed programs is awarded free time on the Dutch Television Network for a monthly program. There is even an organization for tiny and often eccentric splinter groups without 15,000 supporters. If a similar experiment were conducted in this country, groups interested in electronic music, drag racing, handicrafts, camping, as well as the League of Women Voters, the National Association for the Advancement of Colored People, local school boards, theater and drama associations, the Young Republicans (and, who knows, even the Smothers Brothers), could obtain television time to broadcast programs prepared under their supervision.

Or each network might devote a full one-third of its prime time (6 P.M. to 11 P.M.) programming to something other than entertainment or sports. It could be nonsponsored cultural, educational and public-affairs programming. If the networks were required to stagger such fare, then at any given time during the 6 P.M. to 11 P.M. period of greatest audiences the American viewer would have an alternative, a *choice.* There would still be at all times *two* networks with the commercial-laden, lowest-common-denominator mass entertainment of situation comedies, Westerns, quiz shows and old movies. The third, however, would have something else.

It would be wholly inappropriate for me as an FCC Commissioner to insist that broadcasters present only the information, ideas and entertainment that I personally find compatible. The FCC does not have, and would not want, the responsibility for selecting your television programs. But it would be equally irresponsible for me to sit idly by and watch the corporate censors keep from your TV screen the full range of needs, tastes and interests of the American people.

The television-station owner, not the network, has ultimate responsibility for his programming. But somebody has to select his programs, you say; nobody's perfect. You're right. And all I'm urging is that, when in doubt, all of us — audience, networks and Government — ought to listen a little more carefully to the talented voices of those who are crying out to be heard. In short, I would far rather leave the heady responsibility for the inventory in America's "marketplace of ideas" to talented and uncensored *individuals* — creative writers, performers and journalists from *all* sections of this great country — than to the *committees* of frightened financiers in New York City. Wouldn't you? I think so.

I am delighted the networks have raised the issue of censorship in America. I hope they will permit us to discuss it fully.

MILITARIZATION

As civil rights, the Vietnam war, and student protest have
been the dominant political experience of the student generation of the 1960's, World War II was the dominant political experience of the student generation of the 1940's
and 50's. It has been said that World War II was a popular war, in contrast to the war in Vietnam. Yet the consequences of that "popularity," as distinct from its sources,
have rarely been analyzed. The sources of popularity are
easily discerned. The enemy was a symbol of absolute
evil; the federal government, and especially the presidency of Roosevelt, were as popular with most intellectuals
as the administration of Lyndon B. Johnson was to become
unpopular during the 1960's. Indeed, this combination of
Roosevelt and Hitler was to establish the United States as
the ethical center of the universe for most American liberals. But what were the consequences of this combination
of popularity and moral righteousness?

Four of the consequences help explain the militarization
of American life. First, although the rest of the world
might have been somewhat skeptical, the entrance of the
United States into World War II could have been interpreted as a fulfillment of earlier conceptions of the superiority and "manifest destiny" of the country. The
American way of life could serve as a model for the rest of
the world and their "development" would be measured by
the American standard. Thus, America was morally sanc-

tioned, indeed obliged, to extend its "orbit of influence" throughout the world.

Second, the expansion of interests and alliances produced a necessary corollary in a world increasingly divided into spheres of influence by great powers, the expansion of military commitments to resist attacks by large powers against our own expanded military forces, and to quell insurgents within indigenous populations. Therefore, we were "temporarily" required to support reactionary and brutal, but unquestionably "anti-Communist," regimes, whose character, the American public was told, would be changed by the contact with American values and technology. This policy implied that indigenous values and beliefs were worth little, especially as they stood in the path of technological "progress."

Third, the belief in America's ethical leadership, plus the requirements of American expansionism during and after World War II, led to the incorporating of intellectuals and scholars within the bureaucracy of government. This incorporation had begun in the 1930's during the Roosevelt administration. The benign attitude toward the government and its needs had begun during World War II when such agencies as the Office of Strategic Services were staffed by social scientists, many of whom were later to become leaders in the field and to develop such organizations as the RAND corporation.

Finally, as the articles in this section make clear, there was a slow but steady extension of military influence into many civilian institutions. Our first selection, the extraordinary document *Channeling*, exposes the influence of the conscription that continued after World War II on university priorities regarding strength of departments and emphasis upon areas of study.

Channeling is one of ten documents in an "Orientation Kit" distributed in July, 1965, by the Selective Service System. It was later withdrawn, perhaps because it was used by student radicals to demonstrate the manipulative quality of the system. The suppression of the document is easily understood. The document begins with the observa-

tion that the Selective Service System functions to channel
manpower into the military service, and also to channel
youth into civilian occupations. Students gravitate toward
those fields which will allow them to avoid military service.

Other institutions are also affected by "channeling."
Young men are less likely to turn to careers in business enterprises not in "the national interest." In this hierarchy of
values, floral design is of far less value than weapons design. And if the intensity of "the pressure" moves the
young man into certain occupational choices, it may also
direct him into other life conditions that he may not be
ready for. To what extent is the high divorce rate in the
United States attributable to the policies of the Selective
Service System? How many children were born who were
not fully desired by their parents, except as a means for the
future father to avoid conscription? As this document
points out, "Delivery of manpower for induction, the process of providing a few thousand men with transportation
to a reception center, is not much of an administrative or
financial challenge. It is in dealing with the other millions
of registrants that the system is heavily occupied, developing more effective human beings in the national interest."

But what are "more effective human beings," and what
is the "national interest?" One of the most remarkable features of this document is the assumption that "effective human beings" and the "national interest" coincide with the
priorities of the military. Increasingly, this opinion is
being publicly challenged by respected "establishment"
figures. In a critique of the "new American militarism,"
General David M. Shoup, a hero of the Battle of Tarawa in
1943, who rose to become a commandant of the United
States Marine Corps for four years until his retirement in
December, 1963, charges that "America has become a
militaristic and aggressive nation."

General Shoup maintains that as a result of World War
II, the Korean war, conscription following the Korean war,
and the Vietnam war, we have become a nation of veterans
and powerful veterans' organizations infused with military
ideas, codes, and values. He informs us that in 1968 the

total population of veterans of United States military service numbered over 23 million, or about 20 per cent of
the adult population. Moreover, a vast complex of defense
industries has grown up alongside the veteran population,
which, together with it, form an influential public opinion
lobby. Each of the four services has its own association
and additional military associations and organizations perform a variety of functions. The military and its associated
organizations have provided a public opinion climate
which is receptive to a military definition of national interest.

General Shoup's analysis of the military's capacity and
mentality shows that the military work hard, think straight,
and "they keep their eyes on the objective, which is to be
instantly ready to solve the problem through military action while insuring that their respective service gets its
proper mission, role and recognition, in the operation."
Thus, the military are a highly pragmatic force, especially
in a crisis, and can come forward with an apparent resolution more confidently and with greater certainty than civilian appointees and diplomats.

Yet the military are principally concerned with "tactics"
of response to particular situations. Shoup believes that,
unlike some of the civilian policymakers, the military has
not itself been obsessed with the threat of "Communism,"
per se. Military men generally know or care little about
Communism. Rather, Communists can be plugged into
the "aggressor" category in military war games and "defeating aggression is a gigantic combat area competition
rather than a crusade to save the world from Communism." According to Shoup, the militarization of American
life results not so much from large policy objectives, but
rather from a base of narrow practicality. The military requires a basic creed for the defense establishment to build,
grow, and justify its cause.

As the military establishment grows, competition grows
within it for each segment to demonstrate its superior tactical abilities. Such a demonstration cannot take place
without active warfare, because it is only in warfare that
the capacity of the particular branch of service, or weap-

ons systems, may be demonstrated. The social or political issues surrounding a military venture are disregarded by comparison to the functional requirements of prestige and power of the Armed Forces. In this fashion, wars tend to have a self-perpetuating and self-justifying function.

Two of the themes developed by General Shoup are elaborated in the remaining articles of this section. Richard Kaufman, an economist on the staff of the Joint Economic Subcommittee on Economy in Government, reveals that in fiscal 1968, total federal outlays for military and military-related spending were nearly 179 billion dollars, whereas less than 500 million dollars were spent for food stamps, school lunches, and the special milk program, combined. The largest item in the defense budget is procurement — in other words, government contracts. Indeed, one critic, H. L. Nieburg, has called the military-industrial complex the basis for a "contract state" in America.[1] Defense contracting involves many of the large industrial corporations of America, and a company enlarges its share of defense work over the years. As military business has become solidly entrenched, studies of defense contracting have shown that the industry, particularly the aerospace industry, is both inefficient and unreliable. Furthermore, the defense contractor rarely loses. Whatever losses he may incur are usually subsidized by the government — i.e., the taxpayer. The most ominous consequence of a bloated defense budget, however, is in the expanding and sometimes furtive military activities in such areas as foreign affairs, social science research, domestic riot control, and chemical and biological warfare. This military influence ultimately affects the quality of American life as a whole.

For example, students of democracy have argued that independent labor unions foster the institutions of political democracy in American society. Reputedly, labor unions in Communist countries are notoriously government dominated, but the claim is made that in the free, democratic western countries, labor unions are indepen-

[1] H. L. Nieburg, *In the Name of Science* (Chicago: Quadrangle Books, 1966).

dent of external control. But organized labor has been among the most consistent and conservative supporters of American military and foreign policy, and especially of American intervention in Vietnam. There is little difference between the foreign policy of former President Johnson and that of George Meany. Indeed, what we have referred to in this introduction as the military-industrial complex is increasingly labeled the military-industrial-labor complex. Richard Dudman accepts the veracity of this description, and points out that several labor operated institutes in Latin America, Africa, and Asia are largely supported by the Agency for International Development. And not only has the AFL-CIO failed to be independent of government policy, it has on occasion become a de facto part of the United States government, directly dependent for its support on government counterinsurgency agencies.

The industrialists and labor leaders are the beneficiaries and supporters of the system, and the military officers are its tacticians. However, its strategists are those officials in the State Department, Pentagon, CIA, and White House who manage United States foreign relations. These officials are called "national security managers" by Richard J. Barnet. These men are usually trained in law, engineering, or banking, and entered service during World War II. They consider revolution in the underdeveloped world a problem in the management of violence rather than a failure of society, economy, and local politics. Since these men came to power in the midst of World War II, their views of international politics are influenced by experiences in the struggle with Hitler's Germany. Their enemy symbolized absolute evil; they are prone to see all contemporary enemies as symbols of absolute evil and to develop myths of monolithic Communism. "The National-Security Manager assumes that U.S. interests and those of the rest of humanity coincide. Governments and political movements which contest this idea have ulterior and illegitimate motives."

This mythology, as General Shoup puts it, "develops somewhat like a religion," and serves as the ideological basis for the defense establishment's self-perpetuation,

justifying its organizations, its doctrines, its self-maintenance, and its management. There is an interlocking network of ideology, organization, history, and power, which
fosters the contemporary militarization of American life.

SELECTIVE SERVICE SYSTEM   *Channeling*

One of the major products of the Selective Service classification process
is the channeling of manpower into many endeavors and occupations,
activities that are in the national interest. This function is a counterpart
and amplification of the System's responsibility to deliver manpower to
the armed forces in such a manner as to reduce to a minimum any adverse effect upon the national health, safety, interest, and progress. By
identifying and applying this process intelligently, the System is able not
only to minimize any adverse effect, but to exert an effect beneficial to
the national health, safety and interest.

   The line dividing the primary function of armed forces manpower procurement from the process of channeling manpower into civilian support
is often finely drawn. The process of channeling by not taking men from
certain activities who are otherwise liable for service, or by giving deferment to qualified men in certain occupations, is actual procurement
by inducement of manpower for civilian activities which are manifestly
in the national interest.

   While the best known purpose of Selective Service is to procure manpower for the armed forces, a variety of related processes takes place outside delivery of manpower to the active armed forces. Many of these
may be put under the heading of "channeling manpower." Many young
men would not have pursued a higher education if there had not been
a program of student deferment. Many young scientists, engineers, tool
and die makers, and other possessors of scarce skills would not remain
in their jobs in the defense effort if it were not for a program of occupational deferment. Even though the salary of a teacher has historically
been meager, many young men remain in that job seeking the reward of

From a document distributed by the Selective Service System in July, 1965, reprinted here as adapted in a pamphlet printed by Palo Alto Resistance, Palo Alto,
California.

deferment. The process of channeling manpower by deferment is entitled to much credit for the large amount of graduate students in technical fields and for the fact that there is not a greater shortage of teachers, engineers, and other scientists working in activities which are essential to the national interest.

More than ten years ago, it became evident that something additional had to be done to permit and encourage development of young scientists and trained people in all fields. A million and a half registrants are now deferred as students. One reason the Nation is not in shorter supply of engineers today is that they were among the students deferred by Selective Service in previous years. Similarly, Selective Service student deferments reduced what otherwise would have developed into more serious shortages in teaching, medicine, dentistry, and every field requiring advanced study. The System has also induced needed people to remain in these professions and in industry engaged in defense activities or in support of national health, safety, or interest.

The opportunity to enhance the national well-being by inducing more registrants to participate in fields which relate directly to the national interest came about as a consequence, soon after the close of the Korean episode, of the knowledge within the System that there was enough registrant personnel to allow stringent deferent practices employed during war time to be relaxed or tightened as the situation might require. Circumstances had become favorable to induce registrants, by the attraction of deferment, to matriculate in schools and pursue subjects in which there was beginning to be a national shortage of personnel. These were particularly in the engineering, scientific, and teaching professions.

This was coupled with a growing public recognition that the complexities of future wars would diminish further the distinction between what constitutes military service in uniform and a comparable contribution to the national interest out of uniform. Wars have always been conducted in various ways, but appreciation of this fact and its relationship to preparation for war has never been so sharp in the public mind as it is now becoming. The meaning of the word "service," with its former restricted application to the armed forces, is certain to become widened much more in the future. This brings with it the ever increasing problem of how to control effectively the service of individuals who are not in the armed forces.

In the Selective Service System, the term "deferment" has been used millions of times to describe the method and means used to attract to the kind of service considered to be the most important, the individuals who were not compelled to do it. The club of induction has been used to drive out of areas considered to be less important to the areas of greater importance in which deferments were given, the individuals who did not or could not participate in activities which were considered essential to the Nation. The Selective Service System anticipates evolution in this area. It is promoting the process by the granting of deferments in liberal numbers where the national need clearly would benefit.

Soon after Sputnik I was launched it became popular to reappraise critically our educational, scientific, and technological inventory. Many deplored our shortage of scientific and technical personnel, inadequacies of our schools, and shortage of teachers. Since any analysis having any connection with manpower and its relation to the Nation's survival vitally involves the Selective Service System, it is well to point out that for quite some time the System had been following a policy of deferring instructors who were engaged in the teaching of mathematics and physical and biological sciences. It is appropriate also to recall the System's previously invoked practice of deferring students to prepare themselves for work in some essential activity and the established program of deferring engineers, scientists, and other critically skilled persons who were working in essential fields.

The Congress, in enacting the Universal Military Training and Service legislation, declared that adequate provisions for national security required maximum effort in the fields of scientific research and development, and the fullest possible utilization of the Nation's technological, scientific, and other critical manpower resources. To give effect to this philosophy, the classifying boards of the Selective Service System defer registrants determined by them to be necessary in the national health, safety, or interest. This is accomplished on the basis of evidence of record in each individual case. No group deferments are permitted. Deferments are granted, however, in a realistic atmosphere so that the fullest effect of channeling will be felt, rather than be terminated by military service at too early a time.

Registrants and their employers are encouraged and required to make available to the classifying authorities detailed evidence as to the occupations and activities in which the registrants are engaged. It is not necessary for any registrant to specifically request deferment, but his selective service file must contain sufficient current evidence on which can be based a proper determination as to whether he should remain where he is or be made available for service. Since occupational deferments are granted for no more than a year at a time, a process of periodically receiving current information and repeated review assures that every deferred registrant continues to contribute to the overall national good. This reminds him of the basis of his deferment. The skills as well as the activities are periodically reevaluated. A critical skill that is not employed in an essential activity does not qualify for deferment.

Patriotism is defined as "devotion to the welfare of one's country." It has been interpreted to mean many different things. Men have always been exhorted to do their duty. But what that duty is depends upon a variety of variables, most important being the nature of the threat to the national welfare and the capacity and opportunity of the individual. Take, for example, the boy who saved the Netherlands by plugging the dike with his finger.

At the time of the American Revolution the patriot was the so-called "embattled farmer" who joined General Washington to fight the British. The concept that patriotism is best exemplified by service in uniform has always been under some degree of challenge, but never to the extent that it is today. In today's complicated warfare when the man in uniform may be suffering far less than the civilians at home, patriotism must be interpreted far more broadly than ever before.

This is not a new thought, but it has had new emphasis since the development of nuclear and rocket warfare. Educators, scientists, engineers, and their professional organizations, during the last ten years particularly, have been convincing the American public that for the mentally qualified man there is a special order of patriotism other than service in uniform — that for the man having the capacity, dedicated service as a civilian in such fields as engineering, the sciences, and teaching constitute the ultimate in their expression of patriotism. A large segment of the American public has been convinced that this is true.

It is in this atmosphere that the young man registers at age 18 and pressure begins to force his choice. He does not have the inhibitions that a philosophy of universal service in uniform would engender. The door is open for him as a student to qualify if capable in a skill needed by his nation. He has many choices and he is prodded to make a decision.

The psychological effect of this circumstantial climate depends upon the individual, his sense of good citizenship, his love of country and its way of life. He can obtain a sense of well being and satisfaction that he is doing as a civilian what will help his country most. This process encourages him to put forth his best effort and removes to some degree the stigma that has been attached to being out of uniform.

In the less patriotic and more selfish individual it engenders a sense of fear, uncertainty, and dissatisfaction which motivates him, nevertheless, in the same direction. He complains of the uncertainty which he must endure; he would like to be able to do as he pleases; he would appreciate a certain future with no prospect of military service or civilian contribution, but he complies with the needs of the national health, safety, or interest — or he is denied deferment.

Throughout his career as a student, the pressure — the threat of loss of deferment — continues. It continues with equal intensity after graduation. His local board requires periodic reports to find out what he is up to. He is impelled to pursue his skill rather than embark upon some less important enterprise and is encouraged to apply his skill in an essential activity in the national interest. The loss of deferred status is the consequence for the individual who has acquired the skill and either does not use it, or uses it in a nonessential activity.

The psychology of granting wide choice under pressure to take action is the American or indirect way of achieving what is done by direction in foreign countries where choice is not allowed. Here, choice is limited but not denied, and it is fundamental that an individual generally applies himself better to something he has decided to do rather than something he has been told to do.

The effects of channeling are manifested among student physicians; they are deferred to complete their education through school and internship. This permits them to serve in the armed forces in their skills rather than in an unskilled capacity as enlisted men.

The device of pressurized guidance, or channeling, is employed on Standby Reservists of which more than 2½ million have been referred by all services for availability determinations. The appeal to the Reservist who knows he is subject to recall to active duty unless he is determined to be unavailable is virtually identical to that extended to other registrants.

The psychological impact of being rejected for service in uniform is severe. The earlier this occurs in a young man's life, the sooner the beneficial effects of pressured motivation by the Selective Service System are lost. He is labeled unwanted. His patriotism is not desired. Once the label of "rejectee" is upon him all efforts at guidance by persuasion are futile. If he attempts to enlist at 17 or 18 and is rejected, then he receives virtually none of the impulsion the System is capable of giving him. If he makes no effort to enlist and as a result is not rejected until delivered for examination by the Selective Service System at about age 23, he has felt some of the pressure but thereafter is a free agent.

This contributed to establishment of a new classification of I–Y (registrant qualified for military service only in time of war or national emergency). That classification reminds the registrant of his ultimate qualification to serve and preserves some of the benefit of what we call channeling. Without it or any other similar method of categorizing men in degrees of acceptability, men rejected for military service would be left with the understanding that they are unfit to defend their country, even in war time.

An unprejudiced choice between alternative routes in civilian skills can be offered only by an agency which is not a user of manpower and is, therefore, not a competitor. In the absence of such an agency, bright young men would be importuned with bounties and pirated like potential college football players until eventually a system of arbitration would have to be established.

From the individual's viewpoint, he is standing in a room which has been made uncomfortably warm. Several doors are open, but they all lead to various forms of recognized, patriotic service to the Nation. Some accept the alternatives gladly — some with reluctance. The consequence is approximately the same.

The so-called Doctor Draft was set up during the Korean episode to insure sufficient physicians, dentists, and veterinarians in the armed forces as officers. The objective of that law was to exert sufficient pressure to furnish an incentive for application for commission. However, the indirect effect was to induce many physicians, dentists, and veterinarians to specialize in areas of greatest demand and national need rather than of greatest financial return.

Selective Service processes do not compel people by edict as in foreign systems to enter pursuits having to do with essentiality and progress. They go because they know that by going they will be deferred.

The application of direct methods to effect the policy of every man doing his duty in support of national interest involves considerably more capacity than the current use of indirection as a method of allocation of personnel. The problem, however, of what is every man's duty when each individual case is approached is not simple. The question of whether he can do one duty better than another is a problem of considerable proportions and the complications of logistics in attempting to control parts of an operation without controlling all of it (in other words, to control allocation of personnel without controlling where people eat, where they live and how they are to be transported) adds to the administrative difficulties of direct administration. The organization necessary to make the decisions, even poor decisions, would, of necessity, extract a large segment of population from productive work. If the members of the organization are conceived to be reasonably qualified to exercise judgment and control over skilled personnel, the impact of their withdrawal from war production work would be severe. The number of decisions would extend into billions.

A quarter billion classification actions were needed in World War II for the comparatively limited function of the Selective Service System at that time. Deciding what people should do, rather than letting them do something of national importance of their own choosing, introduces many problems that are at least partially avoided when indirect methods, the kind currently invoked by the Selective Service System, are used.

Delivery of manpower for induction, the process of providing a few thousand men with transportation to a reception center, is not much of an administrative or financial challenge. It is in dealing with the other millions of registrants that the system is heavily occupied, developing

more effective human beings in the national interest. If there is to be
any survival after disaster, it will take people, and not machines, to re-
store the Nation.

GENERAL DAVID M. SHOUP   *The New
                               American Militarism*

America has become a militaristic and aggressive nation. Our massive and
swift invasion of the Dominican Republic in 1965, concurrent with the
rapid buildup of U.S. military power in Vietnam, constituted an impressive demonstration of America's readiness to execute military contingency
plans and to seek military solutions to problems of political disorder and
potential Communist threats in the areas of our interest.

   This "military task force" type of diplomacy is in the tradition of our
more primitive, pre-World War II "gunboat diplomacy," in which we
landed small forces of Marines to protect American lives and property
from the perils of native bandits and revolutionaries. In those days the
U.S. Navy and its Marine landing forces were our chief means, short of
war, for showing the flag, exercising American power, and protecting U.S.
interests abroad. The Navy, enjoying the freedom of the seas, was a
visible and effective representative of the nation's sovereign power. The
Marines could be employed ashore "on such other duties as the President
might direct" without congressional approval or a declaration of war.
The U.S. Army was not then used so freely because it was rarely ready
for expeditionary service without some degree of mobilization, and its
use overseas normally required a declaration of emergency or war. Now,
however, we have numerous contingency plans involving large joint Air
Force-Army-Navy-Marine task forces to defend U.S. interests and to safeguard our allies wherever and whenever we suspect Communist aggression. We maintain more than 1,517,000 Americans in uniform overseas in

119 countries. We have 8 treaties to help defend 48 nations if they ask us to — or if we choose to intervene in their affairs. We have an immense and expensive military establishment, fueled by a gigantic defense industry, and millions of proud, patriotic, and frequently bellicose and militaristic citizens. How did this militarist culture evolve? How did this militarism steer us into the tragic military and political morass of Vietnam?

Prior to World War II, American attitudes were typically isolationist, pacifist, and generally anti-military. The regular peacetime military establishment enjoyed small prestige and limited influence upon national affairs. The public knew little about the armed forces, and only a few thousand men were attracted to military service and careers. In 1940 there were but 428,000 officers and enlisted men in the Army and Navy. The scale of the war, and the world's power relationships which resulted, created the American military giant. Today the active armed forces contain over 3.4 million men and women, with an additional 1.6 million ready reserves and National Guardsmen.

America's vastly expanded world role after World War II hinged upon military power. The voice and views of the professional military people became increasingly prominent. During the post-war period, distinguished military leaders from the war years filled many top positions in government. Generals Marshall, Eisenhower, MacArthur, Taylor, Ridgeway, LeMay, and others were not only popular heroes but respected opinion-makers. It was a time of international readjustment; military minds offered the benefits of firm views and problem-solving experience to the management of the nation's affairs. Military procedures — including the general staff system, briefings, estimates of the situation, and the organizational and operational techniques of the highly schooled, confident military professionals — spread throughout American culture.

World War II had been a long war. Millions of young American men had matured, been educated, and gained rank and stature during their years in uniform. In spite of themselves, many returned to civilian life as indoctrinated, combat-experienced military professionals. They were veterans, and for better or worse would never be the same again. America will never be the same either. We are now a nation of veterans. To the 14.9 million veterans of World War II, Korea added another 5.7 million five years later, and ever since, the large peacetime military establishment has been training and releasing draftees, enlistees, and short-term reservists by the hundreds of thousands each year. In 1968 the total living veterans of U.S. military service numbered over 23 million, or about 20 per cent of the adult population.

Today most middle-aged men, most business, government, civic, and professional leaders, have served some time in uniform. Whether they liked it or not, their military training and experience have affected them, for the creeds and attitudes of the armed forces are powerful medicine, and can become habit-forming. The military codes include all the virtues and beliefs used to motivate men of high principle: patriotism, duty and service to country, honor among fellowmen, courage in the face of danger, loyalty to organization and leaders, self-sacrifice for comrades, leadership, discipline, and physical fitness. For many veterans the military's efforts to train and indoctrinate them may well be the most impressive and influential experience they have ever had — especially so for the young and less educated.

In addition, each of the armed forces has its own special doctrinal beliefs and well-catalogued customs, traditions, rituals, and folklore upon which it strives to build a fiercely loyal military character and esprit de corps. All ranks are taught that their unit and their branch of the military service are the most elite, important, efficient, or effective in the military establishment. By believing in the superiority and importance of their own service they also provide themselves a degree of personal status, pride, and self-confidence.

As they get older, many veterans seem to romanticize and exaggerate their own military experience and loyalties. The policies, attitudes, and positions of the powerful veterans' organizations such as the American Legion, Veterans of Foreign Wars, and AMVETS, totaling over 4 million men, frequently reflect this pugnacious and chauvinistic tendency. Their memberships generally favor military solutions to world problems in the pattern of their own earlier experience, and often assert that their military service and sacrifice should be repeated by the younger generations.

Closely related to the attitudes and influence of America's millions of veterans is the vast and powerful complex of the defense industries, which have been described in detail many times in the eight years since General Eisenhower first warned of the military-industrial power complex in his farewell address as President. The relationship between the defense industry and the military establishment is closer than many citizens realize. Together they form a powerful public opinion lobby. The several military service associations provide both a forum and a meeting ground for the military and its industries. The associations also provide each of the armed services with a means of fostering their respective roles, objectives, and propaganda.

Each of the four services has its own association, and there are also additional military function associations, for ordnance, management, defense industry, and defense transportation, to name some of the more prominent. The Air Force Association and the Association of the U.S. Army are the largest, best organized, and most effective of the service associations. The Navy League, typical of the "silent service" traditions, is not as well coordinated in its public relations efforts, and the small

Marine Corps Association is not even in the same arena with the other contenders, the Marine Association's main activity being the publication of a semi-official monthly magazine. Actually, the service associations' respective magazines, with an estimated combined circulation of over 270,000, are the primary medium serving the several associations' purposes.

Air Force and Space Digest, to cite one example, is the magazine of the Air Force Association and the unofficial mouthpiece of the U.S. Air Force doctrine, "party line," and propaganda. It frequently promotes Air Force policy that has been officially frustrated or suppressed within the Department of Defense. It beats the tub for strength through aerospace power, interprets diplomatic, strategic, and tactical problems in terms of air power, stresses the requirements for quantities of every type of aircraft, and frequently perpetuates the extravagant fictions about the effectiveness of bombing. This, of course, is well coordinated with and supported by the multibillion-dollar aerospace industry, which thrives upon the boundless desires of the Air Force. They reciprocate with lavish and expensive ads in every issue of *Air Force.* Over 96,000 members of the Air Force Association receive the magazine. Members include active, reserve, retired personnel, and veterans of the U.S. Air Force. Additional thousands of copies go to people engaged in the defense industry. The thick mixture of advertising, propaganda, and Air Force doctrine continuously repeated in this publication provides its readers and writers with a form of intellectual hypnosis, and they are prone to believe their own propaganda because they read it in *Air Force.*

The American people have also become more and more accustomed to militarism, to uniforms, to the cult of the gun, and to the violence of combat. Whole generations have been brought up on war news and wartime propaganda; the few years of peace since 1939 have seen a steady stream of war novels, war movies, comic strips, and television programs with war or military settings. To many Americans, military training, expeditionary service, and warfare are merely extensions of the entertainment and games of childhood. Even the weaponry and hardware they use at war are similar to the highly realistic toys of their youth. Soldiering loses appeal for some of the relatively few who experience the blood, terror, and filth of battle; for many, however, including far too many senior professional officers, war and combat are an exciting adventure, a competitive game, and an escape from the dull routines of peacetime.

It is this influential nucleus of aggressive, ambitious professional military leaders who are the root of America's evolving militarism. There are over 410,000 commissioned officers on active duty in the four armed services. Of these, well over half are junior ranking reserve officers on temporary active duty. Of the 150,000 or so regular career officers, only a portion are senior ranking colonels, generals, and admirals, but it is they who constitute the elite core of the military establishment. It is these few thousand top-ranking professionals who command and manage the armed forces and plan and formulate military policy and opinion. How is it, then, that in spite of civilian controls and the national desire for peace, this small group of men exert so much martial influence upon the government and life of the American people?

The military will disclaim any excess of power or influence on their part. They will point to their small numbers, low pay, and subordination to civilian masters as proof of their modest status and innocence. Nevertheless, the professional military, as a group, is probably one of the best organized and most influential of the various segments of the American scene. Three wars and six major contingencies since 1940 have forced the American people to become abnormally aware of the armed forces and their leaders. In turn the military services have produced an unending supply of distinguished, capable, articulate, and effective leaders. The sheer skill, energy, and dedication of America's military officers make them dominant in almost every government or civic organization they may inhabit, from the federal Cabinet to the local PTA.

The hard core of high-ranking professionals are, first of all, mostly service academy graduates: they had to be physically and intellectually above average among their peers just to gain entrance to an academy. Thereafter for the rest of their careers they are exposed to constant competition for selection and promotion. Attrition is high, and only the most capable survive to reach the elite senior ranks. Few other professions have such rigorous selection systems; as a result, the top military leaders are top-caliber men.

Not many industries, institutions, or civilian branches of government have the resources, techniques, or experience in training leaders such as are now employed by the armed forces in their excellent and elaborate school systems. Military leaders are taught to command large organizations and to plan big operations. They learn the techniques of influencing others. Their education is not, however, liberal or cultural. It stresses the tactics, doctrines, traditions, and codes of the military trade. It produces technicians and disciples, not philosophers.

The men who rise to the top of the military hierarchy have usually demonstrated their effectiveness as leaders, planners, and organization managers. They have perhaps performed heroically in combat, but most of all they have demonstrated their loyalty as proponents of their own service's doctrine and their dedication to the defense establishment. The paramount sense of duty to follow orders is at the root of the military professional's performance. As a result the military often operate more efficiently and effectively in the arena of defense policy planning than do their civilian counterparts in the State Department. The military planners have their doctrinal beliefs, their loyalties, their discipline — and their typical desire to compete and win. The civilians in government can scarcely play the same policy-planning game. In general the military are better organized, they work harder, they think straighter, and they keep their eyes on the objective, which is to be instantly ready to solve the problem through military action while ensuring that their respective service gets its proper mission, role, and recognition in the operation. In an emergency the military usually have a ready plan; if not, their numerous doctrinal manuals provide firm guidelines for action. Politicians, civilian appointees, and diplomats do not normally have the same confidence about how to react to threats and violence as do the military.

The motivations behind these endeavors are difficult for civilians to understand. For example, military professionals cannot measure the success of their individual efforts in terms of personal financial gain. The armed forces are not profit-making organizations, and the rewards for excellence in the military profession are acquired in less tangible forms. Thus it is that promotion and the responsibilities of higher command, with the related fringe benefits of quarters, servants, privileges, and prestige, motivate most career officers. Promotions and choice job opportunities are attained by constantly performing well, conforming to the expected patterns, and pleasing the senior officers. Promotions and awards also frequently result from heroic and distinguished performance in combat, and it takes a war to become a military hero. Civilians can scarcely understand or even believe that many ambitious military professionals truly yearn for wars and the opportunities for glory and distinction afforded only in combat. A career of peacetime duty is a dull and frustrating pospect for the normal regular officer to contemplate.

The professional military leaders of the U.S. Armed Forces have some additional motivations which influence their readiness to involve their country in military ventures. Unlike some of the civilian policy-makers, the military has not been obsessed with the threat of Communism per se. Most military people know very little about Communism either as a doctrine or as a form of government. But they have been given reason enough to presume that it is bad and represents the force of evil. When they can identify "Communist aggression," however, the matter then becomes of direct concern to the armed forces. Aggressors are the enemy in the war games, the "bad guys," the "Reds." Defeating aggression is a gigantic combat-area competition rather than a crusade to save the world from Communism. In the military view, all "Communist aggression" is certain to be interpreted as a threat to the United States.

The armed forces' role in performing its part of the national security policy — in addition to defense against actual direct attack on the United States and to maintaining the strategic atomic deterrent forces — is to be prepared to employ its *General Purpose Forces* in support of our collective security policy and the related treaties and alliances. To do this it deploys certain forces to forward zones in the Unified Commands, and maintains an up-to-date file of scores of detailed contingency plans which have been thrashed out and approved by the Joint Chiefs of Staff. Important features of these are the movement or deployment schedules of task forces assigned to each plan. The various details of these plans continue to create intense rivalries between the Navy-Marine sea-lift forces and the Army-Air Force team of air-mobility proponents. At the senior command levels parochial pride in service, personal ambitions, and old Army-Navy game rivalry stemming back to academy loyalties can influence strategic planning far more than most civilians would care to believe. The game is to be ready for deployment sooner than the other elements of the joint task force and to be so disposed as to be the "first to fight." The danger presented by this practice is that readiness and deployment speed become ends in themselves. This was clearly revealed in the massive and rapid intervention in the Dominican Republic in 1965 when the contingency plans and interservice rivalry appeared to supersede diplomacy. Before the world realized what was happening, the momentum and velocity of the military plans propelled almost 20,000 U.S. soldiers and Marines into the small turbulent republic in an impressive race to test the respective mobility of the Army and the Marines, and to attain overall command of "U.S. Forces Dom. Rep." Only a fraction of the force deployed was needed or justified. A small 1935-model Marine landing force could probably have handled the situation. But the Army airlifted much of the 82nd Airborne Division to the scene, included a lieutenant general, and took charge of the operation.

Simultaneously, in Vietnam during 1965 the four services were racing to build up combat strength in that hapless country. This effort was ostensibly to save South Vietnam from Viet Cong and North Vietnamese aggression. It should also be noted that it was motivated in part by the same old interservice rivalry to demonstrate respective importance and combat effectiveness.

The punitive air strikes immediately following the Tonkin Gulf incident in late 1964 revealed the readiness of naval air forces to bomb North Vietnam. (It now appears that the Navy actually had attack plans ready even before the alleged incident took place!) So by early 1965 the Navy carrier people and the Air Force initiated a contest of comparative strikes, sorties, tonnages dropped, "Killed by Air" claims, and target grabbing which continued up to the 1968 bombing pause. Much of the reporting on air action has consisted of misleading data or propaganda to serve Air Force and Navy purposes. In fact, it became increasingly apparent that the U.S. bombing effort in both North and South Vietnam has been one of the most wasteful and expensive hoaxes ever to be put over on the American people. Tactical and close air support of ground operations is essential, but air power use in general has to a large degree been a contest for the operations planners, "fine experience" for young pilots, and opportunity for career officers.

The highly trained professional and aggressive career officers of the Army and Marine Corps played a similar game. Prior to the decision to send combat units to South Vietnam in early 1965, both services were striving to increase their involvement. The Army already had over 16,000 military aid personnel serving in South Vietnam in the military adviser role, in training missions, logistic services, supporting helicopter companies, and in Special Forces teams. The investment of men and matériel justified a requirement for additional U.S. combat units to provide local security and to help protect our growing commitment of aid to the South Vietnam regime.

There were also top-ranking Army officers who wanted to project Army ground combat units into the Vietnam struggle for a variety of other reasons; to test plans and new equipment, to test the new air-mobile theories and tactics, to try the tactics and techniques of counterinsurgency, and to gain combat experience for young officers and noncommissioned officers. It also appeared to be a case of the military's duty to stop "Communist aggression" in Vietnam.

The Marines had somewhat similar motivations, the least of which was any real concern about the political or social problems of the Vietnamese people. In early 1965 there was a shooting war going on and the Marines were being left out of it, contrary to all their traditions. The Army's military advisory people were hogging American participation — except for a Marine Corps transport helicopter squadron at Danang which was helping the Army of the Republic of Vietnam. For several years young Marine officers had been going to South Vietnam from the 3rd Marine Division on Okinawa for short tours of "on-the-job training" with the small South Vietnam Corps. There was a growing concern, however, among some senior Marines that the Corps should get involved on a larger scale and be the "first to fight" in keeping with the Corps's traditions. This would help justify the Corps's continued existence, which many Marines seem to consider to be in constant jeopardy.

The Corps had also spent several years exploring the theories of counterinsurgency and as early as 1961 had developed an elaborate lecture-demonstration called OPERATION CORMORANT, for school and Marine Corps promotion purposes, which depicted the Marines conducting a large-scale amphibious operation on the coast of Vietnam and thereby helping resolve a hypothetical aggressor-insurgency problem. As always it was important to Marine planners and doctrinaires to apply an amphibious operation to the Vietnam situation and provide justification for this special Marine functional responsibility. So Marine planners were seeking an acceptable excuse to thrust a landing force over the beaches of Vietnam when the Viet Cong attacked the U.S. Army Special Forces camp at Pleiku in February, 1965. It was considered unacceptable aggression, and the President was thereby prompted to put U.S. ground combat units into the war. Elements of the 3rd Marine Division at Okinawa were already aboard ship and eager to go, for the Marines also intended to get to Vietnam before their neighbor on Okinawa, the Army's 173rd Airborne Brigade, arrived. (Actually the initial Marine unit to deploy was an airlifted antiaircraft missile battalion which arrived to protect the Danang air base.) With these initial deployments the Army-Marine race to build forces in Vietnam began in earnest and did not slow down until both became overextended, overcommitted, and depleted at home.

For years up to 1964 the chiefs of the armed services, of whom the author was then one, deemed it unnecessary and unwise for U.S. forces to become involved in any ground war in Southeast Asia. In 1964 there were changes in the composition of the Joint Chiefs of Staff, and in a matter of a few months the Johnson Administration, encouraged by the aggressive military, hastened into what has become the quagmire of Vietnam. The intention at the time was that the war effort be kept small and "limited." But as the momentum and involvement built up, the military leaders rationalized a case that this was not a limited-objective exercise, but was a proper war in defense of the United States against "Communist aggression" and in honor of our area commitments.

The battle successes and heroic exploits of America's fine young fighting men have added to the military's traditions which extol service, bravery, and sacrifice, and so it has somehow become unpatriotic to question our military strategy and tactics or the motives of military leaders. Actually, however, the military commanders have directed the war in Vietnam, they have managed the details of its conduct; and more than most civilian officials, the top military planners were initially ready to become involved in Vietnam combat and have the opportunity to practice their trade. It has been popular to blame the civilian administration for the conduct and failures of the war rather than to question the motives of the military. But some of the generals and admirals are by no means without responsibility for the Vietnam miscalculations.

Some of the credibility difficulties experienced by the Johnson Administration over its war situation reports and Vietnam policy can also be blamed in part upon the military advisers. By its very nature most military activity falls under various degrees of security classification. Much that the military plans or does must be kept from the enemy. Thus the military is indoctrinated to be secretive, devious, and misleading in its plans and operations. It does not, however, always confine its security restrictions to purely military operations. Each of the services and all of the major commands practice techniques of controlling the news and the release of self-serving propaganda: in "the interests of national defense," to make the service look good, to cover up mistakes, to build up and publicize a distinguished military personality, or to win a round in the continuous gamesmanship of the interservice contest. (If the Johnson Administration suffered from lack of credibility in its reporting of the war, the truth would reveal that much of the hocus-pocus stemmed from schemers in the military services, both at home and abroad.)

Our militaristic culture was born of the necessities of World War II, nurtured by the Korean War, and became an accepted aspect of American life during the years of cold war emergencies and real or imagined threats from the Communist bloc. Both the philosophy and the institutions of militarism grew during these years because of the momentum of their own dynamism, the vigor of their ideas, their large size and scope, and because of the dedicated concentration of the emergent military leaders upon their doctrinal objectives. The dynamism of the defense establishment and its culture is also inspired and stimulated by vast amounts of money, by the new creations of military research and matériel development, and by the concepts of the Defense Department-supported "think factories." These latter are extravagantly funded civilian organizations of scientists, analysts, and retired military strategists who feed new militaristic philosophies into the Defense Department to help broaden the views of the single service doctrinaires, to create fresh policies and new requirements for ever larger, more expensive defense forces.

Somewhat like a religion, the basic appeals of anti-Communism, national defense, and patriotism provide the foundation for a powerful creed upon which the defense establishment can build, grow, and justify its cost. More so than many large bureaucratic organizations, the defense establishment now devotes a large share of its efforts to self-perpetuation, to justifying its organizations, to preaching its doctrines, and to self-maintenance and management. Warfare becomes an extension of war games and field tests. War justifies the existence of the establishment, provides experience for the military novice and challenges for the senior officer. Wars and emergencies put the military and their leaders on the front pages and give status and prestige to the professionals. Wars add to the military traditions, the self-nourishment of heroic deeds, and provide a new crop of military leaders who become the rededicated disciples of the code of service and military action. Being recognized public figures in a nation always seeking folk heroes, the military leaders have been largely exempt from the criticism experienced by the more plebeian politician. Flag officers are considered "experts," and their views are often accepted by press and Congress as the gospel. In turn, the distinguished military leader feels obliged not only to perpetuate loyally the doctrine of his service but to comply with the stereotyped military characteristics by being tough, aggressive, and firm in his resistance to Communist aggression and his belief in the military solutions to world problems. Standing closely behind these leaders, encouraging and prompting them, are the rich and powerful defense industries. Standing in front, adorned with service caps, ribbons, and lapel emblems, is a nation of veterans — patriotic, belligerent, romantic, and well intentioned, finding a certain sublimation and excitement in their country's latest military venture. Militarism in America is in full bloom and promises a future of vigorous self-pollination — unless the blight of Vietnam reveals that militarism is more a poisonous weed than a glorious blossom.

RICHARD F. KAUFMAN   *The Military-Industrial Complex*

Eight years have gone by since President Eisenhower opened the door on the military-industrial skeleton in the closet. Yet only recently has research started to hang some real meat on his bony, provocative phrase, "military-industrial complex." What is emerging is a real Frankenstein's monster. Not only is there considerable evidence that excessive military spending has contributed to a misallocation of national resources, but the conclusion seems inescapable that society has already suffered irreparable harm from the pressures and distortions thus created.

Military and military-related spending accounts for about 45 per cent of all Federal expenditures. In fiscal 1968, the total Federal outlays were $178.9-billion. The Defense Department alone spent $77.4-billion, and such related programs as military assistance to foreign countries, atomic energy and the Selective Service System raised the figure to $80.5-billion. The $4-billion program of the National Aeronautics and Space Administration and other activities intertwined with the military carry the real level of defense spending considerably higher.

To place the defense bill in perspective we should note that 1968 appropriations were less than $500-million for food stamps, school lunches and the special milk program combined. For all federally assisted housing programs, including Model Cities, they were about $2-billion. The poverty program received less than $2-billion. Federal aid to education was allotted about $5.2-billion. The funds spent on these programs and all those categorized as health, education, welfare, housing, agriculture, conservation, labor, commerce, foreign aid, law enforcement, etc. — in short, all civilian programs — amounted to about $82.5-billion, if the space and veterans' programs are not included, and less than $70-billion if the interest on the national debt is not considered.

The largest single item in the military budget — it accounted for $44-billion in 1968 — is procurement, which includes purchasing, renting or leasing supplies and services (and all the machinery for drawing up and administering the contracts under which those purchases and rentals are made). Procurement, in other words, means Government contracts; it is mother's milk to the military-industrial complex.

The Pentagon annually signs agreements with about 22,000 prime contractors; in addition, more than 100,000 subcontractors are involved in defense production. Defense-oriented industry as a whole employs about 4 million men. However, although a large number of contractors do some military business, the largest share of procurement funds is concentrated among a relative handful of major contractors. Last year the 100 largest defense suppliers obtained $26.2-billion in military contracts, 67.4 per cent of the money spent through contracts of $10,000 or more.

Similarly, the Atomic Energy Commission's contract awards tend to be concentrated in a select group of major corporations. Of approximately $1.6-billion awarded in contracts last year, all but $104-million went to 36 contractors. As for NASA, procurement plays a larger role in its activities than in those of any other Federal agency. More than 90 per cent of its funds are awarded in contracts to industry and educational institutions. Of the $4.1-billion worth of procurement last year, 92 per cent of the direct awards to business went to NASA's 100 largest contractors.

In terms of property holdings, the result of almost two centuries of military procurement is a worldwide and practically incalculable empire. An almost arbitrary and greatly underestimated value — $202.5-billion — was placed on military real and personal property at the end of fiscal year 1968. Weapons were valued at $100-billion. Supplies and plant equipment accounted for $55.6-billion. Most of the remainder was in real estate. The Pentagon says the 29 million acres it controls — an area almost in the size of New York State — are worth $38.7-billion. (The official Defense Department totals do not include 9.7 million acres, valued at $9-billion, under the control of the Army Civil Works Division or additional property valued at $4.7-billion.) The arbitrariness of those figures is seen in the fact that they represent *acquisition* costs. Some of the military real estate was acquired more than a century ago, and much of it is in major cities and metropolitan areas. The actual value of the real estate must be many times its acquisition cost.

But the important fact about procurement is not the extent of the Pentagon's property holdings; it is that defense contracting has involved the military with many of the largest industrial corporations in America. Some companies do almost all their business with the Government. Into this category fall a number of the large aerospace concerns — such giants as General Dynamics, Lockheed Aircraft and United Aircraft. For such other companies as General Electric, A.T.&T. and General Motors, Government work amounts to only a small percentage of the total business. But the tendency is for a company to enlarge its share of defense work over the years, at least in dollar value. And whether defense contracts represent 5 per cent or 50 per cent of a corporation's annual sales, they become a solid part of the business, an advantage to maintain or improve upon. A company may even work harder to increase its military sales than it does to build commercial sales because military work is more profitable, less competitive, more susceptible to control through lobbying in Washington. The industrial giants with assets of more than $1-billion have swarmed around the Pentagon to get their share of the sweets with no less enthusiasm than their smaller brethren.

The enormous attraction of military and military-related contracts for the upper tiers of industry has deepened in the last few years as military procurement has increased sharply. For example, G.E.'s prime-contract awards have gone up from $783-million in 1958 to $1.5-billion in 1968; General Motors' went from $281-million in 1958 to $630-million in 1968. While much of this increase can be traced to the Vietnam war boom and many contractors would suffer a loss of business if the war ended, there was steady growth in the defense industry during the fifties and early sixties (in 1964 and 1965, before the Vietnam build-up, there was a decline in prime-contract awards). In the five years from 1958 to 1963 — five years of peace — the value of G.E.'s prime contracts increased $217-million and General Motors' rose $163-million. The same trend can be shown for many of the large corporations in the aerospace and other industries.

What seems to be happening is that defense production is gradually spreading throughout industry, although the great bulk of the funds is still spent among relatively few companies. Still, as the defense budget increases the procurement dollars go further. The geographical concentration of defense production in the industrialized, high-income states also suggests that military contracts have come less and less to be restricted to an isolated sector of the economy specializing in guns and ammunition. Military business has become solidly entrenched in industrial America.

Considering the high degree of mismanagement and inefficiency in defense production and the tendency for contractors to want more sales and therefore to support the military in its yearly demands for a larger budget, this is not a healthy situation. The inefficiency of defense production, particularly in the aerospace industry, can hardly be disputed. Richard A. Stubbing, a defense analyst at the Bureau of the Budget, in a study of the performance of complex weapons systems, concluded: "The low over-all performance of electronics in major weapon systems developed and produced in the last decade should give pause to even the most outspoken advocates of military-hardware programs." He found that in 13 aircraft and missile programs produced since 1955 at a total cost of $40-billion, fewer than 40 per cent of the electronic components performed acceptably; two programs were canceled at a cost to the Government of $2-billion, and two programs costing $10-billion were phased out after three years because of low reliability.

And the defense industry is inefficient as well as unreliable. Albert Shapero, professor of management at the University of Texas, has accused aerospace contractors of habitually over-staffing, over-analyzing and over-managing. A. E. Fitzgerald, a Deputy Assistant Secretary of the Air Force, in testimony before the Joint Economic Subcommittee on Economy in Government, described poor work habits and poor discipline in contractors' plants. In the same hearing, a retired Air Force officer, Col. A. W. Buesking, a former director of management systems control in the office of the Assistant Secretary of Defense, summarized a study he had conducted by saying that control systems essential to prevent excessive costs simply did not exist.

In a sense, industry is being seduced into bad habits of production and political allegiance with the lure of easy money. And industry is not the only sector being taken in. Consider conscription (3.6 million men in uniform), the Pentagon's civilian bureaucracy (1.3 million), the work force in defense-oriented industry (4 million), the domestic brain drain created by the growth in military technology, the heavy emphasis on military research and development as a percentage (50 per cent) of all American research, the division of universities to serve the military and defense industry. These indicators reveal a steady infiltration of American values by those of the military establishment: production for non-productive use, compulsory service to the state, preparation for war. In the process, the economy continues to lose many of the attributes of the marketplace. In the defense industry, for all practical purposes, there is no marketplace.

The general rule for Government procurement is that purchases shall be made through written competitive bids obtained by advertising for the items needed. In World War II the competitive-bid requirements were suspended. After the war the Armed Services Procurement Act was passed, restating the general rule but setting out 17 exceptions — circumstances under which negotiation would be authorized instead of competition. The exceptions, which are still in use, are very broad and very vague. If the item is determined to be critical or complex or if delivery is urgent or if few supplies exist and competition is impractical or if emergency conditions exist or if security considerations preclude advertising, the Pentagon can negotiate for what it wants.

When President Truman signed this law in 1948 he saw the possibilities for abuse and wrote to the heads of the armed services and the National Advisory Committee for Aeronautics. "This bill," he said, "grants unprecedented freedom from specific procurement restrictions during peacetime. . . . There is danger that the natural desire for flexibility and speed in procurement will lead to excessive placement of contracts by negotiation and undue reliance upon large concerns, and this must not occur." Unfortunately, Truman's apprehensions were well justified. Last year about 90 per cent of the Pentagon's and 98 per cent of NASA's contract awards were negotiated under the "exceptions."

What this means is that there is no longer any objective criterion for measuring the fairness of contract awards. Perhaps more important, control over the costs, quality and time of production, insofar as they resulted from competition, are also lost. Negotiation involves informal discussion between the Pentagon and its contractors over the price and other terms of the contract. It permits subjective decision-making on such important questions as which firms to do business with and what price to accept. The Pentagon can negotiate with a single contractor, a "sole source," or it can ask two or three to submit proposals. If one later complains that he had promised to provide a weapon at a lower price than the contractor who obtained the award, the Pentagon can respond by asserting that the price was not the major factor, that the Government simply had more faith in the contractor who won. This, in effect, is how the Army responded to the Maremont Corporation's recent challenge of a contract award to General Motors for the M-16 rifle. The Pentagon, because of its almost unbounded freedom to award contracts, can favor some companies. And over long periods, this practice can lead to a dependence by the Government on the technical competency of the suppliers on whom it has come to rely. For example, the Newport News Shipbuilding Company has a virtual monopoly on the construction of large aircraft carriers.

Typically, the Pentagon will invite a few of the large contractors to submit proposals for a contract to perform the research and development on a new weapon system. The one who wins occupies a strategic position. The know-how he gains in his research work gives him an advantage over his rivals for the larger and more profitable part of the program, the production. This is what is meant when it is said that the Government is "locked in" with a contractor. Because the contractor knows he will obtain a lock-in if he can do the initial research work, there is a tendency to stretch a few facts during the negotiations.

Contractor performance is measured by three factors: the total cost to the Government of the weapon system, the way in which it functions and the time of delivery. During the contract negotiations over these factors the phenomenon known as the "buy-in" may occur. The contractor, in order to "buy in" to the program, offers more than he can deliver. He may promise to do a job at a lower cost than he knows will be incurred or to meet or exceed performance specifications that he knows are unattainable or to deliver the finished product long before he has reason to believe it will be ready.

Technically, the contractor can be penalized for his failure to fulfill promises made during the negotiations, but the Government rarely insists on full performance. The contractor knows this, of course, and he also knows the "get-well" stratagem. That is, he can reasonably expect, on practically all major weapon contracts, that should he get into difficulty with regard to any of the contract conditions, the Government will extricate him — get him well.

The contractor can get well in a variety of ways. If his costs run higher than his estimates, the Pentagon can agree to pay them. (Cost increases can be hidden through contract-change notices. On a typical complex weapon system, the changes from original specifications will number in the thousands; some originate with the Pentagon, some are authorized at the request of the contractor. The opportunities for burying real or phony cost increases are obvious, so much so that in defense circles contract-change notices are sometimes referred to as "contract nourishment.") The Government can also accept a weapon that performs poorly or justify a late delivery. If for some reason it is impossible for the Pentagon to accept a weapon, there is still a way to keep the contractor well. The Pentagon can cancel a weapon program for the "convenience" of the Government. A company whose contract is canceled for default stands to lose a great deal of money, but cancellation for convenience reduces or eliminates the loss; the Government makes reimbursement for costs incurred. An example of this occurred recently in connection with the F-111B, the Navy's fighter-bomber version of the TFX.

Gordon W. Rule, a civilian procurement official who had responsibility for the F-111B, said in testimony before the House Subcommittee on Military Operations that General Dynamics was in default on its contract

because the planes were too heavy to meet the height or range requirements. Rule proposed in a memorandum to Deputy Secretary of Defense
Paul H. Nitze that the contract be terminated for default. At the same
time, Assistant Secretary of the Air Force Robert H. Charles and Roger
Lewis, the General Dynamics chairman, proposed that the Navy reimburse the company for all costs and impose no penalty. Nitze's compromise was to make reimbursement of $216.5-million, mostly to General
Dynamics, and to impose a small penalty.

In a memo written last year Rule made this comment on the attitude of
defense contractors: "No matter how poor the quality, how late the product and how high the cost, they know nothing will happen to them."

There are many other ways to succeed in the defense business without
really trying. The Pentagon generously provides capital to its contractors; more than $13-billion worth of Government-owned property, in-
cluding land, buildings and equipment, is in contractors' hands. In addition, the Pentagon will reimburse a supplier during the life of his contract
for as much as 90 per cent of the costs he reports. These are called
"progress" payments, but are unrelated to progress in the sense of contract
objectives achieved; they correspond only to the costs incurred. The progress payments are interest-free loans that provide the contractor with
working capital in addition to fixed capital. They minimize his investment in the defense business and free his assets for commercial work or
for obtaining new defense work.

Investigations by the General Accounting Office have revealed that the
Government's money and property have been used by contractors for their
own purposes. The most recent incident involved Thiokol Chemical Corporation, Aerojet-General (a subsidiary of General Tire & Rubber Company) and Hercules, Inc. From 1964 through 1967 they received a total
of $22.4-million to be used for work on the Air Force Minuteman missile
program. The Government accountants found that the three contractors
misused more than $18-million of this money, spending it for research un-
related and inapplicable to Minuteman or any other defense program.

The defense industry is perhaps the most heavily subsidized in the
nation's history. Thanks to Pentagon procurement policies, large contractors find their defense business to be their most lucrative. Although no
comprehensive study of such profits has been made, the known facts indicate that profits on defense contracts are higher than those on related
nondefense business, that they are higher for the defense industry than
for manufacturing as a whole and that the differential has been increasing. In a study that compared the five-year period from 1959 through
1963 with the last six months of 1966, the General Accounting Office found
a 26 per cent increase in the average profit rates negotiated. Admiral
Hyman G. Rickover has testified that suppliers of propulsion turbines are

insisting on profits of 20 to 25 per cent, compared with 10 per cent a few years ago, and that profits on shipbuilding contracts have doubled in two years.

The figures cited by Rickover relate to profits as a percentage of costs, a measure that often understates the true profit level. The more accurate measure is return on investment. An example of the difference was demonstrated in a 1962 tax-court case, North American Aviation v. Renegotiation Board. The contracts provided for 8 per cent profits as a percentage of costs; the tax court found that the company had realized profits of 612 per cent and 802 per cent on its investment in two succeeding years. The reason for the huge return on investment was the Defense Department policy of supplying both fixed and working capital to many of the larger contractors. In some cases the amount of Government-owned property exceeds the contractor's investment, which is sometimes minimal. It is no wonder that contractors prefer to talk about profits as a percentage of costs.

Murray Weidenbaum, recently appointed Assistant Secretary of the Navy, found in a study that between 1962 and 1965 a sample of large defense contractors earned 17.5 per cent net profit (measured as a return on investment), while companies of similar size doing business in the commercial market earned 10.6 per cent.

The Pentagon has attempted to answer the critics of high defense profits by citing the findings of the Logistics Management Institute, a think tank that has done a study showing declining defense profits. The trouble with the institute's study is that it used unverified, unaudited data obtained on a voluntary basis from a sample of defense contractors. Those who did not want to participate simply did not return the questionnaires; in fact, 42 per cent of those contacted provided no data. There is no way of knowing whether the group of contractors who refused to participate in the study included the ones making the highest profits.

There is almost no risk in defense contracting except that borne by the Government. If a major prime contractor has ever suffered a substantial loss on a defense contract, the Pentagon has failed to disclose his name, although it has been requested to do so by members of Congress. On the other hand, the disputed Cheyenne helicopter and C-5A cargo plane projects could conceivably result in large losses for Lockheed, the contractor in both cases. Lockheed asserts that it might still make a profit on the C-5A (which is being produced in a Government-owned plant), and denies that it is at fault in the cancellation of production on the Cheyenne helicopter (on which research work has been resumed). Past experience suggests that one should await the final decision, which may be two years in coming, before making flat statements about profit and loss.

In fairness, it ought to be pointed out that Secretary of Defense Melvin R. Laird has talked about a new get-tough policy with contractors. New procurement techniques that would, for instance, require contractors to meet specific cost benchmarks have been announced; increased prototype development is planned; greater public disclosure of cost overruns and performance or scheduling problems have been promised; the production of the Cheyenne helicopter and the Air Force's Manned Orbiting Laboratory program have been canceled. Whether any of these measures will produce real savings has yet to be determined. The Pentagon is famous for its paper reforms.

The defense industry, in addition to providing high profits at low risk, offers fringe benefits for everyone. One of the important advantages for those in procurement, on either side of the bargaining table, is the opportunity for career advancement. There is a steady march of military and civilian personnel back and forth between the Pentagon and the defense industry. It is not considered unusual for someone like Maj. Gen. Nelson M. Lynde Jr. to retire from the Army after being directly involved in the procurement of the M-16 rifle and go to work five months later for Colt Industries, originally the "sole source" of the M-16; nor is it a matter for comment when Lieut. Gen. Austin Davis retires from the Air Force after playing an important role in procurement for the Minuteman missile program and becomes vice president of North American Rockwell, one of the Minuteman's prime contractors.

This is not to say that the interchange of personnel between the Pentagon and the defense industry is harmful in itself or that it ought to be prohibited. There is a problem in finding qualified people, and one would not want to deprive either the Pentagon or contractors of a source of trained manpower. While it would not be fair to condemn the practice and everyone engaged in it out of hand, there is a serious conflict-of-interest problem.

The conflict-of-interest laws apply primarily to military personnel and are easily evaded. Therefore, the solution to the problem does not seem to lie in expanding the legal restrictions. What might help is the public disclosure of the names of high-ranking Pentagon officials who have moved on to jobs in the defense industry and those who have made the reverse trip. The Subcommittee on Economy in Government has recommended that such a list be compiled. It would facilitate scrutiny of the interchange problem by revealing obvious conflicts of interest that should be investigated.

Individuals in the field of procurement naturally have an interest in the continued growth and importance of their field. The same could be said of people in many other fields. What is disturbing here is the opportunity that many officials have to influence procurement policy while in the Pentagon and then benefit from their actions or those of their former associates when they join the defense industry, or, possibly, one of the 16 Federal-contract research centers supported by the Pentagon.

The 16 centers, including the Rand Corporation and the Institute for Defense Analysis, receive at least 85 per cent — and in some cases as much as 99 per cent — of their income from the Pentagon. With contracts totaling more than $300-million a year, they form a kind of halfway house between the military establishment and the defense industry, serving the interests of both.

Last year, Senator J. W. Fulbright, the chairman of the Senate Foreign Relations Committee, obtained from the Pentagon a list of the top officials of the research centers and their prior Government affiliations. Seven center presidents and five vice presidents — including Maxwell D. Taylor, former chairman of the Joint Chiefs of Staff — had once held high posts in the Defense Department. Taylor's salary as president of the Institute for Defense Analysis was reported as $49,200; he also, of course, received retirement pay as a general. The highest-paid research-center officer was the president of the Aerospace Corporation, an Air Force creation, who received $90,000 a year.

In hearings last fall before the Subcommittee on Economy in Government, Senator William Proxmire looked briefly at the Logistics Management Institute, a Pentagon-created research center that worked exclusively for the Defense Department until recently, when it obtained permission to devote 10 per cent of its time to other assignments. Senator Proxmire learned that, of the institute's 18 professional staff members, six came directly from defense contractors, six were formerly employed by research centers or consultant firms whose work was heavily defense oriented and one was a retired Air Force Reserve officer.

More recently, Proxmire asked the Pentagon for a list of the retired regular military officers holding the ranks of Army colonel, Navy captain or higher employed by the 100 largest defense contractors. As of February, 1969, 2,072 retired regular military officers were employed by the 95 top contractors who responded to the inquiry, an average of 22 in each company. The 10 companies employing the largest number had 1,065 on their payrolls, an average of 106, triple the average number they employed in 1959.

Proxmire, in a March 24 speech, commented, "What we have here is almost a classic example of how the military-industrial complex works." His point was that there is a growing community of interests between the military and the large contractors and that it militates against the public interest. Former high-ranking military men have a special entrée to the Pentagon; they have friendships with those still there and may even negotiate contracts or be involved in developing plans and specifications with officers with whom they served, whom they promoted or vice versa. "In addition," Proxmire said, "there is the subtle or unconscious temptation to the officer still on active duty. After all, he can see that over 2,000 of his fellow officers work for the big companies. How hard a bargain does he drive with them when he is one or two years away from retirement?"

The interchange of personnel, according to testimony by Admiral Rickover, has helped spread a business-oriented philosophy in the Defense Department. One might equally well observe that a military-oriented philosophy has been spread in the defense industry. Several kinds of institutional arrangements in addition to the interchange of personnel help bind military power to industrial wealth. Representatives of industry, in such groups as the Aerospace Industries Association, and of the military, in such organizations as the Air Force Association, agree on the basic issues: a large military budget, a high cost base in defense production, no losses, high profits and Congressional and public compliance.

Though ostensibly preoccupied with national security and maintaining a strong defense against potential foreign aggressors, these institutions interpret domestic criticism of military spending as a problem of the highest priority. Witness a meeting of the Industry Advisory Council and representatives of the Defense Department in October, 1968. The Industry Advisory Council is one of a dozen or more business-advisory groups which meet regularly with officials in the Pentagon to discuss matters ranging from foreign policy to the latest proposed changes in armed services procurement regulations. The Industry Advisory Council until recently was called the Defense Industry Advisory Council. Dropping the word "Defense" from its name suggests its concern over public relations. The council's membership at the time of the October meeting included the presidents or board chairmen of Boeing, G.E., Brown and Root, Western Electric, DuPont, Lockheed, Newport News Shipbuilding, Northrop, General Dynamics, Olin Mathieson, Tenneco, Litton and Ford.

The immediate outcome of the October meeting was an outline of major problems facing the Pentagon and industry. The outline and a memorandum from Assistant Secretary of Defense Thomas Morris were circulated to officials on the assistant-secretary level of the Defense Department and each of the armed services. The subject was: "Fundamental Problem Areas: Key areas worthy of joint exploration by D.O.D. and industry in calendar year 1969."

Four major problem areas were listed. The first was how to "maintain public and Congressional confidence in the integrity and effectiveness of defense procurement and contractor performance." Others were how to obtain full compliance with procurement policies by both Pentagon and industry officials; how to maintain a healthy defense-industrial base, and how to increase the effectiveness of the major-weapon-system acquisition process.

The memo, in discussing how to shore up lagging public and Congressional confidence in the defense procurement process, listed some more specific "detailed problems," including these: uniform-accounting-standards legislation; excess-profits hearings; the Truth-in-Negotiations Act; General Accounting Office investigations and audits; investigations of such specific programs as the TFX and the M-14 rifle and statutory profit limitations. In other words, the chief worries of the industry and Pentagon representatives in 1969 are legislation that would tighten controls on procurement and defense profits, the investigation of specific weapons programs and investigations and audits by Government accountants.

The danger of the military-industrial complex lies in its scale. Reasonable men will tolerate a war machine as a necessary evil. It is the size of the machine and its claim on national resources and individual lives that is at issue. What is alarming is the growth of the complex.

The great leap of the military budget in the last few years, from about $50-billion to $80-billion, and its earlier growth, beginning with the Korean war have helped to bring about serious stresses in the economy. Although no one factor can be identified as the sole cause of inflation, it is no accident that the three most recent price surges accompanied sharp increases in military spending, between 1950 and 1953 (the Korean war period), between 1955 and 1957 and since the build-up in Vietnam began. Defense expenditures have contributed substantially to these inflationary trends. The consequent reduced value of savings and fixed-income assets during each of these periods is an indirect cost of defense; the 10 per cent tax surcharge made necessary by the Vietnam build-up is a much more direct one.

More ominous than the economic consequences of a bloated defense budget are expanding and sometimes furtive military activities in such areas as foreign affairs, social-science research, domestic riot control and chemical and biological warfare. In hearings last year on Pentagon-sponsored foreign-affairs research, Senator Fulbright quoted from a 1967 report of the Defense Science Board (a scientific counterpart to the business-advisory groups): "The D.O.D. mission now embraces problems and responsibilities which have not previously been assigned to a military establishment. It has been properly stated that the D.O.D. must now wage not only warfare but 'peacefare' as well. Pacification assistance and

Big Business and the Big Brass

This table lists the top 25 contractors for the Pentagon, the Atomic Energy Commission and the National Aeronautics and Space Administration and the top 25 names on Fortune *magazine's directory of the 500 largest industrial corporations. Note that only five of the 25 biggest corporations are not among the 100 largest contractors for the Defense Department, and one of the five, Union Carbide, is the largest A.E.C. contractor. Also noteworthy is the high coincidence of names on the Pentagon, A.E.C. and NASA lists. The table suggests that defense contracting is extremely attractive to big business.* — R.F.K.

Largest Defense Contractors			Largest Industrial Corporations[d]
Pentagon[a]	A.E.C.[b]	NASA[c]	
1 General Dynamics	1 Union Carbide	1 North American Rockwell	1 General Motors (10)[e]
2 Lockheed	2 Sandia Corp.		2 Standard Oil (N.J.) (25)
3 General Electric	3 General Electric	2 Grumman	3 Ford (19)
4 United Aircraft	4 DuPont	3 Boeing	4 General Electric (3)
5 McDonnell-Douglas	5 Reynolds Electrical	4 McDonnell-Douglas	5 Chrysler (43)
6 A.T.&T.	6 Westinghouse	5 General Electric	6 Mobil (51)
7 Boeing	7 Bendix	6 I.B.M.	7 I.B.M. (30)
8 Ling Temco Vought	8 Holmes & Narver	7 Bendix	8 Texaco (46)
9 North American Rockwell	9 Douglas United Nuclear	8 Aerojet-General	9 Gulf Oil (78)
10 General Motors	10 Dow Chemical	9 RCA	10 U.S. Steel (60)
11 Grumman	11 Goodyear Atomic	10 Chrysler	11 A.T.&T. (6)
12 AVCO	12 Idaho Nuclear	11 General Dynamics	12 Standard Oil (Calif.) (49)
13 Textron	13 Aerojet-General	12 TRW	13 DuPont (38)
14 Litton	14 Atlantic Richfield	13 General Motors	14 Shell Oil
15 Raytheon	15 E.G.&G.	14 Ling Temco Vought	15 RCA (26)
16 Sperry-Rand	16 Gulf General Atomic	15 Lockheed	16 McDonnell-Douglas (5)
17 Martin Marietta	17 Monsanto	16 Philco-Ford	17 Standard Oil (Ind.)
18 Kaiser Industries	18 Kerr-McGee	17 Sperry Rand	18 Westinghouse (27)
19 Ford	19 National Lead	18 Martin Marietta	19 Boeing (7)
20 Honeywell	20 Mason & Hanger	19 T.W.A.	20 Swift
21 Olin Mathieson	21 North American Rockwell	20 Federal Electric	21 I.T.&T. (29)
22 Northrop	22 Homestake-Sapin	21 Catalytic-Dow (joint venture)	22 Goodyear Tire & Rubber (48)
23 Ryan Aeronautical	23 United Nuclear	22 United Aircraft	23 General Telephone & Electronics (41)
24 Hughes	24 Pan American	23 Brown Engineering	24 Bethlehem Steel
25 Standard Oil (N.J.)	25 Phillips Petroleum	24 Honeywell	25 Union Carbide
		25 Control Data	

[a] 100 Companies & Their Subsidiary Corporations Listed According to Net Value of Military Prime Contract Awards (Fiscal Year 1968), Department of Defense.
[b] Annual Report for 1968, Atomic Energy Commission.
[c] Annual Procurement Report, NASA (Fiscal Year 1968).
[d] 500 Largest U.S. Industrial Corporations, Fortune Directory (1968).
[e] Number in parentheses indicates rank among 100 largest Defense Department contractors.

the battle of ideas are major segments of the D.O.D. responsibility. The social and behavioral sciences constitute the unique resource for support of these new requirements. . . ."

Fulbright's reminder that the military's responsibility is "to prosecute war or to provide military forces which are capable of defending against an external attack" might have sounded like naïveté to the Pentagon, but his point is important. Social-science research conducted in foreign countries by foreigners should, if it is to be supported at all, be supported by the State Department, not the Pentagon. Research into socio-cultural patterns or the social organizations of groups or processes of change should not be a military responsibility. Yet the Pentagon does support foreign research all over the world, awarding contracts to G.E. to make projections of "future world environments" and to McDonnell-Douglas to do a study entitled "Pax Americana," later retitled "Projected World Patterns, 1985."

The Army's new domestic "war room" in the basement of the Pentagon is also of doubtful legitimacy. This "operations center" is supposed to help dispatch and coordinate troops for urban riots (maybe that's "pacification assistance"). Even assuming the need for this kind of activity, one can raise the same question that disturbs Senator Fulbright with regard to social-science research: Is this a proper military responsibility?

The most recent example of the Pentagon's "independent thinking," brought to light by the efforts of Congressmen Richard D. McCarthy and Cornelius Gallagher, is the controversial Army plan to transport about 27,000 tons of obsolete poison gas across the country by train to New Jersey to be loaded onto old hulks, towed out to sea and sunk. Both the State Department and the Interior Department have a direct interest in this project, yet the Army did not bother to coordinate its plans with them until long after the plans were formulated.

Such incidents as the construction of the domestic war room and the independent decision to ship poison gas across the country symbolize the drift of power in the executive branch to the Pentagon and show the extent to which military authority has exceeded its traditional limits. Swollen by overgenerous appropriations, the defense budget has become the source of frightening political as well as economic power. Practically freed of the fiscal limitations that restrain other agencies, the Pentagon seems to be able to exercise its will in almost any area it chooses, foreign or domestic, from negotiating a new lease for bases and promising military assistance to Spain (as it was recently alleged to have done) to launching programs of social reform.

The nature of the problem was simply stated recently at a hearing of the House Subcommittee on Military Operations. Testifying was Phillip S. Hughes, deputy director of the Bureau of the Budget. Representative William Moorhead had charged that the bureau was unable to scrutinize Defense Department expenditures to the same extent that it reviews non-defense spending. The budget requests of Government agencies, except the Defense Department, are subjected to an independent analysis and review, which is then submitted to the Budget Director. The director makes his recommendations to the President, subject to challenge by the Cabinet officer concerned. But the Defense Department is treated differently. In the Pentagon, Moorhead said, Budget Bureau analysts must work alongside their Defense counterparts, not independently. The results of this joint review are submitted to the Secretary of Defense, who sends it to the President, subject to challenge by the Budget Director. The result is that the burden of persuading the President to change the budget he receives is shifted from the agency head to the Budget Director in the case of the defense item, but only there. (The Nixon Administration's Budget Director, Robert P. Mayo, testified recently that the defense budget would be transmitted to the President in the future just as other departmental requests are.)

"The most relevant consideration," Hughes testified, "is, in blunt terms, sheer power — where the muscle is — and this is a very power-conscious town, and the Secretary of Defense, and the defense establishment are a different group to deal with, whether the Congress is dealing with them or whether the Budget Bureau is dealing with them. . . ."

The military-industrial complex has become a massive, tangled system, half inside, half outside the Government. Like the Gordian knot, it is too intricate to be unraveled. But like the dinosaur, its weakness lies in its great size. If its intricacy rebuffs us, its grossness is vulnerable; it can be reduced by substantially cutting the defense budget.

This is the only viable immediate solution, for innovations in contractual procedures, regulatory statutes such as the Truth-in-Negotiations Act and such watchdog agencies as the General Accounting Office have not been able to cope effectively with the major excesses in military procurement. The Bureau of the Budget has been in a subordinate position, notwithstanding its recent success in challenging the Manned Orbiting Laboratory funds and its claims to more power over the defense budget. The deck is stacked against those who would sit down across the table from the military-industrial complex.

The only way to change the game is to cut the budget.

RICHARD DUDMAN   *Agent Meany*

To George Meany there are "bad" trade unions (Communist) and "good" trade unions (free, democratic) and never the twain shall meet. The former are agents of the Communist party or Communist government-

From *The New Republic*, May 3, 1969. Reprinted by permission of *The New Republic*, © 1969, Harrison-Blaine of New Jersey, Inc.

dominated; the latter are independent of external control. In fact the AFL-CIO has blurred this sharp distinction by accepting United States government funds to finance the work of three regional institutes it operates among unions in Latin America, Africa and Asia — the American Institute for Free Labor Development (AIFLD), the African-American Labor Center (AALC), and the Asian-American Free Labor Institute (AAFLI). The government pays 80 to 90 per cent of their bills through appropriations for the Agency for International Development.

Now a turn of events has made Meany's distinction even blurrier. Not only do these three institutes accept substantial government support; they also have assumed an additional function as conduits for AID money funneled into various "CIA orphans" — the overseas programs that used to be paid for secretly by the Central Intelligence Agency. Whether it is all the same money, whether CIA still actually directs these activities, and whether the change is just a matter of bookkeeping are good questions to which we can only surmise the answers.

Beneficiaries of this new form of roundabout government financing include the Retail Clerks International Association and the International Federation of Petroleum and Chemical Workers, two of the big affiliates of the AFL-CIO that received money from the CIA conduits in the old days: they performed such tasks as supporting the general strike that helped keep Cheddi Jagen from coming to power when Guyana became independent in 1966. Current enterprises includes developing an oil workers' federation in Japan, financing a retail clerks' union office in Peru and buying membership buttons for a labor union in the Congo. Emphasis is on building up "free" (anti-Communist) unions.

CIA financing was exposed two years ago when a flurry of newspaper stories uncovered a labyrinth of foundations that passed untraceable funds back and forth and subsidized certain favored overseas operations. The new system of funneling aid funds into the labor organizations by way of the AFL-CIO institutes apparently grew out of President Johnson's order of March 29, 1967, prohibiting any further hidden subsidies to private voluntary organizations. He promised to give serious considerations to a proposal that the federal government develop and establish "a public-private mechanism to provide public funds openly for overseas activities of organizations which are adjudged deserving, in the national interest, of public support." A panel headed by former Secretary of State Dean Rusk recommended stopgap assistance for a few such organizations last May, but left the question of permanent financing to the new Administration. Financing of the international labor programs through the AFL-CIO outlets with AID funds is part of that stopgap plan.

This program, begun in mid-1968 with a little more than $1 million annually, was planned in meetings of AID and AFL-CIO officials held earlier that year. Ernest S. Lee, assistant director of the AFL-CIO's Department of International Affairs, made the formal proposal in a letter May 15, 1968, to Rutherford M. Poats, deputy administrator of AID. Lee is a son-in-law of Meany and assistant to Jay Lovestone, the onetime secretary general of the American Communist Party who later turned fiercely anti-Communist and helped labor unions spend CIA money in the cold war rivalry after World War II. As Director of International Affairs for the AFL-CIO, Lovestone heads the international activities of the federation and is said to exercise a partial veto over selection of labor attachés at U.S. embassies.

Lee asked AID to provide $1,300,000 by expanding existing contracts with the American Institute for Free Labor Development (AIFLD), the African-American Labor Center (AALC) and the Asian-American Free Labor Institute (AAFLI).

AIFLD, founded in 1962, already has received $23 million from AID to support organizational and political activities, construction of workers' housing, workers, training schools and other programs throughout most of Latin America. It received $8 million last year.

AALC, founded in 1964 for similar work in Africa, and AAFLI, in 1968 for Asian projects, have been getting about $1 million apiece from AID for their regular programs.

The executive director of AALC is Irving Brown, who worked as Lovestone's agent after World War II to set up unions in Germany, France and Italy as rivals to combat Communist-dominated unions. Among Brown's many "impact projects" financed by U.S. government funds is a visit by three African labor leaders to the United States to attend the 1967 AFL-CIO convention.

Technically, there is no secret about the new financial arrangement for the overseas union organizations. Although there has been no voluntary explanation to Congress or to the public, officials answer questions about it in the greatest detail. An AID "position paper" describing the subsidized work of Brown's AALC says that AID support "must be acknowledged, at least to the host government." This seems to suggest that individual citizens of the host country can just as well be left in the dark.

The same document says that AALC technicians "will consult with U.S. AID mission officers, but they should not become identified as AID contractor employes." It also gives the approved public description of AALC: "a private U.S. labor organization, founded by the U.S. labor movement, working with financial support from private and public funds." An official of the U.S. Embassy or AID mission assigned to watch progress on an AALC project "will work with the AALC technician discreetly and tactfully to retain the union-to-union image. Site visits, when required, will be arranged with the AALC technician and will be as unobtrusive as possible."

Lee's plan, eventually adopted, was that AID would use the three institutes as "instruments to provide financial support to American labor organizations" in developing and strengthening free trade unions throughout the world. His proposed schedule of subcontracts called for $300,000 each to be funneled into the Retail Clerks International Association, the International Federation of Petroleum and Chemical Workers, and the Communications Workers of America, and $100,000 into the Brotherhood of Railway Clerks.

Lee proposed an additional $200,000 be routed through the three institutes directly to groups of unions overseas, without reference to any American unions. These groups were the "clothing and textile workers unions," "entertainment workers unions," and "food, drink and plantation workers unions." These programs have been slower to develop. An additional $100,000 was requested for administrative supervisory travel.

Meany stated the case for independent unionism in a speech March 13, 1951, before the Catholic Labor Alliance in Chicago: "We are totally independent of any government control or influence. At times we may agree and cooperate. At times we may disagree. But at no time can we serve or act as an agency or dependent of our government. It is this entirely independent role of the AF of L which has lent great potency, prestige and effectiveness to our domestic and foreign activities against the Communist scourge."

Things have changed since then, however, and Lee's letter to Poats started right off by saying, "This will confirm our rent discussions in which the Agency for International Development may utilize the American Institute for Free Labor Development, the African-American Labor Center, and the Asian-American Free Labor Institute as instruments to provide financial support to American labor organizations involved in, and capable of, developing and strengthening free trade unions throughout the world." He went on to ask for $1,300,000 in AID funds for allocation by the three "instruments."

Things have changed, also, with respect to union delegations from other countries, with the AFL-CIO as host. In the same 1951 speech, Meany boasted about the number of such visits and said: "These are not government financed delegations. They are strictly independent trade union delegations."

As the financing has developed, some of the allocations have been readjusted, and the current total through June is $1,245,000. This AID money takes the place of interim financing through the International Confederation of Free Trade Unions, which Meany quit when he no longer needed it.

The pattern of financing follows closely a plan proposed and actually applied for a short time to support overseas work by the American Newspaper Guild, which also had been financed by the CIA until the exposures two years ago. When the CIA's role was revealed, the Guild could get no satisfactory answers out of the foundations that had been supporting its overseas work and had been exposed as CIA conduits — the Granary Fund, the Andrew Hamilton Fund, the Chesapeake Foundation, the Broad-High Foundation and the Warden Trust. The Guild's board, declaring that this left a shadow over its international affairs program, directed its officers to sever all connection with the funds.

Hoping to keep up the program, however, the Guild obtained a temporary grant from AFL-CIO emergency funds and additional assistance from AIFLD. Meany at one point told the Guild officers that permanent financing could best be obtained from AID through AIFLD, AALC and a third regional institute soon to be created. This was AAFLI, set up since then and now being used for the pass-through financing of the other union programs overseas. But permanent arrangement for the Guild never jelled. Its officers were told that funds were being curtailed. Some of them concluded that their independence of Lovestone and of U.S. policies made them unacceptable for government subsidy.

"The Guild just didn't fit the mold," one officer says. "It was more concerned with wages and hours and conditions of employment and less concerned with political intrigue." The Guild's overseas program, which included seminars for foreign journalists and union organizing activities, has since been dismantled — but the Guild remains in the AFL-CIO.

There were two basic policy questions when the disclosures of two years ago showed that many of the international conferences, orchestra tours, and publications were actually financed by undercover government funds. The first was whether covert financing was to be continued, considering the damage caused by past exposures and the danger of further exposures in the future. President Johnson chose to call a halt to the secret financing rather than look for new secret conduits.

The second question was whether voluntary organizations can function effectively with any government subsidy, covert or overt. Particularly in the case of labor unions, there are those who believe that both credibility and integrity suffer. They point out that AIFLD has lavishly followed U.S. policy on such issues as intervention in the Dominican Republic, where many local unionists and even many Peace Corps volunteers were bitterly and outspokenly opposed to U.S. policy.

The pro-subsidy argument is that adequate funds are not available elsewhere, and that if the government does not pay the bill, no one will. Whatever the theoretical argument, American officials often do rely on labor organizations that they largely finance, for help in carrying out government policies.

Last year, Philip C. Habib, of the State Department's East Asia bureau, answered complaints about the arrest of South Vietnamese labor leaders by pointing out that Irving Brown of AALC and Fernand Audie of AAFLI were in Saigon and could persuade local labor leaders to rely on President Thieu and Vice President Ky to offset General Loan, the national police chief who had made the arrests.

On another occasion, James P. Grant, then the head of AID's Vietnam bureau, reported that a strike against an American firm in South Vietnam could be settled in a few days in view of the excellent relationship between the Vietnamese labor federation and the Saigon government. The labor federation is heavily subsidized through AAFLI.

Brown has made a special point of extending AALC's operations among African unions into Madagascar and other Indian Ocean islands where American satellite tracking stations are located.

The Nixon Administration apparently has accepted the same formula for subsidizing overseas labor activities. Meany seemed apprehensive when he presided at a meeting of the Labor Advisory Committee on Foreign Assistance last Nov. 12, a week after the Republican victory. The doubt had been dispelled when the Committee met again on March 10. George P. Delaney, the State Department's internal labor affairs coordinator, reported that the new AID administrator, John A. Hannah, had a favorable attitude, and that labor would have a "friend in court" in the Nixon Administration.

Meany observed that he knew Hannah personally and would enjoy working with him again. Then Meany went on to read a letter that Nixon had written to AIFLD's board chairman, J. Peter Grace, president of W. R. Grace & Co. Nixon said he was much interested in AIFLD's work and looked forward to continued cooperation toward their common goals. Gerald P. O'Keefe, acting director of AAFLI, said jokingly that, after hearing about Mr. Nixon's interest in AIFLD and AALC, AAFLI as "number three" would have to try harder to attract the President's attention toward Asia.

A further straw in the wind was the word that Gov. Nelson Rockefeller planned to take Andrew C. McLellan, the AFL-CIO's Inter-American representative, and Joseph A. Beirne, secretary-treasurer of AIFLD, on the first of his trips to Latin America for President Nixon.

RICHARD J. BARNET   *The National-*
                                        Security Managers

I

The continuing American conflict with revolutionary movements arises
from a fundamental clash of perspective on modern political history between those officials in the State Department, Pentagon, CIA, and the
White House who manage U.S. foreign relations — the National-Security
Managers — and the Revolutionaries, who guide insurgent movements.[1]
The conflict is fed by two fundamentally incompatible visions of world
order.

In the postwar period much has been made of the "ideological conflict"
between communism and capitalism.[2] That is what the Cold War is supposed to be about. But in fact many basic perspectives of Soviet and

Reprinted by permission of The World Publishing Company from *Intervention
and Revolution* by Richard J. Barnet. Copyright © 1968 by Richard J. Barnet.

[1] In probing the ideological conflict between the National-Security Manager and
the Revolutionary, we shall be talking about each as if he represented an ideal type.
Reality, of course, is less obliging. One can find in the State Department and in the
White House sharp disagreements on questions of national security, counterinsurgency,
and the proper "posture" of the United States towards the Third World. One need
only look at the polemics from the communist world on revolution, relations with the
capitalist world, and various strategies for change to recognize that revolutionaries
dedicated to radical social change through a radical redistribution of political power
do not all agree with one another. Nevertheless, a reading of a great number of
memoirs, congressional testimony, and analytical writings by National-Security Managers reveals that to a remarkable degree they share common assumptions about the
nature of politics and a common view of the world and how to change it. The same
can be said about contemporary Revolutionaries.

[2] During the history of the Cold War, the ideological struggle has been variously
characterized in official rhetoric as a fight between "freedom" and "totalitarianism,"
between a "world of diversity" and a "world of coercion," and as an "irreconcilable
clash of two systems." While these convictions have fired statesmen to greater struggle, they have not been the basis of policy. The Soviet Union and the United States
have few basic disagreements, for example, as to what present Egyptian society should
look like. They disagree primarily as to which of them should be the dominant foreign influence there, and such policies as each recommends to the Egyptians are designed, to a large extent, to enhance its own role. The revolutionary, on the other
hand, has very definite ideas about what his society should *not* look like, even if he
has few concrete ideas as to how to achieve the changes he would like to see. (See
David Apter, *The Politics of Modernization,* Chicago, 1965.) Unlike either of the
Great Powers, the revolutionary's primary interest is in changing a society. Where
his vision of his society clashes with the American vision there is conflict.

American leaders have always been remarkably similar. To be sure, they have had bitter conflicts over their relative power positions. The United States wanted a role in Eastern Europe that Russia refused to give her. Russia wanted a role in Western Europe and the Middle East which the United States has successfully resisted. They fought to a stalemate in Germany. The two powers have had quite different ideas about how to run their internal societies, but they shared the same general view of the proper role of a Great Power in the modern world.

They competed for power and influence in the Third World. Each put great stress on its military might. Each invested more in the symbols of prestige, like the space race, than in projects that might change the face of the earth. Each developed military, paramilitary, and diplomatic bureaucracies that were mirror images of the other. Neither was interested in exporting its system to other countries so much as using its system as an ideology around which to rally supporters and clients. The United States was as anxious to create a truly *independent* capitalist economy in the poor countries of Asia, Africa, and Latin America as Russia was to establish *independent* communist regimes there. Indeed, the United States has usually not favored the accumulation of *local* capital and the Soviets have frequently opposed *local* revolutionaries.[3] Khrushchev proclaimed that the Soviet aspiration was to "overtake and surpass the United States" in building the affluent society. Today the Soviet government continues to hold up the American Way of Life, the abundant consumer economy, as the goal of Russian communism. Both powers have found that they can coexist comfortably and compete for power and influence without attempting to convert the other. This is an *ideological* conflict like the one between Ford and General Motors!

Between the National-Security Managers and the Revolutionary, however, there is a real ideological clash. While both use a common rhetoric at times — the speeches of Dean Rusk and Fidel Castro alike make repeated reference to "self-determination," "revolution," "freedom," etc. — the American bureaucrat and the revolutionary politician start with radically different pictures of world politics and a set of directly conflicting

---

[3] U.S. policy on making capital available to underdeveloped countries has remained essentially as recommended in the *Report to the President on Foreign Economic Policy,* commonly known as the *Gordon Gray Report:* "In contrast to the large-scale grants required to assist in the recovery and rearmament of Europe, the size of grant aid needed to support development is limited." (*Report to the President on Foreign Economic Policies,* Washington, D.C., 1950, pp. 66–67.) The definition of "limited" has become increasingly stringent as loans have replaced grants. (See David A. Baldwin, *Foreign Aid and American Foreign Policy,* New York, 1966.) Between 1946 and 1965 grants for economic development totaled $1.8 billion out of a total program of economic aid, i.e., unmilitary, of $69 billion. (See "AID Summary Report," quoted in Baldwin, *Foreign Aid,* p. 31.)

interests. They differ fundamentally even in the way they characterize the issues which divide them.[4]

This clash of perspectives is dictated by radical differences in their education, theoretical and practical, and in their personal relationships to politics. The typical National-Security Manager during the last twenty years was trained in law, engineering, or banking. He entered government service in the war. Captivated by a chance to be a participant in great events, he stayed on or, more often, returned from time to time. If he has any firsthand knowledge at all of the Third World, it is likely to stem from a mining venture or the sugar business; or, perhaps, from wartime service in the OSS.[5]

From his vantage point in the national-security bureaucracy, the National-Security Manager sees revolution in the underdeveloped world as a problem in the management of violence. Coming to power in the midst of World War II, he formed his view of international politics from his experience in the struggle with Hitler. The primary problem is aggression. The principal cause of aggression is weakness and instability. Unless aggressors are systematically opposed by "situations of strength," they will strike at their weaker neighbors. Nations act in accordance with Newtonian laws, rushing to fill up "power vacuums" wherever they find them.[6] "Everything that happens in this world affects us," President Johnson told the troops in Vietnam in 1966, "because pretty soon it gets on our doorstep."[7] Stripped of the intellectual counterpoint of the foreign-policy expert, the President voiced the most basic and primitive fears of the National-Security Manager. "There are 3 billion people in the world and we

[4] The terms "revolution," "civil war," and "insurgency" are not precise. A civil war can involve any two or more contending factions in a society. A revolution, as the term is used in this book, refers to an organized effort of a group to overthrow the established order with a view to bringing about a radical change in the economic or social system. Most of the revolutions described in this book were organized by peasant leaders or by middle-class leaders, including military officers, for the benefit of classes hitherto excluded from participation in the political process. Such revolutions should also be distinguished from coups d'état, which are designed to change personnel holding leadership positions without basically changing the political or economic system.

[5] The observations on the careers, education, and background of the National-Security Managers is based on a study I have completed of the four hundred individuals who have held the top managerial positions relating to national security (down to and including assistant secretary) from 1945 to 1967 in the Departments of State, Defense, Army, Navy, and Air Force, the Central Intelligence Agency, the Atomic Energy Commission, and the White House. The complete study will be published shortly.

[6] For a description of official thinking on "balance of power" and "power vacuums," see McGeorge Bundy, ed., *The Pattern of Responsibility* (Boston, 1951). An interpretation of the Cold War informed by the "balance of power" view of the world can be found in Louis Halle, *The Cold War and History* (New York, 1967). Mr. Halle was a member of the Policy Planning Staff during the Truman administration.

[7] *The New York Times,* November 2, 1966.

have only 200 million of them. We are outnumbered 15 to 1. If might did make right, they would sweep over the United States and take what we have. We have what they want."[8]

No one is more aware than the man with the authority to launch the nuclear missiles that the United States has a commanding position in military and economic power. Since 1945 this country, not content with being *primus inter pares* among the nations, has sought not the delicate balance of power but a position of commanding superiority in weapons technology, in the regulation of the international economy, and in the manipulation of the internal politics of other countries. For the National-Security Manager the acquisition of power is both a necessity and an end in itself. The world is too dangerous and present advantages too tenuous to permit a pause in the relentless drive for more power. He accepts the creed which General Douglas MacArthur used to voice, "There is no security; there is only opportunity." Few events in the world can be ignored. No matter how remote a coup, a guerrilla struggle, an arms shipment, or a friendly visit from one foreign leader to another may be, when viewed from the seventh floor of the State Department it must be recorded as either a national asset or a liability.

The world is full of enemies, but the most powerful is International Communism. Most National-Security Managers have not shared Dulles' conviction that communism is the incarnation of the Antichrist, a creed so dangerous to moral health that one must refuse to shake hands with their diplomatic spokesmen to avoid contamination.[9] To the less passionate ideologues of the Cold War, communism is not a disease but an "organizational weapon." John F. Kennedy expressed the sophisticated view of the world struggle in a speech on disarmament two years before he entered the White House: the national-security problem for the United States arises from "a vicious circle of two great powers contending with each other for sway over the destiny of man." It is a struggle "compounded by the new dynamics of an expansive world Communism, armed with revolutionary doctrines of class warfare and modern, methods of subversion and terror."[10] The master planners of the Kremlin and Peking, once in concert and now in rivalry, continually survey the globe probing for weak spots to which they can rush agitators, guns, or rubles for a cheap victory.

Communist intervention in the turmoil of revolution, decolonization, and civil strife threatens the security of the United States, for if the com-

---

[8] *Ibid.*

[9] At the Geneva Conference in 1954, Under Secretary of State Walter B. Smith squeezed Chou En-lai's elbow upon greeting him as a substitute for the proscribed handshake.

[10] John F. Kennedy, *The Strategy of Peace* (New York, 1961), p. 52.

munists succeed in their bid "for sway over the destiny of man," the
United States — as the National-Security Manager sees it — will be reduced to a vestigial enclave. Each revolutionary success, therefore, is
seen as a Russian victory and an American defeat. This conviction is
reason enough to mount a global campaign of containment, for National
Security is its own justification.

But the National-Security Manager is also convinced that he has right
as well as necessity on his side. Communist intervention is illegitimate
because the communist is by definition a foreign agent. Ho Chi Minh's
independence movement, Ambassador William C. Bullitt explained in
1947, was designed to "add another finger to the hand that Stalin is closing around China."[11] Mao Tse-tung too was a Russian agent, according to
Dean Rusk in a speech made two years after the Chinese Revolution,
when he was in charge of Far East operations for the State Department.
Mao's regime was "a colonial Russian government — a Slavic Manchukuo
on a large scale — it is not the government of China. It does not pass the
first test. It is not Chinese."[12] The National-Security Manager has convinced himself that no people ever voluntarily choose communism, a system founded on a set of economic myths and made to work at all only
by the systematic use of terror. Perhaps most of the protectorates of the
Free World are not so free, the National-Security Manager concedes in
the intimate atmosphere of a Task Force or a "backgrounder," but they
are better off than if they had gone communist. And so are we.

II

Since the dawn of the sixties the National-Security Managers have taken
it as an article of faith that the Third World is both the locus and the
prize of the Cold War. "Today's struggle does not lie here," President
Kennedy told Paul-Henri Spaak on a visit to Europe in the last year of his
life, "but rather in Asia, Latin America and Africa."[13] The less-developed
lands, John J. McCloy wrote in 1960, "promise to be the principal battleground in which the forces of freedom and communism compete — a
battleground in which the future shape of society may finally be tested
and determined."[14] The vision of Armageddon that had sustained the
arms race of the fifties, the Nuclear War over Europe, had receded in

---

[11] William C. Bullitt, quoted in Carl Oglesby and Richard Shaull, *Containment and
Change: Two Dissenting Views of American Society and Foreign Policy in the New
Revolutionary Age* (New York, 1967), p. 30.

[12] Dean Rusk, quoted in Ronald Steel, *Pax Americana* (New York, 1967), p. 129.

[13] John F. Kennedy, quoted in Arthur Schlesinger, Jr., *A Thousand Days: John F.
Kennedy in the White House* (Boston, 1965), p. 507.

[14] John J. McCloy, "Foreign Economic Policy and Objectives," in *Goals for Americans* (New York, 1960), p. 342.

the wake of a decade of tacit understandings between cautious adversaries and judicious crisis management on both sides of the Elbe. The prospect of the new Armageddon was more frightening, for its terrain was unfamiliar and its weapons unconventional. The clients to be assisted were volatile. They behaved brutally at home and ungratefully toward their benefactors. Yet the decolonizing world, known in the National-Security Manager's vernacular of the fifties as The Gray Areas, had become the major battleground.[15]

For the National-Security bureaucrat, the Cold War conferred a manageable unity upon the landmass of Asia, Africa, and Latin America, with its two-thirds of the world's population, its staggering set of economic and social problems, and its confusing mosaic of race, culture, and politics. For all their differences, the politicians of the Third World shared a common role in the Great Power struggle, and whatever identity such "local" politicians were accorded in the State Department and the White House rested on that role.

The National-Security Manager still tends to look at the "Underdeveloped World" as a vast Gray Area in international politics. No part of it is of intrinsic interest, unless, of course, it supplies some vital commodity. Otherwise it can capture the official attention in Washington only if it symbolizes some struggle which transcends the minor turmoil of native politics. To the man of the West, Paris and Berlin are important places in their own right, for they symbolize his own historical heritage. But Danang, Santo Domingo, and Kinshasa penetrate his consciousness, if at all, only as battlefields, and then only if the fight is about something sufficiently important. He has almost no knowledge about such places, their people, or their politics, and little personal commitment to them. They represent either sources of strength, strategic or economic, or points of vulnerability. "Vietnam is not the issue," National-Security Managers have frequently confided to critics who question whether systematic bombardment is the best way to secure freedom for the Vietnamese people; "it is the testing ground for the Communist strategy of Wars of National Liberation. If they win here, they will strike elsewhere. If they lose, they will not be so ready to start another."

The National-Security Manager is a global thinker. In themselves, local problems of other countries are not worthy of his attention; it is the transcendent importance of local revolutionary struggles that warrants intervention. Interference in purely domestic matters is still unjustified as a

---

[15] For an insight into the way national-security bureaucrats looked at the Third World, even in the early Kennedy period when "uncommitted nations" were identified as a special concern of the new administration, see Schlesinger, *A Thousand Days*, p. 508, where a task of his fellow White House assistant, Robert Komer, is characterized: "Robert Komer . . . patrolled the gray areas from Casablanca to New Guinea."

matter of law and sound policy. Unfortunately, he hastens to add, the line between domestic and foreign matters has blurred. When political factions struggle with one another in far-off places, their conflict is an expression of a single worldwide struggle. The real contestants remain the same. Only the battlefield shifts. The battle, which takes the form of a series of guerrilla wars, is not about Vietnam or Greece or the Dominican Republic any more than World War II was about Iwo Jima or Sicily. Wherever men struggle for power, one can always find International Communism, the ubiquitous political scavenger, ready to use genuine local grievances as ammunition in a global holy war. Global strategy, more than local conditions, dictates the site of the next engagement between International Communism and the Free World.

At this point let us try to look more closely at the mental set of the National-Security Manager as it bears on the U.S. commitment against revolution. The ultimate bureaucratic dream is the perfect freedom of unlimited power. It is the ability to push a button, make a phone call, dispatch a cable, and know that the world will conform to your vision. The capacity to control, or, as he might put it, to have options, is a much clearer objective for the professional statesman than the purposes to which he would put such power. The guiding stars of the working bureaucrat are not cosmic goals. One can find a few expressions of an official eschatology in flowery speeches on National Purpose, or in the negotiated generalities of the Basic National-Security Policy papers representing the collective wisdom of the foreign-policy bureaucracy. Usually, however, the National-Security Manager prides himself on avoiding theological and "nonpragmatic" speculation. He has faith in his intuitive grasp of the art of *ad hoc* politics. Yet, in developing official policy on U.S. intervention, he is not quite so free as he thinks. Just as he casts his adversary, the Revolutionary — Castro, Mao, Ho — in the inevitable role of foreign agent, so he has picked out a well-worn part for himself. It is the role of the imperial peacekeeper.

III

The National-Security Manager is of course outraged by any such suggestion. To note that America follows in the footsteps of other great powers offends against a basic tenet of his faith: America is exceptional. The nation which sprang from a unique political philosophy at a unique historical moment, singularly blessed by geography, climate, and the inventive energy of her people, never needed to fall prey to the temptations of the European empires, and never did.

The more historically minded of the National-Security Managers are quick to point out that the acquisitions of the imperialist spree of the

McKinley era, such as Cuba and Hawaii, have been either abandoned or incorporated as full participants in the American Union. (Even the imperial settlement of the continental United States does not fit the nineteenth-century pattern. The push to the Pacific was an act of conquest. The Indians were pacified, not civilized; killed or resettled, not exploited.) As late as the mid-forties, he reminds us, the State Department openly sided with independence movements in India, Indochina, and Indonesia and gave support to a radical revolutionary party in China. General MacArthur, the hero of the American Right, used his imperial powers in occupied Japan to sponsor a controlled social revolution in which the landed nobility and the military who had run the country lost their power along with their land. Even in Latin America, where economic penetration under the slogan of "manifest destiny" ran deepest, the United States avoided falling into the colonialist mold. Unlike France or England, the United States did not seek to impose a civilization on those she dominated. Indeed, the countries that most successfully have assimilated the American idiom along with the supermarket and the superhighway are not the backward protectorates where the U.S. military bases dominated the economy, but the developed countries of Western Europe, which, though respectful, if not subservient, in their foreign policies, are not colonies.

The leaders of independence movements at the end of World War II helped to reinforce the National-Security Manager's self-image as an antiimperialist. Ho Chi Minh borrowed the words of the Declaration of Independence to embellish the constitution of the Democratic Republic of Vietnam and like many other revolutionary politicians regularly invoked the name of George Washington. Wendell Willkie reported a seemingly inexhaustible "reservoir of good will" for America among the nationalist leaders of the world.

The National-Security Manager thus feels that both the tradition and practice of American foreign policy set it apart from the classic imperialist model. There is, to be sure, an American military presence on every continent, but it is designed neither to acquire territory, to service the U.S. economy, nor to impose an American Way of Life on others. Its sole purposes are, he maintains, to assure the security of the United States and, where possible, to support those who will work for free societies.

To the National-Security Manager, peering out from the seventh floor of the State Department, the Pentagon War Room, or the Situation Room in the White House, the world looks something like a seething caldron. The eruption of violence makes him acutely uncomfortable, for it threatens a status quo which, if left undisturbed, promises to bring a steady appreciation of America's preeminent wealth and power. Attracted by Litvinoff's prewar rhetoric about the "indivisibility" of peace, with its anxiety-producing vision of the strong losing their power by refusing to help the weak, the Managers have come to feel that when the bell tolls for some corrupt but orderly government in a far-off land, it is indeed tolling for them. Whether the psychological roots of this anxiety are the rich man's guilt in the face of starvation or the terror of the comfortable in the midst of chronic desperation, the national-security bureaucrats have taken the early Leninist dogma that rebellion is contagious and made it an existential fear. Far too sophisticated to accept the "domino theory" in literal terms, the National-Security Manager feels that unless the forces of radical change unleashed by two world wars and the break-up of old empires is held in check, the United States cannot maintain its present preeminent economic and political position.

IV

There must be law and order in the world. Violence cannot be tolerated. With these two propositions the National-Security Manager completes a familiar circuit. The powerful have always invoked the law to protect their power and property, and they have usually insisted on the right to help enforce that law themselves. The Pax Romana and Pax Britannica were primarily arrangements to protect Roman and British interests by creating a system of law and order in which those interests could thrive and by supplying the necessary military power to defend the system. Indeed, the word *"imperium"* itself in Roman times referred to the territory under the jurisdiction of the law of Rome. As a by-product, some other nations derived a measure of security. But that was hardly the primary purpose. The benefits flowing to the "world community" of their day were most unevenly distributed. Some peoples did well under imperial protection. Others were crushed. Since he feels no real responsibility to the world community or to any higher power on earth, because there is none, the imperial peacekeeper necessarily applies and enforces the law in a self-serving way. The higher community which American statesmen purport to serve is largely their own creation. In the early postwar days it was a subservient United Nations. Today it is a self-defined Free World.

The National-Security Manager assumes that U.S. interests and those of the rest of humanity coincide. Governments and political movements which contest this idea have ulterior and illegitimate motives. Far from a simple cynic who mouths idealistic rhetoric to mask economic plundering, the Manager sincerely believes that in opposing Third World revolutions the United States is both pursuing its self-interest and promoting the ultimate welfare of the world community. The fight against insurgent movements is rationalized into a continuing crusade for a decent world, the latest episode in the battle to make the world safe for democracy. What gives plausibility to this characterization is that modern insurgent movements, so U.S. leaders have argued, can be lumped with the Kaiser's invasion of Belgium and Hitler's aggression against Europe, for they are all *violent* challenges to the status quo. If, as the National-Security Managers see it, the inevitable involvement of international communism is the key factor that makes U.S. intervention against revolutions ultimately necessary for national survival, the use of violence by the insurgents is the key factor that makes it legally justifiable and morally right.

Like everyone else, the National-Security Manager looks at the issue of violence from a highly personal perspective. He is selective in the violence he notices and inconsistent in the moral judgments he makes about it. On November 23, 1946, for example, at the very moment when the State Department was preparing a major U.S. intervention against Greek "terrorists," a French naval squadron turned its guns on the civilian population of Haiphong and killed more than six thousand in an afternoon. The United States did not protest, much less intervene. Violence in behalf of the established order is judged by one set of criteria, insurgent violence by another. When established institutions kill through their police or their armies, it is regrettable but, by hypothesis, necessary. When the weak rise up and kill, their violence threatens order everywhere. Sympathetic as U.S. bureaucrats were with the objectives of the Hungarian freedom fighters in 1956, they breathed a sigh of relief when they were disarmed.

The National-Security Manager is aware that violence in other countries has political causes, but he sees no other immediate way to handle it than suppression. Reform, modernization, greater political and social justice are all necessary, he knows, to assure stable regimes where the status quo will not be overturned by force. But how can you begin this process unless the snipers and assassins are first rounded up? Once the wretched of the earth and the cynical politicians who manipulate their misery for their own ends are made to see that violence will not work, they may come to cooperate in finding less dangerous ways to political change.

In the long run, political passions will be cooled by the slow process of opening up new doors of opportunity — a revolution from the top. In the short run, those who are impatient with this prolonged prospect will be taught patience by the arm or the police.

One reason why the National-Security Manager has such difficulty in coming to grips with the problem of political violence abroad is that, like most Americans, he has not confronted the issue in his own country. Until the wave of Negro riots struck American cities in the mid-sixties, he pictured his country as a tranquil island in a sea of violence. Because of its tradition of law and order, the United States was uniquely successful in

avoiding the coups, rebellions, assassinations, and executions that plagued
the rest of the world. The most perceptive foreign observers celebrated
our good fortune. Writing in 1888, James Bryce noted that the poor "have
had nothing to fight for, no grounds for disliking the well to do, no complaints to make against them."[16] Violence never played a role in American
politics, according to tradition, because the system worked so well. Every
few years the doors of opportunity have swung open to admit the lowest,
the poorest, or the most recent arrivals to the national consensus.

There is enough validity to the national myth of equal opportunity that
those who have risen to the top of American society are quite prepared
to accept it. In such a well-regulated society, violence is not a phenomenon of politics, but of crime. Those who resort to it are unwilling to
play a competitive game open to all but are trying to wreck the game and
impose their own rules. The few attempts to practice the politics of violence in America have failed. The Wobblies, the KKK, the Confederacy,
and the Whiskey Rebellion were all suppressed. The National-Security
Manger cannot see why younger societies now undergoing economic
and political development should not also suppress violent challenges
from their own populations. And, in the name of order, the United States
should help.

Behind the myth of unique tranquillity lies one of the most violent
countries in the world. The United States has engaged in eight major
wars and over one hundred minor ones in its brief history, including one
of the bloodiest civil wars in history. In the one hundred years since that
war, we have assassinated our Presidents regularly at twenty-year intervals, missing only Harding and Franklin Roosevelt, who died in office.
(Roosevelt and Truman were both targets of assassination attempts.) The
murder rate is among the highest in the world. Other crimes against persons have reached staggering proportions. The United States spends far
more on instruments of violence and on a class of specialists in violence
than any other country. The stern-faced generals on pedestals in our
parks; the aimless brutality of the animated cartoons; the endless flow of
grenades, rockets, and burp guns to amuse the children; and the bloody
fairy tales of television are random illustrations of the same point. The
nation is held in horrified fascination by violence and those who practice it.

Frightened at the real violence in our midst, we Americans try to deny
it by immersing ourselves in the fantasy of violence. Unlike the real world
of violence, the violence of the fairy tale is either morally neutral or
morally ambiguous. It can be without purpose and without consequence,
like a firecracker exploding inside Donald Duck's tailfeathers. Or it can

[16] James Bryce, quoted in Irving Louis Horowitz, *Three Worlds of Development*
(New York, 1966), p. 80.

be a detective, cowboy, or other symbol of virtuous authority gunning down some depraved villain. In the fantasy world violence is thus either a harmless game or a just punishment. In the real world it is a necessary instrument to protect the public order in the hands of those with a right to use it. In the hands of those without such right it is the manifestation of a social sickness.[17] The National-Security Manager does not grasp or will not admit that there are societies — some, it now appears, even in our own country — where the channels of "peaceful change" have totally broken down or never existed. He professes to understand the causal connection between misery and violence but he cannot accept the legitimacy of the guerrilla, no matter how just his grievance. For the sake of world order he must be suppressed until safer paths to economic development and political justice can be found. As we shall see, the Revolutionary thinks of political violence in quite different terms. The gulf between the American bureaucrat and the radical Third World politician on this issue is a direct reflection of their fundamentally different visions of the process of political change.

The National-Security Manager builds his model of political and economic development for the "less-developed nations," as he tactfully calls them, from his own picture of American political development. Too sophisticated to think that the American system of government or economy is the answer to the problems of the Third World or that, even if it were, it could be simply re-created in present societies, he nonetheless sees the process of change in American terms and believes that American techniques offer the only real hope. Projecting his own conception of the dynamics of American life, he concludes that change is primarily a technical rather than a political problem, one that calls for a slow turn of the wheel rather than a sudden jerk. Under the American System man has gone far to transcend political conflict. The "consensus society," a national myth long before President Johnson made it a political slogan, consists of more open channels of opportunities than have ever been available before in human society. As he sees it, old class conflicts and animosities that have torn apart other societies play no role in the land of the Melting Pot. That there is great inequality in American society is clear, but the faith in equal opportunity is a source of personal contentment and national pride for all but a small minority that is very poor and nonwhite.

According to his vision of social change in America, the United States has escaped class conflict because of its economic system, which makes it possible for each man to contribute to the general welfare by looking after his own. The government, he knows, plays a larger role than we care to

[17] For a compelling analysis of American perceptions of violence, based on comparisons of U.S. and foreign films, see Nathan C. Leites and Martha Wolfenstein, *Movies: A Psychological Study* (Glencoe, Ill., 1950), especially pp. 176–179.

advertise. But its function is to prime the pump and to stimulate the general growth of the economy, not to make a radical redistribution of political and economic power. The economy continues to grow because the system has learned how to harness technology.[18]

Looking at the underdeveloped world, the National-Security Manager assumes that what W. W. Rostow calls a "high-mass-consumption" society is the real ultimate goal of newly decolonized societies and a proper one. The best way to achieve the "takeoff" that can bring a modest version of the affluent society to poor nations is through technological innovation and the education of an entrepreneurial class that can supply the energy for change. The economic system that stimulates entrepreneurship is private enterprise. Therefore, the developing nations' "greatest need," as Chester Bowles has put it, is "private investment to aid the free sectors of their economies."[19]

Capital for the public sector of infant economies is likely to be wasted. It cannot be absorbed because the entrepreneurial classes who could invest it profitably do not yet exist. Corruption, waste, inefficiency, and political in-fighting all guarantee that grants of capital to new governments to be used to build planned economies would end up in Swiss bank accounts. The process of development is slow, but the attempt to speed it up through nationalization, confiscation, or other radical remedies would lead to the disasters of Stalinism. The National-Security Manager takes some comfort from the thought that the military of the Third World, the class that has most directly and handsomely benefited from U.S. aid around the world, are also the most promising entrepreneurs. In Latin America and parts of the Middle East the military have been "modernizing" influences. Furnished with U.S. training and equipment, they are the first in their societies to apply technology to public problems. They are now equipped for "civic action." The Department of Defense explains it this way: "As the interdependence of civil and military matters is increasingly recognized, the social and economic welfare of the people can no longer be considered a non-military concern."[20]

---

[18] For accounts of prevailing U.S. views of development and how to achieve it, see W. W. Rostow, *Stages of Economic Growth: A Non-Communist Manifesto* (Cambridge, England, 1960), especially chs. II and VI; Edward S. Mason, *Foreign Aid and Foreign Policy* (New York, 1964); John Kenneth Galbraith, *Economic Development in Perspective* (Cambridge, Mass., 1962). See also Albert O. Hirshmann, *The Strategy of Economic Development* (New Haven, 1958).

[19] Chester Bowles, "The Developing Nations' Greatest Need," *The New York Times Magazine*, April 12, 1964, p. 15.

[20] For a discussion of official U.S. attitudes toward the role of the military in underdeveloped countries, see Horowitz, *Three Worlds*, pp. 420–425.

EDUCATION 5

The Schools

"Education is the way up" is a classical homily of the American folk wisdom. Like most homilies, it has some truth to it, but also needs to be carefully qualified. One problem is in the significance of "up"; another is in its applicability. "Up" might mean going from the bottom to the top; or it might suggest a fundamental change in social stratification; or it might mean an alteration in values and comprehension. In his article, Edgar Z. Friedenberg suggests that "up" has been narrowly interpreted, and that this interpretation has defined the aspirations of the American school system. The principal goal of the American school has been the inculcation of fundamental skills, the three R's, and an indoctrination of American society's conventional values, from the patriotism of the pledge of allegiance to the racism of the songs of Stephen Foster. Friedenberg concludes that the schools serve to inculcate the unexamined American traditions. If the students "rise" at all, they do so within the boundaries of strictly circumscribed norms.

Friedenberg affirms that the American school is primarily a screening mechanism. His argument, both subtle and fundamental, is reminiscent of some of the more powerful and disturbing insights of Thorstein Veblen.[1] Veblen argued that expenditures for material goods did not necessarily depend on their functional value. For example, peo-

[1] See his *The Theory of the Leisure Class* (New York: Modern Library, 1934).

ple buy Cadillacs and Lincoln Continentals to assert the
high status and economic position of the owner. Friedenberg imposes a Veblen-like vision on the school system. A
school is not a place to learn the graceful use of language,
the cutting edge of logic, or the wonders and power of
science. For some people, of course, that is the outcome.
But for most, the schools as a social system offer an opportunity to obtain from constituted authorities a piece of
paper guaranteeing the conventional capacities of its
bearer, as verified by the bureaucratic and authoritarian
structure of the school administration.

Consequently, the school is predisposed to continually
undermine its own values. As an educational institution, it
is by definition committed to social change and innovation.
At the same time, dependent for its support on the community, it is one of the most conservative institutions.
Schools support the status quo by training people in the
existing culture. And generally they support local systems
of social stratification and prestige.

Although other sociologists have argued that schools
serve as agents of social mobility, Friedenberg suggests
that the schools contribute little to social change or social
mobility. When political pressures arise to alter the structure of social stratification, the schools follow, yet when
pressures dictate otherwise the schools also conform. So
the schools, in Friedenberg's view, reflect the norms and
values of the community and have little independence as
educational institutions. Their certification processes meet
the need that people be designated as having the potential
for occupying certain statuses and fulfilling certain roles.
At the same time they undermine their educational values,
since conformity to norms becomes more valued in the
individual than personal creativity and inventiveness.

In his examination of the New York City school system,
David Rogers elaborates on those issues. Rogers attributes
the stultification and aridness of contemporary education
of the organization of authority in the school system itself.
He describes the New York City school system as a bureau-
cratically centralized machine in which decisions are made
from top down rather than from the bottom up, so that

those with authority in the system are out of touch with the everyday needs of the students in the local schools. This rigid and impervious bureacracy operates within a broader social system, namely "the entire institution of public education, including teacher training, the professional associations . . . the technology of teaching." All of this contributes to the increasing lack of confidence shown toward the public schools in our larger cities. The articles by Friedenberg and Rogers contain underlying assumptions without which they could not have been written — that the society is far from perfect and requires considerable social change; that the schools better serve the community if they operate as institutions of change rather than as institutions protecting the status quo; finally, that the status quo within the schools themselves is socially destructive.

These points are made vivid in Jonathan Kozol's discussion of character education in the Boston public schools. Kozol became a substitute teacher in the Boston public schools in 1964. His book shows how ruthlessly, relentlessly the children he taught were brutalized. The brutality is clear — the rattan is used, the welts are real, and one child is seriously injured in his presence.

In the selection from his book Kozol draws attention to the second problem of the American homily that "education is the way up." If disadvantaged people "rise" in American society, they do so despite the conditions that prevail in the public schools, not because of them. The terror of his book is contained in aspects of the evil he describes. First, these are not schools in some rural county of Mississippi, staffed by white southerners reared on a steady diet of overtly racist beliefs. These are schools in a traditional and liberal area — northeast, urban, and with a history of racial equality. This is Boston, Massachusetts, whose favorite basketball team is integrated and has been coached by an outstanding black athlete, and whose history echoes with revolution and abolition. Yet the second terrorizing feature of Kozol's description may account for the first — it is the banality of the evil he describes. Events in the Boston public schools are not the work of super-tyrants. The teachers and administrators of the Boston public schools who commit children to an early destruction are very ordinary people.

In Kozol's piece we obtain a vivid picture of the school as "an agency of social control." In practice this means the punitive indoctrination of large numbers of students, especially those from minority groups, into their "place" in society. Kozol discusses a booklet published by the Boston public school system entitled "A Curriculum Guide in Character Education." Kozol singles out this booklet because it clearly presents the values which children are supposed to submit themselves. These values emphasize both the importance of obedience and character traits that could not create trouble for authorities or arouse interest in the world of letters and science, nor could they ever be considered meaningful to the students. A lack of response to such books as these causes children in minority groups to be described as "culturally deprived," the measure of the deprivation ostensibly being the distance between them and the values expressed in guides to character education.

The cultural discrepancy between children and schools has led to an increasingly strong demand for community control of schools by black and other minority groups. New York City has experimented in community control, attempting not only to respond to dissatisfactions with teaching materials that are irrelevant and sometimes insulting to the students; but also to investigate the possibility of running the schools from the bottom up instead of the top down. In his article "For Local Control of the Schools" Robert Dentler states that there has been no organized pressure to break into what is most culture-bound in the school curriculum. The teachers' union, from which some innovative ideas might have been expected, has concentrated on improving its own working conditions, and has accommodated itself to the norms and values of the centralized bureaucracy. Instead of trying to change the system, the teachers' union has reinforced it.

Critics of decentralization fear that neighborhood control will lead to an unfortunate parochialism in which each neighborhood would be offering its best — and worst — understanding of the world, its functioning, and its needs. The authors of this section suggest, however, that the so-called broader concerns of the boards of education turn out to be narrow provincialisms enforced by the politically dominant. There seems to be a paradox in America's urban school system: state and city control is educationally regressive, whereas local control may prove more forward looking. The more we support what seems to be universalism, the less we achieve the motivation and interest required by society to sustain the highest educational aspirations. Whatever hope there is does not appear to be in the reconstruction of centralized bureaucracies.

EDGAR Z. FRIEDENBERG   *Status and Role in Education*

The central function of education in a complex society is the allocation of the various credentials that define the status of the bearer and the range of social roles that he may be permitted to fill. The role that an individual comes to occupy in society on the basis of his credentials from school virtually determines his social identity both in his own eyes and those of society. By "credential," of course, I mean far more than a transcript or a diploma; these certainly, but, properly speaking, the credential includes the entire dossier collected, preserved, and transmitted by the school or used by it as a basis for recommendations to those authorities on whom the student's life-chances depend.

Much of the emphasis placed on the credential in modern society is an expression of its commitment to universalistic values. Formal education is expected to further universalism by promoting achievement —

This article first appeared in *The Humanist*, September-October, 1968 and is reprinted by permission of *The Humanist* and the author.

doing rather than being — and appraising it impersonally regardless of the needs of or other claims to consideration by the candidate.

And to the degree that the society is egalitarian as well as universalistic in its values the school will also be expected to admit candidates for credentials to its programs solely on the basis of potential or actual competence in the skills the program demands. Such a society conceives itself as engaged in a continuous talent search, which it is obligated to conduct competitively and impartially for the purpose of maintaining a graded talent pool adequate to its enterprises and, generally speaking, without much concern for what the process does to those who are placed in the pool's shark-infested waters. And it regards the schools as its instrument for this purpose and hardly any other.

The schools' devotion to the task of keeping the talent pool stocked with properly labeled and fairly priced items wins it the public support it depends on, but also involves it in fundamental conflicts both internally and with its community. It affronts those students who dislike being processed and labeled as a product. It creates cynicism and despair among students and educators who perceive that, in any case, the credential is awarded in recognition of qualities quite different from the competences it is supposed to certify. And, because of its universalism, the school's talent searching involves it in continuous, covert conflict with its local community, of which maneuvering over school integration provides the best examples.

School systems in the United States are locally controlled, and local control of education is rooted in local political and status systems. It must therefore often conflict with commitments to universalism in an increasingly cosmopolitan society. The intensity, and hence the capacity for damage, in such conflicts tends, however, to be limited by the steady attrition of real local power in an increasingly centralized society. As the scope of local control is reduced by the application of state-aid formulas, the control of textbook production and instructional services by the mass media, and the push toward uniformity exerted by a geographically mobile population that demands interchangeable schools, the local response tends to become more ritualized as it becomes impotent. This does not make it less acrimonious, but merely more passive, so that conflict serves neither to clear the air nor to exert a clear influence on policy.[1]

But local control remains an important influence on the process of status allocation in the schools because it retains considerable veto power and manages thereby to impose local norms on enterprises of great pith and moment. The character of these norms, and their relationship to more cosmopolitan norms, profoundly affect the outcome of this process. Local assessment of students, on the basis of values that may be unrelated

[1] For a vivid descriptive analysis of this process at work, see Arthur D. Vidich and Joseph Bensman, *Small Town in Mass Society*, Princeton University Press, 1958.

or even negatively related to the abilities that will actually be required of them in the roles for which they are becoming qualified, may largely determine their life-chances. As an extreme example of this process, one may conceive of a beard or long hair ultimately costing a youth his life by occasioning his suspension from school, barring him from college admission, and leading to his induction into the armed services. At the level of higher education, it seems to me fair to observe that the Regents and administration of the University of California, by invoking narrowly authoritarian norms of personal conduct when confronted by the hippy cosmopolitanism of student activists and causing their leaders to be jailed, have managed to make a criminal record an essential part of the credential by which those students of the university who were most deeply concerned about education may be recognized; the Ph.D., surely, is a less reliable index.

Ultimately, what any credential comes to certify will be determined by the play of political forces among the groups who participate in the certification, whether they represent local customs, scholarly interests, or the burden of investment. The school, functioning as a certifying agency, serves partly as the vessel within which these contending forces are contained and reach equilibrium, and partly as one of the forces that contribute to the outcome. School personnel themselves judge students according to norms derived from their position in life that express their values and anxieties as well as — and doubtless far more than — academic standards. A school or university credential is in many ways a political document that expresses the vector sum of a set of social forces that determine what kinds of people will be accredited and on what terms; and hence what kinds of people may legitimately influence policy in a given situation. This aspect of the credential's function may or may not involve the way the competences it is supposed to certify are defined, but this does not usually matter crucially. Our society does not value competence very highly. It depends more on the rationalization of production and maintenance than on craftsmanship for quality control, and learns to content itself with lowered standards in those areas — of which teaching is a prime example — where rationalization does not work.

At the level of general education, I need look no further than the last graduation exercise I attended for an example of unconcern with the relevance of the credential to competence even during the very ceremony at which it is being awarded. At this institution, it is customary for the president of the senior class to make a short speech presenting the senior class gift to the university. The young man who did so stated that, instead of giving the school some costly object, the senior class had decided to spend its money on repairs for a dilapidated old fountain, which, he justly observed, "hadn't ran for several years." He further noted that this was "the most expensive gift any senior class had ever given the university." Nobody even winced.

It is possible, perhaps, to define liberal education in such a way that proficiency in its arts need not exclude either graceless and ungrammatical use of language or an unimaginatively materialistic sense of values, but I do not believe that many of my colleagues at that graduation would accept such a definition. Their conceptions of a college education were pretty conventional. They had simply ceased to expect the degree to mean anything at all in terms of the conventions they still accepted. In less striking ways we have all been living with our disillusionment for years, gradually adjusting to it by ceasing to expect high-school graduates to show any real mastery of the "fundamentals" required for college entrance, expecting employers in turn to retrain our graduates on the job instead of relying on the competences for which we had certified them. Except for the advanced physical scientists, who don't really graduate anyway since they are hired by their own major professor or his colleagues to work in another part of the military-academic complex, employers usually have to retrain graduates, since, if they are hired to work with machines, the equipment they learned on at school is usually obsolete by industrial standards; and if they are hired to work with people — as for example, teachers or lawyers — the ideology they were taught in school is usually so naive as to impede their function and must be unlearned on the job.

School credentials, though they determine access to status and role then, I would maintain, are not thought of as certificates of competence. But they certainly mean something, and something society regards as important. And society is right; the process of allocating this access is indeed vital, at least in the sense that the chorus in *The Mikado* use the word:

> Behold the Lord High Executioner:
> A personage of noble rank and title.
> A dignified and potent officer
> Whose function is particularly vital.

Ko-ko himself, it will be recalled, proved incompetent to perform the duties of his post, but satisfied his sovereign with an affidavit that he had done so and an explanation that the affidavit should not be interpreted literally. His very professional deficiencies proved essential to the preservation of the Royal House, while his symbolic discharge of his function tended to preserve freedom and order in the community. In his case, the personnel-selection system of Titipu worked; it put the right man in the job, thereby ensuring that the job never really got done. And this was exactly what was required.

In the more complex society of the United States, the function of the credential is often analogous, though not strictly so. What we require of a credential is that it reliably designate its holder as a person who will get part of his job done, will provide a symbolic substitute for those aspects of it that cannot be publicly denied without creating intolerable social strain but cannot really be performed without creating even more intolerable social strain, and who will unfailingly and discreetly discharge those of his functions that cannot be included in the job-definition or even admitted to be a part of it, but which the actual power distribution of his community requires. This is really more than was demanded of Ko-ko; for a public executioner's role provides little opportunity for partial fulfillment and hence little complexity. But it is no more than is demanded of a school superintendent as he struggles to reconcile what his community really wants to do about its Negro youth with what is officially required; or of a lawyer, or a business executive — indeed, of the practitioner of any profession old enough to have defined its obligations and its ethics under conditions very different from those under which it must now be practiced.

Therefore, when we award a social role and the status that goes with it to a candidate, we want to be sure that he has some skills that cannot tactfully be attributed to practitioners of the role he is seeking; and these will strongly affect his appraisal, though in disguised or covert terms. Communities want to be sure that teachers will control children whether or not this impedes learning; that policemen will enforce their mores regardless of what may have been formally taught about civil rights, before they hire them for the job. Few communities, however, would rest content merely with the reassurance that new recruits to positions of social responsibility understood the requirements of their position well enough to be willing and able to betray its traditions when these became socially dysfunctional. We demand that the credential also tell us something positive about the incompetence that we require as a part of a candidate's qualifications — about what Veblen calls his trained incapacity, or a horse-trader calls being well-broken. We expect it to assure us that the bearer will respect the conventional limits of the roles it makes available to him. To permit the members of a profession to make the fullest use of their technical powers would spoil the existing fit among society's various roles, impede the operation of its status system, and generate such hostility and mistrust as to jeopardize the place of the profession in the society. What tact and diplomacy do for individuals, trained incapacity does for role-definitions and role-expectations; and the credential must certify to that incapacity. A social worker must not only understand the dynamics of social stratification and of group work; he must be incapable of turning the poor on and using his skills to organize them into an effective political action group if he is to earn a good credential.

This is ironical, but not unusual, and is probably as true of most societies as of our own. What is new is that, in the United States, the accrediting function of the school has expanded so far that it issues not just licenses to enter particular trades or professions, or to continue more specialized education, but what amount to licenses to live. The schools have simply accepted the responsibility of recording and transmitting the kind of judgment of the candidate's personal qualities that a society less guilty about social stratification and less concerned to provide equality of opportunity would have left to private judgment, either of individuals or of cliques. Such judgments still affect recruitment and advancement crucially, even in our society; but they are acceptable as much more legitimate if supported by the credential of an official agency. The school grades students on citizenship and emotional adjustment, but this is less important than the fact that value judgments about the student's acceptability within the social structure permeate course grades as well, and at this level they cannot effectively be challenged as reflecting cultural bias. Similar judgments, as Aaron Cicourel and John Kitzuse have observed in *The Educational Decision-Makers* (Bobbs-Merrill, 1963), also strongly affect high-school counselors' judgments as to whether students should be admitted to a college-preparatory program and hence whether they will ever obtain a college degree at all.

I am not certain whether it would be fairer to say that in this way the school introduces into the student's credential a personal judgment masked as a bureaucratic assessment, or that it depersonalizes its students by in fact reducing what is most human about them to a rationalistic appraisal. Both, perhaps; and either would be bad enough in my judgment. Yet, even granting that these processes occur, it would still be logically possible for the school to alter its assessment according to the role the student was preparing to fill, to leave him with a dossier indicating that he might make a very good scientist but a poor office worker, an excellent revolutionary but a rather unpromising naval officer, and so on. And of course the school does this insofar as it takes account of different aptitudes and levels of performance in various subject-matter fields and records variations in personality among students as it perceives them. I am very skeptical, however, that these ways of accounting for variability and suiting the student to the available opportunities are effective over a very wide range of behavior or personality. Despite their terrifying array of testing and psychological services against which even the Constitution provides little defense, schools usually seem bent on turning out and labeling an all-purpose grind that will keep nobody awake.

This uniformity of viewpoint expresses a school mystique that pervades to a considerable degree every school I have observed, despite differences in location, curriculum, or social class served, even nationality. The mystique seems to be international. Of course there are tremendous differences as well; there are no up and down staircases, or any other kind, in glassy new suburban schools. But sooner or later, if one stays around, the characteristic flavor breaks through. I recall, for example, a five-day visit I made within the past year as a consultant to a high school widely — and justly — esteemed as one of the best in the United States for its academic standards and level of instruction. It had also just opened a magnificent new plant and was run with unusual urbanity. My hosts, or clients, had generously arranged for me to meet with student groups as well as staff under as little supervision as the routines of the place permitted. They could not, however, transcend the routines. There just was no way to permit a group of students to meet with me longer than a period unless we planned it that way — and then they had to. There was no place the students and I could sit together and smoke, even tobacco, while we talked. Nevertheless, after several days I had about concluded that this school was enough like a college in its atmosphere and its intellectual level to make the experience of attending it qualitatively different. Then, on the last day there was a fire drill during the morning, and the façade collapsed. Classes were interrupted, of course. Those like myself who happened to be in the library at the time were turned out hurriedly. The teachers and vice principals who had seemed bright and reasonably flexible during the discussions we had been having during the past four days turned into a horde of up-tight little men, blowing whistles and screaming at the youngsters, who were forbidden to talk as they marched out of the new glass and ferroconcrete structure into the snow. Several of the teachers looked a good deal more turned on, too, than they had during our seminars, now that they were really doing their thing.

Even in this nearly completely college-preparatory high school, its college-bound youngsters were still being assessed and recorded by a staff committed to a pattern of values that disparages qualities our colleges and our society could use a great deal more of. What kind of credential does the student get who refuses to interrupt intellectually exacting work in order to act out an imposed collective civic fantasy? Can he still get into a good college? Or are we going to make do with the talents of those who don't take themselves quite that seriously, or possess quite that much autonomy? What kind of credential does the student get who responds as I did to the principal's insistence that fire drills are required by law with the observation that extreme zeal in obeying the law is itself a *ressentient* way of behaving, and that a school that turns compliance with regulations into a devotional pageant is indoctrinating its students in servility as surely as it would be if it decked its halls with "Support your local police!" banners? This is, after all, a useful insight for a student of the social sciences to have, and one that comes rather easily at least to hippier high-school students; and there is a good chance that those who develop it earlier will make more honest artists and even more effective executives.

And if the school is justified in insisting, for the sake of its own internal order and commitment to the official values of the community, that fire drills take precedence over and must be used to disrupt its regular instructional activities, then where does a youngster turn to get away from this constraint and learn more freely, doing his own thing, unconcerned with fires, neither setting nor fleeing them? What kind of credential does he get? The answer is clear enough; he gets a term in juvenile hall as a truant and a credential that says he is either a delinquent or mentally ill. And, of course, he has even less chance to learn on his own than he has of sneaking through the meshes of school routines.

We must still explain, however, why society has become so rigidly insistent on subjecting all its youth to protracted formal socialization, and why, in any case, it has made the public-school system the single instrument of that process — except for the use of the Selective-Service System, which, in effect, extends the compulsory school-attendance age to 21 or so for middle-class male youth and provides an alternative form of compulsory socialization for school dropouts who are usually of lower status. As Paul Goodman has so often pointed out, our society permitted many alternative ways of growing up until a decade or so ago. Moreover, standardized testing has developed so massively in the United States, both in quality and in the scale of its enterprise, that it would be both simple and economical to furlough young people from school as long as they reported to the testing center for a day or two each year and demonstrated that they were making normal progress toward the prescribed goals of the curriculum. That no such social arrangement is provided suggests very strongly that the achievement of these goals, which must be defined in terms of openly demonstrable competence, constitutes little more than a pretext for compelling the student to submit to schooling and submerge himself in its routines. The content of the curriculum is of little significance except insofar as what is done with it conveys to the student the values, threats, and anxieties whose impact he is required to sustain. In schooling more than any other kind of communication the medium is surely the message.

And the school mystique provides the medium. Those who accept it well enough to emerge after 16 years with a favorable credential can usually be trusted to have sufficiently conventional goals, motives, and anxieties to find the larger social system into which they are released rewarding. To those who have learned to endure and even have fun in a small trap, the big trap built to a similar plan but on a much more lavish scale and with much richer bait looks like freedom. It offers, in any case, all they are likely to have learned to desire or even imagine. "TV dinner by the pool! Aren't you glad you finished school?" the Mothers of Inven-

tion chant, succinctly and sardonically, in "The M.O.I. American Pageant."
Most youngsters probably are.

But saturation of the young with the school mystique has, I believe,
more fundamental functions than creating a respect for our common cultural heritage as exemplified by a desire for gracious suburban living. To
survive the school and earn its commendation and support in gaining
access to desirable roles and status, the student must come to accept as
virtually inevitable certain value-positions that determine his most intimate responses to other people and to his own experience. These responses get built into his very nervous system in the form of an anxiety
gradient, and they set the limits of his life space by limiting how far he
can swing and how confidently he can resist the inroads of social sanctions
on his self-esteem. This, after all, is what socialization means.

Wide acceptance of the value-positions conveyed by the school mystique keeps our social institutions going and reduces conflict; it stabilizes
our society. But this is just another way of saying that the schools support
the status quo, and, particularly, that the restriction of opportunity to
those who come to terms with it virtually ensures that our society, in all
its echelons, will be led by people who either cannot conceive of better
social arrangements or despair of ever getting them adopted, and with
good reason. This seems to me the final irony — the school, by controlling
access to status on terms that perpetuate the characteristics of mass
society, while serving simultaneously as the registrar and guarantor of
competence, holds competence in escrow. And it does not release it until
competence has demonstrated, over a period of years and under a variety
of provocations, that its bearer has other qualities that make him unlikely
or even unable to direct his competence toward major social change. By
placing the school in control of the only legitimate channel to status and
power, we virtually ensure that those who gain status and power will use
them to perpetuate our difficulties rather than to create new and radical
solutions.

The problem is not that the schools are conservative — official social
institutions are inevitably conservative. The problem is in the nature of
what is to be conserved, of the specific social values of which the school
is custodian, and to which it demands adherence as the price of accredita-
tion. What are these values? They constitute a complex and seamless
pattern, but the following emphases are revealing: There is first an anxious
and sometimes brutal intolerance of deep feeling between persons, of
emotional commitment to others. This permeates school routines; love and
loyalty are violations of its code and are severely punished. In some ways
this is evident — the school forbids any kind of physical expression of
affection at the same time that it maintains and supports a teasing attitude
toward sexual attraction; its erotic ethos is basically that of a key club
with unpaid bunnies. Love between members of the same sex, though a

real and valid aspect of adolescent growth, is of course even more brutally punished, and hippiness, which refuses to limit itself by considerations of gender at all, is perhaps most condemned. Calm, gentle, long-haired boys arouse genuinely pathological hatred in physical education teachers.

But it is not only physical love and honest, personally expressive sexuality that get the school up tight. Affectionate regard and care among peers is contrary to standard operating procedure, which prescribes instead jolly, antagonistic co-operation and competition. The school breaks up what it calls peer groups bound together by strong personal ties as cliques, which it sees as anti-democratic and potential sources of resistance and subversion. In class, co-operation between friends is cheating. It is evident that this pattern of values is, or has been, functional in breaking youth to the demands of middle-class life in a mobile society dominated by impersonal bureaucratic structure. But the middle class itself has begun a strong revolt against the emptiness and lack of feeling this way of life imposes; not only is hippy youth primarily middle class, but industrial executives as well as isolated professionals have begun seeking a restoration of feeling and authenticity in group therapy sessions, T-groups, and other prostheses intended to replace the functions that friendship and respect for one's neighbor perform in cultures that do not stifle them.

For lower-status, or otherwise "culturally deprived" youth, the schools' insistence on impersonality is anathema. Murray and Rosalie Wax, in a continuing series of published studies of the effect of imposing formal education on the Oglala Sioux, have made it clear that this issue is the focus of a complete educational stalemate. Sioux children will not adopt American competitive folkways and refuse to respond to the teacher at all; adolescents sit in third grade year after year in derisive silence rather than meet the teacher's terms. Similar difficulties, as the Waxes point out, arise in encounters between lower-status urban youth and the schools; and one wonders why so common and serious a source of educational frustration has not resulted in a more flexible response to the children. But in the allocation of status and role the frustration is functional; it ensures that youngsters, whether Indian, Negro, or just unusually autonomous who refuse to be depersonalized will get bad credentials that will stigmatize them as lazy or slow learners, keeping them down without involving the school in a disagreeable overt conflict about values.

A related, and perhaps even more fundamental, aspect of the school mystique is its support of vulgarity, especially shabby-genteel vulgarity. If there is one single social function of the school on which, more than any other, a mass society depends for stability, it is this: the hazing of potential poets and critics into submission, depriving them of the self-confidence that might have turned them into prophets rather than technologists.

This is accomplished by investing authority in personnel who themselves obviously either do not understand the material they are dealing with or are either intolerant of contradiction or defend themselves by treating the whole issue as a "fun thing"; and by grouping together in class students of such different backgrounds that no meaningful discussion is possible. It is all in *Up the Down Staircase;* but though life in Calvin Coolidge High and its counterparts is sometimes farcical, its social function is deadly serious, and it works. By defining the role of the teacher and school officials as fairly low in status, society ensures that, though there will be many competent teachers, all students will nevertheless be exposed for significant periods of time to the cognitive style and emotional attitudes that pervade life at the "common man" level. The fact that higher-status students are unlikely to accept this view as their own, and that students of whatever social status who feel a need for freedom and personal expression will loathe it as constrictive is all to the good. The school does not perform its integrative function by convincing its students that the way of life of the common man is beautiful and his view of reality profound. Rather, it demonstrates to them, over and over, that the common man is going to win and they are going to lose, no matter who is right, so that if they are wise they will learn to avoid challenging him. The lesson is not that the system is admirable but that you can't beat it.

Most of us learn this lesson; later, if we become professors at a state university we simply assume that we mustn't buck the legislature. Our administrators depend on our having this insight to assist them in their funding. Most of the good credentials go to those who learn it early and well. And in this way a shifting sea of unhappy and resentful people who live by wheeling and dealing keep their society going and avoid breaking one another up in direct confrontation. But the poets become frightened and sound the alarm; they, at least, are faithful to their function:

> Face the day
> And walk around
> Watch the Nazis
> Run your town
> Then go home
> And check yourself —
> You think we're singing
> 'Bout someone else!
> But you're plastic people!
> I know that love
> Will never be
> A product of
> Plasticity![2]

the Mothers sing. And the schools bear some of the responsibility for the truth of their vision of the Great Society.

[2] "Plastic People" is from "Absolutely Free," words and music by Frank Zappa. © 1968 by Frank Zappa Music Inc. All rights reserved.

School officials desperately need more explanations for their failures and more suggestions for reversing such failures than they have received thus far. Some are beginning to realize that time is running out on them, and that they had better reform the schools quickly before ghetto unrest leads to rioting, to demands to take over the schools, and the white middle class exodus contributes to the final downfall of big-city public education.

The temptation in diagnosing how the schools have failed is to search for scapegoats. Actually, the entire institution of public education is to blame, as are the present conditions of urban life that it confronts.

Nobody can make the system work if the bureaucratic structure is not radically altered. State education laws, traditions, rules, and interlocking administrative relationships victimize anybody who comes into contact with the system — parents with legitimate complaints, people applying for teaching licenses, city officials developing community renewal programs, publishers struggling to get their textbooks and readers into the classrooms even after the principals and teachers have accepted them, teachers and principals waiting months to receive needed supplies from headquarters, and pupils in the classrooms. To maneuver through the bureaucratic maze of the New York City school system takes more patience and political connections than most people can ever hope to have.

It is almost impossible to innovate in the institution. Policy statements are only the beginning of the process. Those who make the decisions, even if they were more eager for reform, must negotiate with the professional staff to secure compliance with their directives. They must secure efficient coordination of the actions of all units carrying out the plans, and they must provide rewards and punishments that will ensure of compliance, institute performance measures, and evaluate how the plans actually worked. Legal and bureaucratic constraints, however, limit the power of the superintendent and the board over the headquarters and field staff, and reforms mandated from above are seldom carried out as they were intended.

Chester Barnard, a distinguished writer and theorist on administration, has noted that an order is never an order unless it is obeyed.[1] Barnard was

From *110 Livingston Street,* by David Rogers. Copyright © 1968 by David Rogers. Reprinted by permission of Random House, Inc.
[1] Chester I. Barnard, *The Functions of The Executive,* Cambridge, Mass.: Harvard, 1938, chapt. 12.

pointing to a central component of administrative authority, namely, that it exists only when it is regarded as "legitimate" by those in subordinate positions.

A MODEL OF BUREAUCRATIC PATHOLOGY

The New York City school system is typical of what social scientists call a "sick" bureaucracy — a term for organizations whose traditions, structure, and operations subvert their stated missions and prevent any flexible accommodation to changing client demands. It has all those characteristics that every large bureaucratic organization has, but they have been instituted and followed to such a degree that they no longer serve their original purpose. Such characteristics as (1) overcentralization, the development of many levels in the chain of command, and an upward orientation of anxious subordinates; (2) vertical and horizontal fragmentation, isolating units from one another and limiting communication and coordination of functions; (3) the consequent development of chauvinism within particular units, reflected in actions to protect and expand their power; (4) the exercise of strong, informal pressure from peers within units to conform to their codes, geared toward political protection and expansion and ignoring the organization's wider goals; (5) compulsive rule following and rule enforcing; (6) the rebellion of lower-level supervisors against headquarters directives, alternating at times with overconformity, as they develop concerns about ratings and promotions; (7) increasing insulation from clients, as internal politics and personal career interests override interests in serving various publics; and (8) the tendency to make decisions in committees, making it difficult to pinpoint responsibility and authority are the institution's main pathologies.[2]

Such characteristics are exaggerations of a number of administrative patterns that may not be bad if they are not carried too far. In the New York City school system, however, they are carried to the point where they paralyze the system in the face of rapid social changes that demand new administrative arrangements and programs.

Though the term "bureaucracy" usually has negative connotations in

[2] See Victor Thompson, *Modern Organizations,* New York: Knopf, 1961; Michel Crozier, *The Bureaucratic Phenomenon,* Chicago: University of Chicago Press, 1964; Robert K. Merton, "Bureaucratic Structure and Personality," in his *Social Theory and Social Structure,* Glencoe, Ill.: The Free Press, 1957, pp. 195–207; Chester I. Barnard, "The Functions and Pathologies of Status Systems," in William F. Whyte, ed., *Industry and Society,* New York: McGraw-Hill, 1946, pp. 46–83; James Worthy, "Organizational Structure and Employee Morale," *American Sociological Review,* April, 1950, pp. 169–79; F. L. W. Richardson and Charles Walker, *Human Relations in an Expanding Company,* New Haven: Labor and Management Center, 1948; and Warren G. Bennis, *Changing Organizations,* New York: McGraw-Hill, 1966. My "sick bureaucracy" model was derived from these works.

popular usage, I am using it here in a neutral sense, referring simply to social patterns associated with large scale organizations. There can be "good" and "bad" bureaucracy, and much of my analysis of the New York City school system, using the social science model of bureaucratic pathology, will include examples of "bad" bureaucracy.

The school system is set up to function as a "professional" bureaucracy, manned by more than 59,000 teachers and several thousand administrators and technicians. But the term "professionalism" has been given so many meanings, especially in school–community controversies, that little meaningful communication any longer occurs when school officials and community groups try to resolve their differences.[3] If we use the term in its conventional sense to refer to a combination of expertise and service to clients, the bureaucratic structure of the New York City school system clearly undermines the professionalism of its personnel. Service to clients and to the community are often secondary considerations for school officials who are more preoccupied with their own careers.[4]

This is to suggest, then, that "bad" bureaucracy is often associated with "bad" professionalism in the New York City school system, as, indeed, it is in many large civil service bureaucracies.[5] While it may be appropriate for teachers and supervisors to want a degree of autonomy from client pressures, as many professionals do, on grounds that they are better equipped to do the job of educating than laymen, they may use their autonomy for personal ends that do not include service to the community. Further, professionals who are protected from their clients are likely to be unaware of changes in their clients' needs. And bureaucratic pressures to follow particular curricula, texts, instructional methods, and administrative procedures, may prevent teachers and principals from actually educating. Bureaucracy and professionalism may be incompatible in the New York City schools.

If arresting the failure of the schools were just a question of revamping the bureaucracy, there might be more hope for improvement than there really is. But the situation is much more complex. The entire institution of public education, including teacher training, the professional associa-

---

[3] The term has been used as a slogan by school officials to defend themselves against outside attack ("We are professionals, and you, as laymen, have no right to tell us what to do").

[4] Political scientist Victor Thompson observes in his *Modern Organizations:* "When officials are caught between demands or "rights" of clients and tight administrative controls from above, dissociation from the clients and disinterest in their problems may seem to be the only way out of the dilemma. Client hostility, generated by what appears to be official emphasis on the wrong goals, creates tension. Inconsiderate treatment of the clients may become a device for reducing tensions and maintaining the cohesion of the officials." *Modern Organization,* New York: Knopf, 1961, p. 162.

[5] For social science writings on "bureaucracy" and "professionalism," see Howard M. Vollmer and Donald L. Mills, eds., *Professionalization,* Englewood Cliffs, N.J.: Prentice-Hall, 1966.

tions, and the technology of teaching, contribute to the schools' failures. While teachers and principals may know more about education than most laymen, they don't know very much. There is no codified body of knowledge that educators can learn and apply, as there is in medicine and law. Teacher training institutions reflect this in their curriculum, which is based on questionable and unvalidated principles of education, learning, and child development. The fact that these institutions often disregard the rapid demographic and social changes of the city, incapacitates their graduates further. There is little expertise to apply, despite any myths to the contrary.

Furthermore, the quality of people who go into public education careers is not very high. The situation may well be changing, but traditionally education has attracted the mediocre students in the colleges, often of provincial, lower middle class outlook, a large proportion of whom were women marking time before getting married.[6,7]

This combination of poor training and personal mediocrity is reflected in the limited confidence that many college educated, upper middle class people have in the public schools. Many regard Board of Education personnel as culturally and intellectually inferior, and send their children to private schools.

One has only to review the frustrating and tragic experiences of the system's many victims to realize how bad it is. Consider the case of a Puerto Rican mother with two children in schools on Manhattan's West Side.[8] Anyone who cares to can collect hundreds of case histories like this one:

> In the 5th grade, Billy did not seem to me to be reading as well as he should. In the Spanish Mothers Club at the school, we asked if remedial help could be given. There was only one remedial reading teacher so that only a few children could be helped. Then the Club asked if Columbia students could help. In the meantime I took Billy to Columbia myself for reading assistance. In March I went to see the teacher to find out how Billy was doing. The teacher said "very well." He will soon be reading a 5th grade book. In May I received a letter from the Assistant Principal asking me to come to school about Billy. I was told that Billy could not go to the 6th grade because he was reading on a 3.0 level. I was very upset and angry because it seemed to me that the school had done nothing for Billy. He stayed in the 5th grade for another six months. We continued the tutoring but the school gave him no additional

---

[6] It is unlikely, however, that the situation will change that much, given the irrelevant and tedious education courses that are required for licensing and later promotions, and given the fact that New York City school teachers are at the mercy of the bureaucracy and given little autonomy and responsibility.

[7] W. W. Charters, Jr., "The Social Background of Teaching," in N. L. Gage, ed., *Handbook of Research on Teaching,* Chicago, Rand McNally, 1963, pp. 718–723.

[8] A case study written up for civil rights groups.

help. If I had not found a way to help him, nobody else would have helped him. He is now in 10th grade and still has a reading problem which hurts his other studies.

When he went into the New York School of Printing, he needed algebra and science in order to take an academic program. The junior high school had told him that he would have an academic program. But when he got to high school, they refused to give it to him because he did not have these subjects. It was only through his and my persistence that they finally permitted him to take the academic program.

In kindergarten, Grace could read Billy's first reader. When she went to the first grade, she never received a reader. When I asked the teacher why, she said that Grace wasn't ready yet. In the first half of second grade, she had a good teacher and books. In the second half, a new teacher came in. She did not give her much work. In the third grade, the teacher told me that she was a brilliant child and warned me to be careful. She feared that Grace might be hurt by other teachers. She tried to help her and told me to get her help at Columbia. . . . For 4th grade the teacher tried to have Grace put into a "good" class. She was not successful. Instead, she was put into a class where she fell behind — she read the same books she had read in the 3rd grade. When the 3rd grade teacher asked the 4th grade teacher why she was using the same books, the 4th grade teacher became angry with Grace. In the 5th grade Grace seemed to do better. She had a teacher of Puerto Rican background and read 5th grade books. But in the 6th grade she tested at 4.6. The teacher did not give too much work. When I saw the teacher, he said Grace was "blocked." He seemed to feel it was because we spoke Spanish at home. In February, I noticed that Grace had nothing written in her notebook. She said that they were doing nothing in class. I spoke to the Assistant Principal about it. He looked at two notebooks from the class and saw that I was right. He was sorry about it but seemed to have no reason for it. I asked to have Grace's class changed. They asked me which class I wanted her in. I said a "good class" and they transferred her to a class with a teacher who taught. But this teacher told Grace that she didn't belong in her class. I told her not to worry and she remained in the class, where she did well. In March, the teacher in charge of a new program of teaching Spanish, asked Grace to take the program. Her 6th grade teacher said Grace could never make it. Grace insisted upon taking the program because she reads Spanish. She took the test for the program and passed it. She went on to the 7th grade even though her reading test showed a 4th grade level. She was never given any remedial reading in school.

She is now in the 9th grade and studies Spanish. Grace wants to be a teacher. We've been struggling not to make any mistakes so that she will be able to go to an academic high school. The junior high school wanted her to take General Math. She had to fight to get algebra. We knew enough to fight because of what happened to Billy and we won the fight.

WHY HAVE I HAD TO TAKE MY CHILDREN FOR OUTSIDE HELP? AND WHY DO THEY HAVE TO FIGHT TO GET THE KIND OF EDUCATION THEY WANT? I HAVE LEARNED HOW TO PROTECT MY CHILDREN AND IT IS STILL BAD. BUT WHAT ABOUT THE THOUSANDS OF MOTHERS WHO DON'T KNOW WHAT IS HAPPENING TO THEIR CHILDREN IN THE SCHOOLS?

BUREAUCRATIC CENTRALISM

Many of the pathologies of the New York City school system can be traced to the overcentralization of decisions, combined with the proliferation of specialized administrative units. Most decisions on such matters as curriculum, staffing, budgeting, supplies, construction, and maintenance are made by professionals at central headquarters, several layers removed from the schools themselves.[9] The headquarters personnel who make decisions do not know the problems directly, while district superintendents, principals, and teachers who do have some direct knowledge have never had the authority to adjust, experiment, and innovate, though a few adventurous types have taken it upon themselves to run their schools or classrooms as they see fit, without reference to headquarters.

Like any large bureaucracy that has to establish generalized rules for its field units, the Board of Education has a system of formulas and applies programs to schools as the schools fit into particular classifications — special service, transitional, segregated Negro-Puerto Rican, mid-range, segregated white. The system does not take into account gradations within each category, and so it minimizes its flexibility and effective use and distribution of supplies and personnel. While it may be important for large bureaucracies like this one with so many field offices and operating units to categorize and generalize about situations, they do so here with disastrous results. The categorizations are too gross, and many local variations and problems are overlooked.[10]

The NYC Board of Education is thus the prototype of what students of administration call "top-down" rather than "bottom-up" management.[11] Instead of looking at the particular school and community (with particular ethnic, socio-economic groups, local resources and institutions) and saying

[9] Marilyn Gittell, *op. cit.*, chapts. 4–6; and *Reconnection for Learning;* Cresap, McCormick, and Paget; Shinnerer; and Strayer and Yavner, all *op. cit.*
[10] Interviews with school officials, principals.
[11] See Eliot D. Chapple and Leonard R. Sayles, *The Measure of Management,* New York: Macmillan, 1961. The term "bottom-up" management was originally coined by a business executive, William B. Given, Jr., of the American Brake Shoe Company, in his book, *Bottom-up Management,* New York: Harper & Brothers, 1949.

"here is a school and community, now let's work with parent and community groups to set up an appropriate program," they say "here is a program, now let's see where it can go." Too many schools and communities have their own particular problems that do not fit into standard formulas and programs.

Originally there were valid administrative reasons for centralization — to guarantee uniform standards across the city, to preserve professional autonomy from outside political interference at the local level, to prevent ethnic separatism, and to maintain headquarters control over field officials.[12] Also, the sheer size and geographic spread of the system contributed to centralization. Many headquarters officials distrust field personnel and hesitate to delegate authority.

Another reason for centralization was the complexity of the social and psychological problems the system faced. Numerous agencies have been formed over the years — such as the Bureau of Child Guidance, the Bureau for Children with Retarded Mental Development, the Bureau of Physically Handicapped, the Bureau of Socially Maladjusted Children, the Bureau of Speech Improvement, the Bureau of Visually Handicapped, the Bureau of Community Education, the More Effective Schools Program, the Bureau of In-Service Training, the Offices of Zoning, Integration, and Human Relations to deal with these problems. These bureaus in themselves may be necessary, although they often may obstruct education.

The school budget has also led to increased centralization. The difficulties of getting allocations in the budget for more staff led to the practice of transferring more and more teachers to headquarters. Many were eager to escape the trials and stresses of the classroom and, in some cases, the authoritarian rule of the principal. This practice is now reportedly being reversed, but the net effect of the policy change is still limited. There are still nearly 700 teachers on assignment at headquarters, and federal programs will add to the number.[13] Many teachers at headquarters are engaged in tasks for which they are not trained, in auditing, business affairs, programming, human relations, and demographic analysis. There are also cases of teachers at headquarters who direct and monitor research studies, and some teachers perform jobs that could be done by a lower level clerical person. The existence of such headquarters positions helped drain away many competent people from the classroom, while contributing to incompetent and inefficient administration.[14]

---

[12] Interviews with school officials.

[13] Interviews with headquarters officials.

[14] It may also be true, however, as many informants in the system suggested, that putting teachers into headquarters jobs was one of the few ways to unburden the classrooms of incompetents.

The centralized set-up created other obstacles to efficient administration too. The grouping of units and personnel at headquarters violates many basic principles of rational administration, creating little unity of command, much duplication and overlapping of responsibilities, and confusion on who should report to whom.

Positions and tasks were simultaneously grouped along both divisional (elementary, junior high, high) and functional (curriculum, instruction, staffing) lines.[15] Field officials often receive numerous directives, some of them contradictory, from different sources. A publisher finds, for example, that his curriculum materials are welcomed by the board, the superintendent, and the divisions, yet they are not acceptable to some curriculum official who invokes a state education law to justify his authority. A music teacher wants to serve in a ghetto school, but instead gets assigned to a white, middle class school in Queens. When an opening appears in a southeast Bronx school, the Queens principal will not let her go, threatening to give her a bad rating if she leaves. When she goes to headquarters to plead her case before the deputy superintendent in charge of personnel, it takes her a day before she can reach his secretary, and she never does get to see him. Parents who go to headquarters to inquire about zoning regulations are often shunted from office to office without getting any clear answer to their requests.[16]

This pattern of multiple authority hampers the efforts of field personnel to integrate various programs, confronted as they often are with buck-passing when making requests at headquarters for information, facilities, and support. It results in considerable frustration in securing services and much resentment among community groups, local school board members, and field officials.[17]

Securing Services. In many experimental programs, most of which are in ghetto schools, there are long delays in securing textbooks and supplies.[18] Teachers report that they sometimes get supplies several months

[15] See Cresap, McCormick, and Paget, *op. cit.*, chapt. 2, p. 18; and Strayer and Yavner, *op. cit.*

[16] These are not hypothetical examples, but come from many actual situations.

[17] These pathologies have all been discussed in the many management studies on the New York City school system. Consider the following: "The major problems in the functioning of the existing organization are lack of organizational clarity, multiple assignment of functions, and lack of assignment for some important and vital functions." (Cresap, McCormick, and Paget, 1962, chapter 2, p. 16); "At present, communications within the school system contribute to considerable confusion. Field Assistant Superintendents, principals, and teachers complain about the plethora of memorandums, directives and requests, some of them conflicting, which flow from many different organizational units." (Cresap, McCormick, and Paget, *op. cit.*, chapter 2, p. 18.)

[18] Interviews with teachers, principals, and parent association officials. See also the *UPA Study of Supply Procedures in the Public Schools,* United Parents Associations, February 2, 1968.

or a year late; if they want to receive them in time to coordinate them with their programs, they pay for them out of their own pockets.[19]

There is a special problem for teachers who want to experiment with new books. They are required to follow prepared book lists that are sometimes out of date, and requests for new books are often turned down for unexplained reasons. A music teacher in an élite high school asked the assistant principal to permit her to order some new books that she felt should have been on the list but were not. "Some of the books on the list were out of date ten or twenty years ago," she reported. But the assistant principal told her that it was not within his authority or that of the principal to honor her request.

New materials are essential for curriculum change, and the present system makes it almost impossible to introduce such new materials. Curriculum officials have taken no initiative in encouraging publishers to create new materials, and the bureaucratic difficulties that publishers encounter discourage them from risking their capital in programs for urban children.

Many teachers complain that they can't get simple things like paper or chairs when they need them. "A school representative went to headquarters," one teacher reported, "to get some chairs. We needed them badly. He knew the size he wanted. Instead, they led him into a room with undersized chairs, for much younger kids and said 'take your pick.' He had no choice and finally took the chairs, and the kids have been putting their feet up on the desks ever since. There is no room for them to sit comfortably."[20]

Securing Staff. Staffing is an even worse problem. An NYU report on teacher mobility concludes that the present examination system and personnel procedures are in many respects relics of the past.[21] Methods that produced an adequate supply of trained teachers in the 1930s and forties no longer work in the sixties, when teachers are scarce, and the use of those methods produces ever-increasing percentages of substitute teachers: one-third were in this category in 1967.

[19] A recent study on the Bureau of Supplies by the UPA documents these points well. They found that it frequently took a year, and sometimes up to four years, to deliver supplies requisitioned by the NYC schools. They cited the following illustrations: "In one school movable blackboards ordered for a team-teaching project arrived 2½ years later. In another school 1,500 library books lay unused because there were no shelves in the library on which to place them. When a school sent a letter to the supply bureau requesting certain order forms, the bureau replied that these forms could not be requested by letter, but had to be requisitioned on a form that the school did not have." (*New York Times,* March 6, 1968, p. 50.)

[20] Interview with a teacher from one of the academic high schools.

[21] *A Report of Recommendations on the Recruitment, Selection, Appointment, and Promotion of Teachers in The New York City Public Schools,* Center for Field Research and School Services, New York University, 1966.

Bureaucratic entanglements at headquarters made the problem worse. Several headquarters units were involved in staffing decisions, and principals often had great difficulty in getting teachers and supervisors. Dr. Paul Warner, principal at a newly opened, segregated junior high school in The Bronx, JHS 145, tells the following story:[22] "Upon my designation as principal," he wrote, "I conferred with this bureau [the Bureau of Appointment] and was assured that the new school would receive top priority." Despite the many visits to the bureau he made throughout the summer as the desperateness of his situation became more and more apparent, procedural confusions at headquarters prevented him from making any headway. The bureau assigned him only eight regular teachers for the whole school. The rest were substitutes who had not been highly enough regarded by their principals to be asked back.

An indication of the bureau's inefficiency in the matter was that two teachers requested appointments at 145 but were instead reappointed to their current schools, even though there were many regular teachers serving in these schools in their subject areas. Headquarters thus unwittingly subverted Warner's efforts to open his school fully staffed.

His supervisory situation was also critical. Although it was informal board policy to provide three or four assistant principals to ghetto schools, only one woman, who had served for only one year in another school, was assigned to 145. Warner notes further that "two assistant principals applied for transfer and their applications were properly endorsed, but they were rejected by the bureau because of the current 'freeze' on transfers. The freeze has the clear and tenable purpose of impeding an exodus of assistant principals from special service schools until another list of eligibles appears. However, the freeze should not apply to new schools — particularly special service ones."

Principal Warner's dealings with the junior high school division were even more bizarre. He met with a representative of the division in the spring and inquired about transfers and available substitutes. He went back in July, but Holmes, the division official, did not know at the time what appointments would be made. Holmes was away in August, and when he returned on September 11 he was cooperative but was confronted with the impossible task of sorting out lists of available substitutes and making assignments in the week before school opened.

"I learned," Warner went on to say, "that some high school substitutes might not be assigned. After reviewing the addresses of all substitutes not likely to be reached for high school assignments, I mailed about one hundred letters. Some twenty substitutes responded and most of them

[22] *Staffing of JHS 145: A Review and Analysis,* Paul Warner, Principal, 1966, mimeographed statement.

indicated a desire to join us. However, under the contract, assignment had to be made by Mr. Holmes. It was impossible to reach him by telephone, and he informed me subsequently that he was swamped with a backlog of mail. At one point, I sent him a telegram. Because I was unable to hire these substitutes, all of them took positions elsewhere, many in other school systems."[23]

Warner did receive help from the Board of Examiners, which gave emergency examinations; from the district superintendent; and from the elementary school division, which furnished twelve substitute teachers. Nevertheless, his school had thirteen vacancies as late as October 19. Many people Warner considered competent could not be licensed because they did not meet the minimum course requirements.

Principal Warner understood some of the causes of his difficulty. "Nothing that I write is intended to reflect adversely on the personal qualities or cooperative spirit of the people charged with responsibilities concerning personnel. I found them to be friendly in spirit and cooperative in attitude. I am convinced that our school's extreme difficulties arose from organizational and procedural problems." The fundamental pathology of the system, then, is the source of the trouble, not just the incompetence of particular units or people.

All the pathologies of the system get played out most dramatically in the ghetto schools. Teachers and principals, as well as pupils and the wider community, are beaten down and demoralized by experiences there.

The PEA study of 1955 and the Urban League study of 1963 showed that ghetto schools got fewer services than the others in New York City. The recent Sheldon-Glazier fact book, *Pupils and Schools in New York City*, documents this with reference to staffing.[24] Only 8% of the Negro-Puerto Rican segregated elementary schools had more than 65% regularly licensed teachers, while 68% of the segregated white elementary schools did.[25] While ghetto schools have many more compensatory programs and more expenditures per pupil than segregated white schools, the bureaucracy prevents the coherent, integrated use of these "special services," as extra teachers and staff don't understand each others' role and the frag-

---

[23] Numerous interviews with principals, teachers, and parents suggest that Warner's experience was quite common.

[24] *The Status of the Public School Education of Negro and Puerto Rican Children in New York City*, prepared by the Public Education Association, October, 1955: *A Study of the Problems of Integration in New York City Public Schools Since 1955*, Urban League of Greater New York, September, 1963; and Eleanor B. Sheldon and Raymond A. Glazier, *Pupils and Schools in New York City*, New York: Russell Sage Foundation, 1965.

[25] Board data on educational resources in Bronx schools, analyzed by the United Bronx Parents, indicate that ghetto schools consistently get a higher proportion of inexperienced and substitute teachers than schools in middle class white areas.

mentation is even worse than before. In New York City, compensatory programs for ghetto schools usually mean more of the same. But these schools don't need more of the same. They need innovation, which is what the bureaucracy won't permit.

JONATHAN KOZOL   *Death at an Early Age*

There is a booklet published by the Boston Public Schools and bearing the title "A Curriculum Guide in Character Education." This booklet was in the desk of my new classroom and so, as few things are explicitly stated to you and so much must be done by guessing within these poorly run schools, I made the guess that I was supposed to look at it and perhaps make use of it. I did look at it but I did not make use of it. I kept it, however, and studied it and I have it in front of me now.

The booklet, really, is little more than an anthology broken down according to the values which the Boston School Committee hopes to instill or inspire in a child. This is the list of character traits which the teacher is encouraged to develop in a child:

> CHARACTER TRAITS TO BE DEVELOPED: OBEDIENCE TO DULY CON-
> STITUTED AUTHORITY . . . SELF-CONTROL . . . RESPONSIBILITY . . .
> GRATITUDE . . . KINDNESS . . . GOOD WORKMANSHIP AND PERSEVER-
> ANCE . . . LOYALTY . . . TEAMWORK . . . HONESTY . . . FAIR PLAY.

Two of the things that seem most striking about this list are (1) the emphasis upon obedience characteristics and (2) the way in which the personality has been dissected and divided and the way in which consequently each "character trait" has been isolated and dwelt upon in the manner of a list of favorable characteristics in the eulogy at a funeral or in the citation of an honorary degree during a commencement ceremony. You look in vain through this list for anything that has to do with an original child or with an independent style. You also look in vain for any evaluation or assessment or conception of the human personality as a full or organic or continuously living and evolving firmament rather than as a filing cabinet of acceptable traits.

The section on obedience characteristics begins with the following verse: "We must do the thing we must Before the thing we may; We are unfit for any trust Till we can and do obey." It goes on to list the forms that obedience can take and it recommends a list of "selected memory gems" having to do with compliance to authority. Some of them are good and some are by famous people, but all of them, coming at you this way, out of context, have a killing, dull effect. They come one after another, some good, some dumb, and leave you feeling very obedient:

> Honor thy father and thy mother [is the first one]. He who knows how to obey will know how to command . . . Obedience to God is the best evidence of sincere love for Him . . . True obedience is true liberty . . . The good American obeys the laws . . . Help me to be faithful to my country, careful for its good, valiant for its defense, and obedient to its laws . . . He who would command others must first learn to obey . . . The first law that ever God gave to man was a law of obedience . . . My son Hannibal will be a great general, because of all my soldiers he best knows how to obey . . . Obedience sums up our entire duty . . . The first great law is to obey . . . Children, obey your parents in all things; for this is well pleasing to the Lord . . . Wicked men obey from fear; good men from love . . . We are born subjects and to obey God is perfect liberty. He that does this shall be free, safe, and happy . . . Obedience is not truly performed by the body if the heart is dissatisfied . . . Every day, in every way it is our duty to obey. "Every way" means prompt and willing, Cheerfully, each task fulfilling. It means, too, best work achieving Habits of obedience, weaving. To form a cable firm and strong With links unbreakable and long: To do a thing, at once, when told A blessing, doth the act enfold. Obedience, first to God, we owe; It should in all our actions show . . . If you're told to do a thing, And mean to do it really, Never let it be by halves, Do it fully, freely! Do not make a poor excuse Waiting, weak, unsteady; All obedience worth the name Must be prompt and ready.

Of all the quotations included in this list, I think there are only two which are deeply relevant to the case at hand: "Wicked men obey from fear; good men from love" — this comes from Aristotle. And: "Obedience is not truly performed by the body if the heart is dissatisfied," which comes from the Talmudic scholar Saadia. Both of these quotations are directly applicable to the exact problem exemplified by the kind of school system in which such a list could be seriously employed. If it is true, as Aristotle wrote, that wicked men obey from fear and good men from love, then where else is this more likely to become manifest than within these kinds of penitential schools? One thinks of the pathos of anxiety with which teachers and principals go about their duties, seldom out of respect for their superiors, which in so many cases is impossible, but out of an abject fear of being condemned or of being kicked out. I think of the Art Teacher confiding to me in an excited whisper: "Can you imagine that this principal honestly and truly can stand there and call herself an educator? It's the biggest laugh of the school year." The Reading Teacher, with equal vehemence, talking about my supervisor: "That man doesn't know as much about elementary education as the first-year substitutes do. You'll have to agree to whatever he says and then ignore it when he's gone." To these people, whom they held in deeply justified contempt, both women paid ample lip-service. If ever they were honest, I do not see how they could have avoided holding both themselves and each other in some portion of the same contempt.

Saadia's eloquent statement that "obedience is not truly performed by the body if the heart is dissatisfied" seems also appropriate to the Boston public schools. For the heart *is* dissatisfied here, and the obedience *is* perfunctory, and the whole concept of respect for unearned and unde-served authority is bitter and brittle and back-breaking to children, whether rich or poor, or black or white, within these kinds of schools. Only the authority of visible character demands respect. No other kind deserves it. No child in his heart, unless drugged by passivity, will pay obeisance to authority unless authority has earned it, and authority based upon political maneuvering and upon the ingestion and assimilation of platitudes is an authority which no person, white or Negro, adult or child, should respect. There is too much respect for authority in the Boston schools, and too little respect for the truth. If there were more of the latter, there would be less need of the former and the atmosphere of the Boston schools would not have to be so nearly what it is today: the atmosphere of a crumbling dictatorship in time of martial law. The emphasis both in this one booklet and in the words of the school administration in general upon the need for dumb obedience belies its deepest fear.

Another section of the "Character Education" booklet has to do with self-control:

"Teach the necessity for self-discipline by all people" the teacher is advised. Guide the children through discussion to recognize the necessity of self-discipline . . . Responsible, self-disciplined people are an asset to the community . . . People in a community should live by principle, not by emotion . . . Emergencies are met by disciplined people, e.g., pilots, drivers, teachers, pioneers, policemen, firefighters, doctors, nurses, Ameri-can Red Cross workers, clergymen, astronauts . . . Disciplined people make good neighbors . . ." The teacher is next told to "select many examples of self-disciplined people and discuss events in their lives which exemplify self-control, e.g., Abraham Lincoln, Louis Pasteur, Robert Fulton, Thomas Edison, Charles Lindbergh, Robinson Crusoe, Daniel

Boone, George R. Clarke, Helen Keller, Florence Nightingale, Clara Barton, Dwight D. Eisenhower, Dr. Tom Dooley, Dr. Albert Schweitzer.

The unit on "good workmanship and perseverance" puts forth another list of famous men, several of them the same ones as before. The list in this case is notable partly for the odd discrepancies between the statures of the different people who are involved and partly, simply, for the heavy and thudding and skull-hammering manner in which the whole thing is gotten across:

> Discuss the perseverance and good workmanship of (1) Individuals whose inventions have made our way of life easier, e.g., Gutenberg, Watts, Whitney, Bell, Edison, Howe, Wright. (2) Individuals whose research has made it possible for us to be safer from disease, e.g., Curie, Roentgen, Lister, Pasteur, Salk, Sabin. (3) Individuals who have shown good workmanship in spite of physical handicaps, e.g., Demosthenes, R. L. Stevenson, Helen Keller, Steinmetz, Dr. Tom Dooley, President Roosevelt, President Kennedy, Mayor John F. Collins. (4) Individuals whose artistry has provided us with pleasure, e.g., a. Music — Chopin, Mozart, Schubert, Leonard Bernstein, Arthur Feidler [sic], etc. b. Authors — Dickens, Anderson, Longfellow, Alcott, Stevenson, etc. c. Artists — Raphael, Michelangelo, Millet, Grandma Moses . . .

When I look at this list, I find myself wondering who on earth could ever have put it all together and I also wonder whether anyone really thinks that you are going to teach character, or anything, to children by rattling off a list of all the people in the world or in America or in Boston who have struggled to make good. "Like a postage stamp, a man's value depends on his ability to stick to anything until he gets there." This is quoted from someone by the name of Chamberlain. "Excellence is never granted to man, but is a reward of labor," is quoted from Reynolds. "Do the very best you can today and tomorrow you can do better," says someone named M. Vanbee. Can teachers and children be expected to take this seriously? And who is it who bears responsibility for this soul-drowning dreariness and waste of hours? With material as bad as this, surely it is no wonder that the matter of motivation has become such an overriding factor in the considerations of those who administer these schools. It cannot be unexpected that motivation becomes the all-important obstacle when the material is so often a diet of banality and irrelevance which it is not worth the while of a child to learn or that of a teacher to teach.

This seems to be a central issue. For the problem of motivation is talked about endlessly in Boston, and the point has been made repeatedly in the writings of Miss Sullivan and others that the motivational difficulty has its origin in the children and in their backgrounds, rather than in the teachers or the schools. I think the opposite is true. But the predictability with this wrong assertion has been restated suggests the nervousness which the school administration of this city must experience in regard to its own failure.

"How can we motivate these culturally deprived in-migrant minorities to learn?"

This is the form of the standard question. The blame, in almost all cases, is immediately placed upon the child's background and his family. Then, but only after it has divested itself of prior responsibility, does the school administration come forward to profess a willingness to do what it can. Miss Sullivan, for example, in putting forward the aims of the compensatory program designed for Negro children, presented such an attitude in the following words: This endeavor, she said, "is a preventive program designed to catch undesirable situations in their incipiency, to improve children's attitudes toward school, to inspire standards of excellence which should be carried over into secondary education for all and beyond for many. It is our hope through this program to raise the achievement of these pupils closer to their potentials which have for too long been submerged by parental lack of values."

The last phrase is a defensive one. It suggests that the child be granted full mercy, high pardon and even a certain amount of compassion just so long as it is made absolutely clear ahead of time that the heart of the problem is the lack of values of his parents. I don't think that the Negro parents lack values. I think the people who administer the Boston school system do. To go a bit further, honestly, I do not understand what is implied by such a phrase as "the lack of values" of the culturally deprived. I think that when we are faced with an expression of that kind, we have to ask whose values we are talking about and "deprived" in the eyes of whom? To say that Negroes in Boston are deprived of rights would be an honest statement. It would also be honest to say that they are deprived of good schools and that, along with this, they are deprived of a fair chance, of democracy, of opportunity, and of all the things these words are supposed to mean. But to say that they are deprived culturally, in the face of Boston's School Superintendent, in the face of Mrs. Hicks, in the face of the profound cynicism of the entire system, seems to me meaningless. The phrase "cultural deprivation" has not met with a great deal of favor among Negroes and is, as a consequence, going out of fashion quickly with white liberals. Needless to say, it is still a fervent catch-cry in the Boston schools.

Edgar Friedenberg has written recently that the education and assimilation of Negro people provide American society with one of its last chances "to transfuse into itself a stream of people whose moral vision has been — relatively, at least — preserved and sharpened by exclusion from opportunities for self-betrayal as well as self-advancement." If people regret, as some must, the exclusion of Negroes from opportunities for advancement, there is at least reason to be grateful for an equal exclusion from opportunities for self-betrayal. Too many white people in Boston are compromised, to the point of seeming almost impotent, because they have been, not by others, but by themselves essentially betrayed. There is also the problem of those who, having grown up in low status, are determined, once their head is a little bit above water, to make the next generation of unlucky people pay. One man at my school, the redneck teacher I have quoted often, once said to me in his usual frankness that he had been beaten all around and treated rough and whipped and so on by his parents or teachers or both when he had been a child. To him, this seemed to clear the field for beating others around today. The attitude of many older people in our school system has been consistent with this view: "We had a hard time of it, so why shouldn't they?" This less than gentle attitude is characteristic of a less than gentle city in which the overriding outlook of those who are moderately successful is too likely to be that they have got theirs and the others can damn well wait a while before they get the same. Friedenberg has also written in a somewhat different context that former prisoners make bad jailers. A corollary to this is that former slum-residents make poor landlords. And former Irish boys beaten by Yankee schoolmasters may frequently make ungenerous teachers for little boys whose skins are black. The matter of where the real values lie seems to me to be the final important question of this book.

You can't, obviously, say things like this without bringing down professional resentment on your head. In a school system like Boston's, where there is so little inward credential for service, the outward credential counts for a great deal. For the lack of such credentials, therefore, any straightforward critic is apt to be condemned. Ushers take their usher-uniforms seriously. In Boston, teachers take their degrees and accumulated credits seriously and administrators take their political positions as a palliation for their inward sense of empty space. Mechanical credentials make up for genuine ones in this system and it is precisely in this manner that fragile bureaucracies have often defended themselves and their areas of power from the dangers of real life. That same blunt redneck teacher at my school who spoke with so much honesty on most topics once made this remark to me while we were chatting:

> They talk about the Negroes being culturally deprived. I'm the one who's been goddamn culturally deprived and I don't need anyone to tell me. I haven't learned a thing, read a thing, that I wished I'd read or learned since the day I entered high school, and I've known it for years and I tried to hide it from myself and now I wish I could do something about it but I'm afraid it's just too late.

Few people in Boston have the openness to talk that way. The man who spoke those words will probably be a principal some day. I think he will probably be a much better principal than most, if for no other reason than that he knows so well what he is lacking. But how many other people in our city will ever allow themselves even that degree of insight? And how many of those others, who may have the superficial trappings and the polysyllables of "culture," will ever stop to think of some of the deeper and truer things that culture ought to be about?

ROBERT A. DENTLER   *For Local Control*
                                     in the Schools

It remains an open question whether New York City will be able to reassemble its Humpty-Dumpty public school system, let alone put it back on the wall. And if it must lie forever broken on the ground, it will have been broken not by the quest for neighborhood control and not by the fears of teachers, but by the inexorable, cumulative push of decades of public and corporate neglect.

If all or some parts of the system get back into operation, the great fall may produce important positive changes. We must hope that one of these will be a change in the quality of transaction between the diverse cultures of the poor and the culture of the city school.

Most city public schools appear to operate as local institutions, but in fact they depend for staffing, funds, material supply, and management upon vast structures which go beyond city boards and superintendents to encompass state education departments and federal agencies. And, from the nonpublic sector, they are the creatures of unions of custodians, support personnel, and teachers; and the consumers of the great and growing education industry.

Vast as these intersecting bureaucracies, unions, and corporations may be, they have never come abreast of the growth in scale common to population, technology, or social organization in the cities and states that nurture them. So short of the mark are they in New York City that staffing of teachers is seldom completed in neighborhood schools by opening day each September. New neighborhood schools are never built on schedule. School procurement and supply procedures are no longer sources of graft. But they are now so complicated that school principals in New York City complain that supplies are delivered one and two years behind schedule. Instructional materials are often delivered after the lesson has been taught. Once this would have mattered very little: the same textbooks could be used for a decade without objection. Now, with increasing attention being given to the sciences and social studies, fresh materials, texts, and equipment matter a great deal.

Many improvements began to occur in New York City schools in the late fifties and early sixties. These resulted in part from greatly increased state aid. In spite of substantial increases, however, per pupil expenditures in surrounding suburbs are still, on the average, 30 to 45 per cent greater than those in New York City. State aid, while vast, has never gone to New York City in a way that equalizes expenditures between city and suburb. Indeed, the gap between poor city and rich suburb has widened yearly since 1955.

All of this is important, but it is not the heart of the crisis in New York City education. Indeed, Coleman and Campbell demonstrated in their great study, *Equality of Educational Opportunity*, that student achievement is very weakly associated with differences in dollar expenditures, plant facilities, and administrative practices. Instead, school achievement is a product of socioeconomic background, pupil attitudes, and quality of instruction.

Out-of-school environment and student background are the strongest predictors of in-school achievement, chiefly because these are the determinants of the teacher's expectations. As a New York City teacher wrote in a letter to *The New York Times*.

> Every teacher knows . . . the causative role of this tangle of pathology in the personality of the reluctant learner. And no amount of manipulation of the ghetto child's school experience is likely to modify his pattern of low achievement regardless of the label under which the manipulation masquerades — decentralization, community control or experimentation. For a child hounded by a broken home, poverty, inadequate housing and job opportunities for parents, drug addiction and by manifold other forms of delinquency, marked deficiencies in the qualities vital for success in school such as interest, initiative, and industry are inevitable.

This is the characteristic mind-set of the veteran public school teacher. That a child can be "hounded" by an intact family and wealth is not mentioned.

Public school teachers everywhere tend to reinforce the standard notions about achievement of their middle-class-oriented pupils. Their own success in school resulted, usually, from the fit between their own social class origins, which may spring from parent aspirations as much as from occupational position, and those of their teachers.

New York City public education is of a piece with American public education as a whole, and the national fabric is astonishingly standardized. The public elementary school, regardless of equipment and administrative superstructure, tends to welcome and reward the child who arrives in the first grade speaking standard English, who can be trained readily toward conformity, and who is diligent in his application to conventional school tasks.

The culture of the public schools built up this form between 1880 and 1930. The culture was one that welcomed children from all backgrounds — *if* each child made plain his readiness to absorb the culture of the school. The children of only a small proportion of millions of European immigrants were effectively assimilated by this culture, contrary to popular myth. Those who were not withdrew between the fifth and eighth grades. Those who went on to high school — one in ten before World War I, and one in twenty until the Great Depression — were those who had made the school culture their own.

Many critics of this school culture know little of its history and less about how cultures develop within urban service institutions. They speak glibly about rigidity, insularity, and bureaucratic pathology. They forget that the culture of New York City public schools evolved under persistent conditions of public indifference, short funding, and ethnic and class conflict. Its carriers, the teachers and officers, learned early to toughen themselves against these conditions. Like their counterparts in the professions of nursing and social work, they learned to turn a stern face outward upon a seemingly hostile milieu. Among themselves, they rewarded sheer endurance, and they punished those who revealed to the public a flair for innovation.

CULTURE CHANGES

The culture of New York City public schools has changed since 1930. Having built some things in which to take enduring pride and having attracted increased public attention and better funding, this culture has become less regimented, more respectful of the social origins of its students, and more relaxed in its formalistic demands.

But these changes have all been matters of degree. The basic city school culture is as adient as the essentially medieval culture of the university. What has changed in kind is the situation of the incoming public school student.

The symbol of this transformation is the Negro child from the impoverished neighborhood. The culture which sustains him has its rugged constancies too: His parents hope he will achieve well enough to gain a good job, but they remain suspicious of certain aspects of intellectual endeavor. His relatives and friends assume that the local public school is a necessary yet foreign agent: an essential instrument of growth with some intentions that are culturally subversive.

The culture of the impoverished Negro family and its neighborhood is, like other cultures, wise and complex. The local public school is viewed with suspicion: it is not truly part of the neighborhood; it is inhabited by outsiders whose predecessors did not do well by the neighborhood in previous generations. But this view is masked, for the school is also the safest, quietest, and warmest place for a child to be on a winter day. What is more, some of the teachers are sources of encouragement. Thus the family and neighborhood culture of the urban poor offers a mixed disposition toward its public schools. Each child may select those elements that reinforce his unique hopes and fears. There is room, at least in the first four years, for rationalizing individual success or failure.

Indeed, the views of low-income parents and their children toward teachers, public schools, school materials, and programs reflect a sometimes sanguine, sometimes diffident disposition. This disposition pervades the local public climate, in spite of the keen anger and mobilizing calls of insurgent leaders and neighborhood spokesmen.

Since World War II, this neighborhood culture has changed. The volume of children entering first grade and unable to speak school-standard English has increased. Standards of social control among children in all subcultural groups have also changed. In impoverished neighborhoods, standards of conduct never fitted the demands of the school culture; but the disparity has increased year by year.

For a time, the school response to these changes was clinical. Three times as many Negro children were diagnosed as retarded and were remanded to institutional care as were white children in New York City in the late 1950s. Three times as many were diagnosed as emotionally disturbed or socially maladjusted and were sent to special schools.

But public interest in special education remained low, and clinical facilities were not expanded significantly. The disruptive child — the label for a child who refuses to adopt the standards of social conduct peculiar to schools — became the focus of concern. This was evident first in the 1950s, when slum schools were stereotyped as blackboard jungles. Then the disruptive pupil was seen as a juvenile offender, an adolescent gang member. Today the disruptive child crops out with stereotypical force in the fourth and fifth grades. He is too young to be a gang member, and besides, fighting gangs are themselves passé.

The child of the poor also speaks a different brand of English, if he speaks English at all. He also rejects the mode of docility expected of him;

he rejects it earlier; and his rejection is shared by greater numbers of his fellow students than was the case in the past.

Nor will this child manifest scholastic diligence in the old manner. The busy work of copying, penmanship, crayoning, and recitation, all of them the basis in the past for displaying earnest intent, no longer makes the day for the student. His once latent suspicions are now manifested in disruption or in apathy. This has always been a part of the classroom drama in the slum neighborhood school, but now it can become epidemic.

Few of these changes appear in first or second grade. They begin to percolate in the third and fourth grades and to boil over in the seventh and eighth. New York City principals tend to place their newly recruited teachers in third-grade positions. These teachers (themselves ill prepared for accommodation to the thick-skinned culture of the school) experience something like culture shock as they discover the poorness of fit between their own notions of teaching and the conduct of their pupils. Under the impress of veteran teachers, the shock is converted into traditional interpretations. The new recruit comes to believe that the school "cannot make up" for what is "lacking at home and in the neighborhood."

THE QUEST FOR LOCAL CONTROL

The source of the New York City school crisis is embedded in this faulty transaction between young students and their teachers. The impoverished parents understand this. They also understand that the rise of teacher unionism has seldom had much to do with changing the quality of that transaction. Unionism aims at a struggle for better wages, better working conditions, and enlarged control over the decision process. It does *not* aim directly at changes in teacher training, certification, and assignment procedures that might improve the quality of teacher personnel within poor neighborhoods. Teacher unionism sometimes reinforces what is culture-bound within the city system. It need not do so, but it has, and this trend is apparent to poor Negro and Puerto Rican parents.

The quest for local control as a remedy has grown out of the rise in New York City of new leadership spurred by federal antipoverty programs, by the alienation experienced among civil rights leaders as a result of the failure to secure school desegregation, and by the growth of the black power movement.

The impoverished parent can respond to the call by local leaders for increased local control. The call is tangible; it offers a way to make the neighborhood school an indigenous rather than a foreign agent. It addresses the suspicions he harbors, with good reason, toward public schools. The call is for more than citizen participation or parental involvement. The neighborhood parent has seen the spectator approach before, and it has resulted in little that was useful to him. Local control, in contrast, evokes the dreams of controlling the fates of the education of his children.

With decentralization one might remove or censure an incompetent or culturally indifferent school officer. With decentralization one might hire superintendents and principals who seemed capable of community leadership. With decentralization one could press for the transfer of insensitive or incompetent teachers. The parent has little interest in running the school himself. But he wants to be able to trust its agents and to "throw the rascals out."

Critics of decentralization always point out how dangerous it could be to obligate educators to be highly responsive to local neighborhood needs and interests. They fail to note how dangerous it has been to build a separate school culture which is in many respects highly unresponsive to neighborhood cultures. Of course, an extreme obligation would prove undesirable: little academic growth can occur without tension between teacher and learner. But this tension should be intellectual and it must be grounded in respect for the culture and personality of the student.

Besides, the case for increasing local control is already at hand in the I.S. 201 experiment in Harlem. There, the school culture persists, but it has been richly intertwined with other cultural influences. Language arts, social studies, music, physical education, assemblies, and graduation ceremonies are observably enriched by the efforts of the 201 Unit's Planning Board. Moreover, parents are pleased and excited by new opportunities to take on leadership responsibilities, to aid in teaching, and to do all of the things which have long been customary in white suburbs. These are things which add up to the practice of local democracy.

WHAT THEY WANT

The practice of democracy includes the employing and policy guidance of professionals. Ghetto neighborhood parents have little time to invest in operating their schools from day to day. But they do want to change current relations between paid professionals and themselves.

They want to help select the professional leadership, set some of the goals, and judge the overall performance. What they want is what privileged suburban and small-town taxpayers have had routinely for more than a century.

The enormous historic wrongs that have been visited upon minorities in the United States will not be righted by singling minorities out as peculiar groups and then planning programs *for* "them." Rather, they will be righted when *all* citizens participate in the making of some of the decisions that affect their lives. The era of benevolent patronage is over, and the quest for increased local control over policy-making in big-city education demonstrates this change.

No one believes that decentralization will result directly in better teaching and learning. As with other policy changes, the details of execution will govern the value of the policy. But decentralization *can* repair parts of the old breach between school and community. University men who think this an inconsiderable gain have learned very little from the rise of the alienated adolescent.

The Universities

Much can happen in five years. Irving Howe chided his Stanford University students in 1964 for their scant interest in life outside the offices and suburbs of California:

> I lecture to a class at Stanford, a class of bright-cheeked, good-hearted innocents:
> "Tell me now, apart from grades, politeness and caution: do the questions raised by Ivan Karamazov in his talks with Alyosha seem to you deeply, burningly relevant to the life you expect to lead when you get back to your offices and suburbs in California?" Not many can honestly say Yes. The dull students say No with ease; The bright ones No with disturbance. "But then," I continue, "it means that the past exists for you as something confined to the classroom, an exercise (at best) in piety. I, your odd professor from the east, nevertheless have the impudence to say: I will try to persuade, bludgeon, excite and coax you into believing that Ivan Karamazov's words are burningly important to your life. That is an assumption, you reply, which threatens the whole way of life you have chosen for yourselves. . . . My dears, you are right."[1]

[1] Irving Howe, "Universities and Intellectuals," *Dissent* (Winter, 1964), p. 11.

Somebody, perhaps Irving Howe, perhaps Dostoyevsky, perhaps Bob Dylan, succeeded beyond their wildest expectations. The bright-cheeked, good-hearted innocents were persuaded, bludgeoned, excited, and coaxed into growing beards and sometimes taking to the streets to fight for opinions that become burningly important to them. By the summer of 1969, David Harris, erstwhile Stanford student body president, had become a leader of the resistance and occupied a jail cell as a political prisoner. In five years, student protest had turned many American campuses into arenas of political conflict.

To many people both in and out of the universities, the very idea that the campus might be politicized is abhorrent, for this conflicts with a cherished image of the university as a place of free inquiry, academic values, and "stability," in brief, an institution whose fundamental concerns transcend politics. According to this view, the university is a *community* sharing a common culture; and it stands apart from both internal political conflict and external political influence. A kind of sacredness has been conferred of the university as an institution. In fact, however, the American university has long ceased to be — if it ever was — purely a community of shared values. Faculty and graduate students often confine their interests to specialized aspects of particular disciplines. While the university itself becomes involved in the larger political community without conscious direction, sometimes without intent, and usually without a careful consideration of the consequences of its involvement.

The model of the university as a "neutral" institution probably described its pretentions more closely than its functions, even in the past. Currently, the university is clearly not and cannot be "neutral," if this means, as some seem to think, not at the service of any social interests. Michael Maccoby points out that, as the financing of higher education in the United States has become increasingly dependent upon the federal government, the interests and resources of the university have come to reflect the political priorities designated by this sponsor. The contemporary university is an important cultural and economic resource, but it also administers more fully to some social interests than others, and especially to those interests that provide it with assets. As it is presently organized, the university can hardly be "neutral" in the sense of being equally at the service of all legitimate social interests. The provision of defense research, for example, necessarily aligns the university with national foreign policy and of military strategy, and aligns the university with ordering of priorities concerning defense spending as opposed to social reform.

The scientific and technological functions of the university become politicized by thus entering the service of the political order. Maccoby strongly urges that the scientific community assume the responsibility of determining its own goals as well as the goals of the national polity: "The scientific community has the knowledge, the ability and the prestige to reorient the nation toward 'biophilic' goals. Unless science wakes up to the dangers of acquiescence and objects to priorities set by fear and political expediency, there is little hope of reversing a process which at best leads to waste and stagnation and at worst moral disintegration."

Who makes the policy for the universities? We must distinguish here between decisions and policy. Decisions — whether to hire a member of the faculty, to use a certain building for a certain purpose, to allocate space to one department or another — are usually made by the administration, with the consultation of the faculty, and sometimes even the consultation of students. But major issues of policy, such as the acceptance of large grants for defense research, are usually made by the board of trustees. Ultimate power resides in these boards. Usually, their members are themselves so busy with other affairs that they do not generally interfere with the decision making processes of the university, although that too, has been changing recently. These governing boards vary greatly in composition, attitudes, and interests, according to the institution. Nevertheless a recent survey by the Educational Testing Service (ETS) of more than 5,000 college and university trustees reveals some prevalent characteristics of trustees as a group. From these data, a troubling picture emerges: the trustees are indifferent to academic values and are uninformed about issues and problems in contemporary education. They are convinced that the combination of student and faculty decision making power on crucial academic isues is inappropriate.

These attitudes, of course, change with the university represented. Still, the overall picture is inconsistent with a conception of the university as an integrated academic community. The average trustee has values and interests that differ from most faculty and students, and little comprehension of the problematic character of campus issues. Furthermore, the ETS data show that the few trustees bother to remain well informed about trends and problems in higher education. The vast majority have not read any major books on higher education and are unfamiliar with most of the relevant periodicals.

Trustee systems vary. The Board of Regents of the University of California includes such political figures as the governor of the state and the speaker of the lower house of the legislature. The governor also has appointive power over the regents and may well be the most influential individual in the nine-campus system of the university. The "People's Park" incident in Berkeley is an almost pure example of how a decision made by the Board of Regents and implemented through the channels of university administration can lead to open confrontation and an escalation of violence.

The People's Park incident raised four fundamental problems: bureaucracy, property, work, and power. A university as large as the University of California has, naturally, a master plan. In conformity to this plan the development of the nine campuses of the university will come about at a prescribed speed and in a foreordained manner. When neighborhoods change, when student attitudes change, it becomes very difficult for "responsible" officials to set their plans aside and develop new ones. In only five years American student culture has changed greatly. Spontaneity has come to be strongly valued as bureaucracies have become larger and more rigid. Property is also challenged. In this instance, the property was obtained by the university under its state powers of eminent domain. To those who wanted a user-controlled park, the property appeared to be quasi-public. At the same time, as expressed in the press, television, and radio, many Californians feared that this might set a precedent for people "camping in my own backyard." The students voted to have a user-controlled park; the master plan called for a dormitory. And the regents insists on the dormitory, in part because of the public feeling that rules must be obeyed, and in part because of their understanding of what the university is all about. To them it is a place where people come to work hard in prescribed courses so as to get a leg up on the system. However, to the students, it is becoming a place of experiment and participation; and a user-controlled park allows for experiments with new work and ideas.

Not that experimentation within a university is likely to be a simple and untroubled matter. In her article on the Federal City College in Washington, D.C., Barbara Raskin discusses many of the ambiguities and difficulties in experimentation. The Federal City College was started as a comprehensive, low cost institution of higher education for District of Columbia students, and it was to make the equivalent of a high school diploma the basic requirement for admission. Because of the demography of Washington, D.C.., when the college opened its doors 94 per cent of its students were black. This is not the same kind of institution as the University of California at Berkeley, or any other prestigious private or public university. Here, though, was an opportunity for experimentation, an opportunity for experimentation, an opportunity that is presently being explored. But with opportunity came inevitable divisions among faculty, administration, and students, and these divisions were not based merely on the status of those within the institution. Some faculty members committed to changing academic structures and trying new techniques as these are defined and encouraged in the most prestigious white colleges. Other faculty members believed in a more classical education for participation in a traditional and hierarchically organized white middle class society. Still other students and faculty believed that the ultimate organizational principle for the college, because of social composition, should be the job market. And finally, some believed in training students for militant action in the social, political, and economic system of the country.

Perhaps, ultimately, a university is indeed a "microcosm" of the larger society. At the same time, the Study Commission on University Governance of the University of California at Berkeley asserts that the university ought to be much more. The most important goal of the university as a community, and therefore the best measure of its excellence, is the intellectual growth of its students. Such intellectual growth includes the capacity to use reason not only to resolve problems but to criticize the society around the university. The conclusion of the Study Commission is that the university, despite its rhetoric, has not been true to its own values of community and intellectual challenge:

> We have imperceptibly slumped into a posture in which the demands of external interests — strongly reinforced by economic lures, rewards of prestige and status, and other powerful resources which only those with power can marshal and wield — have increasingly dominated the ethos of the university and shaped the direction of its educational activities.

It is not clear whether the university will ever achieve the lofty vision of the Berkeley Study Commission. In the meantime, we may be sure that the universities will continue to be places of social criticism and social conflict.

MICHAEL MACCOBY   *Government, Scientists,*
and the Priorities of Science

Massive federal financing of the sciences, which in principle should be strengthening American society, in practice threatens to divert science and higher education from their proper goals. In the universities, the influx of government funds has often narrowed rather than broadened the search for knowledge and has resulted in neglect of teaching. In general, the harvest of scientific discovery is disappointing, considering the investment involved, for too often the supervision of governmental agencies has reinforced the trend toward bureaucratized projects which produce trivial, non-controversial findings.

Apart from the effects of federal financing on the universities, one must question the results of concentrating funds in research bearing on national defense. Not only does such concentration hinder the solving of non-military problems; it also diminishes our capacity, as Norbert Wiener puts it, "to react homeostatically to the vicissitudes of the future." Especially important here is the role of the scientific community, as it responds to government support and to the political dictation of priorities; for the worst effects of government influence are aggravated by the willingness of scientists to pursue those goals least likely to arouse division or debate. Consequently, science, rather than serving men, has become increasingly the enemy of life.

FEDERAL SUPPORT AND THE UNIVERSITIES

The results of government financing of university research have been studied systematically by Harold Orlans and summarized in his book, *The Effects of Federal Programs on Higher Education, A Study of 36 Universities and Colleges.*[1] On the basis of 400 interviews with administrators and 3500 faculty questionnaires, Orlans concludes that large-scale, high-level scientific programs cannot survive without federal support, but that the manner in which grants are doled out creates dangers and imbalances. Most of the funds go to a few wealthy universities which

From *Dissent,* Winter, 1964. Reprinted with permission.
Note: This article is based on the Gabrielson Lecture on Government and the Priorities of Science delivered at Colby College, February 14, 1963.
[1] Washington: The Brookings Institute, 1962.

use them to help attract the leading scientists and the best students. (According to a recent report from the House Labor and Education Committee, 90 per cent of the federal funds were concentrated in 100 universities, 38 per cent in ten.) Within the universities themselves, the money goes almost entirely to natural scientists and psychologists, who consequently improve their positions and prestige at the expense of other social scientists and humanists. Even among scientists, government grants carry greater prestige and chance of advancement than do good teaching and individual research outside of the government-financed project system.

Yet, while supporting scientists, government funds have not necessarily opened new scientific frontiers. Orlans states that while the "best" or most well-known scientists can get support for projects of their own choosing, the "average" scientist must do the work the government wants in order to receive its support. And Orlans writes that "The preference of government agencies for 'safe' and 'projectable' rather than venturesome research, and for experimental rather than theoretical work, was noted by many observers."[2]

Although government support has sometimes led to important discoveries, Orlans emphasizes the view, as stated by one professor, that federal financing is creating a higher education that is "nationalized" rather than "universalized." While the universities have some power to resist government interference in regard to educational policies and academic freedom, it remains an open question whether in fact they would resist, should the issue arise with fresh McCarthy-style hysteria. Since the days of McCarthy, government support has grown to the point where not only research but also teaching programs and salaries of permanent faculty members often depend heavily on federal funds. Yet the universities appear to be more concerned with beating one another in the race for money than in banding together to assert their autonomy. Thus, the two main dangers of federal aid, as cited by Orlans: "(1) that academic values and objectives will be surrendered to those of a business enterprise or the more important goals of a nation, and (2) that some form of political control will, indeed, follow federal aid."[3]

FEDERAL PRIORITIES AND THE RESPONSE OF SCIENCE

There is no question but that the federal government now dominates the setting of scientific priorities in the United States. Of the nearly $16 billion spent by the nation on research and development during 1962, over $12.2 billion was appropriated by Congress, most of it in contracts to industry ($5.8 billion) and universities ($4.2 billion). The current

2 *Ibid.*, p. 93.
3 *Ibid.*, p. 292.

federal research and development budget asks Congress for $14.9 billion, continuing that trend which since 1956 has increased appropriations by 10 to 35 per cent every year.[4]

Fifteen per cent of total expenditures in American universities derive from government sources; some private universities, including Harvard, Yale and Princeton, receive a larger percentage of operating revenue than do land grant colleges such as Illinois, Kentucky and Maryland[5]; and in the most heavily supported schools some 78 per cent of the natural scientists receive federal subsidy.[6] The most essential statistic concerning federal involvement in science, however, is that most of the funds spent on research and development (R & D) fall under the military budget. For example, of $9 billion invested by the government in R & D in 1961, $6.2 billion went into national defense, $1.4 billion into space research, $.9 billion to atomic energy, and the remaining billion was divided among smaller programs such as health, agriculture, the Bureau of Mines and the National Bureau of Standards. And of the $613 million spent by the government directly on university research (as opposed to "development"), one-third supported work related to military purposes.[7]

What are the results to science and to the nation of directing so much energy and genius into the arts of weaponry? Why does this trend continue even though, as we shall see, it is economically and morally self-defeating? To answer such questions requires an examination not only of the forces that determine Congressional appropriations, but also of the scientists' motives, the bureaucratization resulting from the project system, and the manner in which political priorities blunt the free spirit of scientific inquiry.

The failure of American scientists to oppose pressures which could reduce their community to a technical bureau contrasts markedly with C. P. Snow's description of the scientific ethos in *The Two Cultures*.[8] According to Snow, the scientist is supremely qualified to set the priorities of society, because his intellectual outlook is molded by his professional method. He is democratic and objective, influenced by considerations of utility rather than established authority. He believes in progress; he is open to new and better ways of doing things.

Snow reports the scientific ideology accurately enough, but his evaluation of it is overly optimistic. For all too often the scientific mind

[4] *Science*, 26 July 1963, p. 339. It is doubtful, however, whether the Congress will appropriate all this money, especially the requests for non-military research which House subcommittees have already begun to cut.

[5] Harold L. Enarson, "Free Universities and National Policy," *Science*, 2 November 1963, p. 582.

[6] Orlans, *loc. cit.*, p. 98.

[7] National Science Foundation, *Federal Funds for Science X* (Washington: Government Printing Office, 1962).

[8] C. P. Snow, *The Two Cultures and the Scientific Revolution* (Cambridge: Cambridge University Press, 1959).

equates "winning" with "progress," and substitutes a belief in personal achievement and the "advancement" of a field for an authentic interest in knowledge and truth. Thus many scientists appear as members of teams out to win contests, concerned more with personal batting averages than with the value of the game or the cost of winning. Scientists with the "game-like attitude"[9] seldom come to grips with the needs of the world they live in, believing instead, as Don K. Price comments, "that the public interest is the same as their professional specialty."[10]

But it is unjust to lump all scientists together, as both Snow and his critics tend to do. There is a great difference between the scientist whose pleasure begins and ends in the elegant development of a device, whether it be a triggering mechanism for a bomb or a new drug, and the scientist impelled by a vision of widening the scope of natural knowledge or understanding human existence. The trouble with the first kind of scientist is that he might do just as well on a project designed to destroy the planet as on one to bring cheap power to the underdeveloped world.

The major problems that arise from government and science are not the fault of either large-scale government support or the scientists' lack of say in setting priorities. As Price points out, scientists in the United States have more influence at the highest levels of government than do those of other countries; indeed, many administrators are themselves scientists. Even the problem of explaining scientific problems to Congressmen might not be insurmountable, if scientists were firm in their convictions. But scientists in general, according to Orlans, are satisfied with the present form of government support; the trouble lies in the very ease with which they accommodate their activities to the going market.

A certain amount of red tape and inefficiency under the project system seems an inevitable price for progress in those fields that cannot be developed without huge financial investments. But it is clear from Orlans' interviews that the quality of scientific work is compromised as much by the scientists themselves as by the agencies, which in fact are often troubled by the lack of courage and imagination in the research projects proposed to them. Thus Orlans quotes from the Proceedings of a *Conference on Academic and Industrial Basic Research* (National Science Foundation, 1961):

> The present atmosphere of the intense competition for jobs, for prestige, and for research grants places too much emphasis on the achievement of quick and fairly certain results at the expense of the slower and more valuable maturing of the scientist. The younger

[9] For the effects of this game-like attitude on military strategy, see M. Maccoby, "Social Psychology of Deterrence," *Bulletin of the Atomic Scientists*, September, 1961. This scientific attitude reinforces the tendency to seek technical solutions while ignoring political realities and long-range unintended effects of policy.
[10] Don K. Price, *Government and Science* (New York: N.Y.U Press, 1954), p. 26.

men have become concerned with making their reputations as quickly as possible; to do this they are forced to choose problems they are sure will yield publishable results in a short time, rather than the more difficult problems with uncertain results. Some of the participants in this Conference felt that the research of younger men is becoming more superficial and even trivial, although in the past it was the younger men who made the deepest and most striking contributions to science.[11]

The best scientists also worry about the trivializing of research. Hans Bethe has noted that with large computers doing so much work, scientists do not think enough: "They lose the inspiration for further research that came from an intimate contact with every phase of the calculations."[12] Professor Melvin Schwartz, a physicist at Columbia, writes that with expensive machines, science becomes assembly-line research. No one tries risky problems because the machine is expensive and he fears wasting money on a worthless result. And no one takes responsibility of accuracy, for it is the machine that does the work.[13]

At the present time the scientific community is receiving from the government more or less what it demands. If scientists were truly determined to attack more important problems, there is no evidence that the government would stand in their way. Professors in Orlans' sample note that agencies such as the National Institutes of Health, the National Science Foundation, and even the Navy with all their limitations, show more courage in backing adventuresome ideas than do private foundations. Similarly, administrators in Washington are more often characterized by breadth of vision than many within universities who measure success — as do scientific guilds themselves — by quantity of publication. Most universities hire and fire purely on the basis of work published, without regard to the work's significance or lack of it.

Yet even if one grants that the scientists — especially the best of them — might claim somewhat more autonomy than they do, that institutions accepting federal funds hoard more independence than they spend, and that the opinions of scientists are heard at the highest levels of government, one must still ask how the scientific community uses its power and influence. Price, in *Government and Science,* suggests that generally American science goes along with fixed political goals rather than trying to influence society toward better goals. He explains that the decentralization of science into private institutions facilitates the carrying-out of

[11] Orlans, *loc. cit.,* p. 98.

[12] Quoted by Sidney Lens, "The Professors and the Pentagon," *The Progressive,* October, 1962, p. 34. Lens also cites the opinions of other eminent scientists that many of the best investigators waste much of their time on administrative work. The quality of science is also diluted by government demands for secrecy and that projects be planned that are easily explained to untrained legislators.

[13] Melvin Schwartz, "The Conflict Between Productivity and Creativity in Modern-Day Physics," *The American Behavioral Scientist,* December, 1962, p. 36.

specific projects, "but not our ability to give integrity and direction to our total effort."[14]

It is a common belief that to improve our society all we need do is give more money and power to science. Price remarks, however, that "We will do well to recognize that a government bureau is tempted to be more concerned with its own status and power than with the purposes of national policy."[15] Since the scientists themselves suffer the same temptation, the two groups unconsciously conspire to promote the kind of work which is most likely to gain congressional support. In other words, although the scientific community may have a great deal to say in setting its own priorities, there is a reluctance to risk power, prestige, and support by clashing with priorities set in advance by the interplay of political forces. Like many other Americans, the scientist does not want to be told what to do, but he will gratefully accept a clue as to what will sell so he can then suggest it himself. The results of this attitude go beyond the concentration of research in safe but unimportant areas. A more serious consequence is that the majority of scientists will search for "interesting" research problems with military significance.

SCIENCE FOR WHAT?

Considering the large government investment in military research, the character of scientists, and (as we shall see later) the government's fear of scientific projects that might radically change our society, there is a real danger that a bureaucratized scientific community, with a naive, games-playing mentality, will ally itself with the military-industrial complex. It is not my purpose to make a wholesale indictment of American science. Clearly, many scientists are aware of the danger I am citing. Orlans indicates that 70 per cent of the scientists he interviewed realize that the present concentration of federal funds in the sciences is not in the "long-run national interest," although over 50 per cent do believe it to be "in the present national interest."[16] What concerns me, however, is not support of science vs. support of humanities, but that the kind of science now supported has a deadly effect on the spirit of scientific inquiry and the pursuit of human-oriented goals.

"Necrophilic" scientists who revel in a science of destruction are probably rare, statistically speaking, but their strong minds and purposive attitude may significantly influence the direction of scientific endeavor.[17] The physicist Ralph Lapp writes that while many scientists accept mili-

[14] Don K. Price, "The Scientific Establishment," *Science*, 29 June 1962.
[15] Price, *ibid*.
[16] Orlans, *loc. cit.*, p. 103.
[17] *Necrophilic* is here used not in the sense of the rare sexual perversion but in a broader definition suggested by Erich Fromm in *War Within Man* (Philadelphia:

tary employment reluctantly, the complex problems of weaponry which now enlist the majority of the nation's scientists also attract the best of the younger men — because these problems are so scientifically fascinating. Lap also refers to the fact that weapons of destruction have traditionally compensated man for his physical weakness and given him the means to master others.[18] Elaborating on man's age-old fascination with weaponry, Lapp quotes from G. B. Shaw's *Man and Superman,* where the Devil tells Don Juan:

> I have examined man's wonderful inventions. And I tell you that in the arts of life man invents nothing, but in the arts of death he outdoes Nature herself, and produces by chemistry and machinery all the slaughter of plague, pestilence, and famine. The peasant . . . eats and drinks what was eaten and drunk by peasants 10,000 years ago; and the house he lives in has not altered as much in a thousand centuries as the fashion of a lady's bonnet in a score of weeks. But when he goes out to slay, he carries a marvel of mechanism that lets loose at the touch of a finger all the hidden molecular energies, and leaves the javelin, the arrow, the blow-pipe of his fathers far behind.

Through science, to be sure, man has found many ways to preserve and extend life. But there is far more to the difference between science for death and science for life than is expressed in the contrast between making weapons and making medicines. Science for life implies research motivated by a profound vision of harmony, of *ecology* in its broadest meaning, of rational inquiry into the interrelation of things — whether it be expressed by Einstein's interest in mass-energy-space-time or by Rachel Carson's concern with protecting the balance of nature from technological assault.[19]

The difference between science for life and other science is not one of method, but of openness to a larger universe of variables. To the "biophilic" scientist, a problem does not end with the supression of a symptom or the discovery of a relationship; the central question is how the cure or discovery affects a wide balance of forces. Such an attitude is easier to observe in the biological than the physical sciences, for example in the work of Hans Selye on stress reactions and the medical possibilities of reinforcing natural homeostatic mechanisms while guarding against destructive side effects and over-reactions by these same mechanisms. Per-

---

American Friends Service Committee, 1963). Fromm shows that necrophilia is characterized by a love of death, a need for certainty, for complete predictability which can result in commitment to force, a preference for machines over living organisms (and the desire to make men into machines). Fromm also shows that the complex overly-bureaucratized and mechanized society conditions the spread of necrophilia. In contrast to the necrophilic attitude, Fromm describes a *biophilic* attitude, based on the love of life.

[18] Ralph E. Lapp, *Kill and Overkill* (New York: Basic Books, 1962). p. 16.

[19] Cf. Rachel Carson, *Silent Spring* (Boston: Houghton Mifflin, 1962).

haps in physics the distinction is more subtle, involving the choosing of problems, the use of techniques as means not ends, and the quest for truth rather than for power. (It is noteworthy that Einstein became one of the very few scientists to refuse political power when President Roosevelt offered it to him in 1939.) The "biophilic" scientist is not so intent on *conquering* nature as he is on discovery or on learning how to employ the forces of nature to create a greater harmony for man within his environment.

I do not mean to insist that the priorities of scientific work be totally determined by social priorities, nor that society does not benefit from science based on mixed motives. The important question is whether the motives are weighted in favor of understanding rather than power, and whether the thrust of scientific work in general is toward life-enhancing goals. As Norbert Weiner points out, science is most useful to society when scientists set priorities themselves, free from political pressures. Science must be allowed to gather information without regard to "historical predictions and prejudgments which belong primarily to one particular age, and may be proved false. . . . Thus the internal life of science must be preserved without a too direct dependence on the policies of the moment, or the official fashions of thought. This means that the scholar must retain for his own efficacy something — not too much — of the ivory tower attitude which it is the spirit of the times to decry."[20]

Yet the government provides massive support mainly for military research and development, and most scientists are neither capable nor interested in setting their own priorities based on pure scientific interest. Unlike Einstein, they are too concerned with worldly power. The question is no longer whether or not the government will support science, but what kind of science will be supported. The average scientist thinks less about the ultimate purpose of his work than about the immediate investigation at hand. As Lapp reminds us, for those fascinated by problems centering "on gyro-mechanisms, on miniaturized electronics, on plasma physics," it is "easy to forget the monstrous machines of destruction to which their work is contributing."[21]

FEDERAL PRIORITIES IN SCIENCE

The bulk of science now supported by the government is not science for life. Much of it is devoted to outright destruction, and much of what

[20] "Science and Society," *Science*, 9 November 1962, p. 651.

[21] Lapp, *loc. cit.*, p. 21. But Lapp also cites Tartaglia, the 16th-century ballistics expert who wrote, " 'One day meditating to myself, it seemed to me that it was a thing blameworthy, shameful, and barbarous, worthy of severe punishment before God and man, to wish to bring to perfection an art damageable to one's neighbor and destruction to the human race. . . .' "

is not — such as space exploration — diverts resources from the alleviation of pressing human problems. It can be argued that some of the research done in military and space programs has contributed to our store of useful knowledge concerning new plasmas, improved communications systems, etc. Yet it is difficult to secure appropriations for direct non-military research into these problems. Furthermore, medical scientists report that although the military services may at first offer to support an investigator's non-military work, once his laboratory is dependent on their funds he may be pressured into military research.

Why is it that the science most readily supported by Congress is either a science for death or a science for leaving the planet, when in fact there is so much to be done in developing our own planet? We do not yet understand the processes of physical and mental disease. We have not solved problems of water and air pollution. Most of the world is impoverished, although for the first time in human history we have the means to eradicate poverty. According to Lee A. DuBridge, member of the National Science Board and President of the California Institute of Technology, we now possess the scientific knowledge to:

> Produce enough food to feed every hungry mouth on earth — and to do this even though the population should double or triple.
> Make fresh water out of sea water and thus irrigate all the world's arid regions.
> Produce enough energy from uranium to light and heat our homes and offices, electrify our railroads, and run all our factories and mills.
> Build houses, buildings, and indeed whole cities, which are essentially weatherproof — heatproof, coldproof, and stormproof. . . .

Yet plans to realize these possibilities awake fears of socialism, despite the fact that they would create a higher standard of living and help solve the problems of the underdeveloped world; while the investment in destruction and space, involving at least as much government control, is rationalized as national security. . . .

Besides blocking economic and scientific development, massive military subsidies increase the chances and the destructiveness of war. Social scientists who might be expected to warn of this danger are often seduced into harmless research by government and foundation grants. Orlans notes that "sociologists complained about the restriction of government programs to quantitative, statistical, and computer analysis to the exclusion of qualitative and descriptive approaches; political scientists about the shying away from political implications which lie at the heart of their field."[22] The same criticisms were levelled at private foundations.

[22] Orlans, *loc. cit.*, p. 97.

Tragically, the behavior of the scientist is being moulded like that of the rat in a Skinner box, who is reinforced only for the right kind of action, so that gradually he learns to want to do what is rewarded and loses interest in what is not rewarded. As Lapp states, "No one . . . is responsible — and everyone is responsible. We cannot single out the scientists, or the politicians, or even the military, as the villains of our danger. We have no recourse but the hard one of disentangling the hypnotic skein in which we are all enmeshed — of finding a way out to rationality."[23]

But the same forces which block humane science and free scientific inquiry also nourish the apathetic and self-destructive tendencies in our society. The new generation of scientists, raised in the shadow of world war and anesthetized by the anxieties of the cold war and the bomb, has little faith that man can control his destructive impulses or that individuals can influence society. Thus scientists alienate themselves from that tradition which stems from the Enlightenment: that through reason and science, man can create a better society. Some of them seem not to believe man wants a better society.

The scientific community has the knowledge, the ability, and the prestige to reorient the nation toward "biophilic" goals. Unless science wakes up to the dangers of acquiescence and objects to priorities set by fear and political expediency, there is little hope of reversing a process which at best leads to waste and stagnation and at worst to moral disintegration and suicide.

RODNEY T. HARTNETT   *College and University*
                                Trustees: Their Backgrounds,
                          Roles, and Educational Attitudes

Only selected highlights from the total compilation of data are presented and interpreted here. The two most important criteria employed in de-

[23] Lapp, *loc. cit.*, p. 22.

From *College and University Trustees: Their Backgrounds, Roles, and Educational Attitudes* by Rodney T. Hartnett. Copyright © 1969 by Educational Testing Service. All rights reserved. Used by permission.

ciding upon what results should be included and what emphasis they should receive were relevance and freshness: relevant to the current higher education scene, preferably to an "issue" still unresolved, and fresh in the sense that the findings must add to what has been previously known about college and university trustees.

Thus, data regarding trustees' age, sex, level of education, income and the like are treated only briefly. On the other hand, the trustees' educational and social attitudes are dealt with in considerable detail, especially those having to do with academic freedom, business orientations, and the decision-making process. Information relating to trustees' familiarity with what has been written about higher education is discussed at some length, whereas the question of "Who shall be educated?" is, by comparison, treated very briefly, and responses to many of the questions in the survey are not discussed at all.

BIOGRAPHICAL CHARACTERISTICS

Data regarding some of the more basic characteristics of college and university trustees conform to previous findings and are not surprising in terms of the nature of the description they provide. In general, trustees are male, in their 50's (though, nationally, more than a third are over 60), white (fewer than two per cent in our sample are Negro), well-educated, and financially well-off (more than half have annual incomes exceeding $30,000). They occupy prestige occupations, frequently in medicine, law and education, but more often as business executives (in the total sample over 35 per cent are executives of manufacturing, merchandising or investment firms and at private universities nearly 50 per cent hold such positions). As a group, then, they personify "success" in the usual American sense of that word.[1]

Most are Protestants, with only 4 per cent being Jewish and 17 per cent Catholic, the majority of the latter serving on boards of Catholic institutions. Trustees also tend to identify themselves as Republicans (approximately 50 per cent overall) and most often regard themselves as politically moderate (61 per cent) rather than conservative (21 per cent) or liberal (15 per cent). Many of them — nearly 40 per cent overall and well over half at certain types of institutions — are alumni of the institutions on whose boards they serve. Of considerable interest is the fact that for the great majority (85 per cent) their current board membership, whether with their alma mater or not, is their only college or university trustee commitment.

[1] Again we caution the reader to keep in mind the purposely very general nature of these summary statements. There is considrable diversity on these characteristics across types of institutions.

EDUCATIONAL/SOCIAL ATTITUDES

Perhaps more important than biographical characteristics for understanding the college trustees is how he feels about prevailing issues that face American higher education. Indeed, the relevance of such information as occupation, income, and the like is its presumed relationship to educational attitudes. Traditionally, this relationship has been taken for granted, and some have drawn the rather reckless conclusions that because the trustee is seldom young his educational attitudes are old-fashioned, that because he is frequently a business executive he will urge that his institution be "run like a business," and so on.[2] One of our intentions in developing the questionnaire was to replace suppositions with facts, to replace easy generalities with "hard" data. To our knowledge, information regarding trustees' opinions on most of these matters has never before been systematically gathered on a national scale.

Academic Freedom. One of the prime areas of interest is that of academic freedom. A number of items in the attitude section of the questionnaire were directed at this issue. These items and the trustees' responses are summarized in Table 1.

TABLE 1   *Extent to Which Trustees Agree with Statements Regarding Academic Freedom*[a]

	Percentage strongly agreeing or agreeing[b]	Percentage disagreeing or strongly disagreeing
Faculty members have right to free expression of opinions	67	27[c]
Administration should control contents of student newspaper	40	51
Campus speakers should be screened	69	25
Students punished by local authorities for off-campus matter should also be disciplined by the college	49	38
It is reasonable to require loyalty oaths from faculty members	53	38

a Statements in table are abbreviated; for complete statements see questionnaire.
b Percentages rounded to whole numbers.
c Percentages do not add to 100 because of those responding "unable to say."

[2] Of course an opposite, and perhaps more dangerous, assumption has also been frequently made: that because one is a "successful" businessman, attorney, dentist, or whatever, he will therefore be a competent overseer of a higher educational institution.

Though the great majority of trustees favor the right to free expression by faculty in various channels of college communication, the more general impression one gets from these data is that the trustees, by and large, are somewhat reluctant to accept a wider notion of academic freedom. For example, over two-thirds of these people favor a screening process for all campus speakers, and nearly half feel that students already punished by local authorities for involvement in matters of civil disobedience *off the campus* should be further disciplined by the college.[3]

These attitudes are extremely relevant to campus problems today. Those who would argue that the trustee holds no authority or influence need only to examine some of the trustee attitudes regarding academic freedom against a backdrop of trustee/faculty conflicts. In the fall of 1968, for example, the regents of the University of California voted to withhold regular college credits for a series of speeches by Eldridge Cleaver (Minister of Information for the Black Panthers, an Oakland-based black militant group, and author of *Soul on Ice*), at the Berkeley campus. The academic senate at Berkeley has recorded its opposition to the regents' "encroachment" in curricular matters, but, at the time of this writing, the trustees' decision stands. There are many cases similar to this one and none should come as a surprise in view of trustee attitudes.

Naturally, trustee opinions about these matters vary considerably, not only across types of institutions, as already suggested, but across other dimensions as well. As an example of this, the academic freedom attitudes reported in Table 1 are presented again in Table 2, this time arranged by geographic region. The diversity is apparent. Notice, for example, that over half of the trustees of institutions located in the South agree that the contents of the student newspaper should be controlled by the institution, whereas only about 30 per cent of the trustees of New England and Mid-Atlantic institutions hold similar views. Similar comparisons suggest that, in general, trustees of southern and Rocky Mountain institutions are most cautious in these matters, whereas trustees of institutions located in the New England and Mid-Atlantic region appear to be the most "liberal." The point of this particular analysis is to underscore the fact that the total sample of trustees could be categorized many different ways — by type of control, geographic region, enrollment, and sex makeup of student body to name but a few — and differences would almost surely appear.

There is an interesting sidelight to the academic freedom data which is not presented in Tables 1 or 2, but can be seen by referring to attitude items 3, 4, 5, 16 and 20 [in Part II of the original report]. Trustees of

---

[3] It should be pointed out that this particular item, dealing with off-campus civil disobedience, is probably more a matter of "in loco parentis" than academic freedom. Nevertheless it is included here since freedom (though perhaps not academic freedom) *is* involved, and the item does correlate with the other four in this table.

TABLE 2

Agreement with Academic Freedom
Statements by Trustees of Institutions in
Different Geographic Regions (in percentages)[a, b]

	New England and Mid-Atlantic	South	Midwest	Rockies	West
Faculty members have right to free expression of opinions	73.2	64.0	64.2	62.6	62.0
Administration should control contents of student newspaper	29.8	51.5	42.0	48.1	44.4
Campus speakers should be screened	58.3	80.9	72.0	77.8	74.5
Students punished by local authorities for off-campus matter should also be disciplined by the college	39.8	63.2	49.5	62.5	44.0
It is reasonable to require loyalty oaths from faculty members	46.4	63.6	52.2	66.1	53.4

[a] Numbers are percentages agreeing or strongly agreeing with each statement.
[b] Statements in table are abbreviated; for complete statements see questionnaire.

public junior colleges appear to be the least freedom-oriented in terms of their responses to these items. At the same time we note that 42 per cent of the trustees of public junior colleges are elected by the general public [item 5 in questionnaire Part III]. Though such an occurrence is far too tenuous to draw any definite conclusions some speculations are hard to resist. In a recent discussion of the matter, Jencks and Riesman remark, "Publicly elected or appointed boards of trustees seem in many ways to cause more trouble than they are worth."[4] This opinion apparently stems from their belief that "budgetary support and review are the only forms of public control that make much sense" and that these functions could just as easily, and more efficiently, be performed by already existing groups (for example, the legislature). As suggested by comments of these same authors in another source, however, we may wonder if their opinion isn't also influenced by the numerous cases in which trustees have campaigned for a position on an institution's governing board on a plank opposed to academic freedom.[5] The public often does not understand the full meaning of academic freedom and is apparently suspicious of it. It is possible, therefore, that publicly elected

[4] Christopher Jencks and David Riesman, *The Academic Revolution.* New York: Doubleday, 1968, p. 269.
[5] David Riesman and Christopher Jencks, "The Viability of the American College," in *The American College* (Nevitt Sanford, editor). New York: Wiley, 1962, p. 109.

trustees may be conservative in these matters, as suggested by the junior college data reported here.[6]

If this is true, it would suggest that publicly elected trustees may not be confronted with the long-standing dilemma facing other governing board members, that is, whether to adopt the role of "protector of the public interest" or that of insulator between the public and the institution. While most trustees — at least at public institutions — appear to vacillate between these two roles, the publicly elected trustee, perhaps by virtue of being elected rather than appointed, is apparently committed to the former.[7]

Education for Whom? Another topic of recent concern to American higher education has to do with the question of "education for whom?" Until fairly recently American higher education was restricted to those of demonstrated academic ability who could afford the high costs that earning a degree required. More recently, however, we have seen a trend toward more flexible selection criteria and an "open-door" philosophy, perhaps exemplified best by the growing number of junior colleges throughout the country. Trustee attitudes toward this phenomenon are summarized in Table 3.

For the national sample taken together, there appears to be general sympathy for the broader-access trend just discussed. Slightly more than 85 per cent agree (with almost one-third *strongly* agreeing) that there should be opportunities for higher education available to anyone who seeks education beyond secondary school, and two-thirds agree that colleges should admit socially disadvantaged students who appear to have the potential, even when these students do not meet the normal entrance requirements. Nevertheless over 90 per cent still regard attendance at their college to be a privilege, not a right. In fact, 68 per cent of the trustees of public junior colleges, open-door institutions if you will, also share the privilege-not-a-right sentiment. In view of the other responses indicating acceptance of the concept of wide accessibility of higher education opportunity, these latter figures seem inconsistent. Several expanations seem plausible, however. It may mean that even trustees of non-selective institutions cling to the elitist model, perhaps thinking that while *other* colleges should employ flexible admissions criteria, their own institution must "maintain high standards." Or perhaps most trustees simply interpreted the statement somewhat differently, wishing only to indicate their feeling that students should not *expect* to be in college but,

[6] The general question of what differences exist, if any, among trustees gaining board membership by different avenues is one of many we hope to pursue in much grater detail in subsequent analyses of these data.

[7] For a more detailed discussion of these roles at both public and private institutions, see John D. Millett, *The Academic Community: An Essay on Organization.* New York: McGraw-Hill, Inc., 1962.

TABLE 3   *Trustees' Views Regarding Who*
                      Should Be Served by Higher Education[a]

	Percentage strongly agreeing or agreeing[b]	Percentage disagreeing or strongly disagreeing
Attendance a privilege, not a right	92	6[c]
Aptitude most important admissions criteria	70	24
Curriculum designed to accommodate diverse student body	63	27
Opportunity for higher education for anyone who desires it	85	11
College should admit socially disadvantaged who do not meet normal requirements	66	22

[a] Statements in table are abbreviated; for complete statements see questionnaire.

[b] Percentages rounded to whole numbers.

[c] Percentages do not add to 100 because of those responding "unable to say."

rather, should feel *grateful* for the opportunity. Or finally, it could mean that trustees favor extending the opportunity for college *admission* to more and more students but, in order to protect themselves and their institutions against "unacceptable" student conduct, feel the institutions must retain the authority to decide who will *remain*.

Business Orienation of Trustees. One frequently hears the assertion that trustees tend to think colleges and universities can function best by imitating the corporation or big business model (the assumption being that such a model is inappropriate and, in the long run, damaging to higher education). Whether such a model is appropriate or not cannot be answered by these data, but we can at least get some idea of whether or not it is a model preferred by the trustees.

It has already been indicated that trustees are frequently business executives. Two additional indices should also suggest such an orientation: first, whether trustees endorse the statement that "running a college is basically like running a business," and, second, the extent to which they feel "experience in high-level business management" is an important quality to consider in the selection of a new president. These data are presented in Table 4.

Inspection of this table makes it clear that trustees who are business executives definitely have a stronger business orientation toward the university than trustees with other occupations. For the total sample, of the

TABLE 4

Trustee Responses to Items Indicative of Their Business-Model Orientation for Colleges and Universities (in percentages)

	Regard themselves as executives of manufacturing, merchandising or banking firm	Agree that running a college is basically like running a business		Regard experience in high-level business management as important quality for new president	
	(col. 1)	(col 2) Business Executives[a]	(col. 3) Others	(col. 4) Business Executives	(col. 5) Others
Total sample	35	49	31	49	44
Public junior colleges	33 (7)[b]	56 (2)	49	45 (6)	46
Public colleges	39 (3)	56 (2)	42	55 (1)	40
Public universities	36 (5)	45 (6)	28	51 (4)	43
Private colleges	36 (5)	48 (4)	29	49 (5)	45
Private universities	49 (1)	42 (7)	23	41 (7)	38
Catholic college and universities	22 (8)	56 (2)	31	54 (2)	43
Selective public	36 (5)	47 (5)	30	53 (3)	38
Selective private	43 (2)	30 (8)	14	31 (8)	25

a "Business executives" includes all those in first column, determined on the basis of their response to the occupation (No. 16) in first part of questionnaire.

b Numbers in parentheses alongside percentages in columns 1, 2, and 4 are within-column ranks (excluding total sample). Rank-order correlation (ρ) between columns are as follows: $\rho_{12} = -.62$ (p. $< .05$), $\rho_{14} = -.40$ (n.s.), $\rho_{24} = +.69$ (p. $< .05$).

35 per cent who are business executives nearly half (49 per cent) agree that running a college is basically like running a business, whereas fewer than one-third (31 per cent) of the nonexecutives accept this view. In fact, of the 16 possible business executives vs. "other" comparisons (eight institutional types by two attitude items) there is only one case in which trustees who are business executives are not also more business oriented. The exception is for public junior colleges, where a slightly higher proportion of nonbusiness executives regard business management experience as an important quality for a new president. Thus, there appears to be validity to the often heard claim that because governing boards are made up of businessmen, the decisions they make about the institutions will reflect this business outlook.

Another finding emerging from the data in Table 4, however, has to do with the relationship between the three indices and suggests that the "business outlook" hypothesis is not so simple. Note that the group having the second greatest proportion of trustees who are business executives (selective private universities) is the group which has the smallest percentage of those executives agreeing that running a college is like running a business and also the smallest proportion regarding high-level business management experience as an important criterion for a new president. Contrast this with trustees of public junior colleges, where a nearly opposite pattern occurs. In fact, the rank-order correlations between columns indicates that, across all types, the proportion of trustees holding business-executive positions is *negatively* correlated with the proportion of those executives endorsing the attitude statements in Table 4; that is, the greater the proportion of business executives on the governing board, the *smaller* the proportion of executives who feel that "running a college is like running a business" and that high-level business management experience is an important quality to consider in choosing a new president. Consequently, even though the "business orientation" is distinctly more prevalent among business executives generally, it would be a mistake to jump to the conclusion that on boards where the proportion of business executives is high, the business orientation will be strongest.

What is the explanation for this befuddling situation? One is at first tempted to speculate about the influence of the nonbusiness trustees on their colleagues' attitudes. While such a possibility should not be lightly dismissed, a more convincing interpretation might consider the varying levels of "executiveness" represented on the boards. We suspect, for example, that the types of institutions having the greatest proportion of business executives (the private universities and selective private institutions) generally have men who are a much different kind of executive than those who serve on boards with the smallest proportion of businessmen (the junior colleges and Catholic institutions). This is probably a case of men simply not being cut from the same cloth, regardless of what may be suggested by the mutual occupational perception of "business executive." This difference, in turn, is reflected in their attitudes about "running" a college, and the high-level executive appears to be more inclined to see it as a nonbusiness undertaking when compared to his probably less prestigious executive counterpart serving on some of the other boards.

The Decision-making Process. One of the complaints most frequently made about higher education by disenchanted members of the academic community is that the wrong people are making the decisions. Many of the campus demonstrators have been claiming, in one way or another, that the university should be run by the faculty and students, not by administrators and trustees. The following quotation, taken from a newspaper article summarizing some of the events at Columbia in the spring of 1968, is not atypical:

> Speakers in buildings and on the lawn . . . called for the "reconstruction of this university," with students and faculty assuming the power now exercised by the president and trustees.[8]

Though the extent to which faculty and students across the country actually feel they should "run" the campus is not known, there are some indications that it is not just a radical minority who desire more participation in the decision-making process. In a survey of faculty opinion regarding participation in academic decision making at one institution, for example, 51 per cent of the faculty included in the survey felt that "the faculty has too little influence on decisions; more of the decision making power should rest with the faculty," and another 44 per cent agreed that "the faculty's role is not what it should be ideally, but it is about what one can realistically expect." Furthermore, 63 per cent indicated that they were either dissatisfied or very dissatisfied with the situation.[9] And a recent survey of college trustees, administrators, faculty members, and students conducted by the American Council on Education, tells us that faculty are almost unanimous in wanting a larger share in academic rule, including greater participation in the selection of their president.[10] Though the former study was done at one university in the Midwest, and the faculty sample in the A.C.E. study consisted only of American Association of University Professors chapter heads (thus making neither sam-

[8] Joel Kramer, "Does Student Power Mean: Rocking the Boat? Running the University?" *The New York Times*, May 26, 1968, section IV, p. 32.

[9] Archie R. Dykes, *Faculty Participation in Academic Decision Making.* American Council on Education, 1968.

[10] John Caffrey, "Predictions for Higher Education in the 1970's," in *The Future Academic Community: Continuity and Change,* background papers for participants in the 51st annual meeting of the American Council on Education, 1968, pp. 123–153.

ple "representative" in any sense), together they provide some empirical support for the claim that there is dissatisfaction with the perceived way in which decisions are reached.

With this information in mind, let us examine the trustees' views of who should have major involvement in deciding various campus issues. Several things are made quite clear by these data, which are presented in Tables 5 and 6.

First, trustees generally favor a hierarchical system in which decisions are made at the top and passed "down." For example, over 50 per cent of the total sample of trustees believe that faculty and students should *not* have major authority in half of the sixteen decisions listed (that is, eight column-one percentage figures exceed 50 per cent in Table 5). The proportion feeling that trustees and/or administrators alone should have major authority in making the decision exceeds 40 per cent in 12 of the 16 decisions.[11] Some of these are particularly interesting. For example, 63 per cent say that the appointment of an academic dean should be made with only the administrators and trustees having major authority, or, to say it another way, 63 per cent feel that the faculty should *not* have major authority in the appointment of their dean. Similarly, 57 per cent would exempt the faculty from major authority in the awarding of honorary degrees, and 58 per cent would exempt them from major authority in policies regarding faculty leaves. To many, of course, these findings come as no surprise. But, surprising or not, they do help underscore some of the very wide differences of opinion among members of the academic community as to who should govern.

Second, there is a perceptible difference in the kinds of decisions trustees feel should and should not involve other groups having substantial authority. For example, the areas that should have greatest faculty authority are seen to be, by and large, academic matters, such as whether or not to add or delete specific courses, or what criteria should be employed in admitting students. Student authority is judged relevant in matters of student life, such as housing, student cheating, fraternities and sororities, and the like.

Third, though the trustees generally prefer an arrangement in which the faculty and students do not have major authority, neither do they want to "rule" by themselves. Notice in Table 5, for example, that with the exception of presidential appointments, they prefer major authority for decisions to rest with the administration alone or with the administration

---

[11] Caution should be used in interpreting Table 7. It should be kept in mind, for example, that the percentages in columns two and three might also include trustees and administrators, and column three might also include faculty members. Column one, then, is the only "pure" combination. Again, the reader is urged to study Part II of [the original] report.

TABLE 5

Proportion of Trustees Who Think That Certain Campus Groups
Should Have Major Authority in Making Various Decisions (in percentages)[a,b]

	Decision should be made by administrators alone (A), trustees alone (T) or trustees and admin. together (TA)				Decision should be made by faculty alone or in conjunction with admin., trustees or both	Decision should be made by students alone or in conjunction with faculty and/or A and/or T
	A	T	TA	(col. 1) Total[c]	(col. 2)	(col. 3)
Add or delete courses	11	1	4	16	65	14
Add or delete degree programs	9	6	18	33	57	3
Rules re student housing	32	2	13	47	6	37
Commencement speaker	29	4	13	46	25	22
Presidential appointment	1	64	5	70	8	1
Determine tuition	10	17	64	91	2	1
Professor's immoral conduct	29	7	28	64	27	2
Tenure decisions	27	7	30	64	30	1
Student cheating	20	0	1	21	39	37
Policy re student protests	16	6	30	52	18	22
Appoint academic dean	22	8	33	63	30	1
Policy re faculty leaves	19	8	31	58	37	0
Admission criteria	17	3	16	36	59	1
Honorary degrees	7	19	31	57	34	1
Athletic program	17	4	22	43	22	24
Fraternities and sororities	18	5	21	44	10	31

[a] Statements in table are abbreviated; for example statements see questionnaire.
[b] Percentages rounded to whole numbers.
[c] Column 1, which is simply a total of columns A, T, and TA, can be interpreted as the percentage of trustees who feel that faculty and/or students should *not* have major authority in deciding the various issues.

TABLE 6 — Percentage of Trustees by Type of Institution Feeling That Various Decisions Should Be Made with Administrators and/or Trustees Having the Only Major Authority

Decision	Total	Public j.c.	Public colleges	Public univ.	Private colleges	Private univ.	Catholic c's & u's	Selective public	Selective private
Add or delete courses	16	31	21	17	14	10	13	13	6
Add or delete degree programs	33	56	42	32	31	25	31	26	18
Rules re student housing	47	54	55	53	46	47	37	48	40
Commencement speaker	46	52	49	46	46	48	44	39	44
Presidential appointment	70	85	72	60	69	70	70	61	63
Determine tuition	91	91	87	88	93	93	88	88	95
Professor's immoral conduct	64	74	70	67	65	60	56	63	54
Tenure decisions	64	79	67	61	67	55	54	63	44
Student cheating	21	26	27	24	19	20	20	14	19
Policy re student protests	52	64	60	61	51	54	45	63	49
Appoint academic dean	63	81	68	57	64	61	61	48	54
Policy re faculty leaves	58	70	65	60	59	54	46	57	48
Admissions criteria	36	56	50	41	33	27	33	47	25
Honorary degrees	57	64	62	48	55	51	60	43	45
Athletic programs	43	49	58	50	41	42	41	48	37
Fraternities and sororities	44	95	48	47	45	47	38	43	44
No. of issues with 50 per cent or more trustees feeling that trustees and/or administrators alone should have major authority	8	13	11	9	8	8	6	6	4

and trustees conjointly. Thus, the "power at the top" model must be modified. Trustees prefer their own power to be singularly authoritative only when it comes to choosing the president of the institution. Having selected him, however, they like to lean heavily on him (and his administrative colleagues) for making the decisions.[12]

Finally, as seen in Table 6, there is a great deal of variation from group to group on these matters. It would appear that trustees of selective private institutions are most inclined to include other members of the academic community in the decision-making process, while trustees of non-selective public institutions are more inclined toward a power-at-the-top sort of arrangement. Notice, for example, that 50 per cent or more of the trustees feel that administrators and/or trustees alone should have major authority in deciding 13 of the 16 issues at public junior colleges, but only 4 of the 16 issues at selective private institutions. The concept of democratic governance or shared authority clearly has a more receptive audience among trustees at the latter type of institution. In fact, the ordering of institutions in Table 6 would correspond very closely to an ordering of institutional types by educational prestige. That is, where prestige is defined by the usual (but not necessarily reasonable) indices of student ability, faculty prominence and the like, it would appear that the greater the prestige of the institutional type, the more likely the trustees are to favor student and faculty involvement in decision making.[13] It can also be seen that, with the exception of the selective public universities, there is public-private division on this question.

It would be easy to get caught in a chicken vs. egg cycle in trying to account for these relationships, and there surely is no simple explanation. But again, speculation is hard to resist, and several interpretations are compelling. The most basic reason for the public-private difference probably comes from the sources of financial support. Because they do not have to answer to a public constituency, trustees of private institutions may be more willing to maintain a looser hold on the reins. Though accountable to the alumni, parents, and "friends" of the institution, such

[12] It should be remembered that these data refer to how trustees think decisions *should* be made, not how they *are* made. They are trustee preferences. As suggested in the introduction to this report, many claim that the trustees' real authority has diminished substantially over the years to a point where the gap between "paper" power and actual power is large indeed. For a more complete discussion of this, see Ernest L. Boyer, "A Fresh Look at the College Trustee," *Educational Record*, Summer, 1968, pp. 274–279.

[13] There is corroborating data for this assertion. In other research currently underway in the Higher Education Research Group at ETS, scores on the Democratic Governance scale of an experimental *Institutional Functioning Inventory* (an instrument which asks for faculty perceptions of their own institutions) have been found to correlate significantly with selectivity, income per student, proportion of faculty holding a doctorate, and average faculty compensation.

groups are basically *for* the institution and are seldom as concerned about its actions as the general public might be of colleges supported by tax money. Thus, trustees of private institutions are less hesitant to involve the faculty and students.

The reason for the prestige difference is not as straightforward but certainly no less important. There is a relationship between institutional prestige and trustee affluence. More specifically, the greater the prestige of the institution, the higher the trustees' income, level of education, occupational status, etc. Such people are probably more inclined to delegate authority and to be less concerned personally about maintaining control over things. Trustees of the more prestigious institutions, by virtue of the characteristics that led to their being selected to such boards, are simply more inclined to a laissez faire attitude regarding student and faculty involvement in campus governance.

In any event, the question "who shall govern" is obviously a very complex one and to be treated thoroughly would require far more detailed treatment than provided by the brief summary of responses reported here. Many faculty who complain about lack of participation in academic governance are actually unwilling to participate themselves and suspicious of other members of the faculty who do get involved. Furthermore, it is sometimes members of the faculty who would prefer to keep authority out of the hands of their colleagues. As one recent example of this, at an institution which is moving from a teachers' college to a large state university, one department chairman opposed efforts to give greater authority to faculty members on the grounds that there were still far too many holdovers on the faculty from the teacher-training days who were not at all interested in reseach and presumably would have slowed the institution's emergence as a first-rate institution.

Nevertheless, it seems safe to conclude that, by and large, faculty members tend to favor a horizontal as opposed to vertical form of authority, whereas trustees prefer a hierarchical arrangement or system of graded authority, imitating, it would seem the "bureaucratic management" model. Though neither of these forms of government actually exist in any pure sense, they still represent what would appear to be rather basic ideological differences between trustees and faculty.

SHELDON WOLIN
JOHN SCHAAR

Berkeley: The Battle
of People's Park

Shortly before 5:00 A.M., on Thursday, May 16 [1969], a motley group of
about fifty hippies and "street-people" were huddled together on a lot 270
by 450 feet in Berkeley. The lot was owned by the Regents of the University of California and located a few blocks south of the Berkeley
campus. Since mid-April this lot had been taken over and transformed into
a "People's Park" by scores of people, most of whom had no connection
with the university. Now the university was determined to reassert its
legal rights of ownership. A police officer approached the group and
announced that it must leave or face charges of trespassing. Except for
three persons, the group left and the area was immediately occupied and
surrounded by about 200 police from Berkeley, Alameda county, and the
campus. The police were equipped with flak jackets, tear gas launchers,
shotguns, and telescopic rifles. At 6:00 A.M. a construction crew arrived
and by mid-afternoon an eight-foot steel fence encircled the lot.

   At noon a rally was convened on campus and about 3,000 people gathered. The president-elect of the student body spoke. He started to suggest various courses of action that might be considered. The crowd
responded to the first of these by spontaneously marching toward the lot
guarded by the police. (For this speech, the speaker was charged a few
days later with violating numerous campus rules, and, on the initiative
of University officials, indicted for incitement to riot.) The crowd was
blocked by a drawn police line. Rocks and bottles were thrown at the
police, and the police loosed a tear gas barrage, scattering the crowd.
Elsewhere, a car belonging to the city was burned. Meanwhile, police
reinforcements poured in, soon reaching around 600. A rock was thrown
from a roof-top and, without warning, police fired into a group on the
roof of an adjacent building. Two persons were struck in the face by the
police fire, another was blinded, probably permanently, and a fourth,
twenty-five-year-old James Rector, later died. Before the day was over,
at least thirty others were wounded by police gunfire, and many more
by clubs. One policeman received a minor stab wound and six more were
reported as having been treated for minor cuts and bruises.

Meanwhile, action shifted to the campus itself, where police had herded a large crowd into Sproul Plaza by shooting tear gas along the bordering streets. The police then formed small detachments which continuously swept across the campus, breaking up groups of all sizes. Tear gas enfolded the main part of the campus and drifted into many of its buildings, as well as into the surrounding city. Nearby streets were littered with broken glass and rubble. At least six buckshot slugs entered the main library and three .38 calibre bullets lodged in the wall of a reference room in the same building. Before the day ended, more than ninety people had been injured by police guns and clubs.

Under a "State of Extreme Emergency" proclamation issued by Governor Reagan on February 5th in connection with the "Third World Strike" at Berkeley late last winter and never rescinded, a curfew was imposed on the city. Strict security measures were enforced on campus and in the nearby business districts, and all assemblies and rallies were prohibited. The proclamation also centralized control of the police under the command of Sheriff Frank Madigan of Alameda County.

Roger Heyns, the Chancellor of the University, saw none of this, for he had left the previous day for a meeting in Washington. His principal Vice-Chancellor had gone to the Regents' meeting in Los Angeles. The Regents took notice of the events by declaring, "It is of paramount importance that law and order be upheld." The Governor said that the lot had been seized by the street-people "as an excuse for a riot." A Berkeley councilman called the previous use of the lot a "Hippie Disneyland freak show."

The next day, May 17, 2,000 National Guardsmen appeared in full battle dress, armed with rifles, bayonets, and tear gas. They were called into action by the Governor, but apparently the initiative came from local authorities acting in consultation with University administrators. Helicopters weaved back and forth over the campus and city. Berkeley was occupied. (The next day one helicopter landed on campus and an officer came out to ask that students stop flying their kites because the strings might foul his rotors. A collection was promptly taken and the sky was soon full of brightly colored kites.)

During the next few days a pattern emerged. Each day began quietly, almost like any other day, except that people awoke to the roar of helicopters and the rumble of transports. As University classes began (they have never been officially cancelled), the Guardsmen formed a line along the south boundary of the campus. The Guard and the police would cordon off the main plaza and station smaller detachments at various points around the campus. Gradually the students crowded together, staring curiously at the Guardsmen and occasionally taunting them. The Guard stood ready with bayonets pointed directly at the crowd. This standoff would continue for an hour or two, and then the police would charge the crowd with clubs and tear gas. The crowd would scatter, the police would give chase, the students and street-people would curse and sometimes hurl rocks or return the tear gas canisters, and the police would beat or arrest some of them.

On Tuesday, May 20, the pattern and tempo changed. Previously the police had sought to break up gatherings on the campus, so now the protesters left the campus and began a peaceful march through the city. This was promptly stopped by the police. The marchers then filtered back to campus and a crowd of about 3,000 assembled. The group was pressed toward the Plaza by the police and Guardsmen and, when solidly hemmed in, was attacked by tear gas. A little later a helicopter flew low over the center of the campus and spewed gas over a wide area, even though the crowd had been thoroughly scattered. Panic broke out and people fled, weeping, choking, vomiting. Gas penetrated the University hospital, imperiling patients and interrupting hospital routines. It caused another panic at the University recreation area, nearly a mile from the center of campus, where many people, including mothers and children, were swimming. The police also threw gas into a student snack bar and into an office and classroom building.

The next day, May 21, was a turning point. More than 200 faculty members announced their refusal to teach; a local labor council condemned the police action; some church groups protested; and the newspapers and television stations began to express some criticism. Controversy arose over the ammunition which the police had used the previous Thursday. Sheriff Madigan was evasive about the size of birdshot issued, but the evidence was clear that buckshot had killed James Rector. The tear gas was first identified as the normal variety (CN) for crowd disturbances, but later it was officially acknowledged that a more dangerous gas (CS) was also used. The American army uses CS gas to flush out guerrillas in Vietnam. It can cause projectile vomiting, instant diarrhea, and skin blisters, and even death, as it has to the VC, when the victim is tubercular. The Geneva Conventions outlaw the use of CS in warfare.

On the same day the Chancellor issued his first statement. He deplored the death which had occurred, as well as "the senseless violence." He warned that attempts were being made "to polarize the community and prevent rational solutions," and he stated that a university has a responsibility to follow "civilized procedures." Heyns made no criticism of the police or National Guard tactics: that same day a Guardsman had thrown down his helmet, dropped his rifle, and reportedly shouted. "I can't stand this any more." He was handcuffed, taken away for a physical examination, and then rushed off to a psychiatric examination. He was diagnosed as suffering from "suppressed aggressions."

In Sacramento, where a deputation of Berkeley faculty members was meeting with the Governor, aggression was more open. The Governor conceded that the helicopter attack might have been a "tactical mistake," but he also insisted that "once the dogs of war are unleashed, you must expect things will happen. . . ." Meantime, the statewide commander of the Guards defended the gas attack on the grounds that his troops were threatened. He noted that the general who ordered the attack had said, "It was a Godsend that it was done at that time." The commander regretted the "discomfort and inconvenience to innocent bystanders," but added: "It is an inescapable by-product of combatting terrorists, anarchists, and hard-core militants on the streets and on the campus."

The next day, May 22, a peaceful march and flower planting procession began in downtown Berkeley. With little warning, police and Guardsmen converged on the unsuspecting participants and swept them, along with a number of shoppers, newsmen, people at lunch, and a mailman, into a parking lot, where 482 were arrested, bringing the week's total near 800. As those arrested were released on bail, disturbing stories began to circulate concerning the special treatment accorded "Berkeley types" in Santa Rita prison.

These stories, supported by numerous affidavits and news accounts submitted by journalists who had been bagged in the mass arrest, told of beatings, verbal abuse, and humiliation, physical deprivations, and refusal of permission to contact counsel. Male prisoners told of being marched into the prison yard and forced to lie face down, absolutely motionless, on gravel and concrete for several hours. The slightest shift in posture, except for a head movement permitted once every half hour, was met with a blow to the kidneys or testicles. On May 24th a District Court judge issued an order restraining Sheriff Madigan's subordinates from beating and otherwise mistreating the arrestees taken to Santa Rita prison.

Despite all the arrests, the shotguns, gas, and clubs, the protesters have thus far shown remarkable restraint. Although both police and Guards have been targets of much foul language and some hard objects, nothing remotely resembling sustained violence has been employed against the police; and the Guard has been spared from all except verbal abuse. At this writing, the only damage to campus property, other than that caused by the police, has been two broken windows and one flooded floor.

After the mass arrests, the Governor lifted the curfew and the ban on assemblies, saying "a more controlled situation" existed. But he warned that no solution was likely until the trouble-making faculty and students were separated from the University. "A professional revolutionary group," he said, was behind it all. Charles Hitch, the President of the University of California, issued his first statement. (Much earlier, his own staff issued a statement protesting campus conditions of "intolerable stress" and physical danger.) The President ventured to criticize "certain tactics" of the police, but noted that these "were not the responsibility of university authorities."

In a television interview, the Chancellor agreed with the President, but added that negotiations were still possible because "we haven't stopped the rational process." A published interview (May 22) with the principal Vice-Chancellor found him saying, "Our strategy was to act with humor and sensitivity. For instance, we offered to roll up the sod in the park and return it to the people. . . . We had no reason to believe there would be trouble." Meanwhile the Governor was saying, "The police didn't kill the young man. He was killed by the first college administrator who said some time ago it was all right to break laws in the name of dissent."

The Governor also accused the President of the University, a former Assistant Secretary of Defense and RANDsman, of "trying to weasel" to the side of the street-people. Two days later the Governor refused the request of the Berkeley City Council to end the state of emergency and recall the Guard — requests, it might be added, that the University itself has not yet made. At this time the Mayor of Berkeley suggested that police tactics had been "clumsy and not efficient," to which Sheriff Madigan retorted: "If the Mayor was capable of running the city so well without problems we wouldn't be here. I advise the Mayor to take his umbrella and go to Berkeley's Munich. . . ."

On Friday, May 23, the Faculty Senate met. It listened first to a speech by the Chancellor in which he defined the occupation of the lot as an act of "unjustified aggression" against the University, and declared that the "avoidance of confrontations cannot be the absolute value." He said that the fence would remain as long as the issue was one of possession and control, and, pleading for more "elbow room," he asserted that the faculty should support or at least not oppose an administrative decision once it had been made. The faculty then defeated a motion calling for the Chancellor's removal (94 voted for, 737 against, and 99 abstained). It approved, by a vote of 737 to 94, a series of resolutions which condemned what was called "as irresponsible a police and military reaction to a civic disturbance as this country has seen in recent times."

The resolutions demanded withdrawal of "the massive police and military presence on campus"; the "cessation of all acts of belligerency and provocation by demonstrators"; an investigation by the Attorney General of California and the Department of Justice; and the prompt implementation of a plan whereby part of the lot would become "an experimental community-generated park" and the fence would be simultaneously removed. The faculty also resolved to reconvene in a few days to reassess the situation.

There is where events now stand (May 26). But pressures from all sides are increasing. A student referendum, which saw the heaviest turnout in the history of student voting, found 85 per cent of the nearly 15,000 who voted favoring the use of the lot as it had been before the occupation. The students also voted to assess themselves $1.50 each quarter to help finance an ethnic studies department previously accepted by the University but now foundering. As of this writing, college students from all over the state are planning direct protests to Governor Reagan. Leaders of the protesters are preparing for a huge march against the fence on Memorial Day. The Governor remains committed to a hard line. All the issues remain unsettled.

What brought on this crisis? Like many of its sister institutions, the Berkeley campus has been steadily advancing its boundaries into the city. Back in 1956 it had announced its intention to purchase property in the area which includes the present disputed lot. Owing to lack of funds, very little land was actually purchased. Finally, in June, 1967, the monies were allocated and the University announced that ultimately dormitories would be built on the land, but that in the interim it would be used for recreation.

The lot itself was purchased in 1968, but no funds were then available for development. Undoubtedly the University was aware of the disastrous experience of other academic institutions which had attempted to "redevelop" surrounding areas. In fact, a short time ago the University announced, with much fanfare, its intention to mount a major attack on the problems of the cities. Despite these professions, the University's treatment of its own urban neighbors has consisted of a mixture of middle-class prejudice, aesthetic blindness, and bureaucratic callousness.

The victims in this case, however, have not been so much the Blacks as another pariah group, one whose identity is profoundly influenced by the University itself. For many years, Telegraph Avenue and "the south campus area" have constituted a major irritant to the University, the City fathers, and the business interests. It is the Berkeley demi-monde, the place where students, hippies, drop-outs, radicals, and run-aways congregate. To the respectables, it is a haven for drug addicts, sex fiends, criminals, and revolutionaries. Until the University began its expansion, it was also an architectural preserve for fine old brown shingle houses and interesting shops. It is no secret that the University has long considered the acquisition of land as a means of ridding the area not of substandard housing, but of its human "blight." The disputed lot was the perfect symbol of the University's way of carrying out urban regeneration: first, raze the buildings; next let the land lay idle and uncared for; then permit it to be used as an unimproved parking lot, muddy and pitted;

and finally, when the local people threaten to use and enjoy the land, throw a fence around it.

Around mid-April, a movement was begun by street-people, hippies, students, radicals, and a fair sprinkling of elderly free spirits to take over the parking lot and transform it. Many possibilities were discussed: a child care clinic; a crafts fair; a baseball diamond. Soon grass and shrubs were planted, playground equipment installed, benches built, and places made for eating, lounging, and occasional speechmaking. About 200 people were involved in the beginning, but soon the Park was intensively and lovingly used by children, the young, students and street-people, and the elderly. A week after the Park began, the University announced its intention to develop a playing field by July 1, and the Park people responded by saying that the University would have to fight for it. Discussions followed, but not much else. The University said, however, that no construction would be started without proper warning and that it was willing to discuss the future design of the field.

On May 8 the Chancellor agreed to form a committee representing those who were using the lot as well as the University. But he insisted as "an essential condition" of discussions about the future of the land that all work on the People's Park cease. In addition he announced certain guidelines for his committee: University control and eventual use must be assured; the field must not produce "police and other control problems"; and no political or public meetings were to be held on the land. Suddenly, on May 13, he announced his decision to fence in the area as the first step toward developing the land for intramural recreation. "That's a hard way to make a point," he said, "but that's the way it has to be. . . . The fence will also give us time to plan and consult. Regretfully, this is the only way the entire site can be surveyed, soil tested, and planned for development . . . hence the fence."

Why did it have to be this way? Because, as the Chancellor explained, it was necessary to assert the University's title to ownership. Concerning the apparent lack of consultation with his own committee, he said that a plan could not be worked out because the Park people had not only refused to stop cultivating and improving the land, but they had "refused to organize a responsible committee" for consultative purposes. In addition, he cited problems of health, safety, and legal liability, as well as complaints from local residents.

The first response came from the faculty chairman of the Chancellor's committee. He declared that the Chancellor had allowed only two days (the weekend) for the committee to produce a plan and that the "University didn't seem interested in negotiations." On May 14 a protest rally was held and the anarchs of the Park, surprisingly, pulled themselves together and formed a negotiating committee. Although rumors of an impending fence were circulating, spokesmen for the Park people insisted that they wanted discussion, not confrontation.

On May 15, the day immediately preceding the early morning police action, the Chancellor placed an advertisement in the campus newspaper inviting students to draw up "ideas or designs" for the lot and to submit them by May 21. The ad was continued even after the military occupation. On May 18, three days after the occupation had begun, the Chancellor announced that there would be "no negotiations in regard to the land known as People's Park," although discussions might go on "while the fence is up anyway." His principal Vice-Chancellor, in an interview reported on May 22, stated that the University had not turned down a negotiating committee.

He also noted — and this was after the helicopter attack — that "the fence was necessary to permit the kind of rational discussion and planning that wasn't possible before." Once more the faculty chairman had to protest that he had not been informed of meetings between the Administration and representatives of the People's Park and that the Chancellor had consistently ignored the committee's recommendations. However, the principal Vice-Chancellor had an explanation for this lack of consultation: "I guess that's because the Chancellor didn't want him to get chewed up by this thing."

Why did the making of a park provoke such a desolating response? The bureaucratic nature of the multiversity and its disastrous consequences for education are by now familiar and beyond dispute. So, too, is the web of interdependence between it and the dominant military, industrial, and political institutions of our society. These explain much about the response of the University to the absurd, yet hopeful, experiment of People's Park.

What needs further comment is the increasingly ineffectual quality of the University's responses, particularly when its organizational apparatus attempts to cope with what is spontaneous, ambiguous, and disturbingly human. It is significant that the Berkeley adminisration repeatedly expressed irritation with the failure of the Park people to "organize" a "responsible committee" or to select "representatives" who might "negotiate." The life-styles and values of the Park people were forever escaping the categories and procedures of those who administer the academic plant.

Likewise the issue itself: the occupants of the Park wanted to use the land for a variety of projects, strange but deeply natural, which defied customary forms and expectations, whereas, at worst, the University saw the land as something to be fenced, soil-tested, processed through a score of experts and a maze of committees, and finally encased in the tight and tidy form of a rational design. At best, the most imaginative use of the land which the University could contemplate was as a "field-experiment station" where faculty and graduate students could observe their fellow beings coping with their "environment." In brief, the educational bureaucracy, like bureaucracies elsewhere, is experiencing increasing difficulty, because human life is manifesting itself in forms which are unrecognizable to the mentality of the technological age.

This suggests that part of the problem lies in the very way bureaucracies perceive the world and process information from it. It was this "bureaucratic epistemology" which largely determined how the University responded to the People's Park. Bureaucracy is both an expression of the drive for rationality and predictability, and one of the chief agencies in making the world ever more rational and predictable, for the bureaucratic mode of knowing and behaving comes to constitute the things known and done themselves.

Now this rational form of organizing human efforts employs a conception of knowledge which is also rational in specific ways (cf. Kenneth Keniston's analysis in *The Uncommitted: Alienated Youth in American Society*, 1967, pp. 253–272). The only legitimate instrument of knowledge is systematic cognition, and the only acceptable mode of discourse is the cognitive mode. Other paths to knowledge are suspect. Everything tainted with the personal, and subjective, and the passionate is suppressed, or dismissed as prejudice or pathology. A bureaucrat who based his decisions upon, say, intuition, dialectical reason, empathic awareness, or even common sense, would be guilty of misconduct.

The bureaucratic search for "understanding" does not begin in wonder, but in the reduction of the world to the ordinary and the manageable. In order to deal with the world in the cognitive mode, the world must first be approached as an exercise in "problem-solving." To say there is a problem is to imply there is a solution; and finding the solution largely means devising the right technique. Since most problems are "complex," they must be broken down by bureaucrats into their component parts before the right solution can be found. Reality is parsed into an ensemble of discrete though related parts, and each part is assigned to the expert specially qualified to deal with that part. Wholes can appear as nothing more than assemblages of parts, just as a whole automobile is an assemblage of parts. But in order for wholes to be broken into parts, things that are dissimilar in appearance and quality must be made similar.

This is done by abstracting from the objects dealt with those aspects as though they were the whole. Abstraction and grouping by common attributes require measuring tools that yield comparable units for analysis: favorite ones are units of money, time, space, and power; income, occupation, and party affiliation. All such measurements and comparisons subordinate qualitative dimensions, natural context, and unique and variable properties to the common, stable, external, and reproducible. This way of thinking becomes real when campus administrators define "recreation" in fixed and restrictive terms so that it may accord with the abstract demands of "leadtime." In a way Hegel might barely recognize, the Rational becomes the Real and the Real the Rational.

When men treat themselves this way, they increasingly become this way, or they desperately try to escape the "mind-forged manacles," as Blake called them, of the bureaucratic mentality and mode of conduct. In the broadest view, these two trends increasingly dominate the advanced states of our day. On the one side, we see the march toward uniformity, predictability, and the attempt to define all variety as dissent and then to force dissent into the "regular channels" — toward that state whose model citizen is Tocqueville's "industrious sheep," that state whose only greatness is its collective power.

On the other side we see an assertion of spontaneity, self-realization, and do-your-own-thing as the sum and substance of life and liberty. And this assertion, in its extreme form, does approach either madness or infantilism, for the only social institutions in which each member is really free to do his own thing are Bedlam and the nursery, where the condition may be tolerated because there is a keeper with ultimate control over the inmates. The opposing forces were not quite that pure in the confrontation over the People's Park, but the University and public officials nearly managed to make them so. That they could not do so is a comforting measure of the basic vitality of those who built the Park and who have sacrificed to preserve it.

But this still does not account for the frenzy of violence which fell on Berkeley. To understand that, we must shift focus.

Clark Kerr was perceptive when he defined the multiversity as "a mechanism held together by administrative rules and powered by money." But it is important to understand that the last few years in the University have seen more and more rules and less and less money. The money is drying up because the rules are being broken. The rules are being broken because University authorities, administrators and faculty alike, have lost the respect of very many of the students. When authority leaves, power enters — first in the form of more and tougher rules, then as sheer physical force, and finally as violence, which is force unrestrained by any thought of healing and saving, force whose aim is to cleanse by devastation.

Pressed from above by politicians and from below by students, the University Administration simultaneously imposes more rules and makes continual appeals to the faculty for more support in its efforts to cope with permanent emergency. It pleads with the faculty for more "elbow room," more discretionary space in which to make the hard decisions needed when money runs short and students run amuck. That same Administration is right now conducting time-and-motion studies of faculty work and "productivity." Simultaneously, both faculty and Administration make spasmodic efforts to give the students some voice in the governance of the institution. But those efforts are always too little, too late, too grudging.

Besides, as soon as the students get some power, unseemly things happen. Admit the Blacks on campus and they demand their own autonomous departments. Give the students limited power to initiate courses and they bring in Eldridge Cleaver and Tom Hayden. The faculty sees student initiative as a revolting mixture of Agitprop and denial of professional prerogatives. The Administration sees it as a deadly threat to its own precarious standing within the University and before the public. The politicians see it as concession to anarchy and revolution. The result is more rules and less trust all around — more centralization, bureaucratization, and force on one side, more despair and anger on the other.

Under these conditions, the organized system must strive to extend its control and reduce the space in which spontaneous and unpredictable actions are possible. The subjects, on the other hand, come to identify spontaneity and unpredictability with all that is human and alive, and rule and control with all that is inhuman and dead. Order and liberty stand in fatal opposition. No positive synthesis can emerge from this dialectic unless those who now feel themselves pushed out and put down are admitted as full participants. But that is not happening. More and more, we are seeing in this country a reappearance of that stage in the breakdown of political societies where one segment of the whole — in this case still the larger segment — determines to dominate by force and terror other segments which reject and challenge its legitimacy.

This dynamic largely accounts for the crushing violence and terror that hit Berkeley. When spontaneity appeared in People's Park, it was first met by a re-statement of the rules governing possession and control of land. When that re-statement did not have the desired effect, the University failed to take the next step dictated by rule-governed behavior — seeking an injunction. Nor did it take the step which would have acknowledged itself as being in a political situation — talking on a plane of equality, and acting in a spirit of generosity, with the other parties. Instead, it regressed immediately to the use of physical measures. In the eyes of the Administration, the building of People's Park was an "unjustified aggression," and the right of self-defense was promptly invoked.

Once force was called into play, it quickly intensified, and the University cannot evade its share of responsibility for what followed. He who wills the end wills the means; and no University official could have been unaware of the means necessary to keep that fence standing. But the administrators did not quite understand that their chosen agents of force, the police, would not limit their attention only to the students and street-people, who were expendable, but would turn against the University and the city as well.

Ronald Reagan reached Sacramento through Berkeley because, in the eyes of his frightened and furious supporters, Berkeley is daily the scene of events that would have shocked Sodom and revolutionary Moscow. All this came into intense focus in the behavior of the cops who were on the scene.

The police were numerous and armed with all the weapons a fertile technology can provide and an increasingly frightened citizenry will permit. Their superiority of force is overwhelming, and they are convinced they could "solve the problem" overnight if they were permitted to do it their own way: one instant crushing blow, and then license for dealing with the remaining recalcitrants. All the troublemakers are known to the police, either by dossier and record or by appearance and attitude. But the police are kept under some restraints, and those restraints produce greater and greater rage.

The rage comes from another source as well. Demands for a different future have been welling up in this society for some years now, and while those demands have not been unheard they have gone unheeded. Vietnam, racism, poverty, the degradation of the natural and manmade environment, the bureaucratization of the academy and its active collaboration with the military and industrial state, unrepresentative and unreachable structures of domination — all these grow apace. It seems increasingly clear to those who reject this American future that the forces of "law and order" intend to defend it by any means necessary. It becomes increasingly clear to the forces of law and order that extreme means will be necessary, and that the longer they are delayed the more extreme they will have to be.

Those two futures met at People's Park. It should be clear that what is happening this time is qualitatively different from 1964 and the Free Speech Movement. The difference in the amount of violence is the most striking, but this is largely a symptom of underlying differences. In 1964, the issues centered around questions of civil liberties and due process within the University. The issues now are political in the largest sense.

The appearance of People's Park raised questions of property and the nature of meaningful work. It raised questions about how people can begin to make a livable environment for themselves; about why both the defenders and critics of established authority today agree that authority can be considered only in terms of repression, never in terms of genuine respect and affection. These questions cannot be evaded. Those who honestly and courageously ask them are not imperiling the general happiness but are working for the common redemption.

It is increasingly clear that legitimate authority is declining in the modern state. In a real sense, "law and order" *is* the basic question of our day. This crisis of legitimacy has been visible for some time in just about all of the non-political sectors of life — family, economy, religion, education — and is now spreading rapidly into the political realm. The gigantic and seemingly impregnable organizations that surround and dominate men in the modern states are seen by more and more people to have at their center not a vital principle of authority, but a hollow space, a moral vacuum. Increasingly, among the young and the rejected, obedience is mainly a matter of lingering habit, or expediency, or necessity, but not a matter of conviction and deepest sentiment.

The groups who are most persistently raising these questions are, of course, white middle-class youth and the racial and ethnic minorities. The origins of protest are different in the two cases: the former have largely seen through the American Dream of meaning in power and wealth and have found it a nightmare; the latter have been pushed aside and denied even the minimal goods of the Dream. But the ends of the protest are remarkably similar: both are fighting against distortions and denials of their humanity. Both reject the programmed future of an America whose only imperative now seems to be: more.

The people who built the Park (there will be more People's Parks, more and more occasions for seemingly bizarre, perverse, and wild behavior) have pretty much seen through the collective ideals and disciplines that have bound this nation together in its conquest of nature and power. Having been victimized by the restraints and authorities of the past, these people are suspicious of all authorities and most collective ideals. Some of them seem ready to attempt a life built upon no other ideal than self-gratification. They sometimes talk as though they had found the secret which has lain hidden through all the past ages of man: that the individual can live fully and freely with no authority other than his desires, absorbed completely in the development of all his capacities except two — the capacity for memory and the capacity for faith.

No one can say where this will lead. Perhaps new prophets will appear. Perhaps the old faith will be reborn. Perhaps we really shall see the new technological Garden tended by children — kind, sincere innocents, barbarians with good hearts. The great danger at present is that the established and the respectable are more and more disposed to see all this as chaos and outrage. They seem prepared to follow the most profoundly nihilistic denial possible, which is the denial of the future through denial of their own children, the bearers of the future.

In such times as these, hope is not a luxury but a necessity. The hope which we see is in the revival of a sense of shared destiny, of some common fate which can bind us into a people we have never been. Even to sketch out that fate one must first decide that it does not lie with the power of technology or the stability of organizational society. It lies, instead, in something more elemental, in our common fears that scientific weapons may destroy all life; that technology will increasingly disfigure men who live in the city, just as it has already debased the earth and obscured the sky; that the "progress" of industry will destroy the possibility of interesting work; and that "communications" will obliterate the last traces of the varied cultures which have been the inheritance of all but the most benighted societies.

If hope is to be born of these despairs it must be given political direction, a new politics devoted to nurturing life and work. There can be no political direction without political education, yet America from its beginnings has never confronted the question of how to care for men's souls while helping them to see the world politically. Seeing the world politically is preparatory to acting in it politically; and to act politically is not to be tempted by the puerile attraction of power or to be content with the formalism of a politics of compromise. It is, instead, a politics which seeks always to discover what men can share — and how what they share can be enlarged and yet rise beyond the banal.

People's Park is not banal. If only the same could be said of those who build and guard the fences around all of us.

BARBARA RASKIN   *Federal City College:*
                                   Militancy in Microcosm

Washington's new Federal City College differs from other embattled campuses in a number of interesting ways.

Its students are predominantly black; its ultimate arbiters are members of the House of Representatives and the Senate; and the conflicts that beset it are pretty much confined — so far, at least — to the faculty, which is roughly half black and half white.

Reprinted by permission from *The Washington Monthly*, April, 1969.

What makes the college of more than parochial interest, however, is its emergence as an unusual, if not unique, battleground for many of the same issues that are swirling through older (and whiter) centers of higher education.

A word of background first:

Currently housed in a large, renovated government building close to the black community it was chiefly established to serve, Federal City College grew out of Congressional legislation introduced in 1966 by former Senator Wayne Morse (D-Ore.) and by Representative Ancher Nelson (R-Minn.). The college was to be a comprehensive, low-cost institution of higher education for District of Columbia students, and it was to be financed through the annual D.C. appropriations from Congress. It's work was to be overseen (some might now say overlooked) by a nine-member Board of Higher Education.

In July, 1967, the Board concluded its search for the first president of Federal City College and appointed Frank Farner, a white professor of education and former associate dean of the graduate school at the University of Oregon. F.C.C. adopted an open-enrollment policy which makes any D.C. resident with the equivalent of a high-school diploma eligible for admission, and it set modest tuition fees: $25 per academic quarter. It decided to offer two degrees: a two-year Associate of Arts and a four-year Bachelor of Arts, with courses in a wide variety of liberal arts and professional fields.

After the college announced that it was ready to receive applications from would-be students, it was surprised by the response: 6,000 applications vs. an initial capacity of 2,000 students. The administration devised a lottery system for admission, by which the 2,000 entering students were almost literally picked out of a hat. When the college opened its doors last fall, the average age of the students was 21 (virtually all of them freshmen); 94 per cent were black; 58 per cent were women; 40 per cent were night students; and 50 per cent were part-time students. Many had worked for several years after high school; in fact, less than one-third entered Federal City College directly from high school.

Power struggles at Federal City College involve several groupings: political moderates, liberals, and militants; educational realists, traditionalists, and innovationists; the faculty, the administration, and the students; and, finally, blacks and whites. These struggles range over such a diversity of highly charged issues that the pattern of allies and opponents is in constant flux. So are the labels.

All this action, plus the building's attractive gold carpets, purple couches, and pink doors create the carnival atmosphere of an ideological circus. Corridors and offices brim with endless discussions about policies and priorities, as students and faculty groups, each with their own set of internal objectives and invisible agendas, thrash out the controversies.

Roughly speaking, there are four (sometimes) recognizable schools of thought on the faculty:

1. The Pedagogic Radicals. They are committed to changing academic structures, trying new techniques, and questioning the ideas of "excellence" as defined and encouraged in the most prestigious white colleges.

2. The Educational Excellencers. They believe in a more classical education, one which prepares students for leadership and/or participation in a traditional, hierarchically organized, white-middle-class society.

3. The Educational Technocrats. They believe that the ultimate organizing principle should be the job market; they believe the college's major goal is to erase academic deficiencies and prepare students for vocations in the workaday world.

4. The Black Studies Militants. They are dedicated to developing in the students instrumental knowledge that will be useful in understanding and changing the social, political, and economic systems of the country.

Although there was no separate Black Studies department when F.C.C. opened in September, the January quarter started with an officially recognized, visibly active program under the direction of James Garrett, a 26-year-old graduate of San Francisco State College, who had helped to organize the powerful Black Student Union there in 1966. He came to F.C.C. as a creative writing instructor and quickly became the symbol and the center of academic and political controversy on the campus.

Joseph Brent, a white professor of history and the elected chairman of the faculty, outlines the controversy in this way: "The problem that divides the teachers at Federal City College is the existence of two fundamentally different cultures — the black and the white. The cultural orientations are stronger than personal, class, social, political, or pedagogic attitudes. The educational objectives of each group are culture-bound, and the basic split over policy stems from the traditional white idea of education as a way OUT of a particular environment, as a catalyst for individual success or mobility. The black militants view education as a means of reaffirming black culture within a pluralistic society and returning students to their communities educated, radicalized, and ideologically committed to social and political change."

Most of the white liberals who joined the faculty were attracted, at least to some extent, by what they saw as an opportunity to pursue unconventional educational policies. They wanted to break away from the exclusively traditional programs, conventional standards of achievement, and rigid, credit-dictated requirements that had alienated students and ignited college rebellions across the country. They advocated the elimination of competitive grading systems and they favored methods which they felt would create a freer and more productive academic community. Many of the white liberals on the faculty assumed that their support of this approach, along with their commitment to black cultural values, would give them a union card into the circle of militant black leaders. Instead, they were hurt and bewildered when many of the black faculty and student radicals turned against them.

While structural and organizational reforms may be relevant to middle-class white colleges, where students feel the need to be liberated from constraining traditions, these objectives seemed incidental, if not downright antithetical, to the black militant goals at F.C.C. Black leaders accused these white Pedagogic Radicals of trying to superimpose their ideas about innovative education without any fundamental understanding of the students' needs. To the militant blacks, particularly in the Black Studies program, collegiate structural reforms were beside the point. They were interested in one end: instilling a black consciousness in students which would ultimately lead them into roles as revolutionary social activists in ghetto areas. The procedural question that concerned them was: what is the most expedient and efficient way of achieving this end? The answer led them toward just the kind of approach that many white pedagogic radicals had thought they were escaping by joining the F.C.C. faculty: traditional, conservative, authoritarian techniques, and a minimum of open dialogue. Donal Jones, a white professor of psychology, predicts that the students enrolled in Black Studies "will eventually get smart to the authoritarian, dictatorial approach and rebel against the rigidities and formalities of the program. Eventually the students will set the militant teachers straight."

He was not alone in his criticism. Many black moderates objected to the materials and methods used in Black Studies and charged that the militants were trying to take over the entire college to train revolutionaries and propagandize the student body. David W. D. Dickson, the black Provost and Vice President for Academic Affairs said: "Black separatists . . . negate academic principles for revolutionary ends." The Educational Excellencers shook their heads over the academically conservative historical focus that the militants advocated, and the Educational Technocrats worried that preoccupation with black consciousness would divert attention from the courses in basic skills which academically undernourished products of the D.C. public school system so badly need. Many of the pedagogic and political disputes deteriorated into personal and racial quarrels. One white faculty member, who plans to resign in June, claims: "The black militants want control over their own programs because they can't meet white academic standards."

Another aspect of the argument between the Black Studies Militants and the white Pedagogic Radicals — and probably the chief one — involved the form and content of courses.

The militants demanded the power to present ideas about black culture, black consciousness, black history, black community development, and black revolutionary unity in all of the courses offered by the college. They regarded the Pedagogic Radicals as "square" representatives of the white system. While they recognized the need for students to develop basic skills, they saw this only as a technical prerequisite for a revolutionary education. They viewed the students as part of an underdeveloped nation that must acquire technical skills for the day when the colonial powers are driven out and the colonized people assume control over their own communities. Black Studies Militants were forced to develop a heavy academic program incorporating technical information and political studies. The staggering amounts of material to be transmitted frequently required ultra-conventional classes and doctrinaire teaching techniques.

Interracial faculty discussions about the meaning and nature of a great liberal arts education illuminated further differences between the white Pedagogic Radicals and the Black Studies Militants. Was a high-powered, high-quality education to lead simply to knowledge for its own sake (presumably)? Or was it to indoctrinate students with revolutionary ideas and an ideological commitment to return to their communities as leaders in social and political struggles? There was agreement on one point: both the white liberals and the black militants wanted to orient educational policies toward breaking out of what they regarded as a morally corrupt white system. Neither wanted a conventional program which instructed students in how to succeed within the system. But while the Black Studies Militants agreed with this objective, they contended that even the best white teachers could not communicate with Washington students because whites do not understand black culture and are not equipped to define or explain it to students who have a high level of urban sophistication.

The militants believe that black teachers — through cultural understanding, linguistic-stylistic rapport, an implicitly natural acceptance of the student's adequacy within his own community — can extract the sense of pride and rigorous self-discipline which is a prerequisite for academic success. The militant faculty claimed that even scientific and professional courses should be taught by blacks, so that the students would not be further colonized by white-system-oriented material presented by white faculty members. The militants wanted the entire student body exposed to the ideas of black unity, black pride, and black power during their freshmen year — that is, before they entered advanced professional training courses. They wanted a first-year program that taught skills and materials but which also encouraged students to bolt the system and establish a new order based on black separatism and nationalism. But here a flashback is in order.

Curriculum planning took place in the early spring and summer of 1968, when only three-quarters of the faculty had been hired and an even smaller percentage were on campus. This group was composed mostly of men and women with strong academic credentials; politically, they were mostly moderate or liberal.

They worked strenously to put together a first-year core curriculum for the entering freshman class. Within this group the Pedagogic Radicals, most of whom are white, provided experimental ideas designed to suit the needs of academically deprived students. They worked toward integrating courses in an innovative, dynamic, tightly unified, interdisciplinary way that would (a) stimulate and sustain the interest of urban black students, and (b) inconspicuously provide remedial help in basic skills. Moderates and liberals, blacks and whites agreed at the time on the need to emphasize subjects dealing with urban problems; and they also agreed that the method of presentation should reflect an essentially black, though non-militant, orientation.

They were aware that traditional college programs elsewhere had failed to interest the students. They were equally aware of the cultural backgrounds of poor inner-city blacks. And so the group tried to develop what they thought was a high-quality but sensible curriculum that responded to the needs of an open-enrollment policy. In the Humanities division, there were two courses dealing with the "philosophy and ideals of man as represented in literature or drama." The courses were called "Man's Quest for the Good Life" and "Man, Ideas, and Society." There was also a course in Communicative Arts that presented "the spectrum of the field in general lectures supplemented by sections on graphics, drama, art, music, television, interpretive reading, and communication theory." In theory, crossing disciplinary lines, integrating materials, and keeping the subject relevant would insure the students' interest and success.

But after classes began, the student body rejected the team-teaching, integrated core curriculum. Accustomed to a substandard D.C. public school system, the students felt uncomfortable or disoriented in open-minded, unstructured classes. They requested "de-integration" of the curriculum and a return to a traditional scheduling pattern, with math offered in one place at 10:00 and English in another room at 1:00. Although the idea of a standard freshman English Composition course had been discarded by the curriculum planning committee, the students asked for basic math and English courses, which they felt were essential for overcoming their deficiencies in basic skills. Thus it became clear that the college had to respond to the needs and demands of a student body that was much more conservative than almost anyone had anticipated.

The outnumbered Educational Technocrats, who had favored a strong basic-skill program in the first place, felt vindicated at the emergence of conservative academic demands from the student body. They had believed all along that F.C.C. should have developed the kind of course which would lead most directly to a diploma, a good job, and an efficient means of "making it." They now stepped up their lobbying for practical, pre-professional programs geared toward equalizing opportunities for blacks in terms of jobs, career promotions, earning potential, and social mobility.

The Educational Technocrats berated the Pedagogic Radicals for having advocated far-out academic reforms. They muttered that such white anti-conformist teachers shouldn't presume to tell the academic have-nots about the valuelessness of a traditional education which D.C. students had never even had the opportunity to reject! A professionally oriented program, the Technocrats argued, did not necessarily exclude high-quality courses or teachers.

Looking back, it appears that the planners had too little time and too little knowledge of the students to construct a realistic program last summer, even though some students-to-be were consulted about their curricular interests. Faculty members who arrived just prior to the opening of the fall term found themselves in team-teaching situations — and in pedagogical or personal conflicts.

But more important, perhaps, the composition and size of the faculty had changed after Congress appropriated supplemental funds last summer for an additional 30 teachers. The faculty, then 75 per cent white, voted in favor of filling all of the 30 additional slots with blacks — to bring the faculty's racial composition up to a 50-50 ratio. What they may not have anticipated was that many of the blacks hired for those 30 positions would be militants.

It is true that a great percentage of the 2,000 students at F.C.C. are obviously, and with good reason, highly career- and job-conscious. Many of them feel at odds with the Black Studies Militants, whose political agitation seems distracting and potentially destructive, as well as with the Pedagogic Radicals, who seem only to make college confusing and complicated for students who want to earn credits, get a degree, and find a good job in the outside world. The needs and rights of these students — "hustlers" is the mildly disparaging term used by their critics — are taken seriously by most of the faculty. Everyone has had to compromise some of his technical experiments or political objectives to accommodate them. Yet the Pedagogic Radicals tremble at the prospect of another conventional college like the ones many of them fled, and the Black Studies Militants plead for the opportunity to expose even the most career-oriented students to some militant ideology. But once again, there is a split as to whether the arguments over traditional programs concern structure and form, or substance and philosophy.

Some time during the fall, when disputes became too obstreperous, the faculty finally began to make some deals. (Donald Taylor says that these squabbles over educational policy occupied so much attention that the militants seized upon the situation to gain political control and power.) The fragile solution to all of these pedagogical disputes has been the development of a sort of academic supermarket which attempts to offer something palatable and profitable to everyone. "Variety" has become the most frequently uttered word around F.C.C., as the administration attempts to accommodate as many different interest groups as possible. Within budgetary limits, efforts have been made to find space (educationally, politically, and socially) for each and every kind of student and for all of the pedagogical and political groups.

There are still disputes as to what such variety will cost, in terms of both money and quality. Will the value of a degree from F.C.C. be deflated by such widespread diversification? As for methods and materials, what kinds of priorities and standards will determine the allocation of funds and faculty to meet the college's highly charged, often contradictory, demands? Will top-quality teachers come to a college where energy is siphoned off into academic and political schisms? Will the administration allow street-wise candidates who lack the usual academic credentials to join the Black Studies faculty? And by whom will such questions be resolved?

When Black Studies was granted autonomy as a department, it also became separate from the other four divisions (Humanities, Social Sciences, Natural Sciences, and Professional Studies). The status and power of Black Studies has still not been completely defined, but the college's board recently declared — after having kept its distance from campus controversies for months — that it would not approve a program "which is designed to encourage separation between the black and white races, or which would increase rather than seek to eliminate racial antagonism or conflict, or which would encourage or condone violence as a means of resolving issues."

The Black Studies Militants have had the chance to develop their own autonomous four-year program, thereby appeasing widely diversified student and faculty interests. But the militants are ambivalent about autonomy because it has separated them from the rest of the college, at least academically. They claim that their separation deprives them of the chance to reach 90 per cent of the students — those who are *not* enrolled in Black Studies. To their way of thinking, this means that all but 10 per cent of the student body has been abandoned to a traditional white-mirror

educational experience. They had hoped to have a crack at "psychologi-
cally liberating" all of the students, across the board.

The academic program developed by the Black Studies program is described in these words:

> If education is to be relevant to Black people, it must have a two-
> fold purpose: revolution and nation-building. If the education of
> Black students is to be meaningful, it must direct these students
> toward the destruction of the forces of racism, colonialism and op-
> pression that continue to drain Black people all over the world; and
> it must develop in them the skills which will allow them to con-
> ceptualize and structure projections of future Black existence.

The first goal — revolution — concerns the psychological and educational liberation ("decolonization of the mind") which they feel students
need to move toward revolutionary confrontation with the system that
oppresses them. The second — nation-building — directs the students
back into their own communities to build black systems, politically and
economically. The curriculum stresses African history and culture in an
attempt to clarify the past, explain the causes of black oppression, and
prepare for a new nationalist state.

Frank Smith, one of the faculty members of the Black Studies Program,
says: "Black Studies represents an attempt to focus on the rebuilding of a
community that is in great need of reconstruction. Because our people are
in need of decent housing, we use that need as a base for establishing
courses in our curriculum. To develop a housing program that responds
to our community, students must study everything from environmental
planning and architecture to actual construction work such as bricklaying.
Such an overall program makes us confront the trade unions, the construction companies, the bank . . . the entire system. In other words, our curriculum comes out of the communities' needs and we answer with
education, as well as social programs. We are offering technical, political,
and cultural courses. We will work closely with the natural and physical
sciences because our community has a need for skilled people in biology,
chemistry, engineering in order to help build and maintain a self-sufficient
black nation."

The non-militant groups of students and faculty live in daily fear that
the Black Studies people will politicize some issue to such a pitch that the
white-southern-controlled House Appropriations District Subcommittee
will retaliate with financial cutbacks, thus endangering F.C.C.'s survival.
Though the militants are not the kind to back away from a good fight, they
are ultimately restrained from such action by a primary determination to
serve the local community's need for an institution of higher education.
It seems doubtful that they will create the kind of ultimate confrontation

that would jeopardize F.C.C.'s existence. They want to preserve F.C.C., even if this means sacrificing some of their own revolutionary agenda. (Here there is some militant factionalism.) So far, however, the unifying cry is "The Brothers Must Stick Together," and commitments to this ideal soft-pedals conflict and forces coalition policies on the major issue — whether Federal City College will be controlled by the establishment-appointed administration or by the Black Studies Militants.

While the Black Studies Militants seem intimidating to others, they themselves live with the fear of their program being extinguished. As a result, the leaders often escalate their demands for self-determination out of self-protective and defensive instincts. Because of great tactical skill in reducing individual dissent and debate, the militants, behind Garrett's strong leadership, have gained victories in many substantive and political battles on the campus.

Andress Taylor, a black English professor who is engaged in a number of different programs at the college, feels that F.C.C. has a herculean-sized mission. "We must see to it that each student achieves a professional goal, but also a new sense of himself as a black American. Each student must succeed academically, but he must also make a psychological identification with himself and his community."

The forcefulness of the Black Studies Militants is a daily demonstration to the students of a vital and important kind of community strength and feeling. The leaders say that the obvious unity and vitality of their group is an important learning experience for students who have had to hustle and compete to survive within their own oppressed communities and that the vigorous camaraderie of the militants affords a glimpse of a future community among all blacks. James Garrett's busy office possesses a special air of glamour that distinguishes it from more conventional offices in the college. Black Studies teacher Frank Smith commented that even the "hustlers" want to be a part of some group. "People interested in increasing their GS rating in government also want to find a place for themselves within a group," he said, "and we are trying to teach the students to be motivated by ideas and ideals of community development that are apart and beyond personal and individual success."

Each day, the Student Government Association, under the presidency of Cornelius Williams, becomes more militant. The radical students feel their primary commitment is to the general community and they strongly believe that the college belongs to the black citizens who need it. After President Farner approved usage of the F.C.C. building for workshops to be run by Mobilization, an outside group composed primarily of white radicals, the SGA vetoed his permission (which Farner had granted in the old tradition of academic freedom), ostensibly to avoid endangering the college through possible adverse publicity. Various other explanations have been made of this student veto. One was that Mobilization leaders should have gone first to the SGA for permission rather than to the college president. Donal Jones's explanation for the veto is that "free-loading white radicals make the black cause more unpopular and suspect. Mobilization could have caused potential losses and the students believe that the college belongs to the black community. Anyway, SDS-type class analysis of America has little relevancy or currency with the black militant racial analysis of where things are at."

The Student Government Association leaders continue making more demands for control over policy decisions and have begun the battle to wrest power away from the administration. In February, Cornelius Williams attacked President Farner for being derelict in not having acquired new buildings to house the additional 2,000 students expected next fall. He accused the administration of failing to provide full curriculum plans for the various degree programs and claimed that the administration, generally, had failed to organize and operate the college effectively. President Farner's relaxed and politically amiable manner apparently energized the radical students into demanding some of his administrative prerogatives, and he was quoted in The Washington Post as saying: "I have not made any policy decisions on my own. That's probably the wrong style of administration for this situation."

Although most of the administrative officials are keenly intent on keeping highly explosive issues under their hat and "at home on campus," the problems besieging the college become more visible and publicized every day. The administration still argues that all the trouble is coming from perhaps 10 per cent of the school and that the militants have become the tail wagging the dog through extremist tactics and insidious politicking among faculty and student. But as time goes by, and the estimated enrollment grows toward the 20,000 students expected in 1975, internal disputes will no longer be private. Thousands of black students will be waiting each year to see whether Congress comes across with sufficient funding for Federal City College. It will provide an interesting spectacle, socially and politically, as the surrogate city-fathers determine financial arrangements for their unruly offspring, who seem neither appreciative nor obedient.

Education and Society:
The Need for Reconsideration

This Commission is the direct product of the crisis of November 1966, when a student sit-in and strike took place. Confronted with the second major breakdown of its governing process in two years, members of the campus community believed it urgent to reassess the political structure of the university and to devise "modes of governance appropriate to a modern American University." We believe, however, that the rigidity and vulnerability of our university's governing institutions is a condition that cannot be treated in isolation. Rather, it should be seen as a reflection of certain basic weaknesses in prevailing assumptions about the university's direction and the nature of the education it provides. Before an assessment of these institutions can fruitfully be made, it is necessary to appreciate that the fundamental problem of the campus is rooted in education. The campus suffers from more than political ills, and more than political prescriptions are required to cure its malaise.

For the past few decades the definition and treatment of our problems have come largely through administrative and organizational means. For the past few years this community has defined its problems in political terms, or at least protested against their existence by political means. Both approaches are inadequate, the first because it has neglected the human dimension of education, the second because it jeopardizes the innocence and candor necessary to educational settings. Although considerable attention of late has been directed toward educational reform and some valuable changes have been made, the existing inertia defies all but the most resolute of reformers. Inertia and discouragement have combined to produce a situation in which fundamental educational problems are discussed only sporadically, and then in so prosaic a fashion as to make education seem a dreary affair when compared to the melodrama of campus politics. What is worse, the attempts to call attention to severe problems through massive student demonstrations have nourished the delusion that a brief period in which students are not massed in Sproul Plaza or milling in Sproul Hall is a sign of institutional health and success.

The inertia of our institutions and our lack of a rooted tradition of educational innovation have had a paradoxical result: they have led to a

From Caleb Foote, Henry Mayer, and Associates, editors, *The Culture of the University: Governance and Education* (San Francisco: Jossey-Bass, 1968). Reprinted by permission.

brave and unwarranted complacency, as though the campus truly believed its official rhetoric that this is a "great university," the peer of any institution of higher learning in the world. We are skeptical, however, that a count of Nobel prize winners, the high national rating of graduate departments, or the presence of a distinguished faculty provide conclusive measures of a university's greatness. These attributes do not in themselves represent a university's ultimate goals, but rather means toward achieving them. In our view, the most important single goal of a university, and therefore the best measure of its excellence, is the intellectual growth of its students: their initiation into the life of the mind, their commitment to the use of reason in the resolution of problems, their development of both technical competence and intellectual integrity.

When viewed in this manner, neither Berkeley nor any other university is adequately fulfilling its primary mission. It is true that many students and faculty are engaged in exciting and important intellectual endeavors; it is true that here and there on the campus, scattered among certain departments and sometimes outside of departments, true communities of learning do exist. Despite these moments of intellectual excitement and pockets of engagement, however, we find an appallingly high rate of disaffection and disinterest. The activist students who have made their dissatisfactions known in an epidemic of protests from coast to coast are but the most visible manifestations of this malaise. High dropout rates[1] and our assessment of what is *not* happening to many of those who complete their degrees add to our concern.[2] Recently, for example, one of Berkeley's largest departments conducted a series of two-and-one-half-hour interviews with sixty upper division majors selected at random.

[1] While the dropout problem can never be accurately reflected by a single figure, it is worthwhile to note that only about 50 per cent of those who enter Berkeley as freshmen receive baccalaureate degrees from the University. More important than number is the fact that this group includes so many of our most promising students. Less than one-half of the men and less than one-third of the women who left were in academic difficulties at the time they dropped out. Moreover, academic achievement aside, to the extent that the dropouts can be described by personality tests, they seem to have characteristics that would make Berkeley a more exciting place to attend and at which to teach. Robert Suczek and Elizabeth Alfert, *Personality Characteristics of College Dropouts,* Cooperative Research Project No. 5–8232, Office of Education, U.S. Department of Health, Education, and Welfare, 1966 (mimeographed). See also *Education at Berkeley,* Report of the Select Committee on Education, Academic Senate, p. 13.

[2] Professor Martin Trow describes students of this kind: "Still others [at Berkeley] and there are many of these on every large campus, have no great passion for education, little interest in or conception of what higher education might be, and exhibit something like the 'wantlessness of the poor,' a passive and even cheerful acceptance of conditions as they are, almost whatever they are." Martin Trow, "The Large Campus as a Context for Learning" (mimeographed paper), p. 3. And compare comments of Professor Michel Loeve, one of the three newly appointed "Professors of Arts and Sciences" at Berkeley. "What happens to the student when he enters the University world? We build some 80 types of cages and we fit the adolescent into one of them — tightly, so he won't take too much initiative . . . without realizing it, we kill their possible selves. . . ." *Campus Report,* November 22, 1967, p. 2.

These conversations revealed that less than 20 per cent of the interviewees could be described as intellectually engaged with their major, while the rest were discouragingly indifferent. The lack of involvement, it should be emphasized, was not confined to average or poor students, but prevailed even among students with grade point averages above 3.0.

We recognize that a university cannot *give* an education to its students, let alone impose it upon them. We believe, however, that it should awaken the complacent and provide a liberating but demanding milieu in which the uncertain and aimless have a fair chance to develop intellectual autonomy. A faculty critic of the Free Speech Movement called attention to this untapped intellectual potential when, noting the "prodigies at work . . . in organization, in research, in writing" that were evoked by FSM, he observed that "many professors have been given quite a start to discover what stores of energy are locked in our students and untouched by the normal routine."[3]

One major source of our troubles is found in the uncertainty and skepticism concerning the proper relationship between the university and society.[4] In the past, a reciprocity existed between them in which society was willing to extend economic support to higher education in exchange for useful knowledge and trained personnel. That relationship was based on the asumption that the existing organization of society not only would allow university graduates to contribute their skills in ways that would be socially useful and personality satisfying, but that the broad goals of society were such as to command general approval. As long as that situation prevailed, it was possible for students to view with equanimity an education aimed at preparation for specified careers. Now, however, they are increasingly critical of the world and of the institutions that shape it. Some of the most thoughtful and serious students have come to repudiate many of the social goals and values they are asked to serve in the university and upon graduation. That repudiation is directed, in part, at the conditions of technological society that seem to threaten human dignity. The new world emerging seems to exact greater conformity, more routinized lives, more formalized relationships among individuals, and a deeper sense of helplessness amid an increasingly abstract world devoid of humane values.

This repudiation could be interpreted as the esthetic posture of traditional collegiate disillusion were it not for the growing belief, by no means confined to students, that contemporary society is afflicted with grave problems that it cannot solve and can only worsen. Racial conflicts have become so intense that conventional solutions seem superficial; the ugli-

---

[3] Nathan Glazer, "Reply to Philip Selznick," *Commentary*, March, 1965. Reprinted in S. M. Lipset and S. Wolin, *The Berkeley Student Revolt*, Anchor Books, Garden City, New York, 1965, p. 315.

[4] For an analysis of this relationship and its consequences, see Henry D. Aiken, "The American University: Part I," *New York Review of Books*, October 20, 1966, p. 12.

ness and squalor of cities seem beyond repair and fit only for the violence that erupts in their streets; the skies are fouled and the land and forests ravaged; above all, the republic seems hopelessly entangled in a nightmare of a war with ever-widening circles of suffering, destruction, and cynicism. Faced with this crisis, many students express intense dissatisfaction with the university, since it provides much of the knowledge and most of the trained personnel required by the technological and scientific society. The university is, as one economist put it, a vital part of the "knowledge industry" and thus it contributes in important ways to shaping society in forms that evoke neither respect nor affection. It is little wonder, then, that many students are no longer content to spend their college years preparing to "take their places" in such a society. Nor is it surprising that many students regard as irrelevant the miscellany of superficial, uncertain choices and professional training that often passes as the curriculum.

Such discontent with the university is deepened by the degree to which the university's atmosphere reproduces the characteristics of the society. The university is large, impersonal, and bureaucratic. The acquisition of specialized skills has often been substituted for the education of persons instead of supplementing it. Some of the most marvelous expressions of human dignity — the activities of learning, inquiring, and sharing that are brought together in education — are being dehumanized. "Instruction" tends to usurp the place of inquiry; specialized "training" gradually commences at ever earlier stages of education; and the tempo of education is stepped up to meet the pressure of enrollment, the resentment of taxpayers, and the competition with other technological societies for national supremacy in the space age. The result is that instead of the warmth and cordiality that are the natural accompaniments of learning, relationships tend to be remote, fugitive, and vaguely sullen.

The lack of intellectual fellowship within the university, the relentless pressures placed upon it as a vital national resource, the resulting premium attached to the production and application of specialized knowledge, and the growing tendency to reinforce and even mirror the society have all contributed to the crisis in American higher education for which "Berkeley" has become "a convenient shorthand name."[5] This crisis goes far beyond the recent upsurge of political challenges to university ruling authorities and sharply illuminates the university's two crucial failures: its failure to develop a student body that respects the value of the intellect itself, and its failure to order its activities according to a conscious conception of its unique purpose of nurturing that intellect.

The failure to generate respect for intellectual activity may be seen in

[5] John William Ward, "The Trouble with Higher Education," *The Public Interest*, Summer 1966, p. 76.

several ways. Many students move routinely and unthinkingly through the system. Many others, while reacting passionately to the failures of American Society, have not linked their emotional reaction to an appreciation of the need for disciplined analysis of these urgent problems and a search for reasoned solutions. The reaction against the narrow, instrumental uses of intellect and of the university has led to a growing tendency to reject all uses of reason, a rejection that leads either to an enervating quietism or to a form of nihilism that admires only the passionate assertion of humanity through direct, physical protest.

The second crucial failure relates to the university's function of providing useful knowledge and expert consultants to assist society in its efforts to satisfy human needs. Somehow this function of "service" has gotten out of hand so that it has come to dominate the direction, form, and tone of the university. These tendencies have encountered very little critical scrutiny from this campus, primarily because the issues have not been clarified and squarely posed. The campus does not possess institutions capable of such critical appraisal, the establishment of general agreement on the nature and value of various kinds of services and the process for determining the priority to be assigned such services among university activities. These issues deserve the kind of discussion and publicity that can best be provided by institutions that permit wide participation by the campus community as a whole. Because such institutions have been lacking, we have imperceptibly slumped into a posture in which the demands of external interests — strongly reinforced by economic lures, rewards of prestige and status, and other powerful resources which only those with power can marshal and wield — have increasingly dominated the ethos of the university and shaped the direction of its educational activities.

Revision of the university's governing structures and processes cannot in itself revitalize the university's intellectual life. Such goals require great changes in spirit and conviction as well as changes in institutions. We can look to the governing process, however, for the most appropriate means of recognizing genuine conflicts of values and functions and for establishing a framework of priorities and relationships for discriminating among the growing tasks and demands placed upon the university either by society or by the institution's own sense of intellectual obligation. Changes in governance also provides means for building communities of a size that human beings can manage and in which they can live creatively. Such community settings provide the minimum conditions through which a large university can enlist the greater involvement of its members in its educational venture.

SOCIAL SERVICES

Health

Surely one of the most basic functions of an organized society is the provision of a measure of physical well-being for its members. In most advanced industrial nations, minimum levels of health and nutrition are now assumed to be part of the benefits of increasing technological capacity and medical knowledge. In those nations much has been done to mitigate the most fundamental social inequities, the social stratification of life and death. Nowhere has this inequity been completely erased. But no other nation at a comparable level of development has done as little in this area as has the United States.

The health services of industrial societies, like their other social services, are established on the premise that there is a level below which the well-being of citizens must not fall as a result of the routine workings of the economy. In capitalist democracies, this means that the state intervenes in the play of market forces to provide at least a minimum guarantee of living conditions, as protection against the contingencies of social and economic circumstance. Such a conception does not develop easily or all at once, but in England, for example, it had become, by World War II, a presumption shared by nearly everyone. Even the Conservative Party, in a pamphlet issued in 1949, stressed that the social services were "designed to give to all the basic minimum of security, of housing, of opportunity, of employment, and of living standards below which our duty to one another forbids us to permit anyone to fall."[1]

In the United States, on the other hand, in 1967 a National Advisory Commission on Health Manpower commented that the health statistics of certain groups in the United States — the rural poor, urban ghetto dwellers, migrant workers, and others — "occasionally resemble the health statistics of a developing country."[2] Moreover, the quality of health care available to the middle classes is erratic, expensive, and in some ways diminishing. Behind all of this is the continuing American refusal to intervene in what remains essentially a market system of health.

Who fails? Industry, more concerned with profit than with the well-being of workers; government bureaucracies with entrenched standards of nonperformance, often the captives of special interests; professional groups jealousy guarding their control over health care.

Coles and Huge argue that the United States, unlike most European industrial nations, has no overall program to support seriously injured workers. Congress sees to it that the disabled worker must run an obstacle course to receive benefits even under existing programs. And the day-to-day reality of trying to wring benefits from company doctors or local welfare officials makes a mockery of the effectiveness of those programs. Other countries with extensive mining industries manage to spend considerably more care and money in trying to make the industry reasonably safe. Ultimately, the problem involves controlling the disregard of such industries for human life and well-being.

The development of such controls may be difficult because of the frequent captivity of governmental agencies by industrial interests. A similar situation exists with re-

[1] Quoted in Asa Briggs, "The Welfare State in Historical Perspective," in Mayer N. Zald, ed., *Social Welfare Institutions: A Sociological Reader* (New York: Wiley, 1965), p. 42.
[2] Report of the National Advisory Commission on Health Manpower (United States), quoted in R. M. Titmuss, "Ethics and Economics of Medical care", in *Commitment to Welfare* (New York: Pantheon Books, 1968), p. 268.

gard to hunger, as Elizabeth Drew writes in "Going Hungry in America: Government's Failure." By a conservative estimate, ten million undernourished people in the country, some of whom are starving. It would take less than two billion dollars to put an end to that. Yet, the government responds with hopelessly inadequate food programs, rationalized with studies that suggest that perhaps the poor do not value food as much as "we" do.

How does this continue? Without any sort of national commitment to give people enough to eat, the right to eat becomes a question of power, and power is what the poor have least of. Their representatives do not represent them; they represent large agricultural interests and local power structures that are then able effectively to capture the relevant government agencies. These agencies are all too often staffed by functionaries more concerned with defending themselves from scrutiny and criticism than with implementing social goals.

The conflict between organizational interests and social values is nowhere more apparent than in the American approach to medical care. A few countries, among them England, the USSR, and New Zealand, have national health service programs through which extensive medical care is provided for all citizens as a matter of right. Numerous other countries have extensive programs of national health *insurance* covering everyone, or almost everyone; among them Japan, Sweden, Norway, Australia, and Denmark. In one way or another, every highly industrialized nation in western Europe (and many others elsewhere) has a broad program of national medical care for the majority of the population. In the United States there is *no* national health program for the population as a whole. Our only national health insurance is that for the aged and pensioners. And special classes of persons are eligible for governmental health care, such as servicemen, veterans, Indians, and a few others.

Our system is largely a private one, then, and the medical care available varies tremendously, depending primarily on how much one is able to pay. And as Elinor Langer remarks, this means in practice that the system contains absurd extremes; at the top, the wealthy can secure what is probably the highest standard of medical care in the world, while everyone else is left at the mercy of an unpredictable system of "unsupervised services for unregulated fees." For the poor, this may mean death rather than life; an estimated 13,000 poor people died in New York alone in a recent year because adequate care was unavailable.

Langer holds that the organized medical profession is a major force in maintaining the system, despite the statement in the American Medical Association's Principles of Medical Ethics that "The prime object of the medical profession is to render service to humanity; reward or financial gain is a subordinate consideration."[3] And again, governmental policy in this area is characterized by weakness and vacillation; the federal agencies are often so solicitous of the welfare of established interests that they retreat from effective insistence on the social value of health.

Health and nutrition are, of course, only two aspects of human well-being; a more comprehensive treatment would include others such as housing. But health and nutrition are basic, and the failure to make adequate provision in these areas dramatically illustrates a more general failure to grant full citizenship to everyone.

[3] Principles of Medical Ethics of the AMA, 1953, quoted in Titmuss, *Commitment to Welfare*, p. 227.

ROBERT COLES
HARRY HUGE

"Black Lung":
Mining as a Way of Death

Towns like Farmington, West Virginia or cities like Harlan and Hazard, Kentucky struggle with enough ironies to make even children a little sociological as they size up the world: "Some daddys here, they make good money, but a lot of them, they get killed in the mines; and if they don't, they have to stop working after awhile, because they can't breathe very good. Then they're as bad off as the rest of us in the hollows. That's where my uncle says." The boy's father was killed in a mine accident in 1963. The boy's uncle has "black lung" and coughs and wheezes and spits up black phlegm and feels short of breath a lot of the time and has chest pains:

> I've had it. I'm an old man at 31. I started in the mines when I was 16, and no one asked any questions. My daddy, he started when he was 11. I was lucky to have a job. Hereabouts if you have a job, you feel like you're lucky and you give the foreman every ounce of energy you've got. Some of our kinfolk, they never went to the mines, and they near starve to death and freeze to death, come every winter. But you know, as bad as it is for them, I'm beginning to think they're better off than me and my brother. They don't see the money we do — if we live and don't get sick — and they can't have the things we buy. But I'd rather have it real, real terrible up in the hollows than end up like my brother — he got killed, in a second, just like that. The roof fell in on him down in the mine. And me, well you can hear me trying to catch enough air to stay alive. I never know when my lungs will just stop working altogether, and that will be the end. It's no way to die, let me tell you. It's no kind of reward for those years down in the mine. I wonder if a lot of people, they know that the coal they use to run the factories, it's all done at the expense of our lives. We get killed down there, or our lungs go and get killed. And then a lot of us, we don't get hardly anything to live on.

The fate of thousands like him doesn't seem to bother us. Yes, we become upset when a particularly severe disaster takes place like the explosion last November 20 that claimed 78 lives in Consolidated Coal Company's No. 9 mine near Farmington, West Virginia. In a matter of

From *The New Republic*, January 1, 1969. Reprinted by permission of *The New Republic*, © 1969, Harrison-Blaine of New Jersey, Inc.

weeks, though, Farmington's tragedy is forgotten; it was just one more in an apparently endless succession, all recorded carefully by the Interior Department's Bureau of Mines. In this century about 100,000 men have been crushed to death, burnt to death, choked to death in the coal mines, and since 1930 around a million-and-a-half serious injuries have been recorded. Over 40,000 men have been permanently or partially disabled — and for every miner officially declared disabled, many more than one has tried and failed to have his hurt, ailing body so recognized. In 1907, 3,242 miners were killed. In 1952, the year President Truman signed a Coal Mine Safety Act which he insisted was inadequate, 548 miners died in accidents. In 1962 another 220 men died underground; and lest anyone suppose that things are getting better, the accident rate per thousand miners has increased since 1952 from 1.37 to 1.50. All in all, then, mining has become more hazardous for the 150,000 or so men who work in about 5,500 deep mines and 2,200 surface ones. Since Harry Truman severely criticized Congress for failing to enact even half-satisfactory legislation to protect the safety of miners, over 200,000 miners have been injured, and today the coal companies continue to confront their workers with awful risks and dangers, more of them than any other major industry in America dares allow. Each month the journal put out by the United Mine Workers spells out the result: 29 killed in August, 1968; 24 in September; and on. Even before this past November more men were killed in 1968 (182) than in 1967 (173).

None of those statistics measures the incidence of "black lung," an insidious disease which gradually destroys the lung's ability to function normally. Every year hundreds and hundreds of miners die of the various complications that come with the disease — called by today's doctors "pneumonconiocis," and by others long ago (going back to 1862) "miner's asthma." The Surgeon General of the United States has said that "conservatively speaking" over 100,000 miners suffer from "black lung disease," which means that most if not all miners have it, suffer every day from it, and in significant numbers die from it; die because, literally, the lungs become increasingly scarred, lifeless, useless — and eventually the time comes for the last breath to be taken. Anyone who has seen a miner waging that battle, fighting for breath as a drowning man does for air, can never forget it.

Because 78 miners died all at once, the Department of the Interior held a conference on December 11, 1968, and those of us there heard speeches and outbursts and accusations and denials and resolutions and confessions and promises of change — but one can only wonder at something else, as a miner did who sat with us in that large, federal amphitheatre:

> That doctor [the Surgeon General] said over 100,000 of us have the damn disease and everyone knows that if you stay down there

long enough, you get it, you get it worse and worse. And you heard him, Corcoran [President of the Consolidated Coal Company], say they had to do something to reduce the dust. But they didn't tell people what it *is*, what the disease we get *is*. How is someone here in Washington or in California or in New York supposed to know what they're talking about — that the mines are full of coal dust, and it gets into your lungs and eats them up, and then you die? Of course, when I first asked the company doctor if anything was wrong, because I was having trouble breathing, he didn't even want to listen to my chest. He just came over to me from across the room and he said: "Look, if you want to stay working, you'd better not complain, you'd better not mention this." I looked at him as though he was a crook or something. Then I guess he just got mad, because he raised his voice at me: "Every miner has trouble with his breathing one time or another. So why should you start complaining. Don't you talk to your buddies? Haven't they all got the same troubles?" And he was right there — we all do. And he was right with the last thing he told me, before I left: "Look, you're better off working than complaining. You'll die faster from not eating than from some coal dust in your lungs." You know what I said? I said, "You're right, doctor." You know why he's right? I could be on my deathbed — from not eating or from "black lung," either of them — and between the doctors like him, and all those lawyers they've got, and the bosses and the county courthouse people, I'd still not get a cent from the company or the welfare people or Washington or anyplace. And every miner knows that.

Three years ago, in Perry County, Kentucky, one of us carefully examined a 37-year-old man who had been digging coal out of nearby land for 20 years. He was of medium height, blue-eyed and with thinning brown hair. Unlike some of his kin, who do what textbooks rather generously call "subsistence farming," he went to the mines: "You either get a job there, or you don't work at all. It's up to you to decide. All I want to do is work, keep working until my kids are grown-up. I don't care what happens after that, but I can't stop working now. We'd starve to death."

The stethoscope picked up telltale sounds in his chest, evidence that the lungs were in trouble. He had twice been hurt in the back by cave-ins, which he dismissed as "nothing," though he never can really forget that miners die each year from just that — a landslide that happens because proper roofs have not been built to cover men who are probing and cutting away at earth and coal. His back gave him constant pain, for all his brave denial that anything was wrong, and even a cursory neurological examination, done in his home, demonstrated that he had sustained an injury to his back, and to the nerves which enter and leave his spinal column all along the back's length. He had something to say about that difficulty, too: "Look, every miner worth anything gets his back hurt, and his legs and his arms also; all he has to do is stay down there long enough. I'd as soon live in pain and have the money, than have my back in shape and an empty stomach.

More recently we saw him, and he was less defiant. He no longer has a job. His "lung problem" made him a "risk" in the mines. For six months he looked elsewhere for work, but found none. His savings diminished. Now he has nothing except some good furniture and a good but aging car, which he cannot afford to drive. His kinfolk bring over food and a little money. He can "always go up a hollow and live with them," which means, in the true spirit of what a "community" is, he will not starve to death so long as the entire Appalachian region doesn't — in some cases, *barely* doesn't. We asked him why he hadn't applied for Social Security payments which are supposed to go to those with "permanent and total disability." He told us he'd tried, tried everything — and anyway don't we know about things like that, in his words, "about the way they operate, the welfare people and their lawyers and the doctors they send you to."

If we don't know "the way they operate," we eventually found out, thanks to miners like him — and to a whole series of welfare hearings and legal proceedings that the one of us who is a lawyer has attended and studied. Unlike Europe's major industrial nations, the United States has no overall program to support injured, seriously injured, workers. In county after county of Appalachia, and all over the country, men like this miner are excluded from welfare. Unless they have some high-priced form of private insurance, they get nothing. Some states provide money for a few months, even a year, to men suddenly unemployed; but eventually that stops, and in a region like Appalachia, where unemployment can be a way of life, nothing goes to men who want to work and can't find jobs — and to sick men, badly sick men, many of whom desperately try to find something to do, even though by rights they deserve a pension and good medical care, neither of which they get.

Congress has made sure that disabled workers don't get Medicare. Congress has made sure that language in the public assistance schemes that are federally supported (for the aged, the blind and children) is extremely restrictive and vague, which means local welfare officials do all the interpreting. In each case a doctor must decide whether a man is "permanently and totally disabled." In most cases the doctor is a "state doctor," appointed and paid by the welfare department. In Kentucky, as in many other states, even if a private doctor makes a particular claim for his patients, a Medical Review Team goes over the forms and has the final say in the matter — and the doctor on that team does *not* examine the patient, but simply evaluates the citizen's claim. Again and again miners

— and of course others, too — go to those county courthouses and get the following kind of treatment:

> I went there and told them I couldn't work no more in the mines, that it was my lungs, they were giving away and I couldn't catch my breath, and the company doctor, he said it was time for me to go. I had some money saved up, and I thought that maybe in a while my lungs would get better and I could go back to work; but they didn't — instead they've become worse. I tried to get a job in a store, and a gas station, too — that my brother-in-law runs. But he says he can't keep going except by himself and with his son at his side, and he doesn't make the money to hire anyone else — and a lot of men, miners like me, fallen sick, come and ask him if he knows of any work around, and he has to say that the answer is no, sorry, he doesn't.
>
> The welfare lady, she let me apply and it's the same old story, over and over again. They sent me to their doctor and he looked me over and listened to my chest and asked me to walk and bend and like that, and said, "o.k., you can go." As I was leaving I asked him if he thought I could qualify, and he said that wasn't my business, to ask him that, but he'd say this much: "You can walk in here and sit and stand and bend and get up, and you can work — not in the mines, but in a store, you could do that, or an office." Then I tried to tell him that a man like me, he can't overnight become an office-man, and besides there aren't those kinds of jobs around here. But he cut me off, in the middle of a sentence. "I know, I know. You all say that." That's what he said.
>
> Well it wasn't long before the news came back that I wasn't "permanently disabled," and so I couldn't get a cent; and that means I can just go and starve to death so far as everyone's concerned — the coal company and the county courthouse people and the Washington people. Of course, if I can get to be 60 or so — that's over 20 years off — I can get Social Security and after that Medicare. But with this "black lung" inside of me and no money, I'll be lucky to hit 40. Yes sir.

Again and again we have heard miners like him and others in Appalachia, too, say that only a "man about to die" will be found eligible for any kind of financial help, all of which has been substantiated by a statistical analysis of the federally supported welfare programs: "The death rates for disabled workers under 50 finally declared eligible for support approximate those of the United States population 70 to 74 years of age. . . . Disabled beneficiaries 50 to 64 years of age had death rates higher than persons 75 to 84 years of age."

Just in case its civilized and humanitarian purposes might be misunderstood, Congress took up the issue of eligibility for Social Security disability payments in 1967 and spelled out exactly what the world's first nation intends for its citizens. The courts — so often these days susceptible to fits of soft-headed compassion — had decided that the Social Security Act requires a claimant to be unable to do the kind of work that is available in his hometown. No, said a coalition of Republicans and Southern Democrats: the claimant must be unable to do any work at all, and if a disabled miner is found medically suitable for a job, say, on the Stock Exchange on Wall Street — well, then, too bad for him and his devious effort to milk Washington of money. In addition, the courts had ruled pain to be evidence of physical or mental impairment; no, said the Congress — because, after all, people in bad pain can still work. What is more, the courts had foolishly defined disability as a man's "practical inability to be hired by an employer," a definition Congress flatly refused to sanction. Applicants — perhaps supplicants is the better word — are either flat on their backs, vitually at death's door, or else they can expect nothing; and lest anyone slip through that tightly woven net, the Congress thoughtfully made its new restrictions apply retroactively to all cases in any state of appeal before the Social Security Administration or the courts.

In the counties of eastern Kentucky and all over the country, welfare departments do nothing to encourage thorough medical examinations. The forms are brief, the doctors are not given standards or even instructions to use as guides. To many miners we have interviewed, the doctors and their examinations are in fact something worse: "It isn't that they're not thorough, the checkups the doctors give. It's that they're used to disqualify us. The one who saw me, he said 'Sure you're sick, but you're not dying.' And if I was dying, he'd probably have said there's no point for the government to be giving money to a dying man."

That is a harsh judgment for a miner to make about a doctor. In nearby West Virginia we found a little more goodwill and charity for doctors, some of whom are now becoming "agitators" — which means they are demanding that adequate compensation be paid to men who suffer from "black lung." (In recent years exactly four men with the disease have been compensated.) We visited Farmington, talked with miners who worked in Consolidated No. 9. We went through the miles of property that adjoin the particular section of the enormous mine that exploded this last November. We talked with company officials, and a number of doctors, both in northern West Virginia, where Consolidated No. 9 is, and in the southern part of the state, where a first-rate team of specialists is studying the nature of "black lung disease" at the Appalachian Regional Hospital in Beckley. One of us went to Charleston and watched a meeting of the Silicosis Medical Board, assembled to consider the case of a 50-year-old miner who had worked in the mines for 31 years, was now obviously sick with "black lung" and had been denied assistance by the Social Security

Administration. The man's doctor was prodded by a coal company lawyer. Couldn't all sorts of things cause the miner's distress? Were specific tests done to determine the cause of his illness? Might not cigarette smoking cause the same kind of damage to the lungs? No, insisted the doctor: "A man could smoke four packs a day and not begin to show this particular kind of abnormality." For all his effort — trips here and there, examinations and more examinations — the miner had received a flat reward of $1,000; he was appealing for more. In one miner's words:

> You go there, they treat you like you're some kind of animal in a zoo; they tell you it could be cigarettes and polluted air and well — maybe the dust that falls down from the moon or something. Then, if you keep after them long enough, they give you maybe a thousand dollars, or maybe if you're real lucky, double or triple that, and then you've had it, brother, for keeps. That's how it is with us. Then you ask if we mind it, doing the work down there.

After the disaster in Consolidated No. 9, we read that the miners frequently endanger themselves by their recklessness, their bravado, their seeming reluctance to heed various rules or regulations. We had been talking to miners in various parts of Appalachia well before that terrible accident in West Virginia and had, on the contrary, been struck with something quite else: the resignation, the stubborn fatalism, the anything-but-casual manner of the men we watched going down those shafts. So we asked survivors of Consolidated No. 9 about their "attitudes":

> Yes, we do a lot of laughing. What else can you do when you go into a gassy mine, a dusty old one like that one? If you start talking about the danger, they'll fine you as a troublemaker. All I want is for my kids to grow up. I don't care if I die then, in an accident or an explosion or from "black lung." One way or the other I'll die from one of those causes anyway. It's just that if I can last long enough, my kids will get some good schooling — and *they'll* never go into the mines.

> Down there, the fans didn't work right. The whole ventilation system wasn't good enough, and they knew it. You bet they did. Now they all say we could have done more and we should have. Well, they knew that a long time ago. You hear it said that mining is dangerous, and there's not much you can do. Well, if they worried about us the way they do about men who go under water to explore, or in submarines, or up to the moon, they could do a lot. If they did what they're *supposed* to do — keep pushing those gases out with the fans and keep the coal dust down, we'd safer. The fact is that in some mines —like with Bethlehem — where the company uses the coal itself, and doesn't sell it, the mines are much safer. Everyone knows that. There's something wrong with the

whole business, if you ask me. You read that it's Gulf Oil and
Mobil Oil and Humble Oil that are buying up these mines. Our
Consolidated No. 9, did you know who owns it? The foreman, he
told us that the Consolidated people, the Consolidated Coal Company, they're one of the biggest owners of the Chrysler Car Company, and that actually it's the Continental Oil Company — I don't
know where they come from — that owns our Consolidated Coal
mines. Even the foreman — and he's a company man — he said
if they can give huge tax favors to the oil companies they can do it
for us, to the coal people, and they could make it a million times
safer — because they know how to. They just don't want to dig
into their profits.

Ironically, poorer coal-producing countries like England and Germany
and Czechoslovakia spend much more money studying ways to make
mines safe — and *do* something about what is discovered. In those nations miners are regularly given x-rays, and immediately withdrawn from
such work when evidence of lung disease begins to appear. They are
given jobs elsewhere; or if injured or disabled, given decent and honorable
pensions as a right. In those countries the mines are ventilated far more
efficiently than are ours, and in some instances miners are given safe and
comfortable masks, and even whole uniforms that preclude any inhalation
whatsoever of coal dust. One very fine physician, Dr. Donald Rasmussen,
whose recent paper in *The American Review of Respiratory Disease*,
"Pulmonary Impairment in Southern West Virginia Coal Miners," is already a classic in the medical literature that has to do with "black lung,"
told us he finds himself ashamed when he talks with Britain or German
doctors:

> They are doing so much more there, preventatively — it's embar-
> rassing to compare notes with them. If we really wanted to do
> something about "black lung" we could. Each mine goes on as be-
> fore; the men fall sick, but stay at work because they have no
> choice — and we see them suffering here, every day. True, a bad
> disaster brings us some attention; but not for long, and pretty soon
> things are back to normal around here, which means thousands of
> miners are slowly getting sicker and sicker and eventually they die,
> of course — many of them still young men.

In 1917, Sinclair's novel, *King Coal,* aroused the conscience of many.
Today miners get much better pay, but what one of the characters in
King Coal says still holds true:

> . . . the frequency of accidents in this district was not due to any
> special difficulty in operating their mines, the explosiveness of the
> gasses or the dryness of the atmosphere. It was merely the careless-
> ness of those in charge, their disregard of the laws for the protection
> of men. There ought to be a law with "teeth" in it. . . .

President Johnson also thought "there ought to be a law," but to no avail as far as the Congress was concerned. What will President Nixon do? Will these thousands of coal miners qualify in his Administration as "forgotten Americans"?

ELIZABETH B. DREW   *Going Hungry in America:*
                         Government's Failure

From time to time during the past few years, there has come to public attention the jarring news that a great many Americans do not get enough to eat because they are too poor. The words "starvation," "hunger," and "malnutrition" have all been used to describe the phenomenon. Each of these conditions is difficult to isolate, or even describe, or to separate from related diseases, because there has been little scientific or official interest in the problem. Yet it is generally agreed, even among government circles, that, at a minimum, ten million Americans are malnourished, and some of these are chronically hungry, even starving, because they are poor.

In 1967, a group of doctors, including Robert Coles of Harvard University, Joseph Brenner of MIT, Alan Mermann and Milton J. E. Senn of Yale, and private practitioners from Yazoo City, Mississippi, and Charlotte, North Carolina, took a foundation-sponsored trip to Mississippi to investigate the problem and returned to tell the Senate Subcommittee on Poverty what they had seen:

> In Delta counties . . . we saw children whose nutritional and medical condition we can only describe as shocking — even to a group of physicians whose work involves daily confrontation with disease and suffering. In child after child we saw: evidence of vitamin and mineral deficiencies; serious untreated skin infestation and ulcerations; eye and ear diseases, also unattended bone diseases secondary to poor food intake; the prevalence of bacterial and parasitic disease, as well as severe anemia . . . in boys and girls in every county we visited, obvious evidence of severe malnutrition, with injury to the

> body's tissues — its muscles, bones, and skin as well as an associated
> psychological state of fatigue, listlessness, and exhaustion. . . . We
> saw children who don't get to drink milk, don't get to eat fruit,
> green vegetables, or meat. They live on starches — grits, bread,
> Kool Aid. . . . In sum, we saw children who are hungry and who
> are sick — children for whom hunger is a daily fact of life and sick-
> ness, in many forms, an inevitability. We do not want to quibble
> over words, but malnutrition is not quite what we found. . . . They
> are suffering from hunger and disease and directly or indirectly they
> are dying from them — which is exactly what "starvation" means.

There is developing, moreover, a disturbing body of scientific information
that indicates a connection between malnutrition in children, in particular
insufficient protein, and brain damage. Seventy-five per cent of the
mental retardation in this country is estimated to occur in areas of urban
and rural poverty.

The situation in the Mississippi Delta has been particularly acute because of unemployment as a result of mechanization, and among other
things, other government programs: controlled planting, and a new one-
dollar-an-hour minimum wage, which led many plantation owners to lay
workers off rather than pay it. Mississippi's welfare program pays an
average of $50 a month to a family with four children, but payments are
made only if the wage earner is old or disabled or blind or has left his
family. Thus there are thousands of families in the Delta with no jobs
and no income.

There are two basic government programs which are intended to improve the diet of the poor — the sale of food stamps and the distribution
of food. The local county chooses one or the other — or neither. Government officials point out that for some time every county in Mississippi has
had one of the programs. In response to the reports that people still were
not getting enough to eat, the Secretary of Agriculture said to the same
Senate subcommittee: "They got some food because they were obviously
walking around. I don't know where they got it.

For some time, in fact, it has been known within the government that
the food programs had serious shortcomings, in the number of people
being reached and in the form of the assistance. In addition, over the past
year and a half or so, domestic hunger has been the subject of a great deal
of publicity. A solution would not be all that expensive: government
studies have indicated that adequate food distribution for everyone who
needed it would cost between $1.5 billion and $2 billion more than the
roughly half billion being spent on stamps and commodities now. (No
one has calculated, in terms of illness and wasted and dependent lives,
what it costs not to provide everyone with an adequate diet.) There were
also short-range and less expensive actions that could have been taken to

alleviate the most severe distress. While it would be inaccurate to say that nothing was done, the response was slow, piecemeal, and, it often seemed, reluctant. More thorough responses, including a national commitment to see that no one was denied an adequate diet because of low income, were considered, and at several points they were almost made. Because of the impact on the lives, every day, of several million people, the reasons why they were not are worth exploring.

The food programs are run by the Department of Agriculture because they were begun not so much to help the poor as to dispose of embarrassing agricultural surpluses. Food packages are distributed once a month to the poor who live in counties which happen to want the distribution and are willing to pay for it. (Only recently, the federal government began to pay for the packages in a few of the poorest counties.) "But," Orville Freeman, the Secretary of Agriculture, has testified to Congress, "that doesn't mean that every person gets it, because a poor person who lives miles away from the distributing point where 100 pounds of food is made available for a month may very well (a) not even know about the distribution; (b) not be able to get there; and (c) not be able to carry it away:" (One congressman replied: "I know dead soldiers who didn't miss out because they lived 10 miles from a recruiting office.")

The commodity packages have only recently approximated what even the Agriculture Department considers a "minimum adequate" diet, but the cheerful assumption is made that they are a "supplement" to a family's food supply. The commodity package has been periodically expanded, to the point where last summer, under public pressure, the Department announced that it would now contain some twenty-two items. The list is theoretical, however; whether the various items actually end up in the package depends on whether they are in sufficient supply and whether the local community elects to include them. It takes tolerance for tedium and some culinary ingenuity to make edible meals of the surplus packages, which until last summer consisted mainly of such things as flour, corn-meal, rice, dried peas, dried beans, bulgur. Formerly they contained thirty ounces of meat for each person for an entire month; now the packages are supposed to contain more meat, dried eggs, evaporated milk, canned chicken, canned vegetables, and some others. The wrapping is to be prettier, and recipes are to be supplied, although many of the recipients can't read.

The food stamp program, in which participants buy stamps which are worth more than the purchase price and use them to buy groceries, is preferred by just about everyone, including the local grocers. Long part of the Democrats' agenda, food stamps were started on a pilot basis in 1961, and were finally authorized by Congress three years later. The stamps are actually a form of income supplement, but that is not the sort of thing that is said out loud, and thus a great emphasis is always placed on how this, too, is to supplement a family's "normal" expenditure for food. It is difficult to divine just what was in the minds of the federal officials who worked out the details of how the food stamp program should work. Each month, a family may purchase a given amount's worth of stamps, depending on their income, in exchange for a given amount of bonus. Somehow, although people in general pay about 18 per cent of their income for food, the poor, under the food stamp plan, are sometimes required to pay as much as 35 to 50 per cent in order to obtain any stamps at all. If they cannot afford that because of the other demands on their income, or if they do not happen to have enough cash on hand on the day that the stamps are sold, they get no help at all. For example, after eight counties in Mississippi switched from commodity distribution to food stamps, some 32,000 fewer people were receiving food aid one year later. In Arkansas, of the 54,531 households on welfare in counties with the food stamp program, only 9700 buy the stamps. This is not peculiar to these states; while some 6 million people are estimated to be receiving either commodities or food stamps now — roughly 3 million under each program — it is seldom mentioned that six years ago even more people were being helped, albeit the great part by the inferior commodities program.

Another quirk is that the bonuses go up as the income goes up, so that the higher-income poor end up with more food than those at the bottom of the scale. The Agriculture Department explains that this is because it would not be wise to give those who are accustomed to being worst off too much too soon. In order to be certified as eligible for the program, families must run the gauntlet of the welfare agencies, many of which are not known for their sympathy toward Negroes. The food programs are sometimes used as an instrument of control: people who participate in civil rights activities or who are needed when it is time for the crops to be picked find that the programs are suddenly unavailable. In many areas, food prices go up on the day the stamps are issued.

When the uproar over these failings developed in 1967, the Agriculture Department made a study of the situation in Washington County, Mississippi. It found, among other things, that more than half of those qualified to receive food stamps were not doing so. The investigators were not, however, greatly perturbed. "In general," they reported, "the study indicates that low-income households in this Mississippi Delta county accommodate themselves to a diet which low-income families elsewhere would reject. . . . It may be that low-income families place less value on food than we think."

The Department of Agriculture should not, in all fairness, be expected to demonstrate dazzling expertise in the needs and life-styles of the poor.

Its essential mission is to nurture the agricultural economy; the poor are somebody else's department. The typical employee in Agriculture has been there a long, long time. He may have come in with Henry Wallace, or he may have been a dirt farmer who was down and out during the Depression, got a government job measuring acreage, moved up through the ranks, and was promoted to Washington when he was in his fifties.

Nobody envies Orville Freeman his job, frequently described as "the worst one in town." Freeman's own official biography says it all: "He has been shot at not only by Congressmen, rural and urban, but also by consumers protesting food prices, farmers protesting farm prices, and dissidents of all job descriptions and all colors protesting food programs and poverty." Freeman is a liberal out of the Democratic-Farmer-Labor movement, where he was a three-term boy-wonder governor. From the time that John F. Kennedy appointed him in 1961, Freeman has probably stirred up less than the traditional amount of controversy for Secretaries of Agriculture. "The Administration wanted him to cultivate the farmers, not the poor or the civil rights crowd," said one of his associates. "His tendency, in the earlier years, when the subject of hungry people came up, was to look embarrassed and change the subject." When it could no longer be ignored, Freeman behaved like a man in a trap. Moreover, he could, and frequently did, claim with justification that during his tenure, through initiating food stamps and expanding food packages, an unprecedented amount had been done toward feeding the poor. His injured pride and his combative nature served to deepen his troubles.

Jamie Whitten, a fifty-eight-year-old congressman from Charleston, Mississippi, chairman of the subcommittee which provides funds for the Agriculture Department's programs and one of the most powerful members of the House of Representatives, does not believe that anybody in this country is unavoidably hungry, "except," he says "when there has been parental neglect through drunkenness or mental illness. You're dealing with people who for some reason or other are in a condition of poverty. If they had the training and foresight of other people, they wouldn't be in poverty."

Whitten has installed a number of employees at the Agriculture Department, and there is little that Orville Freeman does that Jamie Whitten doesn't know about. Whitten expects Freeman to consult him before he makes any policy move, and Freeman has decided it is the better part of wisdom to do just that. The congressman is a skilled legislator, however, and knows better than to stand intransigently against the majority opinion of the House. He hasn't often, in fact, made significant cuts in the food stamp program's funds once the House has approved the program. Neither, if he doesn't like what Freeman is doing, is he likely to cut into crop-support funds of such importance to the farm bloc. Whitten had denied money for work in the general area of rural poverty; Freeman is also anxious not to annoy Whitten to the point where he might cut funds which the Department lends to rural areas to build ski slides and golf courses that Freeman feels are important community programs. After a while, the relationship between a Cabinet officer and his House appropriations subcommittee chairman blurs beyond a rational if-I-do-this-he-will-do-that situation. "He simply becomes part of your thinking," says one former Cabinet officer. "He is an automatic part of all your decisions."

The House Agriculture Committee, which sets the policies for which Whitten's group then provides the money, is, to state it gently, disinterested in the poor. The committee's concerns are sheep scrapie and hog cholera and agricultural subsidies. The members of most committees see to it that the benefits of programs they preside over reach their constituents in full measure, but it is no accident that the home districts of a number of the Agriculture Committee members do not have food stamp programs. "These programs are not desired by the power structures back home," says one close observer, "and that's what elects them. The recipients of these programs don't vote."

The situation is similar in the Senate. In all cases, the Agriculture committees are almost entirely populated by representatives of Southern and Midwestern farm districts, with, in a Democratic Congress, the representatives of Southern landholders in charge. Senator James O. Eastland, for example, is the third-ranking member of the Senate Agriculture Committee and its most important determiner of cotton policy. Last year, the Eastland family plantations in Sunflower County, Mississippi, received $211,364 in subsidies. Despite the slipping popularity of the farm programs, and the increasing urban and suburban orientation of Congress, these men have enough seniority, and serve on enough other important committees, to make their influence felt. To the extent that the Agriculture Department budget is under attack, they try to keep the budget down by curbing the Department's noncrop programs. "Freeman decided as a matter of policy," says one of his former colleagues, "that he was not going to antagonize these men. He checked out appointments with them and went to enormous lengths to cultivate them socially. When the food issue came up and he got caught in his conspiracy with the Southerners on the Hill, his instinctive reaction was to deny that anything was wrong. After all, he was relying on memos from his staff, and they were defending themselves, too."

In April, 1967, the Senate Labor and Public Welfare Committee's Subcommittee on Employment, Manpower, and Poverty went to Mississippi. The subcommittee, headed by Senator Joseph S. Clark of Pennsylvania, was making a nationwide study of the poverty program, and since Senator Robert Kennedy was a member of the group, wherever it went, the press went too. At a hearing in Jackson, Mississippi, Marian Wright, an attractive, soft-spoken attorney for the NAACP's Legal Defense Fund, Incorporated, who had been working in Mississippi, talked about welfare, poverty, and the situation in the Delta. "They are starving," she concluded. "They are starving, and those who can get the bus fare to go north are trying to go north. But there is absolutely nothing for them to do. There is nowhere to go, and somebody must begin to respond to them."

Kennedy and Clark said they would take it to the Department of Agriculture when they returned to Washington. Senator George Murphy went them one better and said that the group should "notify the President of the United States that there is an emergency situation, and send investigators and help in immediately." On the following day, Clark and Kennedy toured the Delta. The cameras were not there when Robert Kennedy sat on the floor in one particularly fetid shack watching a listless child toy with a plate of rice, feeling the child's body, trying to get the child to respond, and trying to comprehend. Until then, the senators really had not known how bad it was.

After they returned to Washington, all nine members of the subcommittee signed a letter to the President describing the situation as "shocking" and constituting an "emergency," and calling for specific Administration action. The White House, after trying not to receive it at all, bucked the letter to the Office of Economic Opportunity, which runs the poverty program, and OEO responded with a press release, its outlines dictated by the White House. The release said there was poverty in each of the senators' home states, too; that the crisis of poverty had been greater before Lyndon Johnson took office; that the Administration had started a lot of programs in Mississippi; that the Congress had cut funds for the poverty program; that "every recommendation in the letter by the Senators has the hearty concurrence of the administration," but there were some legal problems; and "we already know what needs to be done."

The senators' concern and the attendant publicity might, of course, have been seen by the White House as an opportunity to make major moves to correct the problem, just as it had made it a point to get out in front on any number of issues, such as auto safety or home ownership for the poor, raised in Congress. But this time the President was in no mood to be pushed. Neither he nor Freeman believed that the problem was as serious as Clark and Kennedy said, and both saw "politics" in the whole affair. (Department officials say that Clark and Kennedy were taken on a "pre-arranged" tour by "professionals.") The President knew that neither senator had influence with, in fact they had highly angered, the Agriculture establishment on Capitol Hill, and to the White House these were important people not to anger. When he did move, and it was not doubted that he would, it would be at a time and in a manner of his choosing.

The problem of malnutrition had, like most conceivable domestic problems, been put before a secret interagency task force by the White House the year before, as part of the preparations for the Administration's 1967 legislative program. The appointment of the task force, the task force was told, reflected the White House's deep conviction that every American should have an adequate nutritional diet. The task force, headed by Agriculture Department representatives, did not, in the view of the White House, provide sufficient information on either the dimensions of the problem or possible new approaches. Neither presidential aide Joseph Califano, who had hoped to be able to propose a food program nor his new assistant, James Gaither, was familiar enough with the complexities of the food programs to ask the right questions. Therefore nothing of any consequence was proposed. Following the senators' letter, renewed efforts within the Administration to work something out devolved into angry disputes between OEO, particularly Director Sargent Shriver, who accused Agriculture of incapacity to deal with the problem, and Agriculture, particularly Freeman, who accused OEO of trying to damage their Department and take away the programs. It was a classic bureaucratic fight over turf.

There were two basic issues between the subcommittee and the Administration: the price of the food stamps, and the Secretary's authority to declare an emergency in the Delta and send in extra food. After several months of subcommittee pressure and after prodding by the White House and harrassment by Shriver, the Agriculture Department did lower the price of food stamps for those with an income of less than $20 a month to 50 cents per person a month, with a maximum of $3 per family. (This buys $72 worth of food for a family of six, about half what the Department estimates such a family needs.) It also decided to charge all families only half the price in the first month. Prices could not be lowered generally until there was substantially more money for the program, a decision the President would have to make.

The Department resisted the argument that there were people with no income at all who should be charged nothing for their food stamps. For one thing, the Department thought that this was a problem in a small number of cases, and therefore not worthy of great concern. For another, the Secretary believed, as he told congressional committees on several occasions, that the poor could not be trusted with free stamps. "If you proceed, then, to have free stamps," he said, "and you give free stamps to everybody who wants them, what will happen to those stamps? Those stamps, I am afraid, in many cases will be bootlegged. That is what happened back in the 1940s and the 1930s, with the food stamp program. That destroyed the program. The food stamp program was discredited because those stamps became common currency for all kinds of things, from a wild party, to a beer party, to legitimate uses, to buy shoes." Another view of what ended the earlier program was the almost full employment during World War II.

The senators and others argued that the Secretary should have invoked his emergency power to send extra food to the Delta, using money from a special multipurpose fund (known as Section 32 for its place in an agriculture law), as he had used it to begin the food stamp program and expand the commodity packages. The Department argued that it didn't really have the power (despite the precedents), that the money really hadn't been budgeted, that it would be bad precedent and administratively inefficient to distribute free food where there were already food stamps; and there was also that danger that if there were two programs the people might start bootlegging. There was also the problem that the Agriculture committees frown on such use of the money.

As the arguments tumbled forth at one private meeting, Kennedy looked at Freeman and shook his head. "I don't know, Orville," he said, "I'd just get the food down there. I can't believe that in this country we can't get some food down there."

Oddly, the one senator who took matters in his own hands and introduced a bill was John Stennis of Mississippi. The Stennis bill would have provided money for emergency food and medical programs, and required a government study of the true extent of malnutrition. (The government had made almost no studies of malnutrition in the United States; the Public Health Service had not seen that to be its concern. The Pentagon, wanting to know about the connection between malnutrition and defense preparedness of foreign countries, had sponsored several studies of nutrition overseas, and there were minor studies of the eating habits of Eskimos and Indian tribes in the United States.)

The Stennis bill went through the Senate quickly. But his shrewd move to cut off talk about his state was not appreciated by the House Agriculture Committee, which let the bill die. Through other congressional routes, OEO was given $10 million in emergency food money and the Department of Health, Education, and Welfare was ordered to study the extent of malnutrition.

In September of 1967, in the only public statement on the issue he was to make for a long time, President Johnson said that "we want no American in this country to go hungry. We believe that we have the knowledge, the compassion, and the resources to banish hunger and to do away with malnutrition if we only apply those resources and those energies." He ordered the Department of Agriculture to see to it that, one way or the other, every one of the thousand poorest counties in the nation had a food program. The Department said that there were 331 of those counties that did not, and, to give it a little of the old pizzazz, it embarked on "Project 331." As it turned out, it was a full year before each of the 331 was said to have a program, for the Department remained highly reluctant to fly in the face of tradition by using federal money and federal personnel to establish a program if the counties resisted. It was also concerned about what it felt was a bad precedent of having the federal government pay the full costs. In May of the following year, with the Poor People's Campaign beating at his door, Freeman finally announced that this would be done.

Extending the programs to more counties had nothing to do with improving matters for recipients, as in Mississippi. Since greater amounts of money were not committed, it also meant that other less poor counties that were on the waiting list for the food stamp program would have to continue to wait. Finally, sometime after Project 331 was under way it was discovered that Agriculture defined a "poorest" county as one with the lowest average income, rather than one with the largest number of poor people. Therefore, poor people who had the misfortune of living near too many rich people were out of luck. This covered more counties at less expense, and fewer people were helped.

The President's encouraging statement may have been prompted by the fact that by the fall of 1967 the White House had set up another secret task force, which once more reflected their deep conviction, they said, that every American should have an adequate nutritional diet. The task force, now headed by representatives of the Budget Bureau, reported that for another $1.5 to $2 billion and in relatively short time the government could provide that adequate diet to every American. Now, however, and for months to come, the Administration was locked in its fight to secure a 10 per cent income surtax, from Congress, and Congress' demand that there be substantial cuts in government spending in return. "I don't think anyone realizes how paralyzed we became by that fight," says one Administration official. "I don't think even we realized it." With the White House feeling under particular pressure to do something about the cities (the Detroit riot had just taken place), and with their own expertise tending in that direction, Califano's staff that fall concerned itself with devising new programs for jobs and housing. Whatever the limitations of these programs in terms of delayed spending, they at least represented a commitment and an effort at new approaches, which were not made on giving the poor sufficient food. Through it all, Mr. Johnson remained unconvinced that the problem was as serious as the critics said, reluctant to take the fight to the Hill, where he had enough problems, and annoyed that no one could tell him exactly how many people were going hungry. (No one knows exactly how many unemployed or how much substandard housing there is either.)

Moreover, there was now no great public pressure on the White House to act on hunger, as there was on behalf of the cities. During all of 1967

and 1968, only a small coterie made the issue a continuing preoccupation:
Miss Wright; Peter Edelman of Kennedy's staff; William Smith of Clark's
staff; and Robert Choate, a young businessman of some means who took
a sabbatical to become a freelance, largely behind the scenes, and highly
effective crusader on the issue. Of the enormous Washington press corps,
only Nick Kotz of the Des Moines *Register* saw the hunger issue as worthy
of continuing coverage, whether or not it was "in the news." Of all the
lobby organizations, only a few of the more liberal labor groups found the
issue to be of even intermittent concern.

The Citizens' Crusade Against Poverty, an organization with United
Auto Workers backing, was the closest there was to a group with a full-
time concern. Early in 1968, it had established a Citizens' Board of Inquiry, which published "Hunger, U.S.A.," a stinging indictment of the
food programs. Around the same time, a coalition of women's organizations published a study of the federal school lunch program which could
help children of the poor secure a better meal at least while they were in
school. The women's groups found that of the 18 million children receiving free or reduced-price lunches under the program, only 2 million were
poor; another 4 million poor children were not being helped. The Johnson Administration had tried to get Congress to restructure this so that
less would go to the middle class and more to the poor, and Congress had
adamantly refused. On May 21, CBS broadcast a powerful documentary
called *Hunger in America.*

Several members of Congress reacted to all of this with outrage at the
idea that anyone would charge that people in their areas were going
hungry. Representative W. R. Poage of Texas, chairman of the House
Agriculture Committee, wrote to county health officials, the very ones who
would be most culpable, and asked if they personally knew of anyone
in their county who was starving or seriously hungry. No, replied most
of the health officers, and if the people were hungry it was mostly because
they were lazy or ignorant. A few said the food programs were inadequate, but Poage did not emphasize that in his report to his colleagues.

The response of the politicians was understandable. More puzzling,
in light of his professed zeal to get more done, were Freeman's own persistent attacks on the reports. Finding factual errors in the small (they
didn't mention that grandma had a pension of $82-a-month), he con-
demned them in the large. The CBS telecast, he said, was "a biased, one-
sided, dishonest presentation of a serious national problem."

As the Poor People's Campaign, under the direction of the Southern
Christian Leadership Conference, prepared for its March on Washington
in the spring of 1968, strategists for both the SCLC and the federal government knew that, as always in these situations, there would have to be
a governmental response which would enable the Campaign's leaders to

make an honorable withdrawal from the city. First Attorney General Ramsey Clark, then the President himself asked the various government agencies to draw up a list of administrative actions — which would not cost money — which could alleviate some of the difficulties of the poor. A March on Washington by a grand coalition of white, black, brown, and red poor, who would encamp in the federal city, bringing their plight to the attention of the country, had been the idea of Martin Luther King. After Dr. King was assassinated, the leadership of the SCLC under Dr. Ralph Abernathy was in disarray. Goals and tactics became difficult to resolve. Miss Wright, who had moved to Washington, was placed in charge of the Campaign's dealings with the government agencies, and worked exhaustingly for weeks for a semblance of order and progress in the demands and responses. On the advice of Miss Wright and others, the Campaign leaders decided upon hunger as the central, most dramatic issue.

Now the issue was at its highest point of public attention. Most of the government agencies did what they could to respond to the marchers' demands. Agriculture, however, remained defensive. In the end, the Agriculture response consisted of promising to get a food program into each of the thousand counties — which the President had already done nine months earlier; making more commodities available for surplus distribution; regulations to improve the school lunch program; and improved food packages for infants and expectant mothers. Some Administration officials think the poor were not grateful enough.

As it happened, the major reason this response was so paltry was that the White House was preparing one on a grander scale for the President himself to present, probably in the form of a special message to Congress. It would have revised the entire food stamp schedule and perhaps lowered the cost to the very poorest to either nothing or a token amount; it would have expanded the size of the food programs so that many more areas could receive them; and it would have carried a commitment to build the programs over time, to the point where every American had an adequate diet. The Budget Bureau squirreled away some money to go with the message. The thought was that it would be delivered around the time of "Solidarity Day," on June 19, when thousands of others were to come to Washington to join the poor in a climactic march.

A number of reasons have been offered for why the President's Solidarity Day Message was never delivered: the mail in the White House was overwhelmingly against the Poor People's Campaign, and Resurrection City was out of control; Abernathy's final speech was likely to carry a stinging denunciation of the war in Vietnam; and the House of Representatives was going to vote at last on the tax bill the following day, and any move at that point by the President to increase government spending might jeopardize the long-negotiated compromise. The most important reason, however, was that the President simply did not want to be in the position of appearing to "respond to pressure." More startling to many was that after the poor had left town and the tax bill had passed, he still declined to move. He was focusing on the budget cuts that had to be made, annoyed at Freeman for getting out in front of him on the issue, still concerned at appearing to respond to pressure, and convinced that now that some legislation was moving on the Hill, it would be unseemly for him, the President, to appear to be running to catch up.

By this time, things were most uncomfortable for Freeman, and he began to press hard at the White House for help — belatedly, in the opinion of many. His friend Vice President Humphrey tried to help. First Humphrey offered his services as a mediator with the Poor People's Campaign, but the offer was rejected by the White House. Then the Vice President of the United States tried indirect means of communicating with the President. Humphrey wrote to Mrs. Arthur Krim, wife of the President's chief money raiser: "It is just intolerable to me that there is such a problem of malnutrition and undernourishment in the United States. . . . Through it all, there are ways the President could have helped — in approving some of Orville Freeman's budget requests, in supporting legislation on the Hill, and suggesting administrative change — but he has not. The thought came that you might be the person who could say a word or two to encourage him."

On Capitol Hill, a bill to expand the food stamp program was moving forward. Originally an Administration request to make a minimal expansion of $20 million (over the $225 million already authorized), under pressure from urban liberals, who threatened to retaliate against a farm bill that was also in the mill, the bill ultimately authorized the program to grow by $90 million in the first year and more after that. After endorsing a substantial increase in the program, Freeman was reprimanded by both Poage and the White House, but when an increase seemed probable, the White House joined in. More spending for the school lunch program was approved, and a special Senate committee was established to "study" the food problem, with a view to trying to maneuver the food programs away from Agriculture committees.

In the very last days of the congressional session, with the President about to make a routine request for additional funds for various agencies that had fallen short of funds, the machinery around the government — in the Agriculture Department, in the Budget Bureau, in his own staff — geared up once more for a presidential request for more funds for food stamps and a major statement on the issue. Instead, he simply requested the $90 million and in the closing rush Congress gave him $55 million. Wait, it was said, for his farewell messages in 1969.

The failure of the Johnson Administration to make substantial progress toward feeding the poor is viewed by many as its most serious domestic failure. It is the cause of disappointment and even anguish on the part of many people within the government. Orville Freeman, for one, professes himself satisfied: "Everything I suggested from the beginning that should be in Lyndon Johnson's program, or damn near it, I have gotten. If he had gone up to Congress with a big feeding program like a bull in a china shop he'd have been under fire, and what would he have gotten? Some newspaper accolades and plaudits in some liberal magazines, and trouble with Congress."

The food issue is an unhappy example of a great deal that can go wrong in Washington. It is also an example, however, of the dangers of the latest fad of "local control." The food programs are examples of programs that *are* subject to local control — the local governments request, pay for, and run them — with the result that those areas which are least responsive to the needs of the poor can also deny them federally proffered food.

The problem is not nearly so insoluble as the events of the past two years would suggest. First of all, given enough money and flexibility, it is generally agreed the food stamp program is not at all a bad device. Choate, for one, suggests that in addition the program be federalized and computerized, to work as automatically and without continual harassment for the recipient as social security. He and a number of others believe that ultimately the food programs ought to be recognized as income supplements and become part of an income maintenance system. That, however, seems a long way off. When asked by the space agency, the food companies have found ingenious ways to pack meals for astronauts in Tootsie-Roll-sized bars or toothpaste-sized tubes. The Pentagon seems to have no trouble keeping the troops in the field well nourished. There are problems of tastes and habits to meet, but if the food industry were less apprehensive about change, or did less cohabiting with the farm bloc in that great combine they call "agribusiness," a lot more could be done to feed the poor efficiently and inexpensively. The food companies have lately shown more interest in exploring this field — with government subsidies, of course.

Yet so little was accomplished, not because of mechanical or industrial failures, but because of what can happen to men in policy-making positions in Washington. When they stay in a difficult job too long, they can be overwhelmed by the complexity of it all, and they become overly defensive. Man's pride, particularly the pride of a man who can tell himself he has done some good, can overtake his intellectual honesty. Thus, not Southern politicians, not Orville Freeman, not Lyndon Johnson could face the fact when it was pointed out that many people were hungry, that they weren't wearing any clothes. In this they reflected a national trait: it has been easier to stir sustained national concern over hunger in Bihar or Biafra than places at home for which we are more directly responsible. The problems are looked at in terms of the workings of Washington, not in terms of the problems. Decent men could sit and discuss statistical reliability and administrative neatness and the importance of good precedents while people went hungry.

The niceties of consensus politics were more important than the needs of some 10 million people. A new Congress and a new Administration ought to be able to improve on that kind of government.

ELINOR LANGER   *The Shame*
                                            of American Medicine

The success of American medicine is often attributed to the profession's ability to serve the public on its own terms. Why should doctors care if, from the patient's point of view, the terms chosen — solo practice and emphasis on the "doctor-patient relationship" — mean that a doctor performs unsupervised services for unregulated fees? What does it matter to them that the poor are outside the system altogether, treated in charity wards or public hospitals which are the medical equivalent of Andrew Carnegie's libraries, a small concession to charity from an accelerating machine of wealth, power, and influence? In a country proud of its "pluralism" and fearful of "government interference," a monolithic self-regulating profession is taken as a sign of health. Few people are persuaded that medical care is a fit object of social planning: We have no national health policy and we are mostly proud of it.

It has left us in an extremely unfortunate mess. At its best American medicine may very well be the best in the world, as its practitioners claim, which is why retired English kings and Arabian sheiks turn up regularly in our hospitals. But though excellent treatment is usually available to the very rich, the rest of the population finds even adequate services hard to come by. The charge frequently made by critics that ten countries have lower rates of infant mortality and longer life expectancies does not mean that the Peter Bent Brigham Hospital, for instance, is somewhat slipshod; it means that most people will never set foot in any place half so good.

The situation of the poor is particularly appalling. In Boston, a health survey of a public housing project indicated that among individuals over 65, 25 per cent had chronic bronchitis, 20 per cent had chronic nervous disorders, 12 per cent were blind or had visual defects, and that 40 per cent of these were not receiving treatment. In New York, former Health Commissioner George James has estimated that 13,000 poor people died last year because adequate professional care was not available. The maternal mortality rate for U.S. whites (in 1961) was 2.5 per 10,000 live births. For Mississippi Negroes, it was 15.3, more than six times as high. In a South Carolina county, every tenth Negro child died in the first year of life.

The poor are not wholly without opportunities for medical care. But the public facilities that do exist perpetuate a grotesque circle of personal humiliation and medical lunacy. In many cities a mother cannot take a well baby for a check-up to the same place she must take a sick child for diagnosis or treatment. If she suffers from both migraine headaches and pains in her chest she may have to go to two different clinics herself. Clinics (and emergency rooms) are often far away, in a sometimes unfamiliar "downtown." For a suburban mother with a car and a maid such problems would be easy to surmount. For the poor mother it is different. Each clinic visit may take a separate trip. Each trip means, if she is working, a day's lost pay; or, if she customarily cares for her children, an arrangement with neighbors. It means costly taxi fares or time-consuming bus trips. After a long wait in a crowded room arranged like a bus terminal, she may be ordered to go elsewhere or to return another day. She may be asked to undress in the hallways and, thus stripped, to explain her problem to various impersonal functionaries, to what bureaucratic purpose she can hardly be expected to understand. If she sees a doctor at all (no certainty) he will not be the one she saw last time or the one she will see next time. Her medical records may be scattered about the city. She is apt to be submerged in an avalanche of prescriptions and regimens incompletely understood (for there is no one to explain them to her) and often mutually incompatible.

And so the poor, faced with a system that discourages them from seeking care, and beset with other crises that may seem to them more urgent than a nagging cough, have acquired a certain reputation among the professions: They "don't care" about their health, "don't keep appointments," "won't cooperate," "don't do what you tell them," and even "don't mind being sick." The hoariness of this mythology is clear from a recent study of English hospital development by Brian Abel-Smith. He reports that during a government inspection of English pauper hospitals in the 1860s:

> At Kensington and Paddington some of the sick were found washing in their chamber pots. The inspector was told by one medical officer that the patients preferred to wash in this way but he later established that they did this against their will and their former habits at home. Only a few [institutions] provided lavatory paper on the grounds that a very large proportion of the poor were not in the habit of using it. There were, however, numberless instances of closets being blocked with old towels, dusters and dishcloths — and leaves of Holy Scripture. . . . One or more Bibles, and sometimes a Prayer Book, were found in each ward, but in a more or less imperfect and dilapidated state — a circumstance connected with the subject just discussed.

Even the best of the organized health plans have sometimes had difficulty staffing their units in the ghettoes: Disgust is the other face of charity.

But the medical system has not only failed the poor: It is also cheating the middle class. There is a joke popular with medical students: "What are the indications for a hysterectomy? — Two children, a Blue Cross card, and a uterus." Unfortunately, it is no joke. Every review of the quality of medical care has found a high rate of unnecessary and incompetent surgery, of faulty and delayed diagnosis, of sins not only against medical science but against common sense. A famous study by Columbia University's School of Public Health and Administrative Medicine of the medical care of a group of Teamsters and their families in New York City a few years ago concluded that one fifth of the hospital admissions were unnecessary and one fifth of the surgery was "poor."[1]

More than a third of the hysterectomies and more than half the Caesareans were held unnecessary. A study sponsored by the Rockefeller Foundation and the University of North Carolina Division of Health Affairs of North Carolina general practitioners in the 1950s found that 44 per cent were failing to take medical histories, using unsterile instruments, conducting incomplete examinations without using laboratory aids and without having patients undress or lie down or prescribing irrelevant drugs. "The physicians studied came from many medical schools and had exhibited all degrees of academic success," the report stated, "so there is no reason to assume an adverse selection. It can . . . be stated with considerable assurance that in terms of medical education and training the

---

[1] Selig Greenberg, *The Troubled Calling: Crisis in the Medical Establishment,* Macmillan, 1965, pp. 208–210.

physicians who participated in this study are not evidently different from general practitioners at large."[2]

Ethical controls are as lax as the medical ones. Denunciations of fee-splitting issue periodically from the professional associations. But doctors combine to buy pharmacies in medical buildings; take payments for journal articles they have not written endorsing drugs they have not tested; conduct medical and surgical experiments on their patients without telling them; cheat on insurance; and, like the GE executive who went to jail, they retain an honored place among their colleagues and within their communities.[3]

Middle-class medicine is facing a crisis in costs as well as quality. Hospital rates now average over $40 per day and insurance rates have taken off like a rocket. To a certain extent this is the price of technological achievement: A heart-lung machine, for instance, and a cobalt machine for treating cancer may cost in the vicinity of $100,000 each, and each requires a small army of skilled technicians for its upkeep. It also reflects the inroads of unionization on hospital pay scales. Salaries have been so low that in New York, for example, some hospital employees were recently receiving public welfare while holding down full-time jobs. But to a large extent the doctors themselves are responsible for the inflation: An electrocardiograph standing idle for thirty-five hours a week in the private office of a Park Avenue internist is an exceedingly costly instrument, and the costs are reflected in his bills. The inflationary pattern of solo practice is reinforced by the pattern of insurance plans. Nearly 150 million Americans have some, but it covers on the average only 30 per cent of a family's regular medical bills. Hospitalization insurance is easy enough to obtain, but it is hard to buy policies that cover office or home visits, drugs, outpatient diagnostic tests, or psychiatric or nursing care. The payment system common to insurance — so much for a hernia, so much for a tonsillectomy — supports the ideology of solo practice in another way. It encourages both doctors and patients to think of health negatively, as a series of episodic battles against discrete afflictions. In this system the concept of "comprehensive" or preventive care has little place.

The result is poor medicine and poor policy. It is poor policy because it

[2] Herman M. Somers and Anne R. Somers, *Doctors, Patients, & Health Insurance,* pp. 31–32, notes 7, 8 (Brookings, 1961) and Selig Greenberg, "The Decline of the Healing Art" in *The Crisis in American Medicine,* Harpers, 1961, p. 22.

[3] Documentation of links between physicians and pharmaceutical operations can be found in last year's hearings of the Senate Anti-Trust Committee on "Doctor-Owned Pharmacies" and in hearings of the House Government Operations Committee on "Drug Safety." *Science,* Feb. 11, 1966, p. 663, and *The Saturday Review,* Feb. 5, 1966, p. 61, discuss human experimentation. Doctors' abuse of insurance is reported in Greenberg, *The Troubled Calling,* p. 207 ff.

leaves both doctors and patients dependent on hospitalization — the patient, in order to pay his bills, the doctor to collect his fees — and obstructs
development of more rational and humane outpatient, home, and nursing
services that could be more cheaply arranged. The present dilemma
of the hospitals — shortages of services in some areas and underutili-
zation in others — has additional causes: administrative rigidity, regional
competition, desultory Federal supervision, and technological leap-
frogging that has left many small institutions unable to perform modern
services adequately. But hospital-oriented insurance has played a major
role not only in overcrowding many hospitals but in deflecting attention
from their defects. In addition, the system leads to poor medicine because
it subsidizes the costs of catastrophe, not the preventive care that might
minimize catastrophe, and it is flourishing at a time when medical victories over many acute diseases and the growing proportion of old people
have made arrangements for preventive and long-term care all the more
essential. Illness is simply more flexible than insurance. As Anne Somers
pointed out in a recent paper:

> The corollary of this shift [to an aging population] is increasing
> need for long-term preventive, rehabilitative, semi-custodial, and
> medical social services. Most chronic diseases are months or years
> in developing and require early diagnosis if they are to be handled
> effectively. The period of treatment is, by definition, extensive. If
> cure is achieved, there is often required a long post-cure rehabilita-
> tion. Generally, the most optimistic solution is stabilization — for
> example, in diabetes or glaucoma — under continuous life-time
> medical supervision. With such changes in morbidity and disability
> patterns, the distinction between health and illness becomes blurred,
> and the concept of medical need increasingly difficult to pinpoint
> in space or time. Rather there is a continuous spectrum with vary-
> ing degrees of emphasis. It begins before we are actually ill; it does
> not cease when we are discharged from the hospital. Continuity
> and comprehensiveness have become indispensable aspects of effec-
> tive medical care.[4]

The failure of health insurance to deal with this situation is not just a
coincidence. As the Somerses' study makes clear, Blue Cross and Blue
Shield originated in doctors' efforts to protect their incomes.[5] Blue Shield
plans are dominated by local medical societies; Blue Cross plans by hospital representatives. In neither is there much effective public representation. The commercial plans have broken little new ground. In theory,

[4] Anne R. Somers, "Some Basic Determinants of Medical Care and Health Policy:
Trends and Issues." Paper prepared for Seminar on Health Policy, Institute for Policy Studies, Washington; January 25, 1966.
[5] Somers and Somers op. cit., chapters 15 and 16.

health insurance might have been developed by independent groups who preserved some power to supervise the hospitals and private practice: There is growing pressure for such supervision now from regulatory bodies (state insurance commissions) and organized consumers (business and unions). They have begun to feel that their soaring payments for member or employee health plans cannot be justified without questioning both the cost and the quality of the treatment they are buying. But until now, the system has been manipulated by the doctors to prevent outside control. The doctors opposed medicare because they feared that their freedom from review would come to an end under a system of government insurance, and that rising costs would ultimately force the government to institute controls. Medicare is a conservative step, however, whatever the doctors think; for relieving the pressure of the aged (who are bad risks) on the voluntary insurance system will temporarily conceal some of the cracks the system contains. We continue to revolve in a circle of high costs and high rates that leaves millions of people unable to afford insurance at all, and those who have it stuck with unsatisfactory policies which hardly begin to pay their bills. The result has called forth the invention of a new category of social dependency known as "medical indigence": According to a recent study, 80 per cent of the patients in New York's municipal hospitals were people who are not on relief and who normally "manage to cover their ordinary expenses but lack the margin in income, savings, or health insurance to pay the hospital and the doctor when they get sick."[6] If the doctors continue to have their way, they are likely to make medical indigents of us all.

What is to be done? For about thirty years, the "progressive" elements in American medicine — and there are some — have been formulating plans for the reorganization of medical care. These reformers are not an organized group but individuals associated chiefly with medical schools and public health programs who have come together, over the years, in foundation-sponsored and government-sponsored committees and study groups to consider the organization of medicine.[7] Their prescription has three interrelated ingredients. First, they believe that solo practice should be replaced by teams of specialists mobilized into "group practice," thus both enlarging the intellectual and technological resources of the doctors, and lowering costs. Second, they propose that inclusive prepayment plans (providing, among other things, regular salaries for doctors) should re-

[6] Nora K. Piore, "Metropolitan Medical Economics," in *Scientific American*, January, 1965, p. 19.
[7] George Baehr, "Medical Care — Old Goals and New Horizons," 1965, Michael M. Davis Lecture, The University of Chicago, May 13, 1965. Among the most important groups was the Committee on the Costs of Medical Care, established with philanthropic support in 1928. Another major study was produced by the Presidentially appointed Commission on the Health Needs of the Nation in 1949.

place traditional fee-for-service compensation. Third, they urge that hospital services should be expanded and more efficiently organized both regionally (to avoid the inequitable and inefficient maldistribution of expensive, specialized equipment) and within the hospitals themselves (to offer patients a range of flexible services correlated with their needs as these change during hospitalization). There is no reason why the patient who is getting better should be imprisoned in a reign of nursing terror when he could be helping to take care of himself. Increasingly, a fourth design has been prominent: the fusion of now-fragmented health resources — medical schools, hospitals, public and private health agencies — into a coordinated "health industry team," whereby unified, community-oriented planning would replace competition among hospitals; facilities would be carefully reorganized to avoid overlapping and to make a complete range of services easily available in each part of the city.

Some remarkable evidence from a few pilot projects makes plain that medical and economic logic are on the side of these reforms. The Health Insurance Plan of Greater New York (HIP), for example, the largest group practice in the United States enrolls about 700,000 New Yorkers, many of them city employees. They are served by one of thirty-one medical groups located throughout the city, which include both a "family physician" (a G.P.) and a variety of specialists. For $4.50 a month a person can obtain all regular outpatient medical services from eye check-ups to physiotherapy. Hospitalization costs are not included (subscribers are encouraged to join Blue Cross) although full surgical costs are. Physical examinations and other preventive services are offered without cost and without limit. The availability of outpatient care seems to promote both health and economy. Studies have consistently demonstrated that the rate of hospitalization and the length of hospital stays of HIP patients are substantially lower than for patients treated and insured by conventional means.[8] More striking, the health record is better. The prenatal death rate among HIP subscribers, for instance, is lower than among patients seeing private doctors. (The lower rate holds among comparable groups of whites and nonwhites; among families with comparable incomes; and among families where the wage-earners have comparable occupations.) HIP subscribers suffer fewer infant deaths in the first week after delivery; the average weight of infants at birth is higher; the prematurity rate is lower. The record of other group health plans is the same.

In a limited way, it is true, some "reform" has already begun. The influence of the medical schools and hospitals is rising and solo practice is, statistically, on the decline. Nonetheless, the number of people being served by the new arrangements is small. Lying between successful demonstrations of progressive ideas and their wide application are two things.

[8] Somers and Somers, *op. cit.*, p. 177.

The first is the unrelenting obstructionism of organized medicine. In 1943 the Group Health Association of Washington, D.C. successfully brought an antitrust suit against the AMA and the local medical society for conspiring to restrain trade. But elsewhere, from then till now, physicians entering organized groups have found themselves subject to harassments ranging from social ostracism to suspension of medical society privileges. Twenty-three states still have laws prohibiting group practice except in a form approved by the medical societies. In only about a dozen cities is it even possible to enroll in a full-fledged group practice program. In the same way, the profession has bitterly resisted the trend toward including specialists' services as part of hospitalization, insisting that the radiologist who takes X-rays or the anesthesiologist who gives the injection are private personal physicians, equally entitled to that "special relationship" with their patients that permits them to send a bill.[9] Their fear arises from a domino theory of medicine: As radiologists go, so will go the obstetricians, gynecologists, and internists. Group practice will have a beachhead in the hospitals and fee-for-service practice will come to a stop. The Communists will be at Waikiki.

Supporting the intransigence of the profession in the face of change has been the weak and neutral policies of the federal government. We spend billions of dollars on medical research (paying particular attention to the pet afflictions of the aging politicians who appropriate the money) and billions more on hospital and other construction programs. These have succeeded chiefly in proliferating the interests opposed to change. But aside from providing direct medical care to specialized portions of the population (mainly federal dependents), the government has left what is known in the trade as "the delivery of medical care" alone. There is one exception, the Heart Disease, Cancer, and Stroke legislation passed in the last session of Congress. Following the "progressive" model, this calls for regional cooperation among existing health agencies to advance the research, diagnosis, and treatment of the three diseases. But like the medicare bill which promises that no Federal official shall be permitted "to exercise any supervision or control over the practice of medicine or the manner in which the services are provided," the Heart, Cancer, and Stroke Bill promises to accomplish its ends "without interfering with the patterns, or the methods of financing, of patient care or professional practice, or with the administration of hospitals."

Medicare itself may ultimately be responsible for overturning that intention. Experts anticipate that the availability of payment after July 1 will lead to a sudden, crushing demand for medical services that the present disorganized system will be unable to supply. If they turn out to be right, medical care could become a major political issue, and pressure

[9] *Science*, July 9, 1965, p. 164.

from angry consumers could force the government to play a stronger role. But that is not the way it was planned. When federal officials go up to Capitol Hill to testify that the programs they are endorsing will "save us from socialism," the trouble is that they mean it. They are committed to a timid reformism that masks their unwillingness to retrieve power from the very institutions which need to be reformed.

The idea that the government would take the lead in ending the chaos in medical care was subtly undermined last summer. The AMA convention in New York last June was perhaps the lowest point in the profession's recent history. There were hysterical discussions of medicare ("we would be zombies stepping into involuntary servitude if we accept such fascist control") and intense debate about a doctors strike (". . . it is ethical, proper, desirable, moral and legal not to participate in such socialistic schemes"). Peripheral groups of doctors, formed out of concern with racial discrimination, or with foreign policy, or with the economics of medicine, were beginning to talk seriously about founding a rival association. In Washington, the influence of two potential competitors to the AMA — the American Hospital Association and the Association of American Medical Colleges — became increasingly apparent. An influential coalition of physicians centered around philanthropist Mary Lasker had been moving away from its initial preoccupation with medical care. The AMA was in a shaky position and its leaders knew it. After the confusion of the convention, they went to Washington, timorously, to say that they would, after all, cooperate in drawing up the regulations to implement medicare. And the government — in effect, the chief officials of the Department of Health, Education, and Welfare — took them back. They supplied the doctors with new prestige — a visit with President Johnson — and took some advice on medicare rules and the Heart, Cancer, and Stroke Bill. The new guard at the department might have demanded positive evidence of a change in attitude and definite commitments for AMA support of creative legislation. Instead they lost themselves in public celebration of a fuzzy and undependable "partnership." This same concept of "partnership" — solicitude for established interests — is also rapidly obliterating hope of rapid progress in critical areas of environmental health. We pass a bill requiring a mild cigarette-label warning, but prohibit any other warnings on packs or ads till mid-1969. We pass a strong water pollution bill but leave intact a Jeffersonian formula for distributing grants that actually discriminates against the crowded urban areas where pollution is most serious. We permit the poverty program to offer birth control but refuse to let it instruct the unwed mothers who need contraceptives most. We support research on traffic accidents but permit researchers to withhold the names of auto manufacturers with the most treacherous designs. To celebrate partnership is, usually, to celebrate a deal.

In the case of medical care, there has been a deal, and all of us are the objects of it. The system, in which the government has acquiesced, is designed to keep the doctors well-nourished and the middle class quiet. Discontent over the organization of care is diverted into humble appreciation of scientific triumphs. Doubts about the treatment of the poor are smothered by periodic stories of dramatic recoveries on the wards and by the Robin Hood notion that "our" prices are high because the doctors are working charitably for "them." From the system that offers both a cure for our tuberculosis and a salve for our conscience, we will suffer both humiliation and extortion. The middle class does receive better care and consequently has a better chance for survival than the poor have, but in a subtler sense it is equally victimized. The agility of middle-class patients increases their ability to navigate in the system, obtaining supporting diagnosis or shopping around for more compatible, or lower priced, or more fancily equipped, doctors. But none of us can really change the attitudes we encounter, modify the orders we are given, avoid the charges we are told to pay, or look to anything outside the closed shop for comfort or support. It was precisely this condition of dependence that weakened the wariness some government officials harbored secretly during their reconciliation with the AMA last summer: The officials knew that, from a practical point of view, the AMA represents the only doctors we have. The exceptions, the clusters of independents and critics, are too few numerically and too concentrated geographically (in urban centers) to be the base of a reorganized system of medical care.

Nor would the subtler defects of the system be fundamentally affected if there were more renegades. We would be at the mercy of the good guys instead of the bad guys, but the good guys share with the bad an instinctive commitment to the idea of total professional control. There are some exceptions. The Tufts Medical School has set up a health center in a desolate housing project on the edge of Boston that in effect combines group practice with public control. The formula is the standard requirement of the Office of Economic Opportunity — a board composed of members of the local community. But it is working out with the seeming difference that, unlike most mayors, the Tufts doctors enjoy working with the residents in a non-authoritarian fashion and are actually committed to the idea of "community participation" in the process of medical care. No welfare mother is about to start taking throat cultures, but the doctors are trying to share power with the community in a number of non-specialized areas of policy: The residents influenced the design and furnishing of the health center facility for example; more important, they helped to define the conditions of service (including clinic hours, payment, and so forth) and will help in their execution. Tufts also plans to train Columbia Point residents for a range of subprofessional jobs at the medical center, something that may help to reduce the psychological gulf between doctors and patients. The school is planning a similar project in the rural South. In a few other cities, elements of the scheme — the training of the poor as health assistants or the development of neighborhood health centers — are being talked about and tried. But these projects are confined to the poor and far too restricted to be called a trend. For the most part there is reason to believe that as the progressive vision is implemented, the incapacity of the public to exercise control over the medical profession will be not lessened but exaggerated. In the Heart, Cancer, Stroke program, for example, power will reside in Olympian regional coalitions resting on Medical schools, hospitals and public and private health agencies; in New York's controversial "Trussel Plan" the city has in effect turned over the administration and control of municipal hospitals to the private hospitals and medical schools.[10] The progressive vision in medicine is a corporate one, a response to institutional inefficiency and waste, not to personal inhumanity and confusion. But that, in all probability, is where we are heading. If they oil us now and then, and shore up our outworn parts, will we ask for anything more?

Welfare

Most people agree that the current American welfare system is in a mess, but there the agreement ends. Some attack the system as an instrument through which the middle class forces its version of morality on the less fortunate. Others attack it as an instrument through which the shiftless swindle and cheat the hard-working. Still others attack it as a means of pacifying the poor, thereby allowing an unjust economic system to perpetuate itself.

The object of all this criticism is a complicated and cumbersome apparatus which has shown very little important change since the seventeenth century and shows little sign of changing considerably in the near future.

[10] Robb K. Burlage, "Issues of a Changing Hospital System, with New York Case Study." Preliminary study, Institute for Policy Studies, Washington, 1965.

It was suggested in the last section that the extension of social services to all requires conception of *citizenship*,[1] in which all members of the community are to have a *right* to certain levels of well-being. But dominating in the American conception of social welfare is the principle that no one should "get something for nothing." This belief, in turn rests on the premise that poverty is a result of individual failure, a flaw in the moral character. The responsibility is therefore the individual's, not society's; and if society deigns to grant support, it will do so on its own terms.

The ideology of American welfare, then, is founded on a *minimum* concept of society, in which the effect of social forces on the lives and life chances of individuals is de-emphasized, and correspondingly, the responsibility of society as a whole for the welfare of its individual members is downgraded. Thus we tend to feel not only that poverty is somehow immoral, but also that to tamper with it is to interfere with a basic, natural order of things that it would be folly to disrupt. For these reasons, we are very reluctant to support the poor at a level of tolerable comfort, for fear that it would encourage idleness among others and bring the economy to a halt, as well as deeply offend the relevant deities.

The present system of public assistance results from this refusal to tamper with the forces of the market, coupled with a recognized need for *some* support for the poor, if only to keep them from creating a disturbance. The attempt to implement these rather conflicting aims often results in a system of structured irrationality; a system that, for example, spends tens of millions of dollars to be sure that no one is "cheating" the system in one way or another — i.e., costing the taxpayer extra money. Or which systematically destroys normal family life by supporting only the most broken families, thereby putting considerable pressure on fathers to leave the home in order that the mother and children can quality for assistance.

[1] For a discussion of this conception, with special reference to social services in England, see T. H. Marshall, *Class, Citizenship, and Social Development* (Garden City, New York: Doubleday Anchor, 1964).

But if the system is often irrational, it is also systematically discriminatory; in return for granting some support, the welfare establishment assumes the authority to demand of the poor behavior that is not demanded of anyone else. The welfare system combines the worst of two worlds; the laissez-faire neglect of basic human needs in favor of market forces, and the bureaucratic urge to meddle and control. In this way a "dual system of law" has developed: one law for the poor, another for everyone else.

The origins, nature, and consequences of this double standard are explored in the following articles. In the first, tenBroek describes the origins of the American law of welfare in the Elizabethan Poor Laws of sixteenth- and seventeenth-century England. These laws were based on a theory of the causes of poverty which stressed the character defects of the poor rather than the operation of the economy, but which also divided the poor into "deserving" and "undeserving." This division remains with us today, and is reflected in the differences between our programs for the "respectable" poor — such as old age insurance and unemployment insurance, which tend to be granted as a matter of right, without prejudice — and our programs for the "undeserving" poor, the various forms of "poor relief." In these programs, benefits are contingent on "good" behavior, and are accompanied by a host of special provisions and restrictions applying only to those "on welfare."

In effect, according to tenBroek, the law of welfare is part of the *criminal* law: the state responds to the poor not as citizens but as offenders, the implication being that poverty itself is a crime. The use of the criminal law to deal with poverty reflects society's desire to protect itself from the poor, not a commitment to human welfare.

In "Brownleaf's Story," Richard Elman illuminates another aspect of the second-class citizenship imposed on the poor as a condition of support. Brownleaf is expected to be grateful for the opportunity to haul garbage at $17.50 a week, in the name of "retraining; although it seems clear that the actual training involved is minimal in terms of his economic opportunity, and that what is important is that he display a proper attitude, that he learn "the value of a job." Brownleaf's difficulties are especially meaningful when we consider the welfare reform proposals suggested by the Nixon administration: these propose a flat assistance rate coupled with required job training, a program that seems little different from the one understandably rejected by Brownleaf. There is again a double standard: only the poor are asked not only to accept demeaning work at less-than-subsistence wages, but also to like it.

Cloward and Elman consider the possible avoidance of second-class citizenship for welfare recipients. Their main argument is that this can be achieved only through *law;* specifically, through an assertion of the *right* to welfare without the attendant degradation. The assertion of the rights of the poor to this new kind of "property" implies a limitation on the authorities' discretion to wreak their will on their "clients," a condition that amounts to a kind of official lawlessness.

Some of the specific laws mentioned by the authors, such as the residence requirement, the "suitable home" provisions, and "midnight raids" have been or are being challenged in the federal courts as unconstitutional, a promising development. But as all our selections show, the problem is deeper and more pervasive; not simply a few bad laws, but a fundamentally unjust relationship between the poor and the dominant society.

How can alternative relationships be created? The authors emphasize the importance of mounting a legal challenge to the entire structure of American welfare law; overcoming the lack of information that bolsters the power of the welfare agencies; and building a base of genuine advocacy for the poor. But, finally, they suggest that the problem might be solved at its root by a measure of income redistribution in the form of a "guaranteed income" — altogether eliminating the need for the welfare apparatus as we know it.

JACOBUS tenBROEK

The Two Nations: Differential Moral Values in Welfare Law and Administration

According to legend it was Benjamin Disraeli, the eminent Victorian, who first used the phrase which stands as the title of this essay. Taking note of the vast gulf between the classes and the masses, between the rich and the wretched of England in his time, he expressed the shock of his recognition by describing them as "the two nations."[1] It is instructive to remind ourselves that ours is not the first generation to have discovered the existence of that separate and submerged nation-within-a-nation — the Other America — which is inhabited by the poor. The same finding, indicative of a similar quickening of the social conscience, occurred in England in the second quarter of the last century — in the generation of Dickens and Robert Owen, of the Reform Act, and the revised poor law. That recognition occurred also in the United States, where by the middle of the nineteenth century, as Robert H. Bremner has reminded us:

> There was ample evidence that a poverty problem, novel in kind and alarming in size, was emerging . . . a sizable body of men and women agreed that there was no valid excuse, moral or economic, for the presence of want in the midst of plenty; they condemned the bending of human lives to the will of the machine as inhumane and unwise; and they expressed regret and concern at the signs of growing estrangement between social classes.[2]

"It is often said," wrote a pioneering reformer in the 1840's, "that one half of the world does not know how the other half lives."[3]

But the recognition of poverty did not, either in America or England, carry with it the solution to poverty — although, to be sure, it ushered in a host of panaceas, ranging from the romantic socialisms of Owen and Fourier to the revolutionary socialism of Karl Marx. For Henry George, who saw clearly the connection between progress and poverty, the answer

Reprinted from *Orthopsychiatry and the Law* by M. Levitt and B. Rubenstein (eds.) by permission of the Wayne State University Press. Copyright © 1968 by Wayne State University Press, Detroit, Michigan.

[1] Benjamin Disraeli, *Sybil*, ch. 8.

[2] Robert H. Bremner, *From the Depths: The Discovery of Poverty in the United States* (New York, 1956), p. 4.

[3] John H. Griscom, quoted from *From the Depths*.

was to be found in a single tax on land; for Samuel Butler, whose sensibilities were still more outraged, nothing less than the smashing of the machines would bring an end to poverty and exploitation. For many others, probably including a majority of Americans and Britons, the issue was not social and economic but individual and moral: it involved the rescue, reclamation, and redemption of the fallen ones who were invariably the victims of their own vices.

Few of these nineteenth-century perspectives on poverty faced the issue squarely; none of them produced anything like a solution. Vital as it was, the discovery of the Two Nations did not end the cold war between them. Nor has it ended yet, a full century later. To be sure, during the past half-decade we have become acutely conscious of the poverty in the midst of our plenty; we have begun to perceive the agony alongside the ecstasy, and to replace the complacent self-image of the perfectly affluent society with an idealistic vision of a future Great Society. We have made, in the words of President Johnson, a commitment — "a total commitment by this President, and this Congress, and this Nation, to pursue victory over the most ancient of mankind's enemies."[4]

This is a generous commitment and a constructive advance. But we have lately found ourselves, for all our vast resources, unable to fight a "*two*-front war" simultaneously. The homefront war on poverty, officially declared just two years ago, has given way to the overseas war in Vietnam — a shift of emphasis which poignantly recalls the declaration of Franklin Roosevelt a quarter-century ago that "Dr. New Deal" must give way to "Dr. Win the War." We may dare to hope that the violent war in the Asian jungles will be brought to a settlement, sooner rather than later — so that the nonviolent war upon the asphalt jungles of America may be resumed in full force. Meanwhile we may profit from this hiatus if we make good use of the time to take a fresh and serious look both at the problems of contemporary poverty and at the strategies of welfare available to cope with them. Above all, we need to confront ourselves — to face up to our intentions and our institutions. We have not looked hard enough or long enough at our procedures of law and justice, our channels of opportunity and advancement, our resources of voluntary organization and association, our media of communication and information, or our structures of education and welfare. Our tendency in the past has been to leap into the breach before we look, and hence to find ourselves soon grappling with shadows and ensnarled in a tangle of conflicting agencies and ad hoc crusades. "The United States," wrote Robert Hunter as long ago as 1904, "spends more money than any other nation in the world upon statistical investigations, yet we know less about the poverty

[4] Message to Congress on poverty, March 3, 1964.

of the people than almost any other great nation of the Western World."[5] And in remarkably similar language, a contemporary investigator adds: "Poverty has a formidable ally in our own ignorance of what we must do to root out poverty. . . . There is a surprising dearth of hard knowledge about the root causes and dynamics of poverty."[6]

A decade or so ago, at the instigation of the Eisenhower Administration, we were given a "New Look" in public welfare. That look turned out to be scarcely more than an anxious glance. Today we have the need and opportunity to take another new look at welfare — at its premises and promises, its rigidities and flexibilities. As we probe beneath the surface of official rhetoric and regulation, we may discern the outlines of the two nations — the double standard of law and ethics of "separate but unequal," which has pervaded the field of welfare since the enactment of the Elizabethan Poor Laws. Indeed, the field itself, as institutionalized in the programs of social security, is divided down the middle by an iron curtain. On one side of the curtain are the "respectable" programs of social insurance — old age and survivors' insurance, disability insurance, unemployment insurance — programs to which you and I make our regular contributions and from which, when the rainy day comes, we expect to draw our benefits as a matter of right, in dignity and respectability, without fuss or bother. For these programs enact and celebrate the Protestant ethic — with its premium on self-reliance and self-improvement, on initiative and thrift and clean living. These are the decent structures of social security we have built for decent folk — those who can pay their way, those who belong.

This solid and constructive side of the social security system was regarded as much the more important of the two by its original designers in the New Deal Congress and administration. Its title was intended to convey the distinguishing characteristic: that of *insurance*. The payments regularly made into the system by the covered individual are called premiums; and in turn when the "rainy day" comes (the advent of old age, disability, or death), the covered person or his dependents receive regular payments designated "insurance benefits" — not relief, assistance, or charity. Moreover, these benefits may be claimed as a matter of earned right, it is supposed, since they are tied to a system of premium payments related to the individual's wages and work record. The amount of the benefit is fixed in advance in the statute itself, which has the appearance of an insurance contract; hence the benefit is predictable and certain in amount, rather than being contingent upon the investigations and discretion of a social worker. As a consequence of these built-in stipulations, a whole

[5] Robert Hunter, in *Poverty American Style,* ed. S. M. Miller (Belmont, Cal., 1966), p. 85.
   [6] Ibid., p. 40.

host of factors which are conspicuous on the other side of social security are ruled out as irrelevant in the determination of eligibility for social insurance benefits. Among these absent factors are the income or financial situation of the beneficiary; proof that he is in need at all; the status and number of his relatives; the length of his residence; or the vital statistics of his life and livelihood, morals, habits, and general conduct.

No doubt this roseate image of the social insurances, imposed at the outset and encouraged ever since, bears elements of exaggeration and even of fiction. There are, to be sure, numerous qualifications and contingencies which reduce or deny the insurance character of the system. But what is undeniable is that the beneficiary does make a financial contribution, whether it be called a premium or a tax, which is regularly deducted from his wages. From this he derives a real sense of participation and of responsibility — the conviction that he is entitled to the benefit as a matter of right. This impression is itself of crucial importance; whatever may be the actual legal or logical significance of the contribution, it has great political and psychological significance both in terms of the system and its benefits and in terms of the nation's demand that the harshest features of public assistance be avoided. Sustaining the fiction of insurance as far as possible thus has important consequences for the system of social security. And whether or not it is truly insurance, the system does give substantial protection to the individual against a multiplicity of social hazards, arising from economic boom and bust, from industrial employment and technological unemployment — hazards beyond the control of the person no matter how replete with the legendary virtues of the middle class he may be. Perhaps most important of all, because the personal needs and characteristics of the applicant are irrelevant to the determination of eligibility, administrative costs and machinery can be held to a minimum. There is a conspicuous absence of those numerous rituals of surveillance and supervision which constitute a dominating presence on the other side of the welfare curtain in the domain of public assistance.

For on this nether side of the system are the programs intended for those who cannot pay and who do not "belong" — the programs of poor relief, embracing aid to needy families with children, aid to needy aged, to needy blind, and to needy disabled. These programs are the lineal descendants of the Elizabethan Poor Law, and display an unmistakable family resemblance. The sweeping statutes of Elizabeth, enacted in 1597[7] and 1601,[8] contained most of the fundamental features of welfare law and administration, on the poor side of the curtain, which have persisted into our own time. Basic to them was a characterological theory of poverty, which defined the poor as "the victims of their own vices." Thus the

---

[7] 39 Eliz. 1, c. 3.
[8] 43 Eliz. 1, c. 2.

American sociologist and Social Darwinist of the Gilded Age, William
Graham Sumner, asserted that:

> There is no possible definition of a poor man. A pauper is a person
> who cannot earn his living; whose producing powers have fallen
> positively below his necessary consumption; who cannot, therefore,
> pay his way.

For the most part, Sumner went on to emphasize, the pauper was something less and worse than that:

> Under the names of the poor and the weak, the negligent, shiftless,
> inefficient, silly, and imprudent are fastened upon the industrious
> and prudent as a responsibility and a duty.[9]

Sumner's British counterpart, Herbert Spencer, also warned against mis-
placed sympathy on the part of society for those whose sufferings were the
price of its progress and the agency of its purification:

> The poverty of the incapable, the distresses that come upon the im-
> prudent, the starvation of the idle, and those shoulderings aside of
> the weak by the strong, which leave so many in shallows and in
> miseries, are the decrees of a large, far-seeing benevolence . . . the
> same beneficence which brings to early graves the children of dis-
> eased parents, and singles out the low-spirited, the intemperate, and
> the debilitated as the victims of an epidemic.[10]

These lofty sentiments had long since found their institutional expression
in the provisions of the poor law, whose underlying philosophy has been
graphically summarized by Tawney:

> That the greatest of evils is idleness, that the poor are the victims,
> not of circumstances, but of their own idle, irregular and wicked
> courses, that the truest charity is not to enervate them by relief, but
> so to reform their characters that relief may be unnecessary — such
> doctrines turned severity from a sin into a duty, and froze the im-
> pulse of natural pity with the assurance that, if indulged, it would
> perpetuate the suffering which it sought to allay.[11]

It followed that if poverty was the product of wickedness and sin, the
chief obligation of the overseer was to coerce the sinner into changing
his ways. To be sure, there were gross differences among the poor, and

[9] William Graham Sumner, *What Social Classes Owe to Each Other* (New York,
1900), quoted in Hanna H. Meissner (ed.), *Poverty in the Affluent Society* (New
York, 1966), pp. 11–12.
[10] Herbert Spencer, *Social Statics* (1850), quoted in Robert E. Will and Harold
G. Vatter (eds.), *Poverty in Affluence* (New York, 1965), p. 58.
[11] R. H. Tawney, *Religion and the Rise of Capitalism* (New York, 1957), p. 221.

accordingly they came to be divided into the categories of "deserving" and "undeserving." By far the greater number were undeserving — knaves and rascals whose need was not so much for charity as for correction. Until well into our century the principal clearinghouse in welfare was the National Conference of Charities and Corrections. The prime agency of correction was the workhouse, the pauper's hell whose salient characteristics have been preserved in the bleak vignettes of Dickens. Listen to one of his characters — old Betty Higden of *Our Mutual Friend*, who has always earned her way — as she speaks of the poorhouse of Victorian England:

> Kill me sooner than take me. Throw this pretty child under cart-horses' feet and a loaded wagon, sooner than take him there. Come to us and find us all a-dying, and set a light to us where we lie, and let us all blaze away with the house into a heap of cinders, sooner than move a corpse of us there. . . .
>
> Do I never read in the newspapers — God help me and the like of me! — how the worn-out people that do come down to that, get driven from post to pillar and pillar to post, a-purpose to tire them out! Do I never read how they are put off, put off, put off — how they are grudged, grudged, grudged the shelter, or the doctor, or the drop of physic, or the bit of bread? Do I never read how they grow heart-sick of it, and give it up, after having let themselves drop so low, and how they after all die out for want of help? Then I say, I hope I can die as well as another, and I'll die without that disgrace.[12]

And so when she feels age and decrepitude coming upon her, old Betty, her burial money stitched into her dress, avoids the hospitality of the "great blank barren Union House" as if it were the county jail — from which Dickens tells us it differs "in its dietary, and in its lodgings, and in its tending of the sick" only in being "a much more penal establishment." And the author adds: "It is a remarkable Christian improvement to have made a pursuing fury of the Good Samaritan. . . ."

In the gray perspective of the poor law, during the age of Victoria as much as of Elizabeth, there were no social problems of depression and dislocation, of poverty or injustice to be weighed and dealt with; there were only individual wrongs to be righted, personal sins and corruptions to be expiated and corrected. And the proper corrective, in most cases, was some form of punishment.

If all this sounds like ancient history, let me assure you that it is not; much of it is in full force in our own free and affluent society. It flourishes today in the law and administration of public welfare, from the national to the county level.

[12] Charles Dickens, *Our Mutual Friend.*

We see it again, or still, in our dual system of family law — one system for the poor and another for the rest of the community. The two systems differ in origin, content, purpose, legislation, administration, and enforcement. One is legislative in origin and is the product of the poor law. The other is judicial in origin and is the product of conceptions about the family in the civil law. In the family law of the poor, by contrast with the civil family law, divorce is often replaced by simple desertion, made necessary by poverty; marriage, by simply assuming the role of spouse, often made necessary by undissolved formal marital obligations and fostered by family habits and cultural mores of ethnic minorities. Since actual support and the right to custody of minor children is separated and in different hands in the family law of the poor, the whole structure of parental rights and duties otherwise integrated in custody is weakened. Parental right is not necessarily paramount, parental fitness is examined rather than presumed, and the management, morality, and other conditions of the home are subject to the active interest of public officials. In the family law of the poor, the parents' liability for support of minor children is stated in terms of: conditions of eligibility of the children for AFDC; rules about the utilization of family resources, whether income or property, to meet current and some future needs; and the duty assigned the workers to investigate and determine parental ability to pay. The norms of the civil law concerning the relative wealth and situations of parents and children and their standards of living do not apply. In the family law of the poor, liability for child support has been extended to include stepfathers and unrelated adult males living in the relation of spouse, whatever their relations to the children.

We see it all again, or still, in the continued use of the means test to determine eligibility and the amount of the grant — the means test with its accompanying inquisition into the private lives of applicants and recipients, its destruction of incentive, its violation of dignity and personality, its vesting excessive discretion in welfare administrators and case workers always liable to abuse in the control and custodialization of the recipients.[13]

We see it all again, or still, in conditions of probation imposed by the judges that forbid mothers to secure public aid for their children, whatever their need or eligibility; that command them, regardless of ability, to support their children on threat of imprisonment, whatever the need of the children for their care at home, whatever the unavailability of jobs for the unskilled and the socially and economically marginal. We see it in provisions that would make these people moral by the injunction to be "good" — whatever their cultural family patterns and group mores, whatever their individual retardations and instabilities.

[13] Jacobus tenBroek and Floyd Matson. *Hope Deferred: Public Welfare and the Blind* (Berkeley, 1959), ch. 8.

We see it all again, or still, in the denial, by such actions, of the constitutional guarantees of the equal protection of the laws, of due process of the law, of the right of the people to be secure in their persons, papers, houses, and effects, of the right to privacy and the right to counsel.

We see it all again, or still, in night raids[14] and in unwarrantable searches and seizures.[15] We see it in compulsory authorizations by applicants to provide information about the contents of their "trunks, bags and boxes" containing the intimate mementos and remembrances carried into old age and destitution. We see it all again in county resort ordinances conceived in discrimination, adopted in discrimination, applied in discrimination against aid to needy children's families.

Let me give a somewhat more detailed example. Effective March 10, 1960, there appeared this language in the ordinance book of one of our California counties:

> The Board of Supervisors do ordain as follows: Section I. No person shall resort to any office building, or to any room used or occupied in connection with or under the same management as any cafe, restaurant, soft drink parlor, liquor establishment, or similar business, or to any public park, or to any of the buildings therein, or to any vacant lot, or to any room, rooming house, lodging house, residence, apartment house, hotel, house trailer, street or sidewalk for the purpose of having sexual intercourse with a person to whom he or she is not married.[16]

The attached sanctions were a $500 fine, and/or six months in jail.

The coverage of this ordinance is comprehensive. All conceivable places in town, city, and park are on the list of possible locations. Only the fields and irrigation ditches of the surrounding countryside are forgotten; and the moving cars on the open highway. Equally engulfing are the elements of the crime. The city fathers were not content with prohibiting the commission of the act itself. Resorting to the specified places for the purpose of committing the act was made the crime. Nor need the purpose be shared by both parties. An intent in the mind of either one of them is sufficient. In this county, it almost seems a gleam in the eye of youth, summer or winter, or the lightly turning fancy in the spring, is no mere topic of song, jest or poem. It is a heading on the arrest blotter of the district attorney's office.

Almost needless to say, the application of the ordinance was not so sweeping as its geography and psychology. Quite the contrary, its application was selective and discriminatory. Only mothers on Aid to Needy Children and those found with them knew its penal sanctions. The

---

[14] Parish v. Alameda County Civil Service Commission, 242 ACA 665 (1966).

[15] County of Contra Costa v. SSWB, 40 California Reports, 605, 1st dist. (1964).

[16] Tulare County, California Ordinance 719, March 10, 1960.

methods of enforcement were those associated with the law of crimes. Investigation on nothing more than suspicion or gossip, detectives operating in teams, night raids, simultaneous approaches to the back and front of the house, guns conspicuously displayed on hips, securing entry, inmates interrogated at length and notes taken, the entire house searched without any particular care to secure permission, men and sometimes ANC mothers arrested and hauled off to jail — all of this in the presence of the children to many of whom the episode must have come as a frightening and even traumatic experience — all of this, too, in the presence of the constitutions of State and Nation providing for the rights of individuals, the privacy and security of residents in their persons, houses, papers, and effects. All of this in the presence of the Fourteenth Amendment declaring that "no state shall deny to any person within its jurisdiction the equal protection of the laws."[17]

Let me elaborate on the distinction between the two kinds of law. The law and philosophy of welfare holds that problems of poverty and deprivation are predominantly social, rather than personal, in their etiology; that they cannot be solved by criminal sanctions and the threat of punishment but by measures addressed to their conditions and consequences. The law of welfare is not repressive but rehabilitative. The assumptions and objectives of the law of crimes are, however, diametrically opposed. Its preliminary assumption is that persons in deprived circumstances are there either through willful choice or incorrigible deficiency of character. Its ultimate objective is to eliminate the problem by suppression and punishment. Problems of poverty and immorality, of social change and economic depression are perceived by the law of crimes in the same narrow focus of personal responsibility, to be solved by arrest and investigation, by penal sanctions and retributions.

The incompatibility of the law of crimes with the purposes of social welfare is significant in a further dimension. To call the police is to invoke the police powers of the Constitution, rather than its general welfare powers. The police powers are those that deal with maintaining order, preventing vice and crime, securing safety, and protecting health and morals. When problems of poverty are handled under the police powers of the Constitution, poverty comes to be equated with disease, immorality, and disorder. Indeed, historically these have proved to be inseparable conditions. The constitutional powers of police have generally been called upon to protect one part of the community against another — the comfortable against the needy.

A classic illustration is to be found in the case of *New York v. Miln,* decided by the United States Supreme Court in 1837. "It is as competent

17 California Department of Social Welfare, *Report on Tulare County* (September 16, 1960).

and necessary for a state," wrote the Justices in that case, "to provide precautionary measures against the moral pestilence of paupers, vagabonds and possibly convicts as it is to guard against the physical pestilence which may arise from unsound and infectious articles imported, or from a ship, the crew of which may be laboring under an infectious disease." Accordingly, the Court held valid a New York statute designed to exclude the poor and unwanted brought to New York from other states or from foreign countries. The statute was found to be a regulation of police, not for commerce, and therefore within the power of the state.[18]

So, by this doctrine, the constitutional power of the states to deal with the poor is the police power to preserve public order, to quarantine contagion, to protect morals, and to maintain safety; and poverty entails constitutional as well as social degradation. Welfare programs grounded in these conceptions focus on problems of behavior, rely on methods of coercion and emphasize keeping the peace and maintaining public order. They are designed to safeguard the health and morals of the fortunate in the community rather than directly to improve the lot of the unfortunate.

Let me say what public welfare all too often is and should not be; and let me identify some of the consequences.

Public welfare should not be a program designed to solve the social problems of divorce and marital separation, either voluntary or because of imprisonment or deportation — problems which are of course not confined to recipients of welfare aid but pervade the fabric of contemporary society through all groups and regions.

It should not be a program designed to readjust and bring into social conformity all the diverse mores and customs of our various ethnic and cultural groups.

It should not be a program designed to resolve and reform the vexing problems of morality or immorality. These problems exist in the AFDC caseload. They also exist throughout society.

It should not be a police program. It does not appear as an added chapter to the Penal Code. It should not be treated as an adjunct to the police and criminal law enforcement agencies, subject to their purposes and philosophy. The law of welfare is not the law of crimes.

It should not be a program designed to maintain a static pool of labor at the level of subsistence so as to be available to employers on submarginal terms and as needed seasonally. AFDC is not the modern counterpart of the Statute of Labourers of 1348.

It should not be a program designed to classify, symbolize, or stigmatize the underprivileged recipients as a subordinate or extra-constitutional

[18] 36 US (11 Pet.) 357, 369, 1837.

group. The recipients are not second-class citizens entitled only to second-class justice.

If it is not a program to reconstruct and homogenize all the moral and behavioral patterns of minority groups; if it is not a program of sumptuary legislation discriminatorily applied to AFDC families but aimed at the overall problem of raising moral standards, then problems of promiscuity, common-law relationships, and illegitimacy are beyond its scope; and in any event, are irrelevant and improper conditions of eligibility of the children for aid.

If AFDC is not a program by which the public maintains a cheap labor supply for the employers in the community, seeking to escape responsibility for workers in the off-season but to have them certainly available at low wages when the crops are ready to be handled, then administration should not be geared to this purpose.

If it is not a program creating an auxiliary arm of the criminal law, then we should discourage the intervention of district attorneys, police methods, and penal sanctions.

If it is not a program designed to treat recipients as lesser breeds without the constitutional law, then they are entitled to all of the protections of the Constitution: to the equal protection of the laws; to due process of law; to immunity from unreasonable searches and seizures; to rights of privacy; in short, to all the safeguards of minorities and individuals built up through the centuries of Anglo-American legal history.

It will be no swift or simple matter to move from the separate and unequal law of the poor to a system of equal justice and constitutional protection for those who are in need — from the two nations to a single legal commonwealth. For if there is obvious economic interest behind the dual system of law — one for the underdog and the other for the overlord — there is also apparently a deep psychological stake in its perpetuation. Professor Bernard L. Diamond, in a brilliant speculative paper prepared for a recent conference on the law of the poor, maintains that the emotions of love and hate, particularly that of hate, govern the attitudes from which our social institutions of welfare derive.[19] On the one hand society regards its poor, its dependent, and its disabled as helpless children to be nurtured and cared for; on the other hand there is the "fear — deep, primitive, unconscious fear — that the very existence of the poor and weak in society threatens the existence of that society. Punitive sanctions must then be applied to control those whom one fears. . . ."[20] And so, in Dr. Diamond's view, society vacillates in a "typically neurotic" way be-

[19] Bernard L. Diamond, "The Children of Leviathan: Psychoanalytic Speculations Concerning Welfare Law and Punitive Sanctions," *California Law Review,* 54 (1966): 357.

[20] Ibid., p. 362.

tween polar attitudes of accepting concern and hostile rejection toward its marginal groups — its "non-persons." The two sets of psychological attitudes, one based on love and the other on hate and fear, endure in precarious balance with the result that the two nations remain divided, and the dual system of welfare continues in effect. Here, it would seem, is the actual meaning — the psychological truth — of the biblical prophesy: "The poor always ye have with you."[21]

Although it be the Word, it need not be the last word. I suspect that few psychoanalysts or orthopsychiatrists would consider such a "neurotic" state of affairs to be beyond cure. What is needed, at one level of treatment, is the replacement of the old punitive ethic of the poor law with what Erich Fromm has called a "humanist ethic," and what the late Karen Horney described as a "morality of evolution."[22] If such a constructive moral standard in public welfare policy is to prevail over the competing ethic of crime and punishment — symptomatic of an authoritarian moral code and an "authoritarian personality" — it will need the support of many more psychiatrists, many more welfare administrators and case workers, and a great many more Americans. When that support is forthcoming, the democratic dialogue may commence between the two nations, and the path to reunion will be open.

RICHARD M. ELMAN   *Brownleaf's Story*

Brownleaf is a tall thin Negro in his early forties. If you ask him his name, he will tell you it is Brownie, or Brownleaf, but he will never mention his first name. Although Brownleaf lacks one finger on his left hand and has a cloudy yellowish cast in his right eye, he appears to be otherwise physically fit. One day, in a bar near 5th Street, Brownleaf told the following story.

[21] *John* 12:8.
[22] Erich Fromm, *Man for Himself: An Inquiry into the Psychology of Ethics* (New York, 1947), pp. 8–30; Karen Horney, *Neurosis and Human Growth* (New York, 1950), p. 378.

"About six month ago I come back north from my mother's funeral and started living with my family near Chinatown. My mother had ulcers. I worried I might have them too. One day the man comes to see us.

" 'Brownleaf,' he asks, 'how long your family been on ADC?'

"Well, I started telling him how I had been going out pretty near every day to look for employment when I didn't have to go to the clinic, but he says, 'You don't have to put me on, Brownleaf. I ain't going to do anything to you. Just tell me if you ever had a real job.'

" 'It's been a while,' I say, 'even before the last baby and she is now two.'

" 'Well,' he says, 'I guess I knew that. You can consider yourself lucky. You're going to be retrained.'

" 'I never been trained,' I say, 'so how am I going to be retrained?'

" 'It's just a word,' he says.

"I ask him then if I have to go to any school. 'Don't you worry. It'll be easy,' he says, 'you'll get $17.00 a week and your family can still collect the Welfare.'

" 'Just what I got to do?'

" 'Oh,' he says, "it isn't anything you got to worry about. All you got to do is make sure you show me attendance slips. It isn't bad, you know. $17.00 a week, and you will be retrained.'

" 'And I don't do nothing?'

" 'You just do as you are told,' he says, 'and I'll play ball with you. You might even learn something.'

"Well, I don't like the way he puts it, so I ask, 'Suppose I don't want to.'

" 'Don't be foolish, Brownleaf,' he says, 'you have to start learning how to take care of your family.'

"So this man — his name is Santos and he has a twitch in his face — tells me he has made an appointment with me the very next day at three o'clock over at that big building over on 9th Street. He tells me you go see Miss D'Angelo, and then he reminds me about the attendance slips and he becomes real twitchy because he says, 'Goodbye and good luck. If you hold up your end we'll hold up ours.'

"Well, since there wasn't any way I could argue with a white man like that, the next afternoon at three o'clock I drag it over to see this Miss D'Angelo. Now, she was just like him. Big smile. You know. Couldn't be nicer. And she told me first thing how I was going to get $17.00 a week and all I had to do was make sure about the attendance slips.

" 'What you going to train me to be?' I asked her, and she smiles and asks what did I ever do.

"Well, I've been a laborer and a farmer. I also worked in a factory years ago when I lost this finger, and I've been in jail a few times. Nothing much, but I don't lie to her. I told all of these things, and she said then maybe I ought just to take it easy and get a little orientation first. Then she asked me could I read and write, and when I said yes, she said that was good because all I would need now was a new attitude, a little orientation. She was sending me to that big building over on Church Street.

" 'Don't you forget about those attendance slips,' she says to me, and we shake hands with her telling me to report Monday morning at nine o'clock.

"Well, when I go home and tell my friends what they going to do to me, they say you're crazy Brownie. Use your wit because they can't make you do that if you missing a finger, but I say you got to trust people or they won't trust you. So Monday morning I go down to this place to see this man and he reads my little note and then takes me into this room where there are a lot of other spades just like me. And he tells us to write our names on this piece of paper, which he takes away from us. Then he tells us how the government realizes you just can't give men like us money because you also got to give us opportunities. Then he tells us how lucky we are to be taking this retraining because it will mean so long as we remember our attendance slips we'll get $17.00 a week and our families will still collect the Welfare. Then he asks if there are any questions, but nobody raises their hands.

" 'Come on,' he says, 'let's hear them if you have them.'

"So I raised my hand just like in school. 'What we going to do?'

" 'You see this fellow here. He seems very anxious, don't he?' and he looks and finds my name on that slip of paper and he says, 'It's Mr. Brownleaf, isn't it? Well,' he says to me, 'if you're so anxious to begin, Mr. Brownleaf, you go down to that cellar and ask for Mr. Romeo.' Everybody is laughing. Then he says, 'Go on, now. You go on down there quick and don't disrupt this class anymore.'

"So I took my coat and things and go down in the elevator to the cellar, and it's easy enough to find Mr. Romeo because he is in charge of the trash. A little spic with frizzy hair, speaks with an accent. You know. So when I tell him how I got here, he says, 'You're one of the boys from the Welfare, aren't you?'

" 'That's right,' I said.

" 'Well,' he says then, 'you come here to work for the City, you get busy because this is the taxpayers' money. You see that big barrel full of garbage? You carry it over to the incinerator.'

"I look at this barrel and it is one of those great big cardboard things just full up to the brim with nasty things. So I say, 'You going to help me?'

" 'I work here,' he says. 'You here to learn. You do it. Get busy.' And he leans back against the wall and lights himself a Tiparillo.

"Now maybe I'm just stupid old Brownie, but nobody is that stupid, so I say, 'I ain't here to do your work. I'm here to be retrained.'

" 'First you got to learn things,' he says.

" 'What things?'

" 'You got to learn things,' he says. 'You got to learn the value of a job. You got to learn work habits.'

"I say, 'Who you to teach me these things?' But it's awful hot down there in that cellar, so there ain't no use getting worked up.

"I say, 'You just never mind what you think. You and me ain't got no business being like this. You got something for me to do it's one thing, but I ain't here to do your work, you understand?'"

"Seems being nice just didn't help. That Romeo says, 'You get busy or I call the supervisor.'

"Well, I didn't wanut to cause trouble on my first day, but I didn't see why this spic should be bossing me around. So I say, 'If it's that way I'll help you but you got to understand. I ain't going to do it all alone . . .'

" 'Son of a bitch,' he screams at me, 'You pick up that barrel.'

"So I remembered some stuff from when I lived over near the Broadway Casino, and I say, '*Haga la ponienta chica!*'[1]

"Then this guy who was half nigger himself was fit to be tied, and he tells me to get the hell out of there and see Mr. Auerbach on the fourth floor or there will be trouble. I say, 'I don't want no trouble. Who's going to cause trouble?'

" 'Man,' he says to me, 'you don't know what you are doing. You want to be thrown off the Welfare?'

"Now how the hell should I know they would stoop to that? I say, 'Look here, I got a wife and kids.'

" 'We all got,' he says. 'Don't you think I got? You should have thought of them before this . . .'

" 'Give me another chance,' I say, but this guy Romeo won't even let me come near his barrel. He says, 'You go see Auerbach. I don't want you here, you troublemaker . . .'

"So I go upstairs and wait for maybe half an hour outside this office, and then they bring me in to see this little Jewish man and he seems to know all about me, how many kids I got, where I live, what happened downstairs with Romeo, just about everything except my ulcer; and he says he is very angry and disappointed with me.

"He says, 'You think you can walk right in here and be the boss. First you got to learn something. Then maybe we can make you a clerk or something.'

" 'What they put me down there with the garbage for?'

---

[1] Literally, "abuse yourself."

" 'Well,' he smiled, 'you know you got to start somewhere.'

"Then he tells me to go home and cool off and think it over. He says I don't have to retrain if I don't want to, just like I don't also have to collect the Welfare.

" 'What about my family?'

" 'You go on home,' the man says. 'You think it over real good. We'll come to that bridge when we cross it.'

"Well, I went home and talked to my wife and these friends, and we did some figuring together and hell, that $17.00 was just a few cents more than I could get from the Welfare.

"My wife says, 'If you going to work, why don't they pay you a real salary?'

"And my friends all say, 'Use your wits, son. You're a fool if you work for that. They can't make you.' So the next day I don't show up at that place, and along about four in the afternoon I'm having a beer with a friend when Mr. Santos drops by to see me.

" 'Brownleaf,' he says, 'what the hell you trying to do to me?'

" 'You didn't say I was going to be a garbage man. You said I was going to get retraining.'

" 'You know what I got to do here now,' he says, 'I come here. I see you drinking beer when you supposed to be in your class. I got to throw you off the Welfare.'

" 'You can't do that. I know my rights. I don't have to go to work in the cellar for some spic at $17.00 a week.'

" 'Brownleaf, you're too choosy when you got nothing to be choosy about,' the man says. 'So I'm going to teach you a little responsibility.'

"He goes away, and about a week later I get a letter from the Welfare that my case is being closed. That motherfucker really meant what he said. So I'm fit to be tied, and I borrow a dollar from my wife and call Santos down at the Welfare Center and I say, 'You son of a bitch. You doing this to me or the whole family?'

" 'If I had my way,' he says, 'your wife would leave you because you aren't doing her and the kids any good . . .'

" 'How do you know that? You ain't been around all the time. You're only here when you want to see something.'

"Santos is very angry at me now, but he says if I'm still willing to be retrained, he'll give me another chance. He'll get me put back on the Welfare, only I'll have to wait for the next cycle to begin. In other words, for the next two weeks I don't get no Welfare."

Brownleaf lifted his lean body off the bar stool. "Time I got going home," he said. "Kids ought to be back from school in a little while. The wife is out doing work." He winked at me.

"Suppose the Welfare finds out?" I asked.

Brownleaf dropped thirty cents on the bar. "You know what I think?" he said. "I don't believe this shit about cycles. I just think old twitchy is trying to get me. Whichever way you look at it, he's got me. You know," he said, "over there on 4th Street they're training all the young kids. Teaching them how to be carpenters. Teaching them spelling and reading. They don't got that kind of training for people like me. You know, I went down there one time because I got a nephew down there being trained, and I said, "What can you do for me?"

" 'Well,' this nice man say, 'I think you a little too senior for our programs . . .'

"Well," Brownleaf said, looking at me steadily through that cloudy yellow eye, "if I'm too old what they playing around with me at the Welfare? You know why they play around with me like that?"

"No," I shrugged. "You tell me."

Brownleaf laughed. "They think we niggers going to riot. They think we going to kill Whitey. Let me tell you something," he said. "When you get to be my age, that's the farthest thing from your mind. You're toothless and old, and all you want is that sugar tit. Violence . . . that may be all right for the young kids because they don't know any better, but I know better. Who I going to kill? That bunch down there? Don't you kid yourself," Brownleaf said, "You got this sugar tit, you don't want to kill nobody. You just want that sugar tit. Don't seem much of a chance of that so you get angry, but even then you don't want to kill. You just want more of that sugar tit . . ."

"What does your wife say about all this?" I asked.

"She knows what's good for her."

"And your kids?"

"They got nothing against the kids," Brownleaf said. "It's just the fathers."

RICHARD A. CLOWARD
RICHARD M. ELMAN

Poverty, Injustice,
and the Welfare State

PART 1: AN OMBUDSMAN FOR THE POOR?

Americans think of justice primarily in connection with agencies of law enforcement, for such agencies have drastic powers, even over life itself. But at a time when the United States Supreme Court is upholding the right to counsel in criminal proceedings of all kinds and otherwise curbing infringements of individual liberties by law-enforcement agencies, it needs to be said that many other government agencies have only slightly less drastic powers, especially over low-income people. It is no small matter that a person may be arbitrarily defined as ineligible for public relief, no small matter that he may be arbitrarily evicted from a public-housing project. There are few institutionalized safeguards against the potentially unjust exercise of power by governmental "poor agencies," and virtually no place where low-income people can turn for assistance in availing themselves of the channels of redress that do exist.

In America, we continue to define poverty as resulting from all manner of personal devils which must be exorcised with commensurate autos-da-fé. England, by contrast, has moved far beyond the Elizabethan "poor-law" concepts which still dominate much of America's orientation toward the impoverished. Our welfare state is accordingly characterized by a lawlessness, a discrimination by class and race, a disregard for human rights and dignity, and a niggardliness that are recurrent, often routine, if not institutionalized. And if our social-welfare system is regularly unjust, it is because American public opinion about the poor makes it so.

There is a plethora of evidence to support this view. For one thing, America spends as small a proportion of its tax dollar on social-welfare programs as any other major social-welfare nation in the West; further-more, if the changing value of the dollar is taken into account, we spend little more now than two decades ago. For another, the notion that our welfare programs are chiefly for the poor is a persisting fiction. In fact, most of the economic innovations of the last few decades have not sub-stantially aided those for whom poverty is a desperate and constant condition. Social security payments, for example, mostly benefit working-class persons, and not all of them at that.

From *The Nation*, February 28 and March 7, 1966. Reprinted by permission.

The regularly unemployed poor have not, to cite another example, gotten unemployment compensation, for one must have been employed to become eligible. Although this measure may protect a good many working-class people from the worst consequence of unemployment (at least temporarily), it is no great boon to the unemployable or the chronically unemployed. In retrospect, it seems fair to say that the chief function of this benefit is to enable the temporarily unemployed person to avoid the "means" or "poverty" test required of the chronically poor, who struggle daily to establish and maintain eligibility for the dole. Unlike the applicant for public assistance, who is obliged to divest himself of many assets while on relief, the working class person can obtain economic benefits without having his insurance, savings and automobile attached. Working-class groups have not only increased their share in the fruits of the institution of private property through union organization; they have also understood the necessity of finding ways to secure themselves against such tides of economic misfortune as might thrust them back. The programs of the welfare state are one among many mechanisms by which these groups insure the continuity of their status.

Legislation for the poor, by contrast, makes benefits available to as few as possible, and then only under the most trying and degrading conditions. The New Deal established a huge public-welfare program under federal-state-local auspices, but great numbers of our poorest citizens are even now systematically excluded. Every state in the Union has passed laws withholding public-welfare benefits from persons not residents in the state for some specified period of time. In Michigan, for example, some public benefits are available only to people who have lived in the state for five of the nine years preceding application. For decades, residency provisions have penalized the poorest elements in the society, especially rural migrants within our borders and those crossing from Puerto Rico. Efforts to repeal these laws have been stubbornly resisted. New York — perhaps the most liberal state and certainly one of the wealthiest — has barely resisted the temptation to promulgate a more stringent residence law: such legislation has actually reached the governor during the past decade but was vetoed.

Residence laws probably violate the constitutional right to cross state boundaries without penalty. They are not the only examples of legislation governing "poor agencies" which are of questionable constitutionality. Issues of "equal protection" are constantly posed in the welfare structure. One is the requirement that self-supporting relatives (who already pay income taxes to support social-welfare programs) be taxed again to support their indigent kin. "Relative-responsibility" laws have been successfully reversed in some state courts, under the "equal-protection" clause of the constitution, but no cases have yet reached the federal courts where more binding precedents could be established.

Efforts to secure liberalizing legislation founder much of the time, for powerful groups across the country are working to make the social-welfare apparatus even worse. At various times, it has been proposed that desertion be declared a federal offense if a family is receiving public assistance, that sterilization of welfare recipients who continue to bear illegitimate children be made mandatory, and that conviction for a felony be made grounds to deny any form of assistance. Even at a time when many wonder whether automation will not throw huge numbers into enforced idleness, programs of work relief which verge on peonage are continually being put forth. Although many of these proposals never pass into law, a good many do. A number of states, for example, have ceilings on public-welfare grants to penalize large families, ostensibly to depress the birth rate among the poor. In two states, Nebraska and Iowa, courts have declared these laws to be violations of "equal protection" on the ground that the child in a large family needs to eat as much as the child in a small family.

That the legislative framework of our social-welfare system is becoming more humane is, therefore, open to debate. Gains can be pointed to, but there are setbacks; and it must be recognized that some of the most regressive legislation has been passed in recent years. In the late fifties and early sixties, for example, a number of states passed "suitable-home laws" in response to public outrage over disclosures of high rates of illegitimacy on public-welfare case loads. Louisiana passed a law that any woman who had had illegitimate children while on welfare could be denied further aid, and more than 20,000 mothers and children were immediately struck from the rolls. Other legislatures, as in Florida, gave mothers a choice: surrender your illegitimate children for placement (i.e., institutionalization) or be dropped from the rolls. Thousands of mothers elected to give up assistance rather than their children, and the Florida Department of Welfare, calculating to the second decimal place the millions saved, put itself before the public in subsequent annual reports as a model of administrative efficiency and moral virtue. But in Michigan, where a similar law was passed, mothers who chose to leave the rolls found that the state was determined to get their children anyway: after living for a few months in absolute poverty, they were brought into court on charges of physical neglect, and the children were forcibly removed from their homes.

A characteristic of our welfare state is that administrative practice is almost always worse than statute. Broad grants of discretion in doling out benefits are given to administrators because there is no consensus at the legislative level concerning concepts of social welfare. Some measure of discretion is inevitable, for no set of statutes can provide firm guidelines for all the varied circumstances that will be presented for decision. Legislators assume that those who carry out the laws will be reasonable and prudent men, possessed of common sense if not of the uncommon sense to divine the intent of vague and ambiguous statutes. But in areas as controversial as social welfare, the language of statutes may be purposely vague, since greater specificity would reveal more sharply the differences among contending political groups and would thereby foreclose the possibility of any legislation at all. The task of explicating the statutes then falls upon the welfare bureaucracies, so that the political struggle shifts from the legislature to the arenas of administration.

The struggle to control the discretion of the administrator is, for the low-income person, an unequal one. Those he confronts are organized and powerful, whether taxpayers' associations, newspapers, civic groups, professional societies or political actors. They have the resources to maintain constant watch over agency practices, the knowledge to frame issues and put forward policies, and the power to influence and activate sectors of the populace in behalf of these policies. Lacking comparable weapons, the low-income person is merely a refugee from a battle that alternately rages and dies down, shifting from one area of his existence to another. Whether the field of battle is his morals (if in public housing), or his willingness to work (if on public welfare), he is its victim.

Housing for the poor is an instructive case in the operation of administrative discretion. Faced with far more applicants than can be accommodated, housing officials have had to make choices. In the process they have come to be only incidentally concerned about the need of applicants. They have established elaborate screening techniques to rebuff the unworthy, whatever their need, thereby erecting defenses against the continual charge that public moneys are being used to subsidize immorality. Applicants can thus be rejected (and quite regularly are) if they have illegitimate or retarded children, have been separated from a spouse two or more times, are alcoholic, or display what is defined as obnoxious behavior at the application interview. Families on welfare with illegitimate children are shunned — a curious policy by which eligibility for one meager public benefit disqualifies a family for another. And so it is that agencies established to dispense money and other material benefits become guardians of public morality.

But the chief characteristic of public agencies serving the poor is not the punitive use of lawful discretion: it is the exercise of unlawful discretion — the promulgation of administrative rules and procedures which undoubtedly violate either constitutional provisions or the immediate statutes governing departments. No more vivid evidence can be cited of the enormous impact of political pressures upon these agencies. The most flagrant example in a history of flagrant abuses is the "after-midnight raid" on ADC mothers — an unannounced visit, without benefit of warrant, in which a home is searched for male attire that might be taken as evidence that a man (whether husband or not) is available and presumably capable of providing support, or for some suggestion of immoral' activities or child neglect, any of which might justify terminating benefits. (During the past summer, candidates for office in Nassau County — both the Democrat and the Republican-Liberal — asserted the right of the district attorney's office to make such raids; the Conservative candidate denounced the practice.) These actions surely violate constitutional prohibitions against illegal search and seizure. They are, nevertheless, conducted by virtually every welfare department in the country. When an Oakland, Calif., welfare worker refused to take part in a raid in January, 1962, he was dismissed for insubordination, and is now suing for reinstatement through the appeals courts of that state. At one stage of the proceedings, the state argued that people taking public assistance waive certain rights, not the least being the right to privacy.

Another instance of lawless discretion is revealed in the way relative-responsibility statutes are applied (assuming for the moment that they are constitutional). Laws in each state designate the categories of relatives who are to be considered responsible, but administrators expand on legislative intent by instructing staff to seek out additional categories of relatives (and even friends) as potential "financial resources." When such sources of support are located, the applicant may be denied assistance, or his grant may be arbitrarily reduced by an amount presumed to be available elsewhere.

Or consider the administration of New York's "welfare-abuses law," passage of which followed hard on the Newburgh controversy. This statute, a residency law, provides that a person may be denied benefits *only* if it can be shown that he came into the state for the express purpose of securing them. It stipulates that the burden of proof is on the local welfare department, and that emergency relief must be granted pending a factual determination on the issue of motive. As a practical matter, however, the mere fact that an applicant is from out of state is often taken as prima facie evidence of intent to collect welfare. Many thousands of families have been illegally disqualified since passage of the law in 1962.

But administrative lawlessness is not limited to matters of initial eligibility for benefits. Once on the welfare rolls, recipients in need of special grants of many kinds — for winter clothing, furniture, apartment security, for example — frequently fail to secure them. There are at least three reasons. The law states that requests for all grants must be investigated, frequently by a home visit, and overburdened departments cannot always spare the manpower. In addition, under pressure to conserve funds, departments often ignore requests for special grants. Finally, because of high turnover, public-welfare employees frequently do not themselves know what benefits the applicants are entitled to and how these can be obtained for them. For instance, welfare recipients in New York who live in rat-infested buildings can receive a so-called "rat allowance" to cover the cost of keeping their lights burning all night long; few welfare workers seem to know about special grants of this kind and few clients are told of them. By such practices, welfare clients are routinely deprived of substantial cash entitlements.

The American poor may not be able to protect themselves from injustice, but affluent groups can. As governmental powers proliferate, middle-class people are also becoming objects of abuses. Accustomed to having their rights respected, they are calling for restraints against government.

Traditionally, representative democracies have relied upon the legislator to mediate between the citizen and the public agency. With the growth of government, however, this arrangement — never very effective — has become mired down in complaints. To cope with the situation, a European legislative innovation, called the Ombudsman, has been proposed for America. Developed in Sweden more than 150 years ago, this innovation has evolved and spread to all other Scandinavian countries and to a number of nations in the British Commonwealth. Last October, the cause of the Ombudsman got a special boost when the British Labour government decided to establish such an office, even preserving the Scandinavian title.[1] On January 1 of this year a somewhat modified version of the Ombudsman was established in Laval, Canada (a suburb of Quebec City); it is the first in North America.

The Ombudsman is a "justice officer" or "citizen's defender." He is usually a highly respected senior member of the judiciary or a renowned professor in law, and is assisted by a small staff of lawyers. Appointed by and responsible to a legislative body — in most countries where the Ombudsman exists, to a parliament — he is charged to investigate all complaints from citizens. In Denmark, for example, the Ombudsman is obliged by statute "to keep himself informed as to whether any person under his jurisdiction [i.e., any civil servant] pursues unlawful ends, makes arbitrary or unreasonable decisions, or otherwise commits mistakes or acts of negligence in the discharge of his duties." If complaints from citizens are declared valid, the offending functionary is asked to provide redress; if invalid, no reprisals can be taken against the complainant.

Typical complaints involve the right of a postman to have in writing the grounds for a disciplinary action against him (the Ombudsman agreed, saying that governmental agencies should routinely inform

[1] The British action followed the notorious Crichel Down affair, in which the Ministry of Agriculture and Fisheries tried to rid itself of a particularly irksome farmer by ordering his lands to be confiscated, an action which led to a Question before Parliament.

citizens of the reasons for official decisions); the denial of unemployment benefits to a plumber on what he alleged was inaccurate evidence (the Ombudsman agreed, castigating officialdom for not procuring complete and reliable evidence); a businessman's charge that a national bank required him to conduct all his business with them in writing because he had been abusive to bank employees (the Ombudsman referred the complaining businessman to the ordinary courts which he said had jurisdiction); a charge that the grounds for federal grants for road construction made selectively to municipalities each year, had not been explained (the Ombudsman ruled for the complaining municipality, saying that criteria of selection should be published).

Judging from a newly published volume of essays about Ombudsman ship around the world,[2] bureaucratic excesses have been effectively curbed by this legislative officer. The success of the Ombudsman is all the more remarkable because his powers are usually limited to investigation and recommendation. The Ombudsman typically publishes recommendations and can thus embarrass the bureaucracies. Representatives of the press are frequently permitted to comb through his correspondence, and his activities ordinarily make news. He is also empowered to make broad recommendations for new legislation intended to remedy sources of injustice by governmental agencies. And because of the esteem in which he is typically held, his recommendations are nearly always heeded. The Ombudsman's chief strength thus derives from intangibles, the support he cultivates in the press. He cannot, in short, move much beyond public opinion.

Within recent months, a spate of articles have appeared proposing that a parallel complaints office be developed at all levels of American government. Sweden's present Ombudsman, Alfred Bexelius, was interviewed in *The New Yorker*. An article in *Harper's* by Marion K. Sanders suggested that the creation of an Ombudsman might appease Negro demands for citizen review boards to take up complaints of police brutality. In *The New York Times Magazine*, Rep. Henry Reuss of Wisconsin explained his proposal to establish a nonpartisan "Office of Congressional Counsel." Similar bills have been proposed in state legislatures and municipal councils across the country. The general idea has been endorsed by civil liberties groups for both national and local government.

Proponents of American Ombudsmanship would endow the office with an immense purview. "If there are no avenues for correcting maladministration," Congressman Reuss has pointed out in the *Christian Century*,

---

[2] Donald C. Rowat, *The Ombudsman: Citizen's Defender* (with 29 contributors, including Ombudsmen from thirteen countries). Toronto, Canada: University of Toronto Press, 1965, 361 pp. All quotations, unless otherwise noted, are taken from this volume.

"programs for the general welfare, such as Social Security, public housing, and veterans' benefits, are full of possibilities for human injustice." Ralph Nader has listed the following abuses with which an Ombudsman proposed for Connecticut might wish to deal:

> . . . preferential treatment and influence peddling, inadequate or unpublished regulations, wrongful detention, state police over-zealousness or laxity, unjust procedures in agency hearings, arbitrary censorship or secrecy, agency reluctance or refusal to give explicit reasons for decisions, patronage excesses, inefficiencies and delays by state personnel, undesirable conditions in prisons and mental institutions, payoffs and kickbacks in state contracts, and discriminatory enforcement or flagrant non-enforcement of state laws.

Given the growing concern here about governmental abuses, it is possible that various adaptations of this mechanism will presently emerge in the United States. The likelihood that they will protect the rights of the poor therefore deserves careful scrutiny.

Debate about an American Ombudsman has thus far focused on questions of governmental organization: would an American complaints officer weaken rather than strengthen the traditional role of legislators as Ombudsmen en masse; could an institution nurtured in parliamentary systems be successfully adapted to governments marked by separation of powers; would the use of this device not give American courts further grounds for avoiding politically controversial issues in favor of narrowly technical ones? It has been assumed, and not debated, that the Ombudsman's services would be found equally effective by all American citizens. But the poor of our nation still confront special problems of injustice that have been resolved in most other welfare states, and discussions about the Ombudsman have not even approached a full appreciation of this fact.

In the United States, procedures to review the decisions of public departments have been successful when they found support in public opinion. The Loyalty Review Board, to cite one instance, compiled an extraordinary record, only one of its many recommendations having been spurned by a public department. Years after its abolition, the courts held that it had exceeded its legal authority; but its actions were hardly held to be excessive in the court of public opinion. An Ombudsman for the poor will fail for precisely the reason that the Loyalty Review Board succeeded: his recommendations would run counter to public attitudes toward the rights of the poor.

In countries where the Ombudsman has succeeded, social-welfare principles are generally accepted, even by conservatives. Compared with America, the poor in these countries have a tradition of political organization, often radical in ideology. Through political organizations — such as the British Labour Party — the poor have decisively influenced the shape of social-welfare legislation in their interests. By contrast, pressures to reform the welfare apparatus in this country have originated primarily in very limited sectors of the middle-class community, unaided by organized demands from the poor themselves. Deprived of this allied base of power, middle class reformers have had to compromise the interests of the poor. Knowing of the injustice of social-welfare practices, but fearing that disclosures of any kind might arouse a dormant and hostile public opinion, reformers have worked "behind the scenes" and have not attacked the system forthrightly and publicly. They have found it necessary, in effect, to conspire with administrators (tacitly, at least) to conceal the full facts from the public. This accounts in part for the widespread ignorance that most Americans exhibit about the welfare apparatus and its abuses.

In America, then, all faces are turned against the welfare apparatus. Everyone seeks to secure the release of the poor from what is defined as the bondage of "welfare colonialism" or from the psychological entrapment allegedly induced by prolonged dependence on the dole. Only the strategies differ: conservatives would make welfare practices more punitive than they are to deter men from dependency; liberals would lift the poor from dependency by equipping them to become economically competitive. Even the crusade against poverty is a crusade against public welfare; Mr. Shriver has repeatedly stressed that the Office of Economic Opportunity does not sanction "handouts."

Concepts of economic individualism also permeate the civil rights movement. The movement calls upon Americans to strike down historic barriers to individual achievement such that the poor may rise, one by one, into higher economic strata. The Negro is said to want to share in America's wealth on the same idealized terms and by the same idealized means as other groups. Thus consumer boycotts have been organized primarily to enlarge opportunities for the employment of individual Negroes, especially in white-collar positions. Out of deference to this ideology, "compensatory programs" in education and "quotas" in employment have not been pressed hard, for they seem antithetical to a social order based on the theory of open competition and individual merit. This same way of thinking accounts in no small part for the fervor with which so many now embrace the philosophy of the Office of Economic Opportunity — especially as it is symbolized in skills-investment programs like preschool education and youth-employment training. The great mass of poor whose daily lives are controlled by the "poor agencies" thus have neither defenders nor have they organized to defend themselves.

Given these compelling political facts, one derives no reassurance from the observation that Ombudsmen throughout the world cultivate success by carefully selecting cases "of a decidedly nonpolitical nature." Such judicious screening would, in the United States, eliminate from purview most administrative injustices perpetrated upon the poor. It is important to understand, then, that Ombudsmanship is not a substitute for basic reform, and that only reform will produce justice for the poor. The Ombudsman cannot overturn whole systems of law and administrative practice that are rooted in the culture and politics of a nation. He is not a legislature, or a chief executive, or a court of law. He merely polices functionaries in public agencies according to prevailing values: Ombudsmanship, one observer has noted, "cannot cure all administrative ills. It will work successfully only in a country, province or state that is already reasonably well administered. When an administration is riddled with political patronage or corruption . . . a reform of the whole system is required."

And, one might add, when a social-welfare system is rooted in contempt for its beneficiaries, it is also the system that must be reformed, for the injustices spawned are countless. Taking up these individual cases of injustice, there being literally hundreds of thousands to contemplate, is a task that would shortly overwhelm an American citizen-defender of any kind. It would require, if nothing else, an investigatory apparatus as large as the system being surveyed and policed.

Advocates of an American Ombudsman have not been altogether unmindful of the pressures of public opinion to which the office would be exposed, although it is not opinion about poverty that they have in mind. Rather, they point generally to our loose federalism and diversity of national opinion. The Ombudsman has grown up in countries that are relatively homogenous, especially in the factor of race. Economically and racially the United States is among the most heterogeneous countries for which the mechanism has as yet been proposed. Consequently, it has been suggested that early experiments with the office might better be undertaken locally than nationally. There, presumably, one would encounter less diverse population grouping, and the task of cultivating public opinion would be easier.

But group conflicts, along both class and racial lines, are deeper the closer one gets to the local community. In recent years, disputes about integration in education, employment and housing have evoked bitter antagonism at the local level, and local officials have been virtually immobilized because of apparently irreconcilable differences among their constituents. By and large, federal perspectives on social welfare have been more liberal; most local practices would be much more punitive were it not for pressures from federal agencies. At a time when the Congress has been passing historic civil rights legislation, state bodies have been passing residence laws and suitable-home laws, not to speak of regressive laws in other categories, which partly reflect growing racial tensions. In New York, mounting pressure for an unqualified residence law stems from the in-migration of both Negroes and Puerto Ricans, for the high proportion of these groups on welfare rolls makes them vulnerable to attack by conservative political interests. As the Negro continues to strike at the roots of historic patterns of class and racial dominance, tensions will undoubtedly mount, and further punitive social-welfare legislation and practices at the local level may result.

Countries where the Ombudsman has been effective also tend to have high standards of public service. The success of the Ombudsman partly depends upon responsible and responsive government functionaries. America's social-welfare agencies have slowly been professionalizing, and one might see in these improved standards of personnel training an omen favorable to an Ombudsman for the poor. There is reason to doubt that this is so. Professional ideology is rooted in political ideology. Reflecting the values of their culture, American professional groups have not argued for the rights of the poor or for the legitimacy of dependency. Rather they have said that introducing better-trained personnel into the welfare apparatus will eliminate moralistic punitive practices and supplant them by scientific, rehabilitative ones. But whether strategies are puritanical or professional, the poor are still to be lifted from dependency in spite of themselves. Rehabilitative services should, of course, be extended to those who can use them, but submitting to such technical services should not be made a condition for access to economic and other material benefits; and that is how professionals have always seen it. Public housing, for example, now employs many kinds of professionals. If management finds the behavior of a tenant objectionable, he may be required to accept some form of therapy upon pain of eviction. Professionals have thus become new agents in an enveloping fabric of bureaucratic control of the poor and are, if only unwittingly, part of the problem that needs correcting. When an unwed mother makes an application for public housing in New York City for herself and her children, to cite a further example, she is routinely referred to what the Housing Authority calls its "social consultation unit." There professionals employ their higher skills to make a determination of her "suitability" — not her need — for residence in a public project. Thus the rights of the poor are jeopardized as much by those who find legitimacy for their practices in the sciences as by those who find it in the scriptures.

Before an Ombudsman (or any other policing mechanism) can be of much aid to the poor, basic reforms of governmental poor agencies are required.

PART 2: HOW RIGHTS CAN BE SECURED

One form of attack upon the social-welfare apparatus should be mounted in the courts. Undue emphasis has been placed upon securing reforms through legislative action, and insufficient attention paid to legal remedies. Two types of legal action are required: one designed to achieve basic changes in the structure of social-welfare law, and the other to insure that laws are faithfully implemented at the administrative level. Much of the current discussion about extending legal services to the poor is intended to yield the latter objective. The Office of Economic Opportunity, for example, plans to finance legal resources for the poor in urban and rural slums. This program, to be discussed below, will bring lawyers into contact with the poor, where they will be quickly inundated by pressing problems demanding immediate action. Lawyers practicing under these circumstances will doubtless succeed in remedying injustices in one case after another through negotiation and administrative appeal or in the lower courts; they may even on occasion create a major legal precedent to which the welfare apparatus must accommodate. But crucial precedents are usually more efficiently pursued by organizations which do not offer mass services but specialize in finding "test" cases. Such organizations can develop specialized legal expertise in a given field, and can find the resources to pursue issues doggedly and tenaciously through the labyrinth of appeals, at the end of which a binding precedent may finally be established. We need, in short, an "association for the advancement of social-welfare rights," comparable in purpose and function to the NAACP and the ACLU in their respective fields of interest.

The issues of law that require intensive action are both substantive and procedural. As to the first, no aspect of substantive law in the field of social welfare is so murky as that pertaining to the question of whether various classes of entitlements are matters of legal right or public charity. Ambiguity especially surrounds benefits for the poor; most of the benefits directed toward the regularly employed classes having been less plagued. Here again, "social security" is a case in point. It is virtually unheard of that recipients require legal assistance in order to obtain this benefit. The clarity with which entitlements are framed and implemented thus reflects the relative political power of the groups which are their object. In the field of public housing, by contrast, ambiguity is striking. Legislation is written in such a way as to deny tenants any of the rights commonly associated with tenancy in private housing. Apartments can be inspected at will by management; leases are month to month; eviction can occur without recourse to the courts. Charles Reich, a professor in law, has suggested that social-welfare benefits constitute "new property rights" and should be vigorously pursued in the courts until they are so defined under law.

If benefits can be established as rights, to whom then do these rights pertain, and under what conditions? Here again, a variety of substantive issues are posed. Residence laws provide one notorious case in point, for, as we have noted, they appear to violate the historic right to cross state boundaries without penalty. Issues of illegal search and seizure arise from widespread investigatory practices now prescribed by existing legislation or administrative fiat — such as the "post-midnight raids" discussed earlier. It is customarily regarded as within the province of welfare departments to force unwed mothers to be examined regarding putative fathers as a condition for public assistance. Invasions of privacy are taken for granted in a system where no one has rights.

Eligibility for public-welfare benefits has sometimes been made contingent upon one's willingness to perform work for a governmental jurisdiction. One such case, involving male welfare recipients who were jailed for refusing to cut brush in hip-deep snow, was recently struck down in the lower courts as a form of peonage.

Ambiguity about "rights" versus "charity" is also reflected in the absence of adequate procedural safeguards. Under the guise of discharging an ethical responsibility to "protect the confidentiality" of information disclosed by clients, welfare departments have resisted the right of clients to be represented by counsel during interviews, investigations and many types of semi-judicial proceedings. But perhaps most striking is the fact that it is not clear, with respect to many benefits, whether an aggrieved person has the right to do anything more than complain. Appeals procedures, administrative or otherwise, are not often defined in legislation, and administrators do not usually choose to establish them. If a person has a grievance, it is often not known to whom he should turn or whether he must be heard. Until test cases resolve matters of this kind, rights cannot be effectively asserted.

The second form of attack should be a vigorous campaign of communication. Tyranny is not so likely to take root when men have access to information. The authoritarianism of social-welfare agencies is partly made possible by the pervasive ignorance they engender in their clientele. Where ignorance prevails, myths arise to explain what otherwise seems arbitrary and capricious. It is believed by some on the dole in New York City that welfare workers get $50 for each case they can close, for how else is one to understand the hundreds of instances in which recipients are discharged from the rolls for no apparent reason (e.g., "failed to comply with departmental regulations")? Myths serve to order the reality, but they also reinforce ignorance of it. And because recipients do not understand administrative decisions, officials can dismiss complaints out of hand. By converting issues of justice into instances of ignorance, attacks upon the rules are thus deflected and the system remains intact.

One can grant the low education of recipients without supposing that this goes far toward explaining their failure to grasp the workings of the apparatus upon which they depend for survival. Ignorance is a product of the system itself. Our social-welfare state is enormously complex — not because it needs to be, but because it serves our ambivalence toward the poor to make it so. Because, as we have pointed out, statutes are vague and ambiguous as to who can get benefits and strikingly clear as to who cannot, fantastic administrative energy is required to define criteria of eligibility. The resulting proliferation of regulations is incomprehensible even to those who create them. People who need a variety of services (money, housing, health care) must negotiate with an array of autonomous departments, each jealous of its prerogatives, each a complex rules system, each caught up in its own trappings of petty tyranny.

A public department can make itself surveyable to its constituents or can place them under surveillance. Our "social security" agencies assiduously explain themselves, advertising on radio and in newspapers to inform a broad audience of entitlements. They deplore unclaimed benefits and pursue those unschooled in their rights. But the claimants of social security are the once employed and the propertied; they are, in time, the majority of us, and agencies catering to a majority are not unmindful of its influence. Who advertises for clients for public welfare, for public housing, or for any of the "poor agencies"? For every person on the public-welfare rolls, at least one more is eligible but does not apply. Let them find their own way to appropriate agencies and through the maze of procedures that will stand between them and relief. Let them submit without challenge to investigation, for ours is a system obsessed with the fear that benefits will be obtained fraudulently, or by persons of questionable eligibility. No one may certify to his pauperism; it must be proved — repeatedly — and even then the evidence of home visits, interviews, forms and affidavits is not to be trusted. Elaborate patterns of illegal surveillance multiply. It is not thought that clients require information about the system; rather, the system must know about them.

A massive and aggressive program of public information could go far toward eliminating an ignorance that is both produced by and reinforces these barbaric practices. Such programs are by no means novel or untried. Some three decades ago, Britain's National Council of Social Service, a private organization, established a number of "citizen's advice bureaus" which have been operated with public funds since 1949, and are located in churches, settlements, family agencies, unions and elsewhere, close to those who need them most. The central office generates a constant flow of information to the local bureaus: it summarizes entitlements under new legislation, digests changes in administrative rulings, reports the outcome of appeals on one issue or another, and otherwise provides judicious advice and guidance to the users of public services. It has been, from all accounts, a remarkably successful program.

American private social-welfare agencies — despite large subsidies from government — resist making functions of this kind central to their operations. Consonant with American's attitudes toward the poor, private agencies have devoted themselves unceasingly to various forms of moral, cultural and psychiatric uplife. Prior to the depression, they carried on cash-relief programs, using such funds as could be extracted from the well to do. Pressed by heavy demands from their clients, and with relatively little money to disburse, they became experts in making judicious grants, evolving criteria and techniques to distinguish the worthy from the unworthy. They instituted a system of "social-service exchanges" which compiled information on their clientele to insure against the possibility that a few recipients might be pyramiding meager benefits by migrating from agency to agency. When government acted during the depression, many voluntary agencies argued that the new poverty agencies — such as public welfare — should be staffed by experienced social workers who understood how to administer benefits without inducing dependency, that tragic flaw of America's poor.

The mental hygiene movement also penetrated the field of social work during the depression years, and it was not long before private agencies began to draw from Freudianism their images of man, his needs and his susceptibility to intervention. And so the private field progressively turned away from environmental assistance and embraced the new personality manipulations. But the economically dispossessed remained stubbornly oblivious to the subtleties of a psychology that stressed man's participation in the creation of his own problems, preferring to believe instead that they were the victims of arbitrary and capricious outer forces beyond human control. With their traditional clientele thus alienated, a good many private agencies announced that they would welcome opportunities to serve people "in need of counseling and guidance, whether financially dependent or not." By the mid-fifties, many agencies had succeeded in uplifting themselves by attracting a high proportion of middle-class constituents.

The "war against poverty" has again focused attention on the poor, and a new period of uplift has begun. The National Urban League, the Family Service Association of America and the Child Study Association recently joined to establish, with poverty funds, a program called "Project Enable." With the League's access to the Negro ghetto and the technological expertise of the Associations, a vast program of counseling and guidance of parents will be undertaken to improve child-rearing practices so that their children can become upwardly mobile.

It is now being said, curiously, that people are poor because they have no money — but no one has thought to give them any. "Welfarism" has become discredited; all forms of the dole are in particular disrepute. The new uplift stresses a cherished American value — economic advance by individual achievement. But the poor are mostly young or very old. For the old it is too late to advance; and the poverty of the young is so crippling that they are incapacitated for mobility once they come of age. The question of poverty, in short, is being confused with the question of economic mobility. Once again, America finds itself unable to deal just with poverty; it has always had to "save" the poor as well — exhorting them to abandon the immoral ways which cause their condition, or diagnosing and treating them, or launching into the next economic stratum those who could respond to the countdown. Merely to provide money so that all may start from a minimum standard of living affronts our belief in individualism and our faith in the efficacy of professional interventions to which all social problems can finally be made to yield.

Reflecting the culture of which they are instruments, private agencies have by and large failed to act as guardians and proponents of the welfare apparatus. Standards of financial assistance are still very low (even in industrial states, "minimum cost-of-living indexes" are computed, and grant formulas are fixed at two-thirds or less of the indexes); millions of families needing assistance are not being recruited to the rolls; and those who obtain assistance are still not getting all to which they are entitled. Specializing in "information services" may not lay the best basis from which to assert professional status, but it must be said that the poor need allies against the welfare apparatus a good deal more than they require the therapeutic and other skilled services which are the stuff of professional legitimacy.

Power finally belongs to those who are able to define for others their station in life. If men have been led to believe that they have no rights, being told that they do may matter little, for the belief can overwhelm the telling. In New York State, public-welfare agencies distribute a brochure to every recipient describing, briefly and abstractly, the rights of clients, including the right to take appeals from decisions considered unjust. And, as we have shown, the grounds for appeal are abundant.

The third attack, then, must be through the apparatus of appears. In New York City, which contains more than 500,000 welfare clients, and almost half again as many rejected applicants, how many come to challenge the tens of millions of decisions regarding their various entitlements made in any year? For the whole of the city, in most years, there are about fifteen. Granted that the poor have little education and even less money for legal assistance, this is still unimaginably few.

To what interpretation will such a statistic yield? Only, it would seem, to one showing how the welfare system leads the poor to participate in their own victimization. Many welfare recipients endure that status for long periods of time, sometimes handing it down from generation to generation. Eventually, some come to believe that they know a great deal about the workings of the system, as indeed they often do, including ways to circumvent its rules. Those most familiar with the system often end by accepting its premises and thus ascribe legitimacy to its practices.

Doubtless, reluctance to appeal also arises from the fear that petty evasions of the rules will be uncovered during hearings. Nor is this the only instance one could point to in which men have given allegiance to the rules by which they are degraded, to the rules which they covertly violate. The lawless and authoritarian practices of the welfare apparatus thus produce correlative adaptations among clients. For when rights are ignored, men come to live by their wits, meeting caprice with chicanery; or they live witlessly, meeting the arbitrary with acquiescence.

Under such conditions, it will take more than information about rights to make them believable or to lead men to act upon them. If old patterns of accommodation are to be disrupted, there must be a demonstration that rights can be successfully asserted. And that will require advocates willing to pit themselves against an entrenched system. Where, then, are the poor to find these advocates?

One answer comes from the Office of Economic Opportunity, which has been promoting programs of legal services for the poor. Bar associations have rather vigorously opposed this intrusion by government into their part of the free-enterprise preserve, but that resistance may be overcome, for it is difficult to find any but the most obviously self-serving arguments to support it. The plans for "neighborhood law offices" and other legal programs under various auspices are, to be sure, a distinct advance over the present condition. Until now we have preferred to avoid the matter by ostentatiously praising the charity and idealism of those few lawyers in Legal Aid Societies and elsewhere who have resigned themselves to relative poverty by choosing to serve the poor. If, through OEO's largess, the number of lawyers entering the lists against the welfare state can be multiplied five or tenfold or more, it is certainly all to the good.

The plan to expand legal services, however, has several defects. First, it equates the need for advocacy with the need for lawyers. But the great bulk of problems that arise in the day-to-day transactions between recipients and public agencies can be resolved by persons possessing only a rudimentary knowledge of the social-welfare establishment, provided that they are willing to be aggressive and tough-minded negotiators. Such pressure is all the more likely to be effective if back-stopped by the threat of legal action, should redress not be obtained. The existence of legal power is thus more important than its exercise.

Mobilization for Youth, on New York's Lower East Side, has conducted large-scale advocacy programs through a series of "neighborhood service centers" located in store fronts and staffed by professional social workers and case aides. Lawyers train staff members in the basic laws and rule systems governing public departments. The vast majority of problems brought to the centers are then effectively resolved by these nonlegal advocates, the more difficult cases being referred to MFY's legal unit of five full-time lawyers. With poverty funds, neighborhood service centers patterned after those on the Lower East Side are being established in other cities, although it remains to be seen whether the vigor of advocacy which distinguished MFY's program will be matched elsewhere, for such programs are not popular with the governmental officials who control poverty funds. Aside from this question, the point, is that advocacy resources could be greatly expanded if scarce legal resources were conserved for in-service training, appeal procedures, court actions and other matters requiring depth of legal knowledge and experience.

The plan for "neighborhood law offices" also suffers the defect of being an altogether *ad hoc* mechanism. It will thus be dependent for funding on the vagaries of the political process. If the programs generate a great many problems for city government (as they surely will when the job is properly done), pressure may mount to shut off funds. Legal services can also be initiated in stable institutional settings — unions, settlement houses, family service agencies, inner-city churches — and this is slowly happening. Even if such institutions apply for governmental funds to initiate advocacy services, they would be able to carry on with private resources, should public sources dry up. Bar associations, it should be noted, resist the practice of law by organizations, the stated fear being that organizational interests will be "interposed" between client and lawyer. The danger is real, to be sure, for once organizations experience political backlash from the activities of their lawyers, internal pressures for more moderate advocacy may be felt. On the other hand, it is equally real that the reluctance to see nonprofit organizations hire lawyers has had the long-standing consequence of denying counsel to the poor.

In the end, we shall require arrangements that do not make access to advocates dependent upon the vagaries of poverty funding or the interests of private organizations. Once again we may need to look to European countries, where legislative measures — such as Britain's Legal Aid and Advice Act of 1949 — guarantee the availability of lawyers and provide payment for services for the very poor. Clearly, the country is not yet ready to entertain such measures. But some form of socialized law seems inevitable if men's rights are to be secured.

We have stressed reform strategies which take account of the lack of organized low-income political influence on this country. If, however, welfare recipients in large urban centers could be organized to press their grievances through dramatic, well-publicized actions, these strategies would be greatly enhanced. The notion that the poor should participate in the decisions affecting their dependency is not novel. In the depression years, the Workers' Alliance — a union of relief clients and relief workers — performed this important function in New York City. The Alliance staged sit-ins at welfare offices, mass demonstrations and letterwriting campaigns, and succeeded in securing improved benefits from its members.

Recently, groups under diverse sponsorships and in scattered localities have begun to organize around welfare issues. In some cases, as in Syracuse or Washington, they have been organized by professional social workers, using OEO funds. In Newark, Cleveland, Detroit, some parts of the South and elsewhere, they have been organized by newly emergent radical groups, principally SNCC and SDS. One would be hard put to describe these sporadic efforts as a movement, or even a potential movement. They have been isolated efforts to adjust individual grievances through protest.

In some instances, efforts have been made to establish procedures comparable to collective bargaining. If this process is to succeed, it must attract expert allies. A short time ago, for example, a group of Lower East Side Negro and Puerto Rican ADC mothers, represented by an attorney and a social worker, held a meeting with the Commissioner of Welfare to negotiate grievances. The immediate aim of this Committee of Welfare Families, organized through Mobilization for Youth, was to force the Welfare Department to supply its members with winter clothing. The Committee first notified the Commissioner that it had unsuccessfully made formal requests to the appropriate welfare investigators for the necessary cash grants. It threatened to picket if the Commissioner refused a hearing. The Commissioner agreed to a meeting with the Committee, and subsequently negotiated a formal grievance procedure with them. But, throughout the negotiations, the Commissioner continued to insist upon the traditional prerogative to investigate assertions of individual need, rather than to accept the validity of the Committee's assertions. While acceding to the principle of collective bargaining, he reaffirmed the right of the Department to conduct confidential interviews with clients, unimpeded by the presence of other Committee members, lawyers, social workers or translators. "Why should a discussion on why our members are not receiving the winter clothing which is due them contain so much 'confidential' information?," the Committee wrote to the Commissioner recently. And they went on: "If Mrs. John Doe is told by her investigator that her coat received in 1959 or 1960 should last '5 to 8 years,' or if a Mrs. Rodriguez is told that her investigator is too busy with 'more important things, and I don't know when I can get around to see you,' is all this 'confidential'?" Despite bureaucratic tactics of resistance, these efforts at reform — however faltering and few — are needed in a society whose social-welfare apparatus has always had its way with the poor.

And, finally, it should be said that new legislation — such as the proposed plan for a federally sponsored "guaranteed minimum income" — would solve most of the problems cited in these two articles, for it would eliminate their source. Nor should anyone mourn the passing of the local public-assistance agency, if that ever comes to pass. One reason for developing vigorous programs to protect individual rights — whether by information dissemination, advocacy, legal testing or collective action — is to dramatize the need for a new way to distribute income by revealing just how bad is the way that now prevails.

JUSTICE

The Police

In the 1930's, the leading book on the police in the United States was written by a man trained in public administration. The police themselves were rarely considered interesting to sociologists studying crime and social problems. It was not until the pioneering work of William Westley in 1951,[1] that sociologists began to look at police as an object of study, rather than an accepted fact of life. Since Westley's study, a number of field studies of police have appeared, but the literature is still sparse, compared with that dealing with criminals and deviants.

In their studies of the police, sociologists were principally influenced by two theoretical trends. One was the theory of bureaucratic organization. A number of sociologists who had studied business and governmental organizations had observed that structural pressures on those workers in the organization influenced their behavior. Thus, the theory of bureaucracy as developed by Max Weber and as elaborated by such scholars as Blau and Selznick[2] offered students of the police a perspective that was somewhat different from that of legal scholars. Students of the police expected that the police would deviate

[1] William A. Westley, *The Police: A Sociological Study of Law, Custom, and Morality* (Unpublished Ph.D. dissertation, Department of Sociology, University of Chicago, 1951).

[2] See Hans H. Gerth and C. Wright Mills, eds., *From Max Weber: Essays in Sociology* (New York: Oxford University Press, 1953); Philip Selznick, *TVA and the Grass Roots* (New York: Harper Torchbooks, 1966); Peter M. Blau, *The Dynamics of Bureaucracy* (Chicago: University of Chicago Press, 1957).

from the stated rules of legal organizations, just as workers in industrial organizations deviated from those rules. It became the task of these sociologists to specify how the organization of police work shaped the behavior of police, and also to define the consequences that arose from attempts by police administrators to rationalize and control the behavior of the men under them.

A second important influence was the developing theory of social deviance, as propounded by such writers as Lemert, Becker, and Goffman.[3] In this theory the importance of defining the deviant act was stressed. Defining acts as deviant is often a matter of perspective. The classic example is national prohibition, enforced in the United States from the end of the World War I to the beginning of the Roosevelt administration. For approximately fifteen years, the sale of beverage alcohol was considered a crime. It is of course almost a custom in American culture today. Informed by the prohibition experience and by the writings of the sociologists in the social interactionist tradition, these scholars could point to certain aspects of American life today that carry some of the same connotations as national prohibition. Becker, for example, analyzed the "moral entrepreneurs" behind the marijuana laws. Goffman stressed the social definitional character of mental illness.

Two aspects of this view of social deviance were important for students of the police. If definitions of devant acts were central in determining whether or not an individual was to be regarded as a criminal, or placed in some other stigmatic category, then the decision-making processes of people in a position to define others as deviant became important in understanding the "causes" of deviant behavior. The police, as officials with considerable discretion in deciding who was or who was not to be defined as a criminal, thus became an increasingly important subject for study. At the same time, the theory of social organization pro-

[3] See Edwin M. Lemert, *Social Pathology* (New York: McGraw-Hill, 1951); Howard S. Becker, *Outsiders: Studies in the Sociology of Deviance* (London: Free Press, 1963); Erving Goffman, *Asylums: Essays on the Social Situation of Mental Patients and Other Inmates* (Garden City, New York: Doubleday Anchor, 1961).

vided sociologists studying the police with expectations about the relationship between individual acts and social organization. Only the most naive sociologist could go into a police organization expecting that all the rules would be followed to the letter, since no social organization previously studied had ever achieved this goal. So the two theories — social organization and deviance — fed into each other. The sociologists of police expected to find police variation from legal rules, looked to generative factors within social organization, and ultimately saw the police both as definers of other deviants, and as themselves deviant from the rules of their own organization.

Armed with these previous theoretical perspectives, the sociologists who studied police did not believe that police were exceptional individuals. They did not start off with the notion that police were "sick" or "sadistic" or exceptionally "heroic." Rather, they looked to the social situation of the policeman in an attempt to understand his behavior. Several scholars, notably McNamara and Niederhoffer,[4] systematically studied this issue, and found that although the police were quite conventional in their social attitudes, police recruits did not score particularly high on tests measuring authoritarianism. Careful investigation showed that police represent the attitudes of the social groups from which they are drawn. If firemen, automobile mechanics, and electricians were to become policemen, within six months they would probably be behaving in much the same way as the average policeman. The job itself, according to the findings of the students of police, produces attitudes and responses that almost inevitably leave their mark on the working policeman.

The policeman develops what one sociologist has called a "working personality,"[5] which results from certain outstanding features of his role. These features include two

[4] John H. McNamara, "Uncertainties in Police Work: the Relevance of Police Recruits' Background and Training," in David J. Bordua, ed., *The Police: Six Sociological Essays* (New York: Wiley, 1967); Arthur Niederhoffer, *Behind the Shield: the Police in Urban Society* (Garden City, New York: Doubleday, 1968).

[5] See Jerome H. Skolnick, *Justice Without Trial: Law Enforcement in Democratic Society* (New York: Wiley, 1966).

variables, danger and authority, which need to be interpreted in the light of a "constant" pressure to appear efficient. The element of danger seems to make the policeman especially attentive to signs indicating a potential for violence and lawbreaking. He develops a perceptual shorthand to identify some kinds of people as "symbolic assailants," that is, as persons who use gestures or attire that the policeman has come to recognize as a prelude to violence. This makes the policeman a very "suspicious" person.

Second, the policeman is an authority, and as an authority he is always in the position of being challenged. This is especially true when the policeman is required to enforce laws representing puritanical morality, such as those prohibiting drunkenness, laws regulating the flow of activity, such as traffic laws, and laws in communities that have developed hostile relations between the police and the public, such as the black communities in America. Westley found, for example, that police use physical force largely to maintain authority. As one observer of police has put it, "The most serious crime in the books is contempt of cop."

Many people who think about law enforcement regard it as a fairly automatic process: the policeman observes a crime being committed, he makes an arrest, and charges the offender with violation of an applicable statute. But all students of the administration of justice have rejected that pattern in recent years. No one, neither the police nor their critics, denies that the police have enormous discretion in enforcing criminal law. They have discretion in whether or not they will observe that a particular event is taking place, whether actions will be judged on the basis of those observations, whether those actions will be hostile or friendly, and if hostile, they may have considerable latitude in deciding which statute — carrying greater or lesser penalties — is applicable. Police exercise considerable latitude or discretion in the enforcement of the criminal law. Strongly at issue, however, is whether discretion is exercised fairly by police, and if it is not, what remedies the citizen has against the harsh or unfair enforcement of the criminal law.

In the first excerpt in this chapter, from a book commissioned by the New York Civil Liberties Union, the problems of street interactions between citizens and the police are discussed. When the citizen entertains a grievance against police there is very little he can do to press that grievance. There are no outside bodies to whom he can appeal, the closely knit cooperation of police will protect a brother officer, and, if necessary, police have been known to tell a "cover story" or to produce "cover charges" as a way of dealing with a complaint against them.

Perhaps a more fundamental issue is whether there are systematic biases in the perception of police, and systematic developments in the organization of police that reflect these biases. One important development has been the introduction into police work of the tactical patrol force, a unit that is increasingly prevalent in the urban centers of the United States. This force, usually younger, better trained, and more aggressive, is being used to deal with high crime areas and with confrontation and protest. In his article, Nicholas Pileggi presents a portrait of an aggressive, mobile force that threatens to become a major social control instrument of the police department of the future. Pileggi raises one of the most fundamental questions among students of the police: Do we really want a police force that is mobile, highly trained, well equipped, and aggressive? Does this sort of police "professionalism" augur well for the future of a free society that ostensibly values variety and dissent? Perhaps the answer is not so much in whether the police are well trained and well equipped, as in the question of what we mean by "police professionalism." Is police professionalism to be measured merely by patrol cars, communication systems, and a generally higher order of technical equipment; or is it to be measured primarily by the adequacy of the social and political sensitivities developed to deal with the serious problems in our urban communities? Studies of the police conducted by official commissions have found them to be notably deficient on this score.

The thinking that dominates police circles is described in the book review by Irving Louis Horowitz of J. Edgar Hoover's *On Communism* Horowitz regards Hoover as the last of the simplistic puritans. Yet, Hoover remains the classic figure for the American policeman to emulate. And the politics of the American police reflect ever more strongly Mr. Hoover's views on such issues as Communism, civil rights and liberties, and the problems of American cities. The political views of police have recently been described as a "rotten apple" theory of human nature.[6] This theory is, of course, widespread in our society and this complicates our national problems. Under this "rotten apple" view, crime and disorder are mainly attributed to the intentions of evil individuals; human behavior transcends past experience, culture, society, and other external forces and should be understood as wrong choices, deliberately made. Significantly, and contrary to the general intention of the social sciences, such social factors as poverty, discrimination, and the like are excluded as social causes — "poverty doesn't cause crime, people do."

Through people like Mr. Hoover, this view is gaining credence in fraternal organizations of police, police departments, and the country at large. The police are becoming an important political group, who exercise considerable influence in state legislatures, Congress, and the executive branches of the government. The positions that police political organizations take should help to illuminate the answer to Nicholas Pileggi's question as to whether the tactical patrol force is a "gestapo or an elite." And it should also help to understand the complexity of the problem of controlling the police in a society committed to ideals of liberty and freedom.

[6] *The Politics of Protest,* a report submitted by Jerome H. Skolnick, Director, Task Force on Violent Aspects of Protest and Confrontation, National Commission on the Causes and Prevention of Violence (New York: Ballantine Books, 1969), Chapter 7.

PAUL CHEVIGNY   *Force, Arrest,*
                                   and Cover Charges

Arbitrary arrest and summary punishment have been recurring themes [in *Police Power*] and we are ready now to draw up an Anatomy of Street-corner Abuses.

The one truly iron and inflexible rule we can adduce from the cases [mentioned earlier] is that any person who defies the police risks the imposition of legal sanctions, commencing with a summons, on up to the use of firearms. The sanction that is imposed depends on at least three factors: the character of the officer, the place where the encounter occurs, and the character of the person with whom the encounter is had. The police may arrest *anyone* who challenges them (as they define the challenge), but they are more likely to further abuse anyone who is poor, or who belongs to an outcast group.

Members of outcast groups, by their mere presence, seem to offer an affront to order such that the police will themselves initiate action against them by ordering them to move along, breaking into a party, or some similar action. To the police, the ordinary citizen begins to assume the status of a pariah only when he actively defies the police, whereas a member of an outcast group need take no such action.

John McNamara, reviewing "critical incidents" involving police and citizens, in his work with New York City police recruits was "struck by the extent to which the handling of relatively minor incidents such as traffic violations or disorderly disputes between husbands and wives seemed to create a more serious situation than existed prior to the police attempt to control the situation."[1] In many of our cases, the police have gone further and caused a situation to degenerate into an argument when it was scarcely a dispute at all to begin with. McNamara attributes the phenomenon to mistaken assumptions on the part of the police about how they ought to behave toward the public. For example, he found that 39 to 40 per cent of policemen agree with the proposition that "a patrolman can be pretty sure he will gain compliance from a person who appears to be somewhat frightened of the patrolman," as well as with the proposition that "when patrolmen indicate they will use the force necessary to

    [1] McNamara, "Uncertainties in Police Work," p. 168.

gain compliance from a citizen, they are helped considerably if the citizen thinks they are getting angry."[2] These police opinions are so potentially dangerous, and in many cases so catastrophically applied, that it is not enough to think of them only as mistaken assumptions. The reason why policemen act so aggressively as to exacerbate street situations is, of course, that they seek to establish their authority by such transactions. The answers to McNamara's questions indicate that a large percentage of policemen will usually try to obtain compliance by an unconditional demand or the use of force. Many people wonder whether police work attracts young men who already have such attitudes, or whether the police role develops those attitudes in them. Most authorities who have studied the problem intensively seem to agree that the second alternative is the correct one. Police recruits are much like other young men of a similar background; it is police mores and the police role that make them adopt police attitudes.[3]

In the paradigmatic street encounter there are three steps:

1. Police perception of a challenge to authority. In the case of a member of an outcast group this step is eliminated, or at least minimized.

2. Police demand for submission. This is most commonly enshrined in the question, "So you're a wise guy, eh?" In my office we sat through many lengthy and excited complaints listening only for the words "wise guy," knowing well that an arrest would have occurred shortly after they were uttered.

3. Response to the demand. The citizen in effect either admits that he is a wise guy, or denies it by complying with the police demand, if it involves an action like moving along, or by apologizing to the policeman if no action is demanded.

Police in minority and outcast groups, who are the most likely to be subjected to a police demand for submission, at the same time find it hardest to comply with it. The middle-class man thinks nothing of saying, "Sorry, officer," but to the oppressed and downtrodden those words are galling. It is especially hard for a Negro, for whom such an act seems just one more token of submission. The combination of being an outcast (step one) and refusing to comply in step three is explosive; thereby hangs the tale of many police brutality cases.

The police rationale for this three-step process is that people who present a challenge to them are troublemakers, as the police might put it, or symbolic assailants, as Skolnick calls them. They are, quite literally,

[2] *Ibid.*, pp. 226, 228.

[3] *Ibid.*, p. 194; Arthur Neiderhoffer, *Behind the Shield: The Police in Urban Society* (New York, Doubleday & Company, Inc., 1967), Ch. 5.

potential offenders, and so to arrest one of them is at least the ethical (if not the legal) equivalent of arresting a criminal. The policeman will go on to say that he must maintain his authority against those who challenge it, in order to enforce the laws effectively. In short, his authority over others will be lost if he backs down with one person. It inevitably follows that his authority as a policeman is asserted in situations which are personal disputes, or at least have a personal dimension, like nearly all of the cases recounted in previous chapters. In some of those cases, the provocation comes principally from the citizen, and in others, principally from the police. The point is that they are street arguments, not so very different from those which arise every day between private citizens when one insults another or tries to get him to do something he does not want to do. Although it is true that policemen take umbrage very easily, and that they sometimes see a threat where there is none — as in the Bell and Johnson case [discussed earlier] — it is equally clear that in many instances recounted here — such as George Howard's insulting remark [same] — some sort of retaliation was almost inevitable. The chief difference is that one of the parties is a policeman, and for him no dispute is purely personal. It is no accident that in old-fashioned journalistic parlance the officer was personified as "John Law" or the "long arm of the law." Policemen apparently do see themselves as personifying authority, and a challenge to one of them (or to all of them, as in the case of civilian review) is a challenge to the Law. Everybody knows that when you defy the Law, you go to jail.

The apparently irrational and sometimes provocative behavior of the police in street conflicts has often raised the question whether the police deliberately encourage violence or at least disorderly behavior from a troublemaker, in order to show that he really is an offender and to provide grounds for removing him from the street by arrest. This is one of the unresolved questions about police behavior, and one that is central to an understanding of police abuses. If the police react in a rough manner to provocation from citizens, if they in fact themselves behave in a rude and ham-handed fashion, that is one problem, but it is quite another if the police deliberately provoke to violence people they believe to be troublemakers. Westley, in his research on a Midwestern police department, felt that there was a tendency for the police to provoke anyone who was disrespectful until there was an assault, and then to retaliate with violence.[4] Werthman and Piliavin detected the same thing in their work on police treatment of juveniles,[5] and at least one writer in the

[4] Westley, "Violence and the Police," p. 39.
[5] Carl Werthman and Irving M. Piliavin, "Gang Members and the Police," in David Joseph Bordua, ed., *The Police: Six Sociological Essays* (New York, John Wiley & Sons, Inc., 1966), p. 93.

professional journal *Police* has criticized the practice, while carefully labeling it "unusual."[6]

The issue is difficult to resolve with the research tools at our disposal in this book. Investigation of a case by interviews with witnesses, the method almost invariably used here, is a very blunt instrument for getting at anything as perishable as the words of a verbal interchange, to say nothing of its tone. Moreover, since we did not accept cases in which there actually had been an assault on an officer, we might possibly have missed cases of provocation. There is a suggestion of egging on a "trouble-maker" in the Caulaincourt case, where the policeman repeatedly pushed the defendant. In . . . the systematic harassment of Galahad and the hippies in his communal apartment, there is a well-authenticated case of provocation during one of the practically constant raids by the police in April and May of 1967. On that occasion a narcotics policeman dared one of the boys in the apartment to take a sock at him. The mind boggles at what might have happened if he had, but fortunately he simply responded, "No, man, that's not my life."

The consensus among the authorities who have studied the problem is that the police do sometimes try to provoke violence in order to make an arrest. It is logical to think that policemen will try such things on with outcasts, whom they fear and dislike and would prefer to see in jail. One young Negro in a ghetto neighborhood in Brooklyn, who had the reputation of being a "cop fighter," complained that the police would not let him alone. Whenever they saw him on the street they slowed down their cars and asked him if he wanted to fight. In New York City in 1967, however, I think that the challenge by a policeman to physical combat, or even to a public disturbance, is the exception. In my office we did not receive more than a handful of complaints of such deliberate provocation, and it cannot be a widespread problem if there are so few complaints. In most cases, even if a policeman wanted to use such crude tactics, they would not be necessary. The New York police are sophisticated enough in drawing charges and making them stick not to need an actual act of physical violence to arrest anyone. If they feel that a man is a trouble-maker, they can, unfortunately, charge him with resisting arrest, without the necessity of risking injury to an officer.

The worst problem in street-corner incidents is not that of police quarreling with citizens. Most such quarrels, while never admirable, are at least understandable; they are much like quarrels between private citizens. The worst abuse is not even the police hitting people in such quarrels; pugnacious citizens hit others in private disputes every day. The root problem is the abuse of power, the fact that the police not only hit a man

[6] Richard H. Blum, "The Problems of Being a Police Officer," *Police*, January 1961, p. 12.

but arrest him. Once they have arrested him, of course, lying becomes an inevitable part of the procedure of making the quarrel look like a crime, and thus the lie is the chief abuse with which we must come to grips. If the police simply hit a man and let him go, there would be an abuse of the authority conferred by the uniform and the stick, but not the compound abuse of hitting a man and then dragging him to court on criminal charges, really a more serious injury than a blow. One's head heals up, after all, but a criminal record never goes away. There is no more embittering experience in the legal system than to be abused by the police and then to be tried and convicted on false evidence.

Police abuse and consequent conviction on false evidence are a combination which feeds the impulse to riot; once respect for the legal process is gone, grievances can be expressed only by force. Despite these obvious repercussions upon community relations, it is rarely that anyone is abused without being criminally charged, not only because of the rationale for such abuses ("he was guilty anyhow") but because the policeman is likely to get into trouble if he lets an abused person go free. There is nothing to cover a later accusation of abuse if an arrest has not been made.

There can be no doubt that police lying is the most pervasive of all abuses. In most of the cases [reported in earlier chapters], there was a lie whenever there was a criminal trial. If the charge was disorderly conduct, officers lied to create a breach of the peace where none existed. If the charge was assault or obstructing an officer, they supplied blows by the defendant when none had been struck. In the police canon of ethics, the lie is justified in the same way as the arrest: as a vindication of police authority, by proving that defiance of the police is a crime in fact if not in law. A member of a paraiah group, or anyone who defies the police, being guilty at heart and sometimes potentially guilty in fact, deserves to be punished out of hand. Besides, the police dislike such people so much that they consider them unworthy of the protection of the law. By lying, the police enforce these folkways of their own, while preserving the shell of due process of law.

Not surprisingly, police lying is a problem about which little reliable research has been done. William Westley, after breaking ground upon the police use of violence in his first article, went on to open the problem of lying in "Secrecy and the Police."[7] He found that 11 out of 15 men said they would not report a brother officer for taking money from a prisoner, and 10 out of 13 said they would not testify against the officer if he were accused by the prisoner. Comments on police honesty since the publication of Westley's article have often taken the form of avuncular warnings

[7] William A. Westley, "Secrecy and the Police," *Social Forces*, XXXIV (March 1956), 254.

in the professional journals. Richard H. Blum wrote in *Police:* "The conflict of loyalty versus lawfulness is always with the officer, as he is faced with wanting trust, friendship and reliability on the one hand, while wanting to be lawful on the other."[8] Both Blum and Westley deal with honesty about the conduct of a fellow officer; obviously the temptation is even stronger for an officer to cover up when he himself is in trouble, as he usually is when he has abused a citizen.

Once an arrest is made, the police begin to consider what testimony is necessary for a conviction, and what charges are necessary to create pressure on the defendant for a plea of guilty. The Criminal Court is not viewed as a tribunal for the determination of fact, but as a sort of administrative adjunct to the police station for the purpose of obtaining desirable results. Lying is a litigation tool much like, say, investigation. Once the police have arrested a man, particularly under circumstances when charges have been made against an officer, the only real objective is conviction, and the police feel that they have made a mistake if they fail to obtain the conviction, not if they lied to obtain it. The arresting officer who has abused a citizen makes it his business to get out of trouble, as does any other accused party, and his original aim of "preserving police authority" becomes little more than a rationalization. The lie serves the double purpose of preserving his authority and his job.

It seems that there is some sort of folklore or underground standard circulating in the Department, according to which charges are drawn to cover abuses. Lying to cover a mistake and the use of a criminal charge to buttress the lie are such a natural development that it would hardly seem necessary to do more than give a patrolman a hint. Charges are so invariably preferred, however, and the charges are so much alike from one case to the next, that I am constrained to believe that something a little more definite than a hint is at work. At some level in the Department, something close to this standard has been accepted: when a citizen is injured by a policeman, he must be charged with resisting arrest, together with the underlying crime for which he was arrested. If there was no crime, but rather a personal dispute with the policeman, then the defendant must be charged with disorderly conduct and resisting arrest. Other, more serious charges become something of a matter of taste. Experienced men tend to add other charges, in order to increase the pressure for a plea of guilty to one of the charges. I once heard two transit policemen arguing in the hallway outside the courtroom after one of my clients had refused to plead guilty to disorderly conduct in exchange for a dismissal of the charge of resisting arrest. The more experienced of the two was

[8] Blum, "Problems of Being a Police Officer," p. 10.

saying, "You see? He wouldn't take it. I *told* you you should have charged him with felonious assault." These charges — disorderly conduct, resisting arrest, and felonious assault, or all three — together with a story to establish them, constitute the system for covering street abuses. According to a task force of the President's Commission on Law Enforcement, the system exists in many other cities with conditions similar to those of New York, notably in Philadelphia.[9]

It is my guess that the system is perpetuated at the middle level, among the sergeants and possibly the lieutenants. I cannot, of course, be sure, because I rarely hear a reliable account of what is being said at the precinct. However, investigators for a field survey of the President's Commission, covering police departments in major cities outside New York, were able to gain access to the precincts, and their direct observation supports the theory that it is the officers at the middle level who tend to cover for the abuses of the men working under them.[10] This cover may take the form of advice about criminal charges, the system I describe here, or simply of keeping quiet about abuses; in any case, it is characteristic of the extreme solidarity and secrecy of policemen in every city. No doubt the solidarity is as tight as it is because every ranking officer in the typical urban police department has come up through the ranks and shares the mores of the men below him. By the same token, it follows that the introduction of new men at the middle level, specially trained for their jobs rather than drawn from the ranks, would be the most effective way of breaking through the police secrecy. Under present civil service laws, in New York as well as most other communities, it is difficult to alter the system of seniority, but any limitation on the protection of underlings by superiors may be impossible without it.

The Review Board and other institutions in the New York City Police Department do little to discourage the system of cover charges. The Review Board does not hold a hearing until after criminal charges against the complainant have been disposed of, and the charges at a departmental trial are always artfully drawn to avoid any conflict with criminal charges made by the officer involved, even when they have been disposed of. Such tailoring of charges occurred in the Kaplan case [Chapter 6] and the Queens bar case [Chapter 3]. These practices encourage officers to believe that if they can cover themselves by a criminal charge, they will escape censure. If the Department were vitally concerned about seeing justice done, it would make sure that criminal charges were dropped against citizens when a departmental investigation showed that they were

[9] TFRP, p. 195.
[10] President's Commission on Law Enforcement and the Administration of Justice, *Field Survey V*, pp. 189 ff.

unwarranted. Instead, the Department sits back to see whether the officer can make his criminal case stick before proceeding against him.

It is worth mentioning here that the ironclad system of cover charges exists in New York City partly because certain other abuses do not. For example, the New York City Police Department does not permit arrests[11] on "suspicion," a practice allowed by departments in other cities such as Detroit, where 13 per cent of the arrests in 1964 were for "detention."[12] Dragnet arrests for suspicious persons do occasionally occur after serious crimes in New York, but in general, if a city policeman has a defendant in custody, he must try to show probable cause for arresting him, and if he is to account for a defendant's injuries by resistance to arrest, he must commence his explanation with a lawful arrest. Hence the elaborate lies about disorderly conduct. It is because the men at the top of the Department are trying to maintain a façade of probable cause for arrest that the men in the middle and at the bottom go to such lengths to cover their mistakes. To be an oppressor is a tricky business in New York, this most liberal of all possible worlds. In jurisdictions where no attempt is made to maintain the requirements of probable cause, the system of cover charges is correspondingly less deeply entrenched.

Furthermore, in other jurisdictions a policeman can afford to be a little lax in covering himself because he can rely on the district attorney to help him out if he makes a mistake. In the District of Columbia, for example, the authorities have in the past preferred charges of filing a false report against people who made complaints about policemen.[13] In one case from that jurisdiction the District Attorney started a prosecution upon minor traffic charges three months after the events were supposed to have occurred, and solely because the defendant had complained against the police officer involved in the incident.[14] If there is an instance of equal skulduggery perpetrated by any of the five New York City district attorneys, I have not heard of it. The only incident in my experience which approaches these in depravity was a threat by the prosecutor in one of my cases, after he had consented to a dismissal of the charges against two out of three co-defendants, to reinstate the charges against them if they testified in defense of the third. That is an exceptional incident, however, and it is generally up to the New York City policeman to provide his own cover for his mistakes. If he does not make his accusation at the time of the occurrence, the prosecutor is not likely to look upon the case with favor. The system is the policeman's only solution.

If officials outside the Police Department in New York do not participate

---

[11] As distinguished from field interrogation, or "stop and frisk."
[12] TFRP, p. 186.
[13] Ibid., p. 195.
[14] Miller Dixon v. District of Columbia, D.C. Cir. Dkt. No. 21084/67.

directly in protecting police officers, they do so by their silence. The judges, the prosecutors, even the commissioner himself, cannot appear to condone slipshod police work or police abuses. On the other hand, they know that there is such poor police work, and although they would not participate in it, they do not expect to do very much to improve it. The district attorneys go right on taking waivers of damage claims in return for the dismissal of criminal charges, the remedies for abuses continue to be inadequate, and all in all, with some exceptions, the system works nearly as effectively as if all the other officials participated in it. They become parties to the system in the sense that they know, or should know, that the policeman is covering his mistakes by lying and are content to let him go on doing it. They maintain the rigid standards of due process required in a modern liberal society by letting the patrolman vary the facts to fit the case. They have helped to make the policeman the target for much of the hostility in the city by making him do all the dirty work.

Ironically, the vigilance and sophistication of citizens in pursuing what few poor remedies are open to them have probably helped to make the system as rigid as it is. In rural communities and small towns, where abused citizens are satisfied to forget the whole thing if the police will forget it, criminal charges may not be used by the police as a cover, but in New York, where many abused citizens are very likely to complain to the Department and perhaps even bring a lawsuit, criminal charges are almost invariably preferred. One thoroughly puzzled woman who complained of being manhandled in a welfare center by a policeman told me that the officer had later bought her lunch and said that he would like to drop the charges, but he dared not because she might sue the city. She tried to convince him that she would not sue, but he felt that he could not trust her; regardless of the promises she made while she was under arrest, she might change her mind later. The system was too ironclad for him to let her go.

NICHOLAS PILEGGI   *"Gestapo" or "Elite"?*
                                The Tactical Patrol Force

Whether New Yorkers really want a Police Department made up of 28,000 incorruptible, impartial and indiscriminate law enforcers is open to question. For whenever the Tactical Patrol Force moves to clean up a high-crime area, it is not only the muggers and mashers who are likely to find themselves in trouble, but also litterbugs, jay-walkers, domestic battlers and actors filming chase scenes through the city's streets. It is, in fact, this unblinking dedication to the law by the city's 944 resolute T.P.F. members that has brought them numerous citizen complaints, the resentment of their less meticulous fellow officers and the accusations of student, peace and civil-rights groups that they are far more tactile than tactical.

While the only items on their uniforms that distinguish members of the Tactical Patrol from other patrolmen are the chromed T.P.F. pins on their collars, their presence is unmistakable. For instance, when they were sent to rid Washington Square Park of undesirables, which they did in short order, it was not too long before relatively law-abiding residents of the area found themselves charged with walking on the grass, unleashing their dogs and playing chess after dark. At large peace demonstrations, civil-rights rallies and student sit-ins, the T.P.F. is invariably greeted with shouts of "Gestapo!"

A single member of the Tactical Force, Patrolman Melvin Schwartz, "captured" James Coburn, the actor, during the filming of a chase scene for "The President's Analyst." In fairness to Patrolman Schwartz, it should be explained that he was probably as much a victim of departmental sabotage as he was of his own zeal. The precinct in which the film was being made had "forgotten" to tell the T.P.F. men assigned there for the day that a mock chase involving actor-policemen was scheduled to take place. "If they're supposed to be so hot," one patrolman smirked at the time, "let 'em find out for themselves."

The T.P.F., which is not assigned to any one precinct, has as many critics inside the Police Department as out. "Elite!" shouted one Brooklyn desk lieutenant when asked about the adjective often applied to the Tactical Patrol Force. "They're more gung-ho than elite. Why every time I hear they're being sent into my precinct I know I'll be writing up arrest cards

From *The New York Times Magazine*, July 21, 1968. © 1968 by The New York Times Company. Reprinted by permission of Curtis Brown, Ltd.

all night. They'll arrest anybody. They're all looking for nice, fat arrest quotas. One time I sent two of them out to quiet down a little Friday-night family dispute, and they came back with two arrests."

The Tactical Patrol, organized nine years ago as an experimental squad of 75 men, also has its champions, and the hand-picked, eager young men in its ranks make up a showcase unit. Police experts from all over the nation marvel at its exceptional discipline, dazzling mobility and graft-proof personnel. The Detroit, San Francisco and Chicago departments have organized similar units. The T.P.F., many high police officials feel, could very well be the forerunner of tomorrow's decentralized, college-educated urban police department.

Conceived to supplement regular precinct policemen during the peak street-crime hours — 6 P.M. to 2 A.M. — the Force draws its men directly from the Police Academy, long before they can be soured by less ambitious and often cynical veterans. Admittedly unequal to the sum of their hyperbolic press notices — T.P.F. men are not all six-foot, riot-trained judo experts — they are nevertheless considered the cream of the department's young recruits. The drop-out rate is minuscule. In fact, most of the men who leave the Tactical Patrol Force have been pirated away by other outfits. Negroes and Puerto Ricans, who make up 10 per cent of the T.P.F. and, on the average, 4 per cent of other units, are constantly being drained off by the Detective Division and special investigating groups. The T.P.F. men who remain are selected volunteers, willing and eager to work nights and happy to forgo the cozy friendships with local merchants that are the lot of many regular precinct men. They must be large enough to avoid being challenged for size alone, and it helps to have at least some college experience. T.P.F. men are paid no more than regular patrolmen.

The office of Deputy Chief Inspector Charles E. McCarthy, who heads the Tactical Patrol Force, is on the top floor of the Fourth Precinct, a dilapidated, overcrowded brick and stone building in lower Manhattan. At the top of four flights of steep and sagging wooden stairs a large dressing room has been converted into an office filled with old lockers, typewriters, scarred maple desks, flat-back benches and a few windowsill pencil sharpeners. The room serves as the administrative center for the Tactical Patrol Force and looks, as do almost all of its command posts, like a hastily established battlefront bunker. A broken metal door gapes open and a large stencilled hand directs visitors inside. From the tip of the stencilled index finger some precinct critic has drawn a piece of string and a yo-yo.

"Our operation, as anyone can see, does not depend upon a building or station house," Chief McCarthy said, smiling amid the jumble of men, maps and charts. "In fact, our sergeants and patrolmen never even come to this building. They go from their homes directly to the areas in which they have been assigned. Only lieutenants and captains report here early in the afternoon for briefings and then scatter all over the city to deliver instructions and turn out their men at 6 o'clock.

Behind a plywood partition one day recently, five lieutenants were gathered around a desk. Before them were minutely detailed orders pertaining to every movement each of 300 T.P.F. men would make under the command of 20 sergeants in 13 high-crime neighborhoods that night. Above the desk a small red, blue and gold Vietcong flag was tacked to the corner of a bulletin board. The areas to be patrolled by the Force on this rainy night included Greenwich Village, the Lower East Side, midtown and Harlem in Manhattan. T.P.F. men would also supplement regular precinct details in the Bedford-Stuyvesant, Brownsville, Williamsburg, East New York, Coney Island, Borough Park and Crown Heights sections of Brooklyn and the Jamaica section of Queens; but by far the largest detail was being sent to the Morrisania section of the South Bronx, which, statistically, has the highest crime rate in the city.

"Our main operation — 98 per cent of our work — involves fighting street crimes and muggings, purse snatchers, rapes, breaking into cars, the armed robberies of small neighborhood stores," McCarthy said. "Street crimes, however, are not static things. Sometimes a few precincts in Brooklyn are inundated with them, and over we go to supplement the regular patrol. A few weeks later it's Queens or a few weeks after that, as it is now, it's the South Bronx.

Chief McCarthy, 48 years old and the father of eight children, has been with the T.P.F. since its inception. He is a calm man with a relaxed manner and a hushed, gentle voice. His bearing is not military, his jaw does not jut, his bones are thin and his whole approach is far more that of an academician than a naval officer, which he was during World War II.

"You can't measure what a patrolman standing on a corner has prevented," he said. "There is no product at the end of a policeman's day."

There are, however, statistics. In 1967, for instance, the Tactical Patrol made 8,355 arrests, 2,290 of them for felonies. In the first three months of 1968 the Force had a total of 2,059 arrests, including 703 for felonies.

One T.P.F. technique, called the "safety check," is directed at automobiles but often winds up with the arrest of the driver. For one hour every night, usually at a traffic signal, each Tactical Patrolman approaches automobiles with defects for a "safety check." The car might have only one headlight or an obscured license plate or an excessively noisy muffler.

"They need a good, well-lighted spot and great tact to make these checks," McCarthy said. "We've found that an amazing number of the automobiles being driven around the city are stolen or are not properly registered or are uninsured. Quite often they're being driven by young kids without licenses and looking for trouble. Last year, just through these spot checks, we arrested 795 drunken drivers, 572 car thieves and 161 drivers with forged licenses."

Another street crime to which the T.P.F. has given special attention is the theft of packages from parked automobiles. "We usually get two or three of these a night," McCarthy sighed, "and they're invariably addicts. We've arrested three or four in the same night trying to break into the same car before the owner returned."

The Tactical Patrol Force was created to combat mugging, which McCarthy describes this way: "A mugging takes place when only the use of physical force or fear is involved. No knife. No gun. When a gun or knife is used it is armed robbery. Muggers are careful to avoid being caught with a weapon." There were 16,200 muggings reported in New York last year (the National Opinion Research Corporation indicates that about 50 per cent of all robberies are never reported to the police), and 82 per cent of all those arrested and charged with the crime had been arrested previously.

The T.P.F. uses area saturation and a decoy system to capture muggers. In the decoy system, a Tactical Patrolman is dressed like a woman — usually an old, fat woman who wears ankle-length coats. Equipped with a radio transmitter and a big pocketbook, he sits on a bench between two shopping bags. Nearby, also in disguise, a backup team of T.P.F. men waits for the mugger's arrival.

Mashers have been one of the most persistent problems for the decoys. "None of our men are exactly beauties," McCarthy admits, "and yet some park-bench Romeos are so insistent that we have to have them placed under arrest just to get them to let our decoys alone."

Aside from female impersonation, the experience most men gain in the Tactical Patrol Force — the average tour is four or five years — prepares them for a wide variety of police duties. Patrolman Thomas Doyle, for instance, has made more than three times as many arrests as the average patrolman assigned to regular precinct work. The department average annually is between 12 and 15; Doyle made 51 last year. This meant that Doyle had three or four times as much courtroom experience as the average patrolman, having taken his prisoners through more arraignments, hearings, adjournments and grand jury appearances. Thus Doyle and men like him gain practical knowledge quickly. The T.P.F. gives a man 20 years of expertise in five years, so that for 15 more years the department has the services of an invaluably experienced man. Too often men leave the department just when they have gained all of the skills and knowledge that would make them the best policemen.

Doyle, at 31, is older than the T.P.F. average, which is about 24, and a former Westchester County Parkway policeman who quit specifically to join the Tactical Patrol Force. He is married and the father of two daughters.

"I was with the Westchester Department for four years," he said, "but I came here because I wanted a real police job. It was my career and I wanted the activity. I wanted to work with men who I knew felt the same way about it as I did. Working with the T.P.F. is a tremendous challenge. I went to Manhattan College for two years, and then I went into the Marine Corps for three years." He is currently studying five hours a week at a civil service school and plans to take the examination for sergeant when it is given next year.

Fifty per cent of the T.P.F. members have either been to college or are attending college while on the police force. Only one out of six Police Academy recruits is chosen for the élite group, and a high proportion of those chosen are unmarried — most wives want their husbands at home most nights. By the time a young T.P.F. member gets married he is usually ready for a promotion into the Detective Division or to a higher rank; the hours then are not so consistently awkward.

"A man in uniform gets street-wise," Chief McCarthy said. "In very short order our young men, working in pairs with a veteran of two or three years, begin to get the feel of police work. They begin to know what to look for. They notice a man's gait. Is he in a hurry? What's around the corner? It there a liquor store or dry cleaning shop nearby? They learn to be suspicious. Is there unusual traffic in any one building? They begin to spot broken side vents on cars without really looking. They get a kind of peripheral vision that is difficult to explain and difficult to acquire if you're stationed in a quiet precinct. Some men, however, are really very keen, very observant. I can see who they are because their names keep coming up on my arrest sheets all the time."

When asked if some of his men are perhaps a little over-zealous in making disorderly conduct arrests — drunkenness, domestic quarrels, abusive language, etc. — McCarthy reacts sharply.

"To a citizen on the street who is a witness to a disorderly act, that act is as awful as a felony. By letting up on disorderly conduct arrests you slowly begin to find that there is a disregard for all laws. The thing T.P.F. men are taught to do is to keep their posts free of all visible violations at all times."

The selective enforcement of the law, McCarthy feels, creates many more dangers than its impartial and relentless enforcement. However, as one Tactical Patrol member put it, "Sometimes we've got to use a kind of soft-sell approach."

In the Puerto Rican section of the South Bronx, for example, two T.P.F. men walked along Melrose Avenue on a warm summer evening. Small groups of men, a few with cans of beer, chatted on the corners. Others were crowded on stoops. A few guitars and several radios could be heard. Bare-chested men washed their cars at the curb. There was a stickball game going on in the middle of the street, slowing traffic, and youngsters

rode bicycles on the sidewalk. It was, according to the two Tactical
Patrolmen, a classic visual-perception test. ("How many violations can
you see in the photograph — you have 10 seconds.")

"You have to make certain allowances," said the older patrolman,
"certainly in a neighborhood like this. You can't force your mores on the
people. So you let them wash their cars, play stickball. Sure it's forbidden,
but it is a crowded neighborhood."

"You learn quickly," the other patrolman added. "You learn the difference between a peaceful gathering on one corner and the three people
across the street who are quarreling. Quarreling means trouble in an over-
crowded neighborhood, and you have to move in quickly. One trick is
not to attract attention yourself. You walk up to the person or group you
suspect of trouble and ask them politely to walk with you. You talk to
them as quietly as you can as you walk along. It keeps the curious from
gathering."

Since its men are assigned to many different precincts to supplement
regular patrols, the T.P.F. tries to remain as unobtrusive as possible. The
officers find a basement corner or an unused locker room and set up a
portable two-way radio unit that connects them with the Tactical Patrolmen on the street. The problems that have plagued the precinct and
resulted in the Patrol's being assigned there have usually been taken into
account in the detailed daily plan laid out by Chief McCarthy, his captains
and lieutenants. Since the Tactical Patrolmen take orders from their own
command, contact with the precinct is largely limited to the recording of
arrests.

While their basic training is no different from that of other Police
Academy graduates, members of the T.P.F. get some extra moonlight
instruction. Once a month they meet with an officer who teaches them
drilling, crowd control and law. The lectures touch upon recent court
rulings, current criminal fads, such as forging drivers' licenses, and the
latest in department regulations. There is also rudimentary instruction in
sociology and anthropology — two areas no longer suspect among more
advanced police officials.

The T.P.F. men are told, for instance, that large numbers of Puerto
Rican citizens chatting loudly and playing dominoes on the stoop of a
tenement need not be a cause for alarm; that sidewalk speech-making
in Harlem has a tendency to be far more violent in rhetoric than in fact;
that hippies are much more likely to be the victims of a crime than the
perpetrators.

A lot of these instructions are very basic — almost primitive — but the
thrust, at least, is in the direction of uncomfortable knowledge rather than
happy ignorance. Some of the more practical lessons deal with crowd
control, something the T.P.F. does not consider a major part of its responsibility, but one which often concerns it because it is highly mobile.

Tactical Patrolmen are instructed in crowd psychology, handling spectator crowds and how crowds can turn hostile and aggressive.

"Our prime interest when dealing with crowds is to instill in every man the knowledge that he must wait for orders," says Chief McCarthy. "If somebody sees a guy lie down in front of a car, our men must wait. They must never take independent action.

"We look for men with some military experience. In fact, it is a major consideration. It is important because we work more like a highly mobile Army unit than like traditional policemen. Our lieutenants and sergeants are all young. They stay with the same 25-man platoons all the way through their tours so that they know the capabilities and weaknesses of every man in the unit. I cannot overemphasize the closeness of that supervision. If a man is considered a risk, we let him go. A risk, to us, is any man who acts on his own."

Sgt. James Motherway, a pipe-smoking veteran of 15 years in the Police Department and, until his transfer to the Detective Division this month, a T.P.F. instructor, was equally proud of the Tactical Patrol.

"We get the cream of the crop," he said. "They are not afraid of long hours and they have not been worn down by the dull routines that often grind the enthusiasm out of some guys. They don't have to watch school crossings, they don't go to quiet precincts where nothing happens for weeks, they're never stuck on fixed posts in front of embassies, they don't get traffic details, they're not burdened with giving out parking tickets or calling the desk sergeant of a precinct every hour to ask if anything is doing. Our men are on the street blanketing an active precinct with two-way radios strapped to their belts and with the knowledge that they are right there, on the line, in the middle of it, and that if anything more important comes along — a plane crash, a sudden visit from the President, a large demonstration or a disorderly mob — they're the ones who will go. That means so much."

"Wherever our men are working there is always a T.P.F. bus parked outside the precinct," says McCarthy. "On a signal, either by walkie-talkie or by sending a radio car speeding through an area with its dome light flashing and its siren silent, everyone is alerted to head for the bus. The men are given a certain amount of time to make the bus before it takes off, and anyone who misses it has some explaining to do the next day. We can repeat that call for men in every area where we are stationed on any night and bring together between 200 and 400 men at any large gathering — like a Beatles concert, an airplane crash or an unruly demonstration — without stripping the precincts involved of any of their own men.

"We're supplementary, remember, and we also know each other. When we get off those buses we know what has to be done, how it should be done and who is to do what. The sergeants know which men do what best, and the men know each other. It is a much tighter unit, a much more controlled group than could possibly be mustered by drawing men from all over the city to work with superiors they have never seen before."

It is because of the discipline and close supervision in the Tactical Patrol that men can be moved in great numbers anywhere in the city within minutes. The development of this discipline has been one of the unit's extraordinary achievements, and with a few exceptions the T.P.F. has won wide approval for its self-control in handling demonstrations. There was not one charge of brutality, for instance, after the Tactical Patrol Force went into Hamilton Hall during the Columbia University sit-ins this spring and cleared out almost 100 Negro students. A few days later the T.P.F. was sent into a university-owned tenement to clear it of students protesting the school's real-estate policies. Once more the building was cleared without incident and no brutality charges were filed. When Brooklyn College students staged a sympathy sit-in, the T.P.F. again cleared a building without incident.

"When our men are being trained," Sergeant Motherway said, "we explain that they are being put into a situation where they must be prepared to accept abuse. That they must be ready to let it roll off their backs."

The Tactical Patrolmen have been accused, however, of forgetting their training and reverting to primitive nightstick justice. On March 22, for example, when about 3,000 Yippies — members of the Youth International Party — celebrated a salute to spring by taking over Grand Central Station, the T.P.F. apparently lost its cool. A 22-page report from 40 witnesses prepared by the New York Civil Liberties Union, accused the Tactical Patrolmen of brutality and the repeated use of excessive force.

Nicholas Von Hoffman, a reporter for The Washington Post, said: "At first they were pretty nice about trying to clear the station, but then something happened to them and they began to use their clubs."

Walter Stovall, a wire-service reporter who covered the police action that night, recalled: "You could see that many of the policemen really despised the kids. They kept making comments among themselves about how all the kids looked so filthy and scruffy, but every time one of the good-looking girls would walk by everybody would just shut up and watch. Finally, when about 40 kids on top of the information booth began removing the clock hands, the T.P.F. just charged, and all that steaming they had been doing got released.

Roger Vaughn, a Life Magazine staff member, said: "No attempt at verbal communication was made that I could detect. The police simply formed a column of two and charged the information booth as though it was a pillbox containing a machine gun."

Neither the Police Department nor any member of the Tactical Patrol

will comment on the report or the incident; the matter is under study by
the Civilian Complaint Review Board, a departmental body noted for its
prolonged investigations. It is apparent, however, that Tactical Patrol
leaders regard incidents of this type as serious breakdowns of discipline.
Their attitude seems to be that control must be so strict that even groups
bent on provoking the police into rash action, groups whose whole purpose is provocation, cannot succeed.

The Yippie incident aside, much of the criticism directed at the T.P.F.
should be aimed at other police units. During several recent clashes with
groups of citizens, department investigations have concluded, the Tactical
Patrol has handled itself extraordinarily well. After the Columbia sit-in,
for instance, most of the charges leveled against the police for using
excessive force specified plainclothesmen and detectives. After an antiwar gathering in Washington Square Park in April it was also plainclothesmen, under the command of Chief Inspector Sanford Garelik, who were
accused of brutality.

Whatever its shortcomings, the T.P.F. remains the New York City
Police Department's most dependable unit for control of unruly demonstrations. It is considered a vital factor in the department's "area saturation" plan to suffocate incipient riots with masses of policemen. By
flooding a neighborhood with disciplined men, department planners feel
they can contain almost any situation. As part of the plan, the department
has drawn up detailed "riot maps" for more than 100 sections of the city;
the maps show topography, access and escape routes, possible police
mobilization points and all liquor stores, bars, clubs, sewer lines, Con Ed
tunnels and gun stores.

The maps are designed to supply all the necessary information, but
there is no formula for action in the event of riot. Tactical Patrolmen are
trained only to follow orders, and the orders are to be tailored to the
situation. However, Mayor Lindsay's edict on looters — "We will not
shoot youngsters in New York City" — is likely to keep guns holstered.
The T.P.F. has yet to be tested in a major crisis. During the Harlem and
Bedford-Stuyvesant riots in 1964, it had only half its present strength and
played a minor role.

The Tactical Patrol Force is "obviously the metropolitan police force
of the future," says Deputy Police Commissioner Jacques Nevard. He sees
the Patrol as the first in a series of steps that might get police departments
out of the "precinct hangup," and "out of the archaic system that may
have been efficient in 1875, but is cumbersome today."

"Today we must avail ourselves of modern management tools," Nevard
says. "We have 2,500 radio cars, 1,000 scooters, a fleet of radio-equipped
buses, walkie-talkies, high-speed teletype units. The T.P.F. has shown us
what communications and mobility can do, and still we're locked into

the concept of measuring distance by how far a man can walk or a voice can carry. The public still somehow equates protection with a police station rather than a policeman."

IRVING LOUIS HOROWITZ   *Reactionary Immortality: The Private Life in Public Testimony of John Edgar Hoover*

The books of quotations from Lyndon Baines Johnson (*Quotations From Chairman L.B.J.*) and Richard Milhous Nixon (*Poor Richard's Almanack*) were collections done by critics in jest and in jibe. As such, the essential integrity of these two men is left strangely intact. This contrasts markedly with the books of quotations from Chairman Mao Tse-tung and Director J. Edgar Hoover which are in the different category of self-celebration. They are collections of sacred sayings, selected by the author and demonstrating an unabashed thirst for immortality.

Hoover's *On Communism* is a hoary collection of homiletics, polemics, and recollections. It must be judged in terms of the traditionalist American suspicion of anything in the world alien, atheistic, and antagonistic to the American way. But rather than concentrate on some of the interesting theoretical points that could be extrapolated from Director Hoover's wisdom, it is perhaps more significant to examine the actual government documents under review that serve as the justification for the Director's ideologically transparent assumptions. For those who are deeply concerned with what Hoover himself considers to be his most important thought, *On Communism* will bring ample succor; but for those who are more concerned with the implications of his message, the testimonies provide solid evidence of the Director's reluctance or inability to come to terms with changes in the structure of American society, not to mention changes in the Soviet Union.

Obsolescence, intellectual as well as physical, is an affliction common to all organizations and to all men. The three volumes of F.B.I. budgetary requests before the House Appropriations Committee and the excerpts from five decades of Hoover's speeches and writings make it perfectly clear that "waiting for the end" is a malady that overtakes the Right as well as the Left. Through these "works" one sees an almost comic spectacle of the old Right exhausting itself in symbolic battle with the very old Left. The hero is clearly John Edgar Hoover, defender of the American faith; while his nemesis is Gus Hall, the tenacious head of the Communist Party in the United States and the incarnation of the Soviet faith. Hoover now depends on Hall for his very raison d'être; the two men are the Abbott and Costello of American political life.

In these volumes, Communism emerges as an eternal oneness, endowed with the omnipotence and powers generally reserved for evil deities. This allegorical approach to the world has been winning the Director's increasing approval as more intricate models for explaining it are concocted. Hoover tells us that, "Although the names of the Soviet intelligence services differ today from what they were 20 years ago when Joseph Stalin was Premier, the objective of world conquest by Communism has never wavered. The change over the years has been not a change in objective, but a steady intensification of the effort to reach that objective, the destruction of a capitalistic country." By the simple substitution of the word "socialistic" for "capitalistic" in the latter sentence, we have the perfect summary statement of the goals of the F.B.I. under Hoover's tutelage; he clearly thinks of capitalism as a moral movement rather than an economic system. But he is careful to rely on political allies, rather than his own agency, to execute such moral ambitions.

Communism is more than a malodorous vapor emitted by evil men to becloud the minds of good people. It settles and concentrates in geographical locales, surrounding the dwelling place of the good, from which it diabolically awaits opportunities to do them damage. Cuba is only 90 miles from Florida. The evil work of the Mexican Communists takes place in a "concentrated area . . . less than 150 miles from Laredo, Texas." Meetings of indigenous Leftists are not considered part of the internal politics of sovereign nations but rather a ring of evil enveloping the American nation.

Lenin considered imperialism to be the last and highest stage of capitalism. In the same peculiar way, Hoover see Communism as the last stage of moral deviance. Deviance comes from insidious exposure to Communism. We are told that (1) peaceful coexistence is not possible "with a country that every year has intensified its intelligence and espionage operations against this country"; and (2) "there are many gullible people who are against the policy in Vietnam as a result of the propaganda put out by some college professors who are naive and some students lacking in maturity and objectivity and who are constantly agitating and carrying on demonstrations in some of our largest universities." It does not occur to Hoover that the size and strength of the university may be related to the size and the strength of the student protest movement it harbors. Instead, he broadly hints that if only Communist speakers like the perennial Gus Hall and the inevitable Herbert Aptheker were prevented from keeping their lecture engagements on campuses, the innocence of American youth would be preserved.

This strange nature of moral deviationism is particularly well-illustrated in Hoover's nasty handling of Bayard Rustin. Rustin's links with the entire antiwar movement are said to arise from having been "convicted for sodomy" and for violation of the Selective Service Act before World War II. Or again, when he mentions that a Crime Prevention Commission has been set up in a California school, he also expresses regret that people like H. Rap Brown and Stokely Carmichael are allowed to speak to young students. The use of tax funds to support men whose positions he cannot accept is immoral. He speaks of these Negro leaders as "rabble-rousers," as men who live off, rather than in the "so-called" ghettos, where presumably their children can be bitten by "so-called" rats. (Hoover is clever enough, however, to relate the radical protest movement in America to the behavior of black militants, for it is true that militants, in contrast to most black special-interest groups, oppose American foreign policy.)

Together with his fellow septuagenarians Harry Anslinger in the Federal Bureau of Narcotics and Lewis Hershey, head of the Selective Service Commission, Hoover is obsessed by the young. He relates a fundamentalist suspicion of the corrupting effects of secular education to a fearful awareness of the political volatility of university life. Drugs, military service, and radicalism are all loosely associated among some of the younger generation. But it follows for Hoover that the universities have become enclaves of young radical opposition that must be broken.

At appropriation time, Hoover attempts to convince Congress that youth's "corruption" may be attributed to political subversion by offering a list of public appearances made by Communist Party leaders at various colleges throughout the United States. But Hoover's materials indicate that fewer than 70 appearances in all were made by Communist officials at American campuses during each of the three years reported in these hearings. This means that the collective position of the Communist Party is probably heard less often on American campuses than the views of, say, Arthur Schlesinger, Jr., William F. Buckley, or any other major figures on the lecture circuit. Yet the persistence with which he presents his

Communist speakers' chart makes it clear that Hoover considers it an important indicator of what is wrong with American higher education. He emphatically states that although "We all believe in academic freedom, this does not grant license to deliberately present distortions or falsehoods. Communists are not obligated morally or otherwise to seek for or to tell the truth. Some young people are capable of recognizing and exposing propaganda and propagandists. Others are not. This is the dangerous thing, particularly when it is recognized that the Communists in this country are conducting an energetic propaganda campaign to recruit young people to the Communist banner."

More recently, Hoover has extended his concern for education to the high school. Inviting black militants such as Brown and Carmichael to public schools is inexcusable: "They invite an individual of that kind to talk before a public high school composed of youth not at the age yet to properly evaluate what he has to say. He is enough of a rabble-rouser in the so-called ghettoes of the country where there are militant Negro elements that like to hear him expound but to have him spew his venom in the schoolrooms is wrong."

Evidently Mr. Hoover considers colleges and the high schools the institutional framework through which the Communist ideology makes its deepest penetration. What is particularly absurd is that Gus Hall himself reinforces Hoover's charge by indicating that his Communist Party is indeed involved with the leadership of campus radical struggles. And in each year of testimony Hoover cites Hall to this effect without ever once questioning the validity, not to mention the blind conceit, of such a claim. At no point does Hoover challenge the veracity of Hall who, as the leading Communist menace, presumably would not be above lying and deception. Quite the contrary. The implicit contract between them is that neither shall challenge the fantasies of the other. One can confidently expect that an examination of the collective essays of Gus Hall would bear this out in reverse.

What enables the F.B.I. to maintain its preeminent position as defender of American society? What are the ideological bases of its authority and prestige?

First, there is Hoover's legalism. In each of his pronouncements Hoover is careful to stay within the letter of the law. This emphasis on the legitimacy of the law has served to enhance rather than discredit his power. Nowhere in American literature may be found a clearer expression of the agonizing gap between an advocate of justice and a supporter of law. Hoover is a law-lover, there is no question about that. He always distinguishes the lines of responsibility between his offices and those of the Attorney General. However, and this too is a curious fact, these divisions of authority are drawn most sharply in matters of civil disorder involving Negro-white relations and least sharply in matters of civil rights involving political radicals. It would seem that demands for economic integration into the system are more acceptable to the F.B.I. than demands for racial separation by lower middle-class whites.

From the attempts of Attorney General William D. Mitchell in 1932 until the equally courageous efforts of Attorney General Ramsey Clark in 1968 to limit the scope of the Federal Bureau of Investigation, the philosophies of the Attorney General and the Director of the F.B.I. have been at considerable variance. The Attorney General is usually guided by the belief that federal jurisdiction should yield to local and state regulations whenever possible. Hoover has always taken the position that, with the important exception of crimes against the civil rights of Negroes, federal policing of crime is made necessary by the ineptitude, bravura, and limited expertise of local officials. Thus, the peculiar anomaly arises that the principle of states' rights — one of the sacred cows of conservative doctrine — has nowhere been more violated and breached than in extensions of the police power by conservative politicians who, following Hoover, are prepared to waive all constitutional objections in the name of efficiency.

The struggle between the Attorney General and the Bureau Director became openly ideological when Ramsey Clark and J. Edgar Hoover provided the first public testimonies before the special Presidential National Commission on the Causes and Prevention of Violence. In what is now a classic presentation of different positions toward the "law and order" issue, the Attorney General saw the problem as the absence of equity in the distribution of law, and warned against the substitution of order for justice in processing criminal cases. Hoover, needless to say, presented the problem as a breakdown of order in the nation, and the solution as the application of law without regard to the social causes of crime.

Underlying this extreme legalism is the question of Hoover's appropriations. As long as Congress continues to pass enabling legislation granting the F.B.I. jurisdiction in wide areas of national defense, kidnapping, extortion, robbery, et al., Hoover can demand and receive annual increases of funds for his agency, risking only the mildest quaver of protest. This extreme concern for formal law and lack of response to social expressions of discontent is one of the most characteristic features of Hoover's leadership of the Bureau. But it serves beautifully to make the actions of his Bureau appear above reproach.

The second point, one closely related to the issue of legality, might be called bureaucratic competence, or adherence to executive directives. The F.B.I. is an agency that disseminates large volumes of information on Communism and crime, but it is never presented as a policy-making agency. Hoover speaks of acting under "Presidential directives requiring the F.B.I. to ascertain facts pertinent to the loyalty and security risk of employees and applications for positions in the Government service or in activities incident to which the Government has an official interest." These enable the F.B.I. to justify its investigation of the private lives of all citizens who are in any way involved with the work of the Government. Since the directives are general in character, the manner in which they are interpreted becomes of central importance. Here too a significant distinction may be drawn between what is formally sanctioned and what is actually undertaken.

The same demand for bureaucratic competence underlies current calls for professionalization of police work. But Hoover, more clearly than other cops before and after him, understood the opportunities offered by the shift from elective to appointive power in government and the enlarged role of expertise in this shift. In his earlier work, A Study of Communism (1962), Hoover points out that there are many Communist activities "with which the average citizen cannot directly contend." But more: "nor would it be desirable for the average citizen to play a direct role in combating them." The struggle against Communism must be as professional an activity as "the science of espionage" necessitates. "To meet effectively the Communist subversive thrusts, it is essential to employ highly professional counterintelligence measures — measures for which the average citizen is neither equipped nor trained. Modern-day counterintelligence, with its emphasis on professional skills and training as well as its reliance on competent scientific aids, is a task for experts."

A third point, is that the F.B.I., like any agency, has special knowledge. But Hoover chooses to "classify" his special knowledge which puts him in a position to bludgeon any feeble opposition to his budgetary demands with the superior information at his disposal. The secrecy in which special knowledge is held enables the F.B.I. to claim that confidentiality is required for the effective operation of the department. Invariably at these hearings, questions arise concerning matters such as case loads per agent. Perhaps there are vague doubts about the need for an increase in the number of agents, but Hoover has the facts at his fingertips and the Congressmen docilely respond to his information edge. Having accepted the presumptions of the Bureau, they can do little to deny the agency more money. Thus it is that special knowledge serves both as a weapon of organizational supremacy and as an instrument of high-government finance.

A fourth F.B.I. ploy, and again one not often recognized by Congressmen, is the notion of its impartiality. The agency is presented as equally harsh toward all enemies of the nation. But its claims to equal treatment are in fact nonsense. Hundreds of pages are offered on the "Communist conspiracy," only passing references are made to right-wing organizations such as the Minutemen or the John Birch Society. Hoover's only real concern with the John Birch Society is that so many of his former agents openly work for it and indeed make their past affiliation with the F.B.I. a featured selling point. Even under rather obvious prompting to have the F.B.I. go on record with respect to Birch Society activities, Hoover can only work up enough steam to resent the Birchites' jeopardizing the organization's presumed "impartiality." "It is an improper attempt to capitalize on the name of the F.B.I."

But the agency's impartiality has been inadvertently discredited by Hoover himself in discussing where his *other* agents often wind up after leaving the Service. "Seventy per cent of our special agent personnel have been with us 10 years or longer. We do have a problem now and then, but I do not raise any obstacle to it, of large companies and corporations asking some very capable man in the Bureau to take a position in their organization, such as that of vice president. I lost one man years ago who became vice president of the Ford Motor Company. I lost a man just a few years ago who was agent in charge of my New York office and is now a vice president of American Airlines. There are nine Congressmen and one Senator who are former special agents of the Bureau." Just how service in the Bureau equips one for the vice presidency of Ford Motors or American Airlines is not explained — although one might surmise they are used in connection with plant sabotage, record tampering, and union pressures. Thus far at least, vice presidencies seem to be the upper limits of the F.B.I. as a quasi-official placement office.

On the matter of impartiality, too, civil rights and political rights are confused. Hoover has lately been referring to the work of the enemy with respect to the rights of Negroes in the South. The Ku Klux Klan is converted into a right-wing counterpart of the Communist Party. In point of fact its specific modes of operation and its quasi-military character distinguish it most sharply from the debating society that the American Communist Party now represents. This juxtaposition of Right and Left nonetheless provides precisely that aura of impartiality and equal treatment that permits the F.B.I. to claim a nonideological base. Critics of the Bureau have overlooked the fact that what distinguishes the F.B.I. from the Gestapo or the old G.P.U. is precisely the faith in "law" to accomplish the essential tasks of preserving state authority. And in this, in contrast to Himmler or Beria, Hoover is a giant.

These four points, then: legalism, bureaucratism, priestly wisdom, and political impartiality, coalesce to make possible the legitimacy of the F.B.I. in both war and peace. We must now turn finally to the world as it is perceived by J. Edgar Hoover and to what could be called the four fears that the man has as a public figure — for it is clear that for Hoover the world is a perpetually frightening place. This comes through time and

again in his discourses, or better, monologues, before the House Subcommittee on Appropriations.

First, there is his fear of not living up to the images of the F.B.I. as presented by the mass media. Although it is clear that Hoover sincerely
believes his own rhetoric, his notion of cleanliness and sound hygienic
practices is less the outcome of an internalized Protestant ethic than it is
a response to American hero-types generated by the mass media, particularly television. Hoover is so concerned with what he calls good character
and personal appearance that he would "rather have vacancies than employees who do not measure up to those qualifications. He refers to the
television program on the F.B.I. and the model inspector as portrayed by
Efrem Zimbalist, Jr. Young, well-groomed, cool under pressure, courteous
to all friends of America, the F.B.I. agent is strikingly liberated from inner
turmoil, doubt, confusion, or sophistication. Mirror, mirror on the wall,
how would I look, feel and act if I were younger? "Like Efrem Zimbalist,
Mr. Hoover," assures the captive mirror. For Hoover, self-image and
organizational image are one, and "I want our agents to live up to that
special image."

Related to this whole question of imagery and appearance is Hoover's
second bugaboo, namely, sexuality — homo or hetero. The theme haunts
the man in every report. Perhaps its most fascinating expression came in
the statement he issued in response to Congressmen Charles S. Joelson
and John J. Rooney's promptings on the "appearance" of Bureau agents.
"As regards appearance, Mr. Congressman, I certainly would not want
to have any beatniks with long sideburns and beards as employees in the
Bureau. . . . No member of the Mattachine Society or anyone else who is
a sex deviate will ever be appointed to the F.B.I. If I find one in the F.B.I.
he will be dismissed. As to appearance, our special agents in a broad sense
are really salesmen. They interview the presidents of large banks, the
chairmen of the boards of large corporations, longshoremen, and laborers.
They have to sell themselves to them to get their confidence to obtain the
information they need."

What is fascinating, even puzzling, is that it is apparently perfectly
permissible for agents to "sell themselves" in the line of duty but not to
"give themselves" in their private experiences. The dialogue is a sobering
indication that Hoover's traditionalist view of masculine behavior will,
when integrated with other agent standards, presumably provide a bulwark against sexual and criminal deviance generally. Again, the Hoover
hardline seems not so much linked to Protestant beliefs, but to the simple
police notion of the dangers in sexual "deviance."

The third great fear is oppressive Communism, or better still, the Communist Party. Strangely, Hoover displays no ideological awareness or
even concern with the structure of Communist Parties throughout the

world. And in the 1969 report he reveals only the barest recognition of the pluralization of radicalism in the United States. Hoover has a typical policeman's definition of a Communist, namely, a "dues-paying" member of the Communist Party. When asked if Herbert Aptheker was a Communist, Hoover quickly responded, and said, "Yes, and his daughter Bettina is just as much a Communist as he is" — a "dues-paying member," no doubt. Bettina Aptheker, Herbert Aptheker, Gus Hall, etc., the names keep recurring, indicating Hoover's need for a personal embodiment of the Communist evil rather than an analysis of the Party structure. It is not the political role of these poor people (or perhaps their lack of a real political role) but rather their mere existence as "card carriers" that seems so painful and yet so fascinating for Hoover. And since the rhetoric of people changes at a slower rate than the reality of organizational decay, Hoover as political analyst has proven a failure.

The final fear, and perhaps the most frightening, is that of criticism. Not that there's been much criticism in Congress. It is simply impossible for Hoover to accept the idea of being wrong, to acknowledge an improper understanding of an issue, or in any way to reveal a weakness in either his organization or his personal opinions. The testimony provided by Hoover stands as a veritable indictment of Congressional timidity and insipidity. At no point in three years has anyone offered anything but the most sycophantic response to Hoover's testimony. Hoover is always being congratulated, and in turn the leader drops pleasantries on the home towns of the Congressmen before whom he testifies. The city of Monrovia, California, is more frequently cited than any other city or town in America, simply because Congressman Glenard P. Lipscomb comes from Monrovia. This ludicrous conspiracy of mutual flattery serves to deflect criticism and transform the hearings into an annual celebration.

An old postelection gag has the President-elect in the year 2000 automatically reappointing John Edgar Hoover Director of the service, and turning his attention to more problematic choices. This black humor points up the totalitarian essence of the organization. For whether Hoover is in fact the real leader, or just a front man for other more dynamic figures, is less important than an encrusted situation in which he can no more be replaced or be "permitted" to retire than can Mao Tse-tung. Indeed, few doubt that an organizational "crisis" would occur in the F.B.I. were such a retirement to ensue by a means other than natural death. But what must also be realized is that the precipitating cause of such a crisis lies within an organizational situation in which one man alone has been permitted to embody the structure and sentiment of the entire force.

Hoover is one of America's few remaining "symbols" of the pristine age of primitive anti-Communism, a leftover from an age of simplicity, if not of purity. The death of Hoover would only mean the final passing of a policy based on coping with the Bolshevik Revolution as our chief internal menace. The file checks, wiretaps, security clearances would still remain. After all, they are part of the endemic features of a genteel totalitarianism. But without Hoover these interventions into the affairs of private souls would be deprived of their patriotic *telos* and be seen as crude impositions. President Nixon and his advisors also know this to be true. This is why the F.B.I.'s symbol without substance remains stubbornly entombed in his Washington office, while our political leadership hopes that nature disposes of what man seemingly cannot depose.

Criminal Law and Corrections

Criminal law is a principal instrument through which societies attempt to control the behavior of their members. It is a system through which rules of conduct, the sanctions for violations of these rules, and the processes for enforcing these rules are articulated. Criminal law embodies rules, enforcement procedures, and sanctions. The rules of the criminal law determine what legislature says the citizen can or cannot do, subject to a penalty. He cannot murder, rape, rob, possess or sell marijuana, and in some states, he may not fornicate. How do these rules come about? Basically, there have been two models concerning the nature of legislation. In one, all legislation is seen the "natural" embodiment of the collective conscience or social mores — that is, the state tends to mirror the society. This view is popularly attributed both to William Graham Sumner[1] and to Emile Durkheim.[2] Sumner held that many acts of legislation were shaped by mores, and that under such cir-

[1] On Sumner, see H. V. Simpson, and K. Ikeda, "Law and Social Change: Sumner Reconsidered," *American Journal of Sociology*, Vol. 67, 1962.

[2] Emile Durkheim, *Professional Ethics and Civic Morals* (Glencoe: Free Press, 1958).

cumstances the law represented "a crystallization of the mores combined with collective power to maintain the status quo." Positive law became possible when a society attained "the stage of verification, reflection, and criticism." Accordingly, prohibitions begin to replace taboos and punishments are planned for deterrence, rather than revenge. Nevertheless, Sumner was deeply concerned with the deficiencies of customary law. And he insisted that a distinction be maintained between "public morals" and "positive law." He wrote that: "The older abuse was to suppress public morals in the name of positive laws; the later abuse is to introduce public morals into positive law directly and immaturely." Sumner considered whether social control should be left to the mores, or effected by the criminal law. He thought several important considerations ought to influence this question. He wanted to know whether there was adequate knowledge at hand to formulate laws that would achieve desired ends but without undesired and unplanned consequences. He was also concerned with the flexibility of formal enactments as compared with the "elasticity and automatic self-regulation of custom." He also stressed the need for popular support for a particular proposal and for the government in general in order to preserve the legitimacy of enforcement. And, finally, he thought it important to consider whether enforcers have sufficient power to make the affected parties comply with the enactment.

A "natural embodiment" view of legislation is also sometimes attributed to Durkheim. Yet, Durkheim explicitly distinguished between the state and its legislation and collective consciousness or collective morality. He wrote:

> It is not accurate to say that the state embodies the collective consciousness, for that goes beyond the state at every point. In the main, that consciousness is diffused; there is at all times a vast number of social sentiments and social states of mind of all kinds, of which the state hears only a faint echo. The state is the center only of a particular kind of consciousness, one that is limited but higher, clearer and with a more vivid sense of itself. There is nothing so obscure and so indefinite as those collective representations that are

spread throughout all societies — midst religious or moral
legends and so on . . . the representations that derive from
the state . . . are distinguished from the other collective
representations by their higher degree of consciousness and
reflection.[3]

Durkheim's analysis suggests that legal norms are, if not
arbitrary, then certainly not determined solely by such notions as collective consciousness. For Durkheim the state
is an instrumentality that has the potential of making a rational analysis over and beyond the mythic and religiously
motivated manifestations of "intolerance, indignation, and
disgust,"[4] which some propose to include in the criminal
law.

Although Sumner and Durkheim were wary of the legislative enactment of community feelings about moral behavior, legislatures have, in fact, frequently used the criminal
law to "solve" what they perceived to be social problems.
In the first paper of this section, Sanford H. Kadish, a
law professor who served as a general consultant for the
President's Commission on Law Enforcement and Administration of Justice, writes that there has been an excessive
reliance on the criminal law to enforce morals, to provide
social services, and to avoid legal restraints on law enforcement. He feels that this reliance has created acute problems for the administration of criminal justice, partly
because it results in inefficiency, partly because it has induced offensive and degrading police conduct — particularly against the poor and the disadvantaged — and partly
because it has generated cynicism about, and indifference
to, the criminal law. Without the legal enforcement of
morals it would be difficult to have organized crime in its
present forms, and it is quite possible that the attempt to
suppress gambling, drinking, prostitution, and narcotics,
has produced more crime than it has suppressed. Certainly, these measures divert the resources of law enforcement from protecting the public against serious crime.
The most recent figures (1969) project 50,000 arrests in

[3] *Ibid.*, p. 50.
[4] See Patrick Devlin, *The Enforcement of Morals* (London and New
York: Oxford University Press, 1965).

the state of California on marijuana charges alone. The estimated court time alone will cost 75 million dollars, to say nothing of the cost of police and other law enforcement personnel. This investment will take place when there is a great cry for doing something about "crime in the streets." Thus, the legal enforcement of morals is expensive, often irrational, and can lead to consequences never intended by those who are propounding these laws.

Those who advocate the enforcement of morals are often "do-gooders" who see in the imposition of sanctions a means for dealing with what they perceive to be terrible social wrongs. From their own point of view, they are useful and engaged citizens, interested in progress and reform. In the second article in the chapter, Anthony Platt deals with the rise of the "child-saving movement," leading to the establishment of the juvenile court. This movement was heavily influenced by middle class women who extended their housewifely roles into public service and who emphasized the strong public need for properly socializing children. These enterprising women, at the end of the nineteenth century, helped to create special judicial and correctional institutions, for the labeling, processing, and management of "troublesome" youth. Initially, child-saving was intended to segregate youthful offenders from their more hardened elders and, in this fashion, protect the young both from older criminals and from the stigma of a criminal record. In doing so, however, the movement brought attention to and invented new categories of youthful misbehavior, which were labeled quite broadly, and brought many youngsters into contact with law enforcement officials who would otherwise not have been involved. Statutory definitions of "delinquency" not only encompassed acts that would be criminal if they had been committed by adults but also all sorts of vaguely defined new "crimes," such as "vicious or immoral behavior," "incorrigibility," and "truancy," all of which subjected the young — especially those in minority groups — to a more stringent standard of conduct than adults. These sorts of definitions lately have come to be criticized by civil liberties reformers.

In addition to creating new crimes, the youthful offender movement also deprived the children of due process of law in the name of such (then) liberal notions as "treating the criminal rather than the crime." (This idea too, has been attacked recently by lawyers and criminologists.) The children were to be treated by a reformatory system that the child-savers hoped would show that delinquents were capable of being transformed into upright, law abiding citizens. Since treatment and "organized persuasion" rather than "coercive restraint" were employed at reformatories, the institution was distinguished by its policy of indeterminate sentencing. Of course, conditions at the reformatories frequently deteriorated into overcrowding, understaffing, and inadequate facilities and they were distinguished from prisons perhaps more by rhetoric than by fact.

The difference between rhetoric and reality, however, is not limited to institutions for "troublesome" youth. It is a more general problem of the whole "correctional" establishment. Robert Martinson explains that the reform movement in American prisons attempted to mitigate the worst conditions within the prisons and introduce into them "such categories as the Chaplain, the Teacher, the Psychologist, the Vocational Instructor, and presently the Caseworker and Psychiatrist." He portrays the historical development of prisons as a move from an age of humanitarian reform to an age of treatment. It is no longer enough, says Martinson, merely to provide the prisoner with more livable and more comfortable conditions. It is not enough for the prisoner to reform himself. We now feel that "people changing" has become "a skill, a profession, indeed a moral injunction." This new morality, although painted with a veneer of professionalism — which makes it even more difficult to criticize than the simplistic homilies of puritanical legislators and their supporters — is to Martinson even more dangerous, in some respects, than the older moralities. The aims of this new morality are no more successful in accomplishing its purposes; the "deviant" will learn from the process of being "treated" not so much that what he has done is wrong, but rather that an identity outside the conventional culture is more appropriate to him.

Both the old morality and the new morality are demonstrably failures. Martinson describes treatment as "a redoubling of efforts in the face of persistent failure." The increasing penalties for the use of narcotics and marijuana have been associated over the years with an increasing incidence of use. In a rational world, we might assume that evidence would persuade and that expensive and time-consuming failures would be discarded. So, perhaps we must concentrate public attention toward the institutions that seek to control "deviance" and "crime," and attempt to understand how and why they come to organize themselves for failure, and how and why they continue to receive public support in the face of failure. Our social policies toward "crime" — which offer bonanzas to organized crime, create police hostility toward civil liberties, the young, and minority groups, corrupt police, divert their attention from violent and dangerous acts, criminalize the young, and create deviant identities in the guise of "correction" — are probably our most serious "social problems" in justice and correction.

SANFORD H. KADISH   *The Crisis*
                              of Overcriminalization

Since the last war there have been striking achievements in reform of the substantive criminal law. Largely under the impetus of the American Law Institute's Model Penal Code, a number of states have completed

From *The Annals*, November 1967, pp. 157–170. Reprinted by permission of the author and the American Academy of Political and Social Science.

revisions of their criminal codes, and still more are in the process. The importance of this reform for criminal justice cannot be overstated.

But there is a significant feature of substantive law-revision which these reforms have succeeded in reaching only in part. By and large, these efforts have dealt with offenses entailing substantial harm to persons, property, and the state, against which the criminal law is generally accepted as the last and necessary resort. But American criminal law typically has extended the criminal sanction well beyond these fundamental offenses to include very different kinds of behavior, kinds which threaten far less serious harms, or else highly intangible ones about which there is no genuine consensus, or even no harms at all. The existence of these crimes and attempts at their eradication raise problems of inestimable importance for the criminal law. Indeed, it is fair to say that until these problems of overcriminalization are systematically examined and effectively dealt with, some of the most besetting problems of criminal-law administration are bound to continue.

Chapter VIII of *Task Force Report: The Courts,* of the President's Commission on Law Enforcement and Administration of Justice, is an attempt to deal with some of these problems.[1] The Executive Director has chosen to reveal my own hand in its preparation,[2] and I could hardly come now either to praise it or to bury it. Still, it may be said that the controversial character of these issues, and the need to achieve consensus among nineteen Commissioners of highly differing backgrounds and orientation, quite understandably required some reduction in scope and muting in tone and conclusion of my original draft. I note this not in complaint. Indeed, that these distinguished citizens, who, as a group, can scarcely be charged with being immoderate or visionary, were prepared to raise substantial reservations concerning the overextension of the criminal law is itself an event of significance. Still, this special issue of *The Annals* provides an opportunity to present, free of the restraints of the need for consensus, a number of observations and conclusions which appeared to me compelling in thinking about these matters for the Commission. I do this not to disown Chapter VIII, but to add to it. Indeed, I have not hesitated to make use of its substance, and occasionally its phrasing, where desirable, in the interest of making this statement self-contained. In short, whereas Chapter VIII is a version of my original draft, this article is my own version of Chapter VIII, though compressed as far as possible in keeping with the admirable Annals policy of brevity.

[1] U.S. President's Commission on Law Enforcement and Administration of Justice, *Task Force Report: The Courts* 97–107 (1967). This commission will be referred to herein as the National Crime Commission.

[2] *Idem* at 2.

The subjects raising the central issue of overcriminalization cut a wide swathe through the laws of most jurisdictions. In the process of revising the California criminal law, we encountered a mass of crimes outside the Penal Code, matching the Penal Code itself in volume, and authorizing criminal convictions for such offenses as failure by a school principal to use required textbooks,[3] failure of a teacher to carry first-aid kits on field trips,[4] gambling on the result of an election,[5] giving private commercial performances by a state-supported band,[6] and allowing waste of an artesian well by the landowner.[7] Then there are the criminal laws, enforced by state police forces, which have been the primary means used to deal with the death and injury toll of the automobile. Indications are that this response may ultimately do more harm than good by blocking off politically harder, but more likely, remedial alternatives.[8] Problematic also has been the use of criminal sanctions to enforce economic regulatory measures, a matter which I have deal with elsewhere.[9] And there are other instances as well. In this piece I want to comment on the problems of overcriminalization in just three kinds of situations, in each of which the costs paid primarily affect the day-to-day business of law enforcement. These are the situations in which the criminal law is used: (1) to declare or enforce public standards of private morality, (2) as a means of providing social services in default of other public agencies, and (3) as a disingenuous means of permitting police to do indirectly what the law forbids them to do directly.

ENFORCEMENT OF MORALS

The use of the criminal law to prohibit moral deviancy among consenting adults has been a recurring subject of jurisprudential debate. Stephens in the last century[10] and Lord Devlin in this century have urged the legitimacy of criminal intervention on the ground that "society cannot ignore the morality of the individual any more than it can his loyalty; it flourishes on both and without either it dies."[11] The contrary view, vigorously espoused by John Stuart Mill in the nineteenth century,[12] and

---

[3] Calif. Education Code §9255.
[4] *Idem* at §11955.
[5] Calif. Elections Code §29003.
[6] Calif. Government Code §6650.
[7] Calif. Water Code §307.
[8] See the telling account of Moynihan, "The War Against the Automobile," *The Public Interest*, No. 3 (Spring 1966), especially at 21 *et seq.*
[9] Kadish, "Some Observations on the Use of Criminal Sanctions in Enforcing Economic Regulations," 30 *U. Chi. L. Rev.* 423 (1963).
[10] J. F. Stephens, *Liberty, Fraternity and Equality* (1873).
[11] Devlin, *The Enforcement of Morals* 23 (1959).
[12] J. S. Mill, *On Liberty* (1859).

by H. L. A. Hart[13] and many others in recent years, is, in the words of
the Wolfenden Report:

> Unless a deliberate attempt is to be made by society, acting through
> the agency of the law, to equate the sphere of crime with that of
> sin, there must remain a realm of private morality and immorality
> which is in brief and crude terms, not the law's business.[14]

It is not my purpose here to mediate or resolve that dispute. My objective
is to call attention to matters of the hardest concreteness and practicality,
which should be of as much concern in reaching final judgment to a Devlin
as to the staunchest libertarian; namely, the adverse consequences to
effective law enforcement of attempting to achieve conformity with
private moral standards through use of the criminal law.

Sex Offenses. The classic instance of the use of the criminal law purely
to enforce a moral code is the laws prohibiting extramarital and abnormal
sexual intercourse between a man and a woman. Whether or not Kinsey's
judgment is accurate that 95 per cent of the population are made potential
criminals by these laws,[15] no one doubts that their standard of sexual
conduct is not adhered to by vast numbers in the community, including
the otherwise most respectable (and, most especially, the police themselves);[16] nor is it disputed that there is no effort to enforce these laws.
The traditional function of the criminal law, therefore — to curtail socially
threatening behavior through the threat of punishment and the incapaci-
tation and rehabilitation of offenders — is quite beside the point. Thurman Arnold surely had it right when he observed that these laws "are
unenforced because we want to continue our conduct, and unrepealed
because we want to preserve our morals."[17]

But law enforcement pays a price for using the criminal law in this way.
First, the moral message communicated by the law is contradicted by the
total absence of enforcement; for while the public sees the conduct condemned in words, it also sees in the dramatic absence of prosecutions that
it is not condemned in deed. Moral adjurations vulnerable to a charge
of hypocrisy are self-defeating no less in law than elsewhere. Second, the
spectacle of nullification of the legislature's solemn commands is an un-
healthy influence on law enforcement generally. It tends to breed a
cynicism and an indifference to the criminal-law processes which augment
tendencies toward disrespect for those who make and enforce the law, a
disrespect which is already widely in evidence. In addition:

[13] H. L. A. Hart, *Law, Liberty and Morality* (1963).
[14] Great Britain Committee on Homosexual Offenses and Prostitution, *Report,
Command No. 247* (1957) (Wolfenden Report), Paras. 61 and 62.
[15] Kinsey, Pomeroy, and Martin, *Sexual Behavior in the Human Male* 392 (1948).
[16] See Skolnick, *Justice without Trial* (1966), chap. iii.
[17] Thurman Arnold, *Symbols of Government 160* (1936).

> Dead letter laws, far from promoting a sense of security, which is
> the main function of the penal law, actually impair that security by
> holding the threat of prosecution over the heads of people whom we
> have no intention to punish.[18]

Finally, these laws invite discriminatory enforcement against persons
selected for prosecution on grounds unrelated to the evil against which
these laws are purportedly addressed, whether those grounds be "the
prodding of some reform group, a newspaper-generated hysteria over
some local sex crime, a vice drive which is put on by the local authorities
to distract attention from defects in their administration of the city government."[19]

The criminalization of consensual adult homosexuality represents another attempt to legislate private morality. It raises somewhat different
problems from heterosexual offenses, in that there are some attempts at
enforcement. The central questions are whether the criminal law is an
effective way of discouraging this conduct and how wasteful or costly
it is.

Despite the fact that homosexual practices are condemned as criminal in
virtually all states, usually as a felony with substantial punishment, and
despite sporadic efforts at enforcement in certain situations, there is little
evidence that the criminal law has discouraged the practice to any substantial degree. The Kinsey Report as well as other studies suggest a wide
incidence of homosexuality throughout the country. One major reason
for the ineffectiveness of these laws is that the private and consensual
nature of the conduct precludes the attainment of any substantial deterrent efficacy through law enforcement. There are no complainants, and
only the indiscreet have reasons for fear. Another reason is the irrelevance
of the threat of punishment. Homosexuality involves not so much a choice
to act wickedly as the seeking of normal sexual fulfillment in abnormal
ways (though not abnormal to the individual) preferred by the individual
for reasons deeply rooted in his development as a personality. Moreover,
in view of the character of prison environments, putting the homosexual
defendant into the prison system is, as observed recently by a United
States District Court Judge, "a little like throwing Bre'r Rabbit into the
briarpatch."[20]

On the other hand, the use of the criminal law has been attended by
grave consequences. A commonly noted consequence is the enhanced
opportunities created for extortionary threats of exposure and prosecution.
Certainly, incidents of this kind have been reported often enough to raise

[18] Model Penal Code §207.11, comments at 111 (Tent. Draft No. 9, 1959).
[19] Kinsey, Martin, and Gebhard, *Sexual Behavior in the Human Female* 392 (1953).
[20] Chief Judge Craven in *Perkins v. North Carolina,* 234 F. Supp. 333, 339 (W.D.
N.C. 1964).

genuine concern.[21] But, of more significance for the administration of justice, enforcement efforts by police have created problems both for them and for the community. Opportunities for enforcement are limited by the private and consensual character of the behavior. Only a small and insignificant manifestation of homosexuality is amenable to enforcement. This is that which takes place, either in the solicitation or the act, in public places. Even in these circumstances, it is not usual for persons to act openly. To obtain evidence, police are obliged to resort to behavior which tends to degrade and demean both themselves personally and law enforcement as an institution.[22] However one may deplore homosexual conduct, no one can lightly accept a criminal law which requires for its enforcement that officers of the law sit concealed in ceilings, their eyes fixed to "peepholes," searching for criminal sexuality in the lavatories below;[23] or that they loiter suggestively around public toilets or in corridors hopefully awaiting a sexual advance.[24] Such conduct corrupts both citizenry and police and reduces the moral authority of the criminal law, especially among those portions of the citizenry — the poor and subcultural — who are particularly liable to be treated in an arbitrary fashion. The complaint of the critical that the police have more important things to do with their time is amply attested by the several volumes of the National Crime Commission's reports.

The offense of prostitution creates similar problems. Although there are social harms beyond private immorality in commercialized sex — spread of venereal disease, exploitation of the young, and the affront of public solicitation, for example — the blunt use of the criminal prohibition has proven ineffective and costly. Prostitution has perdured in all civiliza-

[21] As recently as August 1966 a nationwide extortion ring was uncovered which used blackmail of homosexuals to extort millions of dollars from thousands of victims, many of whom were prominent personalities in entertainment, business, education, and government. *Time,* August 26, 1966, p. 14.

[22] See Project, "The Consenting Adult Homosexual and the Law: An Empirical Study of Enforcement in Los Angeles County, 13 *U.C.L.A. Law Rev.* 643 (1966).

[23] See *Bielicki v. Superior Court,* 57 Cal.2d 600, 371 P.2d 288 (1962); *Britt v. Superior Court,* 58 Cal.2d 469, 374 P.2d 817 (1962); *Smayda v. United States,* 352 F.2d 251 (9th Cir. 1965).

[24] See Project, *supra,* note 22, at 690–691: "The decoy method is utilized by undercover officers who 'operate' by intentionally providing homosexuals with the opportunity to make a proscribed solicitation. . . . The decoy's modus operandi at a public restroom may be to loiter inside engaging a suspect in friendly conversation, using handwashing or urinal facilities, or even occupying a commode for long periods of time. If the suspect makes a lewd solicitation or touching, the decoy will usually suggest going elsewhere to consummate the act and the arrest will be made outside of the restroom. When a street area is a known rendezvous location for homosexuals and male prostitutes, the decoy will operate by loitering on the street or by using a car to approach the suspect. In bars frequented by homosexuals, the decoy will order a drink and engage in friendly conversation with a suspect. Enforcement in bathhouses may necessitate operation by nude and semi-nude decoys."

tions; indeed, few institutions have proven as hardy. The inevitable conditions of social life unfailingly produce the supply to meet the ever-present demand. As the Wolfenden Report observed: "There are limits to the degree of discouragement which the criminal law can properly exercise towards a woman who has deliberately decided to live her life in this way, or a man who has deliberately chosen to use her services."[25] The more so, one may add, in a country where it has been estimated that over two-thirds of white males alone will have experience with prostitutes during their lives.[26] The costs, on the other hand, of making the effort are similar to those entailed in enforcing the homosexual laws — diversion of police resources; encouragement of use of illegal means of police control (which, in the case of prostitution, take the form of knowingly unlawful harassment arrests to remove suspected prostitutes from the streets;[27] and various entrapment devices, usually the only means of obtaining convictions);[28] degradation of the image of law enforcement; discriminatory enforcement against the poor; and official corruption.

To the extent that spread of venereal disease, corruption of the young, and public affront are the objects of prostitution controls, it would require little ingenuity to devise modes of social control of the blanket criminalization of prostitution which would at the same time prove more effective and less costly for law enforcement. Apparently, the driving force behind prostitution laws is principally the conviction that prostitution is immoral. Only the judgment that the use of the criminal law for verbal vindication of our morals is more important than its use to protect life and property can support the preservation of these laws as they are.

Abortion. The criminal prohibition of abortions is occasionally defended on the ground that it is necessary to protect the mother against the adverse physical and psychological effects of such operations. There seems little doubt, however, that these laws serve to augment rather than to reduce the danger. The criminal penalty has given rise to a black market of illegal abortionists who stand ready to run the risk of imprisonment in order to earn the high fees produced by the law's discouragement of legitimate physicians. As a consequence, abortions are performed in kitchens and private rooms instead of in properly equipped hospitals, and often by unqualified amateurs rather than by licensed physicians. A relatively simple and nondangerous operation on patients strongly desirous of avoiding parenthood is therefore converted into a surreptitious, degrading, and traumatic experience in which the risk to the mental and

[25] *Supra,* note 14 at 247.
[26] Kinsey, *supra,* note 15 at 597.
[27] La Fave, *Arrest: The Decision to Take a Suspect into Custody* 450 (1965).
[28] Skolnick, *supra,* note 16 at 100.

physical well-being of the woman is many times increased. Indeed, the evidence is irresistible that thousands of lives are needlessly lost yearly at the hands of illegal abortionists.[29]

It is plain, therefore, that the primary force behind retention of the abortion laws is belief that it is immoral. One of the serious moral objections is based on the view that the unborn foetus, even in its early stages of development, has an independent claim to life equivalent to that of a developed human being. Even those holding this judgment, however, can scarcely ignore the hard fact that abortion laws do not work to stop abortion, except for those too poor and ignorant to avail themselves of blackmarket alternatives, and that the consequence of their retention is probably to sacrifice more lives of mothers than the total number of foetuses saved by the abortion laws.

While there are no reliable figures on the number of illegal abortions, estimates have ranged from a hundred thousand to a million and a half yearly.[30] Among the factors responsible for this widespread nullification, two appear to predominate. The first is that there is no general consensus on the legitimacy of the moral claim on behalf of the foetus. While it is vigorously asserted by some portions of the community, it is as vigorously denied by others of equal honesty and respectability. In democratic societies, fortunately, the coercive sanctions of the criminal law prove unacceptable and unworkable as a means of settling clashes of sharply divided moralities. Second, the demand for abortions, by both married and unmarried women, is urgent and widespread, arising out of natural and understandable motives manifesting no threat to other persons or property. As with most morals offenses, therefore, sympathy for the offender combines with an unsettled moral climate to preclude any real possibility of enforcement.

Gambling and Narcotics. Laws against gambling and narcotics present serious problems for law enforcement. Despite arrests, prosecutions and convictions, and increasingly severe penalties, the conduct seems only to flourish. The irrepressible demand for gambling and drugs, like the demand for alcohol during Prohibition days, survives the condemnation of the criminal law. Whether or not the criminal restriction operates paradoxically, as some have thought, to make the conduct more attractive, it is clear that the prohibitions have not substantially eliminated the demand.

[29] See the sobering testimony of the Assistant Chief of the Division of Preventive Medical Services of the State Department of Public Health, before the California Assembly Interim Committee on Criminal Procedure, July 20, 1964, quoted in *Task Force Report: The Courts, supra,* note 1 at 5.

[30] See the sources in Model Penal Code, §207.11, Comments at 147 (Tent. Draft No. 9, 1959).

Nor have the laws and enforcement efforts suppressed sources of supply. No one with an urge to gamble in any fair-sized city of this country has far to go to place an illegal bet. And in the case of narcotics, illicit suppliers enter the market to seek the profits made available by the persistence of the demand and the criminal law's reduction of legitimate sources of supply, while "pusher"-addicts distribute narcotics as a means of fulfilling their own needs. Risk of conviction, even of long terms of imprisonment, appears to have little effect. Partly, this is because the immediate and compelling need of the "pusher"-addict for narcotics precludes any real attention to the distant prospect of conviction and imprisonment. For large-scale suppliers, who may not be addicts, the very process of criminalization and punishment serves to raise the stakes — while the risk becomes greater, so do the prospects of rewards.[31] In addition, experience has demonstrated that convictions are difficult to obtain against large, nonaddict, organized dealers.

Our indiscriminate policy of using the criminal law against selling what people insist on buying has spawned large-scale, organized systems, often of national scope, comprising an integration of the stages of production and distribution of the illicit product on a continuous and thoroughly business-like basis. Not only are these organizations especially difficult for law enforcement to deal with; they have the unpleasant quality of producing other crimes as well because, after the fashion of legitimate business, they tend to extend and diversify their operations. After repeal of Prohibition, racketeering organizations moved into the illegal drug market. Organizations which purvey drugs and supply gambling find it profitable to move into loan-sharking and labor racketeering. To enhance their effectiveness, these organized systems engage in satellite forms of crime, of which bribery and corruption of local government are the most far-reaching in their consequences.[32] Hence the irony that, in some measure, crime is encouraged and successful modes of criminality are produced by the criminal law itself.

Another significant cost of our policy is that the intractable difficulties of enforcement, produced by the consensual character of the illegal conduct and the typically organized methods of operation, have driven enforcement agencies to excesses in pursuit of evidence. These are not only undesirable in themselves, but have evoked a counterreaction in the courts in the form of restrictions upon the use of evidence designed to discourage these police practices. One need look no farther than the decisions of the United States Supreme Court. The two leading decisions

[31] Packer, "The Crime Tariff," 33 *American Scholar* 551 (1964).
[32] For a detailed description, see U.S. President's Commission on Law Enforcement and Administration of Justice, *Task Force Report: Organized Crime* (1967).

on entrapment were produced by overreaching undercover agents in gambling[33] and narcotics prosecutions,[34] respectively. Decisions involving the admissibility of evidence arising out of illegal arrests have, for the most part, been rendered in gambling, alcohol, and narcotics prosecutions.[35] Legal restraints upon unlawful search and seizure have largely grown out of litigation over the last five decades concerning a variety of forms of physical intrusion by police in the course of obtaining evidence of violations of these same laws.[36] The same is true with respect to the developing law of wire-tapping, bugging, and other forms of electronic interception.[37] Indeed, no single phenomenon is more responsible for the whole pattern of judicial restraints upon methods of law enforcement than the unfortunate experience with enforcing these laws against vice.

There is, finally, a cost of inestimable importance, one which tends to be a product of virtually all the misuses of the criminal law discussed in this paper. That is the substantial diversion of police, prosecutorial and judicial time, personnel, and resources. At a time when the volume of crime is steadily increasing, the burden on law-enforcement agencies is becoming more and more onerous, and massive efforts are being considered to deal more effectively with threats to the public of dangerous and threatening conduct, releasing enforcement resources from the obligation to enforce the vice laws must be taken seriously. Indeed, in view of the minimal effectiveness of enforcement measures in dealing with vice crimes and the tangible costs and disadvantages of that effort, the case for this rediversion of resources to more profitable purposes becomes commanding. It seems fair to say that in few areas of the criminal law have we paid so much for so little.

One might, even so, quite reasonably take the position that gambling and narcotics are formidable social evils and that it would be dogmatic to insist that the criminal law should in no circumstances be used as one

---

[33] *Sorrels v. U.S.*, 287 U.S. 435 (1932).

[34] *Sherman v. U.S.*, 356 U.S. 370 (1958).

[35] E.g., *Johnson v. U.S.* 333 U.S. 10 (1948) (narcotics); *Draper v. U.S.* 358 U.S. 307 (1959) (narcotics); *Beck v. Ohio*, 379 U.S. 89 (1964) (gambling).

[36] E.g., *Carrol v. U.S.*, 267 U.S. 132 (1925) (prohibition); *Agnello v. U.S.*, 269 U.S. 20 (1925) (narcotics); *Marron v. U.S.*, 275 U.S. 192 (1927) (prohibition); *Go-Bart Co. v. U.S.*, 282 U.S. 344 (1931) (narcotics); *Lefkowitz v. U.S.*, 285 U.S. 452 (1932) (prohibition); *Johnson v. U.S.*, 333 U.S. 10 (1948) (narcotics); *Rochin v. California*, 342 U.S. 165 (1952) (narcotics); *Jones v. U.S.*, 362 U.S. 267 (1960) (narcotics); *Wong Sun v. U.S.*, 371 U.S. 471 (1963) (narcotics); *Ker v. California*, 374 U.S. 23 (1963) (narcotics).

[37] E.g., *Olmstead v. U.S.*, 277 U.S. 438 (1928) (prohibition); *Nardone v. U.S.*, 302 U.S. 379 (1938), 308 U.S. 338 (1939) (smuggled alcohol); *On Lee v. U.S.*, 343 U.S. 747 (1952) (narcotics); *Irvine v. California*, 347 U.S. 128 (1954) (gambling); *Benanti v. U.S.* 355 U.S. 96 (1957) (illicit alcohol); *Silverman v. U.S.*, 365 U.S. 505 (1961) (gambling).

way, among others, of dealing with them. The exploitation of the weakness of vulnerable people, in the case of gambling, often results in economic loss and personal dislocations of substantial proportions. And the
major physical and emotional hardships imposed by narcotics addiction
raise even more serious evils. Still, such a view would scarcely excuse
perpetuating the pattern of indiscriminate criminalization. There are
obvious ways at least to mitigate the problems described; for example, by
narrowing the scope of criminality. In the case of gambling, there is an
overwhelming case for abandoning the traditional approach of sweeping
all forms of gambling within the scope of the prohibition, while relying
on the discretion of police and charitable and religious fund-raising
enterprises.[38] At least, the evil of delegating discretion in such magnitude
as to abandon law can be remedied by a more careful legislative definition
of precisely the form of gambling conduct which the legislature means to
bring within the criminal sanction. In the case of narcotics, our legislatures have tended indiscriminately to treat all narcotics as creative of the
same dangers despite the strong evidence that some drugs, particularly
marijuana, present evils of such limited character that elimination of the
criminal prohibition is plainly indicated.[39] In short, there is much of value
that could be done even if the whole dose of repeal were too much to
swallow.

PROVISION OF SOCIAL SERVICES

In a number of instances which, taken together, consume a significant
portion of law-enforcement resources, the criminal law is used neither to
protect against serious misbehavior through the medium of crime and
punishment nor to confirm standards of private morality, but rather to
provide social services to needy segments of the community. The drunk,
the deserted mother, and the creditor have been the chief beneficiaries.
In each instance, the gains have been dubious in view of the toll exacted
on effective law enforcement.

The Drunk. Using the criminal law to protect against offensive public
behavior, whether by drunken or sober persons, is not the issue here. The
trouble arises out of the use of laws against public drunkenness to deal

[38] The Model Anti-Gambling Act deliberately overgeneralizes the prohibition in this
way even though recognizing "that it is unrealistic to promulgate a law literally aimed
at making a criminal offense of the friendly election bet, the private, social card game
among friends, etc.," on the ground that "it is imperative to confront the professional
gambler with a statutory façade that is wholly devoid of loopholes." 2 ABA Comm'n
on Organized Crime, *Organized Crime and Law Enforcement* 74–78 (1953).
[39] See the review of the evidence in the papers of Messrs. Blum and Rosenthal in
U.S. President's Commission on Law Enforcement and Administration of Justice, *Task
Force Report: Narcotics and Drug Abuse* (1967), especially at pp. 24–26, 126–131.

with the inert, stuporous drunk in the public streets and alleyways, who constitutes a danger to himself and an ugly inconvenience to others. Staggering numbers of these drunks are fed daily into the criminal machinery. Indeed, more arrests are made for this offense than for any other — 35 to 40 per cent of all reported arrests. Not only does the use of the criminal law, therefore, divert substantial law-enforcement resources away from genuinely threatening conduct, but the whole criminal-justice system is denigrated by the need to process massive numbers of pathetic and impoverished people through clumsy and inappropriate procedures. Hearings and trials degenerate into a mockery of the forms of due process, with mass appearances, guilt assumed, and defendants unrepresented. Even if the social and personal problems of drunkenness were, in some measure, helped by this effort, these costs would make the investment doubtful. In fact, however, apart from a very temporary cleaning of the streets by the police, the effort is notoriously unsuccessful. Poverty, rootlessness, and personal inadequacy, which are at the bottom of alcoholism, are scarcely deterrable by the threat of criminal conviction. And rehabilitation in the human warehouses of our city jails is unthinkable.

In view of the detailed accounting of the experience with using the criminal law to deal with the public drunk and the suggestions of alternative civil remedies in the article in this issue by Mr. Stern[40] and in the report of the Crime Commission,[41] the matter need not be further pursued here. But it should be said that no single experience so dramatically exemplifies the misuse of the criminal law.

The Creditor and the Deserted Mother. The bad-check laws and the family nonsupport laws are two other instances in which the criminal law is used in practice to provide social services; in these cases, to assist a merchant in obtaining payment and to assist needy families in obtaining support from a deserting spouse. The issue for legislative choice is straightforward: Is it ultimately worthwhile to employ the resources of police, prosecutors, and the criminal process generally in order to supplement civil remedies, even though such use entails a diversion of law-enforcement energies from more threatening criminal conduct?

Checks, of course, can be instruments of serious fraud for which it is proper to employ the sanctions of the criminal law. However, the typical bad-check laws provide for serious punishment as well for the person who draws a check on his account knowing that at the time it has insufficient funds to cover the check. Usually, the intent to defraud is presumed

[40] See the article by Gerald Stern in this issue of *The Annals*, 147–156.

[41] See U.S. President's Commission on Law Enforcement and Administration of Justice, *Task Force Report: Drunkenness* (1967).

in these cases. Merchants, of course, are aware of the risk of accepting payment in checks, but expectedly prefer not to discourage sales. The effect of the insufficient-fund bad-check laws, therefore, is to enable them to make use of the resources of the criminal law to reduce what, in a sense, are voluntarily assumed business risks. When complaints are filed, the police, or sometimes the prosecutor, investigate to determine if there was a genuine intent to defraud or if the accused is an habitual bad-check writer. If not, the usual practice is to discourage prosecution and instead to assume the role of free collection agencies for the merchants.[42]

The cost to law enforcement is, again, the diversion of resources from genuine threatening criminality. It is not clear that it is anything but habit which keeps states from narrowing their bad-check laws to exclude the occasional bad-check writer where there is no proof of intent to defraud. This would make it more difficult for merchants to obtain payment, but it is hard to see why it would not be preferable to conserve precious law-enforcement resources at the far lesser cost of requiring the merchant to choose between being more conservative in accepting checks and assuming the risk as a business loss.

Nonsupport complaints by wives against deserting husbands are handled similarly. The objective of law-enforcement personnel — the probation officer, a deputy in the prosecutor's office, a welfare agency — is not to invoke the criminal process to punish or rehabilitate a wrongdoer, but to obtain needed support for the family.[43] Instead, jailing the father is the least likely means of obtaining it. As in the bad-check cases, the chief effect on law-enforcement officers is that this duty amounts to still another diversion from their main business. Unlike the bad-check cases, however, here the criminal process is being used to provide a service which, indisputably, the state has an obligation to provide. It is apparent from the economic status of those usually involved that the service amounts to the equivalent of legal aid for needy families. Still, although the service is a useful one, it makes little sense to provide it through the already overburdened criminal processes. Although the obligation is performed by police and prosecutors with some success, it is done reluctantly and usually less effectively than by a civil agency especially designed to handle the service. In addition, it is performed at a sacrifice to those primary functions of protecting the public against dangerous and threatening conduct which only the criminal law can perform.

---

[42] American Bar Foundation, *Pilot Project Report on the Administration of Criminal Justice in the United States,* Vol. III, 570 (1959); LaFave, *supra,* note 27 at 118; Frank Miller and Frank Remington, *Procedures Before Trial,* 335 *The Annals,* 111, 114 (1962).
[43] *Ibid.*

AVOIDING RESTRAINTS ON
LAW ENFORCEMENT

Another costly misuse of the substantive criminal law is exemplified in
the disorderly conduct and vagrancy laws. These laws are not crimes
which define serious misconduct which the law seeks to prevent through
conviction and punishment. Instead, they function as delegations of discretion to the police to act in ways which formally we decline to extend
to them because it would be inconsistent with certain fundamental principles with respect to the administration of criminal justice. The disorderly-conduct laws constitute, in effect, a grant of authority to the police
to intervene in a great range of minor conduct, difficult or impossible
legally to specify in advance, in which the police find it desirable to act.
The vagrancy laws similarly delegate an authority to hold a suspect, whom
police could not hold under the law of arrest, for purposes of investigation
and interrogation.

Disorderly-conduct statutes vary widely. They usually proscribe such
conduct as riot, breach of the peace, unlawful assembly, disturbing the
peace, and similar conduct in terms so general and imprecise as to offer
the police a broad freedom to decide what conduct to treat as criminal. A
New York Court of Appeals Judge observed of that state's disorderly-
conduct statute: "It is obviously one of those dragnet laws designed to
cover newly invented crimes, or existing crimes that cannot be readily
classified or defined."[44] In examining disorderly-conduct convictions, the
Model Penal Code found that the statutes have been used to proscribe
obscenity in a sermon, swearing in a public park, illicit sexual activity,
picketing the home of a nonstriking employee, picketing the United
Nations, obstructing law enforcement, shouting by a preacher whose
"Amen" and "Glory Hallelujah" could be heard six blocks away, and
talking back and otherwise using loud and offensive language to a policeman.[45] But the reported decisions give only a remote hint of the use of
these laws since convictions are appealed only in a minute percentage of
the cases.[46] In fact, arrests for disorderly conduct exceed those of arrests
for any other crime except drunkenness — in 1965, a half-million arrests
out of a total of five million were made for disorderly conduct.[47]

Vagrancy-type laws define criminality in terms of a person's status or a
set of circumstances. Often, no disorderly conduct need be committed
at all. The usual components of the offense include living in idleness
without employment and having no visible means of support; roaming,

[44] *People v. Tylkoff*, 212 N.Y. 187, 201, 105 N.E. 2d 835, 836 (1914).
[45] Model Penal Code, §250.1, Comments at 2 *et seq.* (Tent. Draft No. 13, 1961).
[46] See Adlerberg and Chetow, "Disorderly Conduct in New York Penal Law Section" 722, 25 *Brooklyn L. Rev.* 46 (1958).
[47] U.S. FBI, *Uniform Crime Reports 108* (1965).

wandering or loitering; begging; being a common prostitute, drunkard, or gambler; and sleeping outdoors or in a residential building without permission. Beginning in feudal days, when these laws had their beginning, they have been pressed into a great variety of services. Today, they are widely and regularly used by police as a basis for arresting, searching, questioning, or detaining persons (who otherwise could not legally be subjected to such interventions) because of suspicion that they have committed or may commit a crime or for other police purposes, including cleaning the streets of undesirables, harassing persons believed to be engaged in crime, and investigating uncleared offenses. The story has been told in a number of descriptive studies in recent years.[48]

Both the disorderly-conduct and vagrancy laws, therefore, constitute a powerful weapon in the hands of police in the day-to-day policing of urban communities. Since "penalties involved are generally minor, and defendants are usually from the lowest economic and social levels,"[49] they have proved largely immune from the restraints of appellate surveillance and public criticism. A weighing of the long-term costs of use of these laws against their immediate benefit to law enforcement suggests the wisdom of either scrapping them or at least substantially narrowing their scope.

The chief vice of these laws is that they constitute wholesale abandonment of the basic principle of legality upon which law enforcement in a democratic community must rest — close control over the exercise of the delegated authority to employ official force through the medium of carefully defined laws and judicial and administrative accountability. If I may, in the circumstances, take the liberty of quoting the language of Chapter VIII:

> The practical costs of this departure from principle are significant. One of its consequences is to communicate to the people who tend to be the object of these laws the idea that law enforcement is not a regularized, authoritative procedure, but largely a matter of arbitrary behavior by the authorities. The application of these laws often tends to discriminate against the poor and subcultural groups in the population. It is unjust to structure law enforcement in such a way that poverty itself becomes a crime. And it is costly for society when the law arouses the feelings associated with these laws in the ghetto — a sense of persecution and helplessness before official power and hostility to police and other authority that may

[48] Note, "Use of Vagrancy-Type Laws for Arrest and Detention of Suspicious Persons," 59 *Yale L.J.* 1351 (1950); Foote, "Vagrancy Type Law and Its Administration," 104 *U.P.L. Rev.* 603 (1956); Justice Douglas, "Vagrancy and Arrest on Suspicion," 70 *Yale L.J.* 1 (1960); LaFave, *supra*, note 27 at 87–88, 151–152, 343–363. See N.Y. Law Revision Commission Report 591 (1935): "The underlying purpose [of vagrancy laws] is to relieve the police of the necessity of proving that cirminals have committed or are planning to commit specific crimes."

[49] Model Penal Code, *supra*, note 44 at 2.

tend to generate the very conditions of criminality society is seeking
to extirpate.[50]

I would only add that police conduct undertaken under color of these laws
produces the typical resentment associated with what is perceived as
double-dealing. There is, after all, what can reasonably be taken for
hypocrisy in formally adhering to the constitutional, statutory, and judicial
restrictions upon the power of the police to arrest, search, and otherwise
intervene in the affairs of citizens on the streets, while actually authorizing
disregard of those limitations, principally against the poor and disadvantaged, through the subterfuge of disorderly-conduct and vagrancy laws.

The proper legislative task is to identify precisely the powers which we
want the police to have and to provide by law that they shall have these
powers in the circumstances defined. Amending the law of attempt to
make criminality commence earlier in the stages of preparation than now
generally is the case would help to some degree. More substantial moves
in this direction are exemplified in the attempts to authorize stopping and
questioning short of arrest such as those of the New York "Stop and Frisk"
law and the proposals of the American Law Institute's Model Pre-Arraign-
ment Code. Unfortunately, however, the future is not bright. Increasingly, in recent years, the Supreme Court has been imposing constitutional restraints upon powers which the police and most legislatures
strongly believe the police should have. If anything, therefore, the
temptation to invent subterfuge devices has increased. This is another
of the unfortunate consequences of the tension between the police and
the courts. But until law enforcement comes to yield less grudgingly to
the law's restraints in the process of imposing its restraints upon others,
the problem will long be with us.

CONCLUDING REMARKS

The plain sense that the criminal law is a highly specialized tool of social
control, useful for certain purposes but not for others; that when im-
properly used it is capable of producing more evil than good; that the
decision to criminalize any particular behavior must follow only after an
assessment and balancing of gains and losses — this obvious injunction
of rationality has been noted widely for over 250 years, from Jeremy
Bentham[51] to the National Crime Commission,[52] and by the moralistic
philosophers[53] as well as the utilitarian ones.[54] And those whose daily

[50] *Task Force Report: Courts, supra,* note 1 at 103–104.
[51] Bentham, *Principles of Morals and Legislation* 281–288 (Harrison ed., 1948).
[52] See *supra,* note 1.
[53] Devlin, *The Enforcement of Morals* 17 (1959). It is noteworthy that, as a practical matter, Lord Devlin became convinced of the undesirability of continuing to
consider consenting homosexuality a crime. See Dworkin, "Lord Devlin and the Enforcement of Morals," 75 *Yale L.J.* 986, 987 n.4 (1966).
[54] E.g., H. L. A. Hart, *The Morality of the Criminal Law,* chap. ii (1964).

business is the administration of the criminal law have, on occasion, exhibited acute awareness of the folly of departing from it.[55] The need for restraint seems to be recognized by those who deal with the criminal laws, but not by those who make them or by the general public which lives under them. One hopes that attempts to set out the facts and to particularize the perils of overcriminalization may ultimately affect the decisions of the legislatures. But past experience gives little cause for optimism.

Perhaps part of the explanation of the lack of success is the inherent limitation of any rational appeal against a course of conduct which is moved by powerful irrational drives. Explaining to legislatures why it does more harm than good to criminalize drunkenness or homosexuality, for example, has as little effect (and for the same reasons) as explaining to alcoholics or homosexuals that their behavior does them more harm than good. It may be that the best hope for the future lies in efforts to understand more subtly and comprehensively than we do now the dynamics of the legislative (and, it must be added, popular) drive to criminalize. The sociologists, the social psychologists, the political scientists, the survey research people, and, no doubt, others will have to be conscripted for any effort of this kind. A number of studies have already appeared which have revealed illuminating insights into the process of conversion of popular indignation into legislative designation of deviancy,[56] the nature of the competitive struggles among rival moralities, and the use of the criminal law to solidify and manifest victory.[57] We also have a degree of understanding of the effect of representative political processes on the choice of sanctions and the dynamics of law enforcement by the police.[58] Perhaps by further substantial research along these lines — research which would put the process of over-criminalization by popularly elected legislators itself under the microscope — we will understand better the societal forces which have unfailingly produced it.[59] Understanding, of course, is not control, and control may prove as hopeless with it as without it. But scientific progress over the past one hundred years has dramatized the control over the physical environment which comes

[55] See the quotation from the statement of a representative of the FBI before the National Crime Commission, *supra*, note 1 at 107.

[56] H. S. Becker, *Outsiders: Studies in the Sociology of Deviance* (1963); Kai Erikson, "Sociology of Deviance," in *Social Problems* 457 (J. Simpson ed., 1965).

[57] Gusfield, *Symbolic Crusade: Status Politics and the American Temperance Movement* (1963); Joseph Gusfield, "The Symbolic Process in Deviance Designation" (Ms. 1967).

[58] Westley, "Violence and the Police," 59 *Amer. J. Sociology* 34 (1953); Skolnick, *supra*, note 12.

[59] Under a Ford Foundation grant for a Program of Criminal Law and Social Policy, the Earl Warren Legal Center and the Center for the Study of Law and Society of the University of California (Berkeley) are attempting to undertake studies of this kind.

from knowledge of its forces. It may prove possible to exert in like manner at least some measure of control over the social environment. It is an alternative worth pursuing.

ANTHONY M. PLATT   *The Rise of the*
Child-Saving Movement:
A Study in Social Policy and
Correctional Reform

Studies of crime and delinquency have, for the most part, focused on their psychological and environmental origins. Correctional research has traditionally encompassed the relationship between prisoners and prison-management, the operation of penal programs, the implementation of the "rehabilitative ideal" and, in recent years, the effectiveness of community-based corrections. On the other hand, we know very little about the social processes by which certain types of behavior come to be defined as "criminal" or about the origins of penal reforms.[1] If we intend rationally to assess the nature and purposes of correctional policies, it is of considerable importance to understand how laws and legislation are passed, how changes in penal practices are implemented, and what interests are served by such reforms.

This paper analyzes the nature and origins of the reform movement in juvenile justice and juvenile corrections at the end of the nineteenth century. Delinquency raises fundamental questions about the objects of social control, and it was through the child-saving movement that the modern system of delinquency-control emerged in the United States. The child-savers were responsible for creating a new legal institution for penalizing children (juvenile court) and a new correctional institution to accommodate the needs of youth (reformatory). The origins of "delin-

From *The Annals,* January 1969, pp. 21–38. Reprinted by permission of the author and the American Academy of Political and Social Science.
    [1] This perspective is influenced by Howard S. Becker, *Outsiders: Studies in the Sociology of Deviance* (New York: Free Press, 1966).

quency" are to be found in the programs and ideas of these reformers, who recognized the existence and carriers of delinquent norms.

IMAGES OF DELINQUENCY

The child-saving movement, like most moral crusades, was characterized by a "rhetoric of legitimization,"[2] built on traditional values and imagery. From the medical profession, the child-savers borrowed the imagery of pathology, infection, and treatment; from the tenets of Social Darwinism, they derived their pessimistic views about the intractability of human nature and the innate moral defects of the working class; finally, their ideas about the biological and environmental origins of crime may be attributed to the positivist tradition in European criminology and to anti-urban sentiments associated with the rural, Protestant ethic.

American criminology in the last century was essentially a practical affair. Theoretical concepts of crime were imported from Europe, and an indiscriminating eclecticism dominated the literature. Lombrosian positivism and Social Darwinism were the major sources of intellectual justification for crime workers. The pessimism of Darwinism, however, was counterbalanced by notions of charity, religious optimism, and the dignity of suffering which were implicit components of the Protestant ethic.

Before 1870, there were only a few American textbooks on crime, and the various penal organizations lacked specialized journals. Departments of law and sociology in the universities were rarely concerned with more than the description and classification of crimes. The first American writers on crime were physicians, like Benjamin Rush and Isaac Ray, who were trained according to European methods. The social sciences were similarly imported from Europe, and American criminologists fitted their data to the theoretical framework of criminal anthropology. Herbert Spencer's writings had an enormous impact on American intellectuals, and Cesare Lombroso, perhaps the most significant figure in nineteenth-century criminology, looked for recognition in the United States when he felt that his experiments had been neglected in Europe.[3]

Although Lombroso's theoretical and experimental studies were not translated into English until 1911, his findings were known by American academics in the early 1890's, and their popularity, like that of Spencer's works, was based on the fact that they confirmed popular assumptions about the character and existence of a "criminal class." Lombroso's original theory suggested the existence of a criminal type distinguishable

[2] This term is used by Donald W. Ball, "An Abortion Clinic Ethnography," 14 *Social Problems,* 1967, pp. 293–301.
[3] See Lombroso's Introduction to Arthur MacDonald, *Criminology* (New York: Funk and Wagnalls, 1893).

from noncriminals by observable physical anomalies of a degenerative or atavistic nature. He proposed that the criminal was a morally inferior human species, characterized by physical traits reminiscent of apes, lower primates, and savage tribes. The criminal was thought to be morally retarded and, like a small child, instinctively aggressive and precocious unless restrained.[4] It is not difficult to see the connection between biological determinism in criminological literature and the principles of "natural selection" both of these theoretical positions automatically justified the "eradication of elements that constituted a permanent and serious danger."[5]

Nature versus Nurture. Before 1900, American writers were familiar with Lombroso's general propositions but had only the briefest knowledge of his research techniques.[6] Although the emerging doctrines of preventive criminology implied human malleability, most American penologists were preoccupied with the intractability of the "criminal classes." Hamilton Wey, an influential physician at Elmira Reformatory, argued before the National Prison Association in 1881 that criminals were "a distinct type of human species," characterized by flat-footedness, asymmetrical bodies, and "degenerative physiognomy."[7]

Literature on "social degradation" was extremely popular during the 1870's and 1880's, though most such "studies" were little more than crude polemics, padded with moralistic epithets and preconceived value judgments. Richard Dugdale's series of papers on the Jukes family, which became a model for the case-study approach to social problems, was distorted almost beyond recognition by anti-intellectual supporters of hereditary theories of crime.[8] Confronted by the evidence of Darwin, Galton, Dugdale, Caldwell, and many other disciples of the biological image of man, correctional professionals were compelled to admit that "a large proportion of the unfortunate children that go to make up the great army of criminals are not born right."[9] Reformers adopted the rhetoric of Darwinism in order to emphasize the urgent need for confronting the

[4] Marvin E. Wolfgang, "Cesare Lombroso," in Hermann Mannheim (ed.), *Pioneers in Criminology* (London: Stevens and Sons, 1960), pp. 168–227.

[5] Leon Radzinowicz, *Ideology and Crime* (London: Heinemann Educational Books, 1966), p. 55.

[6] See, for example, Arthur MacDonald, *Abnormal Man* (Washington, D.C.: U.S. Government Printing Office, 1893); and Robert Fletcher, *The New School of Criminal Anthropology* (Washington, D.C.: Judd and Detwiler, 1891).

[7] Hamilton D. Wey, "A Plea for Physical Training of Youthful Criminals," in National Prison Association, *Proceedings of the Annual Congress* (Boston, 1888), pp. 181–193.

[8] Richard L. Dugdale, "Hereditary Pauperism, as Illustrated in the 'Jukes' Family," in Annual Conference of Charities, *Proceedings* (Saratoga, 1877), pp. 81–99; *The Jukes: A Study in Crime, Pauperism, Disease, and Heredity* (New York: G. P. Putnam's Sons, 1877).

[9] Sarah B. Cooper, "The Kindergarten as Child-Saving Work," in National Conference of Charities and Correction, *Proceedings* (Madison, 1883), pp. 130–138.

"crime problem" before it got completely out of hand. A popular proposal was the "methodized registration and training" of potential criminals, "or these failing, their early and entire withdrawal from the community."[10]

The organization of correctional workers through national representatives and their identification with the professions of law and medicine operated to discredit the tenets of Darwinism and Lombrosian theory. Correctional workers did not think of themselves merely as the custodians of a pariah class. The self-image of penal reformers as doctors rather than guards and the domination of criminological research in the United States by physicians helped to encourage the acceptance of "therapeutic" strategies in prisons and reformatories. As Arthur Fink has observed:

> The role of the physician in this ferment is unmistakable. Indeed, he was the dynamic agent. . . . Not only did he preserve and add to existing knowledge — for his field touched all borders of science — but he helped to maintain and extend the methodology of science.[11]

Perhaps what is more significant is that physicians furnished the official rhetoric of penal reform. Admittedly, the criminal was "pathological" and "diseased," but medical science offered the possibility of miraculous cures. Although there was a popular belief in the existence of a "criminal class" separated from the rest of mankind by a "vague boundary line" there was no good reason why this class could not be identified, diagnosed, segregated, changed, and controlled.[12]

By the late 1890's, most correctional administrators agreed that hereditary theories of crime were overfatalistic. The superintendent of the Kentucky Industrial School of Reform told delegates to a national conference on corrections that heredity is "unjustifiably made a bugaboo to discourage efforts at rescue. We know that physical heredity tendencies can be neutralized and often nullified by proper counteracting precautions."[13] E. R. L. Gould, a sociologist at the University of Chicago, similarly criticized biological theories of crime for being unconvincing and sentimental. "Is it not better," he said, "to postulate freedom of choice than to preach the doctrine of the unfettered will, and so elevate criminality into a propitiary sacrifice?"[14]

[10] I. N. Kerlin, "The Moral Imbecile," in National Conference of Charities and Correction, *Proceedings* (Baltimore, 1890), pp. 244–250.

[11] Arthur E. Fink, *Causes of Crime: Biological Theories in the United States, 1800–1915* (New York: A. S. Barnes, 1962), p. 247.

[12] See, for example, Illinois, Board of State Commissioners of Public Charities, *Second Biennial Report* (Springfield: State Journal Steam Print, 1873), pp. 195–196.

[13] Peter Caldwell, "The Duty of the State to Delinquent Children," National Conference of Charities and Correction, *Proceedings* (New Haven, 1895), pp. 134–143.

[14] E. R. L. Gould, "The Statistical Study of Hereditary Criminality," National Conference of Charities and Correction, *Proceedings* (New Haven, 1895), pp. 134–143.

Charles Cooley was one of the first sociologists to observe that criminal behavior depended as much upon social and economic circumstances as it did upon the inheritance of biological traits. "The criminal class," he said, "is largely the result of society's bad workmanship upon fairly good material." In support of this argument, he noted that there was a "large and fairly trustworthy body of evidence" to suggest that many "degenerates" could be converted into "useful citizens by rational treatment."[15]

Urban Disenchantment. Another important influence on nineteenth-century criminology was a disenchantment with urban life — an attitude which is still prevalent in much "social problems" research. Immigrants were regarded as "unsocialized," and the city's impersonality compounded their isolation and degradation. "By some cruel alchemy," wrote Julia Lathrop, "we take the sturdiest of European peasantry and at once destroy in a large measure its power to rear to decent livelihood the first generation of offspring upon our soil."[16] The city symbolically embodied all the worst features of industrial life. A member of the Massachusetts Board of Charities observed:

> Children acquire a perverted taste for city life and crowded streets; but if introduced when young to country life, care of animals and plants, and rural pleasures, they are likely . . . to be healthier in mind and body for such associations.[17]

Programs which promoted rural and primary group concepts were encouraged because slum life was regarded as unregulated, vicious, and lacking social rules. Its inhabitants were depicted as abnormal and maladjusted, living their lives in chaos and conflict.[18] It was consequently the task of social reformers to make city life more wholesome, honest, and free from depravity. Beverley Warner told the National Prison Association in 1898 that philanthropic organizations all over the country were

> making efforts to get the children out of the slums, even if only once a week, into the radiance of better lives. . . . It is only by leading the child out of sin and debauchery, in which it has lived, into the circle of life that is a repudiation of things that it sees in its daily life, that it can be influenced.[19]

[15] Charles H. Cooley, " 'Nature v. Nurture' in the Making of Social Careers," National Conference of Charities and Correction, *Proceedings* (Grand Rapids, Michigan, 1896), pp. 399–405.

[16] Julia Lathrop, "The Development of the Probation System in a Large City," 13 *Charities* (January 1905), p. 348.

[17] Clara T. Leonard, "Family Homes for Pauper and Dependent Children," Annual Conference of Charities, *Proceedings* (Chicago, 1879), p. 174.

[18] William Foote Whyte, "Social Disorganization in the Slums," 8 *American Sociological Review* (1943), pp. 34–39.

[19] Beverley Warner, "Child-Saving," in National Prison Association, *Proceedings of the Annual Congress* (Indianapolis, 1893), pp. 377–378.

Although there was a wide difference of opinion among experts as to the precipitating causes of crime, it was generally agreed that criminals were abnormally conditioned by a multitude of biological and environmental forces, some of which were permanent and irreversible. Biological theories of crime were modified to incorporate a developmental view of human behavior. If, as it was believed, criminals are conditioned by biological heritage and brutish living conditions, then prophylactic measures must be taken early in life. Criminals of the future generations must be reached. "They are born to crime," wrote the penologist Enoch Wines in 1880, "brought up for it. They must be saved."[20]

MATERNAL JUSTICE

The 1880's and 1890's represented for many middle-class intellectuals and professionals a period of discovery of the "dim attics and damp cellars in poverty-stricken sections of populous towns" and of "innumerable haunts of misery throughout the land."[21] The city was suddenly discovered to be a place of scarcity, disease, neglect, ignorance, and "dangerous influences." Its slums were the "last resorts of the penniless and the criminal"; here humanity reached its lowest level of degradation and despair.[22]

The discovery of problems posed by "delinquent" youth was greatly influenced by the role of feminist reformers in the child-saving movement. It was widely agreed that it was a woman's business to be involved in regulating the welfare of children, for women were considered the "natural caretakers" of wayward children. Women's claim to the public care of children had some historical justification during the nineteenth century, and their role in child-rearing was considered paramount. Women were regarded as better teachers than men and were also more influential in child-training at home. The fact that public education also came more under the direction of women teachers in the schools increased the predominance of women in the raising of children.[23]

[20] Enoch C. Wines, *The State of Prisons and of Child-Saving Institutions in the Civilized World* (Cambridge, Mass.: Harvard University Press, 1880), p. 132.

[21] William P. Letchworth, "Children of the State," National Conference of Charities and Correction, *Proceedings* (St. Paul, Minn., 1886), p. 138. The idea that intellectuals *discovered* poverty as a result of their own alienation from the centers of power has been fully treated by Richard Hofstadter, *The Age of Reform* (New York: Vintage Books, 1955); and Christopher Lasch, *The New Radicalism in America, 1889–1963: The Intellectual as a Social Type* (New York: Alfred A. Knopf, 1965).

[22] R. W. Hill, "The Children of Shinbone Alley," National Conference of Charities and Correction, *Proceedings* (Omaha, 1887), p. 231.

[23] Robert Sunley, "Early Nineteenth Century American Literature on Child-Rearing," in Margaret Mead and Martha Wolfenstein (eds.), *Childhood in Contemporary Cultures* (Chicago: University of Chicago Press, 1955), p. 152; see also Orville G. Brim, *Education for Child-Rearing* (New York: Free Press, 1965), pp. 321–349.

Child-saving was a predominantly feminist movement, and it was regarded even by antifeminists as female domain. The social circumstances
behind this appreciation of maternalism were women's emancipation and
the accompanying changes in the character of traditional family life.
Educated middle-class women now had more leisure time but a limited
choice of careers. Child-saving was a reputable task for women who were
allowed to extend their housekeeping functions into the community without denying antifeminist stereotypes of women's nature and place. "It is
an added irony," writes Christopher Lasch in his study of American intel-
lectualism,

> that the ideas about woman's nature to which some feminists still
> clung, in spite of their opposition to the enslavement of woman in
> the home, were these very clichés which had so long been used to
> keep her there. The assumption that women were morally purer
> than men, better capable of altruism and self-sacrifice, was the core
> of the myth of domesticity against which the feminists were in re-
> volt. . . . [F]eminist and anti-feminist assumptions seemed curiously
> to coincide.[24]

Child-saving may be understood as a crusade which served symbolic
and status functions for native, middle-class Americans, particularly
feminist groups. Middle-class women at the turn of the century experienced a complex and far-reaching status revolution. Their traditional
functions were dramatically threatened by the weakening of domestic
roles and the specialized rearrangement of family life.[25] One of the main
forces behind the child-saving movement was a concern for the structure
of family life and the proper socialization of young persons, since it was
these concerns that had traditionally given purpose to a woman's life.
Professional organizations — such as Settlement Houses, Women's Clubs,
Bar Associations, and penal organizations — regarded child-saving as a
problem of women's rights, whereas their opponents seized upon it as an
opportunity to keep women in their proper place. Child-saving organizations had little or nothing to do with militant supporters of the suffragette
movement. In fact, the new role of social worker was created by deference
to antifeminist stereotypes of a "woman's place."

A Woman's Place. Feminist involvement in child-saving was endorsed
by a variety of penal and professional organizations. Their participation
was usually justified as an extension of their housekeeping functions so
that they did not view themselves, nor were they regarded by others, as
competitors for jobs usually performed by men. Proponents of the "new

[24] Lasch, *op. cit.*, pp. 53–54.
[25] Talcott Parsons and Robert F. Bales, *Family, Socialization and Interaction Process* (Glencoe, Ill.: Free Press, 1955), pp. 3–33.

penology" insisted that reformatories should resemble home life, for institutions without women were likely to do more harm than good to inmates. According to G. E. Howe, the reformatory system provided "the most ample opportunities for woman's transcendant influence."[26]

Female delegates to philanthropic and correctional conferences also realized that correctional work suggested the possibility of useful careers. Mrs. W. P. Lynde told the National Conference of Charities and Correction in 1879 that children's institutions offered the "truest and noblest scope for the public activities of women in the time which they can spare from their primary domestic duties."[27] Women were exhorted by other delegates to make their lives meaningful by participating in welfare programs, volunteering their time and services, and getting acquainted with less privileged groups. They were told to seek jobs in institutions where "the woman-element shall pervade . . . and soften its social atmosphere with motherly tenderness."[28]

Although the child-savers were responsible for some minor reforms in jails and reformatories, they were more particularly concerned with extending governmental control over a whole range of youthful activities that had previously been handled on an informal basis. The main aim of the child-savers was to impose sanctions on conduct unbecoming youth and to disqualify youth from enjoying adult privileges. As Bennett Berger has commented, "adolescents are not made by nature but by being excluded from responsible participation in adult affairs, by being rewarded for dependency, and penalized for precocity."[29]

The child-saving movement was not so much a break with the past as an affirmation of faith in traditional institutions. Parental authority, education at home, and the virtues of rural life were emphasized because they were in decline at this time. The child-saving movement was, in part, a crusade which, through emphasizing the dependence of the social order on the proper socialization of children, implicitly elevated the nuclear family and, more especially, the role of women as stalwarts of the family. The child-savers were prohibitionists, in a general sense, who believed that social progress depended on efficient law enforcement, strict supervision of children's leisure and recreation, and the regulation of illicit pleasures. What seemingly began as a movement to humanize the lives of adolescents soon developed into a program of moral absolutism through

[26] G. E. Howe, "The Family System," National Conference of Charities and Correction, *Proceedings* (Cleveland, 1880), pp. 212–213.

[27] W. P. Lynde, "Prevention in Some of Its Aspects," Annual Conference of Charities, *Proceedings* (Chicago, 1879), p. 167.

[28] Clara T. Leonard, "Family Homes for Pauper and Dependent Children," in Annual Conference of Charities, *Proceedings*, 1879, *loc. cit.*, p. 175.

[29] Bennett Berger, Review of Frank Musgrove, *Youth and the Social Order*, 32 *American Sociological Review*, 1927, p. 1021.

which youth was to be saved from movies, pornography, cigarettes, alcohol, and anything else which might possibly rob them of their innocence.

Although child-saving had important symbolic functions for preserving the social prestige of a declining elite, it also had considerable practical significance for legitimizing new career openings for women. The new role of social worker combined elements of an old and partly fictitious role — defenders of family life — and elements of a new role — social servant. Social work was thus both an affirmation of cherished American values and an instrumentality for women's emancipation.

JUVENILE COURT

The essential preoccupation of the child-saving movement was the recognition and control of youthful deviance. It brought attention to, and thus "invented," new categories of youthful misbehavior which had been hitherto unappreciated. The efforts of the child-savers were institutionally expressed in the juvenile court, which, despite recent legislative and constitutional reforms, is generally acknowledged as their most significant contribution to progressive penology.

The juvenile-court system was part of a general movement directed towards removing adolescents from the criminal-law process and creating special programs for delinquent, dependent, and neglected children. Regarded widely as "one of the greatest advances in child welfare that has ever occurred," the juvenile court was considered "an integral part of total welfare planning."[30] Charles Chute, an enthusiastic supporter of the child-saving movement, claimed:

> No single event has contributed more to the welfare of children and their families. It revolutionized the treatment of delinquent and neglected children and led to the passage of similar laws throughout the world.[31]

The juvenile court was a special tribunal created by statute to determine the legal status of children and adolescents. Underlying the juvenile-court movement was the concept of *parens patriae* by which the courts were authorized to handle with wide discretion the problems of "its least fortunate junior citizens."[32] The administration of juvenile justice differed in many important respects from the criminal-court processes. A child

[30] Charles L. Chute, "The Juvenile Courts in Retrospect," 13 *Federal Probation* (September 1949), p. 7; Harrison A. Dobbs, "In Defense of Juvenile Courts," 13 *Federal Probation* (September 1949), p. 29.

[31] Charles L. Chute, "Fifty Years of the Juvenile Court," *1949 National Probation and Parole Association Yearbook* (1949), p. 1.

[32] Gustav L. Schramm, "The Juvenile Court Idea," 13 *Federal Probation* (September 1949), p. 21.

was not accused of a crime but offered assistance and guidance; intervention in his life was not supposed to carry the stigma of criminal guilt. Judicial records were not generally available to the press or public, and juvenile-court hearings were conducted in relative privacy. Juvenile-court procedures were typically informal and inquisitorial. Specific criminal safeguards of due process were not applicable because juvenile proceedings were defined by statute as civil in character.[33]

The original statutes enabled the courts to investigate a wide variety of youthful needs and misbehavior. As Joel Handler has observed, "the critical philosophical position of the reform movement was that no formal, legal distinctions should be made between the delinquent and the dependent or neglected."[34] Statutory definitions of "delinquency" encompassed (1) acts that would be criminal if committed by adults; (2) acts that violated county, town, or municipal ordinances; and (3) violations of vaguely defined catch-alls — such as "vicious or immoral behavior," "incorrigibility," and "truancy" — which "seem to express the notion that the adolescent, if allowed to continue, will engage in more serious conduct."[35]

The juvenile-court movement went far beyond a concern for special treatment of adolescent offenders. It brought within the ambit of governmental control a set of youthful activities that had been previously ignored or dealt with on an informal basis. It was not by accident that the behavior selected for penalizing by the child-savers — sexual license, drinking, roaming the streets, begging, frequenting dance halls and movies, fighting, and being seen in public late at night — was most directly relevant to the children of lower-class migrant and immigrant families.

The juvenile court was not perceived by its supporters as a revolutionary experiment, but rather as a culmination of traditionally valued practices.[36] The child-saving movement was "antilegal," in the sense that it derogated civil rights and procedural formalities, which relying heavily on extra-legal techniques. The judges of the new court were empowered to investigate the character and social life of predelinquent as well as delin-

[33] Monrad G. Paulsen, "Fairness to the Juvenile Offender," 41 *Minnesota Law Review*, 1957, pp. 547–567. Note: "Rights and Rehabilitation in the Juvenile Courts," 67 *Columbia Law Review*, 1967, pp. 281–341.

[34] Joel F. Handler, "The Juvenile Court and The Adversary System: Problems of Function and Form," 1965 *Wisconsin Law Review*, 1965, p. 9.

[35] Joel F. Handler and Margaret K. Rosenheim, "Privacy and Welfare: Public Assistance and Juvenile Justice," 31 *Law and Contemporary Problems*, 1966, pp. 377–412.

[36] A reform movement, according to Herbert Blumer, is differentiated from a revolution by its inherent respectability and acceptance of an existing social order. "The primary function of the reform movement is probably not so much the bringing about of social change, as it is to reaffirm the ideal values in a given society." — Herbert Blumer, "Collective Behavior," in Alfred McClung Lee (ed.), *Principles of Sociology* (New York: Barnes and Noble, 1963), pp. 212–213.

quent children; they examined motivation rather than intent, seeking to identify the moral reputation of problematic children. The requirements of preventive penology and child-saving further justified the court's intervention in cases where no offense had actually been committed, but where, for example, a child was posing problems for some person in authority such as a parent or teacher or social worker.

The Personal Touch. Judges were expected to show the same professional competence as doctors and therapists. The sociologist Charles Henderson wrote:

> A careful study of individuals is an essential element in wise procedure. The study must include the physical, mental and moral peculiarities and defects of the children who come under the notice of the courts. Indeed we are likely to follow the lead of those cities which provide for a careful examination of all school children whose physical or psychical condition is in any way or degree abnormal, in order to prevent disease, correct deformity and vice, and select the proper course of study and discipline demanded by the individual need.[37]

Juvenile court judges had to be carefully selected for their skills as expert diagnosticians and for their appreciation of the "helping" professions. Miriam Van Waters, for example, regarded the juvenile court as a "laboratory of human behavior" and its judges as "experts with scientific training and specialists in the art of human relations." It was the judge's task to "get the whole truth about a child" in the same way that a "physician searches for every detail that bears on the condition of a patient."[38]

The child-savers' interest in preventive strategies and treatment programs was based on the premise that delinquents possess innate or acquired characteristics which predispose them to crime and distinguish them from law-abiding youths. Delinquents were regarded as constrained by a variety of biological and environmental forces, so that their proper treatment involved discovery of the "cause of the aberration" and application of "the appropriate corrective or antidote."[39] "What the trouble is with the offender," noted William Healy, "making him what he is, socially undesirable, can only be known by getting at his mental life, as it is an affair of reactive mechanisms."[40]

[37] Charles R. Henderson, "Theory and Practice of Juvenile Courts," National Conference of Charities and Correction, *Proceedings* (Portland, 1904), 358–359.

[38] Miriam Van Waters, "The Socialization of Juvenile Court Procedure," 12 *Journal of Criminal Law and Criminology*, 1922, pp. 61, 69.

[39] Illinois, Board of State Commissioners of Public Charities, *First Biennial Report* (Springfield: Illinois Journal Printing Office, 1871), p. 180.

[40] William Healy, "The Psychology of the Situation: A Fundamental for Understanding and Treatment of Delinquency and Crime," in Jane Addams (ed.), *The Child, The Clinic and The Court* (New York: New Republic Inc., 1925), p. 40.

The use of terms like "unsocialized," "maladjusted," and "pathological" to describe the behavior of delinquents implied that "socialized" and "adjusted" children conform to middle-class morality and participate in respectable institutions.[41] The failure empirically to demonstrate psychological differences between delinquents and nondelinquents did not discourage the child-savers from believing that rural and middle-class values constitute "normality." The unique character of the child-saving movement was its concern for predelinquent offenders — "children who occupy the debatable ground between criminality and innocence" — and its claim that it could transform potential criminals into respectable citizens by training them in "habits of industry, self-control and obedience to law."[42] This policy justified the diminishing of traditional procedures in juvenile court. If children were to be rescued, it was important that the rescuers be free to provide their services without legal hindrance. Delinquents had to be saved, transformed, and reconstituted. "There is no essential difference," said Frederick Wines, "between a criminal and any other sinner. The means and methods of restoration are the same for both."[43]

THE REFORMATORY SYSTEM

It was through the reformatory system that the child-savers hoped to demonstrate that delinquents were capable of being converted into law-abiding citizens. The reformatory was initially developed in the United States during the middle of the nineteenth century as a special form of prison discipline for adolescents and young adults. Its underlying principles were formulated in Britain by Matthew Davenport Hill, Alexander Maconochie, Walter Crofton, and Mary Carpenter. If the United States did not have any great penal theorists, it at least had energetic penal administrators who were prepared to experiment with new programs. The most notable advocates of the reformatory plan in the United States were Enoch Wines, Secretary of the New York Prison Association, Theodore Dwight, the first Dean of Columbia Law School; Zebulon Brockway, Superintendent of Elmira Reformatory in New York; and Frank Sanborn, Secretary of the Massachusetts State Board of Charities.

The reformatory was distinguished from the traditional penitentiary by its policy of indeterminate sentencing, the "mark" system, and "or-

[41] C. Wright Mills, "The Professional Ideology of Social Pathologists," in Bernard Rosenberg, Israel Gerver, and F. William Howton (eds.), Mass Society in Crisis (New York: The Macmillan Company, 1964), pp. 92–111.
[42] Illinois, Board of State Commissioners of Public Charities, Sixth Biennial Report (Springfield: H. W. Rokker, 1880), p. 104.
[43] Frederick H. Wines, "Reformation as an End in Prison Discipline," National Conference of Charities and Correction, Proceedings (Buffalo, 1888), p. 198.

ganized persuasion" rather than "coercive restraint." Its administrators assumed that abnormal and troublesome individuals could become useful and productive citizens. Wines and Dwight, in a report to the New York legislature in 1867, proposed that the ultimate aim of penal policy was reformation of the criminal, which could only be achieved:

> by placing the prisoner's fate, as far as possible, in his own hand, by enabling him, through industry and good conduct to raise himself, step by step, to a position of less restraint; while idleness and bad conduct, on the other hand, keep him in a state of coercion and restraint.[44]

But, as Brockway observed at the first meeting of the National Prison Congress in 1870, the "new penology" was tough-minded and devoid of "sickly sentimentalism. . . . Criminals shall either be cured, or kept under such continued restraint as gives guarantee of safety from further depredations."[45]

Reformatories, unlike penitentiaries and jails, theoretically repudiated punishments based on intimidation and repression. They took into account the fact that delinquents were "either physically or mentally below the average." The reformatory system was based on the assumption that proper training can counteract the impositions of poor family life, a corrupt environment, and poverty, while at the same time toughening and preparing delinquents for the struggle ahead. "The principle at the root of the educational method of dealing with juvenile cirme," wrote William Douglas Morrison, "is an absolutely sound one. It is a principle which recognizes the fact that the juvenile delinquent is in the main, a product of adverse individual and social conditions.[46]

The reformatory movement spread rapidly through the United States, and European visitors crossed the Atlantic to inspect and admire the achievements of their pragmatic colleagues. Mary Carpenter, who visited the United States in 1873, was generally satisfied with the "generous and lavish expenditures freely incurred to promote the welfare of the inmates, and with the love of religion." Most correctional problems with regard to juvenile delinquents, she advised, could be remedied if reformatories were built like farm schools or "true homes." At the Massachusetts Reform School, in Westborough, she found an "entire want of family spirit," and, in New York, she complained that there was no "natural life" in the reformatory. "All the arrangements are artificial," she said; "instead of the cultivation of the land, which would prepare the youth to seek a sphere

---

[44] Max Grünhut, *Penal Reform* (Oxford, England: Clarendon Press, 1948), p. 90.

[45] This speech is reprinted in Zebulon Reed Brockway, *Fifty Years of Prison Service* (New York: Charities Publication Committee, 1912), pp. 389–408.

[46] William Douglas Morrison, *Juvenile Offenders* (New York: D. Appleton, 1897), pp. 274–275.

far from the dangers of large cities, the boys and young men were being taught trades which will confine them to the great centers of an over-crowded population." She found similar conditions in Philadelphia where "hundreds of youth were there congregated under lock and key," but praised the Connecticut Reform School for its "admirable system of agri-cultural training."[47] If she had visited the Illinois State Reformatory at Pontiac, she would have found a seriously overcrowded "minor peniten-tiary" where the inmates were forced to work ten hours a day manufac-turing shoes, brushes, and chairs.

To Cottage and Country. Granted the assumption that "nurture" could usually overcome most of nature's defects, reformatory-administra-tors set about the task of establishing programs consistent with the aim of retraining delinquents for law-abiding careers. It was noted at the Fifth International Prison Congress, held in Paris in 1895, that reforma-tories were capable of obliterating hereditary and environmental taints. In a new and special section devoted to delinquency, the Congress proposed that children under twelve years

> should always be sent to institutions of preservation and unworthy parents must be deprived of the right to rear children. . . . The pre-ponderant place in rational physical training should be given to manual labor, and particularly to agricultural labor in the open air, for both sexes.[48]

The heritage of biological imagery and Social Darwinism had a lasting influence on American criminology, and penal reformers continued to regard delinquency as a problem of individual adjustment to the demands of industrial and urban life. Delinquents had to be removed from con-taminating situations, segregated from their "miserable surroundings," instructed, and "put as far as possible on a footing of equality with the rest of the population."[49]

The trend from congregate housing in the city to group living in the country represented a significant change in the organization of penal insti-tutions for young offenders. The family or cottage plan differed in sev-eral important respects from the congregate style of traditional prisons and jails. According to William Letchworth, in an address delivered be-fore the National Conference of Charities and Correction in 1886:

> A fault in some of our reform schools is their great size. In the con-gregating of large numbers, individuality is lost. . . . These exces-sive aggregations are overcome to a great extent in the cottage plan.

[47] Mary Carpenter, "Suggestions on Reformatory Schools and Prison Discipline, Founded on Observations Made During a Visit to the United States," National Prison Reform Congress, *Proceedings* (St. Louis, 1874), pp. 157–173.

[48] Negley K. Teeters, *Deliberations of the International Penal and Penitentiary Con-gresses, 1872–1935* (Philadelphia: Temple University Book Store, 1949), pp. 97–102.

[49] Morrison, *op. cit.*, pp. 60, 276.

. . . The internal system of the reformatory school should be as
nearly as practicable as that of the family, with its refining and ele-
vating influences; while the awakening of the conscience and the
inculcation of religious principles should be primary aims.[50]

The new penology emphasized the corruptness and artificiality of the
city; from progressive education, it inherited a concern from naturalism,
purity, and innocence. It is not surprising, therefore, that the cottage
plan also entailed a movement to a rural location. The aim of penal reformers was not merely to use the countryside for teaching agricultural
skills. The confrontation between corrupt delinquents and unspoiled
nature was intended to have a spiritual and regenerative effect. The romantic attachment to rural values was quite divorced from social and agricultural realities. It was based on a sentimental and nostalgic repudiation
of city life. Advocates of the reformatory system generally ignored the
economic attractiveness of city work and the redundancy of farming skills.
As one economist cautioned reformers in 1902:

> Whatever may be said about the advantages of farm life for the
> youth of our land, and however much it may be regretted that
> young men and women are leaving the farm and flocking to the
> cities, there can be no doubt that the movement cityward will con-
> tinue. . . . There is great danger that many who had left the home
> [that is, reformatory], unable to find employment in agricultural
> callings, would drift back to the city and not finding there an op-
> portunity to make use of the technical training secured in the in-
> stitution, would become discouraged and resume their old criminal
> associations and occupations.[51]

The "new" reformatory suffered, like all its predecessors, from overcrowding, mismanagement, "boodleism," understaffing, and inadequate
facilities. Its distinctive features were the indeterminate sentence, the
movement to cottage and country, and agricultural training. Although
there was a decline in the use of brutal punishments, inmates were subjected to severe personal and physical controls: military exercises, "training of the will," and long hours of tedious labor constituted the main
program of reform.

SUMMARY AND CONCLUSIONS

The child-saving movement was responsible for reforms in the ideological
and institutional control of "delinquent" youth. The concept of the born

---

[50] William P. Letchworth, "Children of the State," National Conference of Charities
and Correction, *Proceedings* (St. Paul, Minnesota, 1886), pp. 151, 156.

[51] M. B. Hammond's comments at the Illinois Conference of Charities (1901), reported in Illinois, Board of State Commissioners of Public Charities, *Seventeenth
Biennial Report* (Springfield: Phillips Brothers, 1902), pp. 232–233.

delinquent was modified with the rise of a professional class of penal administrators and social servants who promoted a developmental view of human behavior and regarded most delinquent youth as salvageable. The child-savers helped to create special judicial and correctional institutions for the processing and management of "troublesome" youth.

There has been a shift during the last fifty years or so in official policies concerning delinquency. The emphasis has shifted from one emphasizing the criminal nature of delinquency to the "new humanism" which speaks of disease, illness, contagion, and the like. It is essentially a shift from a legal to a medical emphasis. The emergence of a medical emphasis is of considerable significance, since it is a powerful rationale for organizing social action in the most diverse behavioral aspects of our society. For example, the child-savers were not concerned merely with "humanizing" conditions under which children were treated by the criminal law. It was rather their aim to extend the scope of governmental control over a wide variety of personal misdeeds and to regulate potentially disruptive persons.[52] The child-savers' reforms were politically aimed at lower-class behavior and were instrumental in intimidating and controlling the poor.

The child-savers made a fact out of the norm of adolescent dependence. "Every child is dependent," wrote the Illinois Board of Charities in 1899, "even the children of the wealthy. To receive his support at the hands of another does not strike him as unnatural, but quite the reverse."[53] The juvenile court reached into the private lives of youth and disguised basically punitive policies in the rhetoric of "rehabilitation."[54] The child-savers were prohibitionists, in a general sense, who believed that adolescents needed protection from even their own inclinations.

The basic conservatism of the child-saving movement is apparent in the reformatory system which proved to be as tough-minded as traditional forms of punishment. Reformatory programs were unilateral, coercive, and an invasion of human dignity. What most appealed to correctional workers were the paternalistic assumptions of the "new penology," its belief in social progress through individual reform, and its nostalgic preoccupation with the "naturalness" and intimacy of a preindustrial way of life.

The child-saving movement was heavily influenced by middle-class women who extended their housewifely roles into public service. Their contribution may also be seen as a "symbolic crusade" in defense of the nuclear family and their positions within it. They regarded themselves

[52] This thesis is supported by a European study of family life, Philippe Ariès, *Centuries of Childhood* (New York: Vintage Books, 1965).

[53] Illinois, Board of State Commissioners of Public Charities, *Fifteenth Biennial Report* (Springfield: Phillips Brothers, 1899), pp. 62–72.

[54] Francis A. Allen, *The Borderland of Criminal Justice* (Chicago: University of Chicago Press, 1964), *passim*.

as moral custodians and supported programs and institutions dedicated to eliminating youthful immorality. Social service was an instrumentality for female emancipation, and it is not too unreasonable to suggest that women advanced their own fortune at the expense of the dependency of youth.

This analysis of the child-saving movement suggests the importance of (1) understanding the relationship between correctional reforms and related changes in the administration of criminal justice, (2) accounting for the motives and purposes of those enterprising groups who generate such reforms, (3) investigating the methods by which communities establish the formal machinery for regulating crime, and (4) distinguishing between idealized goals and enforced conditions in the implementation of correctional reforms.

IMPLICATIONS FOR CORRECTIONS AND RESEARCH

The child-saving movement illustrates a number of important problems with the quality and purposes of correctional research and knowledge. The following discussion will draw largely upon the child-saving movement in order to examine its relevance for contemporary issues.

Positivism and Progressivism. It is widely implied in the literature that the juvenile court and parallel reforms in penology represented a progressive effort by concerned reformers to alleviate the miseries of urban life and to solve social problems by rational, enlightened, and scientific methods. With few exceptions, studies of delinquency have been parochial and inadequately descriptive, and they show little appreciation of underlying political and cultural conditions. Historical studies, particularly of the juvenile court, are, for the most part, self-confirming and support an evolutionary view of human progress.[55]

The positivist heritage in the study of social problems has directed attention to (1) the primacy of the criminal actor rather than the criminal law as the major point of departure in the construction of etiological theory, (2) a rigidly deterministic view of human behavior, and (3) only the abnormal features of deviant behavior.[56] The "rehabilitative ideal" has so dominated American criminology that there have been only spo-

[55] See, for example, Herbert H. Lou, *Juvenile Courts in the United States* (Chapel Hill: University of North Carolina, 1927); Negley K. Teeters and John Otto Reinemann, *The Challenge of Delinquency* (New York: Prentice-Hall, 1950); Katherine L. Boole, "The Juvenile Court: Its Origin, History, and Procedure" (Unpublished doctoral dissertation, University of California, Berkeley, 1928). One notable exception is Paul W. Tappan, *Delinquent Girls in Court* (New York: Columbia University Press, 1947).

[56] David Matza, *Delinquency and Drift* (New York: John Wiley, 1964).

radic efforts to undertake sociolegal research related to governmental invasion of personal liberties. But, as Francis Allen has suggested:

> Even if one's interests lie primarily in the problems of treatment of offenders, it should be recognized that the existence of the criminal presupposes a crime and that the problems of treatment are derivative in the sense that they depend upon the determination by law-giving agencies that certain sorts of behavior are crimes.[57]

The conservatism and "diluted liberalism"[58] of much research on delinquency results from the fact that researchers are generally prepared to accept prevailing definitions of crime, to work within the premises of the criminal law, and to concur at least implicitly with those who make laws as to the nature and distribution of a "criminal" population. Thus, most theories of delinquency are based on studies of convicted or imprisoned delinquents. As John Seeley has observed in another context, professional caution requires us "to *take* our problems rather than *make* our problems, to accept as constitutive of our 'intake' what is held to be 'deviant' in a way that concerns enough people in that society enough to give us primary protection."[59] Money, encouragement, cooperation from established institutions, and a market for publications are more easily acquired for studies of the socialization or treatment of delinquents than for studies of how laws, law-makers, and law-enforcers contribute to the "registration" of delinquency.

Law and its implementation have been largely dismissed as irrelevant topics for inquiry into the "causes" of delinquency. According to Herbert Packer, it is typical that the National Crime Commission ignored the fundamental question of: "What is the criminal sanction good for?"[60] Further research is needed to understand the dynamics of the legislative and popular drive to "criminalize."[61] Delinquency legislation for example, as has been noted earlier, was not aimed merely at reducing crime or liberating youth. The reform movement also served important symbolic and instrumental interests for groups who made hobbies and careers out of saving children.

Policy Research. Correctional research in this country has been dominated by persons who are intimately concerned with crime and its control. The scholar-technician tradition in corrections, especially with

[57] Allen, *op. cit.*, p. 125.
[58] This phrase and its perspective are taken from C. Wright Mills (ed.), *Images of Man* (New York: George Braziller, 1960), p. 5.
[59] John R. Seeley, "The Making and Taking of Problems: Toward an Ethical Stance," 14 *Social Problems*, 1967, pp. 384–385.
[60] Herbert L. Packer, "A Patchy Look at Crime," *New York Review of Books*, Vol. 17, October 12, 1967.
[61] Sanford H. Kadish, "The Crisis of Overcriminalization," *The Annals*, Vol. 374, (November 1967), pp. 157–170.

regard to delinquency, has resulted in the proliferation of "agency-determined" research whereby scholarship is catered to institutional interests.[62] Much of what passes under the label of "research" takes the form of "methods engineering," produced in the interest of responsible officials and management.[63] It is only rarely, as in Erving Goffman's study of "total institutions," that sympathetic consideration is given to the perceptions and concerns of subordinates in the correctional hierarchy.[64]

There are many historical and practical reasons why corrections has been such a narrow and specialized field of academic interest. First, corrections has been intellectually influenced by the problematic perspective of scholar-technicians, which limits the scope of "research" to local, policy issues. In the last century especially, penology was the exclusive domain of philanthropists, muckrakers, reformers, and missionaries. Secondly, the rise of the "multiversity" and of federal-grant research has given further respectability to applied research in corrections, to the extent that social science and public policy are inextricably linked.[65] Nevertheless, such research is minimal when compared, for example, with that done under the auspices of the Defense Department.[66] It is quite true, as the National Crime Commission reports, that research in corrections has been unsystematic, sporadic, and guided primarily by "intuitive opportunism."[67] Thirdly, it should be remembered that correctional institutions are politically sensitive communities which resist instrusions from academic outsiders unless the proposed research is likely to serve their best interests.[68] Research which undermines policy is generally viewed as insensitive and subversive, aside from the fact that it helps to justify and harden administrators' suspicions of "intellectuals." The lack of critical research is, no doubt, also due to "the reluctance of scholars to address the

[62] Herbert Blumer, "Threats from Agency-determined Researching: The Case of Camelot," in Irvin Louis Horowitz (ed.), *The Rise and Fall of Project Camelot* (Cambridge, Mass.: M.I.T. Press, 1967), pp. 153–174.

[63] See, for example, Daniel Glaser. *The Effectiveness of a Prison and Parole System* (New York: Bobbs-Merrill, 1964).

[64] Erving Goffman, *Asylums* (New York: Anchor Books, 1961).

[65] Clark Kerr, *The Uses of the University* (New York: Anchor Books, 1961).

[66] "Approximately 15 per cent of the Defense Department's annual budget is allocated for research, compared with one per cent of the total federal expenditure for crime control." — U.S., President's Commission on Law Enforcement and Administration of Justice (National Crime Commission), *The Challenge of Crime in a Free Society* (the General Report) (Washington, D.C.: U.S. Government Printing Office, 1967), p. 273.

[67] U.S., President's Commission on Law Enforcement and Administration of Justice (National Crime Commission), *Task Force Report: Corrections* (Washington, D.C.: U.S. Government Printing Office, 1967), p. 13.

[68] Controversial studies of official institutions run the risk of hampering further academic investigations, as was apparently the case with Jerome Skolnick's study of a California police department, *Justice without Trial* (New York: John Wiley & Sons, 1966).

specific problems faced by those charged with the perplexing task of controlling and rehabilitating offenders."[69]

Politics and Corrections. Correctional institutions have been generally regarded as distinct, insulated social organizations. Their relationship to the wider society is viewed in a bureaucratic, civil-service context, and their population is defined in welfare terms. Prisons and their constituency are stripped of political implications, seemingly existing in an apolitical vacuum. Corrections as an academic specialization has focused on the prison community to the neglect of classical interest in the relationship between political decision-making and social policies. As Hans Mattick has observed:

> There is very little appreciation . . . that this "contest between good and evil," and the whole "drama of crime," is taking place within the larger arena of our political system and this, in part, helps to determine public opinion about the nature of crime, criminals and how they are dealt with.[70]

As the gap between social deviance and political marginality narrows, it becomes increasingly necessary to examine how penal administrators are recruited, how "new" programs are selected and implemented, and how local and national legislatures determine correctional budgets. The crisis caused by white racism in this country also requires us to appreciate in what sense prisons and jails may be used as instrumentalities of political control in the "pacification" of black Americans. Similarly, it furthers our understanding of "delinquency" if we appreciate the motives and political interests of those reformers and professionals who perceive youth as threatening and troublesome.

Faith in Reform. The child-saving movement further illustrates that corrections may be understood historically as a succession of reforms. Academics have demonstrated a remarkably persistent optimism about reform, and operate on the premise that they can have a humanitarian influence on correctional administration. As Irving Louis Horowitz has observed, to the extent that social scientists become involved with policy-making agencies, they are committed to an elitist ideology:

> They come to accept as basic the idea that men who really change things are at the top. Thus, the closer to the top one can get direct access, the more likely will intended changes be brought about.[71]

There is little evidence to support this faith in the ultimate wisdom of policy-makers in corrections. The reformatory was not so much an im-

[69] *The Challenge of Crime in a Free Society, op. cit.,* p. 183.

[70] Hans W. Mattick (ed.), "The Future of Imprisonment in a Free Society," 2 *Key Issues,* 1965, p. 5.

[71] Horowitz (ed.), *loc. cit.,* p. 353.

provement on the prison as a means of extending control over a new
constituency; probation and parole became instruments of supervision
rather than treatment; halfway houses have become a means of extending prisons into communities rather than democratically administered
sanctuaries; group therapy in prisons has justified invasion of privacy and
coercive treatment on the dubious grounds that prisoners are psycho-
logically unfit; community-based narcotics programs, such as the nalline
clinic, disguise medical authoritarianism in the guise of rehabilitation.
Nevertheless, the optimism continues, and this is nowhere more apparent
than in the National Crime Commission's Task Force Report on Corrections, which reveals that, in Robert Martinson's words, correctional policy
consists of "a redoubling of efforts in the face of persistent failure."[72]

Finally, we have neglected to study and appreciate those who work
in corrections. Like the police and, to an increasing extent, teachers and
social workers, correctional staffs are constrained by the ethic of bureaucratic responsibility. They are society's "dirty-workers," technicians working on people. As Lee Rainwater has observed:

> The dirty-workers are increasingly caught between the silent middle
> class, which wants them to do the dirty work and keep quiet about
> it, and the objects of that dirty work, who refuse to continue to take
> it lying down. . . . These civilian colonial armies find their right to
> respect from their charges challenged at every turn, and often they
> must carry out their daily duties with fear for their physical safety.[73]

Correctional workers are required to accommodate current definitions of
criminality and to manage victims of political expediency and popular
fashion — drug users, drunks, homosexuals, vagrants, delinquents, and
"looters." They have minimal influence on law-makers and rarely more
than ideological rapport with law enforcers. They have no clear mandate
as to the purpose of corrections, other than to reduce recidivism and reform criminals. They have to live with the proven failure of this enterprise and to justify their role as pacifiers, guards, warehouse-keepers, and
restrainers.[74] They are linked to a professional system that relegates them
to the lowest status in the political hierarchy but uses them as a pawn in

[72] Robert Martinson, "The Age of Treatment: Some Implications of the Custody-
Treatment Dimension," 2 *Issues in Criminology* (Fall 1966), p. 291.

[73] Lee Rainwater, "The Revolt of the Dirty-Workers," 5 *Trans-action* (November
1967), p. 2.

[74] Henry McKay's "Report on the Criminal Careers of Male Delinquents in Chicago"
concludes that "the behavior of significant numbers of boys who become involved in
illegal activity is not redirected toward conventional activity by the institutions created
for that purpose." — U.S., President's Commission on Law Enforcement and Administration of Justice (National Crime Commission), *Task Force Report: Juvenile Delinquency and Youth Crime* (Washington, D.C.: U.S. Government Printing Office,
1967), p. 113.

electoral battles. They are doomed to annual investigations, blue-ribbon commissions, ephemeral research studies, and endless volumes of propaganda and muckraking. They live with the inevitability of professional mediocrity, poor salaries, uncomfortable living conditions, ungrateful "clients," and tenuous links with established institutions. It is understandable that they protect their fragile domain from intrusive research which is not supportive of their policies.

ROBERT MARTINSON   *The Age of Treatment:*
Some Implications of the
Custody-Treatment Dimension

> Turning back, he asked the pundits about the method they followed in instructing the bird.
> It was shown to him. He was immensely impressed. The method was so stupendous that the bird looked ridiculously unimportant in comparison. The Raja was satisfied that there was no flaw in the arrangements. As for any complaint from the bird itself, that simply could not be expected. Its throat was so completely choked with the leaves from the books that it could neither whistle nor whisper. It sent a thrill through one's body to watch the process.
> — Rabindranath Tagore. In *The Parrot's Training and Other Stories.* (Calcutta, 1944.)

Early students of American corrections noted the profound discrepancy between a democratic society and a severe penal system.[1] Decades of prison reform confidently made use of this contrast. Since approximately 1870, the New Penology has attempted to reform American prisons, reformatories and correctional institutions. The stubborn advance of hu-

From *Issues in Criminology*, Fall, 1966, pp. 275–293. Reprinted by permission.
    [1] ". . . it must be acknowledged that the penitentiary system in America is severe. While society in the United States gives the example of the most extended liberty, the prisons of the same country offer the spectacle of the most complete despotism." Gustave de Beaumont and Alexis de Tocqueville, *On the Penitentiary System in the United States and Its Application in France*, Illinois, 1964. p. 79.

manitarian impulse was ultimately successful in mitigating the worst conditions and introducing within facilities such categories as the Chaplain, the Teacher, the Psychologist, the Vocational Instructor and presently the Caseworker and the Psychiatrist.

More recently the Age of Humanitarian Reform has given way to the Age of Treatment. Simply to make prisons more liveable and inmates more comfortable is now often regarded as archaic. The ideology of treatment has gradually replaced the earlier concern with salvation or simply humanitarianism. Conservative opponents of prison reform must now confront the more complex image of the prison-as-hospital rather than the previous more vulnerable image of the prison-as-country club. Proponents of change have gained footholds within facilities and correctional systems primarily through the incorporation of new categories of professional staff. As the helping professions entered the traditional custodial facilities, research activities multiplied. As legislative investigations declined and prison reform societies disappeared, some of their functions have fallen into the hands of staff research departments.[2] Much recent evaluation research has been delegated to University departments of sociology, social welfare, public health or criminology.

Research aimed at corrections has become entwined with vested professional interests in ideologies, job classifications and pay scales. The discrepancy between society and prison (although reduced) is now mediated through professional organizations and professional allegiances. Prison professionals are also often constrained to disregard or transform accredited doctrine and practice and substitute expedient approximations.[3] The influence of professional ideologies on the workers of the correctional system is generally feebler than for the mental hospital[4] but it is far from non-existent.

The Age of Treatment has of course coincided with trends toward the dessication of publics often summarized as the "mass society." Thus the recent unfocussed concern with Crime on the Streets tends to create a crime anxiety on a nationwide basis but fails to find a persistent, knowledgeable *public* outside the network of professional groups immediately concerned.

Historically, the custody-treatment orientation should be viewed in the context of the congeries of professions which increasingly impinged upon the custodial institutions and which have not settled comfortably into the

---

[2] Thus seriously raising the problem of self-serving research. See Donald R. Cressey, "The Nature and Effectiveness of Correctional Techniques," *Law and Contemporary Problems*, 1958, 23:754–771; and Joseph W. Eaton, "Symbolic and Substantive Evaluative Research," *Administrative Science Quarterly*, 1962, 6:421–442.

[3] See Harvey Powelson and Reinhard Bendix, "Psychiatry in Prison," *Psychiatry*, 14: 73–86, February, 1951.

[4] Anselm Strauss, *et al.*, *Psychiatric Ideologies and Institutions*, Glencoe, Ill., 1964.

correctional harness. It provided a common-sense theoretical measuring stick against which to chart the progress toward "treatment" made in a facility or system of facilities.[5]

THE PROBLEM OF TRANSFORMING MAN

It would be remarkable if the doctrinal and world-political trends of recent years had no echoes within ideologically alive[6] segments of the control apparatus of a major world society. Nor are professionals immune from such trends.[7] Professions vary in the degree to which they are professionally dissatisfied with mankind and especially with its mete of scoundrels, scrooges, and fools. Some professions are oriented through doctrine, selective recruitment, idealistic graduate education, and other means toward useful endeavors to change man. In a nation which has in addition suffered the ravages of prohibition and the "Carrie Nation" syndrome this may be an especially powerful force.

What cannot be reasonably denied is this: we live in an age in which "people-changing"[8] has become a skill, a profession, indeed a moral injunction. Among other things, this is what is new. It should not be confused with the pledge, the moral campaign, or frenzied efforts to publicize virtue historically engaged in by concerned amateurs.[9]

[5] The opaque usefulness of this orientation says nothing of its theoretical clarity, cogency or adequacy. The explanatory power of the scheme, it is argued, has been outrun by newer events and impingements to be described.

[6] Erving Goffman, *Asylums,* New York, 1961, traces ideological aliveness in part to characteristics of the total institution in which the self becomes problematic and therefore subject to conflicting theories.

[7] H. L. Wilensky, "The Professionalism of Everyone?", *American Journal of Sociology,* LXX, 2, finds that solo practice encourages a "client orientation." Wilensky quotes Everett Hughes to the effect that "the quack is the man who continues through time to please his customers but not his colleagues." Wilensky does not deal with what the profession *does* to "serve" the client and attributes deviation from the "service ideal" to workplace pressures. From the point of view of the correctional client Hughes' aphorism might read: "A 'head-shrinker' is a tough professional gent who refuses to do his own time but keeps trying to 'blow my mind'." Such sentiments are sometimes expressed by correctional clients and some staff members as well. Richard Korn, "The Private Citizen, the Social Expert, and the Social Problem, *Mass Society in Crisis: Social Problems and Social Pathology* (edited by Bernard Rosenberg, Israel Gerver and F. William Howton), New York, 1964, cuts across professional distinctions to develop alternate models of the social expert, pp. 576–593, but does not deal at length with the sources of this new tough-minded professionalism.

[8] The term appears in quotation marks in: Robert D. Vintner and Morris Janowitz, *The Comparative Study of Juvenile Correctional Institutions: A Research Report,* School of Social Work, University of Michigan, 1961, to designate "a class of organizations more inclusive than 'treatment' institutions." (p. 659).

[9] In America today the official handling of the addict population has reached such an Alice-in-Wonderland state that the addicts band together and, in solemn conclave, give one another a merciless verbal drubbing aimed at a total transformation of the self. Tight and morally virtuous communities are thereby set up and crusaders are even dispatched to bring word of this new method to prisons and college communities. See

Professionals who work closely with delinquents, drug addicts, parolees and street gangs have recently been dichotomized into the "hip" and the "square." The "hip" professional is excoriated for his criminogenic tendencies, his "voyeurism"! If this view were generalized the "plague" of addiction would be turned back through superior moral karma, anomie[10] reversed by the taut will of the dedicated professional unmoved by the subtle strategies of his shifty client.

If the problem of transforming man takes on such malignant forms when dealing with core areas of deviance, it may be present in less measure in the ordinary, day-to-day life of the professional worker.

In broadest compass, the custody-treatment dimension was developed to explicate what has been happening at the intersection of three processes in modern society suggested by the terms: professionalization, bureaucratization, alienation. It professed to measure, at least grossly, the penetration of professional "treatment" into a sphere hitherto ruled over by the uniformed officer class given the task of manning the correctional institutions of the nation. The penetration of professional workers has been costly. It has proceeded furthest in the larger, well-endowed state correctional systems. It is in these larger complex organizations that one is likely to find civil service, specialized facilities, advanced classification procedures, research divisions. The larger systems, historically, have taken the lead in introducing professional categories and more recently group counseling, and even more recently what has come to be summed up in the term: "correctional therapeutic community." Many threads in American (and world) correctional efforts come to rest in this term. If the Age of Treatment is beginning to give way before an emergent correctional philosophy increasingly dedicated to the transformation of man one is likely to find evidence for it in those systems with the strongest emphasis on combining technology, professional skill, managerial ardor, and rational scientific experimentation for the purpose of "changing criminals."[11] This article suggests that the custody-treatment dimension in-

---

Robert Martinson, "Research on Deviance and Deviant Research," *Issues in Criminology,* Vol. 1, No. 1, pp. 138–45, for a critique of Lewis Yablonsky's, *The Tunnel Back: Synanon,* New York: 1965.

[10] Perhaps the reason Durkheim's discussion of "The Normal and the Pathological," *Rules of Sociological Method,* Glencoe, Ill., 1950, pp. 65–73, rings slightly false to the modern ear is the severe theoretical limit it places on the uncontrolled passions of professional workers.

[11] There is arising within sociology a new school of tough-minded practitioners who wish to change criminals by concentrating on "the properties of groups." See, Donald R. Cressey, "Changing Criminals: The Application of the Theory of Differential Association," *American Journal of Sociology,* LXI:116–120, Sept. 1955; J. D. Grant, "The Use of Correctional Institutions as Self-Study Communities in Social Research," *British Journal of Delinquency,* (1957), 7, 4:301–307; LaMar T. Empey, "The Application of Sociological Theory to Social Problems and Research," Youth Studies Center, University of Southern California, August, 1963; Raymond J. Corsini, "Group

creasingly becomes a hindrance to common sense and social scientific understanding in precisely such a system.

A correctional system is a compromise formation embedded in a larger social matrix. It is the "passive" segment of the apparatus of social control and only in exceptional historial circumstances has it been known to cut partially loose from society at large.[12] Parole systems often permit some extension of correctional influence to post-release life.[13] This influence is normally subject to political boards (Authorities, etc.) which, however, may come to function primarily as *regulating valves* matching in-put, out-put and equalizing inter-system and extra-system pressures.[14]

A correctional system will be subject to a variety of outside pressures differing in degree of access, intensity and persistence. The assessment of these pressures for any particular aspect of the system's operation is an open question to be empirically investigated in the light of organization theory. The notion that a Commonweal organization, simply because it serves the public at large, has no initiative, direction or self-actualizing tendency should be dismissed as a metaphysical postulate. Even the notion that the historical *tendencies* associated with the evolution of correctional systems must be primarily a product of congeries of *outside* social forces is a matter to be demonstrated not assumed. For the larger systems, this view would introduce considerable error. For smaller, single-facility situations in which the facility is extensively pervaded by social pressures, such a postulate might be more economical for research.

In discussing the custody treatment dimension in this historical context, I am suggesting that we are dealing with an *emergent* process in corrections.[15] This does not void the discussion of value or empirical relevance. An emergent trend is not a fatality so long as it is recognized in time to do something about it. I would be less than frank if I were not to under-

---

Psychotherapy in Correctional Rehabilitation," *The British Journal of Criminology,* Jan. 1964, pp. 272–77; and "Convicted Felons as Social Therapists," *Corrective Psychiatry and Journal of Social Therapy,* 9, 3, 1963.

[12] See Raul Hilberg, *The Destruction of the European Jews, Chicago,* 1961; Dallin and Nicolaevsky, *Forced Labor in the Soviet Union,* New Haven, 1955.

[13] Some students have suggested a kind of parole system for mental patients released to the community. See Howard E. Freeman and O. G. Simmons, *The Mental Patient Comes Home,* New York, 1963. The aim of parole would apparently be to increase "performance levels" which the authors assert are too low for the good of society.

[14] A recent study of California's paroling boards indicates that the average time spent per case hearing was: Youth Authority, 8.7 minutes; Adult Authority, 13.7 minutes; The Board of Trustees (Women), 33.6 minutes. See, *The Paroling Boards of the Agency: An Administrative Analysis,* Youth and Adult Corrections Agency, December, 1963, Table 5, p. 158.

[15] "In 1958 less than 5 per cent of the 27,000 persons employed in American prisons were directly concerned with the administration of treatment or training," Cressey, "Prison Organizations," *op. cit.,* p. 1031, paraphrasing A. C. Schnur, "The New Penology: Fact or Fiction?", *The Journal of Criminal Law and Criminology,* 49:331–334, 1958.

line my personal rejection of the perspective of the "transformation of man."[16]

The custody-treatment dimension functions to conceal from view the emergence of a new treatment-authoritarianism and thus inhibits the assessment of the costs as well as the possible advantages of new social techniques. There are historical and social alternatives to the "correctional therapeutic community" available to society. The problem of where to strike the balance can only be decided on the basis of all the evidence.

METHODOLOGICAL ASSUMPTIONS OF THE CUSTODY-TREATMENT DIMENSION

The methodology of custody-treatment appears to play the same *normative* function as did such models as the assumption of the "normality" of full employment and the null hypothesis of "perfect justice" in many recent studies in the sociology of law. It differs from these models in that it compares a hazy and little studied *past* state of affairs (custody) with a hoped for *future* state of affairs (treatment) on the assumption that what will be found in any given setting will be some mixture of the two. The custody-treatment orientation does not compare present reality with some widely held present-day norm (justice) or possible present state (perfect competition), but, on the contrary, it judges the present in terms of a projected future. Unlike other normative schemes it is unable to specify a minimum, a maximum, or the segment of the curve being measured. It implicitly contains a built-in program for reform with no maximum limit except the "logical" one of the total reduction of recidivism.[17] It might be called a methodological utopia, if its implications were not seriously connected with advances in the power of certain social segments, professions, and interests.

Historically and socially there is an intimate connection between social emphasis on the goal of reduction of recidivism[18] and movement "up" the

---

[16] J. C. Spencer, "Problems in Transition: From Prison to Therapeutic Community," in: *The Sociological Review Monograph No. 9: Sociological Studies in the British Penal Services*, edited by Paul Halmost, Keele, 1965. Spencer says: "The sociological problem of the therapeutic community is how to translate the ideology of treatment into a viable social system." (p. 19.)

[17] Logically, if "custody" fell to zero, while "treatment" remained constant, the inmates would all escape. If "custody" fell to zero as "treatment" *increased* the need for the institution would wither away assuming no more input to the system, since all the criminals would be rehabilitated and recidivism would disappear. This "Dimension" is not a mathematical function; it has one foot in an unspecified past and the other in a projected future. Since one can only "measure" the present, and cannot specify the limits of the scale, this dimension contains within itself no limit.

[18] This is only *one* of the present goals of the correctional system but it is clearly gaining precedence over others, i.e., punishment, containment, etc. Historically, the goal of the reduction of recidivism could not become a palpable force until recidivism

custody-treatment dimension. As "treatment" personnel were added to custodial facilities the costs of confinement rose. These costs were partly relieved by the application of community control systems like parole and probation. Given the steady (even advancing) imput pressures on the system, experiments have been made with early release and research divisions began to develop operational research. Academics have begun to develop mathematical models of input, output and feedback. These models aim at the maximization of the correctional dollar. Some proponents propose that social science is to be utilized to transform corrections into a "learning organization," a "self-homing missile directed at the enemies of society."[19]

Much work has to be put into a "natural system" in order to further maximize even one clearly established official goal.[20] But the correctional system has *multiple* official goals. This natural system is also at the intersection of independent police, judicial, legal and legislative systems which limit its freedom in intricate ways. These systems in turn have goals and sub-goals of their own. This has become an obstacle for visionaries who wish to solve the crime problem regardless of the consequences of a particular solution on other correctional goals, the goals of connected subsystems, and the larger goals and values of society. Some technocratic enthusiasts imagine they will solve the problem by optimizing a "mix" of costs, inputs, outputs, and values. Their envisioned matrix is a 20th Century variant of the vision behind Bentham's panopticon; it also pretends to translate human values into "costs." What is apparently envisioned is the transformation of multi-valued correctional settings in the

---

could be accurately *measured*. Before this could be done accurate statistics were needed on a national level. Parole also functioned to provide a feed-back network for information about the parolee. Forty years of sociological analysis in the actuarial line has also helped.

[19] Leslie Wilkins, *Social Deviance: Social Policy, Action and Research,* New Jersey, 1965. One may see what could happen when these academic perspectives are further extended by California's systems engineers. See, *Final Report, Prevention and Control of Delinquency,* prepared for Youth and Adult Corrections Agency, State of California, Space-General Corporation, El Monte, California, 1966. The core of this report is its proposed "Potential Offender Identification Program" which includes a "population planning program" aimed to "reduce the production of potential offenders," (p. 73) who, the report reveals, are heavily concentrated in the Negro and Mexican-American ethnic segments of the States. (Fig. A-11, p. 216).

> The program will begin by requesting completely voluntary participation in recommended action, whether it entails practicing family planning or relocation in some less susceptible area. If, however, insufficient numbers are motivated by counseling, indoctrination, and other inducements, then further incentives will be developed by the committee. These might include use of incentive "bonuses" peer group influences, and social pressures as appropriate for the specific community. (p. 75)

[20] See, Philip Selznick, "Foundations of the Theory of Organizations," *American Sociological Review,* 13:25–35, 1958; and *Leadership and Administration,* Ill., 1957.

direction of single-valued settings, i.e., the reduction of recidivism by all available means.[21]

There are many variants of the custody-treatment dimension and a growing literature devoted to it. In the hands of Donald R. Cressey, it takes the form of polar types; here custody, there treatment.[22] In Vintner and Janowitz, it takes the form of a hypothetical variable which is both cross-sectional and longitudinal. They deliberately arranged specially selected facilities to fall along the dimension for comparative purposes, and made use of the same scheme to measure longitudinal change. Attitude surveys of correctional staff have sometimes pushed a *discontinuance* variable (discrete facilities) into one that becomes continuous for all practical purposes.[23]

Recent sociological discussions of prisons and mental hospitals have attempted to put the custody-treatment dimension aside and proceed to more concrete investigations. Erving Goffman has objected to "junior psychiatry" and has constructed a typology cutting across formal distinctions. Anselm Strauss has objected to those who have "used sociological methods and analysis in the service of psychiatric assumptions and interests." Other authors have also kept close to the correctional setting without perceiving it entirely through the custody-treatment lens.[24] One difficulty with some of these empirical and descriptive studies is that they lack an overall orientation and thus do not tend to cumulate. They are like beads without a string, descriptions of discrete cases which do not add

---

[21] Chadwick J. Haberstroh, "Organization Design and Systems Analysis," *Handbook of Organizations, op. cit.*, sees a conflict between "egocentric economizing" and Barnard's concept of "efficiency" and appeals to "prevailing mores" to account for "the failure of Barnard's concept of efficiency to gain currency in usage." Systems analysis need not insert any particular values into its computer simulations models, although it would appear to have an "elective affinity" for certain lofty, technocratic visions.

[22] Cressey keeps close to the tangled truth about prison organizations. In his hands the polar type of "treatment" is overlayed upon the actual reality of custody to show the conflicts, contradictions and limitations that then occur. Nevertheless, both polar types are figments. His "punitive-custodial" type assumes an equivalence between two tasks of the prison, the "punitive" task and the simple custodial task. *Custodians need not be punitive.* His "treatment prison" is an *ideal* in the *ideological* rather than the Weberian sense.

[23] Kassebaum, Ward and Wilner, *op. cit.* Here, the sliding-scale is moved up a notch. "Custodial" becomes "traditional," while "treatment" is "generally consistent with Gilbert and Levinson's conception of the 'humanistic' orientation." (p. 24). The sole measure of personal proclivity toward "authoritarianism" is a short, ten-item version of the California F-scale. Edward A. Shils, "Authoritarianism: 'Right' and 'left,'" in: *Studies in the Scope and Method of 'The Authoritarian Personality,' Continuities in Social Research*, Glencoe, Ill., 1954, has raised doubts about the conception of a conservative-liberal-radical continuum upon which this scale is based. The F-scale measures something real but it may fail to capture an unfamiliar, emergent, reality.

[24] See, for example, Stanton and Schwartz, *The Mental Hospital*, New York, 1954, Caudill, *The Psychiatric Hospital as a Small Society*, Cambridge, 1958.

to an integrated body of knowledge. To ignore the custody-treatment orientation is not to overcome it.[25]

PROFESSIONAL SOURCES OF AUTHORITARIAN TREATMENT IDEOLOGY

"People-changers" are not randomly distributed either in the population at large or in the professions. One might expect to find more of them in social work than in art, in psychiatry than in philology. Ultimately it is not a question of the distribution of persons but of professional *ideology* and the power to implement it.[26] Since professions are not monolithic there are sure to be ideological factions and differences both subtle and gross. One would expect the applied branches of professions and sciences to contain more than their share.

One must seriously limit a perspective which looks solely toward the seduction of professional virtue by the bureaucratic setting although this is demonstrably one significant process.[27] Of increasing importance is a growing, pervasive cynicism-*know-nothingism* — which reflects, in America at least, the widening discrepancy between a democratic, libertarian past and an increasingly authoritarian present.[28] The relation between an amoral scientism and a debunking know-nothingism lays the ground for the growth of curious reactions, especially among students, intellectuals, and professionals.[29]

One is likely to find the "people-changing" ideology growing in those professional areas in which the client is especially helpless, and thus one

[25] "Overcome" in the Hegelian sense of critique through inclusion moving to a more adequate level where past error is seen as partiality. Present day social science is often eclectic in the sense of substituting statesmanship for creative conflict. Herbert Marcuse, *One-Dimensional Man*, Boston, 1964, deals with some of the sources of this "paralysis of criticism."

[26] See, George Rosen, MD, "The Evolution of Social Medicine," in: Howard E. Freeman, Sol Levine and Leo G. Reeder, *Handbook of Medical Sociology*, New Jersey, 1963, esp. the section "Mercantilism and the Concept of Medical Police."

[27] William Kornhauser, *Scientists in Industry: Conflict and Accommodation*, Berkeley, 1963.

[28] I choose the word "authoritarian" with care. Marcuse's Hegelism runs him into error at many points; the primacy he gives to thought pushes him toward the dissolution of all distinctions.

[29] Religious enthusiasm in modern society is as likely to be associated with professional identities as with religious associations. The growth of professional religiosity may be seen in the new "heretic," the professional deviant who makes the error of appealing to the public over the head of his colleagues. Pertinent examples which come to mind are: Thorstein Veblen, C. Wright Mills, T. S. Szasz, Rachel Carson, Hoxey; medicine; Immanuel Velikovsky; astronomy. Velikovsky's case was so extraordinary as to give birth to a special issue of *The American Behavioral Scientist*, Sept. 1963.

is hardly surprised to find it associated with Skid Row, or aspects of probation, parole, social work,[30] criminology and sociology, with especially interesting forms in the small therapeutic mental hospital.[31] It is vaguely consistent with the growing public ideology of "mental health."[32]

It is at the intersection of congeries of sciences, professions, agencies and institutions that one may see the social roots of a new version of the "medical police" based not on the cameralist presuppositions of mercantilism but on more modern forms. The professions that might be empirically investigated from this orientation would be public health, psychiatry, social work, hospital and prison administration, and their para-professional helpers. The relevant agencies would be those with the more *chronic* relations with clients in which the stubbornness and intractability of the human animal may give birth to impatience, cynicism, and daring dreams. Not all aspects of social control are equally relevant, only those in which clients are stubborn, socially visible and collected together in one spot. Not all social strata are equally relevant, perhaps only those which turn away from white, middle class, Protestant, values. Class is ceasing to be the most salient distinction to make in relation to this "turning away" process. One will find many candidates who are not cheerful and cooperative among the nation's five million alcoholics, one hundred thousand drug addicts, and the increasing numbers of very old people. Ethnic distinctions are not entirely relevant. American political positions are not very revealing.

I am attempting to point to what may be regarded as one of the *prin-*

[30] The custody-treatment dimension shows up once again in: H. L. Wilensky and Charles N. Lebeaux, *Industrial Society and Social Welfare*, New York, 1965. Here the distinction is between the "residual" and "institutional conceptions of social welfare (Chapter VI). More recently, in his foreword, Wilensky warns that "welfare planners must be alert to the danger that in the name of improved coordination of the welfare services, in pursuit of the humane purposes of the welfare state, we may simply subject the underlying population to more efficient surveillance" (p.li). The concept "institutional" may be useful for a broad social survey of American welfare practices but it covers over nicer distinctions useful in the present context.

[31] Especially symptomatic is the frank dissolution of psychiatry into an "ideology of hopefulness" complete with a "leader who is not vulnerable to the upsets of patients." Ezra Statland and Arthur L. Kobler, *Life and Death of a Mental Hospital*, Seattle, 1965, pp. 221 ff. Chapter VII, "An Epidemic of Suicide in a Dying Hospital," makes Orwell's *1984* seem like a pleasant dream.

[32] See the interesting if troubled essay by John R. Seeley, "Social Values, the Mental Health, Movement, and Mental Health," in: *Mental Health and Mental Disorder, A Sociological Approach*, New York, 1955, pp. 599–612. "Like the early church, the mental health movement unites and addresses itself to 'all sorts and conditions of men,' so only they be "for" mental health as they were formerly for virtue and (more mildly) against sin" (p. 606), See also Kingsley Davis' article, "Mental Hygiene and Class Structure," pp. 578–598, *ibid.* Davis sees the "mental hygienist" as a "practicing moralist in a scientific, mobile world" who is vaguely buttressing the "standards of the entire society." He objects to the notion that "the mental hygienist is consciously enforcing alien class standards upon unwilling members of a lower stratum" (p. 596).

cipia media of our society.[33] A relatively "unique" intersection of professional ideology, medical bureaucratization, with forms of chronic alienation gives birth to our "medical police" and its project of halting the *chronic* discontent of our time.

CHRONIC ALIENATION

The distinction between acute and chronic is fundamental to this discussion and cuts across the medical-social spheres. It is usually not sufficiently appreciated that *chronic* illness as a social problem was partially a result of medical progress. The progress in halting acute disease through identifying and coping with specific infectious microorganisms has advanced steadily for the last century. Death by chronic disease — malignant neoplasms, diabetes mellitus, cardiovascular renal diseases — have doubled and tripled.[34]

While acute rapidly-spreading, infectious disorders — like the plague — have had powerful social consequences, they were more in the nature of the pre-20th Century business cycle than the structural unemployment of more recent times. The "plagues" of our day are slow, creeping processes, sometimes not even recognized as problems until they have assumed major dimensions.[35] When recognized they are usually turned over to some specialized agency or congeries of agencies.[36] As illness becomes more chronic, "public health in the community" turns from epidemiology to discussions of the "latent" function of public health in "introducing some degree of rationality into everyday life." Public health now studies

[33] ". . . while the economic, political and ideological spheres (according to the cross-sections taken by different observers) each represent a single dimension of events as a whole, existing reality in fact consists in the mutual relationships between many such spheres and the concrete *principia media* at work in them." Karl Mannheim, *Man and Society in an Age of Reconstruction*, London, 1942.

[34] See, Saxon Graham, "Social Factors in Relation to the Chronic Illnesses," in: *Handbook of Medical Sociology, op. cit.*, pp. 65–98, especially Table 3–1. While deaths from tuberculosis have dropped from 194.4 in 1900 to 6.7 in 1959, cancer has increased from 64.0 to 147.1, heart disease from 345.2 to 519.7. Deaths from motor-vehicle accidents have climbed from nothing to 20.0 in this period.

[35] The public health research techniques summarized in the term epidemiology often raise acutely embarrassing social questions. One interesting recent example is the possible connection between circumcision and a low incidence of cancer of the cervix; another is the relation between the "gay life" and the incidence of syphilis; the smoking-cancer association, is of course, a *cause célèbre*. Value elements enter profoundly in all such situations.

[36] See, Sol Levine and Paul E. White, "The Community of Health Organizations," in: *Handbook of Medical Sociology, op. cit.*, pp. 321–347. One problem with this "community" is "interinstitutional conflict" and, of course, the answer lies in "interagency cooperation." The authors do not deal with the problem of the "unwanted client," the "multi-agency family," and the possibility of vested interest in the continuation of an on-going, chronic, situation.

its own network of functionaries, action programs, and is especially concerned with community power. Ideology is a recurrent problem.[37]

As public health becomes more political, health becomes more politicized, more ideological. The problem of cost has given way to the irrational-rationality of citizens banding together to oppose fluoridation.[38] As the medical profession has gained in income, power and prestige,[39] the problem of quasi-practitioners and "quackery" continues as sub-professionals, non-professionals and religious sects borrow the prestige of medicine.[40]

As one turns toward the addictive substances such as alcohol, narcotics, and the "dangerous drugs," the emergence of the "medical police" is quite striking. Chronic alienation here received a crutch which increases incredibly the stubbornness of the client and his rejection of "treatment." Systems of social control are instituted with little success or even with a reverse effect, maintaining and sometimes increasing the problem they were instituted to solve.[41]

Large-scale industrial societies (especially the democratic ones) must wait until a process has become socially visible to act upon it. The ponderous gears of law, police, corrections and "treatment" only screw down

[37] See, Irwin T. Sanders, "Public Health in the Community," in: *Handbook of Medical Sociology, op. cit.*, pp. 369–396. ". . . public health usually means intervening in the lives of people, often against their will. To date, those in public health have not succeeded in developing for themselves or conveying to the general public an ideology of intervention which jibes with the more widely-accepted beliefs about individual rights and the general distrust of government involvement in daily affairs" (p. 379).

[38] The attempt to dismiss this protracted, nation-wide resistance as a residual "superstition" reminds one of the manner in which the Enlightenment treated the Dark Ages. Yet it resembles the prisoner who "rejects his rejectors," the old codger who would rather die in a Skid Row hotel than live in a nice, clean zoo for old people, the fat businessman who works himself to death despite the doctor's good advice. Perhaps the ultimate in this line recently occurred in Dallas, Texas, where a Negro woman joined hands with her neighbors to prevent the white fire department from saving her six-year-old child.

[39] Drug prices, hospital prices and medical incomes have recently advanced astronomically. See, "The Rising Costs of Medical Care," Chapter 10 in: H. M. Somers and A. R. Somers, *Doctors, Patients and Health Insurance*, New York, 1961. ". . . the net *median* income of doctors rose 85 per cent from 1947 to 1955 when it reached $16,017. The 1959 *median* of $22,100 represents a 153 per cent advance over 1957." (p. 180–181).

[40] See, Walter I. Wardwell, "Limited, Marginal and Quasi-Practitioners," in *Handbook of Medical Sociology, op. cit.*, pp. 213–239. "Of course, such practitioners sometimes do effect cures among those who believe" (p. 230). See also, Ari Kiev, *Magic, Faith and Healing: Studies in Primitive Psychiatry Today*, New York, 1964; and the works of Thomas Szasz.

[41] Prohibition is the classic example. See also, Alfred Lindesmith, *The Addict and the Law*, Bloomington, Indiana, 1965. See, Edwin M. Lemerb, "Social Structure, Social Control, and Deviation," in: *Anomie and Deviant Behavior*, (edited by Marchal B. Clinard), New York, 1966, pp. 57–97. "There is a processual aspect to deviation, whose acknowledgement is forced upon us by the fact that with repetitive, persistent deviation or invidious differentiation, something happens 'inside the skin' of the deviating person" (p. 81).

upon such problems long after they have fixed in areas, ethnic groups, strata, and grey-markets. The deviant person joins the deviant group, subcultures, and even parallel economy. Organized crime enters and sometimes the dialectic of protracted war replaces the processualism of deviance. Since the demand for the product is quite inelastic, the crime has no victim, and an independent judicial system stands as an obstacle to a totally efficient war against crime, an open, pluralistic society may find itself in a tragic, complex circle of effects and countereffects which operates to maintain a given permissible level of the deviance in question. The control apparatus functions in part to maintain this level. In its "war against crime" it is often forced to turn to publicity stunts, public relations, and hokum in response to an impossible task.[42]

There is an increasing recognition of the intersection of the correctional and control apparatus and the career paths of chronic deviants. For example, Wikler notes that the abstinence rate of Lexington patients compares favorably with recovery rates from diabetes, or pulmonary tuberculosis.[43] Chein sees recidivism as a constructive part of the therapeutic process.[44] Parole system use of nalline may in part function to permit addicts on parole to maintain a moderate "habit" on a working class salary.[45] Civil commitment tends to lead to a confinement, abstention, controlled re-addiction, and re-confinement.

One authority asserts: "There is no real cure for the addictive disorders, just as no cure exists for many chronic disease — there is only a slow rehabilitative process which involves continuous support and a changed way of life."[46]

The role of coercion in the "treatment" of the addictions is clearly rec-

---

[42] The World Health Organization argues that "the maintenance of drug addiction is not treatment," *Chronicle of the World Health Organization*, "Treatment and Care of Drug Addicts," 11:323, October, 1957. The requirements of a democratic society may hinder measures which would "ruthlessly stamp out" these practices.

[43] Abraham Wikler, "Clinical Aspects of Diagnosis and Treatment of Addictions," *Bulletin of the Meninger Clinic*, 15 (1951).

[44] Isadore Chein, et al., *The Road to H: Narcotics, Delinquency and Social Policy*, New York, 1964.

[45] See, Robert Martinson, Gene G. Kassebaum, David A. Ward, "A Critique of Research in Parole," *Federal Probation*, 28,3:34–38, Sept. 1966.

[46] Edward A. Suchman, "The Addictive Diseases as Socio-Environmental Health Problems," in *Handbook of Medical Sociology, op. cit.*, p. 139. Medicine and medical sociology is rife with such ideological injunctions. The statement should read: "Given what is meant by "cure" by upper middle-class medical practitioners in the United States *today*, there is no real cure. . . ." Even then the statement would be false. Alcoholics Anonymous, and Synanon certainly "cure" in their own way. So do the Siberian *shaman*, the Yoruba *babalawo*, the Bahalis *yanka* and *barwa*, the Iban *manang*, the Ndembu *chimbuki*, the Australian *margidbu*, the Yemenite *mori*, and so forth. See also, William Madsen, "Value Conflicts and Folk Psychotherapy in South Texas," in *Magic, Faith and Healing, op. cit.*, pp. 420–445. Madsen points to "the high degree of success the *curandero* has demonstrated and the inability of the psychiatrist or physician to communicate linguistically or culturally with this predominantly Spanish-speaking group" (p. 420).

ognized by the World Health Organization, which recommends some form of legal compulsion because "most addicts require some degree of coercion, preferably civil commitment for medical treatment, to force them to desist from what is to them often a pleasurable experience."[47] The ordinary human stubbornness of the old, the weak, the eccentric and the stupid may then be reinforced by the quality of pleasureableness. The "rehabilitative process" must then consist in tearing from the user his habitually pleasurable method for coping with his problems while simultaneously defining his resistance to both the first *and* the second as a "disease."[48]

In American sociology, the recent interest in alienation, social change, evolutionist prespectives, conflict theory and dialectical processes of change provides some context for the discussion.[49]

The use of the term *chronic* alienation suggests something of the process. In the largest sense, we confront the drawing apart of science and man, but in this grandiose form the process escapes definition, limit, or verification. More specifically, we must confront *medical* progress, the lengthening of human life, the healing of the sick, the halt, the blind, the essence of humanistic perspective. The technical, scientific and humanitarian revolution associated with medicine has given birth to special new forms of misery, loneliness, isolation, and suffering.

Science is capable of producing destruction on an unprecedented scale. Today the world is ambivalent about new scientific inventions. The great powers spend large sums on space. In turning toward the stars we may become more impatient with man. The sick joke, the violent gang, the search for flying saucers are associated with a partial turning away from the helpless, the victims, the drop-outs. We are intensely concerned with the invisible reality just beyond our reach. We "cathect" with the starry heavens and leave our neighbors to die on the streets.[50]

We must confront the many ways in which we have kept the chronically alienated socially invisible. There are hundred of thousands if not mil-

[47] *Chronicle of the World Health Organization, op. cit.,* p. 323.

[48] See, *Drug Addiction, Crime or Disease?* Interim and Final Reports of the Joint Committee of the American Bar Association and the American Medical Association on Narcotic Drugs, Indiana, 1963. See also, Henry D. Lederer, "How the Sick View Their World," in: Jaco, *op. cit.,* pp. 247–256. The author sees social reaction to illness moving from denial to acceptance to body interest and dependency to convalescence. Neither *chronic* illness nor addiction would seem to fit this model.

[49] See, for example, Pierre L. van den Berhe, "Dialectic and Functionalism: Toward a Theoretical Synthesis," *American Sociological Review,* 28, 5, October 1963. The specification of a "minimum dialectic" as a "residual" is not very enlightening. If a process of change is dialectical one should be able to show it to be so, empirically. The question of how "residual" it is cannot be settled by an *a priori* logic but only by following the process to its end.

[50] I am suggesting that the space emphasis has shifted mass psychology, literary perspectives, and, perhaps, our attitudes towards those who refuse the gifts of a universal, free education.

lions of little "places" throughout America in which they are systematically tucked away. They are receiving care and "treatment." In these places, small and large, thoughts of mercy killing often arise.[51] Historically, brutal devices have been utilized in "treating" the inhabitants of these places.[52]

The health industry in America plays a most active role in producing chronic alienation. Almost all of the addicting substances are in the pharmacopeia. The opiates, heroin, *aqua vita*, the newer categories of "dangerous drugs" have been medically useful substances. Medical addiction is an important sub-category of addiction. Doctors and nurses have high rates of addiction. The American drug industry has poured hundreds of dangerous compounds on the market. The latest products of the most advanced industry often threaten the health and safety of the consumer.[53]

More specifically, we have to confront long-range demographic processes, such as the increase in the proportions of old people, the reduction of the extended family, the concentration and social isolation of poverty,[54] the transformation of Skid Row from "hobohemia" to a white swamp surrounded by colored areas. We are concerned with the general increase in the use of alcohol, the transformation of the major cities into Negro strongholds, and the keeping alive of the halt, lame, blind, disturbed, eccentric, and deviated.

Two perceptive students of the medical world have discussed the "paradox of medical progress."

> As we preserve life at all age levels, there is more illness, more enduring disability, for the population as a whole. A great shift is taking place in the nation's morbidity and disability patterns. A relative decline in serious acute illness is accompanied by a vast increase in chronic illness of long duration and a high rate of residual disability. The control of many formerly fatal diseases, like diabetes, or disabilities, like spinal paralysis, creates a need for expensive lifetime medical supervision."[55]

[51] See, for example, Harold Orlans, "An American Death Camp," in: Rosenberg, Gerver, and Howton, *op. cit.*, pp. 614–626. "It is in the murder by neglect of decrepit old men that, I believe, the closest analogy is to be found with death camp murders" (p. 626). The author, a Conscientious Objector, recognizes the "humanizing influence" of the CO's, but wishes also to emphasize "the brutalization of CO's by their experience" (p. 625, footnote).

[52] See, Albert Deutsch, *The Mentally Ill in America*, New York, 1949.

[53] See, the muckraking and not altogether reliable report by N. Mintz, *The Therapeutic Nightmare*, Boston, 1965.

[54] Michael Harrington, *The Other America*, New York, 1962, has helped to make the more politically relevant of these areas visible. The new visibility of the poor may also give birth to unanticipated consequences. Urban renewal, the "elimination" of Skid Row, old people's hospitals, foster homes for runaways, villages for the "old folks," recovery houses for alcoholics, Synanon's, and a thousand-and-one clinics and drying-out hospitals are relevant here.

[55] Somers and Somers, *op. cit.*, p. 7.

The term paradox is meant to give a non-objective thrust to the process and to lay the basis for its solution through "Organization: The Perilous Imperative." For the majority of Americans organization implies the general hospital, the medical plan, medical insurance and group practice or some combination of these. For the chronically alienated a future of organization may not look so bright.

It is a symptom of our condition that the *Right to Die* is listed by the Director of the Massachusetts General Hospital as "one of the four major medical problems facing the United States."

> Part of this issue . . . is keeping alive people who, not to put too fine a point upon it, would be happier if allowed to die. . . . Not long ago I heard a minister talk on the various freedoms he would like to see available to all mankind. After reviewing the more familiar ones, he added a new one: Freedom to Die. I beg of you to think that over."[56]

The chronic alienation of the aged, the crippled, the socially useless, should be carefully distinguished from the classical alienation of the worker from his product analyzed by Marx, or the alienation of man from rationality spoken of by Weber. The worker is a force of production, the chronically alienated a burden. The worker reacted to alienation through voluntary association, political and social struggle; the chronically alienated are drop-outs, a burden to themselves, their families, neighbors, and society. The worker had "nothing to lose but his chains"; the chronically alienated, as times goes on, have little to look forward to but death.[57]

Nor is the Weberian perspective too useful. The doctor, the military man, the business man, have been progressively deprived of control over their means of production through the development of the general hospital, the giant corporation, the military complex but they are not deprived of socially useful work. They are valuable. Embedded in the organizations of an organizational society they face problems peculiar to that society, some soluble, some relatively endemic. They fight for autonomy, form organizations, change policies, make alliances, preserve distance, or otherwise carry on the desperate work of the 20th Century.

The modern drop-out tends to be an *organizational reject,* a person rejected from the public school system or deprived of his livelihood at age

---

[56] *Ibid.,* p. 7.

[57] Despite the increase in chronic illness, death as a meaningful experience is progressively blotted out or denied. In sociology, death becomes death *rate.* For example, in the *Index to the American Sociological Review,* 1936–1960, I am unable to find one article on the meaning of death; Julius Gould and William L. Kolb, *A Dictionary of the Social Sciences,* New York, 1964, list *Death Rate* but not death. Perhaps it would be speculative to suggests that the "obliteration" of death is a fitting form of alienation for the chronically ill, and perhaps for all of us, since we are all increasingly faced with this fate.

65. The drop-outs live in the interstices between organizations — Skid Row, the slum, the family mental ward, the small, grey cheerless houses. They are everywhere and nowhere. They are incapable of organizing, for what could they demand? The world does not want their talents, has no need of their advice, sentimentality, sensitivity, their tales of past glories, their non-automated skills.

Pessimism has never been a strong point for Americans and it is increasingly becoming unthinkable in the helping professions to the degree that the clients refuse to become the cooperative, cheerful robots of whom C. Wright Mills often spoke. Americans salt their pragmatism with a strong belief in inevitable, gradually increasing, material and social progress. In certain professions, this boyish optimism is faced with the obstreperous, eccentric, shifty, and nasty temperament of man. An unsentimental, tough-minded stance is called forth, a set of persuasions, inducements, bonuses, incentives, motivations, and coercions. This collective Hickey marches forward looking neither to the left nor the right. Something like that, I think, provides a powerful motor for our collective dealings with the drop-outs and rejects who are incapable of playing the organizational game. These drop-outs, criminals, drug fiends, sexual perverts, are not left alone. To the Ten Commandments we have added the eleventh: Thou Shalt Be Organized!

The custody-treatment dimension is thus associated with a powerful social process — the organization of the deviant, a special bringing to bear of the control apparatus of society on those who are not permitted to drop away from the mainstream.[58]

Chronic alienation tends to evolve a career which takes different forms in the ordinary criminal, the alcoholic, the drug addict, and the very old or ill. This career often seizes upon some substance, mechanism, fantasy, some personal strategy, the aim of which is to cope with a life-plan which excludes meaningful participation in organized society. These coping mechanisms are varied but they appear to have in common the defense of consciousness from the pressures of organized society. Coping mechanisms aim to remove and isolate the reject from understanding his fate: they function to gradually extinguish his autonomy, freedom, and consciousness as a center of decision and responsibility. They may be regarded as a slow form of suicide. This career includes a set of moves, retreats, betrayals and more retreats, which is a different form of "risk-taking" than, say, the act of a soldier, or the accidental death of a hero who risks his life.

[58] Or, perhaps, become downward mobile through chronic illness. See, P. S. Lawrence, "Chronic Illness and Socio-Economic Status," in: Patients, Physicians and Illness (E. Gartly Jaco, editor), New York, 1958, pp. 37–49. "Families which had a reduction in socio-economic status between 1923 and 1943 had an adjusted chronic disease rate in 1943 of 87.2 per cent almost twice as high as the rate for families with an "improved status" (p. 48).

Chronic alienation is broader than that type of deviance prohibited by the legal code. The legal code is no sure guide to the process. It often provides invaluable aid to its workings. Nor am I talking about "deviance" in general. I am speaking of the widow who sips herself to death in the home of her late husband, the obese lady who eats herself to illness propped up on her bed, the businessman who works himself to extinction, the older, divorced woman who spends her former husband's declining fortune in buying a dependent relationship with a psychiatrist. What distinguishes these coping mechanisms is their concentration on relations and strategies which aim at the gradual and progressive obliteration of freedom, responsibility for self, and personal autonomy.

Criminology concentrates on those coping mechanisms for chronic alienation prohibited by the legal code; for society is not content to leave people alone to kill themselves swiftly or slowly. Society intervenes upon this process through personal appeals, the family, the Church, professional help, and legal coercion. In describing the processual nature of some deviance, Lemert distinguished *primary* from *secondary* deviance. Briefly, primary deviance was the pristine deviant act while secondary deviance was the reaction of the deviant to the social reaction called forth by the deviant act. The custody-treatment dimension forces upon us the recognition of further steps in this process.[59]

There has increasingly appeared a new, social reaction to the persistent failure of the traditional social reactions to deviance. The original deviant act has been partially contained, controlled, semi-organized. This process often gives birth to secondary deviance — "rejecting the rejectors," if you like. But this rejecting has become unacceptable to those agents of society rejected by the deviant. They are somewhat in the position of the fanatic who might be defined as a person who, faced with failure, redoubles his efforts. This is what treatment has become or is becoming — a redoubling of efforts in the face of persistent failure.

There is no compelling evidence that this redoubling of efforts has as yet had an important effect on the rate of recidivism. One powerful component of the new "treatment" reaction is the growing social recognition that this is so. To the daily frustrations of the correctional treatment staff member involved in the intimate game of "shucking" the inmate who is "shucking" him, there grows the pressure for results from central office, legislature, and society, and all those who would narrow correctional func-

[59] Edwin M. Lemert, "Social Structure, Social Control and Deviation," in: *Anomie and Deviant Behavior, op. cit.*, pp. 57–97, speaks of "passive social control" and the act of defining behavior so as to "produce change, not to repress it" (p. 91). In the end he returns to "secondary deviation" (p. 97). One difficulty may be the social psychological bias built into the primary-secondary dichotomy. Lemert's essay moves strikingly toward a *dialectical* conception of social deviance.

tions to reducing recidivism. This new urgency within the correctional system is beginning to be called: "the correctional therapeutic community."[60] In probation and parole a similar process *can be*[61] involved in the halfway house, the parole outpatient clinic, gathering parolees together for nalline tests or group counseling sessions, the movement toward smaller caseloads — situations in which the agent of society may tackle his slippery client jowl-to-jowl.

I am not suggesting that this process has run its course or is even a major component of all correctional or medical situations. It has gone further in some areas than others. It is not a fatal drift. It is, nevertheless, a reality. It has laid a powerful basis for even more severe redoublings of effort by those standing in the wings with some new nostrums to sell the despairing but ever-hopeful "treatment teams."

For Marx alienation was the antithesis to the thesis of the unregulated accumulation of capital. The synthesis would be a return of society to man. We cannot comfort ourselves with the words. We know far too much about bureaucracy, the State-party, forced labor, concentration camps, and a good deal more. It should be clear that chronic alienation is a process of death not a process of life. It apparently gives birth to little of social value.

Despite what I have said there are those who will push and preach for the prison to become a "hospital." We are to use the iron compression chamber of prison life to screw down upon the helpless, the aged, the misfits, the liars, the psychopaths, the drop-outs, and those who have almost accidentally got caught up in the correctional stream. We will let these people out on parole only if they agree to continue playing the intimate and tiring games of "treatment" with us. Many practitioners wish only the best for the inmate or parolee and would be happy to see him carrying on a productive and socially useful life. That is really beside the point. If such therapy simply takes the form of a small discussion group, or larger town meeting, it is consistent with a democratic ethic. But to some degree traditional forms of "lay group therapy" are a *turning aside* of treatment

[60] Clemmer's use of the term "community" to refer to a total institution is discussed by George A. Hillery, Jr., "Villages, Cities, and Total Institutions," *American Sociological Review*, 28, 5:779–791. Hillery maintains that villages and cities are on a continuum while the total institution represents a qualitative break. He does not deal at length with the *functions* of using this word, however. For a discussion of the *ideology* of the "correctional therapeutic community" see: Robert Martinson with William J. O'Brien, *Staff Training and Correctional Change, op. cit.*, Chapter 8.

[61] I will repeat this and underline it. *Can be* involved. Any new "treatment" method may involve tertiary methods of dealing with deviance or democratic ones. For example, a "halfway house" may be a small, intense treatment prison or a "sanctuary." See, Robert Martinson, "The California Recovery House: A Sanctuary for Alcoholics," *Mental Hygiene*, 58, 3, July 1964 and *Recovery Establishments for Alcoholics*, State of California, Department of Public Health, April 1963.

authoritarianism through the inertia and perhaps good sense of many correctional personnel. If one is truly serious about "treating" the prisoner, and reducing recidivism, much more effort and work must be put into the system. The screws must be tightened, the hopefulness whipped up, efforts coordinated. All eyes shall be turned to *that rate*, all "uneconomical" expenditures reduced. This must then be coordinated to ever-new levels of dedication and intensity.

SUMMARY

If a gloomy picture emerges from this discussion, it is a result of the method of abstraction I have used. I have also attempted to combine areas often kept apart through academic and professional specialization. Yet there appears to be some gain in explanatory power in so doing.

Chronic alienation affects only a relatively small, though growing, number of persons in all medically advanced societies. It is no respecter of different political systems. The challenge it presents may be met in a variety of ways. In America, the situation noted by de Tocqueville has undergone a complex process of change. The *discrepancy* between prison tyranny and American democracy has been reduced. During the period of humanitarianism, the prison was reformed in a democratic direction. As the age of treatment begins to give way to a more vigorous assertion of the need to transform man, efforts are being made to introduce methods in fundamental opposition to the democratic ethic. These methods are more verbal than actual, more a promise than a fulfillment. Yet they are pursued by many well-intentioned persons with little thought to the consequences.

One important way in which sociology may contribute to the study of crime and the correctional process is to ask some of the right questions. One important question seldom asked in corrections is: what kind of correctional system is fitting for a democratic society? This ethical question may easily be translated into a rich variety of sociological investigations. For example, what accounts for the growth and development of the new treatment authoritarianism? Where are the professional sources of the new emphasis upon utilizing the prison for the transformation of man? Does this new ideology cut across a variety of professions? What are the social forces pressing for making the reduction of recidivism the single goal of the correctional system?

Of course, these questions may be posed and answered strictly within the compass of criminology but some may find it helpful to do so within a somewhat broader perspective. The new emphasis on the control of the use of medical substances has already produced cross-disciplinary areas and subjects. The medical profession is involved in a wide variety of activities in which social control becomes strikingly important. The increasingly chronic nature of many social ailments also tends in this direction. The chronically alienated are not the most powerful segment of a modern population. They are likely to be lost sight of in what appear to be more compelling concerns. Sociology may play a very important function in keeping them before our eyes, in describing their tribulations, and in defending their humanity.